AFTER MANDELA

AFTER MANDELA

The Struggle for Freedom in
Post-Apartheid South Africa

DOUGLAS FOSTER

LIVERIGHT PUBLISHING CORPORATION
A DIVISION OF W. W. NORTON & COMPANY
NEW YORK · LONDON

"*Ek Ken 'n Plek*" by André Boezak, from *Die Fonteyn* by André Boezak, Poem Mooney, Hans Oosthuizen, and Jan van Wyk. Kannaland Produksies, 1996. Translation by Anabelle Oosthuizen. Selections from "Human Rainbow" and "Take My Heart Away" used by permission of Johnny Clegg. Selection from "Higher" by Brenda Fassie, Malcolm Watson, and Rufus Klaas © 1985 EMI Music Publishing (South Africa) (Pty) Ltd.

For information about permissions to reproduce selections from this book, write to Permissions, Liveright Publishing Corporation, a division of W. W. Norton & Company, Inc., 500 Fifth Avenue, New York, NY 10110

For information about special discounts for bulk purchases, please contact W. W. Norton Special Sales at specialsales@wwnorton.com or 800-233-4830

Manufacturing by RR Donnelley, Harrisonburg
Book design by Ellen Cipriano
Production manager: Devon Zahn

Library of Congress Cataloging-in-Publication Data

Foster, Douglas.
After Mandela : the struggle for freedom in post-apartheid
South Africa / Douglas Foster.
p. cm.
Includes bibliographical references and index.
ISBN 978-0-87140-478-7 (hardcover)
1. South Africa—Politics and government—1994– 2. South Africa—
Social conditions—1994– 3. Post-apartheid era—South Africa.
4. Social change—South Africa. I. Title.
DT1971.F67 2012
968.066—dc23
2012003249

Liveright Publishing Corporation
500 Fifth Avenue, New York, N.Y. 10110
www.wwnorton.com

W. W. Norton & Company Ltd.
Castle House, 75/76 Wells Street, London W1T 3QT

1 2 3 4 5 6 7 8 9 0

To Jacob Foster, my beloved son,
who shared the entire adventure

For my parents, Frances and Donald,
who took me to Africa for the first time in 1962

And for Anne Lamott, truest compass
and most certain guide

Contents

AFTER
MANDELA

Bird of paradise, also known as the crane flower, is a perennial pollinated by sunbirds and is native to South Africa. (*Douglas Foster*)

Overture

Baleka Uzohaqwa!

(Escape Before You Are Injured!)

Low-hanging clouds shadowed Cape Town's flat-topped colossus, known in English as Table Mountain and in isiXhosa as *Umlindi Wemingizimu* (Watcher of the South). Streams of fog swept its craggy slopes, wrapping the entire city below in misty ribbons. On the drive from the airport we slowed through brief whiteouts; one minute the view was clear, and in the next it was all pale oblivion. On our left, a stand of trees veiled the massive hillside monument to Cecil Rhodes, the sixth prime minister of the Cape Colony in the nineteenth century who envisioned the imposition of white rule across the continent "from Cape Town to Cairo." This was a place that always inspired big dreams of radical change.

For outsiders, mention of South Africa summoned up memories of the extreme form of racial segregation that held sway here for more than forty years, and also the stunning transition to one-person–one-vote democracy in 1994. A decade later, in March of 2004, I had traveled to South Africa, in part to get a fix on how the grand experiment in creating a different kind of society had worked out. The country, a land of ragged coastline and open savannas where humans first emerged to stand upright on two legs more than two million years ago, was in the midst of a struggle to hang onto the vision of a nonracial, nonsexist, and egalitarian nation promised at its birth.

The emerald waters of Table Bay came into view. If you squinted, you could make out Robben Island, a stark islet far offshore where generations of rebels like Nelson Mandela were once held. This glimpse was superimposed, naturally, over a palimpsest of images from newsreels, photographs, books, and films I'd seen that gave visitors a powerful, and sometimes misleading, sensation of knowing the place already. For my generation, South Africa had symbolized a modern moral fable. For millions of other people around the world, the mass global mobilization against the system of racial segregation known as apartheid had unfolded much like the international campaign to end slavery a century earlier. In demonstrations in the United States for civil rights and against the Vietnam War, students also had hoisted placards with Mandela's image and chanted, "Free Mandela!" because they believed there was an essential link between his freedom and theirs.

Under apartheid (which means "apartness" in Afrikaans), one's identity was established chiefly on the basis of skin color: you were European (white), Coloured (mixed race), Asian (Indian), or Native (black). The vast majority had been governed, for centuries, by the white minority. Now, at last, the natives were in charge. For ten years, the country had been governed by a three-sided coalition including the African National Congress (ANC), the continental's oldest political party; the Congress of South African Trade Unions (COSATU); and the South African Communist Party (SACP).

Political liberation hadn't led to material freedom yet, though. On this first trip, I had brought along with me ten students from the university where I teach, and they were stunned by first impressions. On the drive into Cape Town there were shacks along the highway for as far as we could see. Kids from informal settlements darted out from the side of the road to play chicken to the concrete median strip, where they watched luxury sedans whiz by. We passed, soon enough, into the parallel universe of a gorgeous tourist destination with a world-class convention center. Just off the last off-ramp into Cape Town, at Riebeek Street, there was an Alfa Romeo and Rolls-Royce dealership, where business was brisk.

Up on Long Street, near the hostel where we would be staying, cafes and clubs overflowed with people dressed in designer-label clothes. The image of Thabo Mbeki, Nelson Mandela's successor as president, was plastered on utility poles up and down the alleys and streets. Campaign posters for the ANC showed him dressed in a dark business suit, smiling shyly beneath the governing party's ubiquitous slogan: "A Better Life for All."

An unruly clutch of street kids wrapped in tattered blankets shouted in the background as more fortunate people were ordering skinny lattes and tramezzini. The kids latched onto us before we could find our footing at the curb. "Captain! Master! *Baas!*" they cried, using the old Afrikaans word for white boss. "We're hungry, *Baas!*" It startled us to be implicated, right from the beginning, in the language of oppression.

If you lost track of developments in South Africa around the time Mandela retired as head of state in 1999, its recent history seemed rather disappointing. When Mandela took office, he was depicted as the indispensable leader, using his *magic* to inspire a *miracle*. If you paired the terms *magic* and *Mandela* in a Google search, you would find a million hits. By contrast, the 154,000 entries for his successor, Thabo Mbeki, were stripped of any inference of magic. He was dubbed the *enigmatic* leader who had stabilized the national economy but also had sabotaged the country's effort to control the spread of AIDS.

President Mbeki was the chief architect of the postliberation transition, but his administration was swamped by two world historical forces that might have sunk even a more visionary leader—rapid economic globalization and an unprecedented sexually transmitted plague. South Africa was the only place on the globe where advanced capitalism, AIDS, and political freedom rushed through the door together.

Could the idea of a rainbow people, creating a Rainbow Nation, survive the pressure?

On our third day in Cape Town, the students and I headed out to a demonstration, in a township outside the city, called by the Treatment Action Campaign (TAC). The group was the country's largest and most successful civic organization, responsible for advocating on behalf of HIV-positive people. Leaders of TAC in Khayelitsha had called the protest to raise hell about the rape and killing of an activist who had disclosed that she was infected with HIV. Our guide, hired to show us around, initially balked at taking us to the township. "You never know what *these blacks* will do," he told us. To us, he looked as dark as any African American, but in South African terms he was *coloured*, or of mixed race. It was our first lesson in the tapestry of racial bigotry that extended far beyond divisions between blacks and whites.

We arrived in Khayelitsha just as organizers from TAC were unveiling banners that read, "Once a Killer Always a Killer / Keep Them Away from Our Community," "No Bail for Murderers," "REMEMBER LORNA," and "JAIL THEM FOR LIFE." Within a half hour we had gathered a collection of stories from women who had been raped into AIDS and who together had successfully fought back against discrimination. Our guide stuck close to the car, though, looking quite uncomfortable. He regained his composure only when we left the black township and moved on to another settlement, Mitchells Plain, which under apartheid had been set aside for mixed-race people, or coloureds.

This incident marked the start of a long education for us about ongoing ethnic tensions in the new South Africa. New black acquaintances back in Cape Town volunteered the opinion that coloureds or *brown* people were really *closet whites*. But this sort of tension between blacks and coloureds was only the beginning of the complications we encountered. There were eleven official languages in the country, nine of them distinguishing black groups. The archaic and anthropologically incorrect word *tribe* didn't help in figuring out disparate identities, partly because of the long history of groups fusing together and breaking apart. The correct term, *ethnic group*, sounded rather flat against the emotions threaded through intergroup bigotry.

Leaders of the ANC often emphasized the dangers of "tribalism" and the importance of nonracialism. One of the signal successes of the liberation struggle had been bridging ethnic cleavages, which apartheid leaders had exploited in a strategy of divide-and-rule. As a white outsider, I had set out to avoid old tropes without closing my eyes to reality as it presented itself.

The two most populous groups in the country were Zulu speakers and Xhosa speakers. Within days of our arrival we heard Xhosa speakers muttering about the ways Zulu-speaking blacks were intellectually inferior or especially prone to violence. Non-Xhosa speakers told us, in a similar tone of voice, that there was something suspicious about Xhosa speakers as a group; we were told they were clannish, money-grubbing, and far *too clever* for their own good. Our friends cited as Exhibit A the conspiratorial style of President Mbeki. Just a decade after its founding, inhabitants of the Rainbow Nation, including the young, seemed decidedly *over* the rainbow.

I had set off to South Africa, in early 2004, in part because there was a mystery I had been trying to unravel in nearly three decades working as a journalist: how most people, most often, seemed so imprisoned by the past, while others managed to slip away from history's grasp. In dispatches I had filed from places such as Guatemala, Nicaragua, Peru, and Argentina—as well as from the agricultural valleys and booming cities of my native California—I had covered mass social and political clashes for decades. Without planning it, over the years I had developed a pattern of moving in to investigate what happened in the aftermath of great social convulsions. Other journalists were better at covering wars or blazing conflicts. I tended, instead, to turn up just when the pack of reporters moved on to the next big hot spot. In so many places, I had been drawn to witness the ways people stitched their societies together in the wake of horrific traumas. Perhaps it was inevitable, then, that I should eventually get so hooked on the postliberation story of South Africa.

During the initial visit in 2004, I intended to stay a few weeks before heading off to the Congo. Every time I prepared to leave South Africa, though, something startling would happen. After spending long periods in the country during the next three years, I finally surrendered to the seduction of the place. On New Year's Day in 2007, I put my furniture in storage, packed up my belongings in Chicago, and moved to Johannesburg for the year. By then, it seemed to me that the country was in the process of revealing something of its essence. At the close of that year, South Africa's emerging democracy perched on the edge of a revolution within a revolution. By chance, I had the good fortune to be around when this new fight for freedom began.

Along the way, I had the opportunity to travel with presidents and interview business and political leaders. The discipline I undertook, as reporting for the book proceeded, was to butt the vantage point of the emerging new elite up against that of working people and the poor, giving added emphasis to the voices of those less often heard.

I underscored the experience of the young. The post-transition ANC now governs a country where nearly 40 percent of its people are less than eighteen years old; fully half the population is less than twenty-five. During my travels around the country, a series of individual and group interviews involving hundreds of young South Africans—the children of liberation heroes as well as seamstresses, nurses, mechanics, schoolteachers, gangsters, and the unemployed—shaped my understanding of future prospects for the country.

Six key individuals helped me stitch the general narrative together: Ndaba Mandela, the grandson of the founding president of the country; Thuthukile Zuma, the daughter of President Jacob Zuma and Minister of Home Affairs Nkosazana Dlamini-Zuma; Thomas Maree, son of the leader of the opposition, Helen Zille; as well as three others from more straitened backgrounds—Vunene Mabasa, from a remote town in Limpopo; Gwendoline Dube, who lives in a hardscrabble township south of Johannesburg; and Jonathan Persens, who lives by his wits in the alleys of Cape Town and sometimes sleeps on the lawns near the National Museum.

On a sunny day a few months after I arrived in the country in 2004, I crossed the Grand Parade. It is the vast plaza on the west side of City Hall. A new friend, Gavin Jacobs, had agreed to show me around. He was a tall, lean, mischievous-looking man in his mid-thirties with golden skin and high cheekbones that gave him away as a typical Capetonian. Descended from indigenous San people and from blacks who arrived thousands of years *after* the San, Jacobs was classified under apartheid as *coloured*.

We passed by the colonial-era City Hall, an Edwardian building dwarfed by more modern neighbors. To our right loomed the oddly majestic pentagonal Castle of Good Hope, built more than 350 years ago. The castle once served as a crude stone monument to would-be conquerors—Dutch and British—who had long competed for control of the Cape's first military fort and, through it, dominion over the southern tip of Africa.

"I stood right here on the day Nelson Mandela was released," Jacobs said, stopping abruptly to mark the place.[1] Twirling around, I located the tiny wrought-iron balcony that I had seen several times in video clips taken on February 1990, when Nelson Mandela walked out of prison and was shuttled by car to address the massive crowd here. "There were *tons*, more people than I've ever seen, before or since," Jacobs added. That image of Mandela, wiry and spry but looking dazed and clenching his fist in a revolutionary salute, came back to me. Mandela had begun his speech with the cry *"Amandla! Iafrica! Mayibuye!"* and he called on South Africans to "seize this moment so that the process towards democracy is rapid and uninterrupted."[2]

Craning his neck, Jacobs said that it was impossible to convey the force of emotion that had welled up from the people on that day. The impossible—Mandela's release—suddenly proved possible. The imprisoned hero was free, and it looked like the narrative arc of his life, from entombed martyr brought back to life, might be superimposed as the narrative of the nation, setting the pattern for similar, amazing transformative changes in the lives of his people.

Jacobs squatted, then rose, bringing his palms up toward the sky. Class and racial divisions hadn't seemed to matter any longer on that day, he said. Everything petty and cruel in the culture seemed to vanish—he snapped his fingers—just like that.

He had no memory of the violent clashes between the police and the crowd that had been reported in contemporaneous accounts on that day. It felt, to him and so many others, as if the slate of history had been wiped clean. South Africans could slip from the constraints of their own past and create something new.

We stood for a few moments as if still being jostled by a vast crowd and reinvigorated by past hopes. As we walked on, Jacobs filled in the gaps in his own life from then to now. He hadn't had a steady job, not under white rule and not since the day of his supposed liberation; like most coloured and black young people he was unemployed in the supercompetitive global economy South Africa had rejoined after decades of explicit racial discrimination.

He admitted that his memory of the period 1990–1994 was a little dim. Along with his friends, he had partied hard in drawn-out celebration of national liberation. Right around Freedom Day, that first election day in 1994, Jacobs was infected with HIV during a night of carefree sex. Like one in six young South Africans, he now lived with the virus that led to AIDS. He was a *slow progressor*, which was good news—it meant he had not needed medication yet—but the virus was often at the back of his mind. Jacobs recently had signed up at a school for tour guides, because he figured that he might have a future in telling the story of national transformation he had witnessed firsthand. Then he had flunked out of the program. Why had he failed in the program he had wanted so much to pass? Partly because he hated following anybody else's rules, he said.

Like many of his contemporaries, Jacobs had been surrounded in early life by the spirit of rebellion as people rose up against the police, the law, and the state. He felt rather unsuited for building anything up, even if it was his own career. "I just never can get *traction*, you know?" he told me. On a brightening, sunny day, the kind that steals your heart in Cape Town, he looked a little broken.

Registering my reaction, Jacobs laughed and launched into a riff about how South Africans always beat the odds. "God, you have to love this country!" he exclaimed. "There's nothing like it." An unemployed young man with HIV, he was still celebrating the miracle while heading across a bridge to a train that could take him anywhere if only he had the fare.

Jacobs and I headed off on a day trip to Stellenbosch, a lovely, lush valley planted with wine grapes and the center of production for distinctive Pinotage. I had arranged to meet a colleague from Stellenbosch University, and afterward we hung around the picturesque town. On the way back to Cape Town, we crossed over from the large bubble of privilege back to the hard realities of the Cape Flats. He larded every story he told with loads of details about the history of protest against the old system.

By the time we returned to the hostel in Cape Town, it was nearly dark. From the balcony we could see the harbor. Farther out flashed the turquoise sea. The sounds of hip-hop and *kwaito*, the country's distinctive hybrid genre, rumbled down Long Street.

A sound system in a passing car blasted the voices of a pair of singers, Johnny Clegg and Sipho Mchunu, the "white Zulu" anthropologist and his black partner. They were singing, *"Baleka Uzohaqwa!"* (Escape before you are injured!)—words from an eerie, searing ballad called "Human Rainbow" from their 1988 collection *Shadow Man*. The lyrics shifted from Zulu to English and back again. "*Uwahaqwa!*" (Too late—he is injured!) was the swift reply to the invocation. The chorus went as follows:

> *Same old human story*
> *The saddest winds do blow*
> *While we are trapped in the language of dark history.*

In the kitchen, a domestic worker cranked up her own music. One of the most compelling voices I had ever heard filled the room. When I asked who was singing, she looked startled that I would prove so ignorant. "Brenda Fassie!" she cried, swaying to the chorus. Fassie was the crossover artist from a township outside Cape Town whose ode to Nelson Mandela, "My Black President," struck a blow against apartheid. Now she belted out a post-apartheid message:

> *Higher and higher*
> *Aint nothing stopping us from reaching for the top.*
> *Aint nothing stopping us from reaching for more!*

A chilly wind blew from the sea. The sun fell. Neon lights from surrounding clubs flickered on. Darkness settled in. Johnny Clegg reminded listeners of the persistent effects of oppression while Brenda Fassie crooned her seductive invitation to forget about the country's brutal history: go faster, farther, quicker, she suggested, and don't look back.

It occurred to me that both messages deserved their due. One voice crossed over the other; together they made a discordant, and quite beautiful, duet. It seemed an appropriate augur for the amazing and troubling, puzzling and transformative things bound to happen next.

PART I

Tomorrow's Country

(2004)

We have learnt the lesson that our blemishes speak of what all humanity should not do. We understand this fully, that our glories point to the heights of what human genius can achieve.

—NELSON MANDELA
1994

We are the ones who created the system. The system shouldn't create us. . . . Ultimately, we are in a battle with ourselves.

—NDABA MANDELA
2007

Young men in a job training program hoist a homemade flag of the country made from papier mâché. (*Douglas Foster*)

I.

The Chief

At last, I thought, I get to see a person constantly being described as *enigmatic*. Thabo Mbeki, Nelson Mandela's successor as president of South Africa, was endlessly tagged in this way by journalists and scholars, as if it was dereliction of duty for a politician to be complicated and difficult to read. Since the president was scheduled to make a major address in the Klein Karoo the next morning, I had set out from Cape Town after midnight, heading east.

Thabo Mbeki was the country's second black leader, and he had suffered terribly, in contemporary coverage, by comparison to Mandela. The older man was tall, gracious, and possessed of a blazing smile; his successor was short, awkward, and rather tightly wound. Even some of Mbeki's supporters described their leader as Machiavellian or even paranoiac.

Mbeki had been chief architect of post-transition politics in the country. Through much of the heavy lifting undertaken in the period 1999–2004, during his first term as head of state, his government aimed to turn the extravagant promises made by Mandela's generation into reality for masses of South Africans.

For an outsider, Mbeki seemed like a Rubik's Cube. He was a self-proclaimed modernizer in a government laced with incompetent, corrupt cronies; a critic of world capitalism for the widening patterns of inequality while he embraced conservative macroeconomic policy at home; an avid peacemaker in Côte d'Ivoire, Burundi, and the Democratic Republic of the Congo and advocate of an African Renaissance while he also protected brutal and aging tyrants like Robert Mugabe of Zimbabwe. An advocate of finding "African solutions to African problems," Mbeki had turned his back on medical science in the fight against AIDS, largely on the basis of marginalized views of discredited scientists in the West.

South Africans who feared that the country was on a slide toward catastrophe fingered him for the blame, while plenty of business leaders considered Thabo Mbeki the indispensable force for moving the country forward. To understand the state of the nation's politics in 2004 meant taking a run at understanding *him*.

After leaving Cape Town, I passed a series of towns named for colonial-era generals and governors. The archipelago that stretched from Table Bay to Cape Point, now at my back, once was the source of contention between the Dutch and the British. The Cape was a prized possession back in the seventeenth and eighteenth centuries because control of the sea passage from Europe around Africa meant a measure of control of the trade in pepper (used in preserving foodstuffs) and other spices from India, Malaysia, and Indonesia.[1]

Lush coastal terrain zipped by, exposed by the headlights. Tens of thousands of years ago, indigenous San and Khoikhoi occupied a fairly narrow band of land that lies between the mountains and the sea. The geography shifted, in dramatic steps, across three mountain ranges to the Great Escarpment, from a patchwork of green forest to ever-drier plains before you reached the Karoo, which means "dry" in Khoikhoi.

The first recorded instance of face-to-face contact between indigenous Khoikhoi and Europeans took place here six centuries ago. It happened near Mossel Bay, where I stopped for coffee before turning inland. On a cloudy afternoon in 1488, a small group of Khoikhoi confronted sailors from a fleet commanded by the Portuguese explorer Bartolomeu Dias on the beach nearby. The indigenous people were offered trinkets by the sailors, according to the magisterial history *Frontiers*, by Noel Mostert. They threw stones at the intruders rather than accept the gifts, and Captain Dias snatched up a crossbow to shoot one of the Khoikhoi dead. This victim was "the first indigene to be killed by the white man in South Africa,"[2] Mostert wrote. From that day forward, he added, the Cape of Good Hope "symbolized for many centuries the two great formative frontiers of the modern world: the physical one of the oceanic barrier to the east and its concomitant one of the mind, global consciousness."[3] This same landscape, it seemed to me, represented a third formative frontier now: the place where a new form of social democracy, established in a developing country in Africa, faced its severest test.

Just beyond Herolds Bay, which featured a windswept surfing beach with a stunning break to the left, I headed inland north on the N12 highway through George and on over the winding Outeniqua Pass. The pass was pocked with thick woodland. On the far side of it the terrain opened up, much like the sudden revelation of space in New Mexico or west Texas.

Common pincushion trees punctuated vast open fields, and the valley was spotted with feathery, small bushman grass rippling in the breeze. A vast array of *fynbos*, the squat fine-leafed plants native to this soil, lay interwoven with varieties of aloes prized for their medicinal qualities.

Down in the valley, the Klein Karoo, my destination, was visible in a stretch on dun-colored soil spread across low-rolling hills. The plains were overgrazed by cattle, sheep, and ostrich in the direction of Oudtshoorn. That was the town where President Mbeki was scheduled to open an Afrikaans language cultural festival.

Oudtshoorn was founded by Jewish traders in the 1870s, and it had been the epicenter of a great worldwide Ostrich Boom. The boom went on for thirty years, until the ostrich feather market suddenly vanished around 1910, the same year the Republic of South Africa was founded.

The creation and subsequent collapse of the ostrich feather economy suggested an early lesson about the sometimes-devastating boom-and-bust cycles suffered by people relying on economies based heavily on commodity exports.

To the north of the town were the sacred ruins of indigenous life, the Cango Caves. Thousands of years before in these caves, the San people depicted key events in ochre paint across granite walls. The rock paintings were like a reference library, its sequences registering the arrival of successive waves of intruders, including darker-skinned people coming southward from central Africa; then white colonizers, the Dutch, a thousand years later, with the British right behind.[4] Each successive wave of intruders changed the telling of the history, as if the true story of humans moving through space and time only began once their own group arrived. The paintings made a quieter statement about who had been there first.

East of the town, vast tracts of land lay between two great rivers—the Kei and Great Fish—from which ancestors of Xhosa-speaking blacks had been pushed steadily eastward in a series of wars, as they battled the Dutch between 1779 and 1802, and then faced the British in bloody conflicts from 1811 to 1851.[5] Both geography and demography demonstrated that apartheid wasn't a system sprung full blown from the segregationist theories of National Party leaders in 1948; rather, apartheid was a cultural and political expression deeply rooted in patterns of racial oppression developed systematically during centuries of colonial rule.

Many of South Africa's most grievous contemporary problems could be traced back to a system of legalized theft, rooted earlier in the Native Land Act of 1913. From 1948 to 1990, under formal apartheid, the screws were tightened on black inhabitants in devastating ways. Blacks were pressed into highly constricted areas designated as "homelands," and eventually more than 75 percent of the population was quarantined on less than 13 percent of the land.

The political power won by the ANC in two successive national elections in 1994 and 1999 offered political representation in a parliamentary democracy, but only limited control over land and other key levers of the economy. The party of liberation held little power to redistribute wealth to make up for the stark inequality rooted in this long history. Minority whites, less than 10 percent of the population, still held title to most productive land and fungible wealth.

On the street, and in the townships, people remarked on this double-sided nature of the 1994 liberation by saying that the ANC was in *office* but not in *power*—implying that Mandela and Mbeki had simply become the black faces superimposed on an old and unjust system.

The two men who had served as the country's paramount leaders during the first decade of democracy both spent much of their adult lives forcibly separated from the people they eventually governed—Nelson Mandela in prison for twenty-seven years and Thabo Mbeki in exile for nearly thirty years.

Among their many differences were the ways each man invoked memories of the past. In his autobiography, *Long Walk to Freedom*, Mandela had referred to his childhood haunts with nostalgic affection: "It was in the fields that I learned to knock birds out of the sky with a slingshot, to gather wild honey and fruits and edible roots, to drink warm, sweet milk straight from the udder of a cow, to swim in the clear, cold streams."[6]

Mbeki, on the other hand, was born and raised in Mbewuleni, an Eastern Cape village not far from Mandela's, but he never described his home village in similarly idyllic terms. In a brief autobiographical sketch written in the 1990s, Mbeki recalled an early scene from childhood of men returning to his village, as he put it, "broken by the mines, which then spewed them out to die in the superficially idyllic surroundings of the undulating hills."[7]

Both leaders knew quite well that the national system of migrant labor destroyed relationships in black families for generations. When it came to looking back, though, Mandela claimed a rooted identity in time and place, while the phrase Mbeki used—"superficially idyllic surroundings"—read like an indirect rebuke to his elder's much-celebrated account and rooted his own identity firmly in class struggle rather than in any particular place.

Thabo Mbeki's father, Govan, was a Communist stalwart later imprisoned for decades on Robben Island. His mother, Epainette, ran a shop and was a community organizer who raised the children virtually on her own. Thabo, their oldest son, was bounced from the care of relatives to boarding school and then out of the country entirely, into exile, before he reached the age of twenty.

Revolutionary ideals, and the ties Mbeki developed inside the ANC, became his substitute for family, his only real home. In a comprehensive biography by Mark Gevisser, the author cited the word "disconnect" to sum up the psychic strain of Mbeki's upbringing. *Disconnect* was a word the president himself had summoned up to describe his early life and exile.

He had arrived at the University of Sussex in the early 1960s as one of only two black students on campus. Almost overnight, the future president stepped from an African reality into white British culture in the midst of a generational revolt. Back home, a wave of arrests, trials, and brutal crackdowns marked a period of sustained and effective repression. Well into middle age, he would live a freighted double life of fine pipes, black tea and milk, and worn tweeds overlaid by the news of terrible things happening back home.

Mbeki worked with Oliver Reginald Tambo, the president of the ANC, who at that time was living in exile in London with his wife, Adelaide. He emerged as the self-effacing interlocutor for a movement denounced as *terrorist* by Western powers. As Tambo's chief diplomat, Mbeki mediated between the ANC and its financial backers in the Soviet

Union and Sweden and reached out to grassroots supporters in Europe and the United States.

Mbeki also developed a mixed reputation inside the movement during the 1980s. While he eventually charmed Afrikaner intellectuals, and even shuttled around Europe for secret talks with intelligence agents of the regime, in the camps where guerrillas trained he was suspected of harboring inadequate faith in the armed struggle. Among activists inside the country, organizing from the bottom up under the umbrella of the United Democratic Front, there was a dominant culture of open discussion, consultation, and consensual decision-making; these activists chafed sometimes under the weight of top-down decision-making by leaders in exile.

The secretive, top-down system of decision-making by ANC leaders was rooted, in part, in Leninist-style democratic centralism, but also was reinforced by the exigencies of the time. The white regime in Pretoria had a top-notch intelligence-gathering operation focused relentlessly on its opponents, and the movement was riddled with spies. Drugging, poisoning, biological warfare, letter bombs, and psychological mind games were part of the armory. "For the exiles, paranoia was common sense," a historian of the period wrote. "Pretoria *was* out to get them and its agents were everywhere."[8]

When differences broke out within the movement, adversaries often traced them back to the simplest variables—where you placed yourself in the struggle and the nature of the sacrifices you paid for liberation. Were you in exile? Or were you known by that odd word—*inzile*—invented to describe someone working for freedom *inside* the country? Had you joined Umkhonto we Sizwe (MK), the military wing of the ANC, where you might be subjected to bombing, assassination, or kidnapping by South African military or intelligence forces? Were you a longtime prisoner, or had you been banned, imprisoned, and tortured?

The intensity of one's sacrifice turned into a kind of currency used to measure one's suitability for leadership. Those who differed with

Mbeki over the years often rubbished him, behind his back, as a "black Englishman" who had lived in London and Lusaka while others slogged through the mud on the front lines of the struggle.

In early 1990, after President F. W. de Klerk surprised ANC leaders by legalizing formerly banned revolutionary organizations and releasing political prisoners, top exiled leaders flooded back into a country they scarcely knew. Many, like Mbeki, had been away for decades.

"You suddenly felt you were carrying the whole of South Africa on your shoulders, to try to give people what they expected," one of his comrades recalled. ". . . Coming from exile, you were not even part and parcel of the fabric of your own society. You didn't have a support base that understood you. You were struggling to reintegrate . . . and at the same time you were expected to be focused, to deliver."[9]

The transition from long exile to governing proved a drawn-out affair. More than three years dragged by during intense on-again/off-again negotiations before the country's first nonracial national election was held, in 1994. In negotiations, the ANC had essentially agreed to leave the basic structure of the economy intact in exchange for winning the electoral franchise for blacks. Private property rights would be protected under the new dispensation, and the vast network of civil service jobs in government, held mostly by Afrikaans-speaking whites, would be phased out only over time.

In other words, there would be no quick fulfillment of the demands of the Freedom Charter of 1955, which had been the movement's seminal declaration of purpose for more than forty years; there would be no nationalization of the mines or redistribution of land, or sharing of the wealth. Figuring out how social and economic justice would flow from the decision to extend the right to vote to blacks was left as business for another day.

In later years, outsiders often wondered aloud how it was that Mbeki became Mandela's successor. In the election of 1994, the ANC swamped the National Party, capturing 62 percent of the vote to just over 20 percent for the National Party.[10] After the balloting, against Mandela's better judgment, Mbeki was selected from within the ANC as one of two deputy presidents, serving alongside de Klerk in a Government of National Unity for more than a year. Mbeki also routed Mandela's preferred candidate in internal party elections for the deputy presidency of the ANC, though he would never completely shake the suspicion that the best-possible leader had not prevailed.[11]

A few weeks after the election in 1994, Mandela and Mbeki arrived at Union Buildings, the seat of the country's executive power in Pretoria. They had inherited a government, and country, in a perilous state. Mbeki later reported that he arrived on his first day of work to find the executive offices stripped bare. "There were no pictures on the wall, nor telephones on the desk," his biographers wrote. "The previous occupant's computer had been removed, along with the rugs, glasses, files and teaspoons."[12]

What was far worse was that the nation's economy was in virtual free fall. National debt stood at more than 8 percent; 40 percent of South African workers were unable to find jobs in the formal sector. Gold prices were in flux and manufacturing in decline. The South African economy was completely "buggered" in the words of the country's holdover finance minister.[13] One top Mandela advisor confided, "There was simply no money to do what we had planned. We had to dump our blueprints and start from the beginning."[14]

From the first day of the Mandela presidency, Mbeki served as more than second in command. As early as 1996 President Mandela told people that his deputy was "the real ruler, the de facto ruler." Behind the scenes, there was tension between the two men about everything from human rights policy to matters of style. They worked to keep their differences under wraps, though, holding to party discipline and the ethos of the ANC, which emphasized the value of collective leadership.

When Mandela stepped down as head of state in 1999, Mbeki was elected in Parliament to replace him. Videotape of Mbeki's inauguration in 1999 reveals a young-looking man with a full head of dark hair dressed in a dark business suit and spruced up in a blue tie flecked in red diamonds. He looks impatient as he waited for Mandela to arrive.

On the hillside above the platform where the new president would take the oath of office were sandstone Roman columns of the Union Buildings framing an open-air amphitheater, which linked two wings of the building designed originally to symbolize the two separable white "races"—descendants of Dutch-speaking inhabitants and offspring of English-speaking immigrants. There were no wings designed to symbolize representation of indigenous, mixed-race, or black people.

When Mandela appeared, cheers erupted. The two men embraced on stage, then stood near the edge of it with hands clasped above their heads. They intended to send a strong message about how modern African leaders should manage handovers of power. Cries that appropriated Mandela's clan name rang out—"*Siyabonga, Madiba!*" (Thank you, Madiba!)—were answered by loud shouts of "*Viva Thabo Mbeki! Viva!*"[15]

In his address to the crowd, the new president used a Setswana saying—*mahube a naka tsa kgomo*—to explain that he believed South Africa had only reached "the dawning of the dawn, when only the tips of the horns of the cattle can be seen etched against the morning sky." Elders like Mandela were part of "a generation that pulled our country out of the abyss," he added. Now, it would be entirely up to the next generation to confront the "brutal past that forever seeks to drag us backwards," he added.[16]

This marked a shift, in tone, from Mandela's 1994 inaugural address, in which the country's first president had pressed for national reconciliation. "Out of the experience of an extraordinary human disaster that lasted too long must be born a society of which all humanity must be proud," he said. ". . . The time for the healing of the wounds has come."[17]

The difference in emphasis was frequently exaggerated, however. It was often wrongly reported that Mandela had included in his inaugural speech two lines in Afrikaans: "*Laat ons die verlede vergeet. Wat verby is is verby.*" (Let's forget the past. What's done is done.) If you google this phrase, the barrage of hits from subsequent reports on the inauguration makes it look as though this message was at the heart of Mandela's remarks. In fact, the comments trace back to a single journalist's account as something the new president said spontaneously after his formal address.[18] The Mandela inauguration speech was no invitation to create the new society by forgetting the depredations of apartheid. The lines have been endlessly repeated, perhaps because *Wat verby is is verby* was the line many South Africans, especially whites, wanted to hear.

The new president's maiden address, in sum, had been an exegesis about the dangers of *forgetting*. Mbeki pointed out that colonial rulers and "African predators" had long entrenched a corrosive ideology that "defined us as sub-human." South Africa had been defined, falsely, he pointed out, "as a European outpost in Africa." He called for "a complex process of formation and renewal" in order to "rediscover and claim the African heritage, especially for the benefit of the young."

As Mbeki finished, the new leader looked funereal. He had listed the country's major problems, acknowledging that millions were still in "humiliating suffering." The president mentioned the Comrades Marathon being run that day, likening the work ahead to a race in which "the road is very long, the inclines very steep and that, at times, what we see as the end is but a mirage."[19]

At the moment of his triumph Mbeki insisted on telling this discomfiting truth: a society celebrated around the world as a miracle looked, to rising numbers of its own inhabitants, like a phantom.

Five years since his inauguration, President Mbeki stepped out of his armored car, looking more diminutive than he had seemed on-screen. He appeared short and slight, an elf among national leaders. The president trudged toward the stage, moving more slowly than you might expect from a man of sixty-one. His skin carried a faint, green tinge. His health, like much of his personal life, was the subject of nonstop gossip by journalists. If rumors were correct, the president would already have been dead of everything from cirrhosis to HIV.

The South African Army Band, which had been entertaining the crowd as people waited for their leader to arrive, swung into an up-tempo version of "Rock around the Clock." Mbeki offered the schoolchildren lined up to greet him a slight nod, slipping past a clutch of local dignitaries. His advisors explained his standoffishness as simple shyness. "He's never going to do the Nelson Mandela, saying, 'Oh, how *are* you? Are you *fine*? How is your daughter *Miriam*?'" one of his advisors explained. "He's not like that. Thabo Mbeki is a very, very private person."[20]

The town's Afrikaner mayor extended a quavering hand, bowing. A longtime member of the National Party, he was dressed in a resplendent colonial-era robe with gold medallions strung across the breast. When the mayor greeted Mbeki, he mentioned rising rates of unemployment in Oudtshoorn as something "quite *worrying*." Depending on how you calculated it, unemployment in South Africa stood between 25 and 40 percent. In rural areas like the Klein Karoo, the rate of unemployment was often far higher.

The president nodded, registering the remark. In candid Internet letters Mbeki wrote to the nation each week, he had recently questioned how the statistics were gathered, implying that perhaps the analysts *measuring* the problem were somehow to blame. It irked him that his critics never seemed to weigh the question of what power he had to create jobs. This was precisely the kind of command-and-control authority over the economy that the ANC had explicitly promised *not* to exercise in the multiparty negotiations that led to the first election.

Mbeki made his way to a large, regal chair, settling into the red silk upholstery with a neutral, faraway expression, his head cocked toward the sky and his fingers steepled like a pastor's. Representatives of the country's new multiracial elite mingled onstage behind his perch; they were stand-ins, in effect, for an estimated two million black South Africans who had made their way past racial barriers into the middle class during the president's first term.

Black entrepreneurs, Indian businesswomen, and coloured civil servants alike were part of an emerging bourgeoisie that owed a measure of their success to the man they had come to honor. As president, Mbeki had pushed through controversial affirmative action and Black Economic Empowerment (BEE) programs designed to prod corporations into promoting blacks and cutting fledgling businessmen from underrepresented groups in as major shareholders. He had taken flack for pursuing these programs—from the Right for interfering with the logic of the market and from the Left because those who benefited often were already well connected politically.

Within the president's line of sight from onstage was a much wider circle of people gathered in the middle of a soccer field. Thousands of poor black women and men were penned behind high cyclone fences out on the field, chanting, "*Viva ANC!*" A line of children dressed in faded shorts and raggedy shirts pulled at the wiry links in the fence and hammered little fists across their hearts. The wind kicked up and there was a buzz at the microphone.

In a report card prepared by one of Mbeki's chief aides, the successes of the ANC government had been memorialized: almost R35 billion in social grants, the equivalent of $5 billion, had been targeted to the country's poor over the past ten years. (The exchange rate for the South African rand fluctuated from a low of less than six rand per dollar to nearly eleven rand per dollar from 2004 to 2011, but mostly gyrated in the range of six to seven rand per dollar.)

The percentage of households with access to clean water had risen from 60 to 85 percent, and the proportion of homes with electricity increased from under a third to more than two-thirds.[21] This was undoubtedly good news for people who had lived with no indoor plumbing and no electric lights, but the vast majority of the blacks were still desperately poor and unemployed. It wasn't at all clear how the country's massive new welfare burden, in which there were more grant recipients than wage earners, could be sustained longer term.

At the microphone, the president's voice sounded crisp and clear. Mbeki shifted masterfully in and out of English and Afrikaans as well as isiXhosa, his mother tongue. In a new country with eleven official languages, the president demonstrated fluency in three of them.

His speech was larded with literary allusions and lyrical poetry. Mbeki mentioned the "creativity and imagination of ancient peoples whose magnificent art has survived for thousands of years," and urged his listeners to think deeply about their own changing identities.

"Those who cross the same winding river . . . are arriving at a new place again," he announced. This seemed like a supple formulation: he intended to lead his people to a *new place again*. The president's opponents often complained that he spoke so incessantly about history because he had nothing new to say; the speech was an indirect answer to them about how an appreciation of history should inform the present. Mbeki pointed out that the plains we were sitting in—referred to as Kannaland by the San peoples—should be appreciated for its history but *re-imagined*, too.

"Ancient Kannaland is once more free," the president said, peering up from his text, his eyebrows bobbling. A few of the people sitting near me looked puzzled: *Once more free?* When exactly had people been free across this terrain in the past? Before blacks migrated south from central Africa? Before Dias sailed into Mossel Bay and killed the first Khoikhoi? Before the Dutch settled? Before the British took control and pushed blacks eastward from these plains?

The president didn't specify a date, but he had invoked the spirit of a people long vanished from the landscape as the true touchstone for the kind of freedom South Africa should emulate. He proclaimed, "I'm proud to be a Free Man of Oudtshoorn." At that, everybody stood and cheered.

The roar of the crowd brought me up short. It reminded me suddenly of all the terrible things that had happened since his inauguration. Back when he was deputy president, from 1994 to 1998, Mbeki had overseen a massive series of military purchases under contracts riddled with kickbacks and payoffs. Then, once an investigation was launched in Parliament, as president he had ordered the probe shut down. So much for Mbeki's promise to provide a model of transparent, incorruptible governance of the kind he had advocated in his poignant call for an "African Renaissance."

In the midst of this scandal over the arms contracts, the president's minister of safety and security had appeared live on television to announce there was a plot afoot against Mbeki by three of his longtime rivals—Cyril Ramaphosa, the man Mandela once favored as his successor, as well as Mathews Phosa and Tokyo Sexwale, two former ANC heavyweights who had gone into business after being run out of the government.

Suddenly, South Africa was perched on the verge of a power struggle similar to the kind that had wrecked so many other emerging democracies. The three men who had been smeared pushed back forcefully in public—Mandela voiced his support for Ramaphosa—and they were exonerated after an investigation; it was an early, important corrective to the destructive palace politics of the Mbeki years.

On AIDS, the new president had failed even more spectacularly. In raising questions about what he called "a particular paradigm" about HIV, he had behaved more like a contrarian university lecturer rather than a head of state in a country at the epicenter of arguably the worst public health disaster in human history. Mbeki began his term in office by questioning the narrative offered by medical researchers to explain why South Africa had been hit so hard by the global tide of HIV infection.

Epidemiologists, the scientists who trace the course of infectious diseases, believed that the human immunodeficiency virus (HIV) had jumped the species barrier from chimpanzees to humans in central Africa in the 1930s through blood-to-blood exchange, perhaps during the slaughter of apes. These researchers followed the trail of evidence to understand how the virus had then spilled into an epidemic of acquired immunodeficiency syndrome (AIDS) in the developed world decades later. The disease primarily affected gay men and intravenous drug users in the United States and elsewhere before eventually tumbling back into Africa, where the illness had spread primarily among heterosexuals.

In its unlikely twists and turns, this wasn't an easy narrative to track or accept. Now, more than 70 percent of people living with the virus that caused AIDS around the globe were in Africa. The burden of dying, too, was unequally shared.

President Mbeki frankly doubted that conventional wisdom about the disease was true. As the illness swept across southern Africa, he posed a series of logical questions: Who gained by this interpretation of the situation and who lost? It was classic dialectical thinking, and reflected the tremendous pressures that would be placed on the new government if the conventional explanation proved true.

Mbeki and other party leaders believed that they risked everything if they turned all of the government's attention toward AIDS alone. Much of the nation's limited financial resources—slated for education, job training, and economic development—could be diverted to the purchase of drugs in the battle against a single disease. (Costs for medications were much higher then.)

In the president's view, large drug conglomerates were the only winners in this scenario. The assertion that HIV was spread through sex, what's more, seemed like a barbed affront meant to reinforce racist tropes about supposedly hypersexualized lives of black people. Even though the epidemic already had been brought under control in places where people had more sex than the average South African, Mbeki was enraged by the idea that so many whites seemed to hold that black Africans would find their fates at the intersection of sex and death. In a document the president circulated among ANC insiders, he argued that the clear meta-message of the HIV "theory" was simple: "Yes, we are sex crazy! Yes, we are diseased!"

Mbeki characterized the struggle against the conventional scientific wisdom on AIDS as part of the historic battle for self-determination. "No longer will the Africans accept as the unalterable truth that they are a dependent people that emanates from and inhabits a continent shrouded in a terrible darkness of destructive superstition, driven and sustained by ignorance, hunger and underdevelopment, and that is victim to a self-inflicted 'disease' called HIV/AIDS," he wrote. "For centuries we have carried the burden of the crimes and falsities of 'scientific' Eurocentrism, its dogmas imposed upon our being as the brands of a definitive, 'universal' truth. Against this, we have, in struggle, made the statement to which we will remain loyal—that we are human and African! Because we are human, we shall no longer permit of control by a colonial mother who claims for herself the right unceasingly to restrain us from reclaiming our dignity. We *shall* overcome!"[22]

The president latched instead onto the theory of a small band of dissident scientists being promoted by a group of South African journalists and others, who questioned the link between HIV and AIDS. Rising in Parliament in 2001, Mbeki asked publicly how it was possible "for a virus to cause a syndrome." Behind closed doors with his colleagues, he spun conspiracy theories, claiming among other things that Western powers and the CIA had conspired to create an AIDS panic in South Africa.[23] Some of his closest aides even believed that he was the target of an assassination plot by pharmaceutical companies or the CIA as a result of the questions he had raised about HIV.

"Totally delusional," Condoleezza Rice remarked some years later when I asked if she had ever been asked about these supposed plots. Rice served during this period as U.S. national security advisor, and was later secretary of state, but received no queries from Mbeki and his top aides, with whom she worked closely. "Why would the U.S. want to do that?" she asked, sighing. "There's no plausible explanation—none—of why it would be in the interest of this country to do something like that."[24]

When the new president's skepticism about the HIV/AIDS connection sparked a chorus of condemnation around the world, Mbeki responded, characteristically his friends and advisors said, by clinging more forcefully to his view. World leaders criticized him publicly, and South African activist Zackie Achmat, of the Treatment Action Campaign, even suggested that a modern holocaust was under way.

The president complained to his advisors that he was being treated like a heretic, and the attacks made him all the more certain that malign forces were out to force South Africa to embrace the interests of pharmaceutical companies. His advisors also worried, in turn, about a sense of "despondency" swamping the country, in which mass panic "could result in people being burnt at the stake," presidential advisor Joel Netshitenzhe told me.[25]

Eventually, the president stopped talking about AIDS publicly, having bowed in the end to the entreaties of Netshitenzhe and Nkosazana Dlamini-Zuma, then minister of international affairs. In the end, he silenced himself rather than acknowledge there had not been merit to his argument in the first place. In the run-up to the 2004 election campaign, the national government finally started distributing antiretroviral medications in public health clinics, but the lack of leadership at the top continued to hobble the entire anti-AIDS campaign.

President Mbeki's handling of the pandemic, his involvement in the arms deals, and his dithering over the dictatorial rule of Robert Mugabe in neighboring Zimbabwe were his biggest blunders. The consequences of this trio of catastrophes would reverberate, politically and culturally, for generations.

❖

The country was twelve years into the AIDS pandemic, but on the stage at Oudtshoorn, Mbeki said nothing to the crowd about the plague that had claimed two million South Africans. There was no mention of the current massive rollout of medications in hospitals and clinics. The president provided no information about how the estimated half a million people already in late stages of the disease could get tested, treated, and find appropriate care. Mbeki didn't even advise the youngsters standing in front of him on the soccer field how they could protect themselves.

Instead, he referred to a poem, *"Ek Ken 'n Plek,"* written by André Boezak, a noted local writer. *"Ek ken 'n plek van ooptes / wat ruimte maak vir ons gan,"* it read; *"vir al ons vele foute, ons hartser / en ons pret / 'n dordroë vlakkeland / wat liefhet sonder vrees."* Mbeki recited a version translated from the Afrikaans:

> *I know a wide open place*
> *with so much space*
> *it draws our mistakes,*
> *our sorrows and fun*
> *into its dry flatland*
> *embrace which loves without fear*
> *and holds us dear.*

None of the young people standing in the field was free to leave without fear, however. When he was finished, the president accepted a pair of handsome ostrich-hide shoes and a gigantic, disturbing, dark portrait of a moonless night. He set off on a walkabout in a bubble of bodyguards two rows thick. At the C.P. Nel Museum, the president cocked his head through a long talk about the history of the ostrich from the beginning of time. Once free of this obligation, he nearly galloped back to his motorcade. Mbeki turned, with a forced smile, before sliding back inside his car.

Later that day the president would tell one of his aides that the trip to Oudtshoorn had been among the happiest days of his presidency. The trip, he reported, had convinced him, through the reception he had received from Afrikaans-speaking whites, that they finally accepted him as their leader.[26] It was obvious, from outside the bubble that heads of state travel in, that he hadn't had an honest conversation with anybody all day.

When the motorcade sped off, I strolled past Die Kolonie Restaurant, a clean, airy place with nice curtains in the window and a sign posted offering the best ostrich steaks in town. Throngs of white people streamed past for the opening acts of the cultural festival, having skipped the president's appearance.

In front of Die Kolonie I fell into conversation with two lean fellows dressed in long shorts and buttoned-up shirts. They had been only eleven years old when South Africa went through its transformative change, and in the following week they would cast their first votes in a national election. The young men volunteered that they thought of Nelson Mandela as a great president; they couldn't stand his successor, though.

"It's not racial. But I would never vote for the ANC," Ivan van Rensburg explained. He argued that the government had embarked on a massive home-building program; those houses had gone largely to blacks. The outcome, which stemmed from the fact that the vast majority of homeless people were black, still rubbed him the wrong way. He thought the remedy for a race-based system of oppression looked quite race-based. "I don't remember apartheid!" he cried. "We are being punished for something our forefathers did!"

The two friends had enrolled in engineering courses at a publicly financed university but assumed they would be forced to look for jobs outside the country when they graduated. When I asked about their apparent assumption that they would be discriminated against if they stayed at home, it turned out that the feeling was based only on a general feeling that blacks now had preference in hiring. When I pressed them to detail instances of antiwhite discrimination they had actually experienced, both shook their heads. It hadn't happened, but they felt threatened nevertheless.

When I suggested that perhaps the lack of opportunity was a *generational*, and not a racial, grievance—part of a global challenge in which young people everywhere were getting the short end of the deal—they nodded again. This wasn't something they could imagine discussing with black classmates, though.

"We mingle" across racial lines, "but it's not quite social yet," François Boseq, the other young man, noted. "It's getting better, though. Maybe for our children it will be like in the United States." His friend reared back, nearly shouting, "I don't think it will get better soon. We don't know what's going to happen in this country yet!"

On the drive out of town, I came across a herd of ostrich, a gaggle of ridiculous-looking puffs of feathers on skinny legs skittering off at the sound of a backfiring engine. Back on the road, rows of flimsy tin roofs in ramshackle informal settlements popped up like stands of stunted trees. Low rolling hills broke through to an open view of the Indian Ocean at Mossel Bay, the upscale white town where Dias once answered a flurry of stones with a deadly arrow.

The comparison I reflexively drew—between the shacks and seaside villas—felt quite self-serving, though. Here, after all, was the predictable lament of a visitor in a developing country, allowed to behave as if he were exempt from the conditions he was describing.

The rest of us, of course, were equally embedded in the global system that yielded such stark contrasts. Constraints under which the fledgling democracy operated were imposed as much by decision-makers in Bonn, Geneva, London, Washington, D.C., and Beijing as by those at Union Buildings in Pretoria. The struggle to align democratic governance with economic equity was not just a challenge for the ANC government and the people of South Africa, then, but was instead the central dilemma for the rest of us in a globalizing world.

Hours later, as twilight fell on the outskirts of Cape Town, I drove down a series of harrowing switchbacks on the highway that leads back into town. I watched the lights coming on in the city below, and considered the vans stuffed full of families migrating from the Eastern Cape as they streamed past. The folks inside the vans, and loading into trucks and buses, were part of a swirling mass of people still on the move across the country. Having been wedged for generations inside the constrained boundaries of the so-called black homelands, they were utterly unbound now, looking for liberty somewhere down the road.

Trucks filled with supplies huffed into low gear, engines whining. A string of mini-buses careened into the oncoming lanes to pass me. They jammed ahead, helter-skelter, with horns blaring as the drivers played chicken with cars coming at them from the opposite direction. Then the drivers sped on in blasts of black exhaust, headed toward the country's Mother City, lit up in the distance like Oz.

2.

The Thief

A few months before President Mbeki swept through ostrich-ranching country to accept his honor from the burghers of Oudtshoorn, a young teenager hitched a ride from the Cape Flats into the city. He was part of the churn of people, like the crowds I had seen pouring into Cape Town on my way back from Klein Karoo, relentlessly on the move in search for the better life that had been promised by the ANC. His name was Jonathan Persens, and he was of mixed-race parentage, classified as *coloured* under apartheid categories. He had full lips, thick dark eyebrows, and a prominent, flattened nose.

Jonathan was small boned and angular, and he jutted his breast forward like a boxer anticipating insults. His broad forehead and high cheekbones lent his face an impression of ferocity. When he smiled, his teeth flashed brilliantly, which allowed a fleeting glimpse of the child he might have become had history treated him differently.

The boy was just fourteen years old when he hitchhiked into Cape Town the first time, in late 2003. He was six years younger than the two white young men I had met in the Klein Karoo, but unlike them he had never attended a regular public school and could not read or write.

Jonathan had arrived in Cape Town dreaming that he would become a

famous rugby player. It hadn't registered with him that sports, like everything else in South African society, was race coded. The odds for a future in
rugby were not good for a slight, uneducated coloured boy on the run.
Three years later, in a series of conversations and interviews, we would discuss at length what drove Jonathan to the streets in the first place. In the
intervening years I met hundreds of other young men and women who
found themselves, like him, utterly adrift in the new South Africa.

On the eight-hour drive back from Oudtshoorn I had been trying
to imagine what the country looked like from President Mbeki's point
of view—like a massive collection of headaches. Large swaths of the
country's population had been left out of postliberation benefits. The
new world economic order, characterized most of all by low barriers to
trade, limits on government spending, and unmediated markets, didn't
leave much maneuvering room for political leaders in any one country
who were out to ameliorate historic patterns of injustice.

On my return to the city, I had decided to turn this picture upside
down and consider the situation from the point of view of those homeless kids on the *bottom*. The trace effects of apartheid for them were visible on the streets where the boys begged for food. Seventy-six percent of
black children in South Africa lived in poverty at the time; the compa-
rable proportion of white children living in penury was 2.8 percent.

Nationally, the proportion of children living in homes with at least
one employed grownup had actually *fallen* during Mbeki's first term.
Here was the rub in President Mbeki's claim of leading a progressive
government. As in much of the developing world, South Africa's population was skewed toward the young; half of the country's people were now
twenty-four years old or younger.

There was an important global point embedded in such statistics. If
you wanted to get a preview of what the world might look like in the
future, it was wise to look to the *south*. That was where the bulk of the
world's young people lived. By the middle of the decade, of the 1.5 billion
young people on the planet 1.3 billion lived in developing countries. Over

all, nearly 70 percent of the world's population inhabited land between the Tropic of Cancer and the Tropic of Capricorn. In the developed north, people were aging, whiter, and richer; the population in the developing south was younger, darker, poorer—and increasingly frustrated.

Here, writ large, was worldwide representation of the dynamic that would shape our collective future: the bulge in the population of young people in southern Africa provided the country's leaders with an urgent sort of test. There was a "window of opportunity" for beneficial development in countries like South Africa—but only if there was adequate investment in education and job creation for the young.

This was the argument put forward by demographers in a study for the World Bank. They warned that this window would slam shut in another two decades. The Baby Boom would be followed by an inevitable Baby Bust,[1] and if the right investments were not made in education there would be hell to pay.

Potential consequences were clear from an examination of historic trends elsewhere: Where national governments had designed effective programs for education and skills training when the youth population billowed—as had happened in East Asia in the 1970s—bursts of economic growth resulted.

What the World Bank report called a "demographic dividend" only accrued in countries where leaders figured out how to cash in on it. Otherwise, rising numbers of alienated young people reacted with what analysts euphemistically called "misaligned expectations and social unrest." In developing countries like South Africa, aspirations of this giant mass of youth would either fuel the creation of viable new societies or tear them apart.

When I first met Jonathan in 2007, three years after he had hitchhiked to Cape Town, it seemed to me that he could help me understand how things looked at the bottom. I met him through a social worker whom I had told of my interest in getting to know the population of homeless street children. Gerald Jacobs was the outreach worker at an organization called Homestead, and he recently had talked Jonathan and a group of his friends into coming off the street.

Jonathan was born as apartheid was falling apart, in 1989, and so his existence traced the arc of efforts to create a new kind of country. He had been raised in a far-flung town called Atlantis—not the mythical Atlantis, of course, but rather the flat, dusty settlement north of Cape Town to which nonwhites were "removed" during the apartheid years.

Coloured people and blacks had been sent out of the city proper to windswept, undesirable quarters in the flats, where land was unproductive and there was no industry. It was little surprise that racially delineated, poverty-producing towns of this sort spawned enormous dysfunction, including sky-high levels of alcohol abuse, drug addiction, and violent crime.

We met on a cold and drizzling summer morning at the curb outside a carpentry workshop run by the Salesian Brothers, a Catholic charity. The workshop, on Riebeek Street, was located half a block from the Rolls-Royce dealership just across the street from a gay disco and a shopping mall filled with fine restaurants.

My first impression, when Jonathan finally appeared, was of how painfully gaunt he looked, and how short for a boy of eighteen. He was wiry, seemingly made up of all elbows and knees. He felt famished, naturally, so I took him to a grill across the road.

By crossing the street, we passed an invisible boundary between one universe—of the marginalized—and the parallel world of the vibey, upbeat new South Africa unfolding before our eyes from a table inside the mall. We ordered hamburgers, and considered one another. Perched at the edge of his chair, he dug into the meal, then put it down and forced himself to chew more slowly, determined not to sully his dignity by wolfing the burger down.

In the beginning, Jonathan let me do all the talking. During our initial meeting, he rarely looked at me directly, and answered most of my questions by raising his thick black eyebrows and issuing monosyllabic replies. "*Mebbe*" was his most common response.

By the middle of the meal, though, he opened up a little more. His early upbringing had been quite *hectic*, he offered. He had been told that his father was dead from AIDS. A drug-dealing stepfather had used the boy as a runner in his business, Jonathan told me. When he was only six years old, his mother had been arrested and sent to prison. The sequence wasn't clear, the dates were imprecise, and soon enough I would find out how difficult it would be to verify the facts.

He said that his sisters were parceled out to relatives in the aftermath of the sentencing of his mother to prison. Jonathan was the only child consigned to a state home. When I asked him why he was sent away to a state home instead of being taken in by foster parents, he shrugged his bony shoulders. "Because I was very *rude*," he replied, as if bad manners were the root of all his troubles.[2]

The children's home where Jonathan was sent hadn't seemed like a bad place, as he recalled it. In fact, there was an Afrikaans-speaking white instructor in shop class who boosted his self-esteem by praising his creativity in wood shop. He still remembered with precision the lilt in that man's voice when he had said that Jonathan was quite *clever*.

In the end, though, Jonathan had chafed under the rules of the institution. Everything was so rigidly controlled—when he woke, when he ate, when he went to bed—and he longed to reconnect with his mother and sisters. One afternoon, Jonathan simply walked away from the home, stuck his thumb out at the edge of the highway, and pitched himself into the bed of a pickup truck whose driver pulled over for him.

Jonathan remembered how it had felt to lean into the wind and let all his troubles get swept away. It felt glorious to be on the run. He figured that he would be able to track down his mother and sisters and manage somehow to stitch their little family back together. As the truck neared the outskirts of Atlantis, though, Jonathan realized that he had nothing to offer his sisters yet—no money, no gifts, no thought-out plan for their future. So he had tapped on the window of the cab, motioning the driver to continue on.

Cape Town had presented itself like in a stirring dream: the lights, the wide paved streets, buses, taxis, and music blaring everywhere, not to mention the ocean and all those fashionable people. Compared to Atlantis, it looked like a complete paradise. During his first few nights in the city, Jonathan slept under a large acacia tree near a major intersection. He remembered dozing, then blinking awake to the sound of sleek cars streaming by. A few days later, he happened across an acquaintance from Atlantis, a boy who had also escaped from the children's home. They found a better spot for sleeping, sheltered from the rain, in a ditch beneath a highway.

Jonathan recalled how gloriously optimistic he had felt while living in the ditch. There were no grownups around telling him what to eat, what to do, how to behave, or when to turn the lights out. There were no lights, but that seemed a small price to pay.

As he described the details of his life, I was reminded of the central character in a novel I had been reading—*Thirteen Cents*, by Sello Duiker. Duiker was a rare talent who had won wide notice in 2001 for his debut novel, *Thirteen Cents*, a searing portrait of a deracinated teenager also living beneath a bridge in Cape Town.

The key character in the novel, named Azure after his light skin and blue eyes, is a battered teenager beaten and raped by gangsters partly because they find his indeterminate identity so upsetting. "That's why people have beat you up all your life," a friend tells the young character as he's recovering from a brutal thrashing. "They think you are not black enough."[3] Despite the hardships, Azure learns to adore his adopted city: "The air is warm and smells sweet from all the flowers in the garden. It's my birthday. I'm thirteen. Grow up. Fast," he says.

I was on the verge of mentioning the novel to Jonathan and offering to buy him a copy when I hesitated. If I explained the plot, I figured he would ask me about the author, who after graduating from Rhodes University and launching a brilliant literary career had killed himself. It seemed to me that Jonathan's life was overstuffed already with tragic inflection points, so I kept the sad story of Azure and Duiker to myself.

Not long after Jonathan arrived in Cape Town in late 2003, one of the boys who also slept in the ditch beneath the freeway showed him how to work the streets for cash. When he told me this, he held an index finger up, like a teacher delivering a lesson. "Then he did learn me what I should do," he said softly, referring to his friend. "We did go and *skarrel*." (*Skarrel* is an Afrikaans word that means to hustle.)

Jonathan demonstrated how he had held out his hands to tourists passing by. He looked terribly sad, wobbling his head back and forth as though he might perish on the spot. Clutching at his belly, he used a small, reedy, childish voice to cry, "Don't you have some little small change for my *stomach*?" He and the other boys had roamed around town flush with the coins and bills they took in, buying loaves of bread and roasted chickens.

At first, Jonathan loved his new routine. Sometimes there were wonderful surprises, like on the night when "a whitey, a woman" had handed him fifty rand (a little over eight dollars) outside the gas station on Annandale Street. "She drived a BMW—like a small C4. She was drunk a little bit. She did open her wallet and give it to me," he reported, eyebrows raised.

When people unexpectedly opened their wallets it seemed to him astounding to see how much money was tucked away inside. Jonathan thought of it as perfectly good money simply trapped in there, accomplishing nothing for nobody and almost begging for release. "We were just laughing, smiling, *so* happy," he recalled. "Now we all put the money together. I did think, 'Now we're going to eat! And smoke cigarettes and eat some more.'"

A few older boys had a different idea. They led the younger ones back to the center of the city and tracked down a merchant willing to sell them glue. "Yeah—and that time I did learn to smoke it," he reported. Jonathan turned his profile toward me, narrowing his eyes.

"So, what was it like to take glue the first time?" I asked. Gerald Jacobs had told me already that he thought glue served "like a chemical blanket" for kids out in the cold.

Jonathan squinted, looking skyward. "It's like . . . you *see* a lot of stuff," he said. "When the moon is there . . . ," he pointed at the sky— "N'eh, you smoke on the moon. Then the moon will come close to you. Then you will run!"

The boys had run themselves breathless, flat out in front of the moon, to the steps of St. George's Cathedral. It was the majestic colonial church in the center of Cape Town, around the corner from the old Slave Lodge, where former archbishop Desmond Tutu famously used to denounce the old apartheid order. Just across the way was the colonial mansion called Tuynhuys, where President Mbeki worked when he was in town.

Jonathan had felt blissfully high on the steps of the cathedral that night. It seemed like he and his friends—who felt like his new family— could scratch out a fine existence in this sphere that ran beneath and beyond the world inhabited by proper Capetonians. In his new world, regular inhabitants of the city were like spectral figures, strutting down the sidewalks and floating away in the mist.

He forgot all his worries in the giddy fuzz of the glue. When the boys returned to their ditch, they would sit together, telling stories long into the night. "We will see some lights coming down from the sky— beautiful lights—and like you will see Pope Pius," he recalled. Jonathan inhaled deeply, showing me how the huffing had calmed his normally shallow breathing. These were long, slow, welcome draughts. "I promise you," he said, "you will see the *Pope*."

Only a short drive from Long Street lay a separate jet stream in the cosmos. Kirstenbosch National Botanical Garden, one of the most beautiful spots in the world, nestled across more than thirteen hundred acres in a gorgeous glade. Rolling, neon-green lawns gave way to a breath-taking view of Table Mountain.

At the end of a long and shocking week, I took a cab out to the gardens for a respite. It was dusk on a crisp Sunday afternoon in autumn, and the Soweto String Quartet was just back from a successful international tour. The quartet was scheduled to perform in the gardens as a kind of homecoming gift for local fans.

A stand of Moreton Bay fig trees held up the sky on one side of the walkway. A painterly hillside on the other side was heavily planted in geraniums. King Proteus preened. People poured off the walkways, wedging themselves beside one another on the lawn. Nearly everyone was dressed stylishly, with plenty of Diesel jeans and Benetton shirts in the mix.

Along the edges of the gardens, Jan van Riebeeck, the Dutch explorer who established a permanent station for seafarers here in the seventeenth century, planted a wild almond hedge to ward off local Khoi pastoralists and San hunters.[4] Early settlers, at one point, envisioned dredging a gigantic moat to separate themselves from indigenous peoples, part of a long, sorry pattern of attempting to be *in* Africa but not *of* it.

Here in the garden, class trumped the old divisions. The poor were warded off by the entry fees. Black students were goofing around with white friends from the University of Cape Town. Coloured, or mixed-race, parents were chasing after young children. Even the food was ecumenical: A white couple pulled deli sandwiches out of paper sacks, setting themselves down next to an Indian woman breaking out the curry.

Right behind me two men unpacked their pasta salads, and I assumed they were brothers until they began to spoon. No one missed a beat or took a second look, a reminder that for all of the homophobia evident in the country, the South African Constitution was the only one in the world that explicitly prohibited discrimination against lesbians and gay men.

The scene unfolding before us seemed like an advertisement for the country's tourism board, or like stepping into a segment on *Oprah* about the new South Africa. The opening act was a racially mixed group from the university. They swept people to their feet with a fusion of global pop and *kwaito* rhythms. The lyrics stitched English together between snatches of isiXhosa and Afrikaans, the most common languages, respectively, of blacks and coloured people in the Western Cape. Sentences started off in one language, careened into the next, and finished in a third.

This is what it felt like to enter a truly multicultural and multilingual zone, where everything was all mixed up in the ecumenical way that racist colonists and apartheid advocates always had feared most. "Isn't it *something*?" a coloured woman my age shouted, shaking her fanny and twirling. "It's something *new*."

When the youngsters packed up their instruments, the Soweto String Quartet filed in. They launched right away into the first song: "Mbayi Mbayi," which was a haunting number that memorialized the depredations of apartheid. The song had an upbeat rhythm, with stirring strings; it told the story, though, of the destruction of Sophiatown in the 1950s.

Sophiatown was the vibrant township on the outskirts of Johannesburg, which in many ways was a model for the mixed stew of cross-cultural experience that the new South Africa was supposed to emulate. In Cape Town, too, there was a neighborhood called District Six, from which people also had been removed—to Khayelitsha, Mitchells Plain, and, farther out, Atlantis, Jonathan's home.

Under apartheid, Sophiatown was destroyed and its residents were *removed* to Soweto. "We will shoot them with our cannons," the lyrics said. This crowd was in no warlike mood, though. It was an exuberant explosion. People rose spontaneously and joined hands, creating a long, vibrating line of upraised hands and swinging hips that threaded between blankets all across the vast lawn.

On evenings like this one, it felt clear what kind of change had already taken place, for some middle-class South Africans at least. There was an intimation of the astonishing transformation that might still be possible for larger numbers of their countrymen.

This experience was a needed corrective to much of the reporting that I had been doing in my initial weeks in the country. For decades, South Africans had been held up in an iconic way, as models for the oppressed, as noble rebels, or avatars of reconciliation and forgiveness. Real people don't behave like ideological formulas, of course. They have more complicated lives.

What I had been striving to gather was an un-idealized, but also anti-cynical, portrait. The teenagers dancing around me were around Jonathan's age. It seemed to me that their pleasures deserved as much mention as the troubles he had experienced.

A scholarly study of young people in Cape Town, done in the middle of the decade, had alerted me to the point: "The stories of most South African children and adolescents are not stories of 'failure' or of a 'descent' into marginality," the authors cautioned. "They are the opposite: stories of creativity and at least partial success in tackling challenges."[5]

In the circles of students like those at the concert, and in the burgeoning working class, there were plenty of prosaic stories of creative coping. Couples danced, the concert went on, and I let the music wash over me. For millions of citizens in the new South Africa, I realized, there had been considerable progress in the past ten years. They were as concerned as anybody about whether these advances could be sustained.

Perhaps the tenor and uplift from that idyllic afternoon left such a deep imprint because of an experience I had two months later, when I moved to Johannesburg for several months. I was invited one afternoon to a *braai*, a traditional barbeque, in an upscale suburban home in a northern suburb of the city, Bryanston.

I was accustomed to the simple grid of Chicago, and found the way Johannesburg's roads were organized like a vast wagon wheel of intersecting ovals difficult to navigate. I arrived a little late. New complexes were springing up in a blizzard of construction as whites retreated northward from the slowly integrating neighborhoods closer to the city center.

Past security guards, through an iron-mesh gate, I found the comfortable villa and the family, waiting on me for supper. The motif resembled winter homes in Palm Springs. The place had stucco walls, an open floor plan, a sturdy tile roof, and a large sliding glass door leading to a tidy garden. On the table inside the house, barbequed grilled steak and chicken were set alongside grandma's *bobotie*, a traditional dish of savory meat that combines Dutch and Malay influences.

The guests had been told a journalist was coming to supper, so I encountered a tone of grievance right from the start. Other whites I had met already had complained at great length that whites were unfairly depicted by outside observers while ANC stalwarts were portrayed as angelic figures. Why was it, they asked, that white journalists from America seemed so *antiwhite*? The regular repetition of this complaint brought me up short, for I had to admit to myself that I had little interest in the perspective of the white minority. What had captivated me far more, from the start, were the transformational changes in circumstances for some blacks and coloured people.

One young woman sitting directly across the table from me hunched over her salad, seemingly having read my mind. She spoke up, then, about how difficult it had been for her, as a young white woman in the mid-1990s, to come to terms with the radical changes under way in the country. "We used to know who we were by putting ourselves on one side of the line or the other," she said. "You knew that you were either *Afrikaner* or *English*, that was all."

Here it was, the frank admission that for much of her earlier life the woman hadn't really considered the existence of 90 percent of the population. The long, bitter divisions between descendants of English-speaking colonizers, and Dutch-speaking immigrants, had loomed far larger in her imagination.

She fiddled with her napkin. "It never occurred to me to wonder where black people lived or how they were treated," she confessed, wincing at how she knew this would sound. "The idea that our servants had a whole other life in the townships—I never gave it a single thought."

Now that black people had seized center stage in national political life, it was quite disorienting for her to locate herself as a white citizen in the new dispensation. Before, the aspirations of blacks seemed utterly remote, a little like the unseen bulk of our universe—90 percent of it made up of dark matter cosmologists don't fully understand.

In this respect, there hadn't been much change. She was in her mid-thirties, but she felt she didn't understand blacks—how they saw things and what they wanted to achieve—any better now than before. President Mbeki was a prime example. Where did he get his odd ideas about AIDS?

An argument broke out between the woman's aunt and a friend of hers who was her contemporary, which meant that both were born before 1948, when the National Party had won that pivotal election. (Formal apartheid followed in the late 1940s and through the 1950s.) With a slight lift of her narrow shoulders, the woman's aunt said, "A lot has changed for the better." Her friend felt less sure. "A big part of it just comes down to *hygiene*," she argued, wrinkling her English nose. "They just used to stink." When she registered my look and took a slight elbow from her niece, she shifted course. "But in that regard I'd have to say they've *improved* 101 percent."

In a room full of people, including several white liberals who had voted for the ANC in two national elections, no one felt called to correct her. No one made the point, even gently, that the architecture of privilege virtually ensured that blacks traveling long distances in hot buses, or on foot, in order to get work, might not always reach her elevated standards in grooming.

Stories about crime filled lapses in the conversation. A carjacking would be mentioned, the *bobotie* complimented. An armed invasion of someone's home was reported, and tomato sauce requested. News of the murder of a friend earned hushed tones, but then it was on to news of cricket games. Details of a rape overlapped offers of dessert.

Nobody made explicit, at least in front of me, the obvious racial connotation: if people were assaulted or robbed, there was a high likelihood that the face of the perpetrator would be black. Black people were statistically twice as likely to be assaulted as whites, of course, but the whites in the room experienced the ongoing crime wave as though it was a siege directed primarily at *them*.

Property theft was something understandable, if unpleasant. Family members described the taking of things by robbers as something explained by the fact that the thieves were desperate because they had nothing. Yet, it seemed to them as though crime rates, and the violence that came with crime in South Africa, had tipped into something more sinister.

People huddled around the table talking about black people, by proxy, as if they thought an undeclared race war was under way—a race-based revolution by other means, conducted through armed robbery, carjacking, rape, and murder. While security had always been tight, the systems of alarms and summoning private cops were increasingly elaborate. Walls around the houses were built ever higher. Panic alarms, portable black gadgets with actual red buttons that set off remote signals, were strung like amulets on chains around people's necks. You found women cooking in the kitchen, and men drinking beer in the living room, with these buttons at their breasts.

Whites who had been shut off from black South Africans under apartheid paid an ever-higher premium now to get farther away. They locked themselves up in gated, still-segregated neighborhoods, as if they were the prisoners of the liberated country, and they had decided to become their own jailers.

For decades, apartheid leaders had warned white constituents of the Black Threat and the Red Menace, twin avatars of apocalypse. With the unraveling of the Soviet Union, there was only one threat left. The throngs of desperate boys, like Jonathan, were the new faces of the *swaart gevaar.*

"If we see you, we will follow you," Jonathan remarked to me, in a distinctly cheerful tone. The second time we got together, I asked him to spell out what had happened to him in the years spent living off the streets. He explained the logical steps in his eventual graduation, from begging to something more insidious.

Getting high night after night had broken something loose in him, he recalled. Jonathan mentioned how quickly he had forgotten his initial ambition to become a rugby player. He and his new friends were too busy working during the daytime, raising enough cash to get high every night. The addictive need for money, fueled by the drugs that money brought, led the boys down a well-worn path, from harmless begging to aggressive *skarreling* and, from there, to purse snatching.

Cape Town was so full of easy marks, and it seemed foolish, to him, not to take advantage of the situation. After several muggings, the boys pooled their money to purchase a set of knives. Jonathan picked out a medium-sized blade, wanting nothing showy or too threatening. He also braced himself for the first time he would have to use it.

There followed another series of firsts: the first time he held someone down so other boys could beat him; the first time he stuck a knife into another man's body; the first time a victim screeched in a way that reverberated in his memory. At first, robbing "was fun, just a game," he told me. When he stabbed someone, "it felt good," he went on. The knife had glided in with remarkable ease.

Once the boys saw what could be accomplished with their set of little knives, they jacked up their ambitions. Increasingly violent robberies resulted in markedly larger scores. In telling me about these robberies,

Jonathan emphasized that he never jabbed for the torso or intended to kill anyone, and he made quick slashing gestures at my arms and shoulders to show me that the attack was workmanlike and restrained.

When he told me all this, we were talking in a large dormitory room in a shelter for boys, where he was staying temporarily. It was chilly, in the middle of winter. When Jonathan fell silent, overtaken by moodiness, you could hear the wind wheezing past the window frames.

Haltingly, he ventured on. Jonathan said that things had turned sour between him and the other young thugs one night when they invaded the coastal walk in the beach town of Muizenberg, a half hour's drive over on the Indian Ocean side of the peninsula.

"It was two guys and two womens," he recalled. "We did walk behind them and rob." This episode, unlike the others, had felt "not so good," Jonathan confessed. "Because there was so much stabbing," he added, averting his glance. "I was too scared to stab."

Two couples targeted by the boys were coloured people, and this elemental fact had pricked at his conscience. He had placed himself in the brown man's shoes. I asked, What if the guys had been his cousins, what if the women had been his sisters? Jonathan told me that he wrestled with his conscience over this question all the time. When the boys were finished with each crime, he would regularly promise himself never to do it again. He was a little like an alcoholic after a bender, promising to get treatment only while the hangover raged. But it was also dangerous for him to try to back out of the gang, he pointed out. If he pulled away from the other boys, Jonathan felt the others might kill him because of what he knew.

He slipped, almost effortlessly, into the identity of a full-fledged gangster. In speaking of the robberies, Jonathan had the disconcerting habit of relaying his tales in second person, as if he was among the attackers still and I was one of the targets. "But I did throw stones on you . . . ," he said, before falling silent. "They stab, they just stab." He demonstrated, with thrusts at my thighs, and neck and chest, how awful it must have been.

After their biggest heist, the boys made off with cash and jewelry. All of a sudden, they had money for nice clothes and plenty of real dope. There would be no more low-class glue, but rather ganja—marijuana—and other drugs instead. The boys could afford to go to restaurants and clubs, and buy plenty of booze, having crossed over the invisible line to join other upwardly mobile highfliers in the new country.

Within a few months the boys were quite expert in staking out their marks. They would keep watch outside the homes of wealthy people, catching their owners in the yards or inside the thresholds before they had a chance to set their fancy alarms. The boys were especially keen to invade properties where yards looked well tended and houses were recently painted. They took these as signs that there would be lots of cash inside.

"If we see you are alone, we just follow you in," Jonathan told me. "If you have a lot of money, we force you to turn it over to us. If you don't want to, we will let you feel the pain." This expression—"we will let you feel the pain"—made an impression on me. It replayed, in a loop in my mind, whenever I heard stories about excessively violent thefts.

After another heist in 2005, the boys visited the owner of an illegal gun shop. The stakes were now raised. "Guns everywhere," Jonathan recalled, waving his hand to show how they had been hanging from the ceiling and all along the walls. He bought a small revolver with spinning barrels. Two packets of bullets came with the purchase.

South African criminologist Antony Altbeker described the subculture Jonathan had slipped into so easily. "Violence has become a cultural phenomenon," the author noted, in his book *A Country at War with Itself.* "It is a form of behaviour driven by its own logic, and attractive in its own right, one that is, for a significant minority, an expression of their selfhood, something towards which young men are drawn by the 'enticement, or incitement, of class and peer-group prestige.'"[6]

Like in everything else, there were thoroughly intertwined implications based on class and race. The logic of Jonathan's business interests was clear: follow the money and take it; and most of the money, by the way, was in the hands of whites. Whites—powerful, segregated, money-eyed, arrogant, selfish racists who shared so little and had so much—seemed to think they could *remove* themselves from danger. Ultimately, of course, there was no sure protection behind those supposedly secure walls against a distinctly violent society, where 220,000 murders had taken place since the dawning of democracy.[7] In the years between 1994 and 2004, more than one hundred thousand people were killed in gun-related violence in South Africa, and the proliferation of firearms, and casual acceptance of violence, fueled the carnage.[8]

In the late stages of apartheid, the ANC had called on South Africans to make the country *ungovernable*. Jonathan and his friends, one generation later, were rebels without a cause. No schools had been set up to provide them a context for channeling their rebellious energies to larger, more socially useful purposes. There was no mass national campaign under way to try taming the murderous rage alive in so many youngsters.

I was thinking about this aspect of the country's challenge one afternoon when Jonathan and I were talking. I mentioned that there had been a mass mobilization around the world in the 1970s and 1980s to help South Africans free themselves from the white regime. He knit his thick eyebrows together. "Why did those people do it?" he asked. It seemed inconceivable to him that people way across the ocean would have taken notice of what was happening at the tip of Africa.

A few moments later, I asked him how the political liberation in 1994 had affected him and his family. "Do I feel *free* now?" he said, repeating the question I asked every young person I met. "I'm not *free*!" He added, by way of example, his certainty that if he tried to return to his home community of Atlantis that afternoon he would be murdered by nightfall. This assertion, of course, led to a series of new questions from me about his life back home.

The second example of his lack of freedom was this: he felt sure that if he and his friends marched into any of the good public schools in Cape Town, the ones where so many white children were enrolled, in order to demand they should be educated alongside the whites, "they would shoot us!" He carried a heavy sense of grievance and a firm belief that people like him remained under siege from the remote, overprivileged whites and the police who served their interests.

This was a deep-seated problem in civic life that former archbishop Desmond Tutu periodically raised in his public talks. Archbishop Tutu had just arrived back in Cape Town after a stint of teaching and speaking engagements abroad. I told Jonathan about a recent speech of Tutu's about the challenges of poverty and homelessness.

He squinted, trying to place the person. "You know, he used to preach in that cathedral where you and the other boys smoked glue *on the moon* that first time," I prompted him. Jonathan perked up, then, because he knew the archbishop as a heroic figure. He was "that church guy with the funny laugh," he said. Yes, I replied: Tutu had played a critical role in the fight against apartheid, and he also was a critic of President Mbeki, over everything from the Truth and Reconciliation Commission Report to his policy on HIV.

When I mentioned that I had spent time shadowing the president as he traveled around the Western Cape, Jonathan cocked his head, as if rattled. "President?" he asked. As it turned out, Jonathan had no idea who the guy was in all those posters plastered on utility poles up and down the street back in 2004.

He challenged me, then, in a rather stern voice: "Isn't Mandela still president?" I laughed, thinking he meant to make a joke. He scowled at me, because he took insults easily. He pointed out that everybody still called the founder of the country *President* Mandela.

Then it struck me: he thought Mandela must still be the leader of the country because the promises made by the Old Man were yet unfulfilled. Here, too, was a symptom of the failure by President Mbeki to connect

with his people: one of the boys on whose fate the new president was riding had no understanding of the president's many efforts on his behalf—
or his background and history, or his intentions as a leader. Jonathan
didn't know that Thabo Mbeki existed. Even if his life were at stake, he
would not have been able to repeat the current president's name.

3.

The Rival

The Army Band was marching again. The band looked even more impressive than it had weeks before when its members rolled into "Rock around the Clock" as musical accompaniment to President Mbeki's arrival in the Klein Karoo. This time the band played a martial tune and marched through the center of Cape Town while members of the country's new elite trailed up a blood-red carpet laid over cobblestones toward the majestic colonial columns of Parliament.

It was April 23, 2004, ten years since the election of Nelson Mandela. Jacob Gedleyihlekisa Zuma, the country's deputy president, swept past behind President Mbeki. Zuma was the former chief of intelligence of the ANC's military wing and the president's longtime comrade. For the past five years he had served as the voice of the executive in Parliament by virtue of his role as deputy president.

Unbeknownst to the public, tensions between the two top leaders had been steadily building behind the scenes. Mbeki was limited by the Constitution to two terms as head of state and his biggest critics were lining up behind Zuma as his successor. There was a fierce campaign under way, led by the president's closest friends, to deny the presidency to Zuma. The two men were no longer speaking to one another.

If the deputy president was weighed down by these developments, you couldn't tell by the way he carried himself. Zuma ambled along the carpet in the loose-limbed manner of a natural politician. His gait reminded me of the jiving rhythm of "The Stride," jazz-great Abdullah Ibrahim's sly number. He was a large-boned character with a bullet-shaped head and round cheeks that lent the impression of someone younger than sixty-one. In the anteroom of the National Assembly, a swirl of people rushed up to greet Zuma beneath the vaulted ceiling.

Finance Minister Trevor Manuel, once a leather-jacketed firebrand, strode by in banker's black, having morphed over the past decade into chief manager of the government's conservative macroeconomic policy. Behind him trudged the health minister, Manto Tshabalala-Msimang, a short, rotund woman dressed in delicate red chiffon and weighed down by an alarmingly large hat. They were the alpha and omega of the Mbeki government—the first one sober and super competent and the other an alcoholic who had compiled a disastrous record on AIDS. Both ministers were fully backed by the president, and were also quite popular among the party's rank-and-file.

There were no biographies written about Jacob Zuma, so the details of his background were still little known. His middle name, *Gedleyihle-kisa*, meant in isiZulu "the one who laughs while he endangers you," though it seemed he was the endangered one now. A long list of his pending troubles stemmed from bribery allegations related to the expensive arms deal shepherded through the Cabinet shortly before he took national office. The deals were handled chiefly by Thabo Mbeki, then deputy president, during the waning days of Mandela's presidency, but Zuma was the highest-ranked member of government who had been implicated in corruption in the deals so far.

A businessman friend of his named Schabir Shaik would go on trial later in the year for seeking payoffs from a French arms manufacturer on Zuma's behalf. Whenever family members expressed anxiety about the case, though, Zuma habitually shook his head and urged them to forget it. "It's just *politics*," he would say to his children. This became his consistent line for the next five years as he refused to answer detailed questions about the millions of rand that had been transferred into his bank accounts by Shaik over the years.

Inside the chamber, plush cushioned banks of seats radiated out around a raised dais. If you knew the history, the tableau struck a stunning note: former exiles, guerrilla fighters, and community activists took their seats in the hall that had been refurbished in a last-ditch effort to deny them power.

This was, after all, the legislative chamber rebuilt in 1983 under the direction of former prime minister P. W. Botha to convince the rest of the world that South Africa's white regime was capable of reforming itself. Botha, known as *Die Groot Krokodil*, or the Big Crocodile, had the room designed as a new meeting place for representatives from three "races"—whites, Indians, and coloureds. The apartheid leader had left blacks entirely out of the equation; they were supposed to accept political representation through appointed, dictatorial leaders in designated rural "homelands." The enduring legacy of colonialism and apartheid was that blacks were expected to live forever as foreigners in their own land.

President Mbeki sat beneath the grand domed ceiling in this same chamber, reviewing his text. Directly across from him were his most vocal critics, the aging Mangosuthu Buthelezi and a baby-faced white politician named Tony Leon. The two opposition figures sat knee to knee in adjoining booths.

Buthelezi was the lion of politics for Zulu speakers, a prince in the royal hierarchy who had been a key political power in the country for half a century. At the moment, though, he appeared discombobulated and washed out. Nobody in the hall knew yet that Buthelezi's son lay in the hospital, near death from AIDS. His daughter had already died of it, too. The chamber quieted, and Buthelezi twiddled his thumbs, moving them backward like a man trying to reel time back in.

During decades of white rule, Chief Buthelezi had served as a counterweight to the apartheid regime in his northern coastal province, which is where Zuma came from, too. He refused to accept the idea that black homelands should be considered separate countries, which had made him something of a hero for Mandela. But when the ANC called on people to make the country ungovernable in the 1980s, and Buthelezi had broken with the movement by declaring his opposition to armed struggle, activists organized by the United Democratic Front denounced him as an apartheid collaborator.

After Mandela's release from prison, vicious fighting between supporters of Buthelezi's Inkatha Freedom Party (IFP) and followers of the ANC led to the murders of more than ten thousand people by Election Day in 1994. Buthelezi had been coaxed, by Mandela, into participation in the election at the last minute and then into the Cabinet. He also had served as minister of home affairs during Mbeki's first term.

But Buthelezi had just finished running in opposition to the ANC in the national campaign of 2004, in tandem with the white man to his right, leader of the Democratic Alliance. Now, thanks partly to organizing by Jacob Zuma in their home province, KwaZulu-Natal, the ANC would control provincial affairs, too. Buthelezi would be dropped from the Cabinet and his party would begin a slow, irreversible decline to political irrelevance.

Seated beside Buthelezi, his erstwhile election ally, Tony Leon, bobbed up and down in his seat like an overactive child. Leon was a broad-faced, irrepressible man in his forties dressed in a freshly pressed white shirt and modish suit. Urbane, and given to reciting from memory entire paragraphs of articles in the *New York Review of Books*, he was also English speaking and a Jew, which made him part of an exceedingly small slice of the white minority.

Leon's party had garnered the second-highest proportion of votes nationally, about 12 percent. When he rose to take the oath of office, like the other members of Parliament, ANC members flapped their hands in a gesture of derision.

To Leon's left, in turn, Patricia de Lille sported a wry smile. She had launched the maiden campaign of her fledgling party, the Independent Democrats (ID), in the just-competed campaign and had emerged as a power on the national stage. As a representative in Parliament, de Lille was a courageous whistle-blower. She had spoken out about evidence of kickbacks and payoffs in the arms deal and called on Jacob Zuma to resign his post.

As if on cue, in the Visitors Bay suspended over her head, there was a stir in the section reserved for special guests of the Presidency. A bearded Indian man made his way down the aisle. Reporters in the press gallery elbowed one another to ask, Is it really *him*?

It was, indeed, Schabir Shaik, Zuma's friend and financial advisor whose presence as a presidential VIP seemed odd since he was scheduled to go on trial in October on corruption and bribery charges. Shaik looked rather cheerful, apparently unfazed by the trial to come.

Jacob Zuma appeared equally unflappable as the chief justice of the Constitutional Court, Arthur Chaskalson, gaveled the session to order. Shaik's presence among the VIPs, though, reinforced the idea that the scandal over the armaments deals went all the way to the top.

It was several years later, when we sat down to tea one afternoon, when Zuma delivered the first whopper of the day. "The truth is I never wanted to be president," he said. Three years after I first had laid eyes on him in Parliament, I had finally convinced Zuma to sit down for a chat with me. So much had happened since 2004, and in the intervening years he had been largely walled off from any meaningful contact with journalists or scholars.

This first encounter at his home in Johannesburg was not for a formal interview, but rather to discuss the conditions under which an interview might be granted. From the outset, he wanted me, most of all, to understand that he had never gone looking for a fight with President Mbeki.

Zuma presented himself as a humble man, without any personal ambition at all, who felt that he had been backed into the struggle with the president. He implied that fighting back was the only way that he could protect himself, his family, his friends, and allies from complete ruin.

He looked a little heartbroken when he described the effect of the schism on his relationship with Mbeki. "We were not just close. We were like brothers," he said, narrowing his eyes.[1] Later, he would present the breach between them as something mystifying, caused by a conflation of shadowy events. There was the matter of a mysterious change in Mbeki's personality around 1999. "Certain trouble had started—in *him*—at that point," Zuma exclaimed. Zuma also claimed that he had regularly resisted elevation to national office in the postliberation period, repeatedly turning down entreaties to offer his name for election as deputy secretary-general, chair, and deputy president of the ANC. These assertions, of humility and lack of ambition, were a regular feature of our interviews, from the first until the last, in 2010, when he would say, "I wanted to pull away from the national leadership. [For] very good reasons of mine, which are confidential." It was his comrades who had prevailed upon him each time to offer his name, he insisted, largely because they had not ever fully trusted Mbeki to do the right thing on his own.

Zuma entered the house in a bulky green robe before we sat down to tea. He had just come from an evangelical church service where he was made an honorary reverend. The attention he would pay to evangelicals in the next several years proved to be an integral part of his campaign strategy. Since the country was heavily religious, its people among the most church-going on the globe, he had begun making regular appearances each weekend before congregations of all sizes, especially among the expanding numbers of black evangelical sects. In the pulpit he presented himself as a humble believer, a penitent aware of his own sins, like all good Christian seekers.

Once he had shed the robe, he reproved me in the manner of a disappointed parent. "I'm not important. I'm just a cadre in the movement," he said, studying his hands. It said something about the culture of his party, and about him, that he should begin our conversation by placing such emphasis on his lack of personal ambition. This was a party mantra: leaders were *chosen,* and served as vehicles of the popular will and party doctrine, but they never sought promotion through the hierarchy on their own account. Like the protestations of his antagonists, it always struck a note of false modesty since a massive campaign had been launched on his behalf.

We settled in at the oblong wooden table in the dining alcove, sitting adjacent to one another. Zuma proceeded to study me in an unnerving way, as if to say, "Show me why you're worth the trouble." He knew how to use silence to his benefit. He rose halfway from his chair as if to usher me out already. I pulled my notebook and pen from my briefcase, laying them down between us.

After a pause, Zuma delivered a long exegesis about the terrible treatment he had received from other journalists. He mentioned banner headlines detailing the corruption charges in stories about the arms deals based largely, he said, on illegal leaks from the National Prosecuting Authority. "I didn't think that was *fair,*" he said, turning his palms to the ceiling. What had happened to the vaunted Constitution and the cardinal principal of a presumption of innocence?

There also had even been a secret briefing that was limited to the country's top black editors, where the chief prosecutor, Bulelani Ngcuka, had said that he intended to try Zuma in "the court of public opinion" rather than in the courts. He colored slightly at the neck, looking fierce.

When Zuma paused, I said the obvious: the reason I had come to see him was that I "preferred to make my own judgments about people." He nodded and seemed to relax, perhaps because I hadn't played to his vanity or rushed to proclaim a bias in his favor, as journalists often do to claim a subject's cooperation. I had not denounced Mbeki or criticized South African colleagues about whom he felt so critical.

We agreed that I could come back around for a formal interview, and one led to the next. In the end we met four times for extended conversations in 2007, and then once each year from 2008 to 2010 for additional interviews. Zuma usually began these sessions quite guardedly, offering only vague, truncated replies at first, but eventually settled into a breezy, more expansive attitude. I met his children and introduced him to my son; in time, he seemed to relax.

In our first formal interview, a month later, Zuma told me that everything important in his character was quarried out of the landscape north of the Tugela River. Visiting his homestead meant a ninety-minute flight from Johannesburg to Durban, on the Indian Ocean coast, and then a three-hour drive north to deep Zululand—a consciousness shift from where we sat in a comfortable mansion in the big city.

Zuma had spent his early childhood not far from the rural town of Nkandla, on the far side of the Tugela. The river marked a rough dividing line between territory occupied a century ago by British colonial forces to the south and the traditional homeland of Zulu-speaking people to the north.

South of the river lay sugar-cane plantations, factories, and the biggest cities in what was now called KwaZulu-Natal province. Zuma identified himself as a person from the north side of the river, where whites were always scarce.

By the time we spoke, in 2007, I had begun to notice an intriguing generational difference among South Africans. If you asked the simplest question, "Who are you?" older people from rural areas often named the particular village where they were born. "My name is Jacob Zuma. I come from Nkandla," was the first thing he said when I asked him to identify himself as I turned on my digital recorder.

Younger rural people tended to identify themselves by ethnicity, as

Zulu speakers or Xhosa speakers, for example, or to describe themselves first as South African before citing the name of the place where they were living or the family's traditional home. It was important to Zuma for others to see him as a man of Nkandla.

As a boy, Zuma had herded goats and cattle through the nearby hills, exploring the craggy mountains that surrounded the village. When he mentioned these adventures, he spoke in a hushed tone, as if it was a rather mystical experience. "Up there," he told me a few months later, when I had a chance to visit him at the homestead, was "the land of cobras and honey." He would repeat the phrase—"cobras and honey"—laughing at the sound of it.

Even in doing something as simple as telling his own story, it seemed to me, Zuma placed himself midway between Mandela's sensual romanticism (in drinking "warm, sweet milk straight from the udder of a cow") and Mbeki's astringent historicism (the memory of all those local men "broken by the mines"). Zuma was a master of placing himself right in the middle of things. He had gotten along, and acquired immense power, by fashioning bridges between seemingly irreconcilable forces.

Waxing on about the unparalleled sweetness of local honey, Zuma had a faraway look. The menacing, life-threatening potency of a particularly venomous family of cobras, he implied, provided counterpoint to the reward, the incomparably sweet honey.

Zuma was unlike the two preeminent South African political leaders since liberation. Unlike Mandela, the son of a chief descended from Thembu royalty, Zuma was an impoverished peon. Unlike Mbeki, the son of a respected elder in the movement, he was the child of a domestic worker and police sergeant.

Unlike both Mandela, the lawyer, and Mbeki, a trained economist, Zuma had never had extensive schooling. Nobody had provided for him, or promoted his interests, taken him under their wing, or smoothed his path to success. This was what he presented as the prevalent theme of his early life.

And then? He joined the movement, and everything changed. The general overview of his service to the movement was already known. When he was a teenager, Zuma joined the ANC and attended trade union and Youth League informal schools. In 1963, he was caught trying to leave the country with a small band of comrades and was tried on sabotage charges. Zuma was sentenced to serve ten years in prison for conspiracy, and spent his twenties on Robben Island, where he learned to read and write properly. Once released, he had returned immediately to work in the armed underground. After a narrow escape to Swaziland, his thirties and forties were spent in guerrilla camps preparing for the revolutionary overthrow of the white regime.

It was a remarkable narrative arc—from goat herder to guerrilla commander to chief of intelligence to pivotal civilian leader in a new democracy. Zuma was the one chosen to secretly lead a small delegation of ANC exile leaders back into the country in late 1989, and to begin "talks-about-talks." Those conversations, in turn, set the stage for Nelson Mandela's release and the negotiated settlement that followed.

In the years since, Zuma had risen through the ranks. He was leader of the ANC delegation in negotiations between the governing parties in 1992 and 1993. At key turns he had played an outsize role in party deliberations.

Zuma, by his own account, had weighed in with Mandela on Mbeki's behalf, for example, when it came to naming a deputy president. Mandela had hesitated to accept Mbeki as his deputy, but Zuma and several other party leaders convinced him to do so.

Early in Mandela's term as president, Zuma served as provincial minister in KwaZulu-Natal. In 1997, he was elected deputy president of the ANC and was appointed deputy president of the country by Mbeki two years later. Through the years he had earned a reputation as Mbeki's loyal deputy. This made it especially difficult, even for insiders, to understand how he had ended up in a deadly rivalry with the president thirty years on.

"They were chalk and cheese, tongue and saliva," Mosiuoa "Terror" Lekota, then chairman of the ANC, would tell me later.[2] Beneath the surface, though, there had always been unspoken differences between the two men, particularly in their approach to leadership.

In 1997, the Mandela Cabinet adopted a conservative macroeconomic policy called GEAR (Growth, Employment, and Redistribution Policy), marked by low deficits and high interest rates. Zuma had backed the new policy in public, but he also had listened respectfully to criticism from the Left.

He was always a world-class listener, and this quality had drawn Mbeki's critics to him. For trade unionists and Communists, who formally governed with the ANC in the so-called Tripartite Alliance, the economic policy imposed by Mbeki had marked a historic betrayal of the movement.

"It was simply part of what we call the '1996 Class Project,'" Blade Nzimande, general secretary of the Communist Party, told me in mid-2007. With that incendiary phrase, he meant to imply that right-wing business interests had coalesced around Mbeki after Mandela stepped down as president, blunting the revolutionary potential of the movement. "The 1996 Class Project is a project that pursues a strategy of restoring capitalistic profitability above anything else," Nzimande added, to make his point clear.[3]

The breach within the Alliance over GEAR complicated an intense struggle going on at the time about who should succeed Mandela as president of the party and country. The discussions built to a head before the ANC national conference in 1997, when Mbeki was elected president of the ANC and Zuma was chosen as his deputy president. (Mbeki's chief rival until 1993 had been the charismatic Communist guerrilla leader Chris Hani, but Hani was assassinated in the driveway of his home by right-wing white separatists.)

Influential members of the party elite considered Zuma's rise, alongside Mbeki, as part of a package deal. They would accept Mbeki in the top job only if Zuma was kept close to the center of power in Union Buildings to keep an eye on the next president.

Back in 1997, party leaders most uneasy about Mbeki's politics even had suggested, in discussions among themselves, the possibility of elevating Zuma ahead of Mbeki as Mandela's successor. After all, unlike Mbeki, Zuma had strong relationships with each of the party's contending constituencies—former prisoners, former guerrillas, former activists from the United Democratic Front, former exile leaders, and even traditional leaders and royalty around the country, especially in KwaZulu-Natal.

Like Mandela, Zuma was known as a unifier attentive to the expectations of others. "Activists were talking about pushing for Jacob Zuma even then," recalled one key party leader, Zweli Mkhize, a longtime member of the party's National Executive Committee. "They were saying, 'Zuma is good with people.'"[4] Ultimately, though, most insiders felt that Zuma was too genial and not detail oriented, a rather poor administrator—too much like Mandela, in other words. "Some people thought, 'Oh no, he's going to be like Madiba [Mandela's clan name, an affectionate form of address]. He's not good with systems,'" Mkhize recalled. "They said, 'Now we wanted an engineer, someone who was going to drive things'—and that was Mbeki."

A consensus emerged, as Mkhize and others remembered it: "Let Mbeki run things for two terms, and then have Zuma for one term so he can pull people back together again." In effect, then, party leaders had decided to hold Zuma in reserve as a guardian of the party's cohesion and deepest political values.

In the process, these leaders doomed the relationship between the two men, however. By pairing Mbeki and Zuma in this way, party leaders also set in motion the eventual scramble for power at the top that would eventually threaten the party's stability and endanger the country's fragile new democracy. Thabo Mbeki had been pegged as the *un-Mandela* with the intelligence and skill needed to push the country toward its future. A leader so unlike Mandela, not surprisingly, was pre-cisely what the country got.

Back on the floor of Parliament, before members reelected Thabo Mbeki as president, there was a stirring ceremony first. Baleka Mbete, the choice of the ANC, enjoyed election by acclamation as Speaker. After the vote was taken, Chief Justice Arthur Chaskalson of the Con-stitutional Court ceded the gavel to her. He departed, with judicial robes billowing behind. It quickened the pulse, still, to watch an older white man hand the gavel to a younger woman, the first black African to take up the post.

Behind the podium Speaker Mbete was momentarily overcome. Her slight frame swayed as she paid tribute to her predecessor, Frene Gin-wala, who rose in her elegant sari to acknowledge the applause. The new speaker called for the election of the president. No other name was placed in nomination, and Mbeki was swiftly chosen, also by acclama-tion. For someone tuning in on live television, it seemed like an oddly bloodless ritual, and a rather contained vision of democracy.

Leaders of the opposition party were granted a few moments to give their president some advice. "We celebrate the way the president has come to power as a result of a free and fair election," Tony Leon said, a subtle jab because Robert Mugabe, the increasingly authoritarian leader in neighboring Zimbabwe, had just been installed for another term after a rigged election.

Leon's private assessment of the president and his party was rather bleak. In this ceremonial setting he worked hard to sound gracious. "We are rivals, not enemies," he assured the nation. Chief Buthelezi trudged to the podium next, to urge President Mbeki to lead a more energetic fight against AIDS, without mentioning his own private anguish—the loss of his own two children to the disease.

It was left to the president of the Pan Africanist Congress (PAC), Motsoko Pheko, to play the role of spoiler. Pheko was a tall man with long limbs and a craggy face. "I'm not sure I can cooperate in the diplomatic mood," he announced, after stalking to the dais.

Pheko was clad in a simple African-print shirt, and he stood ramrod straight, like a guerrilla commander in the field. The weak position of his party in contemporary South African politics remained something of a mystery. Once a formidable rival of the ANC's for support of black masses, the party had won just 1 percent of the popular vote in 1994. Since then, it had been ravaged by vicious infighting, and though its ideals had many adherents, the feelings never seemed to translate into votes.

"We find a plutocracy trying to replace democracy with a government of the rich!" the PAC leader announced, raising his lanky arm in the air like a prophetic preacher. His remarks amounted to a tough denunciation of the ANC for having sublimated the needs of the people to the requirements of capitalists. Something odd happened, as he spoke, though. A giggle escaped from among a few of the ministers arrayed behind the president. Zuma clapped a hand over his mouth and Mbeki smirked, looking askance.

The entire chamber filled soon enough with uncontrolled, infectious bursts of laughter. Members of Parliament fell back into their seats and held onto their bellies. They were openly hooting, perhaps remembering the revolutionary rhetoric of their younger selves and coming to terms with how much had changed, including for themselves.

After Pheko retreated, Zuma stood up. The laughter died. "The massive mandate we have received has humbled us," he murmured. President Mbeki then followed his deputy to the podium, where he fumbled with his notes. He closed the ceremony on an odd, stilted note. "We for our part will do our best to encourage government to live up to this responsibility," he said.

On the campaign trail, the president often referred to the burden of historic injustice the country needed to overcome. In the first minutes of his second term, though, he pledged only to *encourage* his government—the people's government, supposedly—to take the country in the right direction as if he had only the power to plead with his ministers to follow him.

Shortly after the president finished his remarks, the MPs bolted toward the doors. In the cobblestone lane, public servants slid into their spanking new BMWs, Volvos, and Toyota sedans and headed off to parties to celebrate the beginning of the third term of the National Assembly since freedom had arrived.

Lingering for a few moments out on the front steps below the grand arched entrance to the chamber, I ran into a member of Parliament, Mampe Ramotsamai. She was a middle-aged woman in a brown leather suit who represented a constituency, assigned to her by her party, in Stellenbosch, the wine-making district.

Ramotsamai admitted to me that she had found the just-completed campaign a rather harrowing experience, in spite of her party's lopsided electoral triumph. She reported a high level of hostility, not only toward Mbeki and the ANC, but also toward the democratic process in general. There were lessons, she thought, hiding beneath the happy outcome. "People just do not know what government is doing, has done, and can do," she said.

We huddled together for a few moments on the steps of Parliament so she could tell me about one incident that bothered her most. On the campus of Stellenbosch University, once the exclusive province of white Afrikaans-speaking intellectuals, she had flagged down a young, well-dressed black student to offer her pitch for the ANC.

Figuring the student for an easy sell, the MP had gently urged him to be sure to vote. He had bluntly asked her to offer "a single good reason" for voting at all. "Here he is!" she recalled, flapping her hands as if she wanted to spank him. "Look where you *are* now! You're standing on the steps of a university that blacks were never allowed to attend before! Because of the movement we led, you're getting an excellent education. *Shame* on you for not voting!"

The MP thought that the essential challenge for her party, going forward, would be confronting this antipolitical turn by the young. Though the ANC had won another victory at the polls, voter turnout had also plummeted, from 85 percent in 1994 to 57.5 percent just ten years later. Four million fewer South Africans had cast ballots in the most recent election than had voted just a decade before.

What's more, a new survey showed that areas with the highest prevalence of HIV were the most demoralized and politically inert. You could hardly blame people who had turned away from formal politics if they were concerned about more urgent, life-threatening matters. If you were ill or employed, and black, how exactly were your interests to be reflected in an election that offered a choice between the ANC and a white-led opposition?

The MP thought there was a message to the governing party embedded in the decision by so many citizens to ignore the election, particularly among the young. This message was simple: your revolution is not working for us. She wondered if the leaders of her party, both of whom she admired, had gotten the message yet.

4.

The Chroniclers

From the doorstep of the four-story building that housed the *Cape Times* and the *Cape Argus*, the city's daily newspapers, Table Mountain appeared shrouded in fog. Off to my right loomed Lion's Head, the stark rocky outcropping two thousand feet up the western side of Table Mountain National Park. In the course of millions of years, sandstone had layered over shale deposited across the peaks more than half a billion years ago. The mane of the lion and its crown jutted through the mist, and its spine sloped down to its rump on Signal Hill.

It was from this direction that Chris Whitfield, the editor in chief of the *Cape Times*, power walked down New Church Street shortly after eight o'clock each morning. He stepped around bedrolls laid out in the doorways by the *bergies*, or coloured tramps, and their white counterparts. Apartheid, in effect, had been a state-supported full-employment system for whites. Now, a tramp's life was an equal-opportunity placement. The strong social-welfare safety net for poor whites had vanished in the newly nonracial country.

The lack of dignity in being forced to sleep on the sidewalk pricked at the editor's conscience, whether it was suffered by a white *bergie* or a black beggar. It seemed to Whitfield that those in need were getting younger by the day. He was a broad-shouldered man with a round, open face, his high forehead tinged with the pink glow of a perpetual sunburn. On his drive into the city center from Rondebosch, a pleasant suburb where he lived with his wife and children, the editor had been engaged in an intense argument, with himself, about the kinds of stories missing from the pages of his newspaper.

Like most newspapers, the *Cape Times* tilted toward urgent alarms about fires or murders—so-called hard news, which often crowded out "softer" feature stories about poverty, homeless kids, immigration, and the AIDS epidemic. "Do we have the depth and quality of journalism to look beyond the row-of-the-day?" Whitfield would tell me later. "I wish I could say that we do."[1]

Here was an old conundrum for journalists posed in fresh circumstances: Our work typically focused on the *new* and *unusual*. Traditional journalism wasn't as effective, as normally practiced, in elucidating *deep*, and *systemic*, and *persistent* challenges. Maybe the enormity of South Africa's troubles—not just AIDS, but also poverty, race, and crime—conflated factors tightly intertwined and swamped the ability of journalists to tease them out.

One example of the kinds of challenges journalists faced was visible to the naked eye from the doorstep of the newspaper building. All along St. Georges Mall, close by the steps of the cathedral where Jonathan and his gang had smoked glue, traders were laying paintings, sculptures, and handicrafts out on top of blankets placed over centuries-old cobblestones.

The presence of so many refugees from Zimbabwe in Cape Town was a reminder of the enormous black African diaspora still streaming into the country. The Zimbabwean traders had turned cast-off hanger wire into colorful sculptures of birds, autos, and radios. One of them was an elaborate, full-sized guitar trimmed in red wire, and fully equipped with strings, ready to be played.

The presence of so many immigrants, and the rising resentment toward them by South African blacks, posed a sticky dilemma. Much of the mass migration to South Africa supported President Mbeki's argument that his country's fate was entwined with the future of the continent. The large numbers pouring across the northern border also testified to one of the president's follies—his controversial "quietly quietly" diplomatic approach toward neighboring Zimbabwe. The rule of Robert Mugabe had thrust millions of economic and political refugees southward.

The aging elevators in the newspaper building opened on the fourth floor, a cavernous expanse that housed the staffs of both the morning *Times* and the afternoon *Argus*. Both papers were part of the chain of morning and afternoon dailies published across the country and run by the international conglomerate led by the Irish mogul Anthony O'Reilly.

O'Reilly's purchase of the Argus Group, the oldest and most established chain of newspapers in South Africa (now called Independent Newspapers), had been brokered personally by Nelson Mandela back in 1993, before he was president. Mandela reportedly wanted to ensure that the country's most influential print media house was pulled out from under the control of white South Africans. The successful bid for the papers had been the first major post-apartheid investment in the country by a foreign corporation.

On our left as we entered was the glassed-in conference room of the *Cape Times*. The room was festooned with copies of posters used on the streets to hawk previous editions. "WHY CHARLIZE STRIPPED FOR ME" was the tease for an article about the South African–born actress Charlize Theron, and it was wedged next to another reading, "MOUSE BURNS DOWN HOUSE."

The screaming headlines were reminders of how print media thrived or died here on the basis of single-copy sales. Unlike newspapers in the United States, which relied more on subscription income, 80 percent of the *Cape Times* circulation was in single-copy sales by vendors in shops, at the curbside, and in the middle of the city's busiest intersections.

Further on, the editor's office was crammed with antique furniture and stacks of previous editions. On the wall behind the editor, front pages reporting momentous events were framed in glass. The burning World Trade Center, from the paper published on September 12, 2001, had pride of place:

MOMENT THE WORLD CHANGED
10,000 Feared Dead in Twin Towers

Hanging next to the story about 9/11, as if in counterpoint, was a front-page headline from April 17, 1994, about the country's first election:

NEXT: THE RAINBOW COVENANT
A Nation Is Reborn
Vote, the beloved country

Whitfield was the coauthor of that momentous article, and like so many journalists of his generation, he remembered, with eerie precision, what it had been like to cover mass rebellions in the late 1980s. He had dodged bullets himself during an armed assault on ANC supporters in the Ciskei, one of the so-called homelands.

The editor remembered earlier times—when newspaper circulations soared, people clamored for news, and journalists felt like an essential part of unfolding history—as halcyon days. "In some ways it was easier to cover the fight against apartheid. Back then, the lines were clear," he murmured.

Now, on any number of issues from poverty and AIDS to electoral politics, the lines looked far fuzzier. President Mbeki regularly ripped the country's media for its supposed "failure to transform," meaning he thought that newsrooms were still far too white and resistant to the ANC's leadership.

This charge, of resistance to transformation, felt especially freighted if you were among the dwindling number of whites still running a major newspaper. In the upper echelons of business, the levers of power were still largely in the hands of white managers, but in government, as in journalism, whites felt a fresh challenge to prove their relevance, aware as never before of their minority status. Like other editors, Whitfield faced a quandary. He pointed out that his countrymen had been forced in the recent past "to stare into some fairly dark places and they didn't want to do it readily again." So the papers, if they covered the country's deep systemic problems in depth, could seem endlessly bleak and depressing.

After the 1994 election, whites had deserted the English-language press in large numbers, and tens of thousands of them departed to Australia, England, and the United States. Hundreds of thousands more left in the intervening years. Many other whites who stayed on seemed to migrate—in their imaginations—as though they considered themselves incidental inhabitants of a post-colonial country in Africa rather than as fully engaged citizens who felt they had a stake in the new democracy.

In addition to pressures like these from readers, editors like Whitfield confronted enormous pressure from the ANC government. Advisors to President Mbeki suggested that the old idea of a "watchdog" role for journalists was outmoded. The notion that the "Fourth Estate" should operate as a check on a "people's government" seemed to them like a vestige of an archaic checks-and-balances design better suited to well-established neo-liberal democracies than a progressive, transformational situation like in South Africa. Shouldn't the media be more of a "guide dog" in an emerging democracy?

President Mbeki's oldest friend and advisor, Essop Pahad, regularly rang up editors, publishers, and political reporters to ream them out. Whitfield recently had returned from a meeting with Pahad, minister in the Presidency, at Union Buildings, in Pretoria. The memory left him flushed a shade of purplish red. "He's a bully," the editor said. "He's always very aggressive towards us. He'll shout and curse and carry on." It worried him that the ANC, with overwhelming dominance of politics, seemed so insecure when it came to criticism.

Media-bashing habits, as it happened, harkened way back in the country's history. Faulting the editors for the tenor of the news was an impulse embedded deeply in the nation's political culture. After the election in 1948, for example, when the National Party had unseated the United Party of Jan Smuts by a narrow margin, those who were voted out of power blamed not themselves but the journalists for their defeat. In a dispatch in the *Star* on the day after the National Party victory, General Smuts was quoted as saying that citizens should "blame me" for the massive rout in the election. "'No,' replied Nationalist leader Ben Schoeman, 'blame the press. The United Party did not know what was happening in the *platteland* [rural areas]. All they knew was what they read in *The Star* and the *Rand Daily Mail*.'"[2]

During the intervening decades conservative politicians who often warned of the Red Menace and the Black Threat also commented on a third danger—the *Engelse pers gevaar*—the dangers posed by the English-language press. Switch the year, and change the other circumstances. Now, President Mbeki and his advisors expressed the view that they faced a *counterrevolutionary* stance by "white-controlled" media institutions.

In a submission to the Human Rights Commission, during a controversial investigation of racial bias in the media in 2000, the ANC decried the way the South African media had built up the image of Nelson Mandela as a saintly exception to the prevalent pattern of "venality and incompetence" among black leaders. The portrayal of Thabo Mbeki, by contrast, was of someone "manipulative and calculating," and the governing party felt this was a logical extension of racist premises.

"Why is it that these sections of the media seem to have taken the decision that it is necessary to propagate lies, at all costs!" the submission continued. "The answer to this is that the racist paradigm dictates that facts seen to be inconsistent with the white stereotype of the African savage should not be given such weight as would negate this stereotype." Coverage of Mandela's successor, the ANC argued, was corrupted by the assumption "that the Africans, necessarily with the exception of Nelson Mandela, are: corrupt, anti-democratic, dictatorial and contemptuous of the population."[3]

In the ensuing debate over whether journalists should operate as guide dogs or watchdogs in an emerging democracy, there was a third kind of dog—the lapdog—frequently mentioned. While President Mbeki and ANC stalwarts saw media coverage overall as viciously antigovernment, opposition parties tended to the opposite view—that the media was in thrall to the ANC.

That's what I discovered one morning after the election, when I walked over from Newspaper House to Parliament to check in with the leader of the opposition, Tony Leon. When I asked Leon to offer an assessment of the quality of political reportage, he placed his large head in his hands, rocking dolefully from side to side. "Sclerotic" was the nicest thing he said. "Look—in the sale of the newspapers to Tony O'Reilly, the expectation was that he would appoint black editors who will be supporters of the government. And this is what he has done," the opposition leader added.[4]

Leon argued that the ANC government had used its vast budget for spending on print advertising to influence editorial coverage. Government was now the most lucrative source of advertising. He considered the publicly held South African Broadcasting Corporation (SABC) far worse. "On SABC, it's all just a parade of ministers," he complained. He thought, in general, that President Mbeki had plunged the country to "an incredibly low water mark, as bad as when the state of emergency was declared," and that the media was complicit in a race to the bottom.

When I returned to Whitfield's corner office in the newspaper building, the editor looked up from his work. "What kind of *dog* am I today?" he asked. When I told him that he had been turned into a lapdog, he shook his head. If the media were in President Mbeki's pocket, Whitfield protested, they certainly wouldn't have editorialized against the president's policies on AIDS and Zimbabwe.

The country was in the midst of historic change, and journalists were part of the transformation they were chronicling. The editor thought they deserved a little respect as they struggled with the complications of the task.

Right outside Whitfield's office was the cavernous newsroom that served the separate staffs of the *Cape Times* and its afternoon sister newspaper, the *Cape Argus*. Promptly at eleven o'clock in the morning on the day before the election of 2004, I had watched the *Argus* staff jam into the glassed-in conference room around a massive oak table. Some of these reporters had been around long enough to remember "Whites Only" signs that once hung above the doorway and set apart the bathrooms.

Now, the editor in chief was a coloured man; his female news editor was white; her deputy editor, in turn, was a coloured woman who remembered what it had felt like to grow up in a society where everything was regulated by racial classification. Seated to the right of her was the paper's chief political editor, a brawny, brooding black man named Joe Aranes, who told me that he originally went into journalism because "media was an excellent site of struggle."[5]

Clustered at the far end of the table sat more experienced, predominantly white staff members. In the intermediate sections of the table sat a clump of coloured reporters, while black newcomers generally positioned themselves near the doorway, pitched away slightly from the table as if a little unsure of whether they fully belonged.

Shortly after the planning meeting began, a rousing debate broke out about how to enliven coverage of the balloting. The news editor already had assigned a few reporters to track down major politicians as they voted. Heads flagged, eyes rolled, and several reporters complained that this was an extremely limp trope—tracking down politicians and trying to get them to say something interesting as they put ballots in a box. The reporters wondered how, if they felt bored *covering* these kinds of set pieces, they could expect readers to feel excited *reading* their dispatches.

One of the younger members of the staff, Murray Williams, suggested a novel idea—finding especially interesting *nonpoliticians* to interview about the significance of the election. Williams wore an open-collared, pressed shirt and had a new notebook on the table in front of him. Several of his colleagues chimed in, fired by the notion of doing something new. Reporters began ticking off the names of middle- and upper-class neighborhoods in the city where well-known writers, architects, and theater people lived, suggesting poll-side interviews with Pieter-Dirk Uys, the famous cross-dressing satirist known as Evita Bezuidenhout, among others.

From the far end of the table a coloured reporter protested: "That's all very nice for us to spend time in the wealthy districts, eh? Who are we going to interview in *Khayelitsha*?" Khayelitsha was the burgeoning township on the outskirts of the city my students and I had visited on our second day in the country. The coloured reporter, Zenzile Khoisan, set his chin and glared. He had high cheekbones, a gigantic blue pen sticking out of his pocket, long-sleeved black cotton shirt buttoned tightly beneath his Adam's apple, and a fierce expression. Radicalized as a student in the 1970s, Khoisan was forced into exile in Lesotho and Botswana during the struggle years. He had spent time in New York City, where he worked as a correspondent for radio station WBAI. After returning to South Africa in 1994 to vote, he joined the staff at Bush Radio before signing on as senior investigator for the Truth and Reconciliation Commission.

Part of the reason he had applied to work at the *Argus* was to help explain to readers why the revolution he had supported for so long seemed to be on the verge of sputtering out. Khoisan hitched up his black jeans. The idea that people living in the townships were worth less attention than readers from suburbia stirred an unconcealed sense of grievance. He ticked off for his colleagues the names of other townships surrounding the city, where blacks and mixed-race people still lived. "Aren't they having an election there, too?"

An edgy, uncomfortable silence followed. Williams stiffened in his seat. The implication that he had meant to ignore the concerns of black readers seemed a low, and unfair, blow. "That's a very good question, Zenzile," he shot back. "So maybe you can tell us what important non-politician lives in Khayelitsha."

Silence descended again. The two reporters considered one another unhappily. Nobody around the table, including colleagues sitting between them, intervened. The bosses at the table didn't pick up on the rather reasonable challenge that Williams had just framed. Here was a chance to generate names of township residents who might be worth interviewing, such as athletes, activists, small businesswomen, or even musicians like the famous singer Brenda Fassie, whose home was in one of them. The moment passed, though, as assignments for the day were made and reporters headed out, some for the cushy suburbs and others for the townships.

The next day, Murray and Khoisan put in a long day and night of election reporting. Williams would tell me later that I had missed the essential point of his exchange with Khoisan: "Unlike in the United States, where you never talk about race," he said, the *Argus* newsroom had long since moved past old racial divisions. The reporter argued that the push-and-pull between him and his colleague was only a consequence of healthy, creative tension. He considered Khoisan a friend.[6]

When I looped back to Khoisan a few months later, though, he whistled across the phone line, long and low. "An election is a war" was the way he put it. "It's a war and Murray was taking up our time talking about *fluff*—Evita and so on. All those intellectuals and celebrities he

mentioned were white people. They don't represent the average person."
The central problem with South Africa's media, Khoisan added, was class
and not simply race. "There's too much of a revolving door, from media
to business to government," he argued. Now there was pressure to focus
attention squarely on the emerging black bourgeoisie. "Whites prefer to
cover the new black elite because they identify with them," he continued.
"I want to cover the street urchins, because they'll actually determine if
we live or if we die."[7]

When he had first started working for the paper as a freelance
reporter, Khoisan felt the success of South Africa's democratic experiment pivoted on the ability of journalists to explain the country to itself.
"Readership was up. The danger was palpable. The paper had sex appeal.
You felt like every journalist was about to enter Alcoholics Anonymous
or Divorce Court because we never went home. That gave the paper its
energy," he recalled.

More recently, though, stories had been shortened and dumbed
down, which was part of a worldwide trend. There was a light, bright
tone imposed on stories. This betrayed the dominance of "whites,"
Khoisan felt, not only "in the sense of color only" but also in the more
ethereal "sense of their point of view." From his vantage point, journalism was poised at a tipping point. "We're still operating as if the major
work of creating a democracy here has been accomplished and as if we're
just working out the kinks. That's totally untrue," he added, his voice
breaking slightly. "The situation is still very fluid."

Past a massive taxi rank, shy of the majestic, worn-around-the-edges
City Hall in Johannesburg, was the intersection at Sauer Street where
two venerable institutions squared off. The national headquarters of the
African National Congress, called Luthuli House, occupied one side of
Sauer. The headquarters of Independent Newspapers, publisher of the

Cape Town dailies as well as the nation's oldest national paper, the *Star*, shadowed the other side of the street. Up the way sat the ancient Chamber of Mines, and just short of Gandhi Square stood the luxurious Rand Club. There was neat symmetry, with politics, commerce, and media all quite visible in a power triangle.

From the second floor of the Independent building, Moegsien Williams, the country's most influential editor, had his back turned to the street. He was originally a Capetonian, a former activist/journalist who had been a pioneer in integrating the top management of formerly white-dominated publications. In the years since he had moved to Johannesburg, the editor had become the city's biggest promoter, calling it "Gold Reef City."

Williams managed a staff of reporters covering news for a diverse group of readers—black, white, Indian, and mixed-race people from a wide span of class backgrounds, including unemployed blue-collar workers and newly minted professionals. He was a solidly built, soft-spoken man of fifty-two years, dressed in a cream-colored shirt and neatly pressed slacks. At his hip an oversized holster held a gigantic cell phone that trilled constantly.

The Muslim son of a laborer, Williams had come of age in journalism during the hard-charging 1970s and 1980s. After dropping out of college, he had wobbled from mainstream media to radical alternative publications, *Grassroots* and *South* among them.[8] Since Freedom Day, though, he had shot to the top of the heap, editing one Independent Newspaper group daily after another before taking the plum editorial spot at the *Star* in 2001.

Like most of his colleagues, Williams was unashamedly pro-ANC and an ardent pro-Mbeki partisan. He considered AIDS and Zimbabwe "blind spots" of the president's in an otherwise admirable record. Jacob Zuma, on the other hand, he thought of as a throwback and an embarrassment.

As for the critiques from opposition leaders like Tony Leon, the editor waggled his head, waving a dismissive hand. "[He] thinks it's so easy for us because we just go over to Luthuli House and take our orders," he said, cocking a thumb at the direction of ANC headquarters. "Tony Leon will never know the immense pressure we're actually under."

Those pressures were chiefly commercial, he explained. The *Star*, 108 years old, faced competition from two new dailies, an upscale newspaper called *This Day*, a breezy, open, and sexy read that appealed to the new generation of cosmopolitan twenty- and thirty-somethings, and a new tabloid, the *Daily Sun*, which had caught fire with poor and working-class people. The *Star*, in other words, was being nibbled from both ends.

In the doorway to his office, Williams paused. He said that he wanted his newspaper to "allow this city to talk to itself." The editor ambled off through the newsroom, crossing worn carpets on a meandering trip from his office to OPS, the meeting room where decisions about the next edition were being made. Weaving between the desks of reporters, Williams admitted that they were underpaid, undertrained, and overworked.

The Independent Group already had slashed the number of reporters at the paper in half since its purchase of the papers and also had shut down its acclaimed academy for aspiring journalists, which was responsible for producing some of the best known and most talented of the country's political correspondents. The need for journalism training was immense, and yet the company had backed away from the challenge.

Many staff members in the *Star* newsroom, including whites whose mother tongue was Afrikaans, struggled to write well in English. For some black reporters, English was a third or fourth language. The public education system most journalists came up through was still, ten years on, a colossal mess. Even college-level training in journalism was uneven. A recent industry-wide survey had revealed shockingly low levels of general knowledge among young reporters. For example, a majority who had already worked from two to five years in newsrooms could not answer this question correctly: "If 4,000,000 Zimbabwean citizens indicated that they were going to vote, and 2,000,000 indicated that they were not going to vote, what percentage of Zimbabwean citizens will vote?"

Reports about the survey had spawned a new word—*juniorization*—which was shorthand for the departure of more experienced journalists either to retirement or to higher-paid employment in business or government. The fresh replacements, who were younger and less educated compatriots, could hardly be expected to have the same depth of field or expertise. Juniorization turned into a one-size-fits-all code phrase that also served as a cudgel against current inhabitants of newsrooms without having to mention that so many of the *juniors* were black.

There was a crisis building in media companies, Williams acknowledged. Everyone agreed that newsrooms ought to reflect the demography of the country and that this transformation could provide a turning point for the project of national reconstruction. "But if we don't succeed in transforming this country and affirming the majority—and if the majority of the people don't have a stake in its survival—everything will be lost," he murmured. He pointed over his shoulder at the reporters behind us. "The young black reporters there are the future custodians of a free press in this country."

In the operations center, the *Star*'s editorial team gathered around a long conference table in an airless room lit by fluorescent tubes. They snapped to attention when the boss walked in. He found them discussing pop icon Brenda Fassie, who had been hospitalized in a coma. Fassie was the dynamic singer whose music I had heard for the first time shortly after my arrival in Cape Town. "Higher and higher!" she had crooned. Now she lay near death after a drug overdose.

There had been a massive national reaction to Fassie's collapse akin to the mourning in the United States when Elvis Presley died. She was the superstar singer who had been the breakthrough *kwaito* artist of her time and was especially beloved because she had beaten the odds, rising from a township upbringing to achieve fame even under the old regime. Fassie had been the queen of the fast crowd, a mistress of misbehavior who reminded me of Janis Joplin in her prime. She had married, divorced, and weaved in and out of sexual relationships with women as well as men.

The well-known critic Njabulo Ndebele wrote that the singer's widespread popularity flowed from the fact that she had always been in sync with the spirit of her times. When the call had gone out in the 1980s to make South Africa ungovernable by the white regime, Ndebele felt that Fassie's voice entered "the public arena as ungovernable, the ultimate expression of personal freedom. She brought the experience of freedom very close."[9] The scholar concluded his essay on a reflective note: "Unbridled freedom, though, like the political strategy of ungovernability, can burn the one that wields it."[10]

The editors at the *Star* had been riding their reporters all day for more information about the singer's drug-taking binge, one of them asking if anybody had a line on the woman who was her most recent lover. Icons of the South African musical world, such as Hugh Masekela and Miriam Makeba, had joined younger stars, including Zola and Simphiwe Dana, at the hospital in an ongoing vigil. President Mbeki visited her bedside, too, generating an above-the-fold story with a giant headline.

Brenda Fassie's death a few days later would plunge many in the newsroom into a serious funk. They wondered aloud why some of the most successful breakthrough black artists in the country were dying in such great numbers. Creative people everywhere lived too hard, drank like fish, got high too often, and skated on the edge, but it didn't seem as though their country could afford to squander so many talented people.

Next to the story of Fassie's tragic end, nothing fixed the concentration of the editors in the room like the country's bid to host the 2010 World Cup soccer tournament. The bid had been front-page news for weeks. South Africans were among the most sports-crazed people on the planet, and since the World Cup had never been played on the continent before, tension that surrounded last-minute politicking (and suspected bribe-making) in designation of the next host country was on the rise. A bid two years earlier, to win rights to host the extravaganza in 2006, had been quashed at the last moment by a lobbying blitzkrieg from Germany.

This year's selection for the 2010 host country was just a few days away. Every media outlet in the country was in a feeding frenzy, with the media chasing scraps of information. President Mbeki had headed up the massive, expensive lobbying drive to win the games, staking the nation's dignity and honor on the outcome. The *Star*, like the rest of the country's mainstream media, was the leader's faithful cheerleader.

Williams had chosen to lead the morning's paper with a headline, in type big enough to announce a war, above photographs of each of the judges for the international soccer federation. Jovial Rantao, the paper's deputy editor, noted ruefully, "The last bid we lost in the final twenty-four hours." As he said this, he hunched his shoulders as if the prospect of another loss would be too much for him to bear. Williams laid out his instructions crisply: "We need to get our readers into Zurich, into the war room" in Germany, where the lobbying was taking place. The paper's best sports writer was on the scene. "Can he get insight into what Madiba is doing?" the editor asked.

The delegation to Zurich included Nelson Mandela, former arch-bishop Desmond Tutu, and actress Charlize Theron, among dozens of others. The paper's sports editor voiced an unwelcome concern: What if the South African bid for the World Cup failed? What should be the backup plan for all the space they had slated for coverage? The editor in chief pivoted his head stiffly, like a turret on a tank. "We're going to win," he said slowly. "We need to prepare our readers for a celebration."

There was no Plan B. National unity, and even the country's sense of its own destiny, were wrapped up in the campaign to win the World Cup bid now. South Africans were awaiting the return of a feeling of experiencing a *miracle*—as so many had felt back in 1994—in the middle of their so-far un-miraculous liberation.

Given the challenges facing the country that had proved intractable—

poverty, violence, and AIDS—it was hard to begrudge the hope so many people harbored for another stunning symbolic victory, even in sport, for the country that liked to think of itself as thriving against exceedingly long odds. It wasn't at all clear that South African political leaders and media arbiters had their priorities straight when they lavished attention on a world soccer spectacle and expressed "AIDS fatigue" when it came to the country's burgeoning sexually transmitted plague.

5.

The Doctor

By the middle of 2004, there were two basic approaches to HIV/AIDS among South Africans I met: nearly complete denial or utter fixation. In the larger group, the people I met at political functions, in newsrooms, and in the cafes all shied away from confronting the scope of the tragedy. At a party, there would be a passing mention, attended by a few squirms and followed by a swift steer of the conversation elsewhere.

The scale of the epidemic, and its intractability, yielded a curious self-muting silence. It was as though giving the virus more than passing mention would be an unlucky omen. Among a voluble minority of activists, doctors, and nurses, it was quite the obverse; they operated like human antidotes to this infection of denialism.

One of the doctors treating patients right in the heart of the epidemic, a Cape Town physician named Ashraf Grimwood, fell into the second category. "Hurry up," he said to himself, nearly vibrating in the driver's seat of his Volvo sedan. Dr. Grimwood was a trim, soft-spoken man dressed in a long-sleeved shirt and creased brown slacks. As we set off on rounds among public health clinics that he was helping prepare for the rollout of antiretroviral medications under way at last, the doctor expressed a crackling sense of exasperation. His appointment book, cracked open between our seats, contained a blizzard of notations about people he needed to contact in far-flung clinics.

Grimwood headed HIV treatment operations for an organization called Absolute Return for Kids (ARK), a nongovernmental group funded largely by British hedge fund investors. ARK was organized around a single, clear aim—to identify HIV-positive parents and keep them alive long enough to raise their own children.

We jammed across the flats east of Cape Town, past lush vineyards that produced world-class grapes for Muscadel, Sauvignon Blanc, and Pinot Noir. Not far from luxury resorts along the peninsula the craggy cliffs of the Hex River Mountains loomed. This was the terrain where cattle-herding Khoisan people had resisted the encroachment of early settlers.

There was a sudden, rainy squall, and we shot through the Huguenot Tunnel onto an immense open plain. The sun broke through puffy cotton clouds, casting a yellow glow across the valley. Golden-hued grass and feathery reeds bent in the breeze.

Grimwood said he couldn't register the beauty of the landscape anymore. "I know that will make me sound terribly dull—but I just can't *see* it," he said.[1] He was too busy fighting the pandemic and didn't want to feel distracted. So, we returned to the bleak statistics: one in eight South Africans living with HIV, and two million people dead from AIDS already.

The doctor pointed out that the death toll suffered in the United States on 9/11 was about the number of deaths from this disease every seven days in his country. "We have that scale of loss each *week*," he said, slapping an open hand against the steering wheel. "That's why I think it's so astounding, at this stage in the epidemic, that so few people have any sense of *urgency*."

When I asked Grimwood about the likely effect of the national election on the belated rollout, he nearly exploded. Any mention of President Mbeki or of his minister of health, Manto Tshabalala-Msimang, set the good doctor off. He considered Deputy President Jacob Zuma "next to useless," too, as chairman of the National AIDS Council. The net effect of misdirection on AIDS from top national figures, in addition to mass unemployment and crime, which he considered cofactors in the spread of HIV, had been to turn him into a strident critic of the ANC. He admired the leader of the Independent Democrats, Patricia de Lille, because she wasn't afraid to take on the president about his AIDS policy.

There was just a day left before AIDS medications would finally be available in public health clinics across the country, so the doctor was racing to make sure that nurses, health promoters, and other doctors in the clinics he served would be ready for an onslaught of patients. Over the previous week we had hopscotched from one side of South Africa's southernmost province to the next—from the Atlantic Ocean to the Indian Ocean, from coastal clinics in the south to rural towns in the north.

Grimwood took me to the clinic in Somerset West, where one of the first cases of full-blown AIDS in South Africa had turned up in a gay man in 1988. The first wave of AIDS in South Africa, like elsewhere, had mostly taken the lives of homosexual men. Their marginalized status explained, in part, why the National Party had responded in such a desultory way to early signs of the epidemic.

In the early 1990s, the spread of HIV in sub-Saharan Africa took a distinctive turn: by the time Nelson Mandela was sworn in as president, it had tipped into a generalized epidemic which included large numbers of people infected through sex between men and women.

By the middle of the decade it was clear to infectious disease experts that the course of AIDS in southern Africa would be quite different from what it had been in the United States and Europe. Widespread poverty, high rates of rape, and a swirling mass of people on the *move* in the wake of liberation created a cascade effect. HIV swept across the region with cruel ferocity.

Grimwood hated how his country's leaders had fumbled so badly in response—and how they continued fumbling. HIV had arrived in southern Africa ten years after its spread across the Northern Hemisphere. In theory, then, there had been time to anticipate the course of its spread and head off the catastrophe. "Incredibly stupid and mystifying" was the way the doctor characterized the response of the governing parties, first the National Party and then the African National Congress. Neither one had shown leadership.

When I mentioned that President George W. Bush's $15 billion initiative, known as the President's Emergency Program for AIDS Relief (PEP-FAR), had recently been funded by Congress, Grimwood pointed out that a portion of the initiative originally was budgeted for "advocacy of abstinence," a provision subsequently dropped.

The mantra of the World Health Organization in regard to HIV was "ABC"—Abstain, Be Faithful, and Condomize. The doctor said bitterly, "Your president can't even get past A in his ABCs!" His own mantra, offered in place of ABC, was Prevention, Testing, Treatment. If people learned their HIV status, educated themselves about how to prevent infection, and had an opportunity to treat those already sick, there was a chance for saving masses of people from infection and death.

The doctor felt so confident about this prescription for stopping the epidemic because he had seen it work firsthand in another part of the globe. For seven years he had taken residency training in indigenous communities in Australia, and he had been on hand just as the virus threatened to tip into an epidemic there. The risks of rapid spread were high, but the interventions undertaken had been robust and effective. Explicit information about how the virus spread was widely distributed; clean-needle exchange programs were rolled out to reach intravenous drug users; community health advocates publicized the dangers of unprotected sex through peer-to-peer counseling; and the use of condoms was promoted heavily. "In Australia we put the lid on the epidemic," the doctor said, putting the accelerator to the floor. "We could have done that here, too."

When Grimwood returned home to Cape Town in 1992 after his residency, he remembered feeling giddy initially. Nelson Mandela had been released from prison and apartheid was being dismantled. His sudden shift in tone, so upbeat, reminded me of Gavin Jacobs's romantic account of events at Cape Town City Hall back in 1990. The doctor had seen the campaign to vanquish AIDS as a logical extension of the freedom struggle. In order to free South Africans, they needed to be protected from this disease, too.

At the time, pregnant women treated in public health clinics were testing positive for HIV at a rate between 1.5 and 3.0 percent, the tipping point for epidemic status. Like hundreds of public health advocates around the country, Grimwood set to work, helping draft a national plan to tackle the spread of HIV.

A master plan, unveiled in 1993, was quickly endorsed by all major parties, including the ruling NP and the powerful ANC. It was a reasonably aggressive strategy, the doctor recalled. "What *happened* then?" I asked. "*Nothing*," Grimwood hissed. In his last year in office, President F. W. de Klerk failed to push for the plan and Parliament did not press for it as a priority.

In the midst of the transition to power, and in its aftermath, President Mandela had not moved on the HIV/AIDS front either. While president, he made not a single major address about the epidemic. A little like Bill Clinton, he would spend much of his post-presidential life working hard to make up for this catastrophic lapse. In the mid-1990s, much of the hard early work in diagnosing the illness, and then raising private funds to treat people afflicted by AIDS, was carried out by individual doctors and nurses and by nongovernmental groups like Doctors Without Borders. In the midst of the crisis, the country's largest and most effective civil rights organization, the Treatment Action Campaign (TAC), mobilized in a mass campaign for access to treatment.

In the waning years of the Mandela presidency, treatment advocates began to clash openly with the government. In 1999, President Mbeki's incoming administration turned down calls from doctors demanding access to the drug nevirapine for use in HIV-positive pregnant women, who were at risk of passing the virus to their newborn babies. Leaders of TAC sued to force the Ministry of Health to provide the medications. Mbeki's minister of health eventually gave in, but only when the Constitutional Court ordered her to do so, in late 2001.

The memory of the bitter battles with the ANC government left the doctor feeling mystified and angry. These days, the national health minister was more likely to speak about the hazards of smoking, or of illnesses like malaria, tuberculosis, or diabetes, than HIV. She increasingly talked about the importance of nutrition, or the health benefits of consuming beetroot, lemon juice, olive oil, garlic, and African potatoes in combatting immune deficiency. The minister spoke of *choices*, as if lemons were as effective as pharmaceuticals in fighting the plague.

While the government delayed treatment, HIV flourished. By 2004, the likelihood that a pregnant woman coming into a public health clinic would test positive for HIV was nearing 26 percent, a threefold increase in a decade. This was a tragedy of hard-to-fathom proportions. More than one in four pregnant women being tested in public health facilities, in other words, were carrying the virus that led to AIDS a decade after Liberation Day.

A news bulletin from the South African Broadcasting Company (SABC) came over the radio: the rollout of medication was under way in the largest hospitals in Johannesburg at last, and the wards were swamped with patients. "Finally!" the doctor exclaimed. At last, it seemed to him that the media were giving the national struggle against the epidemic the attention it deserved.

Grimwood considered journalists as guilty as government officials in failing to alert the public about what could have been done to staunch the pandemic. There were few health and science correspondents at daily and weekly newspapers, and even fewer general assignment reporters who incorporated news about HIV into news dispatches or feature stories.

The epidemic was presented by much of the media, much of the time in a simplistic format, as though it was a she said/he said drama. The minister would make another foolish remark, and journalists called up TAC's Zackie Achmat to denounce her. It was the laziest imaginable way to cover a public health emergency and led to predictably disastrous results. This dreary pattern suggested that the pandemic had become so ubiquitous, so much a part of the backdrop in South African life, that journalists no longer knew how to cover it.

The doctor pulled off the highway, tucking into a tarred parking lot at one of tens of thousands of public health clinics around the country. He fetched his medical bag and snatched up a batch of flyers written in English, isiXhosa, and Afrikaans that explained how the highly activated antiretroviral medications, designed to control the replication of HIV inside the body, actually worked. We made our way across the parking lot and entered the clinic. Suddenly I felt a slight wave of heartsickness, right in the doorway of the examining room.

It felt cowardly to register a personal reaction there, but the epidemic was not just a point of professional interest. I had already lost friends and colleagues in the first two waves of the epidemic back home, and my ex-partner was ill with the virus. In the first few months of my stay in South Africa, I had fallen for another HIV-positive survivor. In the new relationship, as in the old one, we often went for weeks without mentioning the specter of HIV. It was a kind of dance, this knowing but also constant forgetting in a rhythm that allowed us a sense of balance against the wily and deadly threat. Here, writ small, were the ingredients for denial of a kind that had rolled out, ahead of treatment, for an entire population across this country.

The first patient of the afternoon bowed her head as she walked in. We were in a small, narrow examining room, with the doctor seated behind a stained wooden desk. The desk was covered with report forms, gauze, and fresh syringes. The patient was a slender, thirty-two-year-old black woman in a red and white head wrap. Her children, aged thirteen, five, and one, had been parked on benches in the reception room outside because their mother didn't want them hearing about her diagnosis yet.

Grimwood explained the science to her, mentioning how the virus sabotaged the immune system by attaching itself to the surface of disease-fighting T cells and destroyed their effectiveness. HIV cells mutated rapidly against attack by the immune system, slowly eating away at the T-cell response over an extended period, sometimes as long as ten years before patients fell ill. His patient considered him soberly.

Doctors assessed the seriousness of the infection, he explained, by measuring the reactivity of T cells, the so-called CD4 cell count. The normal count was 700 and above. The doctor glanced at the woman's latest lab results, which showed that her CD4 count had plunged to 154. That explained why she had been losing weight, sweating through her duvet at night, feeling completely ground down and listless. Her skin was a dull gray.

The patient struggled to smile, and out came a grimace instead. "My whole body is itching, Doctor," she said. "It feels like something bad is moving inside."

Grimwood nodded, reassuring her. Beginning tomorrow there would be supplies of medication at the clinic for the first time. He ran through a checklist of things the patient needed to do before she could receive the drugs: Had she gotten counseling about the disease? Had she joined a support group? Had she learned about antiretroviral medications?

The doctor also asked if her husband was healthy. His patient took a sudden intense interest in the cracked linoleum. Shyly, she revealed that the father of her children was sick now, too. His coloring had changed recently, but he had refused to come along with her to the clinic. "He says there is no problem, there is no such thing as HIV," she said softly. The doctor advised her to insist on using condoms when they had sex because if she got reinfected with a different strain of HIV, especially a strain resistant to the medication, her condition could deteriorate quickly.

After she left the room, Grimwood turned to me. "That husband is the biggest obstacle we're up against," he said. Men typically delayed testing and showed up at the hospital only in the final stages of the disease. Their wives and partners often hesitated to share the diagnosis when they tested positive for HIV, fearing abandonment or worse.

HIV exposed all social fault lines, from gender inequality to the connection between virulent diseases and poverty. Among other things, the high incidence of tuberculosis among poor people made treatment for HIV more difficult because where a patient was infected with both, the treatment regimen had to be carefully sequenced and well monitored.

The doctor knew that if his patient started antiretroviral treatment, she could suffer serious side effects, including nausea, rashes, loss of feeling in her limbs, night sweats, and nightmares. If she fell ill, she would need her husband's help to get through it. If the husband got sick, too, it would be harder for her to stay healthy and care for their kids.

If he had his way, Grimwood would place both parents on treatment simultaneously. But how could he tend to somebody who wouldn't even show up to hear his advice? He wanted to heal entire extended families. "The most important step we can take for those children is to make sure their parents stay alive long enough to raise them," he said, standing to greet his next patient.

The doctor's chief aim in his consultations on this day was to normalize discussion of the disease. Because AIDS was sexually transmitted, it had always seemed like "a calamity one brings on oneself," as Susan Sontag had written during earlier outbreaks of HIV.[2] Treatment of AIDS as a special category of illness only complicated the fight against it. "Infectious diseases to which sexual fault is attached always inspire fears of easy contagion and bizarre fantasies of transmission," the writer had explained.[3]

When AIDS first attracted wide notice in the 1980s, a conflation of fact and fantasy was part of the fight against the disease then as well. As it happened, I was living in the San Francisco Bay Area at the time and had only recently come out as a gay man. I remember vividly how the word of a new, deadly, sexually transmissible disease spread in the first place. People whispered about the new "gay cancer" sweeping through communities around the country.

On first encounter, early theories that the illness might be sexually transmitted sounded like an urban legend—as it had, fifteen years later, to President Mbeki. Key symptoms of the new disease were severe wasting; lesions from Kaposi's sarcoma, a syndrome commonly suffered by elderly Jewish men; and early dementia. At the time Federal researchers were denounced by some gay activists as "sex-phobic" repressives, part of a vast conspiracy of homosexual-hating bureaucrats.

President Ronald Reagan refused for several years to speak of the epidemic, in part because mentioning the strange illness meant having to acknowledge the presence of so many gay men in American life. Only when the actor Rock Hudson, one of the president's close friends, died of AIDS in 1985 did the president mention the disease publicly; in this, there were also shades of Thabo Mbeki and the deep-seated resistance to speaking up or fully accepting what the South African president called a "certain paradigm" about AIDS.

Like South African media outlets, the American mass media repeatedly failed its public, proving clueless in the early stages of the epidemic about how to serve the most important information needs of readers and viewers. Newspapers, magazines, and broadcast networks remained maddeningly vague for several years about how people could protect themselves from infection by the virus. For far too long, general mass media informed its users that HIV was spread through "bodily fluids" rather than using taboo but useful words—penis, anus, vagina, semen, vaginal fluid, unsterilized needles—that would have helped people understand how to protect themselves.

Like in southern Africa later, crazy theories rushed in to occupy the void left open by public officials and the press. Periodic scares about the dangers of kissing, or being served by a gay waiter, or examined by a gay dentist, fanned needless panics. I remember the rumors, amplified by gay media outlets, that the disease was the result of a CIA-sponsored bio-chemical warfare agent accidentally released from the laboratory. Extreme expressions of stigma, in other words, shaped the thinking of people facing unprecedented catastrophe.

Back in 1987, when I was editor of a national magazine called *Mother Jones*, I published an early excerpt from *And the Band Played On*, a land-mark account by journalist Randy Shilts about American politics and AIDS. "The bitter truth was that AIDS did not just happen to America—it was allowed to happen by an array of institutions, all of which failed to perform their appropriate tasks to safeguard the public health. People died and nobody paid attention because the mass media did not like covering stories about homosexuals and was especially skittish about sto-ries that involved gay sexuality," Shilts wrote.[4] "In those early years, the federal government viewed AIDS as a budget problem, local public health officials saw it as a political problem, gay leaders considered AIDS a public relations problem, and the news media regarded it as a homo-sexual problem that wouldn't interest anybody else."[5]

Not long after the story ran, Shilts and a mutual friend joined me for dinner and a long conversation about the unfolding epidemic. We met in a greasy spoon called American Chow, a few blocks from the run-down building where the magazine had its headquarters. Spring had broken in northern California, and it was early enough in the evening that shirtless men from the neighborhood were passing by the large picture windows.

Sighs of admiration from around our table alternated with grim speculation about what would happen if HIV spilled out of the discrete communities hardest hit so far—gay men, intravenous drug users, and sex workers—into the so-called general population of heterosexuals. This was precisely what several key researchers had been predicting—and it was what happened later in South Africa.

As I remember it, Shilts said something like, "I hope it does happen, and I hope it happens *soon!*" He leaned forward over his dinner, and I recall the shiver that ran through me when he said it again. Shilts himself looked stunned by the idea he had just expressed. He thought progress in stopping the spread of AIDS would only be made if straight people were also dying from it.

This feeling revealed something terrible about the level of fear that engulfed gay men at the time. If only the disease was stripped of its stigma as a *gay disease*, the thinking went, there would surely be a rapid, mass mobilization to find a cure, develop treatments, and launch a national prevention program.

In Africa, though, the epidemic had raged on as a result of HIV infection spreading primarily between heterosexuals. And, yet, the same pattern of reactions—denial first, obfuscation next, and delay after delay—seemed startlingly familiar even in this radically different context.

As I watched one patient after another come into the little clinic's small examining room, I thought that the course of the epidemic here had proved my friend wrong in the end. I would have liked nothing better than to call him and continue the argument we had begun back in the restaurant, but Shilts had died of complications of AIDS back in 1994. He had been an out, proud gay man—the first correspondent to work openly in a major metropolitan daily newspaper in the United States—but though we were colleagues and friends for years, he had kept his HIV-positive status a secret. There was a closet deeper than sexual orientation, as it turned out, and more fundamental than the divide between gay and straight. AIDS everywhere spawned a hypertrophic form of stigmata that proved to be a particularly devious trump card held by the virus.

Race complicated the matter further here in South Africa and there in the United States. The virus exploited all preexisting social, psychological, and political fault lines. In the clinics we visited, first in 2004 and in subsequent years, there was a particularly pernicious twist: the epidemic hit disproportionately at black South African communities, for reasons no one entirely understood. Blacks were infected at far higher rates than whites; ethnicity and longtime stereotyped assumptions about sexual behavior of blacks hampered efforts to have meaningful public conversation about the disease. In addition to all the other burdens loaded onto a public health catastrophe, there was an air of breathless anxiety about seeing phrases like *sexual behavior, out-of-control epidemic*, and *race* in the same sentence.

As in earlier waves of the disease in the United States and Europe, conspiracy theories burgeoned. One young man in a township told me, in tones of issuing a news flash, that AIDS was a chemical weapon aimed at the black population as part of a conspiracy to control the sexuality of black people. Another friend claimed the whole thing was a phony set-up—he called AIDS the American Initiative to Demonize Sex. A third friend confided that white people had a cure for AIDS that they used selfishly only for themselves and their kind. Had I heard about it? He watched me for signs that I was keeping this essential knowledge from him.

Among health professionals there was plenty of judgemental moralizing, too. Dr. Grimwood's own colleagues were mostly white and Indian doctors, he told me. He confessed that even they considered AIDS "a disease of low morals." They thought of it differently than other illnesses because it was transmitted through sex. His response was quite pointed: "Fuck that. It's a distortion and distraction." Grimwood paused, before adding, "And, also, fuck *them*."

That reference to AIDS as a "disease of low morals" returned to me months later when I dropped in on LifeLine. It was the national call-in crisis line in

Johannesburg, funded mostly by the South African government, which served as a nerve center for responding to otherwise unexpressed anxiety about the disease. The project sponsored toll-free calls that tumbled in around the clock from people all over the country. Listening in on those conversations provided a vivid chronicle of the private worries and idiosyncratic decisions people were making about how to cope with the disaster.

The center was housed in an office building in the working-class neighborhood of Braamfontein, not far from the new bridge named for Nelson Mandela. Its operation sprawled across an entire floor. There were sixty-eight counselors working at thirty-eight stations, answering questions, during each four-hour shift, in all eleven official languages.

The counselors said that the number of callers seeking information about HIV and AIDS had spiked considerably when the rollout of medications began. The number of callers was up sharply from 2003, when 1.2 million calls poured in. Phones bleeped constantly throughout the room, which meant all of the counselors had to keep their heads bowed toward their computer screens to check on information and record the nature of the inquiries. They punched up one difficult call after another, and I listened in as they attempted to correct all kinds of pernicious ideas.

A male caller asked if it was true that AIDS was a manmade disease and its cure was being held under wraps at a secret location. Another announced that he knew for certain that HIV attacked only black people, not whites. Older white callers required an extra measure of the counselors' patience. "Whites will usually say, 'I'm calling on behalf of my *uncle*.' They don't want to associate with this disease. So you have to pretend you're looking up answers for the person's *relative* and not themselves," a staff member complained.[6] Whites often also inquired about the race of the counselor, not wanting to discuss something so personal with a black person. Even the threat of a fatal disease hadn't broken through racist constraints.

A sixteen-year-old from KwaZulu-Natal province called in because she had given birth to a baby who had tested positive for HIV. The baby had not gained weight, had painful sores inside her mouth, and thrush had spread all over her body. When the counselor confirmed to the mother that this meant she was undoubtedly also infected with HIV, the young woman wept into the receiver. It was open-mouthed bawling you could hear several feet away.

A seventy-year-old woman whose son had died recently at the age of forty-eight wanted advice about how to speak with her daughter-in-law. She hoped that if the younger woman got treatment she would be spared her son's fate, but she also found it hard to broach the topic because she felt guilty that it was almost certainly her son who had infected his wife. An eight-year-old boy called to make sure he understood the gritty details about how semen ejaculated into the vagina or anus could spread infection. He was the youngest caller of the day, but as it happened also the best informed.

A steady buzz of sympathy radiated out into the hallway. A call came in on the next shift from a middle-aged black man from the Eastern Cape. His question initially flummoxed the counselor who took the call. The caller was a local chief from a rural area who had married five wives. This traditional leader was looking for advice about how many times a month he should make love to each of them. He wanted to know if the frequency of sex affected the relative risk of the rampant disease.

The counselor took a quick breath and explained that multiple con-current romantic relationships—which had been one of the big contrib-uting factors to the rapid spread of HIV in central and southern Africa—certainly increased the risk of infection. But if you assumed that all five wives, and the caller himself, were free of HIV now (he sug-gested everyone get tested together), and if you presumed that none of them had unprotected sex outside their circle going forward, they all could remain HIV free. The frequency of sex with each wife would not matter. The counselor recommended that the chief use condoms as added security, though.

When the counselors' shifts ended, I tagged along to debriefing sessions they held. I had noticed earlier in the day how carefree the young counselors looked as they ambled into the building on their way to work, bopping to the beat of music on their iPods like a cross section of twenty-somethings anywhere. Now they trudged in slow motion, with flat expressions on their faces. "People call and they say, 'In my province there's no rollout yet.' They're so sick and there's no treatment available to them," Puff Pitso reported. He was a sturdy black man dressed in a brown cloth cap, gray windbreaker, and blue jeans.

More sorrows tumbled out as the others reviewed their work one by one, going around a circle they had formed. Princess Nkosi straightened her bright-orange fleece pullover and reported on her toughest inquiry of the day. A call had come from a sixteen-year-old girl who had just received results from an HIV test. She was involved with an older lover, a wonderful man, she claimed—he was her "one and only"—and that's why she found it impossible to accept the idea that he had passed the virus on to her.

"How had it happened?" she had asked. Wasn't HIV only something *prostitutes* got? Princess cradled her pretty face in her hands. "I think maybe she went off to kill herself," she murmured. "We often don't know what happens after they hang up."

June Nkosi, a black man with an oval face dusted by a light beard, attempted to raise his colleagues' spirits. He asserted that younger callers seemed less resistant than their older brothers and sisters to the message about using condoms. It was the older boys who complained that having sex with condoms was "like eating candy with the wrapper on."

Nkosi felt that the experience of seeing so many people fall ill had now frightened young people into protecting themselves. Another counselor sitting across from him looked askance. "Are young people really getting the message?" she asked. That question was key, of course. If South Africa had any hope of creating an "HIV-free generation," the country needed an effective mass prevention campaign. There was no way the country could medicate itself out of the epidemic.

Activists from another nonprofit organization known as loveLife had taken up this challenge as a singular calling. They had designed a public health information campaign to inspire a massive shift in sexual behavior among the young. The campaign involved the use of modern marketing techniques, including billboards, public service announcements, a magazine called *Uncut*, a call-in center, and the construction of meeting halls around the country where young people could discuss their generational challenges.

David Harrison, the CEO of loveLife, was a tall, diffident man with a messianic streak. When I stopped in to check out his organization's call-in center, he told me that he thought South African teens were switched off to traditional public health messages. Any effective effort now must treat young people not just as "passive recipients and victims and carriers of HIV" but as makers of their own destinies, he argued.

"Young people are at the forefront of designing South Africa's future," Harrison went on. "In four years we'll be at the tipping point to send rates down, in the right direction."[7] In order to do so, the country needed a dramatic, massive shift in perspective—and the mass mobilization of young people.

Everywhere I went in the middle of 2004, including clinics and hospitals around the country, I encountered a sudden burst of optimism even in the midst of these dire conditions. At Helen Joseph Hospital, in Johannesburg, I caught up one morning with the woman in charge of infectious disease control, Sister Sue Roberts. She was the endlessly energetic, white-haired woman in rubber-soled shoes who never had time to sit down to talk.

We managed a brief exchange before she broke away down an overcrowded hallway, saying, "Excuse me, excuse me, *excuse me!*" On this particular morning, she had caught sight, from the corner of her eye, of a stick-thin woman in a wheelchair who had fallen into convulsions. The woman appeared impossibly thin, like a Somalian refugee in the midst of food shortage; she held up a bony hand, her fingers trembling, uttering a hideous screech. Roberts was able to revive her, then examined her briefly and sent her off for emergency care.

On our walk back through the throngs of patients, Roberts recalled how terrible things had seemed when she first took charge of the infectious disease unit under the old regime in 1991. "I wasn't even allowed to display condoms," she said. At long last, now her clinic could provide antiretroviral therapy. "Now the frustration is that we're being swamped," she added. Success with the medication required strict adherence by the patients, because if patients started taking the drugs but then stopped because they felt better, the virus would mutate and develop a resistance to the medication. "You can do great things with antiretroviral medications," she added. "But you can also go badly wrong," Roberts said.[8]

In the anteroom of her clinic, people were waiting for refills of their medications. They were the lucky ones who had been in the first wave of people placed on medication. Among them were newly saved workmen, nurses, teachers, accountants, and shopkeepers. Glancing down the long corridors of the hospital, they could see, beneath the fluorescent lights, hundreds of people lining up who served as a frightening reminder of the dire condition of their earlier selves.

"I can show you the difference the medication makes," a pretty middle-aged woman in a red cloth coat volunteered. "I know that it's pretty hard to believe otherwise."[9] Ursula Maynier was a coloured woman who had lived most of her life in Johannesburg. She lifted her purse from the chair beside her so I could sit down, and pulled out an official government identification card with a recent photo.

On first impression you would have thought she was showing you the picture of the invalid who had fallen into a convulsion out in the hallway. Spindly and haggard, the figure in the photo had averted her glance as the picture was taken. The eyes were dead, the cheeks were concave, the eye sockets were sunken, and the forehead was pinched in a pained expression.

Just a few months later, though, here was Maynier, the same woman, sitting in a stylish pink blouse and black slacks looking as healthy as me. She was one among many "little Lazarus stories," as Sister Sue Roberts referred to the people so recently snatched back from the brink of death. More than half of the patients in this clinic who tested positive for HIV had CD4 counts of 200 or less, which then was the marker used to designate full-blown AIDS. One in five of them had CD4 counts of 50 or below, which meant their immune systems were quite ravaged and they were less likely to recover fully, even with treatment.

When Maynier had arrived for her first appointment earlier in the year, she had a paltry CD4 count of 54. There had been a delay in getting the right treatment because when she had initially fallen ill her sister had dosed her with beetroot and carrot juice, taking her lead from the health minister's advice.

Clarence Maynier, Ursula's husband, happened upon us at this point. He was a broad-shouldered motor mechanic in a brown button-up sweater. Settling into the chair beside his wife, he grasped her hand as if they were newfound lovers. The couple had been together since they were teenagers, except for a hiatus of a few years leading up to the time Ursula fell ill. They had two grown sons, and when they had separated, it was over differences accumulated during a long marriage.

"I think we had an argument. What was it about?" she said, wrinkling her forehead. He murmured, "I don't remember." Clarence seemed to grip her hand more tightly. After she started dating another man, she reported matter-of-factly, her new partner passed the virus on to her. Her husband had never asked whom she had been dating and she didn't volunteer a name.

When their sons had told him that Ursula was ill, Clarence had promptly quit his job, returned home, and set up a motor shop in the garage next to the house so he could make a living while also tending to her. Ursula Maynier's hair had fallen out and thrush covered her entire body by the time she arrived at the clinic. The itching, she said, had nearly driven her mad.

"To be honest with you, I thought it might be another six months and she would be gone," Clarence Maynier recalled, averting his glance from her. Once doctors at the clinic reviewed her case and changed her medication, though, the itching subsided. She rapidly recovered. "I started walking again!" she exclaimed.

As she stood up now, she insisted that the story of her illness included a positive side. It was the kind of offhand thing commentators some-times said about the pandemic. Normally, I resisted accepting bromides about revelation-through-suffering, often offered by religious leaders, that had the effect of robbing people of their right to experience trauma, and express sorrow, in their own distinctive ways.

Ursula Maynier spelled out the manner, though, in which she felt that her illness had served as a huge wake-up call for her sons, who were nineteen and twenty-four. She hadn't kept anything from them, she said, sparing none of the embarrassing details. As a responsible mother she had felt obligated to supply her sons with condoms and booklets about "safer sex."

Her relationship with her husband, too, was strengthened in the stress of her close call with death. They had never felt closer, she added, smiling at him. As for the questions President Mbeki had raised about the "theory" of HIV and the government's long delay in providing treat-ment, Ursula Maynier told me softly, "I leave it in their hands. All I can tell you is that if I hadn't started treatment in April, I wouldn't *be* here to tell you what I think."

When they rose to leave, Clarence Maynier turned to me. "There must be a cure for this," he said. "There must be a cure. It's like leprosy. One day it will be like leprosy—we don't have it anymore." This was the prevalent mantra—"There must be a cure!"—echoing around the coun-try from patients and doctors alike.

It was an expression of hope against experience, unfortunately. Since HIV mutated so rapidly inside the body, it wasn't possible to devise a vaccine like those that had been effective against polio and hepatitis. Besides, there were four different types of the virus, called clades, and the type commonly found in Africa was different from the type more common in the United States and Europe. In this sense, there were multiple HIV epidemics under way around the world. Nobody knew when, or whether, a vaccine would be produced. It would take an all-out attack on AIDS, from every angle, rather than a single remedy, in order for South Africa to have a fighting chance against it.

One morning a few weeks later, I caught up with Dr. Grimwood again, this time in an examining room at Red Cross Children's Hospital in Cape Town. It was one of the clinics where he regularly saw patients. A beautiful six-year-old child slipped past the door after I entered, and he promptly began tearing around the room.

This boy was one of those unlucky children literally born into the epidemic through infection in the womb. When his HIV status was discovered, though, he was fortunate enough to be placed on medication. Otherwise, he would almost surely be dead by now, as half of all untreated HIV-positive newborns perished by the time they turned two.

This boy had morphed from a sickly child who once looked like a sack of bones into a perfectly healthy kid. That meant he was capable of normal bad manners. He sat briefly in the doctor's chair. Leaning over, his finger upraised, he informed Grimwood that the examination should be conducted with dispatch because there were children out in the hallway he intended to beat up.

The doctor scowled at the boy, barking that he should sit still and learn to behave himself. He responded by clambering across the examining bed. Finally, the boy settled down. Tests revealed that his T-cell count was back to within the normal range. This meant that HIV was still present in his body, hiding in reservoirs, but undetectable in his blood. His appetite was fully returned, evident by his fat cheeks and the slight bulge at his waist.

When the checkup was over, he barreled to the door with his mother in hot pursuit. The doctor watched them scurry down the hall. "*That's* what keeps me going," he said. "He's like a normal kid, playing like a *normal boy*. He's healthy enough to be a real pain in the neck again. This is what I'm living for."

The ministrations of thousands of activists, community health workers, nurses, and doctors were in the process of mass reclamation of hundreds of thousands of lives. The doctor regretted that the entire effort had been complicated so thoroughly by President Mbeki's misdirection. He dreamed of a real national campaign against the epidemic, led from the top by a different leader.

"We still have a whisper of a chance to beat the epidemic," he said. Here was the urgent heart of the story, its essence largely missing from mass media and formal politics. There was a shout, and a curse. The doctor looked longingly, proudly even, down the hallway at his rude, fully revived, indefatigable young patient.

6.

The City

The Nelson Mandela Bridge was an elegant, two-lane, single-span structure arching above the city's old, rusted-out central rail yard. Like its namesake, the bridge stitched together two halves of the metropolis, connecting Johannesburg's traditionally white northern suburbs to its revitalized Africanized heart. The Mandela Bridge represented the way South Africans were expected to digest the indigestible—the legacy of apartheid—by bringing together communities that were still economically, socially, politically, and culturally worlds apart.

Now you could drive straight across the bridge, after visiting the campus of the world-famous University of the Witwatersrand, into the midst of downtown streets swarming with hawkers and traders. Within eyeshot of the bridge, the M1 highway curved, like a quarter moon, around the central business district. The highway shot south, linking more than three million people living within the city limits, residents of the metropolis of Johannesburg, with an even larger number who made their homes in settlements originally established for blacks in the *south*ern *west*ern *town*ship of the city (hence, So-we-to).

If a city could sue for libel and defamation, it seemed to me that Johannesburg had a case to make. A popular tourist guide set South

Africa's most important city up for dismissal in this way: "Fast-paced, frenetic Johannesburg has had a reputation for immorality, greed and violence ever since its first plot auction in December 1886. Despite its status as the largest and richest city in the country, it has never been the seat of government or national political power."[1]

When I initially set off to South Africa, relatives and acquaintances typically asked how much time I would *get* to spend in Cape Town and how many days I would be *required* to work in Johannesburg. Everybody asked if I was sure I would be safe. "You'll hate it. It's a real *pit*," a long-time friend, a foreign correspondent, told me. "Hope you get out alive."

So imagine the surprise I felt as I discovered the city's underreported pleasures. Whenever I flew into the city, it emerged from beneath clouds puffy as gray elephants, so beautiful that it was difficult to describe. Yellow-tinted mounds of tailings from abandoned gold mines marked long stretches of open land to the south of the city; a vast bed of lush green sage and forest ringed it to the north. It was a city with the largest number of trees in any urban area of the world, but you rarely read anything about the terrain, partly because outside observers required that references to "leafy suburbs" be muted in their admiration because of the illicit nature of their splendor—they were located on the white side of town.

Johannesburg was perched on a high-altitude plain, once flat and sparse before the gold rush of the 1880s. Now the city had a profusion of oaks, poplars, acacia, puzzle bush, karee, weeping wattle, blue gums, pines, and jacarandas. The trees were classified these days either as *indigenous* trees or as *aliens* (like the jacarandas), which the government had set out to limit because they depleted precious water supplies. The juxtaposition of gold-tinted earth and a massive green belt gave the city an eerie, otherworldly cast. In the angle of light that fell in late afternoon there was often a reddish glow.

On one of my first evenings in town in 2004, I took a stroll around Zoo Lake, the bucolic area due north of the Mandela Bridge. This large pond with the outsize name was famously deeded to the city on the condition that it should be open to people of all races. It struck me how such simple, straightforward insistence by a property owner had created a gathering place for mixed company. Geese complained along the water line. Couples shifted their weight in rowboats dotting the water. Here was a glimpse, as sappy as it sounds, of one of several possible futures for the globe.

I soon discovered that older people called Johannesburg by its proper name, Egoli (Place of Gold), Kwandonga ziyaduma (Where the walls thunder), or Shishisburg.[2] The city had other names, of course, like Jewburg, a symptom of persistent anti-Semitism, or Sodom and Gomorrah, which is how the Boer leader Paul Kruger once referred to it.[3] Younger people shortened the name and made it more intimate and poetic. They called the city Joburg or Jozi, shorthand for an identity that crossed lines of ethnicity, language, culture, and class among young people caught up in a dizzying kind of life in the fastest-growing urban center in the country.

Jozi was the capital of the smallest province in the nation, called Guateng, but it was also the most populous of the nine provinces. One in five South Africans lived here, one in eight of all jobs in the formal sector were located in the area, and 20 percent of all the country's exports originated from the province.[4] Johannesburg felt, to me, a little like Manhattan, Chicago, and Los Angeles all rolled into one—a mammoth modernizing, hybridizing, genre-defying force in South African life.

Jozi was both a figure of speech and a habit of mind. The city was "at once an outpost of western 'civilization' and a point of entry into another reality, a parallel kingdom of African consciousness," Rian Malan, the South African journalist, had written.[5] Past and present were quite visible here. This was the place where black Joburg identity and its musical accompaniment, *marabi* jazz, developed. It was the city where evolving attitudes about everything from interracial sex to union organizing to lesbian and gay liberation presented the old order with its severest tests. The central delusion of the apartheid system was that you could endlessly exploit cheap labor from black Africans and forever insulate whites from exposure to black people and black culture without setting off an explosion. Apartheid-era distinctions between whites, coloureds, Indians, Asians, and blacks always seemed more fungible and impracticable in this cosmopolitan setting.

Johannesburg burst into existence as an urban space almost overnight, in 1886, and there still wasn't a humble bone in its civic body. The city was founded right after the discovery of gold—actually a *rediscovery*, because indigenous people had mined gold here generations earlier. Now, the city tumbled into a shape-changing force in national life, reinforcing its status as financial capital of the continent. If you drew a line from downtown to the big banks, on to the headquarters of the political parties, around to corporate offices of the biggest transnational corporations, and then out to the burgeoning informal settlements coiled around exclusive suburbs, you began to grasp the reach and significance of Johannesburg.

Up the road to the south of the Mandela Bridge were studios where new music genres and dance styles were being invented every week. The country's fashion sense, scholarship trends, business opportunities, and new political ideas flowed from its galleries, workshops, think tanks, and research universities. Production houses for popular drama, just north of the bridge, had shifted into overdrive to slake the appetite for television soap operas about upwardly mobile business types.

Wildly popular shows, such as *Generations, Isidingo, Rhythm City*, and *The Lab*, offered a reflection of new ways South Africans thought about urban life. Scripts for the shows treated brand new problems, like the burden of escalating debt among the so-called black diamonds, newly ostentatious showoffs. The soap operas that glorified this group of the newly rich also revealed burbling anxiety about the corrosive effects of materialistic "white culture," presented between advertisements for the latest automobiles and electronic gadgets. Edgy new capitalists were, for the most part, portrayed in these dramas as frazzled and ambitious characters who had sold their souls as black people while clamoring to get ahead.

On the other side of the Mandela Bridge were legions of people entirely shut out of what President Mbeki called the country's "first economy." The city center was an increasingly black, African, working-class place. The growing population of traders from the informal "second economy" showed how divided the two worlds remained. Joburg's central business district was like a collecting point for cowherds from the rural provinces, migrants from smaller cities, and entrepreneurs from all over Africa.

Nigerians hawked cell phones, Somalis offered sodas, Rwandans put woven baskets out for sale, and more Zimbabweans poured in every day. The derisive, widely used term that South Africans used for these migrants was *makwerekwere*, which was a nonsense word intended to mimic incomprehensible speech. Wide use of it posed a warning about the rising antipathy toward immigrants from the north.

In the revived arts district known as Newtown, on the other hand, a spirit of pan-Africanism pressed in the opposite direction—*pro-makwerekwere*, in a sense. Here, you found radical mixes of dress, style, food, and rhythms. If you thought of yourself as someone who belonged in Newtown, it was easy to make a further leap, thinking of yourself as an *African* first rather than as a South African distinct, disconnected, and markedly different from people living in the rest of the continent.

At the Market Theatre, the modest space with faded hallways and worn banisters at the edge of Mary Fitzgerald Square, post-apartheid drama had been invented; postliberation theater was on offer there now. In the Horror Café nearby, spoken word and hip-hop sessions presented multilingual and cross-cultural expression. In late-night sessions, prose poems started out in isiXhosa, appropriated a bit of slang from Sepedi or Sesotho, lapsed into English, wedged in an expression from Afrikaans, and somehow landed coherently on an exuberant and defiant note.

At the Dance Factory, across a wide plaza from the cafe, choreographers from Soweto, such as the visionary artist Gregory Maqoma, combined traditional moves and postmodern forms in movement. In clubs like the Bassline and Carfax, packed to bursting on most weekends, distinctly South African fusions mixed jazz, rock, and hip-hop; they blew all night long.

These sights and sounds added up to a distinctive sensibility that scholars tried to capture. "Johannesburg has the potential to become the equivalent of New York on an African scale—a place of sedimentation of the world's cultures," the African theorist, Achille Mbembe, suggested. In a prescient essay entitled "Why Am I Here?" he explained that, as a Cameroonian intellectual, he found in Joburg an exemplar of the emerging "diasporic nation."[6] Mbembe pointed out that young and middle-aged intellectuals and entrepreneurs arrived in Johannesburg every month, in spite of the fulsome warnings they certainly had heard about the city's sky-high rates of robbery, assault, and murder.

Jozi looked, to some of us, like the place where the future of the planet was in the process of being invented. In order to fully arrive, Mbembe suggested, the city's residents would have to figure out how to "jettison the hierarchical logics of yesterday: the White giving orders, the Coloured at the counter, and the Black at the bottom, lifting heavy loads, cleaning and smiling at the countless petty humiliations he or she has to endure in order to make a living."[7]

Wasn't that the essential agenda everywhere—jettisoning race-based hierarchies? Mbembe wrote, "To become a 'universal nation'—such is South Africa's Idea, its call in the history of our modernity. But, for the moment, South Africa is not conscious of its Idea. . . . It is still encumbered by the burdens of its countless wounds." In order to arrive at the proper destination, in other words, the country would have to live up to its promise: "It needs to set itself free from the prison of 'race.'"[8]

On an unseasonably hot autumn day I rode into Soweto, due southwest from the city. I had awakened early in my rented room in Melville, the hippieish neighborhood a few miles north of the bridge, on the day when the international soccer federation, known as FIFA, would announce whether Morocco, Egypt, or South Africa had won the competition to host the World Cup in 2010. It seemed inadequate somehow to watch the announcement on television; I could have done that online from my home in Chicago. So I headed out to the township, because I wanted to see the reaction to the announcement from working-class people.

In circles of academics in Johannesburg and Cape Town, critics of the government's World Cup bid worried about the billions that would be required for stadiums, transportation, security systems, and accommodations for visitors. Extravaganzas of this type, like at the Olympics, produced net losses for host countries. Wasn't this a diversion, a needless carnival, when the country needed to bear down on AIDS, crime, and employment?

Among average citizens, though, sentiment had been running heavily the other way. All over the country, people were gathered around wall-sized screens in parks and community centers set up for those who wanted to watch the announcement live together. The sights along the M1 highway on the way south provided a refresher about how the architects of apartheid had separated people along racial lines for decades.

Behind me, high rises downtown receded in the rearview mirror. Ahead, barren, rocky terrain revealed itself in the once-empty buffer zone created to set off the city and its northern suburbs, where blacks did the menial labor, from the far-flung communities where they were supposed to huddle together by dusk.

The burden of this history, after decades of enforced apartness, still fell disproportionately on blacks. Workers were forced to travel enormous distances on public transportation each day in order to deal with the geography of discrimination known as *spatial apartheid*. Soweto, founded in the early 1900s, grew rapidly from 1948 to 1990 under the old system. It was hard to see how the goal of a nonracial society would ever be fully achieved without a major shift in the patterns of everyday life, from housing to transportation systems. How could you create a unified national identity upon an unchanged social geography embedded in colonial rule and thoroughly encrusted during apartheid?

Past the turnoff to the Apartheid Museum, the highway crossed over a slight ridge made of mine tailings. Ten minutes later I exited onto the flat, dusty streets where houses sat cheek to jowl. Soweto was a vast expanse; the homes in different sections ranged widely, from solid constructions of lumber and brick in Orlando West to the ramshackle lean-tos of Diepsloot.

For generations, blacks had been boxed in together, which meant that lawyers like Nelson Mandela had lived alongside garbage men and the unemployed. Now, upwardly mobile blacks were settling in formerly white neighborhoods, Mandela himself in a mansion in an exclusive community north of the city.

A planting spree in recent years had greened the township, with saplings sprouting everywhere and providing shade on the streets that radiated out from the Hector Pieterson Memorial. The sprawling township, celebrated around the world for the Soweto mass uprising in 1976, was bustling. On this day, the community was fired up again, this time not in protest of the government but rather in anticipation of the decision to be made by international soccer officials in Europe.

At the Mofolo Cultural Bowl, a small park bounded by a massive, raised outdoor stage, I joined a gathering crowd. Across a vast lawn, parents gathered with their children, the kids dressed in frayed shorts and faded shirts, the adults in fleece pullovers and cargo pants. Arches atop the stage were painted light blue and crowned by enormous white letters that spelled out *JOBURG*.

The massive projection screen was tuned to a live shot at the world soccer federation headquarters in Zurich, Switzerland. Below the screen were signs of greeting: "Welcome to the sensational city. *Breathe the life, feel the pulse*." Below the platform was a makeshift altar, with flowers, wreaths, and posters set out to memorialize the life of Brenda Fassie. Passersby dipped their heads as though genuflecting.

Kwaito and hip-hop stars took the stage, crooning lyrics freshly minted for the occasion. The songs were not likely to stand the test of time, but they spoke to the moment. Each one, not surprisingly, concerned religious invocation of deities—soccer and God, soccer and Mandela, and soccer and love of country. Off to the side, halfway up the hill, I watched the entire bowl fill up with people. Little children sitting on the sparse lawn in front of me rocked their heads to the music, holding their hands in their laps.

Between performances, a man in a white windbreaker made a public service announcement about HIV. He asked, "What is a condom?" and held a packet up and ripped its wrapper open, letting the rubber nipple dangle in the breeze. A child of about seven years onstage beside him answered dutifully: "It's for sex." Small kids shouted detailed answers about how you put condoms on the penis properly (pinching it at the end to keep the air out) and why it was important to use one every single time.

Then a hunky hip-hop star took the stage to plead with what he called "two great powers"—the Lord and Nelson Mandela—to convince the world federation's board members to do the right thing. A massive screen behind him flickered on to the image of a luxury sedan pulling to the curb outside federation headquarters. The local crowd turned wild: Mandela, his hair brilliant white against an ornate yellow silk shirt, had arrived in person to hear the verdict.

The screen switched to a view of the audience inside the hall, as everyone rose from their seats to applaud him. The children at Mofolo also leapt up, flapping their arms and clapping as if the father of their country might be able to see and hear them.

The announcer on television pointed out that the 2010 World Cup would be the first on African soil no matter which finalist won. Our emcee onstage asked everyone present to stand and hold hands. We joined in one looping chain across the grass, like born-again Christians at a Holy Roller service. My pale hands were firmly grasped on each side by black men, both of them unashamedly trembling. Onscreen, Federation president Sepp Blatter rattled on for what seemed like an eternity, detailing the process by which hosts of the World Cup were chosen. Finally, he waved the envelope and did a slow reveal: South Africa.

Over the decades I have attended hundreds of mass rallies and sports events all over the world. But never have I experienced anything like the explosion of human energy released at the moment of the announcement. The crowd looked to me as though it was levitating off the ground. Staccato bursts of fireworks yielded string confetti that blanketed everybody. There was a cacophonous roar that rolled on and on.

A frenzied amount of hugging ensued, and not just fraternal pats on the back, either, but rather intense and tender embraces between strangers. It felt like being in the midst of an expression of ecstatic pride in a collective accomplishment. The crowd greeted the news as if the FIFA judges had cast a vote of confidence in the South African experiment.

When the noise subsided, I turned to the tall, lanky young man on my right. Bongani Mdakane had grown up in Soweto. He said the moment was the happiest of his life. He had a narrow, oval face fixed just then in a terribly earnest expression. The young man told me that he thought it was fate that he had ended up standing next to a journalism professor. Bouncing on the tips of his toes, he added that he would like nothing more than to join the ranks of my profession. "I've got the will, and the spirit to do it. It's the only thing I want to do," he told me, tapping his chest. "It's the thing that moves me—in *here*."

Mdakane was a Sotho speaker who had been only a teenager by the time liberation arrived. Like so many young people from the underclass, he had faced stiff barriers to advancement. Raised in the household of a hardworking but underpaid single mother, Mdakane had not been able to afford college tuition. Recently he had lost his job in construction, and his hopes of getting the training he needed were receding.

The young man described this conundrum without a stitch of self-pity. Looking around at the boisterous crowd, he said, "I'm from Soweto and I'd like to report the truth about what's happening here. But if I can't finish my studies because I don't have any money and I also can't get a job, how must I proceed? How can I get noticed? How can I get the training? How do I get *started*?"

These questions seemed especially urgent now that the eyes of the world would be so intently fixed on South Africa in 2010. The distance from the cramped, ramshackle house the young man shared with his brother and three friends to the sleek glass-and-concrete headquarters of the largest media companies, in the northern suburbs, could be crossed in a twenty-minute drive. But the divide, of course, was no simple matter of geography; there were so many cultural, social, and psychological dimensions to the act of crossing the bridge, especially if you were coming to it from Mdakane's direction, that needed to be taken into account.

In Johannesburg, especially in the middle of Newtown or walking around Zoo Lake, there were days when everything seemed possible. You only had to *breathe the life, feel the pulse.* It wasn't clear yet, though, how Jozi's essential constituent parts—from Soweto through the City Center and on to the northern suburbs—would be fitted together in a new way.

How do I get noticed? How do I get started? If you multiplied Bongani Mdakane's questions by millions, you understood why there were so many young people longing for a new leader unencumbered by old battles and unburdened by old ideas. Young people were on the lookout for their own generation's Nelson Mandela, perhaps someone whose name we didn't know yet. That person would become a leader in his or her own right, here in Egoli, the city of gold.

7.

The Grandson

On a craggy hilltop overlooking the lovely, low rolling hills of the Eastern Cape, I got my first close look at the men of the Mandela clan. It was autumn of 2007, and the sun beat down relentlessly on the birthplace of Nelson Mandela. The elderly founder of his country had returned at last to Mvezo, the landscape of his earliest memories, accompanied by a band of grandsons. The consecration of Nelson's grandson, Mandlasizwe, as the new traditional leader of the village marked a moment to recognize how terrible the intervening years had been for his family, especially the year 2004.

The Mandelas were the closest thing to national royalty in South Africa, but they were not immune from either personal tragedy or the broad effects of the turmoil that surrounded them. Mandela himself had been the subject of a series of exposés that had sullied his image. The ANC, the party he had devoted himself to building up for the past sixty years, was awash in charges of corruption and now faced its most serious split in generations because of the emerging battle between Thabo Mbeki and Jacob Zuma.

For the elder Mandela, the installation of his grandson as traditional leader of Mvezo was a respite from other unwelcome news. It was an opportunity to close the circle, in a sense, marking a return to the family's traditional place of origin. Once the formal ceremony was over, and the installation complete, I followed the new *nkosi*, or chief, down the rocky path toward a memorial platform that marks his grandfather's birthplace.

There, I tapped Ndaba Mandela on the shoulder. He was Nelson's second-eldest grandson and he shared a father with the new chief but had a different mother. He turned, with a puzzled look. I asked if he intended to survey the surrounding countryside and stake a claim to leadership in a neighboring community now that his brother was Mvezo's *nkosi*. Swirling around, he whispered, "Are you *mad*? Man, I'm a total *Joburg boy*."[1]

From the first time we spoke, through conversations for the next five years, Ndaba asserted a thoroughly cosmopolitan identity. As a young child, he spent several years living with his grandmother, Evelyn, in the rural Eastern Cape. But the rest of his life was formed through a childhood spent in Soweto and an adolescence in his grandfather's house in suburban Johannesburg.

From the village, Ndaba and his younger brothers would travel with their grandfather back to Joburg. In making that trip they would limn the country's cultural topography—from poorer to richer, from rural to urban, and from isiXhosa to English speaking. They crossed these boundaries without thinking much of it, from the world of uneducated people who daubed themselves with mud, called *amaqaba*, to the growing city dominated by *amagqoboka*, or educated Christians.

It was quite a complicated trip, which I understood better in the weeks that followed. Ndaba met me for dinner back in the city, and our conversation led to a series of interviews that revolved around the sense of destiny he felt as a Mandela heir. His feeling about his destiny had firmed, in the aftermath of the heart-stopping tragedies within the family in late 2004.

At twenty-two years old, Ndaba was a dead ringer for his grandfather at the same age. He had a high forehead, haunted eyes, a wicked smile, and an oval face. The young man carried himself with the kind of upright bearing that marked him as a member of the clan; his voice sounded the same staccato beat as his famous grandfather's.

Nelson Mandela had announced, by the time I arrived in the country in 2004, that he wouldn't sit for any more interviews. In a sense, Ndaba offered me a distinctive angle for understanding this essential part of the modern South African story. "I live with him, so I even know how he *feels* now," the grandson said, inviting me to come visit him in the mansion he shared with his grandfather in Houghton, an exclusive neighborhood due north of downtown.

Just thinking about the distance between Soweto and Houghton that had been traveled by the *Old Man*, as he called his grandfather, inspired a rather philosophical mood. "Here is a man who came from *nothing*," Ndaba continued. "He, himself, was a young boy running around on the farms of Xhosa-land and he became something he himself never imagined!" Here was the prevalent story about Nelson, the amazing arc of his experience.

The other key point Ndaba felt it was important to get across right away was his strong feeling that it was now up to his generation to stop relying so heavily on the elders. His grandfather's generation, he pointed out, had carried the weight of the liberation struggle, creating the possibility of freedom. Now, the contours and character of that freedom were up to the young. They would have to tackle the demands of politically liberated people who were now seeking economic justice.

What did liberation mean if only a few representatives of the liberators lived, like himself and his grandfather, in luxury while so many others remained mired in poverty? "We are the ones who created the system," he said, his voice rising. "The system shouldn't create us. There's a greater thing out there at the end of the day. Ultimately, we are in a battle with ourselves." The next generation had an inherited responsibility to carry the struggle forward. "Why must you be a sheep?" he added. "You must be a *leader*."

By the time we met for the second time, in the winter of 2007, revi-sionist accounts of his grandfather's political career had begun emerging from the work of scholars and commentators. Much of it he described as profoundly unfair. Criticism came from some of President Mbeki's aides, who regularly rubbished the record of Mandela as president in a bid to shore up the reputation of the current leader.

Careful scholars took a more nuanced view: In *Mandela: A Critical Life*, historian Tom Lodge made the case that Nelson Mandela's most important achievement had been his insistence on reinforcing "institu-tional bases of power" and avoiding a cult of personality. "Mandela neither demanded nor received an entirely unconditional devotion," Lodge added.[2]

On the flip side, the historian noted that Mandela had overseen a massive political demobilization of the country's population while he served as president. Electioneering, and then top-down diktat, replaced bottom-up, community-based organizing. The liberation insurgency, which, in turn, had created the pressure that forced the white regime to the negotiating table in the first place, had been allowed to wither away. The result was a political system in which "the institutions of liberal democracy" depended on "the protection afforded by highly authoritar-ian forms of charismatic authority."[3]

Many of the biggest problems in South African politics could be traced directly back to the Mandela years. He established a pattern of attacking critical black journalists as agents of the opposition; he appointed a collection of cronies to high office based on struggle creden-tials instead of competence; and he even had protected a member of his own Cabinet, Stella Sigcau, against charges of corruption, subsequently expelling from the ANC the whistleblower, Bantu Holomisa, whose main offense had been to come forward with evidence of the minister's having taken a bribe. The Old Man parlayed contributions to party cof-fers in exchange for personal intervention on contributors' behalves and failed to enforce essential distinctions between personal favors, party business, and government policy.

Even so, there remained a tremendous residual glow around Mandela's image, as I had noticed at Mofolo Cultural Bowl in Soweto. In the wake of that celebration, the elder Mandela began rather systematically preparing people for his own demise. He started telling directors and staff members at his charities, for example, to prepare themselves for the inevitable. "Everybody dies," Mandela told one of them, sounding almost cheerful. It caused a jolt whenever he said something like this, but he regularly repeated it, almost like a mantra, in his impish, soft-spoken way.

For Ndaba, the inevitable beckoned. Perhaps because his grandfather had served as the central stabilizing influence of his life, much as he had for the country, he did not like revisionist histories about his grandfather's achievements that were making the rounds. He didn't care, either, for talking about the Old Man's warnings that he would die soon.

The third time we met, Ndaba parked his car in a slip two slots down from the sedan that his grandfather and his wife, Graça Machel, used whenever they were home. His ride was a souped-up, bottom-market hatchback, a Toyota Tazz, with small wheels to allow the chassis to stay slung stylishly low to the road. His friends sometimes dogged him, at the glitzy clubs where they partied, about why he wasn't driving something flashier. Even the cop who recently had written him a speeding ticket razzed him: "'Hey man,' the policeman had said, 'Tell your grandfather to fix you up with something better.'" Ndaba presented the purchase of the Tazz as a considered decision, though. He thought that his choice of a modest car signaled a measure of respect for other people. He did not want to rub anybody's nose in his own good fortune, which was an accident of birth, after all. He genuflected in the direction of the car. "That's why I love to drive my Tazz! Joburg is very materialistic—*very* materialistic . . . but that's not what life's about. This doesn't make me who I am. You're a lawyer. You're a president. So what? It's about how you treat people. *Seriously.* Are you a good person? Are you healthy? Not just physically, but is your *spirit* healthy?" This, he added, was the most important lesson he had learned from his grandfather.

Among Ndaba's own circle of friends, many of them children and grandchildren of liberation figures who had now become part of the emerging black elite, too many were beholden to "bling-bling Westernization," in his view. They had chosen to "enslave themselves to the big car," he went on, repeating the phrase for emphasis.

Ndaba believed that excessive materialism and outsize greed among privileged blacks had produced a moral crisis for his generation. Crass money-grubbing was squeezing out a sense of public mindedness and generational mission in South Africa.

While he had nothing against people who earned decent salaries so they could care for extended families, the sharp turn away from public service among the young in the past decade had been quite extreme. I asked how many of his cousins were actively involved in politics. "None, I would say," he murmured. They were reluctant to venture into political life for fear of being compared to the Old Man, Ndaba added; many of his cousins also felt the family had already paid a high enough price for a record of public service.

The house where Ndaba lived with his grandfather was located not far from a second mansion that served as headquarters for the Nelson Mandela Foundation. Their home was a grand, two-story place with large dining and living rooms and an expansive porch off the kitchen with a view of the garden. The backyard was shaded by tall, resplendent trees, and there was an expansive, peaceful glen, especially quiet because of the thick security walls that buffered sounds from the street. In the middle of the yard was an S-shaped swimming pool with crystal clear water.

It was a long way from the village in the Eastern Cape or the prisons where Nelson Mandela had been held, to the mansion in Houghton, the Beverly Hills of Johannesburg. The comic performer Pieter-Dirk Uys, in his drag persona as Evita Bezuidenhout, sometimes vamped on this twist of fate; he played on the title of Mandela's famous autobiography *Long Walk to Freedom* by referring to Mandela's journey as "The Long Walk to *Houghton*."

On our right was the main house, and on the left was the freestanding apartment where Ndaba stayed now that he was older. Inside, he could pull the door closed and crank up his music. He punched up the volume for profane lyrics from Snoop Dogg and blasts from Kris Kross on *Da Bomb*. Bob Marley was among his biggest heroes, he said.

"Who else do you admire?" I asked. "Marcus Garvey, Martin Luther King, and Steve Biko," he replied in a flash. When I pressed the point, he said that his own grandfather wasn't in his pantheon of heroes because it felt awkward to lionize your own kin.

He paused, then raised his hand, palm out. "My dad is actually my biggest hero," he corrected himself. This statement struck me with particular force because Makgatho Mandela, Nelson's second son, had not been known for any particular public achievement. When I asked him to tell me more about his dad, he said that he thought Makgatho Mandela was a model man in that, above all other things, he had remained fiercely protective of his own children.

Inside his quarters was a large television monitor mounted on the wall opposite a plush cream-colored couch. Ndaba rubbed his bare feet against the carpet, channel surfing with the sound on mute while we talked. As he bounced back and forth between ESPN and MTV—where Beyoncé was doing what Beyoncé does best—it occurred to me that he knew as much about American pop culture, and sports, as I did.

He followed my hometown basketball team, the Bulls, as closely as South African soccer and rugby. In the process, he displayed a supranational appetite for world culture that marked the privileged classes of his generation. Ndaba considered Johannesburg his home, but life in South Africa's biggest city only whetted his appetite for something larger. "We're living in a global village, yo," he pointed out. "I definitely am looking forward to working my way around it."

When I asked questions about this larger world, Ndaba seemed completely at ease. When I turned to more personal matters, though, he was far more cautious. Heavy eyebrows presided over narrowed eyes. Ndaba looked wary when we ventured into family matters. I didn't blame him; the Mandela children and grandchildren had had plenty of bad experiences with writers and filmmakers circling around, and asking apparently innocuous questions, then publishing stories portraying them as arrogant and greedy fools.

From the beginning of our conversations though, it seemed clear that Ndaba, like his entire generation, was in the process of picking and choosing which lessons from history, personal and otherwise, to carry with him into the second decade of democracy.

Ndaba hadn't met his grandfather until shortly before the Old Man was released from prison in 1990. Nelson Mandela had been the perennially absent patriarch of the family, largely out of touch and, surprisingly to me at least, largely out of mind. "My parents didn't discuss him much," Ndaba recalled.

Born in 1982 at Chris Hani Baragwanath Hospital, the sprawling and bedraggled public facility in Soweto, Ndaba was the second son of Makgatho Mandela, who was, in turn, the second son of Nelson. His mother came from an impoverished township family, too.

Throughout his early childhood, neither his mother nor his father had worked in regular jobs. Makgatho Mandela supported his family during his father's incarceration by "doing some things that were legal and some things that were illegal—which I won't discuss," Ndaba told me. Theirs was a common story among the offspring of freedom fighters who were off in exile or in prison for decades during the apartheid years. It was also the pattern among the offspring of poor and working-class South Africans who had struggled to stitch together livelihoods in hardscrabble surroundings. In the details of these stories were traces of largely unheralded private costs, through shredded relationships and wounded psyches, of the liberation won in 1994.

As a young child, Ndaba remembered, he was an itinerant, bounced from one relative's home to the next. He spent several years at his grandmother's house in a small village in the Eastern Cape. She was Nelson Mandela's first wife, a devout Jehovah's Witness whose faith had conflicted with her husband's political activism. Ndaba remembered his granny, Evelyn Mase, as a reassuring influence on the children. "She was a special woman, very religious," he recalled. "We would pray twice a day every day and go to church on Saturdays and Sundays—for *three hours!*"

Tucked inside this anecdote was a useful corrective for outsiders who thought of the struggle for freedom as a transformative experience for the majority of the South African population. Only a small minority engaged directly in the liberation struggle, of course; the rest were largely bystanders to the war for freedom waged on their behalf. Women bore the brunt of the effort to hold families together.

During thin times, his grandmother kept her extended family alive by running a country store. Whenever his father was around, Ndaba remembered, he helped manage the store. "He always provided everything, just like a parent should," he said. "For my birthday he would always buy a sheep and we would slaughter it together."

Soon enough the five-year-old boy was uprooted again, this time to live in Durban with the family of his grandfather's mentor, Walter Sisulu. Sisulu was also imprisoned on Robben Island alongside Ndaba's grandfather. As soon as Ndaba began to settle into the new household, though, he was whisked right back to Soweto. There, he lived under the roof of Nelson's second wife, Winnie Madikizela-Mandela. By then, she was a much-lionized, and quite controversial, leader of mass resistance to apartheid.

In these sudden shifts of landscape, Ndaba adopted an eclectic set of cultural sensibilities. By the time he was seven, he had attended a fundamentalist Jehovah's Witness school while living with his grandmother, a

Muslim elementary school in Durban while living with the Sisulus, and a private Catholic school back in the township.

"You go from praying to Jehovah every day and now you go to Muslim school and you have to pray to Allah during the breaks," he explained, snapping his fingers twice. "I'm washing my feet." He snapped again. "I'm in Joburg at a Catholic school, and I'm taught that I have to confess my sins to the Father."

Why he was bounced around so much, from religion to religion, school to school, and city to city, was never explained to him. By the time he got back to Soweto, apartheid was on the ropes, though. Even a boy could feel it. Residents of black townships responded to the ANC's call to "make the country ungovernable." Ndaba remembered the smell of tear gas wafting through his schoolyard as well as the sensation of walking down the street only to encounter his grandfather's image plastered everywhere.

This was how he first had gotten to know Nelson Mandela—as a larger-than-life character—much as I had learned about him myself. Ndaba remembered thinking that this iconic figure, this Mandela elder, was a fantasy who existed mostly in his neighbors' imaginations. "People would be screaming, 'Mandela!'" he recalled. It felt quite odd to have strangers chanting his own last name. The armored tanks called Hippos would arrive to chase after demonstrators, and he would hustle home.

At the time, leaders of the ANC were busily stressing the nonracial character of the liberation struggle. From a street-level view on the wrong side of the tanks, though, Ndaba viewed the fight as completely racially based. "At that time it seemed like it was just blacks versus whites," he recalled.

The grandson first met his famous grandfather later that year, in the middle of 1989. The family was allowed to gather as a group to celebrate

Nelson's seventy-first birthday. He had been imprisoned since he turned forty-four. The family met behind the walls of Victor Verster Prison, near Cape Town.

Ndaba had a child's-eye view of these events. He was stunned to find his grandfather living so comfortably. "Obviously, I had an idea of what prison was supposed to look like—with the gates and the bars and the lockup," he recalled. "[But] he had a pool, a kitchen, and a sitting room." (The little house inside prison walls was a far cry from the conditions Nelson Mandela had survived on Robben Island and Pollsmoor Prison.)

"Finally we met him," Ndaba recalled. "It was: *This is your grandfather*, this old man. And he met our parents while we watched videos. When I left I had this perception that prison is a good place. This is where I want to go. One day I want to be in prison 'cause I want to have a chef and have the latest electronics. I didn't understand this was a political prisoner about to come out."

I asked him whether he had a sense of the important role his grandfather had played in the country's history. Ndaba looked at me with a slight grin, knowing what was expected of him. He had been only six years old, though. To his credit, he resisted the temptation to invent a more satisfying, but inauthentic, answer. "Not really, to be honest," he replied.

In his autobiography, the elder Mandela summoned up a memory of this reunion as a "grand and happy occasion." It was a "deep, deep pleasure," he wrote later, to be with his family again after twenty-six years. He added, "The only pain was the knowledge that I had missed such occasions for so many years."[4]

When Mandela was finally released, in February of 1990, he told the family that he wanted to return home to Soweto. He had spent his first night out of custody in the little house on Vilakazi Street, where he had lived with Winnie and their daughters before going underground. "That night, and every night for the next weeks and months, the house was surrounded by hundreds of well wishers. People sang and danced and called out, and their joy was infectious. These were my people, and

I had no right to deny myself to them," Mandela wrote. "But in giving myself to my people I could see that I was once again taking myself away from my family."[5]

The elder Mandela soon left Soweto, and much of his family, behind. Ndaba's grandfather immediately took up a heavy schedule. The aged leader traveled the globe to address massive, adoring crowds all over the world, including one where I had seen him, in 1990, at the Oakland Coliseum in California. The place, I remembered, had been packed with a cheering throng, and I remembered Mandela thanking international activists who had supported the struggle against apartheid. He had invited us all to come witness the millenarian, nonracial society the ANC intended to create. That invitation had stuck in the back of my mind through the intervening years, and partly explained, I realized, why I found myself here now.

In the next couple of years, life for the rest of the Mandela family had revolved around the effort to fashion a new sense of normality. Ndaba and his parents moved into the family home on Vilakazi Street, the one so recently reclaimed but then abandoned by his grandfather. At first, the boy felt overjoyed to be living with his parents. For as long as he could remember he had yearned to live under the same roof with them.

In the beginning, he said, it felt like a dream come true. "I think he was a good father," he said now, of his dad. "He did what he could." His mother, Ndaba added, "lived to laugh, to have fun, to play pranks." These were descriptions he wanted to have me memorialize—of his father as a dutiful parent and his mother as infectiously high-spirited.

On the other hand, they were also fierce alcoholics. As far back as he could remember, Ndaba had gotten used to stumbling over empties of Gordon's Dry Gin. His face froze in a faraway look, and his voice grew husky. His parents were always deeply in love, he said, but they were also clearly ill suited for one another.

During the next year, when his grandfather was elected president of the ANC and became the party's choice as head of state of the country, Ndaba's father barely scratched out a living. There was ongoing tension between the elder Mandela and his son about this.

"The Old Man had a very huge expectation of my father," Ndaba said. "He had left, gone to prison, and come back. Obviously because he was now this revered leader, he thought his son should make something of himself. He wasn't fair, and I don't think he was looking at it objectively."

He leaned back into the couch, casting his eyes to the ceiling. He was counting backward, recalling that he had turned twenty-two years old, and his father would have been only a child when his father— Ndaba's grandfather—went underground. Makgatho Mandela had been just a young man when his father was arrested, tried, and imprisoned.

The grandson blamed his father's struggle with alcoholism entirely on these events. "It must have been real difficult to adjust," he said. "All of a sudden, you have to provide food for yourself. You have to survive, you know? And you can imagine, at that age you're influenced by a lot of negative forces. That's when you start to drink. That's when you smoke." He thought his father's long spiral downward could be traced directly back to a feeling of abandonment. "How else could he cope?" he asked.

But his grandfather never seemed to understand why his son couldn't shrug off his alcoholism and ganja habit. Ndaba's father, in turn, never discussed with his son what it felt like to have a political figure, an icon of struggle and an international hero, in place of a father.

Inside the family house on Vilakazi Street during the following year, there often wasn't enough money to afford more than rice and tomato broth for dinner. Ndaba paused when he told me this, lost in thought. "I was living in a seriously broken home," he admitted, with a sigh, straightening up then as if startled by the thought. "My father was very abusive, mentally and physically, to my mother." Since the walls in the home were quite thin, he was often awakened deep in the night by the sounds of his parent's quarreling.

Just when it seemed that things couldn't get worse, his grandfather had intervened. Nelson Mandela sent his personal driver along one afternoon to fetch his grandson. The boy had shut the door on the driver, refusing to go initially. In retrospect, Ndaba realized that the summons to his grandfather's house was part of a plan to convince his father to leave Soweto and to study for a law degree in Durban. "My grandfather wanted to send my father back to school," he recalled. "[He thought my father would ask,] 'Who's going to look after your child?' [The answer was,] 'I'll look after your child.'"

At this point in the story, Ndaba paused, then added, with an angry edge, "And what about the *wife*? We don't care about your wife. She'll fend for herself." It angered him still that his mother hadn't been treated with more respect within the family. His grandfather, his grandfather's wife, and the rest of the clan, for that matter, hadn't attended to the needs of her and the other half of his family—the Radebes, of Soweto.

When the driver reappeared the following afternoon, Ndaba jammed his few belongings into a paper sack. His father had advised him that he could go live with his famous grandfather. So, he was chauffeured away from Vilakazi Street, traversing the old apartheid-era geography from the cramped house in the township to a mansion in Houghton where his grandfather lived.

The new home was located on a tree-lined street in the middle of an enclave inhabited mostly by families of white bankers, CEOs, and moguls of various kinds. In the beginning, it felt quite disorienting to Ndaba. You didn't see people on the street, and boys didn't run together in gangs like they did back in the township. Instead of playing together, children were cloistered behind high security walls and locked indoors.

The driver pulled into the driveway of the massive house, and Ndaba remembered a rather muted welcome. "It was like, 'There's your room, and there's your grandfather' (who you hardly see, by the way, because he's always traveling)," he said, his voice clipped. The grandson allowed that it had taken him a number of years to understand the ways of the Old Man.

Ndaba's younger brother, Mbuso, born in the interim, was the first to join him in Houghton. Then their older half-brother, who would later become a chief—Mandlasizwe, or Mandla as he was informally known—moved in as well. When Andile, the youngest of the four grandsons, was born, all three had lobbied their grandfather to bring him out of the township as well. In this way, they had formed their own tight-knit band of brothers.

When I asked Ndaba where he was on the day his grandfather was inaugurated as the first black president of the new South Africa, back in 1994, he replied, "Oh, we all *went*." He had been at Union Buildings at the world-famous event broadcast all over the world, but he couldn't summon clarifying details or articulate any deep emotional resonance with the ceremony. For a few months he had even lived in the official presidential residence with his brothers, where he remembered watching the World Cup on a large television set.

In so many ways, it seemed as though Ndaba's new experience in the world overlapped only tangentially with his grandfather's universe. For one thing, the newly inaugurated president was known for his advocacy of racial reconciliation. Ndaba's own experience, all through adolescence, was of living in a new country riven by the old patterns of racial prejudice.

At their newly integrated schools, Ndaba and his friends were regularly embroiled in racially motivated fistfights. Slurs from white boys were answered with fists, and often there were unprovoked attacks on the white boys, too. "We all became very antiwhite," Ndaba reported. "We had a little clique, a little gang, and we would constantly be fighting with the authorities, and constantly be fighting with a group of white boys—because that's what the struggle was for us at the time. We thought, 'We are the ANC, the black majority. And we are going to fight against anybody who opposed us.'"

This kind of racial tension, visible in the next generation, was an intense subject of concern in the circles of families I had gotten to know in Johannesburg. In workplaces and schools, and even in upwardly mobile communities, students were rarely integrated socially or culturally, even when they attended schools that were mixed.

Frequently during this period you overheard parents wondering why there was so much ongoing racial tension between the youngsters now that apartheid was officially over. I had seen their children roll their eyes because they were tired of being expected to behave like totems of the Rainbow Nation rather than real people.

For his part, Ndaba identified more with the antiestablishment spirit of the township than with the mannered behavior of the new, emerging black bourgeoisie. The refined, buttoned-down style of newly rich blacks seemed to him a shameful exercise in turning oneself *white*.

Back then, he said, he had not entertained the idea of becoming a doctor or a lawyer. Instead, he had identified with the global, generational spirit of rebellion captured in hip-hop, a style that also described a political stance in his circle of friends. "You had hip-hop emerging, and those guys seemed to be going against your conventional professions—a doctor or lawyer or anything like that," he explained. "I was down with the Kris Krosses and the Snoop Doggs." Ndaba lived in luxury, in other words, but at the same time felt captivated by the music of radical rebellion.

"You were just getting this feeling that, as a black man, you know, the system was not really with you," he added. Repeatedly, he got caught in trouble at school for fighting and smoking dope. Since his father had trained as a lawyer by this time, he represented his son once, when he was nearly expelled from school. Ndaba flashed an open-faced smile. "They gave me a suspended expulsion—one more warning!" he recalled. He joked: "I'm a born rebel. It's not my *fault*!"

I asked if he thought the spirit of rebellion was in his DNA, and he vamped on the theme: "Yes, of course. My circumstances! My *environment* made me this way!"

In the middle of 2003 Ndaba's mother fell seriously ill, at the age of forty-six. During the previous few years she had been in an alcohol and drug treatment program, the costs underwritten by the elder Mandela. But when she had withdrawn from treatment, Nelson Mandela washed his hands of her.

"I was a little angry for awhile," Ndaba admitted. "Because you'd ask my grandfather, 'Hey, why can't you help my mother?' and he'd say, 'Oh, I tried to help her. I put her in rehab. I bought her a house. I furnished it. She was staying there with a nun. And still she wants to go back to Soweto and drink. There's nothing I can do for her!' Here's my father—how many times has he been in rehab? Three, four times, before he got his act together. You know what I mean? Here you care about your son. But then, what about your grandchildren's mother?"

Not long after she left the program and returned to Soweto, Ndaba visited her with his older brother, Mandla. The two brothers found her in terrible condition—quite weak and feverish. They took her to a private hospital on their own, and there Ndaba learned the truth about his mother's deteriorating condition. A doctor brusquely blurted out the news that she had AIDS.

"I was just *broken* right there," Ndaba recalled, gnawing on his lower lip. "I was angry," he added. "I shouted at her: 'Why didn't you *tell* me?'" He was now ashamed of this initial reaction, but I admired the fact that he didn't make himself out as a hero. Here was the way these exchanges happened in so many households: the revelation that someone had been infected with HIV brought an assumption of blame down upon the victim.

As Ndaba remembered it, his mother turned over on the examining table after he shouted at her, curling into a defensive ball. "She was just quiet, as if she was ashamed, you know?" he murmured. His eyes filled with tears. "Sometimes you just don't want to *remember*, man."

Ndaba's mother died of complications from AIDS three months later. By the end of the following year, his father also fell ill. The children didn't immediately make any connection. This was how it had happened in too many South African families: one parent perished, only to be swiftly followed by the other. It was the pattern that Dr. Grimwood had set out to disrupt by providing antiretroviral medications to the parents of young children.

Makgatho Mandela, as it happened, was already receiving antiretroviral treatment for HIV, paid for under private medical insurance. But his immune system had been weakened by other illnesses. There was a constellation of health problems, and late in 2004 they created a cascade.

When Ndaba's father was admitted to the hospital in serious condition, for treatment of pancreatitis and a gall bladder infection, that was the way Nelson Mandela learned that his son had been infected years earlier with HIV. Both alcohol abuse and AIDS were ferocious social levelers; his son's illness proved that you could be a complete unknown or one of the most beloved and powerful people on the planet, and it made little difference when you found yourself, frightened and powerless, at your child's bedside.

After being admitted to the hospital, Makgatho improved briefly. There was hope that he might pull through. The elder Mandela and his grandson, along with the brothers and other relatives, sat at the bedside, as in a vigil. Nobody talked much in the hospital suite, Ndaba recalled. "My grandfather is an African man, you know," he pointed out, shrugging. "We don't talk much about feelings."

In his autobiography, the elder Mandela recorded the depression he had suffered during the early years of his imprisonment after he learned, via a letter, that Makgatho's older brother had been killed in an automobile accident. In my reading of the book, I highlighted this statement: "It left a hole in my heart that can never be filled."[6] It reminded me of what Ndaba told me about losing his mother: "I was just *broken* right there."

On the day we spent discussing the more recent tragic events, I was reading a recently published book by the historian Padraig O'Malley, *Shades of Difference*. It was a cross-genre biography/autobiography of Mac Maharaj, Mandela's longtime comrade, and it began with a preface, written in Mandela's name, that amounted to a humbling self-critique.

He put it this way: "The question each of us raises on occasion when we are alone with our own thoughts: What did we do to the people who loved us, our spouses, children, family? What price had they to pay for the choices we imposed on them?" Because of the timing, Mandela must have been thinking of his ailing son. "The fact is that in many cases we inflicted irreparable damage on those closest to us . . . ," he went on. "Our sudden reappearance interfered with the rhythms they danced to. We were unable to dance with them."[7]

In Ndaba's darkening room, I read out to him the entire passage from his grandfather's essay. He reared back, seemingly stung; his grandfather had never said anything remotely like it directly to him.

Makgatho Mandela died after surgery on January 6, 2005, at the age of fifty-four. It struck me, as I spoke to Ndaba about his father's final days, that his dad had been about the age I was now. Ndaba was two years younger than my own son; perhaps that explained a surge of protectiveness toward him that swept over me now.

I tried to imagine how life would have unfolded for my son absent his parents in his early twenties, and then I realized this was the repeated pattern, not the exception, in the Mandela family story. Nelson had lost his father to a sudden illness around the age of nine; Makgatho had lost his father in the struggle against apartheid in his teens. And Ndaba had lost his father, too, to the plague that had swept across the country, in his early twenties.

The immediate cause of his father's death had been uncontrolled bleeding following surgery to remove his gall bladder, but his HIV status was the key complicating factor. After his son slipped into a coma, the elder Mandela convened a family meeting to discuss what would be said publicly about the tragedy.

One of his daughters argued that the family should pin the loss on the immediate medical cause—the gall bladder surgery—rather than the underlying infection. "There were disagreements, there was a discussion," Ndaba recalled. "A few suggestions were put out on the table. An older cousin suggested we say he died of pneumonia—or whatever." But he and his brother Mandla lined up behind their grandfather. "My grandfather said, 'No, we should say AIDS killed him.'"

Within hours of the death, reporters were summoned into the garden right outside Ndaba's room. News photographers recorded the tableau. The Old Man looked ancient. He was seated in a chair, with his wife, Graça Machel, standing by his side and grandchildren fanned out around them.

In photos of the gathering, the patriarch seemed swallowed up in grief. His daughter Makaziwe, Makgatho's sister, stared at the lawn. Directly behind them, Mandla kept his hands clasped one over the other as though trying to pen himself in. Next to him stood Ndaba, standing stiff as could be with his mouth drawn down in a stricken pout.

That's how he looked once again as he remembered the scene. "I was happy we were standing in front of the media as a family," he said, haltingly. "The family was there. As much as I was sad—devastated—it was a good thing we were there together."

For Ndaba, and for his brothers, the following months were an emotionally trying slog. They were highly privileged kids, part of the most-lionized family in the world. But now they were also AIDS orphans, like millions of other children in the country. During the intervening years, Ndaba found it difficult to concentrate on his studies. It was hard to imagine that ordinary things mattered anymore. "I was so worried about my siblings," he remembered. "So, at times you didn't dedicate as much time to the books as you might want." He referred to himself in the second person when talking about this period in his life. "There were times when you didn't really care," he admitted.

The experience of his parents' deaths had insinuated itself into his most intimate thoughts, even including the way he thought about sex, relationships, and marriage. Increasingly, Ndaba told me, he felt wary of all personal attachments. It could be difficult to judge whether you were being approached as a human being or simply as a person attached to the Mandela name.

He had decided not to emulate his grandfather or father in at least one respect. "I do not want to get divorced," he said. "If I do get married, I will try my utter best. I will try it once. But I will learn from my father, and his father, and his father—[they had] four wives, three wives, two wives. I do not want to go through that same process. I've seen the consequences."

Ndaba felt haunted still by the loss he had suffered, but also was reluctant to admit it because he knew you could multiply his experience by tens of millions. There was a deep sense of having been crushed by paralyzing grief right at the moment of everyone's supposed freedom— "the simultaneity of new life and new death," as one scholar put it.[8] Many people found the accumulation of such deep anguish quite difficult to bear, especially when it felt as though they were being dismissed or mocked by the regular public celebrations of their putative liberation.

Ndaba struggled to control himself as he tried to explain the elements of the difficulty, faltering several times and then regaining control over his voice. He looked a little shell-shocked, so I turned the tape recorder off and apologized for making him revisit that period in his life.

I packed up my things and hurried off. Past the security guards and the metal detector by the gate, I felt a slight sense of being shell-shocked myself. Ndaba's story had led me to think about the regenerative capacity of some human beings for absorbing incredibly high levels of trauma— even turning these experiences into something constructive—while others were swamped by sorrow and never recovered from the pain.

In my own life, I had learned the lesson, several times, about how long-forgotten catastrophes could sometimes reassert themselves and sink you all over again. For a long while, I sat slumped over the wheel of my rental car, my mental circuits flooded with images: the faces of children and their mothers in the AIDS wards I had visited; smoldering heads of recently slaughtered goats smoking on grills outside township shacks; Jonathan's face as he told me about the muggings he had committed. These images slid, dreamlike, into another cascade of faces, one set of triggers leading to the next—my sister first, then a close friend of mine, both of whom had killed themselves; the sight of the wasted body of a friend who died in the early years from AIDS.

The faces of public figures flickered, too—Malcolm X and President John F. Kennedy, both assassinated when I was a child. Martin Luther King Jr. and Senator Robert F. Kennedy were murdered five years later. Having lived through these events, in life and politics, inspired a sort of watchful skepticism that had suited me for a career in journalism. In this moment, though, I wondered if I was the right chronicler for the modern South African story. Since I had been part of a generation that learned, the hard way, to anticipate the future in quite apocalyptic terms, I worried that I would not register quieter indications of new beginnings and welcome change.

For Nelson Mandela, his grandson told me, winning the hosting rights to the 2010 World Cup had been the sole bright spot in an otherwise wretched year. Nelson's first wife, Evelyn, had died in May of 2004. Her passing underscored how many of his contemporaries—Walter Sisulu, Govan Mbeki, Oliver Tambo, and Joe Slovo—were already gone. The Old Man's schedule was crammed with obligatory appearances at the funerals of fallen comrades. International news agencies took the hint by striking deals for access to land right around Qunu so they would be able to broadcast live from his burial in his village.

Government communications experts drew up plans for an elaborate state funeral for the elder Mandela. SABC and e.tv, the public broadcaster and the nation's independent national news operation, commissioned dozens of hours of documentaries about his life, set to be aired when he passed.

Once these preparations were complete, Mandela surprised everybody, himself included perhaps, by remaining very much alive. He announced his "retirement from retirement," which was a play on words to emphasize that he was really stepping away from a public role this time.

The main problem, from a political and cultural point of view, was that the vast majority of South Africans were ill prepared for his departure. As if to drive the point home, there were dire predictions of disaster whenever rumors popped up that Mandela had died. The anxiety was expressed most intensely among right-wing whites. Visiting their online chat rooms provided a quick submersion into whacky paranoia. Bloggers drew regularly upon the prophecies of an Afrikaner mystic named Siener van Rensburg to predict that Mandela's demise would set off the mass killing of whites.

Apocalyptic warnings had several common features: when Mandela died, supposedly the news wouldn't be announced right away so that seventy thousand armed blacks could be smuggled into the city of Johannesburg in vans and buses in order to conduct a slaughter. On one right-wing message board, a contributor calling himself "Afrikaner 777" summed up the situation this way: "Mbeki has gone on a country wide rally where he drums up blacks against whites by blaming all [their] current problems on 'apartheid.' Apartheid has not existed for 10 years yet they still blame their CURRENT problems on our white children. White girls 15 and younger are becoming the black man's favoured rape victim so they can spread AIDS amongst us."

The writer had placed quotation marks around the word *apartheid* on its first mention, as if the historic fact of systemic discrimination was in doubt. He had also layered over the *swaart gevaar* with the racist vision of the threats from rape and AIDS. As long as Mandela was alive, the racist concluded, there would be no final catastrophe.

In the wake of the election, and in anticipation of Mandela's death, the country seemed caught in a kind of limbo. This point was driven home for me as I began to trip over the remarkable plasticity in the meaning of the word *now*. It took a while to realize—as I waited for someone who had told me, "I'll see you *just now*," on the phone—that my caller had not the slightest intention of actually arriving to meet me at any point in the foreseeable future.

This was no racially tinged complaint about people keeping "African time," because in my experience the flexible use of the word *now* crossed all lines of race and class. Whites used the word in precisely the same way. "I'll see you *now*," as it turned out, meant "I'll see you *later*"—in some cases, days or weeks further on. In order to distinguish a more proximate *now* from the *now* that meant later, my middle-aged friends simply repeated the word as in, "I'll see you *now now*." Signaling even greater immediacy needed more emphasis, as in "I'm coming *now now now*," as if the word had real potency only if you repeated it three times, as in a magic spell.

It was hard, at first, to tell whether this linguistic twist meant anything. I interpreted it as a sign that people had been waiting so long for change that they had invented a new set of interstices—between *now* and *now now* and *now now now*—to keep faith in the eventual, possible arrival of a much longer *n-o-w*.

The word hardly ever came up among young South Africans, I noticed. It was as though *now* in its fluid state had lost potency from overuse. *There* now occasionally substituted for *now*. To let me know that Jacob Zuma might arrive at his home in the conceivable future, for example, one of his younger aides told me, "He's *there*," which in this particular case meant that he had been placed in a motorcade and was on his way. Young people all over the world were accustomed to being maligned by their elders because they failed to grasp the concept of delayed gratification, but this country had taken the articulation of deferred dreams to an extreme.

In South Africa, where half the population was twenty-four years and younger, the young actually had exercised enormous forbearance. They had grown up hearing a gazillion rhetorical flights of fancy about the supposedly millennial society created in their names, and yet they had not rebelled, in any organized fashion. The increasingly urgent question, as I soon discovered, was the next logical query, taking into account the untimely death of *now*: When, then?

PART II

The Stalled Revolution

(2005–2006)

Water always flows downhill. . . . If you need to get water to the poor who live uphill, then you must put in place special measures to pump the water there. We should never apologize for seeking to reverse the course of history.

TREVOR MANUEL, MINISTER OF FINANCE
2005

They hold this carrot out—*democracy!* Mandela's era must have been the spring rain, but we never got to summer. The rain came down and we got into the mud. Sixteen years! . . . I'm not sure our sons will ever eat the fruits of this democracy.

SANZA DA FANATIK, DJ AT YFM
2006

Informal settlements, like this one in Cape Town, are visible signs of both endemic poverty and the ongoing swirl of internal migration. (*Douglas Foster*)

8.

Inside

Countries sometimes slid into spirals that looked an awful lot like clinical depression in individuals: first came the emotional belly flop when expectations had risen too high followed by a dispiriting fall after which one simply could not get up again. That was the mood in South Africa in 2005, the year after the national election campaign. The ANC had gone all out in the year of the campaign to convince the public that the "better life for all" that had been promised was still within reach. After the party's unprecedented triumph at the polls, though, it was clear that the ANC, and the government, were thoroughly distracted by a fierce internal fight going on at the top.

There were reasons to cheer the successful completion of a third nationwide election, especially if you considered that in much of the rest of sub-Saharan Africa, national governments were still dominated by authoritarian personalities and one-party rule, as in Angola, Zimbabwe, Sudan, and Uganda. South Africa had an independent judiciary, free media, and an established legislature. Rates of growth in gross domestic product (GDP) had risen from 3 percent to more than 4 percent in 2004 and topped out above 5 percent in 2005. Enrollment in secondary-school education soared, millions of new homes had been provided to the poor, and the numbers of people reached by social welfare payments expanded rapidly.

All the same, continued high unemployment, violent crime, and an uncontrolled spread of HIV brought people back to ground. These seemed like the intractable triad standing in the way of national progress. "If only the ANC knew how to govern as well as it knows how to campaign!" a friend told me in March, shortly after my return from teaching for seven months back in Chicago. These problems were deep-seated, and not matters of simple good governance alone. The Gini index, used to measure income inequality across populations, showed that South Africa scored far worse even than other middle-income developing countries in Africa, such as Kenya and Nigeria. The index for the country had been heading in the wrong direction—toward a wider gap between rich and poor—since Liberation Day, in 1994.

Widespread violent protests over the failure of government to deliver jobs and services broke out more frequently after the election. By the middle of the decade, people were regularly marching on government offices and stoning the homes of ANC local councilors, having revived the *toyi-toyi*, that stiff-legged bouncing dance of defiance that had been used against the former apartheid government. Many people had turned on the *people's government*. Barricades went up on the roads leading from townships to exclusive neighborhoods. Residents of a poor community called Happy Valley, in Cape Town, emptied human sewage from the buckets they were forced to use in place of plumbing. They had decided to force whites who were passing by in their shiny automobiles to at least witness the humiliating conditions under which they lived.

You didn't have to be a progressive to register the rising seriousness of these problems. An editorial in *Business Day*, South Africa's equivalent of the *Wall Street Journal*, warned, "There seems to be little substantive change taking place in our boardrooms, and offices, on our factory floors, and even on our sports fields. . . . We need meaningful and substantive transformation. It is the only thing that will ensure our survival as a country."[1]

In his annual address about the country's finances to Parliament, Finance Minister Trevor Manuel made the case for more radical change. Pointing out that the South African economy had grown during the decade at a rate of a little more than 3 percent, which was well below the overall rate of growth on the continent, the finance minister conceded that his government needed "to confront the challenge of making our growth pro-poor." During the debate following the speech, he also said, "If we want to ensure that the opportunities don't favour those who already benefited from apartheid, then we must put in place special measures to ensure that the opportunities are pumped to where the disadvantaged are. We should never apologize for seeking to reverse the course of history."[2] While the Left—the trade union movement and the Communist Party—urged a dramatic reversal of economic policy the minister had overseen in order to accelerate radical change for workers and the poor, it was clear that a single medium-sized developing country could not reverse global trends on its own. Rates of inequality were rising worldwide.

In the country's best-selling tabloid, the *Daily Sun*, a darkening public mood was reflected in sensational reports about crime, car accidents, and witchcraft. One dispatch revealed that, in the midst of an upswing in reports of the burning of homes, and occasional killing of suspected witches, the police were called in one morning on an emergency basis when a clutch of chickens was supposedly witnessed wearing the traditional clothes of Tsonga-speaking people. The chickens were suspected of being *tokoloshes*, or gremlins. A police captain was quoted as saying, "The chickens in the old woman's yard were not headless and were not wearing anything." The story's final, clinching line was this: "The chickens were taken to the police station for their own protection."[3]

In another story in the tabloid, music legend Hugh Masekela complained that a coarsening of the country's spirit had taken place during the first decade of democracy, largely because South Africans accepted acquisitive, money-grubbing values from the West. In articulating this line of thinking, the musician reminded me of what Ndaba Mandela had said about his friends. "If we are not careful about our freedom it will be lost," Masakela argued.[4] Even Nelson Mandela did not escape criticism on this score. You might have thought that the country's founder would be shielded from critical commentary so soon after suffering such a profound personal tragedy.

In a page-one exclusive in the *Sunday Times* in early April, there was shocking news: "Ugly Feud Erupts over Mandela Money."[5] Court filings in a case brought by Mandela against his lawyer pulled the veil away from highly priced "Mandela artwork," then on sale in South Africa and England. Ismail Ayob, his longtime lawyer from the Robben Island period and former close friend, claimed that Mandela hadn't painted the pieces. He also offered details about large gifts to Mandela from wealthy patrons that he had divided up among his children or funneled to the ANC.

The lawyer produced a startling "picture of Mandela as a senile, money-grubbing opportunist," as the *Star* put it.[6] Even the editor who had published this story worried about the larger implications. "We've got this precious resource in this country—the reputation of Nelson Mandela," Moegsien Williams, the newspaper's editor, told me. "Some of us are afraid that we may be in the process now of throwing that resource away."[7]

As if on cue, the Rain Queen suddenly died of undisclosed causes at the age of twenty-five. She had enjoyed a very brief reign. Queen Modjadji VI was living in the royal kraal, just a five-hour drive north of Johannesburg. By tradition the queen carried the responsibility of interceding with the ancestors to keep precious water flowing in a dry land. She had served as head of an unusual matriarchal clan and was allowed as many lovers as she desired—a rare case in which a woman was offered polygamous liaisons among South African indigenous cultures. The queen instead had taken an American-educated husband and lived with him in royal quarters, which had turned many of her people against her.

In the wake of her sudden death, wildly competing theories circulated—that she had been poisoned, that she had been cursed, and that she had died of AIDS. It was hard for outsiders to pin down the truth of what happened to the Rain Queen because her 400,000-strong community was notoriously close-knit. "There is no written form of Khelovedu, the language spoken by the Balobedu," the South African writer Liz McGregor reported. "The most common words used in response to any question about the royal family are: 'It's a secret.'"[8]

On the day Makobo was named queen, it rained heavily, a sign of pleasure by the ancestors. Now, the region settled into a long, punishing drought. This seemed like an augur for the country in the middle of a dispiriting decade.

In the midst of these quite cosmic troubles, more mundane bad news dribbled in. The long trial of Schabir Shaik, Jacob Zuma's friend, came to an end. On May 31, 2005, the verdict was delivered live on television. This was a symbolically important event in the history of the young democracy, for the trial and verdict were seen as an opportunity to test the fairness and strength of the judicial system when quite influential people were involved.

As the proceedings began that morning, I pulled a chair up close to a tiny television at the lodge where I was staying. I figured it would be a short affair, perhaps an hour or two. Instead, the verdict took six hours to explain in a judgment spread out over two days.

The judge, Hilary Squires, bore a passing resemblance to Ichabod Crane; he was gaunt, with a receding silver hairline, and had a serious nose. Once he dispatched the preliminaries, Squires laid out the evidence and his reasoning. After summarizing the basis of the prosecution's charges against Zuma's ally, the judge put his finger on the heart of the matter: "It may be convenient to set out the nature and extent of what is regarded as corruption."[9] That seemed like a reasonable place to begin. The judge had reviewed six thousand pages of documentation and testimony by forty-four witnesses in order to distill things down: "So the giving of a benefit is corrupt when it is done with the intention of influencing the recipient of the benefit to perform or disregard his duty."

Formally, the case brought against Schabir Shaik focused primarily on allegations of bribery, fraud, and corruption. He was the businessman I had seen in the VIP section of Parliament in 2004, when President Mbeki was elected to his second term. The prosecution served as a kind of trial by proxy of Jacob Zuma. Evidence submitted by the prosecution showed a steady flow of large sums of money from Shaik to the deputy president. It followed logically, if not strictly as a matter of law, that it took two to tango (or in this case, three—the foreign company that offered the bribe, Shaik as the interlocutor who sought it, and Zuma as the politician who received the money).

"The overall dispute in count 1 is, of course, whether the payments admittedly made to or on behalf of Jacob Zuma were made 'corruptly,'" Judge Squires explained. "That is to say, were benefits made with the intention of influencing him to use the weight of his political offices to protect or further the business interests of the accused?"

Much of the case revolved around what the judge called a "mutually beneficial relationship" between the businessman and the politician. Sworn testimony centered on the arms deal scandal, which in turn stemmed from a series of purchases from military suppliers in the waning days of the Mandela presidency. Judge Squires noted that a year after the election of 1994, the ANC had found itself deeply indebted, to the tune of R40 million. The judge mentioned that in the competition for contracts to supply new armaments for South Africa there had been thirty-seven hopeful "aspirants," including some of the most powerful multinational arms suppliers, such as British Aerospace and German Frigate Consortium.

Foreign makers of military hardware and software had been backed to the hilt by their own governments in competing for the contracts. Large amounts of money from contractors and subcontractors to supply the South African Navy and Air Force with frigates, submarines, and fighter aircraft apparently had been skimmed off to fund the 1999 and 2004 election campaigns of the ANC. Of course, all around the world, weapons acquisition programs were notoriously laden with pay-to-play corruption. Arms manufacturers regularly larded the cost of production for tanks, warships, and fighter jets with ever-more ingenious forms of commissions, offsets, and contributions designed to land lucrative contracts—bribes by another name.

By the time Squires finished reviewing the evidence the following day, he had summarized quite nicely how the decisions about what to purchase, and from whom, had left such a bad smell behind. In the larger scheme of the country's needs, military spending of this kind looked like a bad bargain. Investigative reporter Paul Holden would later piece together the record of budget allocations to demonstrate that, by 2008, the South African government had spent R43 billion of taxpayer funds on the arms deal over eight years, but only R8.7 billion—nearly five times less—to combat AIDS and sexually transmitted infections, and a comparatively measly R6 billion for student financial aid.[10]

The judge reviewed evidence showing that Zuma had played a crucial role in gaining footing for Shaik on a contract won by the French company Thomson-CSF, which had bid to provide the control consoles for the new frigates. Zuma, as a government official, had vouched for Shaik's bona fides as an acceptable Black Economic Empowerment business partner in the transaction.

Relevant to a discussion of the deputy president's direct participation in the deal was the charge that Shaik had solicited a R1 million bribe from the company on Zuma's behalf in order to secure his help in protecting the military supplier against damage from a Parliamentary probe launched into the deals. The testimony, in other words, tied Zuma both to illegal steering of a contract to a firm paying Shaik and then to the attempt to cover up the crime afterward.

The judge remarked that the prosecution was complicated by the fact that millions of rand paid to Zuma by Shaik "effectively constituted a type of retainer by which [Shaik] agreed, expressly or implied, to pay these many expenses over this period to Zuma or for his benefit or to make cash payments to him as and when he needed such financial help, while he, in return, would render such assistance as he could to further the accused's interests, as and when asked." There was no single payment for an act in his official capacity, on Zuma's part, that could be pinpointed as a strict quid pro quo. The defense had characterized everything, by contrast, as simply the record of a series of gifts and loans from one friend to another.

Through much of Judge Squires's reading, Schabir Shaik was visible in a little inset on my television screen, looking increasingly funereal as the judge talked on. He was dressed in a gray suit, white shirt, and brown tie. Two of his brothers sat behind Shaik—Yunis, an ANC stalwart, and Mo, a former intelligence agent with the armed underground who had served President Mandela in the National Intelligence Agency, had been ambassador to Algeria under President Mbeki, and had been a close comrade of Zuma's as well.

A third brother, Chippy Shaik, a former top-level appointee in the Department of Defence, had been knee-deep in arms deals negotiations but had left the country. Before being dismissed from his post, the prosecution contended, Chippy Shaik had supplied his brother with inside information about the awarding of the contracts.

The trial showed how struggle credentials, mixed in with family ties, were in the process of being translated into quite lucrative business deals under the new dispensation. Schabir Shaik was a longtime financial backer of the ANC, and Mo Shaik had been in the trenches with Zuma. Two years earlier, Mo Shaik had set off a political and media storm when he publicly accused Zuma's nemesis, the national prosecutor Bulelani

Ngcuka, of having been an apartheid-era spy. An inquiry commissioned by President Mbeki found no foundation for the charge, however.

On the witness stand, Schabir Shaik argued that he was guilty only of devotion to the movement and loyalty to his longtime friend. He insisted that he had lent and had given money to Zuma solely because his former comrade suffered from such heavy financial burdens. The deputy president had eighteen or more children to support and no savings.

Judge Squires expressed puzzlement at Zuma's inability to live within his substantial government salary. The deputy president had bought luxury cars and commissioned new construction on land he acquired for a homestead near the village of Nkandla without any apparent regard for the costs. A pattern of financially reckless behavior had forced Shaik to urgently raise cash, even on several occasions when his companies were deeply indebted, raising questions about whether Shaik's loans and gifts could have simply been the charity of a friend.

Concerning the purported bribe from the French arms manufacturer, Shaik claimed that payments solicited from the company were meant as contributions to a charity set up in Zuma's name rather than for any other purpose. He offered an odd twist in his testimony, claiming that the payment had been camouflaged as a business expense only because the French executives were allowed to *bribe* politicians to win contracts in the arms business but not to provide donations for good causes.

Judge Squires announced that he found a certain "hollowness of his explanation." The judge pointed out that President Mbeki himself had successfully sought funding for a school library from the same company. The judge wondered why Shaik had embarked on so much subterfuge, to cover up the payments, if his intentions had been honorable.

Squires noted that Shaik had sent an encrypted fax to the French company detailing arrangements for payments and setting up an elaborate system under which Zuma met with top executives and signaled his acceptance of the terms of these payments with only a nod so he wouldn't be forced to explicitly incriminate himself.

In general, the judge concluded, Shaik's explanation for these events was "not reasonably possible, it is nothing short of ridiculous and we reject it as false." Viewers of the nationwide broadcast could see Shaik, in the little inset, reach over to take a long drink of water. When Judge Squires pronounced him guilty, on two counts of corruption and one of business fraud, Shaik looked ashen.

In his closing remarks, the judge also dismissed the attempt by the defense to portray the agreement to funnel money from the French arms supplier to Zuma through Shaik as anything but an intended bribe punishable under the nation's Corruption Act of 1992. Zuma had not been charged as a codefendant in the case—a curious omission—but his actions had figured prominently in the evidence. Within minutes of the verdict, a law professor, who had been standing by to comment for the independent news broadcaster e.tv, proclaimed that the judgment would prove "earth-shattering for the deputy president."[11]

Zuma wasn't anywhere near the Durban courthouse. As it happened, he was in Pretoria, serving as acting president because President Mbeki had flown to Washington, D.C., for a meeting with President George W. Bush and National Security Advisor Condoleezza Rice. Zuma would tell me later that he had fully expected his friend to be acquitted on all charges, though. Neither he nor his advisors had prepared a plan in case Shaik was convicted.

Eight days later, on June 9, Shaik would be sentenced to fifteen years in prison and ordered to pay a large fine. In the meantime, the political verdict from the country's unofficial commentariat was unanimous: Jacob Zuma was now finished as a factor in the political life of the country. "CHARGE ZUMA" read the banner headline in the *Star* the day after sentencing. "Zuma must now do the ultimate political act of honour," the paper's deputy editor, Jovial Rantao, wrote. "He should fall on his sword and ask Mbeki to appoint a successor."[12]

The only notable voices raised publicly in Zuma's defense belonged to a quartet—trade union chief Zwelinzima Vavi, Communist Party leader Blade Nzimande, ANC Youth League president Fikile Mbalula, and Young Communist League leader Buti Manamela. They would stand by him in concert, and by doing so they had saved Zuma from otherwise certain eclipse. The four leaders on the left portrayed Zuma as the victim of a vast right-wing conspiracy launched by fat cats close to President Mbeki.

The deputy president himself expressed an even more outlandish argument, linking the Shaik verdict to apartheid-era injustice. "In 1963 I was sentenced to 10 years in prison by Justice Steyn here in Pretoria," he announced, in reference to his earlier trial on subversion charges. "It was a political trial. I listened to Judge Squires and there was nothing different to what I heard 42 years ago in terms of the political judgment."[13]

In these three simple lines, Zuma made it clear that he would pull out all stops in his own defense no matter what the consequences were for respect of an independent judiciary. In the wake of the Shaik verdict, he had simply smeared the judge because of a decision he didn't like. It was the beginning of a series of statements, and steps he would take politically, that would seriously challenge the integrity of the judiciary over the following six years.

Just a week and a half after the Shaik verdict came in, President Mbeki brought three of his most trusted advisors together. They were Essop Pahad, the president's closest friend; Mojanku Gumbi, his long-time legal counsel; and Joel Netshitenzhe, the head of government communications. The four advisors swiftly agreed that the crisis around the deputy president had reached a tipping point. One of them argued that if Mbeki failed to fire his deputy, and Zuma became president as a result, the country "could end up looking like Nigeria or Italy."[14]

There wasn't any second-guessing or expressions of personal feeling about the decision, according to the participants. "It was a clear call," the president's press spokesman, Bheki Khumalo, would tell me later. "Judge Squires's comments had established the link to corruption."[15] Netshitenzhe, as government spokesman, summoned reporters after the meeting to announce that President Mbeki would explain his decision on Zuma to a Special Sitting in Parliament the following day. That meant Zuma's fate would be announced, like the Shaik verdict, live on television.

A week earlier, Zuma had turned up in the East Rand, a wide swath of working-class communities set atop abandoned gold mines on the outskirts of Johannesburg. This was where violence between supporters of the ANC and Inkatha Freedom Party had lurched out of control during the early 1990s, costing the lives of thousands. Zuma arrived at the theater in the East Rand to join Zulu King Goodwill Zwelithini at a performance of *House of Shaka*, a musical production about the life of Shaka, the most revered Zulu warrior-king. The play, written and produced by Mbongeni Ngema, centered on Shaka's indefatigable determination.

By turning up, Zuma was explicitly casting himself in the king's image as the preeminent Zulu-speaking political figure of his time. The significance of seeing the country's two most prominent Zulu-speaking men—former pauper and current king—preening at one another was lost on no one. The two men danced on stage together, after which the king announced simply, "We support you fully."[16]

Here was another signal of the risk of a broader cost to pay within the ANC, in cross-ethnic solidarity, as a result of the Mbeki/Zuma split. Political commentator Xolela Mangcu warned that the confrontation between the president and Zuma created "a recipe for the worst kind of tribal politics within the ANC and in our society at large."[17]

It was mystifying, as the tension built, why President Mbeki kept silent about the gathering dangers. It also seemed odd that the president, who had such a reputation for mastery of internal party dynamics as well as such a long history of working with Zuma, would have misjudged his longtime comrade so badly. Mbeki apparently had expected his deputy to slink away, resigning his office, rather than fight back. It was a colossal miscalculation, one that would bring the party and the country to the brink of the most serious political crisis since the ANC took power.

The prospect of an impending bitter and public break between the president and the deputy president came as quite a shock, even for the people closest to the principals. Zuma's children felt particularly perplexed. "I didn't think there was anything [bad] going on between my dad and the president. Remember, Thabo Mbeki had *picked* my dad [for the deputy presidency]," Thuthukile Zuma, his daughter, reminded me during our first interview in 2007.

On the day I had gone to Zuma's home to try to convince him to interview with me, in April, Thuthukile, known as Thuthu, was doing her homework at the dining room table. We fell into conversation while I waited for her father. A few weeks later I invited her to my house in Melville for lunch. That was the first of five long taped conversations about her life.

Thuthu's mother, Nkosazana Dlamini-Zuma, was then the minister of international relations and a powerful party leader in her own right. Once married to Zuma, she was a close ally of Mbeki's, so the fight had a family feel to it. "Mummy and the president are close, too. They're comrades," Thuthu told me, furrowing her brow at how intimate the breach between the two men had been. Suddenly, now, their quiet rift was out in the open. "As you'd drive home there were headlines everywhere," she recalled. "Every day was something new, and it was always terrible!"[18]

Thuthu Zuma was a teenage beauty, with an appealing angular face, long tidy dreadlocks, and espresso-colored eyes that flashed when anyone criticized her parents. By the time I met her, she had begun studies in anthropology at the University of the Witwatersrand. The first thing I noticed was her quietly assertive manner and plainspoken lack of guile.

Back in the midst of the troubles that had befallen her father two years earlier, she recalled, it had felt surreal to watch his sudden eclipse. "I just thought the whole thing was, like, *Swak*, you know?" she said, using a word that meant a total bummer. "I thought it was unfortunate the way it happened. It wasn't fair. My dad hadn't been found guilty of anything!"

For the family, the entire scandal seemed like a mystifying disruption of the main story line the ANC grandees liked to tell: the party was a movement but also a *family*. Thuthu, and the other children of returning exiles, often heard the accepted narrative of the country's liberation, which centered on the intense and selfless loyalty the comrades showed one another through decades of sacrifice.

She was born in London in 1989 while her mother was in exile. At the age of one, Thuthu was moved to the newly liberated country along with her mother and three older sisters. Raised in Durban, she had mostly happy and tranquil memories of her childhood.

The large apartment where her family lived was presided over by her *gogo*, her maternal grandmother, like in so many South African households. Both parents were often away, traveling on party business. Thuthu summoned up only a fuzzy awareness of the violent clashes that had broken out between ANC supporters and Chief Buthelezi's followers, which cost an estimated ten thousand people their lives, around this time.[19] There was a loaded rifle hanging above the front door, as she remembered it. Occasionally, strange men called on the telephone to threaten that they were on their way to kill everyone in the house.

But she insisted that she hadn't ever felt at risk. When police officers showed up to escort her and her sisters to school, "I just thought our parents were just too busy to take us and so the police were nice enough to do it."

The most bothersome thing about carrying the Zuma name that she remembered was when children at school gossiped about her father. Strangers always seemed to know more about his romantic life than she did. When her parents split up around 1996, and her mother subsequently filed for divorce, there were stories in the newspapers before either of them spoke to Thuthu about it.

Divorce wasn't common among Thuthu's friends, and her father had two other wives without having ever explained to his children how polygamous marriages were supposed to work. For Thuthu and her sisters, it was hard to reconcile the multiple wives, and multiple families, with life in a modern South Africa.

Whenever Thuthu and her sisters accompanied their father back to his homestead at Nkandla, in rural KwaZulu-Natal province, the differences between his own rural identity and the cosmopolitan existence the girls enjoyed became quite clear. On one visit to Nkandla when she was little, Thuthu remembered her father's senior wife, Sizakele Khumalo, instructing her to give up her seat in favor of her *brother*. Until that moment, she had been unaware that she even *had* a brother. What's more, Thuthu had never before been told to make way for a boy. She and her sisters followed him out into the yard after the meal. "Who's your daddy?" they asked. And when he replied, "Zuma," they explained that he was their daddy, too.

Thuthu described a kind of doubleness in her father, a purposeful flexibility he had constructed for himself. His two-sided identity—as rural man of the soil and also as part of the urban elite in Joburg—allowed him to behave, like a bilingual/bicultural person. He was a translator able to explain divergent sections of the country to one another.

Her father regularly moved between at least four residences around the country. In addition to three official marriages, he kept multiple affairs going in an ever-expanding circle of temporary liaisons. His senior wife managed his homestead at Nkandla; his wife Kate had lived in his official residence in Pretoria until her suicide in 2001; and Thuthu's mother divorced Zuma before he became deputy president. He seemed to treat his family units much as he had managed operatives in the armed underground, as though they were semiautonomous circles of agents best left in the dark about one another.

An incident in 2005 made this aspect of Zuma family life quite clear. In the midst of the Shaik trial, Thuthu and her sisters stopped by their father's house in Cape Town one morning to visit him. In the living room, they came across a clutch of Father's Day greetings, signed in the names of children they didn't recognize. Because there were other people in the room, Thuthu slipped her father a note that read, "Do you have other children—*young* children?" Her father glanced at it, raised his eyebrows, and jotted down a quick response: "Yes." That was all they said about the matter, her father supplying simple confirmation, with no explanation made or introductions offered.

When I asked Thuthu to write down the names and birthdates of her siblings and half-siblings, she listed nine children, including herself—exactly half of the number of children, by my count, who claimed Zuma as their father by then.

Thuthu and her sisters felt a little like aliens at Nkandla. They couldn't speak Zulu well and they knew next to nothing about the traditional customs that informed their father's behavior. Like Ndaba Mandela, they were completely cosmopolitan creatures with the kind of modern, feminist, and globally recognizable values that made the country's traditional leaders so nervous.

She thought their father could skate expertly across all these kinds of differences. By the same token, she felt that young South Africans lived in conditions, more complicated by the day, that her parents' generation would never understand. "Our parents' generation *lived* politics. But for our generation—look, apartheid's over, thank the Pope," she told me. "Apartheid was a long time ago. Geez, let's get over it and move on."

By then, Thuthu was in the midst of a serious internal dialogue about her own politics and identity. In her early teens, she had lived most of the time with her mother in Pretoria, where she had attended an exclusive private school for girls. The students at the Pretoria school were predominantly white, and they had ostracized her. What she had found even more painful, though, was the rejection she had faced from a small clique of black girls who were Setswana speakers.

Like many young cosmopolitans whose cultural affiliations had gotten frayed, Thuthu felt cast into social limbo. This feeling of alienation only intensified in adolescence. When she moved several years later to Cape Town, she transferred to an elite high school where most of the other black kids came from settlements outside the city. "The other black girls thought I was a *coconut*" (meaning brown on the outside but white on the inside), she recalled. "My generation is [supposed to be] free of the past. But the past has left its mark."

In reflecting on this period later, Thuthu thought she had successfully shaken herself out of her coconut status only after going to work, as a volunteer, for a child advocacy organization. As a volunteer working in black townships, Thuthu had met many children her age who were living in utter poverty. "You're asking kids, 'What are your problems at school?' And the kid is like, 'Insecurity, because other kids sell drugs at school, and if you don't buy you get bullied!' Hard-core things like drugs and promiscuity and prostitution."[20] She noted that her generation had come of age in the time of AIDS and was forced to face the hazard of contracting a fatal disease at the moment of sexual initiation.

By the middle of the decade, AIDS was the leading cause of death among South Africans aged fifteen to twenty-nine. The disease spread especially fiercely where people were hungry. "It's scary when you think of how many people are suffering, how many people are in need of *upliftment*," she pointed out. "The gap between the rich and the poor is big and I don't see it getting smaller," she said. "That's going to be the challenge of our generation."

News of her father's legal troubles swamped almost everything else by the middle of 2005, however. On June 16, the day of President Mbeki's address to Parliament, Thuthu said that her father revealed no sign of nervousness. This was the face he regularly showed the world: implacable, genial, loose, and carefree. "He was totally *chill*," she recalled. "But then, he's *always* chill."

Her father had counseled his kids not to pay heed to any of the bad publicity, including articles detailing the money he had taken from Shaik and the allegations of corruption. "[He said,] 'No, nothing is going on, I haven't done anything shady. *It's just politics,*'" Thuthu recalled. "In our family we've learned not to worry unless things actually *go* wrong."

The morning of the president's broadcast address to the National Assembly, Thuthu and her sisters helped their father pick out a proper tie. "I didn't get a sense of bitterness or anger—but then, my dad is not a bitter person," she said. "He left to go to Parliament. None of us went with him. I went off to school. We said, 'We're here for you.' He was like, 'For sure.'"

In the speech he delivered, President Mbeki explained that he had seen fit to "release" Zuma from his duties, as if he was doing his deputy a favor by firing him. Looking stressed, the president said that he had the responsibility to demonstrate "respect for the integrity and independence of the judiciary and presumption of innocence of any person, pending findings of the courts."

Zuma would claim, later, that Mbeki had tipped his hand with the following line: "Unambiguous as the judgement may be about an assumed unsavoury relationship, the Deputy President has yet to have his day in court."[21] Since prosecutors had not announced their intention to file charges against him yet, Zuma took this statement by the president to mean that Mbeki would press on for a new criminal trial, this time with Zuma in the dock.

One might have thought this day in June had been quite difficult for him. It was a live-on-television shellacking, and a public repudiation, however nicely worded, by the leader of his party and country. If Zuma was bothered by the spectacle in which he had lost his official position and his state salary, it was not apparent to those around him. "[When it was over], he came back, had lunch, had tea, joked, and laughed," his daughter reported. He appeared completely unperturbed. Perhaps that was because he and his allies were so well prepared for the next stage in his contest with the president.

Two weeks after Zuma had been fired as deputy president, I stumbled on a rather surreal scene. The ANC's National General Council, an important party conclave, convened on a university campus in Pretoria. When I entered the auditorium where the meeting was being held, I was surprised to find Jacob Zuma sitting directly to the left of Thabo Mbeki on the dais as if nothing had happened—no breach, no firing, no deepened struggle for power between them.

In the wake of his sacking as deputy president of the country, Zuma had announced he would take a leave from his party post, too. All along, he insisted that he would bow to the discipline of the ANC.

Zuma had been formally charged with corruption by this time. The wife of his chief antagonist, prosecutor Bulelani Ngcuka, had been made deputy president of the country in his place. There was a daily drumbeat of headlines that rubbed his nose in his fall from grace, which helped to explain his growing antipathy toward journalists. Editorially, every major media outlet had supported Zuma's firing. "The Emasculation of Zuma," read one fairly typical, gloating headline in the *Star*.[22]

Yet, here and now, he was cradling his head in his upturned right hand and fixing his former boss with a wary expression. President Mbeki's body was angled away from Zuma, his eyes on the angry crowd. The president wore a yellow, short-sleeved shirt beneath his sports coat, as if he hadn't been able to decide whether to show up in the guise of a regular comrade or as the country's preeminent leader. The rivals were seated beneath a massive banner that read:

A PEOPLE'S CONTRACT

TO ADVANCE

THE FREEDOM CHARTER

In the aftermath of Zuma's firing, as it turned out, rebellion had broken out among delegates representing the ANC's rank-and-file. They had demanded that Zuma's privileges as deputy leader of the party be restored, making it clear that while Mbeki had the prerogative to oust Zuma from government, it was in their hands to decide whether he would be dismissed as leader of their movement, too.

I had stumbled into this historic event quite by accident. Having arrived late for the opening ceremony, I had missed the instruction that this session was closed to the press, and at the entrance to the auditorium bumped into Winnie Madikizela-Mandela, who had shown up late as well. We fell into conversation while approaching security and the guards must have assumed that I was part of her entourage. Nobody checked my credentials, and after she slipped away to find her designated seat, I filed in to witness the insurrection under way.

There was a surge of hooting and jeering from all sides. It was hard for me to make out much of it because I spoke only a few words of isi-Xhosa and isiZulu, unfortunately. But the gist was quite clear. Delegates were upbraiding Mbeki both for the undignified way he had treated his deputy and for his haughty manner in dealing with them. One comrade after another took the microphone to lambaste the president for his pattern of dictatorial behavior.

Delegates were dressed in khaki vests and sweaters pulled down over canvas pants and varied shades of denim. Scattered among them were people wearing T-shirts emblazoned with Jacob Zuma's photograph and words in big block letters: "INNOCENT UNTIL PROVEN GUILTY." The president looked cornered, small, and shaken. He was certainly the most powerful man in the country, but at that moment he was under sustained verbal assault. It reminded me, for some reason, of video I had seen of leaders submitting to public shaming during the Cultural Revolution in China.

Sitting rigidly in his chair on the dais, Mbeki listened with a slack expression. Directly behind him sat his minister of health, Manto Tshabalala-Msimang, wincing like someone in severe abdominal pain.

Beside her, top-level Cabinet members showed no expression. Not one of them rose to defend their leader while I was there.

Other ANC events I had attended over the previous three years were highly choreographed affairs where party members faithfully parroted the line of the day. Here, a buzz of disaffection wafted across the floor and forced its way into the attention of party leaders. These delegates were in open rebellion; they passed a series of substantive resolutions, including one to strip the president of the right to appoint provincial premiers and ANC officeholders at the local level.

At one point the chair, Minister of Defence Mosiuoa Lekota, admonished a delegate who had taken the microphone. "Comrade, you are out of order," Lekota said. "We have moved past participatory democracy and we are taking up the resolution on transformation." The subtext of all further discussion circled back to the question of participatory democracy—and how ANC leaders would respond to this revolt against Mbeki from the party's rank-and-file.

After twenty minutes or so, a party apparatchik noticed me watching the proceedings. He angrily demanded my credentials and hustled me out of the hall. A few hours later, I returned, when journalists were allowed back into the hall again. By then, all of the hooting and jeering and protesting were long over. In place of the angry delegates, a decorous crowd stood in front of the stage, applauding their leaders. Mbeki and Zuma were chatting amiably with one another on the dais as if nothing had ever gotten in the way of their once-close friendship.

After the journalists were seated, a representative from the Women's League rose to praise the president for all of his wonderful work to advance the cause of gender equity. "Congratulations to you, Comrade President!" she gushed. Then the delegates stood together, clapping, as if Mbeki was a conquering hero. It was Potemkin village material, a measure of how uniformly distrusted the media were and how wary ANC members still felt about debating their differences in public.

There was no question that something seismic had just occurred away from the prying eyes of reporters, though it had resulted in Jacob Zuma's remarkable *reappearing* act. Mbeki and his aides, looking depressed and discomfited, left the auditorium. One of them told me later that the president had never felt so humiliated. This meeting had been the nadir of his political career, and perhaps his entire life. The aide himself, he admitted, had gone home and wept. The revolt he had witnessed, he said, was a signal that the party he loved was hopelessly divided and seriously adrift.

Outside the hall, on a beautiful patio, trade union leader Zwelinzima Vavi stretched his tall frame and preened. He held the opposite view. "What happened in there was *historic*," he said. He thought the ANC had been saved just now from a hijacking by conservative forces around the president. The party of liberation had been placed back in the hands of its members. Even years later, Vavi would point to this event in 2005 as a signal achievement in the history of South Africa's young democracy, quite aside from whatever one thought about Zuma's history or abilities. "The ANC was just learning what it meant to disagree—and to actively disagree—something they had not practiced in way too long," he would argue. "There was too much [kowtowing] before that—bow, offer respects, take the pain, and move on. That meeting, in my view, signaled the emergence of a new kind of ANC member who could say no to the leader and still succeed."[23]

In either interpretation, the ruction set off by Mbeki's sacking of Zuma tipped now into the most rancorous period since the party's founding in 1912. It was a fight, both sides believed, for the *soul* of the party, and that partly accounted for its ferocity.

In a prescient article in *Business Day*, political writer Vukani Mde warned of a nation that could be splintered in devastating ways along lines of rural/urban and class interests because of the emerging battle between its two top leaders. He warned, in particular, about the reflexive bias against Zuma's supporters in elite media, judicial, and scholarly circles. "In the new South Africa, it seems, the only open prejudice permissible is that based on class, and the only people we can patronize are our class inferiors," Mde wrote. "Zuma is loved not because he is 'left' or 'populist' or 'nice.' . . . Ordinary people see in the public excoriation of Zuma by the state, the business lobby, ANC elites and their ideological handmaidens in the media evidence that 'people like us' are under attack. Ignore this psychological dimension of the Zuma phenomenon at your peril."[24]

An escalation of rhetoric followed. At a Youth Day rally in a rural province, the crowd chanted, *"Phansi ngo Mbeki! Phambili ngo Zuma!"* (Down with Mbeki! Up with Zuma!)[25] At the first court date for the arraignment of Zuma on criminal charges of corruption, he was thronged by supporters who hailed him as their savior. A handmade placard held up at the rally read, "I am Thabo Mbeki, prince of the G8, loyalist of the liberals, the betrayer of the poor, the enemy of the revolution; I released Zuma of his duties."[26]

This new political storm arrived in the midst of an economic downturn and the hottest period of civil disturbance since the fall of apartheid. Public eruptions ranged from skirmishes over limited housing allocations to the burning of a public library in the Free State.[27] The final years of apartheid had been marked by rolling mass protests to make the country ungovernable. Now the people's government scrambled to keep the lid on, as its older generation of leaders tumbled into a dangerous, dirty, disruptive, and quite selfish brawl.

One afternoon out in Soweto, my new group of students and I were shown around by Jo-Jo Tsheola, a slender man born one year after the mass uprising that made the township famous around the world. On June 17, 1976, high school students had gone on strike against the government's decision to change their primary language of instruction from English to Afrikaans. The young people had been met by a vicious, armed crackdown. Thousands of them, most in their teens, had clashed with soldiers and police and were fired on for their trouble.

My students fell into a hush as Tsheola told the story and led us past the famous intersection where a fourteen-year-old teenager named Hector Pieterson had been shot to death by soldiers. The photo of Pieterson's limp body, held in the arms of his older sister, was one of the iconic images of the struggle years that had helped turn the world against the white regime. It felt different, *chilling*, one of my students murmured, to reconsider the significance of this killing right on the spot.

The Mandela home in Soweto, where Ndaba Mandela once lived with his parents, had been turned into a museum. Inside, we tripped over one another in the narrow passageways that ran between small rooms. Our guide led us back outside, saying that he thought outsiders held a skewed view of Soweto. He thought that Americans, in particular, mistook the township for a ghetto "like the ones where *you people* put your blacks inside."[28]

Tsheola wanted us to understand that Soweto was bigger, and more variegated, than we had imagined. Pointing out the comparatively nice houses nearby belonging to former archbishop Desmond Tutu and soccer magnate Irvin Khoza, he called them "high class." Back when he was growing up, Tsheola said, a young black man had plenty of role models—professionals and political leaders—living close by. Now, a key mark of success was having enough money to leave township life behind. We passed a big billboard sponsored by De Beers, the diamond conglomerate. "DEMOCRACY IS FOREVER," it said, an advertising gambit by the diamond company to associate itself with the country's changing politics.

Our guide took us on a walk through Credo Mutwa's village, built decades ago by the doctor-sorcerer, who still regularly consulted the country's new leaders and top businessmen. Tsheola offered us a hushed account of Mutwa's powers, a reminder of the multisided streams of identity and belief. He was a Christian, but he also believed in the power of traditional healers to cure illness as well as the potency of *muti*—herbs and symbolic artifacts used to heal people.

The world *was* increasingly flat, as author Thomas Friedman argued in his book. But Credo Mutwa's continued hold on a young South African's imagination also pointed up the power of emerging, hybrid forms of identity, where the peaks and valleys of divergent differences still had not been fully mapped.

Just up the street from the Mandela home was a restaurant on Vilakazi Street, where we stopped for lunch. The restaurant was a clean and bright place with a varied menu of ribs, fish, and chips. It was set at the top of an incline, with a view of hillsides in the distance formed by tailings from abandoned gold mines.

Over our meal, my students peppered Tsheola with questions. He ducked his head shyly and admitted that most of his friends were still scrambling to find a toehold in the new South Africa. Some worked as aspirant tour guides, budding musicians, basic carpenters, and would-be laborers.

He briefed us on the difficulties, which started with the challenge of getting a decent education. The public schools, including those right down the street that had been the center of the dispute in the uprising of 1976, remained a shambles, even after eleven years under the new government.

Despite enormous expenditures by national government, the school system was still trapped in a kind of echo chamber imposed by history. Black students were saddled with undereducated teachers who had been taught, in turn, under the segregated system of Bantu Education. A vast achievement gap between blacks and whites, in written English, math, and science, persisted, foreshadowing future inequality even as the economy grew.

While growth in GDP in the country was up, the unemployment rate in South Africa (23.3 percent) was far worse than in Ghana (11 percent), the Sudan or, for that matter, the West Bank (16.5 percent) and Egypt (9.7 percent). The number of South Africans actively seeking work had ballooned to eight million. More than two-thirds of job seekers were between the ages of fifteen and thirty-five.

Tsheola traced Soweto's ongoing troubles to what had happened in the township during the late stages of apartheid. He was just a child when the ANC called on masses of supporters to make the country *ungovernable*. Poor people had borne the brunt of the violence that followed, he said.

"Nelson Mandela was responsible for people dying, too, you know," he added, drawing startled looks from the students. Tsheola said he couldn't understand why people lionized the leader, celebrating the results of the revolution, but then demonized the insurgents who had kept the rebellion hot.

He remembered Soweto during his youth as an often-terrifying place. The neighborhood was full of gangsters who only posed as activists; thugs regularly used political justification as a cover for drug dealing, arms running, and other crimes. Men and women had been *necklaced*—burned to death with gasoline poured into a tire placed around their necks—right before his eyes, he said.

In 1986, Winnie Mandela famously had supported this practice at a rally outside Johannesburg. "Together, hand in hand, with our boxes of matches and our necklaces, we shall liberate this country," she proclaimed.[29] "We all did it," Tsheola said, which struck me as a refreshingly honest but also searing four-word proclamation.

After we got back on our bus, I leaned across the aisle between us to ask Tsheola which party he had supported in the 2004 election. He paused, grimaced, and looked away. Given the criticisms he had offered of the ANC government, I thought he might be a supporter of the Pan-Africanist Congress, whose leader I had heard criticize the government as a tool of the new ruling class at President Mbeki's reelection the previous year in Parliament.

"I've never voted," the young man confessed. I quickly did the math: he would have been one year shy of being old enough to vote in 1994, when Mandela headed the ANC list. In two subsequent national elections, and two municipal rounds, since then, he had never exercised his political rights, though.

"Wait a minute," I said, pointing in the direction of the monument to Hector Pieterson. "How could you *not* vote?" The young man offered a shy smile. "Why vote?" he replied. "As a Sotho speaker, what do the elections have to do with *me*?" The government, he said with an edge, was "nothing but a *Xhosa Nostra*." This reply silenced me. "Politics is *politics*," he went on, drawing out the word as though it was another language.

None of his young friends had voted in the most recent election either. They considered politics nothing but a racket "that excludes all but the Xhosa." As an example, he pointed at the way Zuma was being treated. Leaders of the ANC had warned against ethnic cleavages for nearly a century, but now the split at the top would certainly exacerbate them.

Postelection surveys showed that millions of people had decided not to participate in elections. The ANC had triumphed in 2004 with nearly 70 percent of the vote, up from 66.4 percent in 1999. This apparent rise in support masked the fact that increasing numbers of eligible voters had stayed away from the voting booth. The ANC under Nelson Mandela had won 12.2 million votes in 1994. From a larger potential electorate ten years later, the party led by Thabo Mbeki drew 10.8 million votes. More than 5 million South Africans were newly eligible to vote from 1994 to 2004, but only half of potential young participants had registered.[30] This amounted to a surge in antipolitical sentiment. The fight between Mbeki and Zuma was likely to hasten the turn away from formal politics by the young.

In the midst of the burgeoning political crisis, I went out for drinks one night with Mondli Makhanya, the young, influential editor of the *Sunday Times*. I had been shadowing him for several weeks in the paper's newsroom and had been struck by the triumphant pose he had taken on the day the president dismissed Zuma. "It works! This country *works*," he had told his staff while watching Mbeki's speech, which signaled that he thought Zuma's sacking meant the country's political system had passed an important test in jettisoning such a powerful and corrupt leader. After work, we drove out nearly to the end of Jan Smuts Avenue, parking at the Piazza Centre. We headed out onto an expansive deck behind a bar and restaurant that had the best view of Jozi's orange- and yellow-tinted blaze of lights. It was a crisp, clear winter night, and Johannesburg was showing off again. We looked out over high-tone suburbs where new construction signaled expansion of an integrated middle class. This vantage point presented a bracing, encouraging view of the progress under way.

Digging into a plate of grilled jumbo shrimp, I told Makhanya what the tour guide had said to me about the dominance of the "Xhosa Nostra." I summarized my reading of the polls and emerging understanding, from my interviews, of the apolitical turn by the young, including the children and grandchildren of the new black elite. Weren't these worrisome danger signs?

It seemed to me, I said, that resurgent ethnic tensions might upend the whole democratic experiment. Makhanya was a big-boned man with a boyish face. He had once been an ANC loyalist, but now he was more committed to building a dynamic, representative, courageous media. "No, no, no, no!" he protested. "There are signs that we have become a normal society—like yours." He pointed out that voting turnout typically dropped off after two or three elections, and he felt that ethnic-based campaigning simply wouldn't work in South Africa.

The editor complained that there were only two narratives Americans, particularly American journalists, seemed to recognize—the *miracle* and the *cataclysm*. First, he complained, we exaggerated some event and then acted surprised if the underlying reality proved more complicated. Inflation/deflation: this was the cycle that passed for thoughtful coverage.

Makhanya had never thought of the transition to majority rule in the mid-1990s as a miracle—he had lived through it, after all, and it had felt like a complicated mix of hard-won victories and periodic setbacks rather than something magical. He felt, in a similar vein, that the nation wasn't on the verge of a catastrophe now. South Africa was, instead, a nation engaged in wobbling progress, often inching ahead and sometimes faltering. "Maybe we'll even become more boring in the next few years," he said.

"Wait a minute," I replied, ticking off myriad ways in which the country seemed quite abnormal, including its persistently high rates of AIDS and crime. "Those are just vestiges of apartheid," he said, neatly encapsulating a kind of double vision that seemed to be required of anyone running a South African media operation. When somebody mentioned the terrible things that were happening, people traced the causes back to the stark inequalities and systemic brutality of the old era. At every emerging sign that things were getting better, they reveled in the possibility that South Africa, at long last, would become a little boring, and ever more *normal*.

9.

Outside

ere's what *normal* felt like to a band of kids living on the streets in Cape Town circa 2005: In a ditch beneath the freeway, Jonathan and the other boys in his gang gathered to sleep, having graduated from begging for coins to snatching purses to armed robbery. He was the homeless boy from Atlantis who had hitched a ride into the city two years earlier in order to seek a better life. The gang clustered together against the evening chill, told jokes, and shared a roasted chicken. The boys huffed lighter fluid while passing around spliffs of ganja.

Suddenly, things tipped from cool to quite tense. An argument broke out between an older member of the gang and a spunky child named Oupa. The smaller boy had refused demands to share his stash of glue with the bigger boy. After Oupa had lain down, drifting off to sleep, the angry older boy splashed him with lighter fluid and flicked his cigarette on top. "The small one don't want to give the big one," was the way Jonathan explained it, hunching up his shoulders as if girding against the memory. "He did light it and then he did throw the match at him," he continued. "Then he did *cook*."

I thought of what the tour guide in Soweto had told us about the psychic cost of watching so much violence being perpetrated during the struggle years and tried to match Jonathan's even tone.

"Did the older boy kill him?" I asked.

"Yes," Jonathan replied.

"And you saw that?"

"Yeah," he said, shrugging again. He cocked his head, surprised that I should be so ignorant about this widely known affair. "Didn't you know? The whole *Parade* knew—*everyone* knew that," he said with a hint of condescension.[1]

Jonathan's comment brought back the memory of his reaction when I had laughed because he did not know the name of the current president. Here was turnabout, and a reversal of roles: Jonathan was the expert about the world he occupied. Oupa's death had clearly worried him. He began to wonder if he might be the next boy to *cook* one night. The incident was also a test of loyalty and faith. The younger boy had been killed so casually, and Jonathan had loved him deeply, like a brother. But the older boy who had ignited the flame was a brother, too. How could he mourn the first without turning on the second?

It was several years since this killing when Jonathan and I had met for a series of interviews in 2007. Months later, after our first meeting on a street corner outside the carpentry workshop he attended, he showed me landmarks of his Cape Town life—the stretch of walkway with a view of the ocean where he liked to stroll, the ditch beneath the freeway where he slept, and the Parade, that same vast plaza where my friend Gavin Jacobs had been part of the massive crowd gathered to greet Mandela on the day of his release in 1990. The sight of the Parade reminded Jonathan not of Mandela, but of Oupa's execution. As we skirted its edges, he explained to me how he had been taught to *skarrel* for money, buy glue, and pinch jewelry, purses, and wallets from tourists.

From the beginning, I understood that Jonathan was no exemplar of the next generation of South Africans. He was an outlier in many ways, a marginalized individual of the kind foreign journalists often found it easy to caricature. When in doubt, we chroniclers reached for the grittiest tale of crime and sexual exploitation. Social pathology, like soft pornography, made for gripping reporting and compelling reading. Capturing the meaning of Jonathan's life was an exercise fraught with the temptation to exploit or titillate, as Susan Sontag pointed out in *Regarding the Pain of Others*: "Being a spectator of calamities taking place in another country is a quintessential modern experience, the cumulative offering by more than a century and a half's worth of those professional, specialized tourists known as journalists."[2]

It was always harder to render the complicated push-and-pull tales of more representative lives. This was an issue that scholars at the University of Cape Town raised in a comprehensive study of young people growing up in post-apartheid South Africa. Young women and men of the country had inherited a legacy of inequality, racial inequality, AIDS, and violence, in other words, but they also had witnessed a recent history of dramatic, partly successful change. The scholars concluded, "More than a decade into the new political dispensation, young Capetonians aspire to the possibilities denied to their parents. They participate in creating a society that in some respects is conducive to the achievement of their dreams, yet remains unequal, difficult and often dangerous at the same time."[3]

The story of change in the lives of young South Africans was full of nuances while Jonathan's tale seemed quite stark. Systemic conditions threatened to produce a rising number of boys like him, though. More than one hundred thousand children were threatened with death from preventable diseases each year in the new South Africa,[4] and one in six had already been infected with HIV. While larger numbers of students from low-income families were going to school and on to college, dropout rates remained high. The burgeoning population of poor, unemployed youngsters posed a stark warning about the future.

In the aftermath of the election in 2004, the national Cabinet held several long meetings focused on the need to do something transformative for teenagers. Ambitious new initiatives were launched, including a supercharged R372 billion program known as the Accelerated and Shared Growth Initiative for South Africa (ASGISA), which aimed to break the cycle of poverty for the young.

Mbeki's Cabinet was well aware that economic growth alone would not substantially improve the picture on its own. Even if the country's growth rate surged up to 6 percent, orders of magnitude higher than its current rate, presidential advisor Joel Netshitenzhe figured that many young people from marginalized communities still would not be affected in a meaningful way.

This was the intersection where race, class, and age discrimination were thoroughly, frustratingly intertwined. While blacks accounted for 79 percent of the country's population, they made up 84 percent of South Africans up to fourteen years old. Seventy-nine percent of South Africans aged thirty and over were employed, but only half of those twenty-four and younger who were looking for work could find jobs.

In an address to the National Youth Commission in 2005, the president's advisor suggested that the needs of young South Africans would receive their due only with a more interventionist government in a "developmental state."[5] A key goal of the current national initiative was to align the schools and the skill-training programs with the needs of employers in an increasingly globalized economy.

Anyone aware of the homeless street kids knew the effort was desperately needed and long overdue, but there were few signs of its effects yet on the street corners where the kids hung out. From Jonathan's perspective, these programs offered negligible benefits. He lived outside the margins, and nothing in the new national effort reached him.

Far more visible, from Jonathan's vantage point, were the periodic efforts made by city officials and the police simply to get him and his friends away from the tourists. Sometimes, the police, or the security details hired by local merchants, swept them up and drove them out of the city center in vans, only to dump them near the beach on the Indian Ocean side of the peninsula.

That was how Jonathan's gang ended up skulking around the beach near Muizenberg one summer night. The boys had not been in town long before they caught sight of an elderly man headed home. "The guy going into his house now—it's like a *madala* [an old man]," Jonathan told me, falling into present tense as he did when telling me stories.

The boys surrounded the old man, gave him a stiff beating, and swarmed around his house. When they found only a few pieces of gold jewelry and pocket change, they banged on him more fiercely. "When I'm seeing that he's bleeding, then I stop," he said, sliding his eyes in my direction. "But the other one who had a knife, he just stabs. The *madala* don't want to talk. That's why we did go like that."

When the *madala* finally gave in, revealing that there was a case filled with cash taped behind the toilet bowl in his bathroom, the boys rejoiced. Jonathan stretched his arms wide to show me how vast the fortune had seemed. It was certainly a glorious haul. The inconvenient rub was that the sound of the old man's howls still reverberated in his memory years later. Even as he told the story to me, Jonathan winced.

The way he described it, the voice was a high-pitched, desperate, wheedling sound of a man begging for his life. He turned his face away when he told this part of the story. The experience was so terrifying that he decided never to rob again. When he told the other boys he had had enough, he worried that they would kill him as a security risk. "They wanted to kill me—almost," he reported softly. "But I had one friend who liked me, and he said, 'Don't kill him, leave him.'"

In deciding to withdraw from the gang, Jonathan had taken on a new set of problems. He wondered how he would he make his way in the world now. How would he eat, who would he hang out with, and where would he live? That's when he remembered the outreach worker at a program called Homestead, which was geared toward homeless kids living off the street.

The counselor's name was Gerald Jacobs, and he had come around regularly to see the boys, offering them a warm meal and a bed out of the cold. Jonathan recalled Jacobs once told him that Jonathan had the power to decide what kind of man he would become. It was an audacious proposition. Jonathan had decided to put Gerald's offer to the test. He had come off the streets and Jacobs helped him get enrolled in the carpentry training.

At the end of our tour around town, Jonathan and I stopped in at CNA, the combination bookstore, magazine stand, and stationery shop. I thought it would be good for him to have a journal in which to jot down things when they happened. If he continued to meet with me periodically, the journal would provide me more depth of field as well as more specific details of the intervening events of his life. I also thought writing in a journal would be useful for him, too, as he dealt with traumas like the murder of Oupa. So, I bought him a thick, hard-covered notebook of the kind I liked to use and offered him a couple of pens. Jonathan flipped through the pages, his eyes wide, smiling at all the blank pages. He put the pens away in his pants pocket, and ambled off to meet up with some new friends from the carpentry workshop, his notebook proudly tucked, like a trophy, beneath his arm.

On my next trip to Cape Town, I stopped by to speak with Gerald Jacobs, the man who had talked Jonathan into leaving the streets in the first place. Jacobs worked for a small nongovernmental charity that served homeless youth. In the spring, he had decided to move Jonathan out of the city to a hostel run by the charity in Khayelitsha, the black township where I had covered the demonstration by the Treatment Action Campaign back in 2004.

Jacobs was a wry, taciturn guy with inky black hair partly hidden beneath a brown felt workman's cap. He had a quiet, laid-back style and a brutal glare, which, I noticed, he turned to good effect on the most rambunctious guys when they got out of line. The shelter was a riot of activity, and Jacobs held himself upright like a barroom fighter, balanced on the balls of his feet in a wide stance, hands fisted at his waist. He spoke to the boys in a sympathetic voice, though, soothing rather than threatening.

In my reporting around the world, I had never met anyone who seemed so expert at navigating the herky-jerky thought processes of adolescents in trouble. He felt that in order to get homeless kids off the street you first had to figure out the underlying reasons why they found themselves there. It was like treatment for any other addiction, he reasoned. "All of the boys here have that one issue, that issue that you have to overcome," Jacobs said.[6] So many of the boys, once they were off the street, told him harrowing stories of loss—siblings, parents—and he endeavored to "be that lost brother, be that lost father" that many of them yearned to find.

He thought that much of what passed for social work with homeless children, in which adults lectured street kids about the dire effects of ignorance, alcoholism, drug abuse, and violence, was empty and even harmful evangelizing. It wore on his nerves to hear so many counselors invoke the example of Nelson Mandela when trying to inspire the boys to change their ways, for example. He thought that proselytizing based on unrealistic dreams was just as oppressive to the boys as maintaining low expectations and insulting them. Both approaches inspired potent feelings of self-loathing, which wasn't helpful in pushing the boys toward something better.

The fact that so many poor children were flooding into the cities was completely understandable, according to Jacobs. "It's a legacy of apartheid," he said. "You land at Cape Town airport and twenty minutes later you're confronted by children living on the streets. It's only natural that kids are going to move to the better areas. As people lose their cultural moorings, they're drawn to the city. People come. Kids want to be financially independent, and in their case that means hustling for money on the street. It's *capitalism*!"

For Jacobs, the struggle to salvage lives of kids on the street was the next logical extension of the movement for justice. "We are not fighting now for the vote. We are fighting for something else now," he said. "What's your hope for Jonathan, then?" I asked. He turned his head, unsure of how to put it simply. "When speaking with the boys, I try to make a point about acceptance," he replied, pausing then because he didn't want to suggest that poor boys should learn their place by lowering their sights.

He believed that any realistic plan for young people had to acknowledge the reality that most South Africans would remain quite poor for quite some time, though. This meant that the value of honest work, and maintenance of dignity in the face of these conditions, needed to be reinforced in their less celebrated lives. "It's okay if you live in a shack, you know?" he said, summoning up the message he often delivered to the boys. "We want you to be happy with yourself, and we want you to be responsible. I want you to know what made you run to the street, and not let the same thing happen when you have a child. Who cares if you're a sweeper on the street, you know?"

The important thing, Jacobs insisted, was whether the boys learned how to inhabit their humanity and align their principles with the way they conducted their lives. These seemed like remote, but quite decent, ambitions for Jonathan. "He could be working in a factory and raising a family," he said. "I can really see a bright future for him."

Perhaps Jacobs was so skilled at understanding the homeless kids because he was in his early twenties and had grown up on the Cape Flats. There, coloured people had been wedged in together during apartheid. He understood the attraction to the streets, telling me that his friends from the old neighborhood had felt they had only one real choice to make in life—which gang to join.

Like Tsheola, the man in his twenties we had met in Soweto, Jacobs believed that the rebellious culture of the struggle years, replete with the call to armed resistance, had left a deep imprint on generations to follow. The legacy of rebellion, among other things, reinforced the idea that doing well in school or striving to be successful in business signified *selling out*. "Don't try to be white" was the cardinal injunction he remembered hearing from older boys when he was a teen.

The credo of the flats, as Jacobs interpreted it, was this: "Accept that you are coloured, and accept what society says about you, and *stay right there*." Unlike Jonathan, though, Jacobs had grown up in an intact family, as the youngest child. His mother was a domestic worker who juggled four jobs to keep her children in decent clothes, and his father was an equally hardworking bricklayer. Jacobs figured that his parents' encouragement to study had motivated him to steer clear of the trouble some of his closest friends had gotten into.

After high school, he had landed a decent job with a large insurance company, and was poised to loft himself into the middle class. Then, late one night after a crushing breakup with his longtime girlfriend, he had been struck by a religious epiphany that it was his mission to bring homeless kids off the streets. "It was like I woke up from a long sleep," was the way he remembered it. Kneeling in prayer, he asked for clear direction from God, and the next morning he found himself applying for the job at Homestead.

Jacobs was the person who had suggested that I try to speak with Jonathan. He figured that if I managed to get under the boy's skin, I could gain a richer understanding of the pull of the street. He considered Jonathan's case among the hardest he had ever worked on. In their earliest exchanges, the boy had resisted all of his entreaties. "I made this choice with him not to be too confronting," Jacobs recalled. "You have to be patient, you have to wait—be for him, in other words, that brother or father that he didn't have." He kept entreating the boy to answer the question, "What would you like to *become*?"

Finally, Jonathan had asked to stay at the shelter for a few nights. Then he started coming around more regularly. "He would tell me that his mother drinks, he didn't have a home," Jacobs recalled. "I could tell that there was this boy hiding in there—this boy inside the street tough. This guy who I was dealing with on a day-to-day basis was the street child. To walk with a group, you have to become one of them; you had to prove yourself. I knew that one day this boy underneath that shell was going to come to the fore."

In a Hollywood version of this story, here was the apogee: the unlikely hero, fallen into degradation, would be struck by an unexpected epiphany and discover inner reservoirs of character. This was the narrative, writ small, that international admirers of South Africa wanted for the country, too. It was the softhearted narrative I wanted for Jonathan as well. But real lives rarely traced such a reliable arc, or shook out so quickly or so cleanly.

The hostel where Jonathan was staying when I next caught up with him was located in a compact house in a township twenty minutes southeast of Cape Town off the N2 highway. By the time I arrived, it was mid-afternoon. The hostel was in the midst of Khayelitsha, the second-largest black township in the country, twenty-eight square kilometers of flat, crowded terrain wedged in between the airport and False Bay.

Jacobs had moved Jonathan there because he wanted to begin weaning the boy from the temptations of the bright lights, fast money, and easy marks in Cape Town. He enrolled the boy in a new project to teach the boys how to make belts because Jonathan enjoyed working with his hands.

When I pulled in past the cyclone security gate at the entrance to the compound, he strolled out to the porch. The difference in his demeanor from our last meeting, a few months earlier, was striking. Jonathan looked calmer, cleaner, and much happier. He showed me through the shelter as if it was his own, waving in a proprietary way at the dining hall, the just-swept hallways, and the workshop space where the boys were learning how to weave and work with leather.

Jonathan stood proudly before his assigned metal locker, which was a battered thing pocked with dents and limned with rust. The locker, clearly, was a tiny symbol of normality. He volunteered a complicated explanation of what had happened to my gift of the notebook and pens. He had been faithfully recording daily events in the notebook as we had agreed, he said, but another boy had stolen it. Then he remembered—no, no, no—a rival, rather, had *burned* the book for some unexplained reason.

In the interim, Jacobs had filled me in: Jonathan couldn't read or write, and it had struck me, when he told me this, how foolish I had been to offer a journal and pens to a prideful boy without finding out first if he could use them. Illiteracy helped explain, too, why the name Thabo Mbeki had been so unfamiliar to him.

In the sparsely furnished dormitory room, we settled in on a thin, stained mattress spread across a battered metal frame. The first time we met, Jonathan responded to nosy questions in a monosyllabic monotone. This time he swung his lanky legs out in front of us, cross-examining me casually about where I had been recently. From where we sat, you could see bed after bed after bed placed head-to-toe—artifacts of the scope of the challenge the government faced in providing for children like him.

Casually, Jonathan mentioned that he had continued participating in armed robberies around the city long after I might have supposed. Even after Jacobs had talked him off the street in 2005, it hadn't been easy to turn off the temptation of easy money, he explained. So, had he done many robberies during that period? "It was every day. Every day go and rob. Come back, sleep. Go and rob, sleep," he said, making it sound like an arduous factory shift.

Then, a sudden calamity had occurred that had convinced him to stop. Out on the Parade near City Hall one afternoon, Jonathan was grabbed by the cops and arrested on suspicion of snatching a gold neck-lace from a young woman. He professed that it was actually one of his partners-in-crime who was responsible for the mugging, a claim later confirmed to me by the boy who had done it.

But Jonathan had refused to snitch on his ex-friend. "We are like that," he told me, as if explaining a geometrical principle. "If the cops get me, and we—me and you, we're together—we can not *mpimpa* each other," he said, meaning rat the other boy out. "Why must I *mpimpa* my friends?" He was promptly sent off to a detention center for older juve-niles to await a hearing.

On the way to the center, in the back of a police van, Jonathan remembered carefully weighing the choice he knew awaited him—which gang must he join behind bars. The major gangs operated as freely inside the juvenile detention centers and adult prisons as they did in communi-ties like Atlantis. His choices ran from bad to worse, he realized.

The so-called 26s were known as "money lovers," he explained, and the 27s were celebrated for bloodthirstiness. He had been told that you had to kill a person in order to join them. The "agges," the 28s, worried him most. "He's looking for your *ass*," he said, his mouth drawn, face flushed. "If you want to be a 28, you have to give your bum to him."

Jonathan had an uncle who had been in the 27s. He had been taught from a young age the slang used exclusively by its members. On reflection, he figured the 26s seemed like the best fit for someone like himself. "Yeah, I am a money lover," he told me, in a tone of someone revealing which church he had joined. He considered this gang affiliation almost fated, something natural for a young man on the street, especially a coloured boy. "The coloured people, they just run for the gold," he announced. "We coloureds love gold. When we have the gold, we don't worry."

He seemed to be in the midst of an identity shift. When Jonathan had arrived in Cape Town in 2003, he mostly hung out with other coloured boys. But in the Homestead shelter in Khayelitsha, he had befriended Xhosa-speaking black boys. He had never developed the kind of prejudice against blacks that was common among mixed-race people in the Western Cape.

In fact, Jonathan now figured that black Africans on the whole were made of a sterner character than his own people. He had taken on a dismissive stance toward coloureds. "Black people don't love gold, they don't love money," he explained. "They just love themselves and their work and their kids."

Inside the juvenile center, his eyes were opened—by fear. At night the younger boys clustered together in their rooms, hiding from rapists. In frequent public debates about the high incidence of rape, and child rape, in the country, much of the focus had been placed, quite properly, on the preponderance of sexual violence directed at girls. But young and adolescent boys lived in terror, too. They were sexually abused inside and outside of jails at eye-popping rates.

It was likely that rapes in which males were the victims were drastically underreported because of the shame associated with having been on the receiving end of penetrative sex. A self-perpetuating cycle of abuse seemed like the unhappy, perhaps inevitable result: just as children beaten or neglected were more likely to lash out at their own offspring once they were adults, boys and young men who had been raised where rape was so widely practiced were more likely to commit sexual assaults, on other boys as well as girls.

During long, tortured overnights in the juvenile center, Jonathan took stock of his own life. He was sixteen years old. If he continued with the path he was on, in two more years, when he turned eighteen, he would surely end up in prison. Jonathan was scrappy and explosive, but also small and slight. He decided that he needed a drastic change of direction before his next birthday in order to avoid disaster.

To his surprise, counselors at the center helped him and the other boys with basic literacy and craft skills. A black counselor named Rasta taught him how to juggle. Jonathan excelled at juggling, and it was the only thing he could remember that he had done for the pure pleasure of it. He mimicked the motions for me, his hands dancing in the air.

Before he was taken to a hearing, Jonathan had slipped away from his group on an extramural outing to the beach. "I *schlepped* away," was the way he put it. Having paroled himself, in effect, he eventually made his way back to Homestead. Once there, he told Jacobs that he felt more resolved than ever to stay out of trouble.

Later in the year, when Jacobs put together a soccer club for home-less kids, Jonathan was not among the best players he might have recruited, but when it came to choosing members of the team, Jacobs put him on the roster anyway. Jonathan had risen to the challenge, practicing intensely and swiftly improving his skills. When an opportunity arrived to bring the boys to London on an exchange program, he had a chance to go. In the weeks before the trip to England, though, he had suffered a wither-ing anxiety attack. Along with the only other coloured boy on the team, Jonathan tried to back out, but Jacobs nagged him to make the trip. Even-tually he reeled the boy back in. "You must come to London with us," Jacobs insisted.

Then, as they prepared for the trip to England, word arrived that Nel-son Mandela would be willing to greet the boys at his offices in Johannes-burg. The whole episode with the father of their country unfolded in an overwhelming whirl. As Jonathan sat in the plane waiting on the runway for takeoff on his first flight ever, he was swept by primal fear. He knew that planes took off and landed every day, but he had never known any-body well who had flown in one before.

No one had thought to explain the mechanics of winged flight to him or the other boys. He wondered how it was possible for the plane to get off the ground. Jonathan snatched desperate, rabbit-like breaths as the engine roared. He shut his eyes tightly to screen out the sight of the plane shuttling down that runway and hurtling into space.

Ciko Thomas was a broad-shouldered man in his mid-thirties. He seemed, to me, the apotheosis of Jonathan's dreams. He had a genial baby face that belied the hard work he had done to achieve mind-bending success as a black entrepreneur in the new South Africa. Thomas had come from a working-class family in the Eastern Cape, but by the time I met him he had been lofted into the stratosphere of the new black business elite.

As a young businessman, he had been helped along in a significant way by President Mbeki's affirmative action policies, which, as Mbeki's aide Joel Netshitenzhe had told me, were designed to create a new black *patriotic bourgeoisie*. This was how Thomas himself described how it had all happened: "Boom! I found myself, at the turn of the millennium, with unbelievable opportunity."[7]

Shortly after returning to Johannesburg following an interview with Jonathan, I stopped by the auto dealership owned by Thomas. His story was like the flip side of the street child's, so perfectly turned that it was hard to believe it could be true.

The VW car dealership was located not far from the Nelson Mandela Bridge. I had driven by it often on my way to the University of the Witwatersrand, where I had a small borrowed office in the journalism department. Several friends had mentioned Thomas to me during the previous few months as an important part of the story of young South Africans, but it had taken scads of emails and phone calls to settle on a time to get together because he was so frenetically busy.

His perch in the dealership was a modest office overlooking the showroom, with all of the new models visible from the street through newly cleaned floor-to-ceiling windows. A well-thumbed copy of *Foreign Affairs* lay open on his desk to a piece about the rising importance of India. For businessmen like him, the big question was how entrepreneurs in South Africa could mark out space for growth and prosperity in the new global system, where China dominated manufacturing, India claimed much of the offshore service industry (like call centers), and Brazil was responsible for a large proportion of worldwide agricultural exports.

Thomas was dressed in an open-collar white dress shirt and sober dark-gray suit with polished wing tips—thoroughly turned out, but not overtly flashy. Unlike government officials, media leaders, and other corporate executives I had been interviewing, there was no coterie of personal assistants to order around. He greeted me, then excused himself briefly to heat water in the kitchen and prepare tea for us, which he brought in himself on a tray.

I had been reading about the company's fast growth, and how Thomas and three of his closest friends from business school—dubbed the Gang of Four—had made history back in 2003 by launching the first black-owned BMW dealership in the country. Trade in high-status BMWs was fueled by rising consumptive appetites among the expanding black professional class. Three years on, the partners had added the VW dealership to cash in on the "whole buying chain"—from the black worker considering his first economy car to the successful superstar who wanted to flaunt her bling.

Thomas had grown up not far from Port Elizabeth, an industrial port city on the Indian Ocean in the Eastern Cape. Steven Biko, the famous black nationalist and antiapartheid leader who was murdered while in police custody when Thomas was a child, came from the area. So did one of President Mbeki's closest friends and advisors, Saki Macozoma, the controversial chairman of Standard Bank. "Saki was our political idol," Thomas said. "He made sure the Soweto fire—the student rebellion in 1976—burned in Port Elizabeth." The banker once had been a church activist and supporter of the ANC. At the dawn of liberation, though, Macozoma had embraced black capitalism as the surest route to freedom. It was his example that helped inspire Thomas to make his own entrepreneurial future.

He had put himself through college in Cape Town, and then moved on to Johannesburg, where he earned an MBA. As it turned out, his timing was pitch perfect: Major corporations in the country were under intense pressure from the government to diversify their executive ranks, and he landed a post at South African Breweries and Unilever. Large companies also cut groups of black businessmen in on new investment deals under Black Economic Empowerment (BEE) legislation pushed by President Mbeki. These policies were partly responsible for an 8 percent increase in the number of black middle- and top-level executives in South African businesses by 2001.

Even with this kind of support from national government, though, the launch of the new business had been quite tricky. When the Gang of Four bought the BMW dealership, Thomas was recently married. He described the launch as a stomach-clutching period. "There were constant reminders that put the big risk [of failure] right up there," he said. He and his friends all worked "without a net," as he put it. Unlike their competitors, none of his partners came from families in which members had owned property, managed a large enterprise, or attracted investors before. As young owners, without family money or networks, the partners "were undercapitalized, and we didn't know what we were doing when we started—a dangerous cocktail," he reported.

Success had hinged on healthy expansion of the economy through 2005 and the loyalty of newly enriched black buyers. One prominent businessman, Thomas recalled, had even driven all the way to Johannesburg from Durban, a distance of more than five hundred kilometers. The two of them had taken a long walk together, and then chatted over coffee, before the deal was struck. "It felt almost like I was reconnecting with a grandfather," Thomas said. When they were done communing over family, politics, philosophy, and the older man's advice about the best way to live, the client had bought two BMWs—an X5 for himself and a 6-series for his wife.

A boom in BMW sales was just the tip of a sustained burst of consumerism, fueled by well-paid government officials and new corporate executives—the so-called black diamonds whom Ndaba Mandela had criticized for losing themselves in ill-considered debt. Mandela had told me, "People are losing touch. There aren't as many people who are passionate, and compassionate. One of the things I learned from my grandfather is the compassion he has for people. We are being taken away from that. The system is taking us away from that."[8]

When I raised this criticism with Thomas, he nodded and put his cup down. Then his smile died. Thomas mentioned the long history of blacks being forcibly marginalized from the consumer economy for much of the nation's history, and spoke of the double standard in casual fun that was being made of the black diamonds. When a white professional bought a BMW, he pointed out, nobody blinked. So why should a fuss be made because an upwardly mobile black professional should buy one?

The purchase of a nice home or automobile meant something different for black people, Thomas insisted. "There's a lot of self-actualization needed for us, coming out of apartheid," he said. "Physical items show off the newly self-actualized state. There's nothing stronger than a car to drive that message home. A house and a car are the two clearest signals that you are okay, you are healed."

The businessman argued that if the vast majority of South Africans were to embrace the need for a mixed economy, then blacks needed to see visible results in things acquired by people who looked like themselves. How, otherwise, would they aspire to follow Macozoma's example, and his own?

The urgent need to move farther, and faster, in this direction had struck him with added force the last time he had returned to the Eastern Cape. Thomas shuttled back and forth from Jozi to Port Elizabeth, dropping off or fetching his six-year-old daughter from his parents' home. She was in the regular care of her grandparents. Like so many children of the new elite, she attended school under the supervision of her grandmother, her *gogo*, "back home."

Johannesburg—the Place of Gold—was the preferred destination for ambitious young black professionals, but many of them balked at raising their children in the city because they felt certain that the Joburg's excesses were a danger to the values they wanted to see instilled in the young.

Whenever Thomas returned home, he was confronted by increasingly bald expressions of envy from childhood friends. Only a handful of boys he had known growing up had graduated from high school or had taken advantage of the changing environment under the postliberation dispensation. He noted that the Left attacked those who had become rich through Black Economic Empowerment programs as a "comprador, parasitic" class. "A society that suspects a capitalist class worries me," he murmured. "In a normal society, those differences wouldn't cause horror or amazement."

It concerned the businessman that leaders of the Communist Party and the trade union federation were pushing Jacob Zuma as the country's next president. "What kind of leadership is that?" he asked, turning his palms up. "I mean, what kind of leadership is that for the *future*?" Zuma seemed utterly compromised as a public servant by the charges of corruption.

Thomas felt that the ANC, the party his parents had supported as long as he could remember, risked throwing away its reputation if it sent a message that "bad morality is rewarded." He would remain confident, until late in 2007, that the party of liberation he so admired would come up with a better candidate to succeed Mbeki when the national conference was held in Polokwane.

Thomas thought that the first order of business for South Africans ought to be a radically improved public education system. "Whilst all this other crap is happening, we still have to remain globally competitive," he said. "We have to deal with those realities. Either we take the high road and play along with the rest of the kids in the global playground or we become an inwardly focused society—and then we're in for a hiding."

Everywhere the businessman looked—in China and India especially— skills training and educational reform had driven rapid development. "In a developing country, the only surefire way for poor people to rise beyond their circumstances is education. It's as simple as that. It's as dead simple as that," he said. "Once you've got reasonable competence in math and English, you've got a good fighting chance. And if you don't, you've got odds heavily stacked against you."

Down below, in the showroom, black salesmen in this black-owned car dealership showed off new models to black customers, which in much of the world, including the rest of Africa, might deserve little mention. In South Africa, where for so long blacks had been denied the right to own land or start businesses, or to prove themselves capable in the way Thomas and his friends had done, the business of selling cars seemed less prosaic.

Children peered into the showroom through the tall windows, copping a quick double take when they spied the black owner. Black salesmen and black customers wrangled over prices. Thomas gathered our cups, removed the tray, and headed back to work.

At the headquarters for the Nelson Mandela Foundation in Houghton, about a ten-minute drive from the VW dealership and just blocks away from the home where Ndaba Mandela lived, a bus carrying the homeless street kids cruised across the wide brick driveway past a raised security boom. It was the first time Jonathan, or any of the other children, had been in Johannesburg, let alone inside a majestic mansion. When the door of their bus opened, the boys were given a stern warning from police officers: "This is *Nelson Mandela* you're meeting—you don't mess around. You walk where we tell you to walk. If we catch you in a place you're not supposed to be, we're going to *arrest* you."

The boys fell silent, chastened by the threat, and filed wordlessly into a large auditorium to settle sober-faced into their seats. By the time Mandela arrived, they were sitting on their hands. He scanned their somber faces, and protested, "It doesn't look like they're happy to see me!" Here he was at last—*President* Mandela, with his pillow of brilliant white hair on top of his world-famous face. The minute he was seated, he cracked his first joke: "I know Cape Town very well," he said, trilling his *r*'s. "Because I stayed there for twenty-four years," he added, leaving a beat for the punch line—*"on Robben Island."*

In video of the event, Jonathan could be seen sitting in a row of the boys and listening as Jacobs explained to Mandela that the team recently had been playing outside day-care centers and reformatories.[9] Mandela cocked his head, straining to hear, then sat up abruptly and launched into a speech delivered in a clipped, urgent tone. "But tell me, are you *studying?*" he asked the boys. They sat up a little straighter.

"One thing that you must realize, and accept fully, is that in the present world you must have education," he went on. "It's hard to *rise* through the best levels of education, but that is the price you have to pay if you want to be a leader today. Today there can be no leader without education!" I thought of Jacob Zuma, and of the boys in the room who had not had a chance to stay in school.

Each of them lined up, at the end of this impromptu pep talk, to shake Mandela's hand. "This is Jonathan. He's from Atlantis," Jacobs announced. Mandela took a long look at the lanky, lean coloured boy. "I see," the elderly man replied. He promptly rattled off a few questions in Afrikaans. His was proper Afrikaans that he had learned from his jailers, while Jonathan spoke a patois from the Cape Flats. Jonathan stood, frozen and mute, with a fixed grin on his face. He failed to summon up a single word.

As the next boy came up to greet Mandela, Jonathan sat on the armrest beside the old man. "You know what your name means?" Mandela asked the next boy in line, who was a tall, soft-spoken boy named Thandisizwe. "Love my country," the boy replied, sotto voce. "You're speaking very softly!" Mandela complained. Thandisizwe tried again: "*Love my country!*" The old man beamed. "Love my country. That's *accurate!*"

Jonathan told me later that he hadn't "really known nothing" about Mandela before they met on that day in 2005. All the same, he had noticed an unfamiliar calm settling over him in the Old Man's presence. That's why he had draped himself over the back of the elderly man's chair, settling his palm over his shoulder. The whole thing was engraved in his memory as the moment when the man he had been told was the most important person in the world asked him—Jonathan Persens—to tell him his name.

In the wake of this visit with the iconic hero of the country's liberation, he and his mates set off for the competition, and a tour of London. They played well, and most of the boys behaved themselves, Jacobs would tell me later. Jonathan was one of the few exceptions. He proved to be a handful for his minders, often wandering away to explore the city without chaperones.

To him, seeing England was like entering a fairy tale. London was so clean and orderly, the public parks tidy and shockingly green. It was a surprise to him to find wealthy white people living inside city limits without having high walls constructed around their homes. He and another boy snuck away on bicycles to link up with a group of local girls. The girls were entertaining, he reported later. They flattered him, and urged him to come back to see them again soon. They were remarkably *easy*, he said.

On the flight home Jonathan carried himself with the swagger of a seasoned traveler. The roar of the airplane engines didn't scare him at all this time. The shelter the boys returned to inhabit, though, felt smaller, more worn and shabby than he had remembered. Some of the boys crowded back into their rooms at the shelter, but others scattered across the city.

The breakup of his team triggered memories of other dissolutions, such as that of his own family. In the weeks that followed, he visited Jacobs nearly every day to discuss some detail or other about the trip. Jacobs thought that Jonathan was clinging to memories of the adventure because he wasn't sure how he would make his way in life now. He had taken a taste of a quite glamorous existence, and he was forced to face up to his limitations in a new way.

"He was very sad," Jacobs recalled. "He said, 'I miss my family'—and he meant our group." Jacobs pressed him again to construct a reasonable plan for his future. In a way, he was encouraging the teenager to jettison the past and transform himself, much in the way the nation was expected to change.

Jacobs asked Jonathan whether he would ever go back to the streets. "And the boy stood there, and he didn't hesitate," Jacobs told me later. "As soon as I asked the question, he looked me right in the eyes. 'Never,' he said. 'No—*never.*'" He repeated the phrase again, bristling with excitement. To Jacobs, it sounded like a perfect piece of music. Later, he would remember it as among the happiest moments of his career.

10.

Upside Down

Mantombazana Tshabalala-Msimang, known as Manto, was the country's minister of health. In anticipation of her arrival, a large white tent had been erected on the peak of a hill in the center of Alexandra, the community also known as Alex. It was a sprawling township just a twenty-minute drive north of downtown Joburg.

Alexandra always had been a stronghold of support for the ANC. Looking due west across the intervening valley you could see elegant glass office towers and new shopping malls glinting in the sunlight in nearby Sandton, which was like the Rodeo Drive of the city. There, the malls were filled with Italian fashion, German appliances, sushi joints, and fine delicatessens. It was close enough to see the spires from Alex.

On the field below, boys were playing soccer. Beyond them, uneven rows of low-slung shacks meandered into the distance. Townships like this one had been home to important leaders of the ANC and centers of resistance to white rule. Among others, Kgalema Motlanthe, the ANC secretary-general who later became the country's deputy president, had grown up in the heart of it. For the past dozen years, the inhabitants of Alexandra had voted for the ANC by overwhelming margins. Now, its population was increasingly restive, fed up with unfulfilled promises. One day, when the governing party is voted out of office in South Africa, intimation of the ANC's defeat will come most tellingly from communities like this one.

As the minister's motorcade pulled in, children rushed to get a closer look at the most controversial member of Mbeki's Cabinet. She was a short, squat woman with straightened hair and a fixed expression of dismay. The children sang, "Who told us our Manto is coming?" At the ceremonial reelection of Mbeki as president in Parliament, where I had watched her cross the red carpet the year before, she had seemed sober and at ease. Now, she fairly vibrated with an edgy impatience.

The minister's staying power as a national figure puzzled many of her critics. President Mbeki's backing was assured because she had done his bidding on HIV by articulating positions that he supported but about which he had silenced himself. Her marriage to Mendi Msimang protected her, too; he was the ANC treasurer who knew all the secrets about how the party raised and handled its money. She also had appeal at the grass roots, though. At party conferences, she always placed high on the ANC list of officeholders, at least in part because of her role in the struggle years.

Tshabalala-Msimang had been in the small group of young people sent into exile in 1961 along with Thabo Mbeki, spending much of her time in Russia, where she had trained as a doctor. Until her appointment as health minister in 1999, she was a specialist on health issues in the National Assembly. Earlier in the decade, she helped draft the robust plan to halt the spread of the HIV epidemic that Dr. Grimwood had described to me the year before. When the president appointed her health minister, however, she had earned her reputation as an aggressive, and doctrinaire, denialist. She had questioned the safety of antiretroviral AIDS medications, criticized treatment advocates as stooges of the global drug manufacturers, and argued that poor nutrition and poverty were underlying causes of the disease.

At the International AIDS Conference in 2002, the minister por-

trayed her government's anti-medication stance as somehow heroic, snapping to the health reporter from *Newsday* that a court decision ordering
the government to supply treatment to pregnant women, to interrupt the
transmission of HIV from mother to child, had forced her into a corner:
"'I must feed my people poison,'" she was quoted as saying.[1]

Worse yet, she said that the pandemic "could also be a God-given
opportunity for moral and spiritual growth, a time to review our assumptions about sin and morality."[2] Here was a classic, and cruel, exercise in
demonizing the victims. More recently, she announced that eating garlic,
olive oil, beetroot, and African potatoes would slow progression of the
disease.[3] A historian wrote that the minister "enthusiastically prescribed
an alternative therapy that sounded more like a salad dressing than treatment for a sexually transmitted disease that kills around 600 South Africans a day."[4]

On this day, the minister was wearing a large yellow sweatshirt that
read across the front, "*Vuka* South Africa" (Wake up, South Africa). She
was on the third stop of a road show that would take her all over the
country. I followed her into the tent and squeezed into a seat in the second row next to a tall, weathered, elderly woman. Along with other
officials, the minister took a seat in front of two oversize billboards
reading:

ONLY 30 MINUTES OF PHYSICAL ACTIVITY A DAY
GOOD HEALTH STARTS WITH GOOD NUTRITION

Laid out in front of the long dais were apples, African potatoes, pineap-
ples, tomatoes, and squash. If you closed your eyes, and forgot where you
were, the advice she offered would seem quite unremarkable. It was the
same message you would expect from a health official anywhere in the
world. She mentioned that one-fourth of the country's children spent
more than three hours of each day watching television, and warned

about their addictions to tobacco and booze. "Only responsible drinking and no smoking whatsoever," she said, punctuating the air with an upraised finger.

Rapid urbanization had led to changing diets and the dire health effects of fatty fast food, the minister pointed out. Diabetes and high blood pressure were on a steep rise. Children should be taught to swim and how to play "indigenous games," and adults could "walk up stairs instead of taking the lift." Her advice amounted to nostrums. She drew herself up to her full height. "Please sit up straight—stomach in, buttocks out." We all dutifully did so.

For those overdoing it with fast food, she recommended steering away from Nando's, the country's popular fried-chicken outlet. "Use that money on seeds, plants, vegetables, spinach in the garden." Drink ten glasses of water a day, she demanded. Finally, she suggested a novel thought: "You should leave the car at home and walk to the store." Instead of using the floor polisher, women should do what she did each week in her own house. She sounded more missionary by the minute. "Get down on your hands and knees to polish the floor by hand," the minister crooned, making manic swirling motions with her small, fat hands.

At that point I happened to glance at the old woman sitting next to me. She had begun releasing big puffs of air. "Does she think we have *cars*?" she murmured, her thin voice nearly lost beneath the amplified voice of her leader. "Does she think we have wooden floors?" Like many of her neighbors, this woman lived in a two-room shack with a splash of cement over a dirt floor. Wherever she went it was thanks to her very own feet. It took no self-discipline for her to pass up restaurants where she couldn't afford to eat. As for the minister's well-meaning suggestion to replace fast food with homegrown vegetables, the old woman had no access to seeds or soil, and no yard in which to tend the luscious-sounding veggies.

The only health problems in her family, the woman told me when I turned to ask, were linked to a lack of food, clean water, and adequate sanitation—and *this thing*, which is how she referred to AIDS. As the minister nattered on, the elderly woman held her hands at the ready, prepared to applaud anything that made a modicum of sense. Everything she had heard about the minister convinced her that she was in the presence of a heroic figure. "I thought she was good, she's for the children," she explained.

But the performance she was witnessing was hard for the old woman to fathom. When the minister finished, she sat down, having failed to mention the most urgent health concerns in the community, including the rising levels of tuberculosis and HIV infection—which, together, complicated the treatment for both diseases. The minister of health had said nothing about this, either.

As the program ended, it occurred to me that if you rolled back the calendar and imagined an official from the old apartheid regime behaving in this obtuse and high-handed way, there would have been a riot. It stunned me that Tshabalala-Msimang had gotten away with it.

The minister and other officials set off on a march around the township, accompanied by a large sign that read, "Healthy Food, Regular Exercise, Healthy Lifestyle." A crowd followed behind on the brisk three-kilometer walk. Women called out to her from their shacks: *Manto!* She waved, offering a wiggle of the hand. When the road bottomed out in a little valley, we passed an old cemetery. It was a mammoth collection of tombstones. There were no fresh mounds because this cemetery, like so many others, was already full.

Just a thirty-minute drive due south from the township, the M1 freeway led to Chris Hani Baragwanath Hospital. Within its sprawling grounds the year before I had watched the rollout of HIV medications. So in July of 2005, I headed back to the hospital for a tour of Harriet Shezi Children's Clinic, a center for children infected with HIV.

The head nurse, Sister Sylvia Mtshizana, greeted me inside the doorway. She was a thin black woman with a narrow, angular face drawn down to a severe chin. The nurse made a sour face when I mentioned that I had attended the minister's event in Alexandra. "The minister of health has caused a lot of damage by confusing people about what the best course of treatment would be," she said. "That minister uses the power of her position to lead people in the wrong direction. I've had a few patients who said, 'I will try the alternatives first, I've heard about the alternative of nutrition.' People have died because of the emphasis on nutrition and alternatives."[5]

Unlike many of the younger nurses, Sister Sylvia did not see HIV as an insurmountable plague. She remembered when people also had felt hopeless in the face of TB outbreaks, and remembered how the disease had been tamed with a robust public health campaign. The same thing, she felt sure, could happen in the management of AIDS.

Leaning on a crutch, she hobbled off across the waiting room. It was a large space with sunshine streaming through big windows, rivulets of light playing across clusters of tiny plastic chairs. Everything was miniature, with an eye to a child's comfort.

In her no-nonsense lilt, Sister Sylvia said that the chief obstacle in vanquishing the disease was disinformation and stigmatization. "People still think if you get HIV it means you're sleeping around," she reported. As a nurse, she found it outlandish that this disease should be treated differently than any other simply because it was sexually transmitted.

While making our way to the examining rooms, we passed the office of the clinic's founding director, Dr. Tammy Meyers. She had curly graying-brown hair and an open expression. When she had started the clinic in 1997, she told me, it was the first in the country to exclusively treat rising numbers of infants born into the epidemic.

Meyers founded the children's clinic because during her medical training in the mid-1990s, on a fellowship at a clinic in Harlem, she had seen how the rate of children born with HIV was slashed to nearly zero through aggressive interventions. This had been a signal, rare, early success in dealing with the epidemic in the United States and Europe. She also studied how to safely place children on antiretroviral treatment.

The track record in dealing with these early pediatric AIDS cases suggested a course of action in order to avoid an even greater catastrophe in South Africa. Since the virus passed from mother to child through blood exchanged in the womb or during childbirth, or through breast milk ingested during the first months of life, pregnant women with HIV were treated with medications to suppress the virus and lessen the chance of infecting the baby.

In the United States, babies of HIV-positive mothers were routinely delivered by Caesarian section to minimize the chances of infection at birth; the infants were placed on milk supplements, rather than being breast-fed, to further cut the risk of exposure. By contrast, in South Africa hundreds of thousands of children had been born into the illness already; tens of thousands of them were newly infected each year. This was a most disturbing twist in the African AIDS pandemic—that the fatal disease should be passed by mothers to children even though this result was entirely preventable.

When Meyers returned to Johannesburg in 1996, she launched a study to test the HIV status of children hospitalized at Baragwanath. It turned out that the percentage of hospitalized children with HIV had risen from about 1 percent to more than 30 percent over the previous six years. So the doctor founded her clinic, but in the face of resistance. Her colleagues were worried at the time, she said, that too much emphasis on a single disease might swamp the entire edifice of the country's teetering public health system. Her counterargument was straightforward enough: "If we don't tackle this essential part of the problem, we'll sink the whole thing anyway."[6]

Dr. Meyers felt that a focus on pediatric AIDS was crucial because up to half of untreated HIV-positive children would die by the age of two years; an estimated 98 percent would perish by the age of five unless they received treatment. It had taken a major lawsuit by AIDS treatment activists in 2000, followed by a decision in favor of them by the Constitutional Court in 2002, to force the minister of health to provide medication to prevent mother-to-child transmission. By then, the numbers of infected children had escalated, and hundreds of thousands of youngsters, including newborns, needed urgent medical care.

The challenges for the doctors, in these early years, were immense, Meyers recalled. For one thing, antiretroviral medications had been developed with adult patients in mind. "People were very nervous about treating kids. The whole discussion about side effects made them *more* nervous," she acknowledged.

Meyers was wedged behind her desk, with a mammoth government report on her lap and a draft of a funding proposal on her computer screen. "There was another thing out there about kids that people don't address directly—this feeling that children are not economically *viable*," the doctor admitted. Bluntly put, the question was this: If you could keep someone alive only for the first ten or twenty years of life, was that necessarily a social good? For Meyers, it was a despicable point of view. Was a human life only worth saving if that person would live long enough to be economically productive?

Despite fears spread by the health minister, among others, the rate of adverse side effects of the medications among children turned out to be less of a problem than most doctors expected. "The biggest surprise was that we had relatively little toxicity," the doctor reported. Even in children with devastated immune systems, some with close to zero infection-fighting (CD4) cells, there were remarkable recoveries. These were the littlest of the "little Lazarus stories" that now began to shape the modern narrative of AIDS. The survival rate was a tribute, in part, to Meyers's prescience and stubbornness.

On the other side of the clinic, a little girl was banging away on the door of the counseling room, trying to get the attention of her mother. Her mother, in turn, was purposely ignoring her daughter because she didn't feel ready to explain to her six-year-old that both of them were ill with AIDS. The two counselors in the room, who were, like the patient, black women from Soweto, set up an easel with this unhappy summary:

1. Sex

2. Blood to blood

3. Mother/child

Here was the trifecta of ways for HIV to pass from one person to the next. On poster board placed next to the easel was a list of medications available in public clinics and this sober reminder: "It is not a cure."

One of the counselors delivered a stern lecture about the importance of strict adherence: The pills need to be taken right at eight o'clock in the morning and precisely at eight o'clock in the evening. If the timing was off, or days were missed, the virus would develop resistance to the medication. Like so many other young parents, this mother would need to juggle management of her daughter's disease as she began treatment herself. It was the double burden of the way so many South African women discovered they were infected—by diagnosis of their children first.

The following week I drove back to the clinic so I could observe the second meeting of a new group Meyers had launched for adolescent girls living with HIV. This was the complicated kind of good news: there were now enough surviving adolescents to form a support group for them. When I arrived, the girls were gathered around a table in the counseling room. They all looked healthy, though most of them were small for their ages because HIV in children causes stunting.

A board game called Magical Maze Journey had been set out in front of them, but they paused between turns for a short discussion moderated by their counselor, Yvonne Mahlangu. She raised the subject of boyfriends, and suggested they begin discussing ways to break the news to someone they were dating that they were HIV-positive.

"Once you begin to menstruate, this means you're eligible to fall pregnant," she pointed out. She was rewarded with double takes. "Huh?" said one of the oldest girls in the group, an exuberant teenager named Gwendoline Dube. "I didn't *know* that." She had onyx-colored hair and a firm chin, which she pressed forward as if to make her point. "I really didn't know it."

The counselor, the mother of a teenage girl herself, understood the importance of impressing upon this group the essential facts about reproductive life. If you asked, they would say they knew it all. Or, alternatively, they would insist they didn't need the information yet. None of the girls around the table admitted to having a boyfriend. When Gwendoline chimed in to report that many of her friends at school were already engaging in sex with older men, the counselor perked up. Mahlangu knew that teenagers often found it easier to raise questions about "a friend" with a certain problem than to talk about themselves.

As it turned out, Gwendoline reported, her friend said that a boyfriend was constantly "pressurizing" her to have unprotected sex. "Boyfriends nowadays like to have sex," she informed the younger girls. "My friend said, 'I love him!' but I told her, 'I know you love him, but you have to protect yourself, too.'" The counselor nodded, reinforcing the idea that girls take power in deciding whether they will engage in sex. She added that she favored full disclosure with boys who expressed interest in romantic liaisons.

The girls considered her silently, looking dubious. They had heard stories of women ostracized in the communities or even murdered for revealing their status—like the woman whose killing we had learned about from activists in the Treatment Action Campaign in Khayelitsha.

"I understand it's difficult, but I think we have to develop a strategy," Mahlangu said. "Because you're not going to wait until he's about to put a ring on your finger to tell him, are you?"

The other younger girls headed off for a drink of water, but Gwendoline stayed behind to speak with me. She confided that she was different from many of the other girls in that she hadn't been born with HIV. "My uncle raped me," she reported, her chin up and eyes flaring.[7] Only thirteen years old at the time, Gwendoline had been raped repeatedly by her uncle while she was living with her grandparents in Zimbabwe.

She told the story simply, without much emotion, describing how her uncle often had stayed out drinking in the bars late at night. More than once he had returned home to force himself on her in the room where she and a younger cousin slept. He had warned her that he would kill anyone she told about the sexual assaults, so she had kept the torment to herself.

Gwendoline had not told her parents, even when she returned to the family home in Orange Farm, a black township south of Johannesburg. When she first fell ill with overlapping flu viruses, rashes, and debilitating aches and pains in the year that followed, she was brought to Meyers's clinic in order to be examined. In the same counseling room where I had listened in as another mother wrestled with the question of how to tell her daughter that they both had AIDS, Gwendoline's mom waited with her to learn the results of the blood test.

When the nurse revealed that she already had full-blown AIDS, "I thought I was cursed," Gwendoline said. She thought of suicide when she heard the news and seriously considered it in the following year. "I thought it just was the end of my world," she said.

As a result of the quiet, consistent support of her mother, though, Gwendoline battled her depression and started treatment on antiretroviral medications in 2004, the first year they were available free of charge in public health clinics. The early days of her treatment were quite difficult, she said. She suffered side effects, like persistent nausea and heart palpitations. After notifying the nurses of these reactions, she was placed on an alternative therapy and her condition improved. Before long, she felt nearly normal physically again.

Back in her neighborhood, though, she felt constrained in talking about the rapes and also the disease borne by it. At school, she was elected peer health educator by her classmates, but she still hadn't mustered the courage to tell even her closest friends that she was HIV-positive. "I'll do it when I get older," she told me. In terms of relationships with boys, she felt wary about giving her secret away.

Older men were courting many of her friends. "So many girls at school are involved with taxi drivers, just because they want to get around—just for them to buy you something," she said. This pattern of early sexual debut with older men, who traded money or gifts for intimacy, spurred the spread of HIV to ever-younger girls. "I think the virus is spreading because of poverty," Gwendoline said. "Teenagers want to look like celebrities, want to wear fine clothes like them, and that's making us fall in love with bigger men."

She straightened in her chair, crossing her legs primly. During the years after the rapes she had been in and out of school. Now, she wanted to excel in her studies because she knew she would need good marks to live up to her ambitions. Nobody could say for sure how long her life could be extended, she pointed out. Gwendoline hoped for at least twenty years; maybe she would live into her thirties. When I asked about her ambition, she did not miss a beat. "I want to be a pilot," she replied. "And I want to be a doctor, too."

The other girls began trickling back into the room while we were talking. The younger girls looked at Gwendoline, smiling when they heard this last remark. What an audacious thing she had just said! To me, it seemed an exquisite expression, quite a relief from all the bitter material I had been gathering. This teenager planned to become a doctor to treat other children suffering from HIV; but she also wanted to become a pilot for good measure—to be able to fly away from all the trouble she had seen.

At the 2006 International AIDS Conference held in Toronto the follow-ing August, I came across the minister of health, face-to-face, once again. In the intervening year she had continued on her stubborn way, encour-aging a German vitamin magnate named Matthias Rath to ramp up his operations in South Africa as a supposed contribution to the fight against HIV. The vitamin magnate, in turn, had spent much of his time attack-ing Zackie Achmat and the Treatment Action Campaign, denouncing them as tools of multinational pharmaceutical companies. Leaflets repeating these accusations were circulated in townships across the coun-try, and the attacks tumbled into lawsuits and countersuits. The effect was to sap energy that might otherwise have been spent fighting the epi-demic. (Not incidentally, Rath was a foil, drawing fire from TAC that would otherwise be directed at the minister or the president.)

The international conference, held every other year, was a vast bazaar of HIV advocacy mixed in with celebrity-star appearances and scientific exchanges about prevention and treatment efforts around the world. On this occasion, the minister had ordered health department officials to pack the South African stall in the exhibition hall with lemons, garlic, potatoes, and plenty of beetroot, as if determined to provoke more ridi-cule of her own position.

In meeting rooms at the convention center, hundreds of new research findings on prevention, treatment, and care for people living with AIDS were presented in a blizzard of briefings. Ministers of health and top infectious disease experts from hundreds of nations were on hand to debate the most effective approaches to staunching the epidemic.

Tshabalala-Msimang, however, had forbidden her top HIV/AIDS specialists to attend. She skipped most of the groundbreaking presentations, including one showing that HIV-positive patients needed antiretroviral treatment when their CD4 counts dipped to 350—not 200—in order to restore more robust function of their immune systems. This was precisely the kind of research that could guide a more effective campaign against AIDS, ensuring more effective treatment, and higher survival rates, among those who tested positive for HIV.

From the first day, the minister was the focus of repeated attacks by international public health officials. She missed hearing most of these slights in person and was also absent when more successful HIV prevention and treatment programs, in places like Brazil, Thailand, and Botswana, were discussed. The minister even swept in late for a well-attended morning panel on the final day of the conference, where a large auditorium full of delegates heard Mark Heywood, the treasurer of TAC, discuss the highly effective AIDS program in China. In the end, he compared the Chinese program to the desultory response, and ongoing crisis, in South Africa.

The minister plopped down in a seat directly in front of me, glaring at Heywood as he was speaking. She melodramatically took a tape recorder from her purse and flipped it on. "If we had had the will, we would have saved hundreds of thousands of lives," Heywood said, undaunted.

Behind me, a few rows back, sat Dr. Grimwood, the doctor from the Western Cape whom I had followed around during the rollout of antiretrovirals to public clinics in 2004. "This is how she is!" he whispered. "You see what we're up against?" The doctor placed his head in his hands as Heywood ticked off numerous opportunities that the Mbeki government had missed in fighting the epidemic.

Heywood showed several graphs of national HIV prevalence rates for South Africa on an overhead monitor. The line marked a startlingly steep climb, all during the first twelve years of democracy. "This shows the perverse reality that more people die in my country between the ages of twenty and thirty than between the ages of sixty and seventy," he said, sounding mournful.

He looked out at the crowd, then fixed the minister with his gaze, and called on her to resign. A standing ovation followed, a raucous out-pouring of support from health advocates, representatives from other governments, and South African delegates alike.

Dr. Sanjay Gupta, moderator of the panel on which Heywood was featured, broke through the cheering to ask several times if anybody in the room from the South African government wished to respond. The minister and her advisors offered not one word in their own defense. Meanwhile, she seemed to find the whole episode hilarious. Her shoulders bobbled as she giggled in an odd, high-pitched tone.

When the session ended, a line of doctors, nurses, academics, and activists took the stage holding up signs repeating a demand that the minister resign or be fired. Sipho Mthathi, secretary-general of TAC, carried a sign that said, "Political inaction is a crime against humanity."

The minister gathered up her purse, scurrying off. I ran ahead, jogging to catch up with her before she reached the door. She rounded on me, wobbling and clearly tipsy. The smell of alcohol was on her breath. "I won't talk to you *here*—only back home," she barked. Breaking into a lopsided grin, she shouted, "There's nobody in Toronto who can ask me to resign or fire me! I don't answer to Toronto!"

Of course, she was technically correct. The minister served at the pleasure of a democratically elected president, not international health officials, doctors and nurses, or treatment advocates. She had survived in office already, for six long years, because President Mbeki found her pliant.

The tenure of Manto Tshabalala-Msimang as minister of health would surely go down as the party's biggest self-inflicted mistake. It was an error all the more terrible for having been made as an expression of public will by an elected governing party in a supposed people's government, in an emerging democracy.

The mistake resulted in, tragically, unforgiveable consequences for masses of South Africans like Gwendoline Dube. And it would be a blot forever, in the annals of history, on the reputation of the ANC.

II.

On the Air

Adozen years into the epidemic, HIV still received rather begrudg-
ing notice in newspapers and on the air while gossip about political
figures—especially those involved in the fight between Mbeki and
Zuma—got outsize coverage. With the exception of a coterie of excellent
health reporters at major newspapers and the model work of an independent group known as health-e, few journalists stepped up to the
challenge of chronicling the epidemic in depth. Political leaders took refuge in the argument that the entire country had fallen into "AIDS
fatigue," as if that was a good excuse for their own inaction. In a similar
vein, media managers complained that if they put a story about HIV on
the front page, sales declined. Less than 2 percent of coverage in print
outlets in South Africa, during this period, concerned AIDS—and this in
a country with the largest number of HIV-infected people in the world.

Nowhere was the squandered opportunity more pointed than at the
South African Broadcasting Corporation (SABC), the protean media
outlet with the broadest and deepest reach across the country. An estimated twenty million South Africans, more than half the population of
adults, tuned in to the corporation's radio stations. Six million viewers
watched its television programs. On the staff of its far-flung operations,

though, there was no special unit of reporters and producers established to ensure that the pandemic was covered in accordance with the scale of its impact.

The corporation's broadcast center was a gleaming, blue-tinted colossus that dominated the skyline in the Auckland Park district of Johannesburg. From its conference rooms you could look north all the way to Pretoria, the nation's executive capital. The corporation broadcast 250 news bulletins in eleven official languages every day, plus two additional indigenous ones, !Xu and Khoi, making it the most influential media entity in the country. Under the old regime, SABC was considered a mouthpiece of the government. The relevant question, under the new government, was whether it could be fashioned into a real, distinctly South African media entity that operated according to the broad public interest.

The corporation's director of news and current affairs in 2005 was Snuki Zikalala, a former guerrilla commander who preferred to be addressed as *Dr.* Zikalala in honor of the Ph.D. he had received at Sofia University in Bucharest while in exile in Bulgaria. After I had been monitoring the corporation's broadcasts for a year and a half, I asked for permission to shadow him for a few weeks in order to understand how editorial decisions were made.

On the morning I arrived in his office, I planned to begin by questioning his paltry record in covering AIDS. ("No, no, we have a good record on it—lots of coverage," Zikalala would tell me later, when I finally got a chance.) As I walked in, though, I received a sharp reminder, reminiscent of my days as a daily newspaper reporter, about how breaking news could squeeze out something even as important as the ongoing public health catastrophe.

On the right side as I entered Dr. Zikalala's cavernous office, there was a large plasma screen perched high atop a counter. The news chief had it set to the Sky News channel. A bulletin flashed onscreen about a terrorist attack in Great Britain; three simultaneous explosions had gone off around London and untold numbers of people were dead or maimed. Incoming video, much of it taken on cell phones, was blurry. Partial and distorted images transmitted a sense of immediacy and also the raw fear sweeping through the British capital. Battered, bloodied victims were carried up from the subway where one of the bombs had gone off.

The news chief worked his phones to make sure his staff was on it. He was dressed in a stylish brown sweater with interlocking squares, brown twill slacks, and shiny black Oxford shoes. Zikalala had a broad, unlined face with a shaved head and blunt chin. Normally, he told me, he objected to the unquestioning way newsmen responded to stories about violence. The old mantra in newsrooms around the world was *if it bleeds, it leads*. "If it bleeds, it doesn't necessarily lead on *my* broadcast," he said.[1]

News of this particular terrorist attack would dominate broadcasts around the world, though. "Okay, so that's our lead story tonight," he said, eyes on the screen. Part of the draw to the bombing story for South Africans, of course, was the country's own colonial history; 40 percent of whites were English speaking. But there was something deeper, too, it seemed to me: a poignant twist in the fact that there had been a sudden and somewhat mystifying outbreak of violence in the north.

In this sense, it was reminiscent of the reaction to the 9/11 attacks from the South African perspective. There was a kind of reversal of roles from the apartheid years, when South Africa was the source of breathless reports from New York or London about brutal clashes and hard-to-track enmity. What in the world was happening up there in the supposedly civilized world?

The news chief had 630 permanent staff and more than 600 people under contract to help him gather and present the news, making him the most powerful media manager in the country. Like many other new leaders in charge of big institutions, Zikalala had been a disciplined cadre in the struggle, with a record of fealty to the ANC. His family had been among the vast numbers *removed* a half century earlier from Alexandra, the township ten miles north of his office where I had seen the minister of health holding forth. Winnie Mandela herself had recruited him into the armed underground when he was only a teenager, he told me.

At the age of twenty-two, he had gone off into exile in Botswana, where he served in Umkhonto we Sizwe (Spear of the Nation), the armed underground, under the command of Jacob Zuma. At one point during those years, Zikalala was part of a plan to park a truck filled with explosives in the parking garage below the complex, blowing up the very building in which we were now sitting. "We'd planned on bringing it down," he told me, looking sorry that he had made this revelation.

For me, it had odd resonance to the story we were watching. A few years after the bomb plot was scotched, Zikalala left the front lines to work and study in Bulgaria. He had earned a master's and doctorate in journalism.

The subject of his thesis was the operation of the SABC by the white regime. The research had only fed his appetite to be in charge one day inside the building he had once plotted to obliterate. "I'd always wanted to get into that building because I knew what you could *do* inside it," he told me—"not for propaganda," he added quickly, but rather in the service of a potentially powerful force "in *nation building*."

The selection of Dr. Zikalala as the news boss in 2004 had sparked a debate over the proper role of the public broadcasting service. Should it be more like a state broadcaster, a mouthpiece for the government, as it had been under apartheid? Or should it have far greater autonomy, like the Canadian Broadcasting Corporation?

Behind his back, critics in the newsroom referred to him as "Comrade Snuki" and accused him of ruling through intimidation. They felt he made SABC a mouthpiece for the ANC government, and accused him of blacklisting commentators who disagreed with the party. Zikalala wasn't even particularly beloved in circles around President Mbeki, I soon discovered. "Appalling" was the response from one of the president's top aides when I asked him to evaluate SABC news. "I find what's going on there is a shame."

In listening to the broadcasts, and watching the news, on SABC in the previous eighteen months, I had found especially puzzling how mixed the picture seemed. If you spent days paying full close attention to its broadcasts, you found on the corporation's airwaves a confounding mash-up of incisive, clever, solid journalism and also the worst kind of mind-numbing crap.

There were shows like the *After Eight Debate* with John Perlman, among the liveliest programs heard on radio anywhere in the world. In a series of interviews in 2005 with Finance Minister Trevor Manuel, for example, Perlman pressed the minister for explanations on the twists and turns of national economic policy. (He would later leave SABC after revealing, in a live broadcast, the existence of a blacklist promulgated by Zikalala.) Documentaries on a series called *Special Assignment*, about everything from corruption by local officials to health scams directed at HIV-infected people, were first-rate productions with correspondingly high ratings. These shows demonstrated SABC's potential to produce excellent, in-depth journalism.

What drew more notice from critics were frequent examples of using a dynamic medium in precisely the wrong way—showing and airing important officials *reciting* things from text, Mbeki style, with their head down and going on interminably in muffled monotones. "A parade of ministers!" was what Tony Leon, the leader of the opposition, had called the SABC's coverage of politics.[2]

When I broached these kind of criticisms with Zikalala, he raised his hands with his palms out. "The criticism comes from white editors," he said. "This is a contest over terrain." His answer seemed an odd response from a news executive, since I had explicitly mentioned the critique of politicians and not other journalists. Among his critics elsewhere in the media, those I had in mind were mostly black. "They can't believe that a black man can run this big organization!" the news chief went on. "They *can't* [believe it]. You see, whether we like it or not, white South Africans will never change. Very few have changed so far."

Zikalala volunteered as his prime enemy the last remaining white editor of a daily national newspaper, Peter Bruce at *Business Day*. Under his leadership, reporters at the paper had kept a watchful eye on the inner workings of SABC, partly as a result of the fact that he had hired talented former producers who had been pushed out by Zikalala. Karima Brown had been an influential producer at SABC and now she was *Business Day*'s chief political correspondent. When I ticked off a list of independent-minded black reporters and editors, like Brown, who also had complained about Zikalala's leadership, the news chief slumped back in his chair.

"They are black writers, but where do they get their authority from?" he asked. The whole objective of his critics, he insisted, was "to try and preserve the little white domination that they had before. They look at us, as black people, as being corrupt. And as people who cannot deliver— people with no credibility. And it's a deluge of reports aimed at undermining successes of South Africa."

Here were shades of the kind of reaction one got from President Mbeki, and his aides, if you criticized the leader: he was the elected black president, they were eager to point out, and if you found fault with him, they argued, it was because you couldn't accept leadership from a black person. This was a simplistic, dangerous tautology.

The news chief fixed me with a stern expression. His main goal was "to make the SABC a true public broadcaster," he insisted. After all, he added, he had seen what happened in Bulgaria when the ruling party controlled the media. "Being a rebellious person, I hated that," he had told another interviewer a year earlier. "Despite my socialist ideals, I could see there was no freedom of expression in the media, and I hated the authoritarian controls."[3]

As we made our way through the warren of hallways that run through the building, Zikalala slammed the standards that informed most news gathering in the country. The heads of every other media operation in the country were in the business of "destructing the mentality of South Africans," he claimed. He ticked off his points, flicking at his fingers. "They'll talk about rape, they'll talk about crime. They'll talk about witchcraft—which I don't believe is there. They'll talk about sex. But those things don't add any value to my life, or to the lives of South Africans." That was the sort of thing that you saw clearly in the decadent West, he added. It was all but "smash-and-grab journalism," Zikalala complained.

The idea that SABC should be part of a media practicing a social role as "watchdog" he found particularly insidious. "I ask myself, 'Whose watchdog?'" he went on. "Currently, they are only watching the government, they're not watching the private sector. . . . Why should they only watch the government? Why didn't they become watchdog of the private sector as well?" This was a perfectly legitimate question, but the way the news chief raised it seemed like an excuse to toady up to government. Zikalala said he had set out to make room in the liberated South Africa for a new kind of journalism that he called "developmental" journalism, to go along with a developmental state.

No media outlet was hotter among young people in 2005 and 2006 than Yfm. It was the spectacularly successful postliberation radio venture that had stolen attention away from more traditional outlets like SABC. Young South Africans, like young people all over the world, were busily migrating from traditional news sources to other venues.

The station was located just a short drive from SABC, up the boulevard named for Jan Smuts on a hillside in the upscale Mall of Rosebank. The mall was a collection of sleek corridors and boutique shops crammed to the hilt with world music and imported clothes—Diesel jeans, Benetton blouses, Uzzi underwear. The complex was crowned by a movie multiplex, which specialized in popular Hollywood releases.

In a studio directly downstairs from the movie theaters, two of the country's best-known DJs produced a radio music-plus-chat show that was the essence of distinctly South African popular political culture. They were Sanza da Fanatik and Rudeboy Paul. Beginning in 2005, I had started dropping by the studio during their show periodically because they were fun to spend time with and it helped me take the pulse of generational cleavages in the country. Rudeboy and Sanza had the comic verve of *The Daily Show* with Jon Stewart mixed with the racial political consciousness of Cornel West.

When we first met, I mentioned that I had come straight from shadowing Zikalala at SABC. Sanza wrinkled his broad nose, fluttering his hands. "What does *that* uncle know?" he asked. He was a reed-thin man in his thirties with eyes that flashed when he was angry. His on-air partner, Rudeboy Paul, was a dozen years younger and had baby-smooth cheeks and a laid-back stoner's mien.

As they opened the show, Sanza fidgeted with his mic, standing in his broken-down brown leather shoes like a stand-in for the angry young people of his generation who had helped make the country ungovernable. Rudeboy Paul, his dreadlocks swept over his shoulders, considered his older partner with affectionate but puzzled cool, as if standing in for those who were too young to have been on the ramparts.

Rudeboy punched up a song and crooned his welcome in dulcet tones. Sanza replied, "I'm on *fi-yah!*" Yfm had eighteen million listeners nationwide, with demographics heavily skewed to the young. The station's founders had developed the plan for the station while working at SABC, but top executives there had been too hidebound and conservative to foresee Yfm's potential.[4] Advertisers initially felt quite leery, too, about investing in a vehicle that would reach a rambunctious, edgy, young, predominantly black audience. So it had taken a kamikaze-like effort by its founders to get the station launched.

Sanza had been among the founding core group of poets, rappers, and political activists who created the station's distinctive sound. With a blend of *kwaito*, house music, and hip-hop, Yfm gathered an audience nobody had served before. The station made nearly instant celebrities of the starting lineup of DJs, all of whom had grown up in the townships, among them DJ Fresh, Bad Boy T, and Sanza. The most popular DJ on the station's airwaves had been a frenetic, wisecracking, beloved phenomenon named Fana Khaba, known as Khabzela, who died of AIDS at the age of thirty-five, in 2004.[5]

I had begun listening to Yfm because I liked the eclectic mix of music and because it seemed like one of the few venues for young people to engage with one another across big divides—from the white kid in the suburbs who loved listening to Thandiswa Mazwai, the heartbreakingly beautiful young black South African singer with the flutelike voice, to the black youngster from Soweto who wanted another cut from Amy Winehouse. Between the songs, the DJs added value by way of news, information, and political analysis.

One morning, in mid-2006, I came back to the studio, arriving to find Rudeboy Paul and Sanza standing outside of the sound booth, looking anxious and expectant. They were waiting for a guest, long-exiled South African writer Lewis Nkosi, one of the legendary writers for *Drum* magazine in the 1950s. Nkosi had left the country more than three decades earlier.

"Uncle Louie, we have been waiting for you *so* long!" Sanza told the older man as he huffed into view. Rudeboy chimed in, "What's taken you so long, Uncle?" The writer, spry, mischievous, and in his seventies, wrapped his arms around both of the younger men and explained himself.

After exile in Zambia, Nkosi told them, he had moved to Europe in the 1960s. "Oh yes, and *love!*" he explained. "It's about love." He had fallen for a Swiss woman and he belonged in Geneva now, the writer said. It was a reminder that, from the political diaspora of activists and intellectuals created during the forty years of apartheid, there were large numbers of people who had never come home.

Nkosi visited regularly, and this time he was back in Johannesburg with his first novel published in decades. The book, *Mandela's Ego*, told the story of a Zulu-speaking *isoka* (a great lover) made impotent on the day Nelson Mandela was captured in 1962. It was a rollicking tale, and I had stayed up through much of the previous night to read it. Two things had struck me most forcefully in the midst of it—the main character's searching intelligence and the visceral, sexualized fury beneath his superficial amiability.

"Betrayed, hobbled, finally in the custody of his gleeful pursuers, his hero . . . [was] brought low like himself," Nkosi had written.[6] The central character remained sexually impotent for the twenty-seven years his hero was shut away in prison.

Once they were on the air, Sanza said, "I like the way you weave the story, Uncle." The phone lines lit up right in a cascade of calls. Lulu from Diepsloot wanted to know if it was true, as the book said, that the great father of the country had once stolen a pig. "Yes, indeed he did," Nkosi replied. That brought a series of colloquies with young listeners, which raised, for the writer, a big idea he had been reflecting on now that he was home.

"I like the idea of contingency in history," he mused. "There are *accidents* in history, you know." Nkosi suggested that his young listeners consider what might have happened if Mandela had *not* been captured on that day in 1962, had not been held against his will through much of his life, had not been shut off for so long from people clamoring to be led by him. What kind of history, he asked, might have unfolded then?

"The youth of today are testing this democracy," Sanza said. "What are you seeing in us, Uncle?" The writer beamed at Sanza. "The first thing we have to know about culture is that culture is not independent of politics," he argued. "The second thing is, if you turn over your space to others, you run the danger of other people misrepresenting you." This

notion was central to the DJ's concerns, too. He had an expansive passion for African food and cuisine, and specialized in the nonofficial
accounts of the struggle for liberation, as told from the bottom up.

After the show was over, when Nkosi left for his next reading, Sanza
and I wandered over to a coffee shop in the courtyard. He had been wound
up to meet his hero, but now felt a little deflated. He said that it had been
far easier in the late 1990s to excite listeners about the prospect of politics,
broadly understood. That was when the sound at the station was entirely
fresh, and nobody knew if Yfm would become commercially viable.

Now, the wheels were turning, and he felt the place was less vibrant
by the day—a direct result of being such a commercial hit. There was
pressure to lighten up and drop politics from the show. There was even
pushback, on this score, from young listeners. "The kids complain sometimes," he admitted. "They say, 'You make us think. Give us the other
DJs—they know how to just have fun.'"[7]

The DJ thought that politics needed to be marbled into popular culture if either sphere was going to amount to anything. But what if the
next few generations remained relentlessly apolitical? As he listened to
the voices of young people who phoned in to his show, he began to think
that a truly new kind of society—a democracy worth the name—would
require a thoroughgoing cultural revolution.

"They hold this carrot out—*democracy!*" he keened, swirling the
dregs of his coffee. "Mandela's era must have been the spring rain, but we
never got to summer. The rain came down and we got into the mud.
Sixteen years! Nothing but the mud. I'm not sure our sons will ever eat
the fruits of this democracy." He looked stricken suddenly, all the *fiyah*
momentarily snuffed out.

Back at SABC, there was a different kind of generation gap in evidence
emerging among the staff. It divided the older former exile who was in

charge of running the news operation from his younger subordinates, some of whom were pressing for freedom of expression from *inside* the corporation walls.

When I arrived for a second conversation with Snuki Zikalala one morning in June of 2005, I found that he had slipped away without notice for a meeting with members of the corporation's board of directors. So I wandered downstairs to the television newsroom unannounced, and there I came across Jimi Matthews, the well-respected head of television news.

Matthews was busy boxing up his things because the news chief had finally succeeded in pushing him out of his job. He was a tall, well-built coloured man from the Western Cape, the son of a talented movement poet. He had covered much of contemporary news from Africa as a cameraman and helped document the fall of apartheid and the founding of the new nation.

In the moment, he didn't attempt to hide the pain he felt at giving up a job he called "the biggest news job in the country." Matthews also believed, though, that it was impossible to continue producing fair broadcasts under the thumb of his boss. "The SABC's biggest challenge over twenty years was credibility," he murmured. "If we lose it now, it's going to be very difficult to get it back."[8]

The television chief was no card-carrying member of the ANC, but he had been a stalwart supporter of the governing party. His conversation was peppered with references to *our party*. As head of television news he had been accused of bias by the leader of the opposition, Tony Leon. "They only think you're independent if you *criticize* the ANC," he said heatedly. "There's nothing from the apartheid era that I want back— *nothing*. When the government delivers, we should also be there. It may not be news that people in middle-class homes recognize as news, but it *is* news when kids who had to cross a crocodile-infested river to get to school have a bridge to do it now."

This general fidelity to the movement, and to the party, had not provided him protection from the pressure exerted by Zikalala. "I just tried to introduce the idea of critical distance," Matthews said. "I really don't understand, given the enormous power it has, the desire of the ruling party to be in charge of every institution, public or private."

In the coming months there would be a stream of other SABC executives leaving key jobs after similar conflicts. Pippa Green, the powerful head of radio news, soon joined the exodus after clashing with Zikalala over how to cover the burgeoning crisis in Zimbabwe.

Matthews had developed a theory about why the news chief clashed so often with his younger underlings. He believed that a person's essential style and values were grounded in one's experience in his twenties; the older man's method of running things was gruff and authoritarian, and Matthews thought it reflected his role in the armed wing of the ANC.

The best journalism never flowed from the top down in command-and-control environments, he pointed out. The best journalism was, by its nature, reflective of complicated, daily lives of ordinary people, and it was most often produced by flexible organizations run by people who understood that news should be allowed to bubble up from the bottom. "There's a monster called 'developmental journalism,'" he went on. "Journalism must contribute to our democracy—no argument. But that's come to mean you contribute by not criticizing."

As I spent the next several days following Zikalala through his daily paces, it struck me how little of his time was actually spent considering editorial questions like this one. The news chief spent far more time chasing money. While officials regularly placed pressure on SABC to cover events and contribute to "uplifting" the country, the government actually provided less than 3 percent of the budget. The vast bulk of expenses to keep the whole operation going, up to 75 percent of revenue, came from commercial advertising. In this sense, the pressures on the broadcaster were much like the pressures faced by commercial ventures such as Yfm.

President Mbeki's Cabinet had propounded social democratic goals for SABC, but then it had imposed tight constraints on its finances in a strictly capitalist model. The corporation's resulting heavy reliance on advertising had significant practical consequences. Most South Africans fell into the bottom half of the country's economic categories, which meant they earned less than R3,000 a month per household. More than 80 percent of blacks were trapped at the bottom rung, while 98 percent of whites still earned salaries that placed them in the top half. It was difficult to see how any media outlet could faithfully reflect the needs of the working class and the poor if it was forced to rely so heavily on commercial advertisers pandering to those with disposable income.

Zikalala told me that his proudest accomplishment so far was establishment of a proper presidential press corps. He had recently hired a second correspondent to expand SABC's coverage of President Mbeki. His selections for the team demonstrated how little concern he had for "critical distance," which Matthews advocated. The news chief's first hire had been Miranda Strydom, a former government spokesman known for her avid affection toward Mbeki.

"I'm not the president's lapdog," Zikalala told me, unprompted, in explaining his choice. "But the president is the president of this country, and I believe he should be given the respect he deserves." In his view, other editors purposely undermined the president. Mbeki, he pointed out, recently had brokered a peace agreement in Côte d'Ivoire. "No one cared!" he said, turning his palms to the ceiling. "They criticize him. But what has he done? He's *succeeding.*"

When we got back in Zikalala's office, his newest hire was waiting for instructions about how to cover the president's upcoming trip to Europe. The new correspondent smiled at me. For a moment I had trouble placing him. Then it struck me: Dumisani Nkwamba was a young man I had met the year before in Oudtshoorn when he was doing advance work for President Mbeki. Now he had been selected by Zikalala to *cover* the president for SABC television.

Nkwamba was a smart, energetic lawyer who had gotten into journalism originally as a translator for Venda-speaking audiences. But I also remembered the conversation we had had in Oudtshoorn while we waited for the president to arrive. The SABC's newest correspondent had advised me not to rely on the South African media accounts in coming to a judgment about Mbeki; he had criticized reporters for their habit, at press briefings, of asking tough questions. He had told me he thought the leader was "too brilliant" to be subjected to such treatment. Whenever the president was finished talking, Nkwamba had assured me, he "felt more than satisfied."[9] He was an acolyte, not a chronicler, and he was the news chief's latest hire.

In the afternoon, Zikalala drove us out to an exclusive resort, Saxon, in the northern suburb of Sandton. I had hoped we would wrap up our day together on Constitution Hill instead, because that was where trade union leader Zwelinzima Vavi would deliver a major address in honor of Chris Hani. Hani was the revolutionary hero and former chief of the Communist Party murdered by assassins in 1993; he had been a longtime rival of Thabo Mbeki's. Praise of the Hani legacy sometimes constituted thinly veiled criticism of the president. Instead of going to Constitution Hill, though, we headed off to an exclusive gathering of the country's top black businessmen with the country's minister of trade and industry, Alec Erwin.

From the entryway of the resort we were ferried in a luxury sedan past mammoth reflecting pools and well-tended gardens. The executives clustered around tables wedged full of canapés, mini quiches, and deep-fried jumbo shrimp. Inside the briefing room, around an enormous oval conference table, Minister Erwin told the businessmen that there were new economic opportunities the government intended to make available to the emerging class of black entrepreneurs.

Government officials expected to maintain a strong hand in partially privatized utilities like Eskom, the electricity provider; South African Airways; and Denel, the public/private arms manufacturer, he said. The minister added, though, that some state-held companies would be privatized soon and prime land also would be offered for sale. "We will sell some very interesting companies in the next eighteen months," he added, smiling. In those instances "we're extremely well disposed" toward using the sales as a way to spread the wealth to black entrepreneurs.

Sitting next to me was a man who I thought bore a strong resemblance to Walter Sisulu, Nelson Mandela's mentor and a lionized leader of the liberation generation. As it turned out, he was Walter's son, Max Sisulu, the youngest of a powerful set of siblings. His sister, Lindiwe Sisulu, was a member of Mbeki's Cabinet, and her name sometimes appeared on short lists of potential future presidents.

Max Sisulu was head of economic policy development at the ANC and previously had worked as director of Denel. His wife, Elinor, was a critic of Zimbabwean President Robert Mugabe and was among those who had been blacklisted from the SABC airwaves by Zikalala.

At the beginning of the meeting with the minister, Sisulu had sat down beside me, shuffling his feet slightly through the formal remarks. Now, hours later, he raised his hand because he had an unsettling question to ask. "Maybe it's the socialist in me," Sisulu began, adding that he had been thinking of the proper role of the private sector in achieving national objectives. "What *is* black business at the end of the day—besides getting *deals*, I mean?" he asked, pointedly.

I thought of what presidential advisor Joel Netshitenzhe had told me—that the president hoped to create a new *patriotic bourgeoisie*. Minister Ervin smiled and shuffled through his notes. The younger men around the table glanced at Sisulu, as if he was a brother from another planet. They were too polite to laugh, as the members of Parliament had done to their critic from the Pan-Africanist Congress the year before, when Mbeki had been reelected as president.

Nobody around the table offered an answer. Did the policy outlined by the minister have anything to do with social change and economic justice? Or was it merely a slightly camouflaged play to enrich supporters of the ANC who would, in turn, contribute to the party?

By the time we got back to the newsroom, word was out that the trade union leader, Zwelinzima Vavi, had used his lecture about Chris Hani at Constitution Hill to launch another intense verbal attack on President Mbeki. In the process, he also had lobbed a verbal grenade at the SABC. "Workers have not fought so hard to liberate the SABC from the shackles of apartheid only to end up being subjected to the same oppression," he had said, likening the broadcaster, and the news chief's approach, to the state-controlled media in Zimbabwe. "When dictatorship arrives, it does not beat drums. It is only when people wake up in the middle of an untenable situation that they realize it is too late."[10]

Zikalala was clearly stung by the attack, he later admitted. "I was hurt, to be honest with you," he said. "I had worked with Vavi. . . . But it was much more political than anything else. They felt that I've taken sides with the president." Over the next few months and years, the news chief increasingly would be caricatured as the instrument of his master's voice. In the coming period, every move he made would be seen as evidence of a decision he had taken to side with Mbeki over Zuma.

Like so many other institutions in the half-changed country, including the police, intelligence agencies, government ministries, Parliament, and the judiciary, the SABC had been caught up to damaging effect in the struggle for control of the ANC. Matthews, the departing head of television news, even felt a little sorry for his former boss. "In the past he was more aligned with JZ [Zuma], so this is a difficult period for him," he said. "SABC is probably the most politically contested institution in the country."

On the final day I spent with Zikalala, June 27, 2005, it was the fiftieth anniversary of the Congress of the People, the mass gathering in 1955 that had produced the Freedom Charter, the ANC's original proclamation of principles. To mark the occasion, Parliament had moved its operation from Cape Town into the hardscrabble community of Kliptown, where the convention was originally held.

From home that morning, I tuned in to watch the opening session before heading to the broadcast center. Coverage of the event had begun, normally enough, with reporters setting the scene in stand-ups on the spot. An SABC reporter asked a prominent historian, "Was it a miracle . . . ?" and the historian replied forcefully, "No, because that means it can't be explained." Then the screen inexplicably faded to black.

There was dead air for quite some time. Somebody in the control room apparently had flicked the wrong switch. When the screen came back to life, in place of the special session of Parliament a paid-television segment on vacuum cleaners popped up. The segment showcased Bagless Stick Sharks from a company called Verimark. "Wow, that's amazing!" a woman shouted, showing off the astonishing suction capacity of her gleaming machine. Similarly cheerful advertorials for funeral and life insurance policies, called "Dignity Plans," followed.

When I showed up at the news chief's office a half hour later, I expected to see a massive search launched for the responsible party. But Zikalala appeared unflappable as ever. He admitted that he had received an angry message from Parliament Speaker Baleka Mbete, but said he hadn't gotten around yet to investigating how the blooper had happened.

In his regular morning conference with top news executives of the corporation, Zikalala didn't even mention the snafu. Perhaps he didn't want to draw attention to the fact that he had just sacked an experienced television professional and had replaced him with someone who knew nothing about broadcasting. The news chief, instead, instructed his staff to prepare for the upcoming conference of the ANC. As the conversation began, he turned to whisper to me: "You see, I don't micromanage at all—no, no, no."

He also told his staffers that he had heard complaints from Zuma's advisors because there hadn't been footage on SABC showing the large crowds outside the courtroom where Zuma had appeared for a hearing in connection with the corruption charges. "They said we sanctioned Zuma," he told his underlings. "I'm not saying we should play it up. We should reflect reality—that's all I'm saying."

Several of the participants looked puzzled. It wasn't at all clear to them what they should do. Of course, any attempt at "reflecting reality" was going to get harder by the day at SABC. As a loyal member of the ANC, and an acolyte in the past of both leaders, Zikalala would soon face a bedeviling choice of which leader to side with when their split sharpened even more. In this environment, the corporation increasingly would leave it to others to deliver breaking political news. The news chief insisted, to the end, that the broadcaster could still play the role of *nation builder*.

It seemed like a spectacular cock-up. Zikalala was smart enough to know that his listeners and viewers longed for an unblinkered view of reality, but his loyalties led him elsewhere. His pronouncements were a snarl of contradictions, and there was no question, in the end, about which commitment for him created the strongest pull—toward the party's interest over the interest of the general public.

It wasn't clear now whether there would be a broadcast service worth saving by the time the all-out, scorched-earth battle between the ANC's top leaders finally ground to its finish. The coring out of the SABC's journalism talent was only the first step in a long march in a sustained ANC assault on the capacity of South African media to participate in building a liberated, and also free, nonracial, nonsexist, egalitarian country.

12.

On the Ground

As the country settled into winter, in 2006, Jacob Zuma plunged into the most painful period of his life. This said something about the depth of the current crisis, since he already had been a prisoner, a guerrilla, the target of assassination attempts, a survivor among comrades who had perished in the struggle, a man who had been left through divorce by one woman he loved and abandoned through suicide by another, the object of widespread scorn and derision after the Shaik trial, and the person now caught in the vortex of an enormous crosscutting series of pressures. The onslaught he stood against now was like none I have ever seen a public figure endure anywhere in the world. He sucked up much of the oxygen in political culture for most of the year.

Zuma had been formally charged with corruption after being fired as deputy president of the country, but that was the least of it. Now he had been arrested and tried on a count of forcible rape. The charge had been leveled against him in late 2005 by a woman half his age. She was the daughter of a former comrade, and claimed that he had sexually assaulted her in the guest room of his own home.

Most observers figured, as a result, that Zuma was past what South Africans called his "sell-by date." Even in the unlikely event that he was acquitted of rape, it was hard to imagine how he could reclaim his status as a popular leader. How could he present himself as the leader in a modern nonracial, nonsexist society if there was evidence of both dishonesty and violence against women?

On the last day of the trial, I managed to talk my way past security into the courtroom. I wanted to hear the verdict read out by the judge on the spot and see the reaction for myself. I arrived in time to see Zuma enter the courtroom in a dark suit and a powder-blue shirt, dressed as though for a funeral. His shoes were polished to a high sheen. It was 8:30 in the morning, just a year after his sacking by Mbeki, and he looked contrite. Zuma had once been the second most powerful man in the country, but now he faced the possibility of returning to prison, this time on account of a sex crime. Under a hammering cross-examination about everything from his manner of wooing a potential bedmate to his HIV status (negative, he insisted), he had been portrayed by prosecutors as a lecherous buffoon.

When I had last seen him onstage the year before, at the party meeting where the rebellion against Mbeki had taken place, he had looked puffed up by his remarkable political comeback. But, standing near the defendant's table in the courtroom, Zuma seemed small and vulnerable. A headline in the *Star* after Mbeki had fired him as deputy president said that he had been *emasculated* by his sacking. As in Lewis Nkosi's novel about Mandela's imprisonment, the commentary around Zuma was often wrapped in the language of sexual prowess. In any case, he seemed all tucked in now, utterly mild and meek.

Several hundred people were stuffed into the small wood-paneled courtroom at Johannesburg High Court for the reading of the verdict. As he made his way to the defendant's bench, women in the public gallery where I was sitting sang, "Zuma, My President!" When he turned to face them he raised his hands, pressing them together in greeting, like Gandhi.

In two months of testimony his advocates had pitched his version of the defense to the gallery—and, through them, to large crowds gathered outside the courtroom each day in wild demonstrations on his behalf. Zuma had employed a coterie of the best criminal lawyers in the country to fight the case. Like in the political trials of the past, there was a legal strategy, which unfolded inside court, and a political strategy, for explaining what was happening to the masses rallied outside.

Zuma's accuser was a thirty-one-year-old black woman, known pseudonymously as Khwezi. Her real identity was widely known, but the pseudonym was intended for her safety. As it emerged in testimony, she was the HIV-positive daughter of Judson Khuzwayo, one of Zuma's former comrades. Every snippet of information presented at trial built on this cringe-worthy basic scenario.

The accuser's father had died while in exile. Khwezi claimed that she had always considered Zuma as a surrogate father. She testified that on the night of November 2, 2005, she had gone to Zuma's home in Johannesburg to seek his counsel. After a long evening, and a discussion about her troubles with life and men, she claimed that he had advised her, among other things, to become less picky in her search for a husband.

After retiring to bed, Khwezi testified, she had awakened in the middle of the night to a terrifying sight—the image of her respected father figure looming naked over her. In order to help the judge understand that having sex with Zuma could not have been consensual on her part, she added that she was a lesbian.

Testimony on behalf of the defense, like in so many rape trials, had been designed primarily to obliterate the accuser's credibility. The defense had submitted rafts of telephone text messages, some of them sexually explicit, that the woman had sent to her supposed father figure.

The chief defense lawyer, a formidable litigator named Kemp J. Kemp, surprised Khwezi on the stand by producing sections of her personal journal, from which he quoted extensively concerning her sexual fantasies. Four men called by the defense claimed that she had falsely accused each of them of rape in the past.

On the stand Zuma had insisted on speaking only in Zulu, a move intended to cast the trial in cultural terms. For cosmopolitans, his sudden assertion of status as a Zulu man reinforced doubts about him, since he had used English in his public role for the last twelve years. In the optics of a political campaign to restore his credibility with party members and the public, though, it proved an effective move. Here the black liberation hero, looking sober and speaking colloquial Zulu, had responded to withering and belittling questions put to him, in English, about things that people in traditional communities simply didn't ask one's elders to discuss.

These questions about his sex life had been posed by a brisk and brilliant prosecutor, a younger white woman named Carin de Beer. In the dock, Zuma testified about several things he had noticed during Khwezi's visit—she had arrived at his house in a short skirt and changed into a wrap called a kanga, worn with no underwear on. This line of defense was the oldest canard in sexual assault cases. Under questioning by his own advocates, he was claiming, in effect, that he was the one who had been seduced. He had felt obligated as a Zulu man, he said, to satisfy her.

The long trial unfolded against an uncertain backdrop. Even Zuma's most stalwart supporters felt far more comfortable defending him against corruption allegations than having to stand by him when the charge was rape. Privately, key allies were furious. They couldn't understand why— after they had rallied on his behalf to force the ANC to take him back as deputy president of the party—he had put everything at risk over a casual canoodle.

Even in retrospect, Zuma would acknowledge no fault, a tendency he shared with Mbeki. He cast the rape case only as part of the shadowy conspiracy to destroy him politically. "I was shocked by how some comrades turned [on me]," Zuma would tell me later. "They said that I had a hidden agenda. That made me realize *they* had a hidden agenda."[1] He typically presented everything as threads in a single weave, from the sacking to the corruption charges to the allegation of rape. "That was a staged thing," he said, and his voice dropped to a whisper. "As soon as I [heard] that somebody reported rape, it was clear that this was a *plot*."

Rather than nursing any hurt, he swiftly settled on a strategic response, by his own account. "I knew that there was a campaign against me, and from that point I knew that in order to meet this I've got to move very carefully," he explained later. "I couldn't, just because of anger, move blindly. I did not get excited and I was determined to defend myself. I think the forces against me began to expose themselves. And once they exposed themselves, with time and because of their desperation, they failed to hide this from the people."

In the midst of the rape trial, Zuma and his key strategists created their own grand narrative to counter the state's case. The trial, they contended, was just another sign that Zuma's enemies were ratcheting up the pressure on him. It was one more test of the people's hero. This latest test, the awful nature of the allegations aside, supposedly showed that his opponents would stoop at nothing in order to knock him out of public life.

"I never believed the rape story," Siphiwe Nyanda, a key Zuma supporter, told me later. Nyanda was former commander of the armed underground and, after 1994, chief of the South African Defence Forces. On the day the rape accusation became tabloid fodder, he recalled that he had immediately rushed from his office to meet with Zuma. "He looked so ashen. He was so distressed," Nyanda recalled. The rape allegation had a curious effect in the end, Nyanda explained. "That case convinced me there were sinister forces at work," he said. "I thought we would have to get to the bottom of this."[2]

Trade union leader Zwelinzima Vavi had laid the groundwork already for this line of interpretation in connection with the corruption charges. Vavi had spoken out forcefully against the raids conducted in August of

2005 on Zuma's homes and office, and the offices of his lawyers, as "apartheid-style" assaults and as an attack "on the revolution itself."

The raids were all part of "a classic attempt to drag the working class into a war whose terrain and outcome have been predetermined by neoliberals using their control over key components of the state machinery, in this case in particular the judiciary," the trade union leader insisted.[3] In other words, the charges against Zuma were part of the broader struggle, not a mere legal case against a flawed individual. This approach was adapted by others to the rape charge.

On the stand, Zuma had expanded on this idea, even accusing by name several comrades—former Minister of Justice Penuell Maduna, who had been in office when the corruption case was initiated; former National Prosecuting Authority director Bulelani Ngcuka, who had pursued the fraud and bribery charges against Shaik; and the minister of intelligence, Ronnie Kasrils, who employed a friend of the woman who had accused Zuma of rape in the first place.

Minister Kasrils issued a withering public reply, but it was largely lost in the ensuing war of words. Zuma fanned the frenzy further by asserting that he was the victim of "crucifixion by the media." At every opportunity, he suggested there was a shadowy conspiracy against him by unseen forces that were abetted by the press.

Perhaps not surprisingly, then, the mood around the courthouse during the trial often turned ugly. Supporters of Zuma had burned effigies of his accuser and gotten so riled up one day that they attempted to stone a woman wrongly assumed to be her. "Burn the Bitch!" was the slogan emblazoned on homemade signs and chanted during the days of her testimony.

In testimony inside the courthouse, one embarrassing admission after another had tumbled into the record. Even though Zuma knew Khwezi was HIV-positive, he explained that he hadn't used a condom because there were none at hand. A big challenge in HIV prevention work was convincing men to use condoms, of course; Zuma had been, until recently, the most highly placed government official in the country charged with leading the national effort to rid the country of HIV infection. AIDS treatment activists complained that he had undercut the campaign by his own widely publicized misbehavior.

After intercourse with the young woman—which Zuma estimated had taken twenty-seven minutes—he testified that he had gone to his own bathroom to take a shower to lessen the risk of becoming infected. Since HIV was a virus spread through blood, semen, and vaginal secretions, you couldn't respond rationally by *washing*. In exposing his own ignorance, Zuma reinforced it among sexually active men who admired him.

His legal defense also had relied on the crudest possible implication— that the encounter was the victim's fault, a particularly corrosive line of argument in a country where the rates of violent rape were astronomically high. Representatives of the One in Nine Campaign, so named because an estimated one in nine South African women had been sexually assaulted, rallied to sing, in protest: "Jacob Zuma, your penis has gotten you in trouble."

The trial provided Rashomon-like images of him. Within polite circles of professionals, the trial fanned rising fears about Zuma's character and judgment. There was consternation about antediluvian attitudes he had expressed in the dock, not to mention the misuse of generational power and the assumption he seemed to hold that women found him irresistible. Among township residents and among rural people I sought out, especially young rural men, though, three pieces of testimony were most firmly remembered when the trial was over: the fact that the woman had presented herself in a short dress at Zuma's home; that she had changed later into a kanga without underwear underneath; and the estimate that the former guerrilla leader, now in his sixties, had offered that he lasted *twenty-seven minutes* while having sex.

The trial on rape charges certainly damaged Zuma's reputation among people who were least likely to back him. In other ways, though, it also sharpened his image as a lusty and earthy leader, and a recognizable type (unlike Thabo Mbeki) among the people who constituted his core of support.

When Judge Willem van der Merwe entered the chamber, he bowed toward Zuma's lawyers and the chief prosecutor. He prefaced his remarks with an introduction in fluent unaccented Zulu. When the judge switched back to English, he commented with an edge, "Mr. Zuma understands English perfectly well." This seemed like a bad omen for the defendant in terms of how the judge assessed his behavior at the trial and his overall credibility. The judge was a balding man with full cheeks. He delivered his decision in a singsong cadence, as though offering a lecture on ancient history.

As he began reading, a strikingly beautiful woman slipped into the seat beside me. She was dressed in an open-necked white blouse and a sleek black leather jacket. Clutching a Kleenex, Ranjeni Munusamy looked like a mass of nerves. Her legs kept vibrating up and down and her lips moved soundlessly the whole time. "I'm praying," she explained, flapping her large hands. "I'm Catholic, so I'm repeating what my mother taught me."

We didn't know one another, but I recognized Munusamy instantly: she was the former journalist who had placed herself firmly in the Zuma camp. As a political reporter for the *Sunday Times* years earlier, she had written a story about suspicions that the national prosecutor, Bulelani Ngcuka, was an apartheid-era spy. After her editor, Mathatha Tsedu, had refused to publish the account, she had leaked the exposé to a rival newspaper, *City Press*, and was fired from the staff of the *Sunday Times* for her trouble.

The story she had pursued surfaced an explosive accusation long bandied about concerning Ngcuka, the clear import being that the national prosecutor was out to get Zuma now in a continuation of his role as an agent for the other side. When the ANC had operated in exile, such an accusation could get someone killed, of course.

One of the secrets of the apartheid regime's long lifespan had been its regular success in turning ANC members and leaders into informants. The history of the movement was laced with heartbreaking betrayals of one comrade by another, beginning with the raids on Liliesleaf Farm in Rivonia, back in 1963 when so many leaders of the party were sent off to trial and prison for much of their lives thanks to information supplied to authorities by a snitch.

In postliberation South Africa, there had been no systematic squaring of accounts on this score, to allow party members to come to terms with the pattern of sabotage and betrayal by insiders. Many comrades suspected by others of breaking under questioning, or trading information for favors, had never been confronted in a forum that allowed them to reply. Around these comrades, there was a recurrent buzz of gossip and backstabbing even as they took important roles in the new government.

In the storm of accusations and counteraccusations that followed publication of the exposé about Ngcuka, Mandela's old friend Mac Maharaj and the former MK intelligence operative Mo Shaik, brother of Schabir, had stepped forward to back Munusamy's account. They claimed to have evidence that Ngcuka was, in fact, a turncoat.

In response, President Mbeki commissioned a retired judge to probe the accusation. After a series of hearings the judge cleared the prosecutor of the allegations, and Maharaj and Shaik were both discredited. The journalist who had raised the stink in the first place, now sitting next to me, had been widely vilified by her former colleagues as a Zuma apologist in the consuming media storm.

Since then, Munusamy had served as an on-again/off-again media spokesperson for Zuma. Her manifest nervousness at the moment led me to understand how uncertain his followers actually felt, right until the verdict was announced, about whether their leader would secure an acquittal.

Through the long trial, she confided, it had been Zuma keeping her spirits up rather than the other way around. She told me that on many days after the most damaging testimony was offered at trial his inner circle would reconvene at his home. In Munusamy's telling, Zuma routinely greeted them all with a smile, thanked everybody for coming, as if he was hosting a party, and then offered a small joke told at his own expense. "He never seemed down, his energy never flagged, and never lost faith," Munusamy added, a characterization that reminded me of what Thuthu Zuma had said about her father.

As the hours ticked by in court, Judge van der Merwe droned on. Munusamy's leg kept gyrating. In his elaborate encapsulation of the long trial, the judge kept circling back to apparent inconsistencies in Khwezi's testimony. Though his accuser had claimed Zuma as a father figure, for example, it turned out she had had only spotty contact with him from 1990 forward. There was also that troubling evidence of her making unproved accusations of rape in the past.

Finally, the judge pointed out that the defense lawyer had asked Khwezi point blank if it was conceivable, in the moment they began having sex, that Zuma thought it was consensual. The accused had admitted it was possible he had misunderstood. "She did not object when he came to her room. She did not object when he said he would come again later," the judge said. He mentioned, too, that Khwezi had not called out when Zuma had climbed into bed with her; at no point did she ask him to stop penetrating her; Khwezi also had remembered hearing Zuma offer to pull his penis out before ejaculating and calling her *sweetheart* when he did.

At last, the judge said, "I find that consensual sex took place." Suddenly Munusamy stopped vibrating in her seat. She pulled a Kleenex from her pocket and began to weep. Zuma turned then, in our direction. You could see that his face was flushed, with a little current of darkening color at the nape of his neck.

The judge looked up then, and fixed Zuma with a stern expression.

He quoted a bit of Rudyard Kipling: "If you cannot control your body, and your sexual urges, there you are." Given the history of white men telling black men where they could live and work and with whom they could have sex in South Africa, this was a rather pointed denouement. "The accused should not have had sex with a woman so much younger," the judge went on. "It is inexcusable that he did."

When the judge stopped talking at last, Zuma's relatives, friends, and supporters jumped to their feet. Crowds of supporters outside the court exploded in celebration, too, as word of the acquittal spread. *"Awuleth' Umshini Wam'"* (Bring Me My Machine Gun) broke out in overlapping choruses. Traffic in the streets of downtown Johannesburg came to a halt.

The crowd outside the courthouse was in a triumphal mood. It was as if by beating the rape charge Zuma had achieved something admirable, reinforcing his status as the people's hero. The judge had taken pains to point out that a not-guilty verdict was no proof of his innocence; Zuma's defense was not a "superior version" of what had happened, he explained; only two people, after all, knew for certain what had occurred in that spare bedroom. From the start, the onus of proof had been borne by the State, and the defense had simply provided "a reasonable possibility that his version is true," the judge had said. On that basis, he was obliged to acquit. This distinction was lost on the crowd.

Zuma's legal troubles were far from over. Right outside the courtroom doors, the head of the Jacob Zuma Trust estimated that it would cost R12 million to underwrite an aggressive defense in the upcoming corruption trial. Even if he then managed to beat the corruption rap, it was a considerable stretch to imagine him prevailing now in a battle with Thabo Mbeki to become the next president of the ANC. That was how things appeared from the vantage point of Johannesburg—but I wondered how things looked if you ventured outside major cities. His supporters fanned out around the country, determined to create what the trade union leader Zwelinzima Vavi called a *tsunami* on their leader's behalf.

Tall highveld grasses burnished by golden highlights bent in the breeze, and baobab trees revealed themselves against a steel-gray skyline. Branches arched every which way like jazz dancers in a game of Freeze. It was just a month after the verdict in the rape trial when I set off from Joburg before dawn, purposely blasting myself out of the bubble of cosmopolitan life.

Leaders of the ANC Youth League had scheduled a rally in rural Limpopo province, and it would be the first major speech by Zuma since his acquittal. Beautiful expanses of open plain gave way to makeshift villages, which looked like temporary rest stops for the streams of migrants headed in the opposite direction.

Along the highway, youngsters lined up, waiting for rides, with a few worn belongings stuffed into ragged satchels. They were local expressions of a massive global phenomenon involving hundreds of millions of people in motion around the world. These large conglomerations of people were flowing out from the countryside and headed into the city in overlapping diasporas that crossed lines of ethnicity, class, language, and culture. More people in South Africa had launched themselves into this migratory swirl than ever before. In many ways, governing the country meant attempting to keep up with this swirl of internal wandering. At the moment, I was headed in the opposite direction.

On the outskirts of Polokwane, the provincial capital, a massive billboard came into view, emblazoned with the ANC's ubiquitous slogan, "*A Better Life for All.*" The city coiled around the N1 highway, which ran straight north into Zimbabwe.

Turning off the highway, I headed due east into rolling hills of scrub brush and dwarf trees. The air was blessedly clean of even a trace of the city's heavy layer of smog, and the view resembled the gently rolling landscape of the hill country of rural Texas.

In a curvy stretch along the narrow side road leading into the hills, a rickety cart loaded half full with firewood appeared right in front of me, and I slammed on the brakes. It looked like a message from another century, or a reminder of another South Africa.

The cart was in the process of being yanked forward by a mangy, slow-moving ox. A wiry, ghostly old man clutched at the reins with gnarled, tightly closed fists, his mouth hanging open to reveal a few orphaned teeth. To keep from panicking the ox, I slowed at the next curve in the road and waited.

At that moment we were both overtaken in a flash by a long motorcade. Sirens from the police escorts keened; blue lights swirled along the tops of the cars. They all whipped past at shocking speed. The old man yanked at the reins and snapped a whip to prod the ox onto the shoulder of the road. There, his cart perched on the precipice while the VIP escort thundered on. When it was past, the old man snapped the whip at his ox and inched back onto the road.

Another twenty minutes on, off a paved road and up a deeply rutted dirt lane, I found the village where the rally would be held. Bungeni was sprawled along the ridgetop, its main drag ankle-deep in silt. The road ran along the edge of the town, connecting clusters of tin-roofed shops and ramshackle bars, called shebeens. Mobs of men clustered at the entrances of the bars for their midday drinks. They shouted and poked at one another, ogling the ladies passing by.

Right in the middle of the town stood the soccer field, which was set in a bowl with an expansive view of the surrounding countryside. At one end of the field was a massive stage festooned with banners, and beside the stage a brilliantly bleached white tent offered the local elite shelter from the sun. Above our heads clouds shaped like elephants trekked across a sky streaked with neon blue.

The rally had been advertised as a commemoration of the life of Peter Mokaba, a militant Youth League leader from this area who was most widely known for his famous chant, "one bullet, one Boer." Mokaba also had been instrumental in promoting Thabo Mbeki as the best possible successor for Nelson Mandela, but he had died of complications from AIDS during the president's first term.

Rather than wait near the stage for Zuma's arrival (he had been hustled off to a private luncheon), I threaded my way through the gathering crowd to the soccer field. Heads swiveled and a murmur followed behind me. I must have looked quite odd, as the lone white person around, in dress pants, with a digital camera slung around my neck. "*Umlungu?*" a woman asked in a disbelieving tone of voice. "*Ina,*" her companion answered with an air of wonder—Yes, it was indeed a pale person out there wandering aimlessly in the field under a punishing sun.

Before I reached halfway across the expanse, a band of boys overtook me. "Hey hey hey—*sir!*" they shouted. The boys looked ripe for adolescence in their raggedy T-shirts and torn pants. Their gangly bodies formed sharp angles, like a haphazard collection of elbows and knees.

One of the boys asked where I was from. When I told him that I lived in the United States, his buddy chimed in, "Hey, do you know *Eminem?*" Here was one of those small-world moments: in a village without running water, where few people had electricity or indoor plumbing and none of the kids owned so much as a transistor radio, hip-hop turned out to be our common reference.

"Sure, Eminem's my neighbor," I replied. The boys looked nonplussed, checking one another out for the proper reaction. "Yep, he's the neighbor on one side and my neighbor on the other side is 50 Cent," I added.

Quickly, the joke registered. The one boy had mentioned a white rapper because he thought that would make it easier for me to relate; I had matched him with a reference to a black superstar. The boys broke up in giggly cacophony as we walked on together, the two older ones repeating the exchange to the younger boys in Xitsonga.

The older boys were named Talent Mabundla and Vunene Mabasa. They had just turned twelve, which meant that they had arrived on the planet right between the time of Nelson Mandela's election and his inauguration four years later as president. One of their younger friends, the boy in long pants and worn sneakers, was barely eleven. The smallest pair of their companions were born in 1996, the year the country's new Constitution was ratified.

They were, in other words, part of the so-called Born Free generation celebrated for having been spared the bad old days of apartheid. The boys pumped me for the details of my travels around the country. None of them had traveled outside Bungeni, except for two brief trips—once to hear President Mbeki speak at an ANC campaign rally in Polokwane in 2004 and once, the year before, to watch a play at the Market Theatre in Johannesburg. They had been shocked out of their minds by the size of the big city. There was an awed register in their voices as they talked about it, as if they were talking about a visit to Oz.

Suddenly, sirens sounded, and behind us the motorcade roared up over the lip of the ridge, careening down into the bowl behind the stage. We all turned to watch the motorcade arrive. "What do you think of him, of Jacob Zuma?" I asked the boys.

"We *love* Comrade JZ [pronounced 'Jay-Zed']," Talent replied, craning his neck to get a better look at his hero. "We really, *really love* him." Through a gap in the crowd we caught a glimpse of Zuma as he exited his armor-plated BMW. His shaved, bullet-shaped head emerged first. When he stood up, there bloomed the widest possible smile. Surrounded by bodyguards, he ambled loose-legged toward a throng of ululating women.

Vunene was a lanky, slender boy with an almond-shaped face beneath a thatch of jet-black hair. Scuffing his ratty tennis shoes in the grass, he glanced at Talent, who jabbed an index finger at my chest. "What do *you* think about him?" he asked then, turning the tables on me.

"I don't understand yet why you love him so much," I admitted. "I'd like to understand why."

The boys cocked their heads, as if to allow them time to consider things from my point of view. Talent checked out his sidekicks. "Because JZ is a good person," he put in at last, punctuating the air with an upraised finger, "and also because he doesn't have any *apartheid*."

At first, I thought there must be a language gap, some nuance I had missed between an idea thought up in Xitsonga and the phrase that had just been spoken in English. It occurred to me that the boy had used a word that signified a historical period as a way of describing a person's character.

"Okay, so what about the president?" I asked, testing the hunch. "What do you think of *him*?"

Abruptly, both of the older boys looked skyward while the two younger kids shyly considered their bare feet. "Mbeki's good," one of the littler boys squeaked.

"*Maybe* he's good," Talent corrected him, sounding suddenly angry. "Yes, he's all right as president," he added. "*But he has a little bit of apartheid*."

By way of explanation, Vunene offered a long account about the rally in Polokwane, where President Mbeki had promised everyone that they would receive water and electricity if the ANC was returned to office.

Voters had responded by giving the party nearly 70 percent of the vote. But most of the promises were yet unfulfilled. "Mbeki can *lie*," Talent said, with a sudden edge. He swiveled to point at clusters of houses and shacks in each direction. "He said there would be water and electricity, and there isn't."

Zuma had been sacked the year before, so he apparently wasn't being held to account for the failures of government. In fact, it seemed that his dismissal reinforced the idea that President Mbeki had wobbled off track. Zuma had been reinvented, in a sense, as an outsider.

The boys' other beef with the president boiled down to this: they thought he favored the rights of girls and women over the needs of boys and men. They had heard, for example, that Mbeki preferred to be succeeded by a woman. What kind of man said such a thing? The smaller boys shook their heads as if someone had just told them the 2010 World Cup wouldn't be played in South Africa after all.

Talent volunteered that it would be terrible to have a woman as president. The younger ones piped up with various explanations why:

"They're too weak."

"Women talk too much—way too much."

"And they're lazy, aren't they?"

"They're afraid to fly."

Here was a mix of raw, unfiltered reasons for adoration of Zuma: he "had no apartheid"—which meant, more or less, that he took no guff from white people—and also he knew why boys ought to stand together against the girls.

On stage, a string of officials from the struggle generation lowered themselves into chairs behind a long table. I broke away from the boys then, to make my way back to the stage, and almost immediately regretted it. Up front, at the podium, one speaker after another took the microphone and commenced the longest series of speeches I have ever had to sit through.

Over the next two hours, the speakers warned the large crowd of a shadowy conspiracy that had supposedly been unleashed to destroy the entire liberation movement. One leader likened the Scorpions, the anticorruption strike force under the direction of the National Prosecuting Authority, to a band of right-wing saboteurs. "We are still not in charge of the country, Comrades," a Youth League officer warned. Here was the refrain again: the ANC is in *office* but not in *power*.

A fiery university lecturer and leader of the Young Communist League, David Masondo, chanted, "Away with capitalism—away! Forward to socialism—forward!"—and this was a reminder that South Africa was one of the few places in the world where membership in the Communist Party was growing.

By the time Zuma bellied up to the podium, much of his audience had already flagged in the heat. Everyone who owned an umbrella had it open against the punishing sun. "I am not perfectly healthy," he announced, which struck a jarring note since his HIV status had been an issue at the trial.

If you took a second look, Zuma did appear rather drawn and lethargic. He proceeded to deliver an uninspired text about the political contributions of former youth leader Peter Mokaba during his lifetime. Soon enough, the crowd buzzed with a crosscurrent of its own conversation. People talked with one another through Zuma's exegesis about life on Robben Island, and the rigors of guerrilla training, and the beauty of sacrifice in the struggle.

At long last, as if taking pity on everybody, he closed with a flourish: "The ANC will rule until the Son of Man comes back!" he cried. His audience snapped to attention. Their leader seemed to have awakened from a restorative sleep. He swayed from side to side, a stocky man with rhythm, boogying as if he had just shed an uncomfortably tight suit.

The audience broke into the chorus of his struggle song: *"Awuleth' Umshini Wam'!"* For twelve years now, the party's leaders had portrayed the ANC as stewards of an exemplary experiment in democracy. I wondered what could be gained from encouraging boys as young as Vunene and Talent, the post-apartheid generation, to raise imaginary Kalashnikovs now as part of the struggle to secure what hadn't been won through the ballot box.

When Zuma's entourage finished dancing and singing, they left the stadium. There was a storm of dust raised by the long line of departing luxury cars. The children of Bungeni cleared the field, their voices fading as they hiked up the hill. The elders of the village closed their umbrellas, setting out stiff-legged on the long march toward home. On the way uphill, I chatted with several of them. They made it clear that they respected Zuma, though they were aware their better-educated, higher-income relatives in the cities thought differently. City slickers enjoyed lampooning this leader as a clueless country bumpkin. But when rural people like them heard their city cousins sneering at Zuma, they said, it felt as though they were being laughed at too.

Zuma was someone who looked, and danced, and laughed, and sang in a familiar way. In his plainspoken earnestness, he didn't seem so haughty, and high and mighty, like Thabo Mbeki. This, as it turned out, would be Zuma's biggest trump card in the campaign he mounted to topple the president. He was running, in effect, as an anti-Mbeki and a true son of the soil. Now, all his skills as an organizer, underground operative, intelligence chief, and politician would be tested in an all-out, increasingly nasty struggle for power with Zuma's comrade, the president.

PART III

The Pivotal Year
(2007)

This place [Nkandla] made me who I am. How can I forget? If I can't identify with it, I'm like a South African who's floating in the air. This makes me to be on my feet, on the ground, as a South African who grew up *here* in KwaZulu Natal, who is a *Zulu* with Zulu traditions, and with Zulu values pushed into myself.

—*JACOB ZUMA*
2007

My generation is free of the past. But the past has left its mark. The gap between the rich and the poor is very wide and I don't see it getting smaller. That's going to be the challenge of our generation.

—*THUTHU ZUMA*
2007

Thabo Mbeki (left) and Jacob Zuma (right) face off on the dais at the African National Congress convention in 2007. (*Greg Marinovich / Storytaxi.com*)

13.

Cape Town

When I caught up with President Mbeki, in the middle of 2007, he was on a campaign-style swing through Cape Town for what his advisors called an *imbizo*. The national election was three years behind him and the next national campaign wouldn't happen until 2009. In a normal time, this would be a period for a focus on governance, not canvassing, but it was no normal time.

The president was under increasing pressure to demonstrate his popularity within the ANC and to repair the damage to his own standing already done through his internecine battle with his former deputy. At the end of the year, at a national party conference, top leaders would be subject to election. Supporters of Jacob Zuma were lobbying for the ANC to dump Mbeki.

It was a gray winter morning and the president looked thinner than when I had seen him in ostrich country three years earlier, and at official functions in the intervening years. He was dressed in a white T-shirt worn beneath a bright-red workman's shirt with a blue collar, tucked beneath a spiffy, formal blue suit jacket. A delegation of provincial and national officials and a scrum of journalists had begun the morning with him on a short drive north of the city, heading to a residential treatment

center for drug addicts. Table Mountain, Table Bay, and the leafy suburbs of the city were at our backs.

The rehabilitation center was an impressive new building trimmed in
dark wood with expansive windows. Local officials confided that it had
been finished in a rush so it would stand open in time for the presidential
inspection. The premier of the Western Cape, Ebrahim Rasool, was at
Mbeki's elbow, and they were surrounded by the national ministers of
education, housing, and local government.

Taking up the rear in the official delegation was the leader of the
Democratic Alliance, Helen Zille. She recently had upended ANC
expectations by winning in the municipal elections the year before. Now,
as mayor of Cape Town, Zille was the politician ANC officials feared
most. She had managed to gain a significant post, with executive authority, in one of the country's best-known cities and she also was an unrelenting and astringent critic of the governing party, as she demonstrated
when I drew near. "This whole *imbizo* is nothing but a state-sponsored
political rally," she said. "You have to decide whether to participate or
not—and if you don't, that becomes part of the story."[1]

At the speech in Oudtshoorn, three years earlier, President Mbeki
had held himself apart from the people. Here, as if forcefully making
amends, the president seemed desperate to reconnect. In local branch
meetings of the ANC around the country, Mbeki was regularly pilloried
for having lost touch with the grass roots. The unions had launched a
massive national public-sector strike, which amounted to a month-long
show of power and a rebuke of his policies.

Those were only the public manifestations of anti-Mbeki organizing.
Beneath the surface, there was intense skirmishing that spilled into weird
spy-versus-counterspy shenanigans. Documents, including emails, pur-
porting to show a top-level conspiracy under way against Jacob Zuma by
Mbeki supporters, were leaked to the newspapers. Most or all of the
emails were apparent forgeries, but the whole episode deepened a paranoiac atmosphere among top officials.

One key Mbeki supporter, the banker Saki Macozoma—he was the hero of Ciko Thomas, the businessman I had met—complained to me that agents from the National Intelligence Agency recently had stumbled all over themselves in staking out his home, tapping his phones, and following him around the city. The banker had caught them in the act of following him around, he said. "I said directly to them, 'If this is how you protect the country, then we're fucked because you are so incompetent!'" he exclaimed.[2]

Macozoma was upset both at what the agents had been trying to do and at their clumsy performance in pursuit of misguided aims. He attributed their behavior to "Zuma's long tentacles in the National Intelligence Agency," apparently activated in the service of intraparty conflict. Intimidation of Zuma's allies had sometimes been equally blunt.

Zuma was convinced that the president and acolytes like Macozoma were prepared to use the police, the national security agencies, the criminal justice system, and the media to settle the scores with him. A strange, classified document known as "Browse Mole," commissioned by the country's National Prosecuting Authority, was sent to Zwelinzima Vavi, the trade union leader, and through him it was released to the media. Browse Mole was a wild mix of suggestive allegations layered over partly confirmed facts suggesting, among other things, that Zuma had solicited money from Libya and Angola to fund an anti-Mbeki insurrection.

Suddenly, the entire political elite, so widely praised around the world for its supposed maturity, was caught up in an orgy of backstabbing. The country's most pressing problems seemed to slide off its leaders' radar. Mbeki's advisors hoped that this presidential *imbizo* would yank the focus of media coverage back onto the efforts of government to solve the problems of ordinary South Africans. It was also his considered effort, planned by his closest aides, to burst out of the presidential bubble.

Mbeki's stop at the drug treatment center was planned to showcase programs in the Western Cape designed to grapple with the area's high rates of drug addiction, especially among the young. When apartheid ended, the country's borders had been opened to the rest of the world. Strict controls on who could enter South Africa, and where they could go inside the country, had been eased considerably in the mid-1990s. In the midst of joyous returns of freedom fighters and exiles, the country also was subjected to a sudden flood of less desirable imports—organized crime, pornography, and drugs.

During the first decade of democracy, South Africa turned into the chief transshipment center for illegal narcotics between South America, Africa, and Asia. The rates of addiction to a wide range of drugs inside the country soared. The government had been working hard to develop "south-south trade" between South Africa and the so-called BRIC powers—Brazil, Russia, India, and China—in the legal economy. Massive amounts of money and illegal drugs flowed along parallel routes in the shadow economy. Profit margins in the narcotics trade were enormous, and so was the corrupting power of the drug barons. Jackie Selebi, the national police commissioner, was a close ally of President Mbeki's and a hero of the struggle years, but he was also a close friend of one of the country's biggest suspected drug kingpins.

The facility Mbeki was touring was built to serve seventy-five adults and twenty-five children, a rather small gesture considering the scale of the need. There were hundreds of thousands actively searching for drug addiction treatment in this province alone. In the central meeting room a twenty-one-year-old addict named Bongani Mataka welcomed the dignitaries with a song. Once Mataka finished his performance, provincial officials outlined the government's official antidrug strategy. It was based on the tired, traditional, three-pronged effort of most failed programs: reduce supply, dry up the market, and rehabilitate users. The government had made little progress in any of these three categories. The twin reasons for failure so far were past patterns of oppression and current patterns of incompetence.

Here, as in every other facet of South African life, the war on drugs was coded by race. Black communities were plagued by marijuana with especially potent concentrations of THC, and Mandrax, a powerful sedative. White addicts mostly used heroin, ecstasy, and party drugs. The use of a psychostimulant known as *tik* had taken hold with particular ferocity in coloured townships (as in Asia, where its use had overtaken heroin).[3]

Tik was a methamphetamine, first produced in Japan a century earlier, that produced intense, brief highs that increased confidence, aggression, violent behavior, psychotic breaks, and memory loss—a drug perfectly tailored, it seemed to me, to amplify the country's epidemic of violent crime.

Officials in the room said, one after another, that they were particularly concerned to stem the tide of drugs, and drug-related violence, before the World Cup tournament in 2010. "The drug lords are way ahead of us," the provincial minister of health told the audience. Uncontrolled outbreaks during the competition could deeply embarrass the government and wreck the reputation of South Africa as a tourist destination.

There was an apparent disconnect between the formal briefings and the honored guest. President Mbeki appeared puzzled at the repeated mention of the drug tik. Finally, he brought his chin up from the voluminous notes he had been taking. "What is *tik*?" he asked. A nervous shifting in seats followed. The methamphetamine epidemic had swept into the country several years earlier, and there had been lengthy takeouts in major newspapers and broadcasts.

You could hear a sharp intake of breath. Thabo Mbeki prided himself on his penchant for independent research and mastery of detail. If it appeared that the president didn't know the name of a drug, it would only add to accumulating evidence that he was out of touch. His press spokesman, sitting a few seats away from me, visibly flinched.

Seated to the president's right, Mayor Zille leaned over to fill him in. She was a tall, willowy white woman in a brown cloth coat and stylish turquoise scarf. Her expression, as she had listened impatiently to officials claiming they were making gains in the war on drugs, was that of an irritated school principal. In May, Zille had been elected leader of the Democratic Alliance, replacing Tony Leon. She promptly had begun dismantling her party's reputation as a whites-only preserve by recruiting and promoting young, black leaders. What's more, she had bona fides as a progressive white. Zille had worked for a few years as an investigative reporter for the *Rand Daily Mail* in the 1970s, and she had investigated the police murder of Black Consciousness leader Steven Biko. She was militantly anti-ANC now, but in her case that didn't connote any difficulty in collaborating with black people.

At Mbeki's side, Zille reeled off from memory the chemical ingredients of the drug and sketched its dangers. I knew, from my own reading, that it was a methamphetamine once used to treat weight gain and attention deficit disorder in the United States. Tik was equivalent in its addictive power to crack cocaine, and the high it produced was intensified by the way Cape Town boys used it—heating the drug in light bulbs with the filament removed and inhaling the smoke with glass straws. The sound of it firing in glass had given the drug its name.

Mayor Zille told the president that kids could manufacture tik on their own from cold remedies containing ephedrine or pseudoephedrine available over the counter in pharmacies. She added that a "Chinese triad" recently had moved into the area to supply heroin and other opiates, in exchange for abalone taken by poachers along the coast.

When the mayor was finished, the audience burst into sustained, unscripted applause. Unlike other municipal and provincial officials on hand, she had managed to connect the dots between the direct experience of Capetonians who felt overwhelmed by drug use and the set of larger forces driving the drug economy. She had gone further, suggesting a reasonable approach to countering the dealers with force that seemed commensurate to the scale of the challenge.

At the end of the formal presentations, the moderator turned to the president for a formal response. Mbeki waved her away. Breaking protocol, he beckoned the young addict who had opened the event to come forward again. The president huddled with Mataka near the podium. Mbeki placed a consoling hand on his shoulder and whispered in his ear. In the moment, the president looked like a concerned uncle advising a troubled, but favored nephew. The scene reminded me that Mbeki's own son had disappeared in murky circumstances while he was in exile. This would be the only time, in the years I followed the president at close quarters, when I observed him looking comfortable in the presence of a young person.

He whispered a question, raised his ghostly white eyebrows, and returned to his seat. "The president has asked me to explain how children get in trouble in the first place," Mataka said softly. He explained that he had started using drugs from sheer boredom; out in the Cape Flats, there were no playing fields, no after-school programs, and no jobs for teens. His friends first turned him on to Mandrax, a form of methaqualone. From there, as if moving from elementary school to the upper grades, he graduated on to tik.

After he had become addicted to the drug, Mataka said, it was only a short step to armed robbery. He knew that he was breaking a taboo of his law-abiding parents when he began robbing people. "That first robbery, it was like I was breaking up with my family," he remarked. But the boys he hung out with had stolen a gun in one of their robberies. Then, they had used it in a series of home invasions in the exclusive white neighborhoods of Somerset West. The logic of this spiral reminded me of the stories Jonathan had told me, of course.

The young addict had just been released on parole after serving time in Pollsmoor and Victor Verster prisons, the last two places where Nelson Mandela was incarcerated. Inside those prisons he had learned to record and mix music. Mataka turned to tell the president that he only hoped his ambition as a poet and DJ would help him find his way to freedom. When he stopped talking, Mbeki gave him a thumbs-up, but looked quite chastened.

The president rose slowly, murmuring into the microphone that it was important to recognize "there's a whole chain that works up to recovery." He scanned the audience, registering the presence of representatives from the ANC Youth League. "I hear the youth structures are preoccupied with *other* things," he quipped. The implication was clear: Shouldn't the Youth League launch an urgent campaign to reclaim the lives of young people lost to alcohol and drugs instead of turning the entire organization over to the campaign designed to topple him?

Mbeki noted that in Johannesburg there were thirty-one police districts but one-third of the city's crime was committed in only two of them—Hillbrow, once the center of the city's bohemian culture, and Alexandra, the township north of the city. Most violent crime took place on the weekends, from late afternoon on Friday until midnight on Sunday, and all of it was conflated with drunkenness and drug use. "Imams and priests ought to go to taverns and shebeens," he mused. "They should say: I represent the Almighty and you can't defy the Almighty!" The president was a secular nonbeliever, so it was startling to hear him place his bet on an otherworldly force. All day, he seemed stunned by the scale of the problems that had careened out of his control.

Mbeki made his way out of the hall, and his entourage proceeded in luxury cars and buses on to Delft, a primarily coloured community, and ended up in Khayelitsha, one of the country's largest black townships. In the township, officials filed in beneath an enormous tent where every inch was occupied by residents waiting to see them.

There was a huge response from the crowd, particularly when Mbeki appeared, and an equally loud cascade of booing aimed at Mayor Zille.

When she took the microphone, the mayor explained, in serviceable isiXhosa, her intention "to provide jobs, electricity, and water." As she spoke, Zille was nearly drowned out by jeers. The crowd heckled her, flicking their hands in disgust. She continued speaking, unwavering at the mic, evidently unimpressed by the heckling. When she returned to her chair, Mbeki did something quite unexpected: he rose and embraced the mayor, in effect paying credit to her courage.

From the floor, meanwhile, all sorts of accumulated hurts, wounds, disappointments, and sorrows poured out. It was testimony of the disaffected and disappointed. People asked: Where were the new and better houses promised during the election campaign? How about the jobs? What did the government intend to do about the terrible schools?

Every problem that a citizen faced in dealing with unresponsive bureaucracy was wheeled out for the president's attention. At a long table, secretaries took down the complaints in voluminous records, for Mbeki had promised that he would return one day soon to report on progress.

Near the entrance to the massive tent, I buttonholed the premier of the Western Cape, Ebrahim Rasool. When I asked him about the raucous criticisms about terrible service delivery by local government, he offered a slight smile. The premier said how gratified he was by the turnout and by the content of the discussion.

When I cocked my head, he added, "No, for *sure*," ticking off a list of the kinds of problems raised by the people inside the tent. Then he contrasted these concerns to the sorts of challenges that had been raised in the township, at a similar meeting, five years earlier. In meetings back then, Premier Rasool claimed, every voice had been raised about the lack of food and shelter. Once people had food and a roof over their heads, naturally their attention turned to other demands— education, transportation, jobs. "We've made progress," he insisted, urging me to take stock of everything that had been done, not just what remained to be accomplished.[4]

Inside the tent, President Mbeki brought the event to a close. "The reason we come to an *imbizo* is to listen to you, to hear what people think, to understand what the problems are," he said. "We have come not to talk. We have come here to listen." In conclusion, he offered advice about the apparent need for people to lower their expectations of government.

"Remember that the government has no factories, this government has no mines, this government has no farms," he went on. "Government can only try to encourage people to open businesses so they can employ people." His voice took on a sharper edge. "Everyone is asking about employment. But, why aren't they opening businesses themselves?"

It was a sobering challenge from the person considered a protean figure by so many in the crowd. On this occasion, the president presented himself in searching, quite humble terms. Throughout the day, it seemed to me, Mbeki had been signaling that his powers were tightly circumscribed. In so many ways, he made it clear that he wouldn't be able to respond to the demands being made of him.

The president spoke as if his main role as leader was to analyze current circumstances clearly rather than to chart a new direction in response to the changing conditions. He departed on this discordant note, which was especially unsettling for the masses of people who had been told, just one year earlier, that the ANC knew how to deliver "a better life for all," and that the Chief could lead them there.

A month later, I returned to Cape Town to check in on Mayor Zille. When I arrived for our scheduled appointment, she was headed into a bunker. Outside City Hall, an angry mob of armed policemen had gathered, and they were demanding to meet with her. Instead, she was hustled into the emergency command center in the basement of the new building, situated on the edge of the central business district.

The mayor was dressed in a festive white turtleneck sweater and a baby-blue silk sport coat, but she looked rather sour. A police blockade of the N1 highway, the country's main traffic artery, had snarled traffic in Cape Town all morning. It was the latest in a series of protests by the Cape Town police force in a year of rising discontent among city employees. She had come across the blockade, after a flight from Johannesburg, on her way from the airport.

When the mayor had been caught in the traffic, Zille responded characteristically enough by pulling out a bullhorn to personally order the officers to clear the road. Then she popped back into her car, called in to a live radio show and commanded the police to disband. They had cleared out of her way, but then had followed her into town in a convoy.

I had threaded my way through the police to reach the mayor's office, and now joined the klatch of aides trailing behind her into the bunker. "How am *I*?" she snapped when I greeted her. "I'm *fed up*— that's how I am."

In the hi-tech Crisis Management Center for the city, the mayor sat across from local and regional police officials at a mammoth oblong table. The police chief, Bongani Jonas, who preferred to be addressed as "General Jonas" because he had served in the ANC's guerrilla army, was a big-boned black man who was a holdover from the previous administration.

An air of obvious suspicion and distrust flickered between the two officials. When one of the chief's deputies mentioned that protestors were demanding that the mayor come out of the building to accept a memo from them, Zille balked. "I'd like to know what *you* are prepared to do to enforce the law," she said, looking at the chief.

A provincial police commissioner held up a finger, replying in a soothing tone of voice, "I want to point out that we've got people in bulletproof vests and guns on both sides. We don't want any bloodshed." The mayor blinked twice, audibly grinding her teeth. "This is what sticks in my craw," she shot back. "We're being held hostage by people who are supposed to uphold the law and are in fact breaking it. Then we're told we can't enforce the law because it might cause bloodshed!"

When the commissioner's assistant suggested that the crisis might be defused most effectively by mollifying gestures, the mayor pressed her point. "This is getting into the area of undermining government. It's coup stuff." The police chief did a double take, as if he thought the mayor had taken complete leave of her senses. Behind her back, her take-no-prisoners style had earned her the nickname "Godzille."

Within a matter of hours the confrontation would be defused peacefully and the police officers would eventually disperse. In the afternoon, the mayor asked for videotape of the event so the protestors could be identified and administrators could begin the process of firing them for cause. The trade union federation COSATU would announce its intentions, in turn, to make Cape Town "ungovernable" on September 1, harkening back to mass civic disruption of the kind used against the apartheid regime.

"Never a dull moment in Cape Town," Zille said as we left the basement. We headed to a Council executive meeting that had fifty-four items listed on an agenda attached to 991 pages of documents. Cape Town municipality now made up a metropolis of three million citizens, Zille pointed out. It took in the city center, its suburbs, and also far-flung townships and informal settlements. As mayor, she had set out to demonstrate that the opposition party would make city government efficient, transparent, and honest. Zille believed this was the essential first step in making the eventual defeat of the ANC at the ballot box at least imaginable.

After the meeting, we repaired to her office in City Hall. From the window, there was a splendid view of Table Mountain, shrouded by clouds in the distance. Right below her office, across from the African Jewelry Market, stood a taxi rank where blue-collar workers waited in jostling queues to snag their long rides back to the townships at the end of the day.

On the other side of the market stood the squat colonial-era City Hall, where Mandela had given his first public address on the day he was released from confinement. Large posters on the inside of her door outlined the mayor's biggest plans: 2010 Transport Projects and Prioritised 2010 FIFA World Cup deadlines. Directly behind her was an oil portrait by Isabel Thompson of a boy turning right and a girl going left, painted in sedate shades of black and white.

In an earlier conversation in her office, Zille had explained to me that she identified closely with "the vision of the ANC" during the late stages of apartheid. She added swiftly, "Although I've never, ever, been a Marxist and so I couldn't identify with the nationalization clauses of the Freedom Charter." The turning point in the development of her current politics came shortly after the ANC was unbanned, in 1990, she recalled. "The more I became involved in political organizations, the more I was alienated by the hegemony of a particular way of seeing the world, by the Marxist rhetoric and by the dismissal as reformist of anybody who didn't accept that point of view."

In Black Sash, an organization of antiapartheid women to which she had belonged, Zille thought that she could make out three identifiable strands across the spectrum within the ANC: a "Black Africanist" contingent; a "very strong Marxist grouping"; and a "tiny, tiny" centrist liberal group, where she thought she belonged.

A few years after Mandela's election in 1994, she went over to the opposition. "The next step of the struggle seemed to me to be in the schools," she said. As a mother with children in elementary school, then, she took up the cause with special passion. Zille believed that the ANC government had wrecked what was working in public education in the name of making the whole system more egalitarian.

What's more, she thought that robust competition between parties on a range of issues, including crime, HIV, and economic development, would help South Africa avoid the experience of so many other postcolonial countries in Africa ruled by authoritarian one-party states. "We're a much better society than we used to be. But a democracy depends on checks and balances," she said.

Zille had served in the provincial legislature and then in the National

Assembly, as a specialist on education. In municipal elections in 2006, opposition leader Tony Leon had pressed her into service as a mayoral candidate. "I was conscripted," she admitted, sounding a little sorry about this part of her story. Few people, least of all herself, had expected that she could win.

"I tell you, it was like the dog that caught the bus!" she exclaimed. "Then I had to figure out what to do with this tire I had in my mouth." For much of the first year as mayor, she had concentrated on city services and finances, promoting a relentless corruption-busting image. (In the end, Police Chief Jonas was forced out of office under a cloud.)

At every step of the way, Zille had been denounced as a white interloper. In one township meeting she was the target of a chair-throwing melee. The mayor's response was to keep broadening the appeal of the Democratic Alliance across racial and class lines, and to build coalitions with other minority parties. "Look, the fact of the matter is that we have to get beyond race obsession," she told me. "Unless we get past it, we can't have a real democracy."

I posed a blunt question: What did she think were the chances of building a real multiparty democracy in South Africa? Partly as a result of her experience as the elected chief executive of Cape Town, the mayor felt alternately buoyed and discouraged.

The internecine struggle between Mbeki and Zuma over control of the ANC worried her deeply, though. "If Zuma takes over, you can forget all their talk about reforms," she said. "It will be criminalization, cronyism, and corruption." The mayor believed that Mbeki had run out of ideas and energy. "A realignment of politics has to happen," she said. "The best outcome would be if someone who had our values emerged within the ANC and drove out the Stalinists."

Zuma was aligned with the trade unions and the Communist Party, and would not take on the Left. "I don't think he has what it takes anyway," she volunteered. "He's congenial, nice, very pleasant. But the people he gets tied up with! That's where the problem is. It's fine for him to have multiple wives and so forth, because that's a part of his culture. But then he has to support them in the manner to which they've become accustomed, and you can't do that on a public official's salary."

After our conversation, we rode out to Somerset West, in the Prius she had chosen as her official automobile. There, she gave a speech to local officeholders from around the country, including several other big-city mayors. The route back into Cape Town took us past cheerful, leafy, sunny South Africa of the kind once featured in travelogues. The upscale neighborhoods were filled with majestic stone homes, and she pointed to one where one of her supporters lived.

Then, in a flash, we came upon informal settlements made up of recent arrivals from the Eastern Cape. She wagged her finger. "This is Europe. This is Barcelona," she said. And then she let out a little shriek: "Aii! Four hundred thousand families on waiting lists for housing." Here were contradictions that belied President Mbeki's efforts at poverty alleviation but also posed a quandary for an opposition enamored of market forces. Here, also, was the legacy of apartheid made visible, in the intertwining influence of race and wealth that made it difficult to imagine the Democratic Alliance seriously contesting for the presidency as long as it was led by a white person.

Zille told me that when she had met Thabo Mbeki for the first time in 1989, at a conference in Bermuda, she was working as a journalist. She remembered his wonderful rapport with people. "He was thoughtful and reflective," she recalled. "It was because of my conversations with him then that I reported that we could have a peaceful transition." She had never gotten to know Jacob Zuma nearly as well. "There's profound knock-on evidence he doesn't have the judgment for the job," she insisted.

The mayor realized that the contest for power between the two men might prove to be a boon for her own party. "We need a shift that is most conducive to getting from the politics of race to the politics of ideas," she said. She named Cyril Ramaphosa as the candidate at the head of the ANC list who could crush the opposition. This was a price she was prepared to accept for the good it would do South Africa, however. Then, again, she corrected herself: "Thabo had tried to drive out the Left, and failed."

When I described my trip in 2006 to Limpopo, and quoted the teenage boys who had described President Mbeki as someone who "had a little bit of apartheid," adding how much they "loved Comrade JZ," Zille tumbled immediately to the deeper meaning of what the boys had told me. She sank back into her seat, deflated. After a long pause, she replied softly, "I don't know where the way *out* is. Those attitudes make me depressed about the future, because it shows fundamental differences in our cultures."

The mayor had pursued her political career so far on the assumption that class, racial, ethnic group, language, and cultural differences would narrow over time in the new South Africa. But, what if the gap widened instead? "Our worst nightmare is that we could do all the right things and the ANC continues to grow anyway," she mused. "Zuma takes over, and the Inkatha Freedom Party folds into the ANC."

She grimaced, and went on. Thabo Mbeki's floundering presidency provided a warning about the dangers inherent in trying to hold, and use, power beyond your welcome. "Errors of judgment snowball on you," she pointed out. "No political leader stays popular forever. And the more powerful you get, the quicker the wheel turns." She shot up straight in her seat then, perhaps thinking about how quickly the wheel could turn on her, too.

In spring of 2007, I received an invitation from President Mbeki's staff to an event in Pretoria. The ostensible purpose of the celebration, held at the presidential guesthouse, was the launch of a book, *Fit to Govern: The Native Intelligence of Thabo Mbeki*, written by a volatile personality and combative writer named Ronald Suresh Roberts. Large corporations and one of the country's biggest banks had contributed the costs of producing and distributing the book.

The author's title was a play off the headline of a feature story in the *Weekly Mail* way back in 1996, in which the editors had posed the rude question: "Is Thabo Mbeki Fit to Rule?" His book was intended as a definitive response to the question. In it, the president's critics were assailed by name as racist reactionaries if they were white, and "black assistants" of colonialist interests if they were black.

Every position Mbeki had ever taken, including his stand on HIV/AIDS, was repurposed in Robert's account as trenchant analysis by a far-seeing and perhaps even unblemished political seer. The celebration and the official launch of the work seemed more bizarre, unsettling, and revealing even than key assertions of the book itself.

As the event got under way, guests were ushered along a red carpet up the stairs past heavy security into a massive reception hall filled with many of the nation's most powerful people, including the deputy chief justice of the Constitutional Court, Dikgang Moseneke; soccer star Lucas Radebe; mining magnate Patrice Motsepe; and Cyril Ramaphosa, Mbeki's rival in the 1990s, whose brother Douglas Ramaphosa was the businessman who had arranged corporate sponsorship for *Fit to Govern*.

On the left side of the hall, close to a slightly raised platform, President Mbeki sat by himself on a couch. His minister of justice was perched nearby, across from his longtime friend, Essop Pahad. I had entered the room with Ferial Haffajee, editor of the *Mail & Guardian*. She was friendly with Roberts, but in that day's edition she had published a crude Zapiro cartoon that showed the author with his head nearly enveloped in Mbeki's ass as the president was saying, "That's far enough, Ronald." Haffajee had been wondering on the drive north from Johannesburg if she should come at all and what kind of reception she would get.

As we took our seats, Bheki Khumalo, the president's former press spokesman and the night's emcee, announced that the purpose of the evening—and of the book—was to expose "the historical roots of this negative attitude about the president" from the media. Khumalo put it down as a clear struggle between the movement and the media over who should "set the national agenda."

Roberts took the microphone next to denounce the country's media in quite bitter terms, which seemed strange since he had such a large voice in regular commentaries and essays. "This book speaks truth to power," he said. "It speaks truth to *media* power."[5] The author argued, among other things, that journalists, South African and international alike, had fallen in with the "dominant global ideology"—white liberalism—and therefore never would be able to fully accept an authentic black intellectual as the country's paramount leader.

In the book, Roberts had quoted Mbeki commenting on his own manuscript, which gave reading the text the feeling of being inside an echo chamber. "I am completely at one with you that the best way to assess our 'fitness to rule' is to counterpoise the ideas/concepts we have expressed with/against the 'fitness to rule' of South African liberalism, as pronounced by the DA and its acolytes, of various sorts," Mbeki had written.[6]

For an intellectual biographer promising to explain the president's approach to governing, the book and his talk seemed remarkably backward-looking. Why, eight years after coming to power as head of state, did Mbeki and his supporters still feel so intensely insecure?

The president's bulldog, Minister Pahad, followed Roberts to the microphone, hauling with him a big stack of newspapers that he had tucked under his arm. Pahad quoted from the articles, and belittled the country's best-known journalists. He dismissed Mondli Makhanya, the black editor in chief of the *Sunday Times*, as "a colonial creature." The president broke into a broad grin, laughter rocking him from side to side.

The psychic dissonance of the whole scene only deepened. Corporate executives quaffed cocktails and wolfed down hors d'oeuvres alongside government ministers. In the elegant guesthouse, originally built for use by white segregationists, the new elite listened as their preeminent leader, the second black president in the new South Africa, was described as a visionary figure who, in spite of his considerable efforts, was still wildly misunderstood.

His biographer had put this misunderstanding down, as the president apparently did, to the insidious influence of "settler" thinking transmuted through the politics of liberals cluelessly embraced by "black assistants" in the service of deeply racist but subtly manipulative whites.

It was a cliché to cluck over the dangers of unchecked power, and Roberts's book provided a deft deconstruction of Lord Acton, whose line about "absolute power" was regularly misquoted. As the author pointed out, Lord Acton was a supporter of slavery, an adherent of the infallibility of the pope, and an agent in the colonial oppression of Africans. As the author and the president signed copies of the book, it occurred to me that there were powerfully distorting effects of accumulated *powerlessness* too.

President Mbeki was the current embodiment of a movement that had carried an enormous burden of disempowerment over a century of dismissal, exile, imprisonment, torture, humiliation, and penury. In the moment, he seemed like a leader who had not shed old patterns of thinking, continuing to behave like an outcast even though he was now the most powerful man in the country.

An appreciation for the ebb and flow of power, an understanding of when it was time to cede it after exercising it for a time, had eluded Mbeki. From a distance, and up close, it was all the same; there was no evidence of a generosity of spirit. As the president and his closest acolytes drank, invited guests began to slip away. The president looked like someone trapped in an old movie. It wasn't clear whom he was arguing against any more.

Even from the vantage point of the emerging black elite, the sentiments expressed that evening inside the presidential guesthouse seemed increasingly irrelevant. For people at the bottom, desperate and hungry, the celebration was an affront, an orgy of self-indulgent pity when the full attention of a more grounded, and more measured, leader was desperately needed.

14.

Atlantis

Right after President Mbeki's *imbizo* in the Western Cape, I had tracked Jonathan Persens down at the shelter where he was staying in Khayelitsha, and it was during this visit that we had had our tense moment because he hadn't recognized the name *Thabo Mbeki*. The battle for control of South Africa by its two top political leaders was taking place in an alternative planetary system where he was in orbit. Jonathan was much more concerned about the recent outbreak of violence between gangs operating in the Cape Flats. Several of his uncles were enmeshed in the gang known as the Americans, and Jonathan worried constantly about their safety. "We don't know why they are fighting," he told me, turning his palms up like a penitent.[1]

An hour into our interview, Jonathan turned his face toward the wall in his dormitory, hiding his eyes as he delivered the recent, most terrible news: the shack his mother had been occupying had burned to the ground. That was all he knew from a friend who had passed the news onto him. He wondered if his mother had burned to death in the fire. So many of his fantasies about the future revolved around her, and around the idea of building a house for her and his sisters.

I asked why he hadn't gone to Atlantis already to find out what had happened to his mother. Returning to Atlantis, he replied moodily, would mean putting his own life at risk. "Why?" I asked. Jonathan filled his cheeks with air, letting it out in a low whistle. He watched me with narrowed eyes, as if realizing how much I had to learn, still. I suggested that we go to Atlantis together. He considered me with a slack-jawed expression. "Then you will be dead too," he said coldly.

In order to explain, Jonathan backed up then and filled in the blanks he had left out of the story of his childhood. Soon, the whole catastrophe tumbled out. "Everybody knows me in Atlantis. I did work for everyone," he said, before reverting to second-person address of the kind he had used in our earlier interviews: "When you ask me to do something, you give me a gun and say, 'You go and shoot that one there.' I would go and shoot him."

He explained that he had been trained as a hit man—or a hit boy— by a grownup in the family. This was a distinctly different telling of his story. Before, Jonathan had presented his life of crime as an accidental sequence, like a gear that had slipped by chance—from glue sniffing to mugging to armed robbery. In this retelling, he presented himself more like an active agent, not just the victimized sidekick of older gangsters.

The trouble he faced had begun long ago, he told me. "No, I just did shoot a lot of guys," he said. "A gangster must have a gun. I would go and shoot him. And then I will come back on a bicycle. I will just take a bicycle, go there, and then I will put the gun there," he added, pointing at the back of my head. "I will shoot you, then I will put the gun away and ride back slowly, like nothing did happen." This was the reason, he said, why he would never be allowed to go home.

The way Jonathan talked, so nonchalantly, led me to think about how my own role—the *you* in his telling—kept changing: I was the older man who gave him the gun and sent him out on a job, but then I was also the victim with the muzzle of the weapon placed behind my ear. My lack of a reaction to Jonathan's cool, uninflected description also made me realize how desensitized I had become, in the past few years, to hearing about the infliction of terrible pain. In the previous few months I had fallen into the habit of shrugging off terrible stories friends told me, like the one about the columnist I had met once who was robbed and viciously beaten in his home, located not far from my own. Or the account I had read about the murder of a friend's next-door neighbor; she was a middle-aged white woman scalded to death with boiling water by intruders who were convinced that she had money hidden in her house. It was disorienting to realize that, in the calm gathering of this *material* I found myself identifying with both victim and victimizer—both the person knocked to the floor and the robber wielding the gun.

Deeper into the conversation, Jonathan also revealed, for the first time, that he had fallen in love with a girl named Tracy. She was training to be a nurse back in Atlantis. He felt sure, beyond any doubt, that she would be his one and only forever. He guessed that they would marry when he was twenty-one; he swiftly amended his prediction—no, make that seven years from now, when he was twenty-five. By then he expected that his life would be entirely sorted out. He would have learned a trade by then, though he doubted whether the skills he was learning in the workshop would provide him a path out of poverty.

"But I did leave that—*leave*," he assured me about his former life of crime. "Now I am free. I don't know what will happen exactly. But I just want to work for my own money—not *take* any more." Here was a profound epiphany, it seemed to me: "I want to, when I finish here, I want to *work*," he added, stretching the word out as if it was multisyllabic. "I don't want to work with gangsters any more." I asked what kind of work he envisioned. He and his best friend, Edward, had decided to write songs together, Jonathan said.

He had no iPod and he was moving around so much that he rarely landed in a place where he could listen to music. But, as he escorted me out, Jonathan promised to show me some of the lyrics he and Edward had been working on during my next visit. When he migrated to Cape Town four

Mass outpourings of support for the African National Congress in the first national election in which blacks were allowed to vote swept Nelson Mandela into the presidency in 1994, part of a transfer of power celebrated around the world. (*Per-Anders Pettersson / Getty Images News / Getty Images*)

Thabo Mbeki (left) was chosen by Mandela (right) as deputy president of South Africa in 1994. Mbeki was elected president of the ANC in 1997, became head of state in 1999, and drove the proportion of votes for the party to a historic high in the election of 2004. (*Odd Andersen / AFP / Getty Images*)

Thabo Mbeki (left) was defeated in a contest over the presidency of the African National Congress in late 2007 by Jacob Zuma (right), his former deputy, and resigned his post as head of state in 2008. Zuma led the ANC list in the next national election and was elected president of South Africa in Parliament in 2009. (*Bongiwe Mchunu*)

"Say No to HIV-AIDS" reads the graffiti on the wall, one of untold numbers of activist interventions designed to make up for inaction in the fight against HIV/AIDS in the Mbeki years. (*Shelly Banjo*)

Dr. Ashraf Grimwood, a Cape Town physician who had participated in the campaign to control the AIDS epidemic in Australia, spearheaded a similar effort on his return to South Africa in the early 1990s. (*Douglas Foster*)

President Thabo Mbeki resisted provision of antiretroviral medication to South Africans with HIV/AIDS in a policy overseen by the minister of health, Mantombazana Tshabalala-Msimang, who called the treatment "poison." (*T. J. Lemon*)

Skyline of Johannesburg, known as Gold Reef City, the most populous metropolitan center in South Africa. (*Shelly Banjo*)

Thuthukile Zuma, youngest daughter of Jacob Zuma and Nkosazana Dlamini-Zuma, in 2007, as she was beginning her studies in anthropology at the University of the Witwatersrand. (*Douglas Foster*)

The Mandela grandsons—Ndaba, Mbuso, and Andile—at the home they shared with their grandfather. They are the children of Makgotho Mandela, Nelson's son, and both their parents died as a result of HIV/AIDS infection. (*Douglas Foster*)

The meandering river below the village of Mvezo, the birthplace of Nelson Mandela, in what is now the Eastern Cape province, where Mandela's grandson Mandla became *nkosi*, or head man, in 2007. (*Douglas Foster*)

Children of Mvezo line up in front of a struggle-era photograph of Nelson Mandela in anticipation of a Christmas Day meal provided by their new leader, Mandla Mandela. (*Douglas Foster*)

Chief Mandela handing out bread to children at the end of his first year serving as *nkosi* at Mvezo. (*Douglas Foster*)

Jacob Zuma with one of his younger children at his homestead near the village of Nkandla, his birthplace in KwaZulu-Natal province. (*Douglas Foster*)

Sizakele Khumalo, known as MaKhumalo, is President Zuma's senior wife. She is shown here in front of her home. (*Douglas Foster*)

Zuma (right), shown with his brothers Joseph Zuma (left) and Michael Zuma (middle) at a ceremony to invoke the help of the ancestors in the campaign to make him president of the African National Congress and the country. (*Douglas Foster*)

Jacob Zuma after vanquishing Thabo Mbeki in the contest over the presidency of the ANC at the party's National Conference in Polokwane, in late 2007. (*Bongiwe Mchunu*)

A massive crowd in Limpopo province during the national election campaign of 2009. (*Douglas Foster*)

Zuma in a shirt emblazoned with the image of Nelson Mandela, dances for the crowd while Julius Malema, leader of the ANC Youth League, looks on. Once the closest of allies, Malema and Zuma split, and, after a series of confrontations, Malema was ousted and expelled from the ANC in 2012. (*Douglas Foster*)

Vunene Mabasa, who dreams of becoming a doctor, with his mother, Elizabeth, and his younger sister outside their temporary quarters in Bungeni, Limpopo, the country's poorest province. (*Douglas Foster*)

Gwendoline Dube, a young woman who hoped to become "a pilot and a doctor," with her mother at their home in Orange Farm, south of Johannesburg. (*Douglas Foster*)

Jonathan Persens, a homeless young man from Atlantis, in the Eastern Cape, with his mother, Susan, on the day of her eviction from the home behind them. (*Douglas Foster*)

Gwendoline Dube, hunting for a job in Mary Fitzgerald Square, in Newtown, shortly after the FIFA World Cup games in 2010 that brought South Africa enthusiastic international acclaim. (*Douglas Foster*)

Thuthukile Zuma, daughter of President Zuma, shortly before a rally at the University of the Witwatersrand against the xenophobic violence that resulted in riots and murders aimed at African immigrants to South Africa. (*Douglas Foster*)

A sign recommending a return to the principle of *ubuntu*, which means respect for individual dignity and the collective good, in Newtown, outside Sofiatown Restaurant, one of the many places where Gwendoline Dube could not find work. (*Douglas Foster*)

years earlier, he had wanted to be a star rugby player; now he hoped to find his purpose in life as a megastar.

I thought of Gerald Jacobs's admonition that impossible dreams were often the biggest obstacle in helping reclaim lives lost to the street. It would have seemed cruel to second-guess Jonathan's ambition now, though. He and Edward were working on the moves to go with the music and the lyrics, he said. On the stoop of the shelter, Jonathan swayed a little as if he might dance. He stopped himself, saying that Edward could perform these moves better, and I could see the act the next time I came back.

In the car, threading my way through the narrow roads out of Khayelitsha, I listened to a disk of Johnny Clegg and Savuka. The song "Take My Heart Away" came on: "To dance the sun beyond the tides of war and peace / To put silence stained by crimes to flight," they sang.

> *Sing me the first and the last man's glory*
> *Sing me the songs that taste of freedom*
> *Thread me through with your sacred needle*
> Liyeza, liyeza, liyeza, ilanga lami seliyeza

It was painfully lyrical, and quite moving given what Jonathan had just told me. The singers crooned the last line, which meant "It's coming, it's coming, my day is coming."

These same streets, connecting the same townships to Cape Town proper, looked entirely different if you were white. The quality of this difference was something I had begun to understand through a series of interviews with white teenagers around the country. The conversations led me, in turn, back to a decision I had made to try to profile Thomas Maree, the youngest child of Mayor Helen Zille.

Ever since I had met with the mayor for the first time the previous

February, I had been planning to interview her son as well, partly because he was about the same age as Jonathan. All year, I tried to reach the mayor's son, even fantasizing about putting the two of them in the same room together. They seemed like phantoms, eliding past one another in the same time and place.

Thomas Maree had just turned eighteen and he still lived in the family home, which was located an easy ten-minute drive from the Grand Parade, where Jonathan hung out when he was in the city. They were two young men born in the same part of South Africa in the same year, but Tom's life had unfolded in a happier parallel universe. He was the beloved younger child of a pair of boys who had been raised in an intact family living in the perfect home in a pristine neighborhood.

All through 2007, including half-a-dozen trips to Cape Town, Thomas Maree had eluded me, however. I had begun trying to reach him on a cell phone number his mother had passed on to me. This particular number, as it turned out, belonged to a phone that had been stolen from him at knifepoint some weeks earlier. The mayor didn't know this because her son had not told her about the robbery. It was only one in a series of phones that he had been forced to hand over to muggers in recent months, and he didn't want to worry his mother.

The mix-up with the cell phone wasn't my only problem in tracking him down. Whenever I called the house phone in my hunt for him, he was regularly reported to be out practicing rugby, playing rugby, clubbing with friends, or listening to music in a dive somewhere to support his older brother, who played in a popular indie rock band. Thomas was harder to track down and interview than Jonathan, a boy with no fixed address and nothing to gain from answering my questions.

When I finally caught up with him in early December, Thomas had just returned from an extended graduation celebration with his best friends. They had partied around the clock in a coastal town at Plettenberg Bay, a resort on the Indian Ocean in the shadow of the Tsitsikamma

Mountains. We finally met in the rambling, comfortable home in the university district of Cape Town where the family lived.

Thomas was a tall, broad-shouldered young man with blond hair and the classic slouch of a teenager. He looked appropriately bulked up after the break, with the sun-kissed face of someone enjoying an extended South African summer. Having completed high school, Thomas had just sent off applications to study economics and law at two prestigious universities— Stellenbosch University, in the middle of a wine-growing part of the province, and the University of Cape Town, where his father was a respected professor in the sociology department.

The house, which the Maree/Zille family had occupied for as long as Thomas could remember, was located on a pleasant, leafy suburban lane not far from the Baxter Theatre, a famous Cape Town playhouse. It was a comfortable, unpretentious home with high ceilings, large rooms, and a steady stream of people bustling through, including his older brother's friends and the companions of a seven-year-old boy, Xulu, who was the son of the family's longtime domestic worker.

Thomas referred to the boy as "my younger brother" and to the domestic worker as "my second mother." His *first* mother, the mayor, was away so often that, he confessed, it was sometimes easier to confide in Grace, including things that he figured would "never, ever be shared with my mother."[2] As he showed me around the house, it occurred to me that this was the sort of place, set behind a thick wall and gated driveway, that Jonathan's pals were often casing out in their never-ending quest to foil ever-more elaborate security systems.

In a quiet corner in the living room, I asked the mayor's son the same question I had asked every young person I had interviewed that year: "You're living in a country that people died and fought to make free. So, how free do you feel?" Thomas raised his eyebrows, leaning forward with his forearms settled on his thighs. "I feel I'm at the pinnacle of what it means to be free," he replied. "The financial problems that a majority of people in this country face, I *don't* face. I'm free to control my own destiny and pursue whatever I want to pursue in life."

He spoke in trim sentences and well-parsed paragraphs, and it was clear he wanted me to understand, right off, that he hadn't screened out the poverty or missed the point of his own relative privilege. Quite the contrary: he volunteered his view straight away that there were terrible human costs from the country's rank inequality, rooted in its history.

"Even if you're driving towards the airport, you see how real the poverty is for people living in the squatter camps. And how the cycle of poverty is like a trap that's very hard to get out of," he went on. "That's a reflection on most people's so-called freedom." Deep structural patterns of inequality, and the death of the spirit they caused in people trapped in poverty, were clearly "the legacy of apartheid," Thomas said.

If the country was ever to escape this plight, he felt sure the South African government would need to adopt far more radical policies. He had read, for example, about what the United States had done in the Depression of the 1930s, involving a massive investment in jobs. The piecemeal, ameliorative policies of the Mbeki government clearly weren't working. "It certainly is a huge problem our generation has to face up to, this legacy of apartheid—especially divide-and-rule strategies and separate development," he said. Thuthu Zuma had said something similar.

Thomas added his worry that apartheid-era divisions carried through to the present day, and were registered in the current tensions between black groups, blacks and coloureds, and blacks and Indians. This concerned him even more than the divisions between blacks and whites. He felt the problem of "Zulus versus the Xhosas, represented in the struggle between Mbeki and Zuma, could wreck the nation." Violence along these lines might tear the governing party apart, and then plunge the country into catastrophe.

He glimpsed intimations of these conflicts even at his school, Westerford High School. He remembered that Thuthu Zuma had been one year ahead of him there. The student body was diverse, and on the surface, he said, there had been a stab at achieving nonracialism. But he added that there had been no real social basis for full integration. "You still see the tendency of kids to stick to their own racial group," he pointed out.

Thuthu Zuma already had told me about her mixed experiences at Westerford, and I realized, as Thomas was talking, that she hadn't mentioned him or any other whites in her class. For his part, Thomas remembered Thuthu as "a clever girl" who had seemed amiable enough. She had rubbed him the wrong way only when his mother came to speak once at a student assembly. On that occasion, Thuthu had forcefully challenged Zille's stand on affirmative action. He noted stiffly, by contrast, that when *her* father had come to speak to the students, he had clapped for him and kept his own mouth shut concerning the many questionable things the elder Zuma had said.

In Thomas's own circle of close friends, all white, the emergence of Jacob Zuma as a possible president stirred considerable consternation. One of his closest friends had already announced to the group, "If Zuma is elected, I'll fly." In restaurants and private homes, I had heard plenty of whites telling me the same thing. They thought Zuma had the potential to become the stereotypical African dictator hungry only for power and money. They assumed that his rise to power would signal the end of their country as an exceptional place on the continent. If Zuma took office, it would not be the South Africa as they imagined it.

Thomas intended to stay in the country no matter what happened, so it saddened him, naturally, to realize that his closest friends would respond in this way. "If Zuma becomes president there will be a lot of immigration to Australia," he predicted. If his friends left, they would become part of a massive generational exit of talent that the country could scarcely afford. The urge to go reflected mostly "fear of the unknown," Thomas admitted. "We realize we don't understand the views of the majority of blacks towards him."

Current politics didn't occupy much space in conversations with his best friends, he continued. When he and his buddies hung out, they spoke mostly about girls and sport. Thomas was a big fan of hip-hop—the Notorious B.I.G., Tupac, and the emerging South African group Skwatta Kamp—but most friends in his circle were inclined to American-influenced indie rock, especially the songstress Jamie T.

As we talked, text messages and phone calls began to ping in. One of his closest friends was turning eighteen that day. His entire mob was headed for a night out, in the clubs on Long Street. Thomas was thinking about whether he should take along his new, cheaper cell phone, a replacement for the more expensive one lost in the latest robbery. The whole mugging situation didn't seem like a big deal to him. The less said, the better.

When I pressed, he described with precision what the robbers had looked like. He also summoned up a recollection of the shape of the guns on the day when his car had been stolen, right here outside the house, in the driveway, a few months earlier. "Crime is always on my mind when I go out," he admitted.

Whenever he was held up, he did not resist. Afterward, he sometimes mused over alternative scenarios. Thomas imagined heroic sequences in which he overpowered his assailants, disarmed them, and held onto the phone, the wallet, the car. It wasn't worth it to risk your life over material things, though. The sort of theft that generated such casual mention among his friends, and whose details were often kept from their parents, was perpetrated by boys and men who he understood "were running on empty stomachs."

Thomas described the crime wave in the Western Cape as a phenomenon of "crystal meth combined with poverty." I briefly told him about Jonathan's plight, and the stories told by the young addict at the treatment center President Mbeki had opened. "That's *it*," Thomas said, nodding. He could rattle off the crime stats, and reel off many of the most cogent details.

"In the Western Cape, we have some of the highest murder rates in the world!" he exclaimed. "It's a violent crowd." He shrugged, and gathered his keys. If you stayed alert, and kept track of where you were going, things would be fine. He was in the habit of planning an "escape route" to use, whenever he was out, if things went suddenly sour.

Cape Town was still a beautiful place, he said, and a country of huge potential, he added. "From apartheid, there's only one way we could go!" he said. Thomas felt an almost religious faith that the sort of freedom he enjoyed would be much more widely shared by other young South Africans one day. He understood the apparent irony: a middle-class white boy, like whites generally, had been liberated the most so far in the South African freedom struggle. After centuries of efforts to upend the old systems of white privilege and liberate the black majority in the process, his sense of limitless opportunity marked such a stark contrast with the experience of so many blacks his age.

In the week before my visit with the mayor's son, I went on a wild goose chase to find Jonathan. He had left the shelter in Khayelitsha months earlier, and I couldn't find him in any of his usual haunts on the street. At the Homestead shelter in town, Gerald Jacobs said he hadn't heard from Jonathan recently, either. Even the friend who had been collaborating with him on the hip-hop songs had no clue about where he had gone.

Jonathan seemed to have vanished after falling out with everyone. When I stopped by the carpentry workshop where he had been registered for more classes, I learned that he hadn't tipped his hand even to his instructors. Several homeless boys told me that he had abandoned the city to make his way back to Atlantis. I found this hard to believe given that he had told me he "would be dead" if he ever went home to look for his missing mother.

One morning I set off for Atlantis anyway, armed with just a phone number for one of Jonathan's aunts. I didn't speak Afrikaans, and the aunt didn't speak English, but I thought she had made me understand that Jonathan had been seen in the community. So I invited an Afrikaans-speaking acquaintance along to serve as interpreter, and we set off to find him on the first Sunday in December.

Once we reached city limits, it was striking how little time it took to get to Atlantis from the cottage near Sea Point where I was staying. Listening to Jonathan's stories during the previous year, I had been left with the impression that his home community lay a great distance away. Now, in forty minutes, on a well-paved road, we crossed over from neighborhoods Mayor Zille had described as "a little Brussels," to the dusty flats of the township where Jonathan had spent his infancy.

The first stop I made in the township was at his grandmother's house. She was an open-faced, nearly toothless woman who launched into a series of questions about the United States. Had I really come so far in order to speak with her grandson? She marveled at the improbability of it. Jonathan's aunt appeared, and she offered general directions to a shack where she thought he might be staying temporarily with his mother.

Back and forth along the circuitous roads through the township we traveled looking for him, with dimming hope. I thought this might leave me off the hook as a storyteller, though. If Jonathan vanished without a trace, then the reader would be allowed to imagine any range of possible outcomes for him.

Around a curve, he suddenly appeared. Jonathan was perched on the seat of a battered, dented old Stingray bicycle. Looking slight and wiry for someone about to turn nineteen, he considered me with a puzzled expression. He did a triple take. Finally, his face split open in a boyish grin. "I can't *believe* you!" he shouted. He took off pedaling like a mad man, then, leading the way to a shack situated in a cul-de-sac.

Jonathan rushed into the shack and came popping straightaway out again. He reported that there was trouble brewing inside the house: the friends of his mother's who had offered her shelter had announced just now that they were throwing her out. He fidgeted, darty-eyed, checking out the neighbors and glancing up and down the street. "We can't stay here right now," he said gruffly. So he climbed into my car, and we drove out to a fast-food stand about a kilometer away.

The last time I had seen Jonathan, he had told me how dangerous it would be for him to return to Atlantis. If I accompanied him, he had said, I "would be dead," too. After I bought us lunch, I challenged him to explain this contradiction. He leaned deep into the car seat, studying his hands, and began talking quite haltingly.

Not long after I had visited him in Khayelitsha the last time, he said, he had received news from a relative that his mother survived the fire. This welcome revelation had strengthened his resolve to go home, no matter the consequences. "If you can just go home, talk to your mama, then everything is all right," he said softly.[3]

Jonathan explained that in order to ease his return, he called upon his uncle, a gang leader known as Evil, or Dr. Evil. "He is not *too* evil," Jonathan assured me. He said that he had asked Dr. Evil for assistance in untangling a thorny problem. Here was the trouble, as Jonathan explained it: he had been accused of killing a prominent member of a gang known as the Bad Boys.

His explanations often backed up on themselves, from present to past and then in one spinning circle inside another. Jonathan allowed that he had been in possession of a gun used in the killing, but he swore that he hadn't been the one to fire the fatal shot.

After checking out his story, he said, Dr. Evil had backed him up. Gang members subsequently fingered a different suspect for the killing. This particular boy, Jonathan reported, was then snatched off the streets and strung up by baling wire from a lamppost. His face betrayed no emotion. It was simply a description of the ugly fate he had narrowly escaped himself.

We fetched fried chicken and burgers, and ate and talked in the sweltering car, with the windows rolled up tight because Jonathan was afraid of being overheard. It wasn't good in Atlantis, he said, for anybody to hear you talking about these things with an outsider. Now he began speaking more freely about both the past and the present.

"When did you do these shootings you were involved in?" I asked. Initially, he misunderstood my question. "From ten until one," he said. "What?" I asked, placing my face near his. "From ten 'til one o'clock," he replied as if describing his schedule at the carpentry workshop. It was my turn for a triple take.

"How old were you?" I pressed on. That was what I had been asking—when he had started working as a hit man, not what time of the day was best for an execution. Jonathan glanced at me, frowning. "My first time where I would shoot a gun I was five years old," he recalled. He explained that a different uncle, a security guard, had lent him a gun because there were bullies in the neighborhood who regularly beat him up. He had been small for his age, and the uncle intended the gun to serve only as a protective equalizer.

"A big guy was beating me every day by the school," Jonathan said. He would steal the boy's pocket money in order to buy drugs. On the day Jonathan struck back, "he was smoking," he remembered. "I just picked his money out of his pocket. And then I did shoot him. Then I did run away."

As we finished our lunch, other detailed accounts were offered, though it was sometimes hard to follow the chronology. Jonathan said he had been part of a group of five boys when he was quite young who were regularly sent on their bicycles to do the dirty work for the gang known as the Americans.

It had been a regular occurrence, he said, your average hit-and-run job. Each of the boys was paid well, Jonathan said, and it was a windfall, like winning the lottery, for a poor boy in the dusty streets of Atlantis. Because they opened fire all at once, no individual had to take responsibility for a particular kill, he added. Jonathan took care to make clear that he never knew if it was his bullet that actually caused a death, as if this made a moral difference. "But not *now*. Not any more," he put in, with sudden force.

Before, I had seen the narrative arc of Jonathan's life as a scrum of terrible deeds explained by a history of awful abuse he had suffered. It hit me that Jonathan had decided he could trust me enough to reveal that he had continued working as a paid assassin all along, including during the time I had gotten to know him.

"Why didn't you tell me all of this before?" I asked. He lifted his eyebrows and glared at me. In one of our earlier conversations, he had explained why he was a person of few words sometimes: "When I'm quiet I don't want to speak . . . because I don't want to let my anger out, I just keep it quiet when I'm angry," he had said. Now he let the silence settle.

"Jonathan, how many people do you think you've shot in your life?" I asked.

"I don't know how much," he said.

"Hundreds?" I pressed.

He paused, doing some sort of calculation in his head. "It's not the hundreds. Over fifty," he allowed.

He leaned in my direction. "Last night they wanted me to shoot a Beretta," he confided. So, this hit-man role of his had continued until this very week. Jonathan said that he had never had such a fine revolver in his hands before. He found the gun sleek and beautiful, a marvel to behold.

When the boys had driven by to pick him up around eight o'clock the night before, they had showed off the gun as a kind of enticement. He said that he had examined the Beretta, was quite impressed, but had turned them down. "I don't want to kill people any more," he said as he finished eating. "It's not good for me. If I sleep, I dream about it." His face clouded. "It's too hard to tell it," he added.

He figured that it was only a matter of time, if he continued on his current path, before the police caught up with his gang. If he was arrested next time, and bullets were traced back to a gun he carried, he risked spending the next few decades behind bars in overcrowded prisons where young men like him were routinely raped and more than half of the inmates lived with HIV. Practical considerations blended with more cosmic concerns. "I don't want to go to jail," he said. "Also, I don't want to go to hell."

Jonathan also had recently had his first experience holding a steady job. As part of an initiative launched by the provincial ANC government, he had been working with a team of young men. They were building a sports field in Atlantis. He squared his shoulder and preened as he told me about the work, sitting up straight for the first time. This was clearly a subject he preferred discussing.

The work was hard, poorly paid manual labor, but Jonathan felt proud of the fact that the field he was building could make a big difference in his community. It would be the place where younger kids from Atlantis could train in track. Maybe a future running sensation, like the star sprinter Caster Semenya, would come from his dusty, run-down town. Perhaps the nation's next great national soccer star would learn to score goals right here in Atlantis.

He was earning only R1,700 a month (about $240), less than what he had told me he would be paid for just one night's assignment with the gang. Jonathan considered the wages pure and honest money, a distinction he wanted to draw for me now. By working every day, he had gotten a glimpse of how life might be different through the simple, steady exercise of labor for earnings. If he could keep it up, stay off alcohol and glue, he thought that he would be able to save enough money to buy the "Wendy house" he dreamed of providing for his sisters and his mother.

Why, I asked him, did he feel so strongly that this was his responsibility—to provide the house and stitch the family back together again when the adults in his life had not managed it? "Because why, I am the only boy," he said. "And they are only girls. And I have to look after my family."

Ducking his head shyly, and turning his face away, Jonathan said there was another reason he had decided to leave behind the life of an assassin. "I was sleeping and I was dreaming about God," he explained. It was the first conversation we had had where any mutation of religion came into it. "Dreaming about *God*?" I asked, remembering the time Jonathan had described to me his experience of being high on glue and the vision he had—of the image of the moon chasing the boys up the steps of St. Georges Cathedral and the visage that came to him of Pope Pius in the flesh.

"Yes, how it was in heaven—yeah," he offered hesitantly.

"Tell me about the dream then," I suggested.

This was how Jonathan explained it: He had been sleeping on a scrap of cardboard in the kitchen when he experienced the sudden sensation of out-of-body travel; pulled upward, he had watched himself asleep in the little kitchen down below as he floated away from Earth; that's when he realized that he was close to heaven. A vast throng of people had been arrayed up there; at first he could only make out their shapes. As he drew nearer to them, though, the faces came crystalline clear.

"They were just standing there, the people who we did kill," he murmured. The men were expressionless, and they considered him with open, neutral expressions. All of a sudden he felt himself falling back to Earth from a great height. Wind whooshed past his ears. When he landed back inside his own body, it was with a powerful thump. The wind was knocked out of him. Jonathan had opened his eyes and howled in terror, waking everyone in the house.

He looked wide-eyed now, as if overtaken by the same kind of trance. "So, I think that's a message from your conscience, you know," I offered, feeling entirely out of my depth. "Yes," he agreed instantly. That was why he had turned the boys away when they came around the night before with the offer of a new, shiny Beretta. "I did say to them, 'I'm not going to do that any more,'" he assured me.

Did he tell them about his dream? "Yes, I did," he said. He had told his buddies the whole tale. What did they make of it? "Hmm?" he mused. "They did say nothing. They did just ride." Before my arrival, he had heard that his group of friends had caught up with their quarry in town. They had shot him to death, right in the front seat of a taxi, not far from Mayor Zille's office. "Didn't go—yeah," he said, nodding at his good judgment and better fortune.

When we drove back to the shack, Jonathan's mother was waiting for us outside. Susan Persens was a tall, angular woman with a shy smile. Deep lines pitted her forehead and wrinkles ran across her cheeks. She wore a skimpy white top over a tight pair of blue jeans. Her hair had been colored and straightened and then brushed back from her forehead in untidy clumps.

The minute she was inside my car, and out of her son's hearing, she began talking unprompted about his childhood. We drove a short way off so we could talk out of sight of her neighbors. Her earliest memory, she said, was of her son as a toddler. She remembered him cowering behind her legs, because his stepfather beat him if he complained of being hungry. "He was a boy who wouldn't fight with other kids," she recalled. "He would always run away and not fight back."[4]

The bullying he suffered took place outside the home, and inside as well. She explained, "If Jonathan asked me for bread—he was small—I still cry about it to this day," his stepfather would chase him and attack him. "He is only a child asking his mother for bread!" she cried. Her husband predicted that Jonathan would amount to nothing and would end up a gangster.

When I asked why she had stayed for so long with someone she considered a monster, Jonathan's mother cursed and shouted in Afrikaans. Tears streamed down her cheeks. "*Omdat hy is my man, ek wil mos se daai is my man ek wil hom mos nie skei ni!*" she cried. Three times! Three times!

She had left him three times, she insisted, but each time she also had returned. "He, me *man!*"

Right around the time Jonathan turned seven years old, she volunteered, a horrible thing had happened. "The sodomizing business," she added. She said that when her son was little, he and other kids regularly hung out at a particular house down the street. A neighbor, a single man, had the only television set on the block, and naturally he drew a crowd. One night, after the other children had gone home, Jonathan was raped, his mother claimed.

"He was seven years old, very small—I'm still not over it." She took him to a hospital the next day, where the wound was closed with four stitches. "Up to today, he's never spoken at all," she said, looking a little uneasy about having shared this story.

Many things fell into place if this was true, including Jonathan's penchant for stormy moods, sudden anger, and his fear of the 28s. His mother felt it was nothing short of a miracle that Jonathan had survived the trauma. "He became withdrawn and he didn't want to attend school," she explained. *"Dis so dat hy n straatkind geword het."* (This is how he became a street kid.) It bothered her immensely that she still saw the rapist around town. "Now he walks around like you and me, but my child is still broken."

Then, she shifted course. Suddenly, everything was coming out right, she assured me. Somehow, Jonathan had landed a normal job and was planning to build her a house. It would be big enough for everyone, including her mother, his granny. "He feels strongly that we must be together, that's why he wants to put up this dwelling, you know, and have us back as a family," she said, beaming. "He's more relaxed now. He thinks like a man. He surprises me all the time."

What were the biggest surprises? Her face split open, in a lopsided grin. "My bungalow," she said. The way she talked about the house you might have imagined that it had been built already and they were preparing to move in. "He told me the other night, 'Mommy, I feel that we need to come together again. . . . I'm going to build a house for us,'" she recalled. "I already told Jonathan that I won't drink any more. I will take the road forward with him. [He] is my inspiration."

When Susan Persens was done talking, she sank back against the seat and promised that she could get her drinking completely under control. I thought of the burden Jonathan carried, not only to save himself but also to serve as the protector of all of the women in his life.

We drove back to the house, where we found Jonathan waiting for us on the stoop. Mother and son stood in front of the shack. They had been told, once again, that they would have to leave before nightfall. Jonathan had on a blue-and-white baseball cap and a black, long-sleeved shirt over a bright white undershirt. He was wearing cotton, drawstring pants. When I raised my camera to take a picture of them, he hooked his left arm across his mother's shoulders. She smiled, keeping her lips closed to hide the missing teeth. Jonathan flashed a magnificent grin.

I told Jonathan that I was headed back to the United States in a few weeks, so I would not see him until the following year. "Is it far?" he asked. "Yes, further than London and across the ocean, too," I replied. We shook hands, like acquaintances at a wedding reception. As I drove away, I could see him and his mother, their faces pressed together. I had no doubt they were talking again, with rising excitement, about the house Jonathan intended to build just as soon as he had the money to pour the concrete foundation and raise the wooden frame.

15.

Johannesburg

Jacob Zuma's impressive home in Johannesburg lay in a pleasant, leafy suburb just a fifteen-minute drive north of the city center by highway. The bungalow that Jonathan planned to build would be far more modest, of course. In Zuma's own teenage years, the prospect of owning such a fine place had seemed similarly remote. On the afternoons I met Zuma at his place, I usually steered clear of the crowded thoroughfares, instead taking a meandering back route from the artsy neighborhood of Melville, where I lived. I traveled up and over the misshapen rocky outcroppings called *koppies* that broke up the city's skyline. The gardens around these homes, glimpsed only when the metal security gates swung open, were lush and spectacular. Evergreen asparagus fern brushed up against pineapple lily and neon-blue squill.

On the ridgetop by the Westcliff Hotel, the upscale traditional colossus painted brilliant pink, there was a spot where flowering jacaranda ran as far as you could see when the mauve-blue bell-shaped flowers came into bloom. Each time I returned to the city, its physical beauty impressed me all over again—lunar landscapes to the south and west, forested suburbs to the north, and the peculiar angle of gold-tinted light on winter afternoons.

The city had worked itself thoroughly under my skin, ever since I had seen it for the first time in 2004. That's why I decided, three years later, to move there for the year. In early January I flew back to South Africa and rented a spacious house at the corner of Sixth Avenue and Fourth Street in Melville, one of the rare neighborhoods in the metropolis where you could walk to the shops and restaurants, meet friends at a bar, go out dancing, and stumble home safely.

There were tall trees on the street where I lived, a magnificent garden behind the thick security walls, and large windows along every side of the house. The rooms were huge, with creaky wooden plank floors and high ceilings with elegant molded patterns and there were two big fireplaces in the parlor and the study, to help take the edge off when autumn arrived.

Within a few months, I felt thoroughly at home and completely engaged in the work. Every day, it seemed, there was some astonishing adventure, or a surprising twist in an interview or two. Mostly, my method of reporting, to the extent there was one, meant ambling around with my notebook out and tape recorder ready, just letting the country reveal itself to me.

Zuma's home lay on the east side of Jan Smuts Avenue, in a district known as Forest Town. The community featured large yards, big entryways, and expansive living spaces. The house, bought for him by a supporter, sat within easy jogging distance of a lush forested area that included the Johannesburg Zoo, the Military Museum, and Zoo Lake. It had the advantage, in security terms, of being on an easily patrolled dead-end lane butting up against the M1 highway.

His house was surrounded by high, thick security walls topped with electric security sensors. Threats to his well-being were endemic—considering the country's astronomical rates of armed home invasions—but they were also particular. Zuma had a host of enemies, some of them operatives in the police and national security agencies. Also, in nearly every small village, medium-sized dorp, and large metropolis in the country now there were entire strata of civil servants and government appointees who owed a debt of gratitude to the current president and might feel threatened by the possibility of a change at the top.

A plaque on the wall outside his home said, "Idyll Wind," but the house itself hardly had seen an idyll moment. Already, it had served for nearly two years as the epicenter of the planning to oust the sitting president of the republic. The home was the current gathering point, too, for friends and family—his twenty or so children as well as assorted mistresses, former aides, current supporters, and a bevy of lawyers.

When he opened the front door for our first formal interview, in late May of 2007, Zuma offered me a quizzical look, as if I had surprised him by actually turning up at the appointed time. We sat down at the long dining table, exchanging a few sentences about recent headlines—including about a supposed assassination plot against him in KwaZulu-Natal—when a phone call came in from a niece who needed money. Then we got started, and an advisor interrupted. One of his wives called. He had text messages arriving, with electronic burps, on one or another of several cell phones he carried.

Zuma operated a number of partly overlapping systems in each domain of his life. He had multiple schedulers, a collection of private cell phone numbers, and his own system for figuring out who could call on which number. He seemed to employ circles of people, sometimes on the same matters, who didn't know what others were doing.

In working out details of meetings like this one, in fact, I had learned to plan redundantly, arranging our meetings through at least two of his assistants. I never fully sorted out whether he was simply disorganized—as some of his friends claimed—or simply carried forward the engrained habits of an intelligence chief. Zuma was the collecting point of scraps of information, and everybody else seemed in possession of only fragments.

The layout of the house helped tell the story of his most recent troubles. The front door opened up to a large spare anteroom. Straight ahead, in an alcove, was the large oblong table of polished blond wood around which political strategy was laid out in late-night meetings. To the right, a wide staircase led to the bedrooms upstairs. To the left was the guest bedroom where the pseudonymous Khwezi had testified that Zuma raped her. Further on were the side doors from the driveway where agents from the National Prosecuting Authority had burst into his house one year earlier, setting off a tense, armed standoff with his bodyguards. In that raid, agents had seized computers and documents here, at his home in Nkandla, at the offices of his lawyers, and in the office at Union Buildings he used as deputy president. The operatives from the elite band of organized crime fighters known as "The Scorpions" collected thousands of pages of material in addition to the files that had accumulated already during the Shaik trial.

Charges against Zuma, for corruption, bribery, and tax evasion, had been formally filed shortly after Mbeki sacked him from his job as deputy president in 2005. Then the case had been struck off the rolls, when the prosecution subsequently announced that the state was not ready to go forward. Ever since, perhaps by Mbeki's design, Zuma operated in a kind of limbo, knowing that the case could be filed again any day.

His cheeks looked full, and his skin was unlined, except for one scar, a horizontal slash above his right eyebrow from a wound he had suffered while stick fighting as a child. Zuma appeared robust for a man in his mid-sixties, far healthier than he had seemed the previous year, when I had watched his performance in Bungeni Stadium. The color was back in his face, and he was closer to fighting trim. Tinted wire-rimmed glasses shaded his heavily lidded eyes.

In the scant feature profiles about him, Zuma was most often lazily contrasted to President Mbeki. The president was routinely described as urbane and intellectual, and Zuma as personable, and even charismatic, but also bumptious. The more time I spent around both of them, though, the more I felt he had an unearned reputation for charisma only because the president was so inward-turned. Zuma flashed no megawatt smiles, like Mandela, nor did he convey an impression of deep intimacy, like Bill

Clinton. He wasn't particularly friendly in close quarters or an effective speaker on the stump. What recommended him, chiefly, was that he behaved more or less normally, unlike his former boss.

In a similar vein, I had decided that the common assumption among journalists that Zuma wasn't smart was rooted in the fact that he had no formal education and had learned to hold his tongue. He passed the sugar, reminding me that lemon in my tea would curdle the milk, and asked a second time if I wanted some biscuits.

Mbeki's closest advisors felt certain that Zuma would fail in a head-to-head contest with their boss. Joel Netshitenzhe, an exiled hero in his own right with a long history of service at top levels of the party and government, told me repeatedly during 2007, the pivotal year, that he was confident rank-and-file ANC members would turn against Zuma once he was re-charged on corruption counts and went on trial.

"You cannot have one law for everybody else and another law for ANC members," he pointed out.[1] But Mbeki supporters like Netshitenzhe hadn't counted on Zuma's wily skill as a backroom operator, which had been brought to bear on the president's behalf in the past, being turned into a cudgel to be used against them now.

On the surface and from a distance, the prospect of Zuma becoming the next president of South Africa seemed quite dim in the middle of 2007. From the outside, this possibility also looked like an exercise in devolution: from Nelson Mandela to Thabo Mbeki to Jacob Zuma.

Letters to the editor in newspapers characterized Zuma as ruthless, corrupt, and dictatorial. Letter writers warned that he would turn out to be South Africa's Robert Mugabe. The rally I had attended in Limpopo province in 2006 had put me on notice that things looked differently from elsewhere in the country, however, particularly in rural areas where the most devoted core of pro-ANC voters still lived.

At a mass ANC rally in Mpumalanga province the previous January, I had also learned, in a twist that left me flummoxed, how Zuma's messy legal problems could be used for building support on his behalf. I had driven to Atlantic Stadium for the celebration of the ninety-fifth anniversary of the founding of the party, and watched closely as the two leaders were brought into the stadium together. They had held hands and danced on the stage.

While the speech-making began, I wandered out into the field, and quickly discovered that delegates weren't keen on being forced to choose between them. "It looks like they've sorted things out," one delegate had told me, visibly relieved at the prospect. His name was Sonnyboy Dorriri, a gold-mine worker from Harmony Mines. As a mineworker and grassroots ANC activist, Dorriri didn't know who was responsible for all the nasty talk of a schism. He shrugged when I mentioned testimony offered in the Shaik trial about bribes Zuma allegedly had taken. The mineworker argued that Zuma simply had shouldered the blame in order to protect others in the party hierarchy. Bribery was a way of life, he added in a singsong voice. "Don't forget that the ANC itself was built on corruption," he said. This was what opposition politicians argued all the time; it was startling to hear a delegate to the mass celebration of the ANC's founding say the same thing.

Some party insiders kept predicting, in interviews with me, that the two leaders would eventually arrive at an accommodation. "Zuma will receive a nice package on his way out," one Mbeki supporter predicted. "The man will have some very nice shoes." Others found it hard to believe that the two men would insist on a fight that could otherwise split the ANC from top to bottom, scramble the political calculus on the continent, and threaten the stability of their much-praised new democracy.

After all, there weren't policy or political differences between them, and so the depth of their enmity caught even other top party leaders by surprise. "From the inside, if you walked into a meeting of the National Executive Committee on an average day, you would not be able to detect the conflict you'd seen [portrayed] in the media," banker Saki Macozoma, a confidant of the president's, told me. "On one level we handled this division in the organization with great difficulty because it was so foreign—and there is a certain denialism of the problems we have."[2]

Macozoma was the chairman of Standard Bank who had served as a role model for the young black auto magnate, Ciko Thomas. Like other members of the party hierarchy, he found the two-faced quality of the rivalry quite unsettling. "When the NEC [National Executive Committee] says we want to discuss the differences between the president and deputy president, both of them say, '*But we have no differences amongst ourselves!*'" Macozoma recalled.

He waggled his head, mimicking first one of them, then the other, spot-on in alternating voices. "Then we say, 'No, we don't believe you because we see this and that [problem].' Thabo will say, 'I have no difference with Jacob Zuma of any kind other than that I don't believe he should be in the Cabinet.' And Zuma will say, 'I have no difference with Thabo, he's been my brother all these years, except for the fact that I should be in his Cabinet. He's unfair to me.' Now, what are you supposed to do with *that*?"

The behavior of the leaders of the movement was frankly dysfunctional. It had led to a systemic breakdown, Macozoma acknowledged. "Everywhere I go, I'm asked by people in the branches, 'Why are you people in the National Executive Council not *leading*? Firstly, you don't tell us the truth about what is going on. Secondly, you don't lead on these things so that we can understand what impact it has had on the organization.'"

He had leaned back in his elegant stuffed armchair and raised his palms, too, to show that he thought the masses were right on. Like the mineworker, he grew increasingly unsettled as time for the National Conference drew nearer. Macozoma felt increasingly uneasy about what might happen there. He knew his comrade, Jacob Zuma, well, and the prospect of his rise to run the country left him visibly rattled.

Outside the inner circle of comrades, little was publicly known about Zuma's personal history, however. No extended feature stories or full-length biographies had been written yet. That's why, in our second discussion in his home, I asked him to tell me about his upbringing and the forces that had shaped him. "My name is Jacob Zuma. I come from Nkandla," he began, identifying himself on tape for my transcriptionist.

Right from the start, he paid tribute to a trio of women—his own mother; his father's senior wife, whom he called his "older mother"; and his uncle's wife. "Three of my mothers had an impact on me," he explained.[3] They had looked after his physical well-being, making sure that he was fed. The second enduring influence, he said, was his father, primarily for his absence. "I don't know my father properly. I only have a shade of him," he added.

Zuma closed his eyes, summoning up a wispy memory from when he was about four years old: His father, a police sergeant, was a heavyset, slow-moving fellow who had been sitting by himself on a stone out in front of a house where a party was under way, and he had risen from the stone, playfully trying to grab the children, little Jacob included.

"We were laughing and turning around. He was trying to catch us," he recalled. Later a woman from the village told him that she had predicted his father would die soon, because it was a sign that death was hovering when children fled from a man.

"The next thing I remember is the day my father was being buried," he said. "People were crying. So we played at crying by putting saliva on our eyes." He mimicked the motion for me. From an early age, Zuma had learned the importance of demonstrating the correct response when a calamity happened—and also the value of feigning emotion if such a display was required.

Then he was the barefoot, fatherless boy of the village who hadn't been sent to school because his mother couldn't afford to pay the fees. Earning a pittance by herding cattle and goats through the nearby mountains, Zuma loved being off in the forest. During the early years, he felt closest to his uncles and his brothers, offspring of his father's other wives. "When my father was gone, they took the place of the father," he added.

All through his childhood Zuma nurtured a few lofty ambitions he had felt too shy to share with anyone at the time. Near his uncle's place, there was a Christian mission, he remembered. "I got interested in education. I really wanted to go to school," he said. He laughed at the outlandishness of this idea. "I wanted to be three things: I wanted to be a teacher. I wanted to be priest. I wanted to be a lawyer." He winced a little at the memory. "I ended up not doing any of them."

But when Zuma's oldest brother, a trade unionist, had joined the ANC, he clamored to be allowed in as well. They were the only ones, among countless siblings and cousins, who were drawn into the fold. Then, as now, his home village was territory dominated overwhelmingly by the followers of Chief Buthelezi. It was risky business to be identified with the ANC if you were a peasant from his area.

I asked Zuma why he turned out so differently from other children. "The influence of my elder brother came in, of course," he said. "But there was already something in the *basket*," he added, pointing to his head. "What was in the basket was the Bambatha War."

What Zuma meant was a historical event, the mass uprising of Zulu warriors near his home village in 1906. It was an awful massacre with pride of place in the country's revolutionary history. The Bambatha uprising began as a local rebellion against imposition of the poll tax, designed by colonial administrators to force indigenous people into systems of paid labor. The battle broke into warfare when Zulu King Dinizulu, successor to Cetshwayo, rejected imposition of the tax.

The resulting conflict turned into the last sustained, quite lopsided combat between white militias and Zulu-speaking people and ended in mass slaughter. Zuma spoke of this war nearly thirty years before his birth as though it had happened recently, though. "When I was growing up there were some people who saw it. Who *saw* it, yes," he told me, excitedly. "There were two old people, and when the war was fought they were only in their teens. They were in fact captured by the British at the end of the war."

Two aging survivors of the uprising, as it happened, lived out their days in the village. He remembered sitting beside the other children at night, listening to these two survivors tell their stories around an open fire. "They would talk about the people who'd died and how the women used to cook for the warriors," he told me. The two survivors of the slaughter described how they had smuggled food to outgunned warriors, and acted out the scenes of carnage as brave Zulu fighters who stood up until the very end against the vastly superior firepower of the British.

"We would sit around listening to the fairy tales," was the way Zuma put it. "And we wanted them to repeat these stories all the time. Fairy tales stick to the head of kids. This one *stuck*." He paused, as if looking for a way to put the stories into context. "I then understood that the White Man had actually taken the rights and the land of the Black Man," he volunteered. It was no great leap from his admiration for the Bambatha warriors, to a similar feeling of fealty to the organization that was founded six years after the massacre—the precursor of the ANC.

When Zuma was quite young, his mother moved a few hundred miles to the south, out of the gyre of Zulu country. She worked as a maid in Durban, and in his teens he lived with her for a few years in Cato Manor township, a rough-and-tumble community on the outskirts of the city. Afterward he moved in with a cousin in nearby Greyville.

This was the part of his life he rarely discussed, but it was certainly as influential in his political development, and in shaping him as a leader, as his earlier childhood had been. "I would see the ANC volunteers marching," he recalled. "And I would be nearby, listening."

While he was still a teenager, Zuma worked odd jobs—washing dishes, gardening, sewing sacks, and cleaning up in shops owned by Indians. In his spare time, he attended informal liberation schools set up by labor unions, socialists, and the Youth League. At these liberation schools, at last, Zuma could exercise his hunger for learning. There, he heard about the history of national liberation movements that were sweeping to power across the rest of Africa.

In 1958, at age sixteen, Zuma signed up as a member of the ANC Youth League. "Around the same period, I joined the trade union movement, the South African Congress of Trade Unions," he said. "This was important because there were study groups—labor theory, to understand trade union history, too."

By this time, he said, everything synced up in his mind. "The Bambatha War, now it made good sense. That was the important landmark, ending armed resistance in South Africa. It was a war that convinced everybody that you needed to fight with new methods," he added. "How we had been divided! If you fight [divided], at different levels, you can't win. You have to fight, instead, on a national level."

In the early 1960s, Nelson Mandela and other young leaders of the Youth League had provoked a long, noisy argument over the party's longtime commitment to the principle of nonviolence. In South Africa, Communists called apartheid "colonialism of a special type," and it looked to Mandela and his allies as though nonviolent resistance to the apartheid system would never bring it down. Others, including senior leaders of the party, resisted this idea, feeling that violence could never be justified.

Zuma, along with a band of young men he knew, fell in on Mandela's side of the argument. He remembered, in study group sessions, considering the example of Mau Mau guerrillas who had launched a campaign to drive white settlers out of Kenya. It had dawned on these young men that they had the power to launch a similar kind of armed rebellion at home.

"We were studying Mau Mau tactics [and] wanted to start it," he explained. Zuma and his closest comrades planned to collect Bush knives and machetes and stash them in the hills, at some point in the mid-1960s. "We used to cross the bluff as if we were going to a picnic" in order to scout locations for stashing caches of arms, he remembered.

Over long months of discussion and gathering weapons, they had worked out a simple plan. They would travel into Durban one Saturday night and launch a sneak attack. The strategy they discussed was straightforward enough: "We'd get there on a Saturday, park, and start butchering everybody," he explained, without emotion. "Once they called the police, we would disappear. We would run off to a hiding place to conduct the war."

Zuma had never spoken of this period to a writer before. Given his earlier reticence to be interviewed, it startled me a little that he offered up the story so unadorned. In the postliberation period, marked by all of the rhetoric about reconciliation and peaceful negotiation, there hadn't been much reflection concerning the earlier history of struggle and the stark terms brought on by the necessity of armed conflict.

In this case, as the young recruits were on the verge of carrying out the planned attack, they sent an emissary to seek approval from ANC leaders. Party elders immediately shut them down, Zuma pointed out. As I listened again to the tape of our discussion that evening, winding and replaying it to make sure I had heard him right, two things struck me most forcefully—first, that his earliest notion of a proper revolution had featured the indiscriminate slaughter of white civilians, and, second, that his band of young hotheads had abandoned their worked-out plans so readily when superiors in the underground ordered them to do so.

Here, it seemed to me, were two consistent strands of his character and career, which had been filled with periodic reckless behavior reined in by dictates of the ANC hierarchy. Zuma's oscillation, from outrageous impulse to strict party discipline, seemed an apt reference, as far back as you could trace it, for the arc of his life.

In subsequent talks months later, we moved chronologically, from Durban to prison, and from exile to his return home in 1990. Then we spoke of his eventual rise as deputy president of the country. Whenever we were interrupted by pressing business, or a family member, he made jokes about how much time it was taking to answer my questions. "Hey, this fellow has been taking my story for a whole year!" he remarked to one of his advisors, after our second talk.

But I also got the impression that this kind of methodical review of his past was useful to him, and certainly far more enjoyable than consideration of his current troubles. As he unspooled aspects of his formative experiences, they offered foreshadowing of what kind of leader he would become; he was instinctively secretive beneath a veneer of amiable sociability.

The habit of keeping big secrets, which required a high level of compartmentalization for any personality, had begun way back in Nkandla. In his late teens, he had courted Sizakele Khumalo, a beautiful young woman aged seventeen, from a neighboring village. It had taken him two full years to persuade her to choose him as her lover. During those years of courtship, and in the decades to follow, I noticed, he told Khumalo nothing about his political ideals or commitments or the possible implications for their life together.

Zuma had regularly walked for about two miles through rocky terrain to prove his seriousness. Yet he never thought to tell the young woman he loved so much of the danger he was courting. "Politically I was very advanced," was the way Zuma explained this decision. "Politically, she wasn't anywhere."

In July of 1963, when he was only twenty-one years old, he was arrested with a group of young men on their way to sneak out of the country for military training. His girlfriend learned that he had become an underground MK operative only from a radio news broadcast on SABC. After Zuma was held in detention for six months, he was tried and convicted on subversion charges.

At his sentencing to ten years' imprisonment on Robben Island, Zuma recalled feeling exuberant. "As we walked out of the court, I thought,

'That judge, he will do those ten years himself,'" he recalled. His bedrock belief, at the time, was that the MK, or Umkhonto we Sizwe, would spark a successful armed revolution and, within just a few years, overthrow apartheid.

Zuma instructed his lover not to visit him while he was on Robben Island, partly because he didn't want her to see him behind bars and also because he figured he would be home soon enough. Even the location of the prison had an apartheid-era subtext. White activists were placed behind bars on the mainland. Though the common cells on Robben Island, where Zuma was held, were integrated, with blacks, coloureds, and Indians crammed in together, black prisoners were treated worst; they were dressed in short pants rather than full pants and fed pap, a starchy dish, and little meat.

There were long days of pounding rocks in the lime quarry during his decade on the island prison, but Zuma never complained about this to me. Instead, he credited manual labor for his being in such good physical shape in his sixties. In prison, he also learned how to read and write in English. Zuma pursued studies in political theory from a famous party militant named Harry Gwala.

Thabo Mbeki's father, Govan Mbeki, was imprisoned on the island, too, and he proved to be a heavy influence on Zuma as well. The elder Mbeki was a widely respected Communist revolutionary. In many ways, he became a surrogate father figure, ideologically and otherwise. Govan Mbeki's own son, of course, was in exile by then, in London.

At the time, Zuma fell in with the "ultra-leftist Gwala camp," according to one of his closest friends. Zuma was among the prisoners who believed the ANC's goals "could only be achieved through a socialist revolution,"[4] Ebrahim Ismail Ebrahim recalled. Ebrahim was a stalwart Indian activist from Durban who had been prominent during key turns in the movement's history. He had participated in the Defiance Campaign of the 1950s and was an elected delegate to the Congress of the People in 1955, when the original Freedom Charter was drafted.

Banished by the apartheid regime, Ebrahim had also been sentenced to two long terms for subversion—the first for fifteen years and the second for twenty. He had shared a cell with Zuma along with twenty-eight other men for ten years. Like Mandela, he had spent much of his adult years behind bars. He would be among the very last political prisoners released from Robben Island, in 1991.

When I first met with Ebrahim, a few months after beginning my talks with Zuma, he was working in Luthuli House as the international relations coordinator for the ANC. He was a genial man with a broad balding forehead, and quite vigorous for someone in his seventies. He remembered Zuma as a thin, Zulu-speaking activist who couldn't speak English well when he entered the common cell they shared, on December 30, 1973. At first, Ebrahim recalled, they had difficulty communicating, because Zuma's English was so sketchy.

They also disagreed politically. Inside the movement, at the time, there was a long history of debate about whether the ANC was inherently a Communist organization. Militants clustered around Govan Mbeki and Harry Gwala believed that the aspirations articulated in the Freedom Charter necessarily meant that national liberation could be achieved only through socialist revolution. Mandela and others took the other side of the argument: the ANC was a broad church, not a Communist Party.

Ebrahim characterized Zuma as part of the "ultra-leftist forces" at the time. In spite of this, they had forged a close friendship. He explained that Zuma had endeared himself to his comrades because he was a master storyteller. Even forty years on, Zuma's longtime comrade pulled himself to the edge of his chair as he told this part of the story.

Zuma had successfully eased the crushing boredom of imprisonment for every prisoner who could hear his voice, Ebrahim recalled. He would tell his cellmates tall tales about the Bambatha uprising, and follow up with folk history about the great Zulu kings, Shaka and Dingane. He discussed anything that made a good yarn.

"He would start telling a story at breakfast," Ebrahim said. "Then he would take a break at lunch, and continue for the rest of the day." Zuma also crooned Zulu folk songs in a surprisingly resonant voice and taught the men fundamentals of Zulu dance.

Zuma himself had neglected to mention any of this to me. He had breezed past the story of his years in prison, noting only that he had done the time without receiving a single visit from the outside. He had forbidden not only his girlfriend, but also his mother and his brothers, from coming to see him. It was only when Zuma was released from Robben Island, at the end of 1973—when he was already in his early thirties—that he learned that the girlfriend he left behind in the early 1960s had waited all that time for his return.

"Ten years she waited!" he told me, his voice rising. A muted cry caught in his throat. He paused to bring his emotions under control. It sounded as though he might even weep. Here was a side of the wise-cracking, cool, and careful man that I hadn't seen before. "I said to myself, 'If I don't marry this woman, then I wouldn't know what kind of woman I'm looking for as a freedom fighter,'" he added.

Zuma had proposed to Khumalo the instant he returned home. He also promised her that his days of political activism were over. In fact, he went right back to work right away for the armed underground.

Just eighteen months later, around the time his new wife became pregnant, Zuma was forced to flee the country because of a security breach within the ranks. He remembered receiving a warning unexpectedly, and having to pull the van he was driving off to the side of the road. He stepped out of the van, making his way on foot to the border with Swaziland.

"By that time, I had been prepared politically to face surprises," he said. "I was mature enough to know that life can determine its own direction." The betrayal by one of his comrades was the largely unmentioned subtext. There were so many informers in the movement, so many comrades who broke under questioning, that a general climate of conspiratorial thinking took root.

The immediate result of this security breach, though, was to wipe out all of his painstaking work in creating a network of armed saboteurs in the province. "My heart was bleeding," he said. "Now I'm going to stay in exile for decades, which I did not want," he explained. "To me, the effectiveness of those in exile had not been the maximum, because of lack of access to the country."

Now, Zuma and his wife would be forced apart for another prolonged period. Shortly after he left, she miscarried, Zuma said. They lost forever the chance to have a child. He eventually sent for Khumalo, and she traveled to the border to meet him, but she was intercepted by border officials just inside Swaziland and then was detained for forty-two days by the South African police.

"She comes back and takes a decision. Never, never again am I going to attempt to go abroad," Zuma remembered, looking sad. "She sent a message saying, 'Sorry, I appreciate your attempt. But I can't go through this again.'" Sizakele Khumalo would wait for her husband, again, for more than fourteen years.

By the time Zuma told me this, it was after dusk. Nobody had turned the lights on and there were shadows across the table between us. Several times that afternoon, he had listened to me pose a question only to protest: "No, no, no, I'll tell about this in my *own* book. It needs the proper context."

Zuma steered me away from any details about his activities underground, too. "Any clandestine operator—you don't give the *dates*," he lectured me. "We did some things you need to forget, so if you're arrested you won't remember. That's a life I usually don't talk about in interviews." You might have thought it was 1987 instead of twenty years later.

He also felt wary, it turned out, about being precise concerning his romantic life in exile—when he met and married Kate Mantsho, a stewardess, for example, or how he arranged to marry Nkosazana Dlamini, a doctor, an ANC stalwart, and Thuthu's mother. "My own personal life is a long story in itself," he said. "I try not to talk about it halfheartedly. It has a lot of emotional things in it."

When I persisted in asking questions, suggesting an alternative every time he dismissed a query, he offered a little more. For example, he described Khumalo, his senior wife, this way: "People look at her and say how much I sacrificed. They don't look at *her*!" he said. "She represents all the women who sacrificed but are not known. They are in the quiet. Only in a few cases—Mandela, Sisulu—were the wives part of the movement. The majority of the people, the wives, are not known. They suffered in silence. I want to tell the story some time of that extraordinary woman in my life," he added, with considerable emotion.

In the intervening years, the suicide of his second wife, Kate, and the divorce from his third wife also had spilled his most excruciating private anguish into public view. Khumalo was shy, and she didn't speak English. When I asked him about their romance, he volunteered an expression of fierce attachment to her. He called her the most beloved woman in his life.

When he was forced into exile in Swaziland, Zuma said, he had argued strenuously with higher-ups, including Thabo Mbeki, that he should be allowed to cross back into South Africa, to continue operating clandestinely. Mbeki had refused his request, saying that it was too risky. The movement could not afford to lose him to prison once again. Zuma bristled at this decision, he admitted, and even made one unauthorized foray into Natal on his own. In the end, though, he bowed once again to party discipline. "The organization had spoken," he explained, sounding grim. "The ANC had spoken. I had no alternative. I had to obey."

Through the mid-1970s, he operated in neighboring states, overseeing the training of others in the armed underground. During the next decade and a half, he also rose through the ranks, to the post of chief of intelligence.

This part of an underdiscussed period in his life was even less openly mentioned. Like others in the top ranks of the ANC, Zuma had refused to give testimony before the Truth and Reconciliation Commission. Around the world, the commission's hearings in South Africa had been celebrated as a model for exposing atrocities and helping interrupt cycles of retribution.

But the commission's investigation at the time had proved quite controversial inside the party. Leaders in the inner circle believed that President Mandela had erred in allowing the commission to examine the misdeeds of the ANC forces. The commission's final report in 1998 documented the long history of extrajudicial kidnappings and killings by the regime's police agencies, and investigators also found proof of murders committed by Pan-Africanist Congress and ANC guerrilla forces.

The report included criticism of the MK, in which Zuma had been a leader, for "gross violations of human rights in certain circumstances and against two categories of individuals—suspected 'enemy agents' and mutineers." Zuma was personally implicated in the incarceration, beating, and torture of an MK soldier named Thami Zulu. The suspected turncoat died shortly after his release from the kind of jail the armed underground operated in guerrilla training camps and elsewhere in the frontline states.

The commission found that "individuals were charged and convicted by tribunals without proper attention to due process being afforded them, sentenced to death and executed."[5] Like so many leaders of his generation, Zuma never felt moved to apologize or explain anything he had ever done in the name of the ANC. When I asked him later about the case, he bristled. "People wanted to believe I was responsible, but I was not. Mine was not to arrest and keep. My [job] was intelligence," he said, concerning the Thami Zulu case.[6]

In the larger scheme of things, Zuma also believed that the commission, and especially its titular head, Archbishop Desmond Tutu, had "missed the point" in holding soldiers and leaders of the liberation struggle to account. He suggested, in a later conversation with me, a hypothetical case in which a civilian woman with a baby strapped to her back appeared in the midst of a critical military operation.

"Soldiers would silence that woman—whether it was any side. It could be a critical, vital mission that would tilt the balance. . . . And in the eyes of Tutu, that's what do you call it? Gross violation of human rights." Zuma shrugged it all off, as if such an allegation was inconsequential. His fundamental distrust of ex post facto examinations of decisions made in wartime, like judicial review of actions taken on behalf of the movement or the party in general, had been set firmly, as in concrete, a long time ago.

If Zuma's basic personality was shaped by his life underground, construction of his public persona was forged in a time of radical change and negotiated settlements. In the 1980s the Berlin Wall came down and the balance of forces for revolutionary movements around the globe had changed forever. The Soviet Union, longtime financial backer of the ANC underground, unraveled. Both sides in the long, cruel conflict in South Africa finally turned to the possible benefits of a negotiated settlement.

"The regime had the state, and police power. But political power? They had zero—very little, except from minority whites," was the way Zuma explained it. "On our side, we had political power and support, [but not] military power." In late 1989, he was part of the first small delegation of exiled leaders secretly ushered back into the country to set the stage for formal negotiations.

When I asked what had surprised him the most about the country he found on his return, he looked a little irked. It took me a moment to realize that it was the word *surprise* that had offended him. As a former intelligence chief of the ANC, I supposed, you never admitted having been taken unawares.

"I operated in the forward areas," he said stiffly. "My major task was to interact and engage the situation. It was my task from the ANC!" He added, in case I had missed his point, "In a sense I was very informed about what was happening in the country."

Zuma flew back to South Africa in a small plane with a delegation that included Penuell Maduna, a longtime comrade. "I come back from Africa, which is not developed," he murmured. "Potholes all over. The first day we drove from the airport to Pretoria. We were in the car—the police and the intelligence people who came to fetch us. First thing that I noticed is that everything was all quiet in the car. And I said to Maduna: 'What do you realize is different?' He couldn't catch it. And I said, 'It's the absence of the potholes.'"

Two things struck me about this anecdote. The first was that the battle that now had him in its grip involved so many longtime comrades; Maduna was the minister of justice who had backed Bulelani Ngcuka's investigation of Zuma. The second reference that stood out for me was his comment about coming "back from Africa"—as if South Africa wasn't located on the continent.

It sounded like a variation on the hubris some whites expressed about being in Africa, in Cape Town or Durban or Joburg, but not being *of* Africa. The earliest colonists had dreamed of a canal that would physically separate their outpost from the rest of the continent, and what had apartheid been, in the end, but an effort to enforce an artificial, unsustainable apartness?

In this limited sense, white colonizers and some black revolutionaries shared an implicit belief in the country's exceptional qualities. In the future, this kind of belief would morph into the assumption that the ANC was an exceptional force in an exceptional place, which, in turn, deserved extraordinary status as the new governors of a model state.

During the time we had been meeting periodically for a series of interviews, Zuma's supporters had begun a village-by-village fight to bring Thabo Mbeki down. Trade union chief Zwelinzima Vavi publicly called on millions of workers to flood the rolls of ANC branches so they could vote for new leadership. The goal was to create an "unstoppable tsunami" of support for Zuma, he said.

Another ally, Communist Party leader Blade Nzimande, added that the campaign was bigger than Zuma himself. "Zuma, like it or not, has become a symbol, in himself. This is a ripe moment, and it either galvanizes you or makes you afraid," Nzimande told me, as he brought his party's membership to bear.[7]

Likewise, in the Youth League, its leader, Fikile Mbalula, pledged to bend every effort on his hero's behalf. The three aligned groups worked together, in a completely synergistic way, in order to further Zuma's cause.

The president, his advisors, and supporters all were preparing for a colossal battle, too. They were fanning out around the country to convince branch members of the value of Mbeki's continued leadership. In his conversations with me, Zuma betrayed no anxiety. He said little about his relationships with Vavi, Nzimande, and Mbalula, never tipping his hand about who controlled campaign strategy.

In our earliest discussions, Zuma claimed that he and President Mbeki were once "closer than brothers." Bit by bit, though, he exposed a different view, perhaps reflecting his view that the president had betrayed him, for reasons he considered quite mysterious.

He intimated that Mbeki had taken advantage of Zuma's own reluctance to engage in an open fight that might hurt the ANC. "It's not fair because he knows I'm disciplined and won't do anything to hurt the party," he said. "I was shocked by how comrades turned," he added. "They said I had a hidden agenda. That made me realize *they* had a hidden agenda."

Before we could flesh out what he meant, he stirred, suddenly conscious of the time. "We must stop there, my brother," he said, forcing himself from his own chair and sighing. He still had ahead of him a long night of meetings with key supporters. On my way out past his coterie of security agents I recalled that Zuma had played a key role in delivering the deputy presidency of the ANC to Thabo Mbeki back in 1994, by weighing in on his behalf with Mandela. He had been one of the strategists who had created an "unstoppable tsunami" for the Chief. In some respects, then, the battle he undertook now was a struggle to unwind a part of his own legacy.

In late October of 2007, I returned one lazy Sunday morning to the Zuma home for breakfast and a game of 30 Seconds with Thuthu Zuma and her sisters. It was the cusp of spring, after a cold winter, and bright sunlight had burned away the morning chill. Their father was traveling, giving a speech in honor of the memory of Oliver Tambo. In his absence his home looked like an entirely different place than when I had visited previously.

The bodyguards were gone, and there was no security check or pat down in the driveway. The front door had been flung open to the fresh air, and from the street you could hear the rising and falling of the young women's voices. The four sisters were running wild in the kitchen. Sausages had burned in a pan over a flame turned on high. The domestic worker observing this mess shook her finger at them, laughing.

One of the sisters, Nokuthula, known as Thuli, was the spitting image of her mother, Foreign Minister Nkosazana Dlamini-Zuma. As I came in, she was razzing her older sister, Gugulethu, for having acted so haughty while receiving an award the previous night. It was for a film she had produced about women living with HIV.

Gugulethu, known as Gugu, was taller than the rest, and she accompanied everything she said with dramatic swings of her arms. She was an actress, after all. Thuthukile, or Thuthu, was the youngest of Dlamini-Zuma's daughters, and she had a hard time getting a word in edgewise. Standing next to them was Duduzile, known as Dudu, whom I had wanted to meet for some time. She was the eldest Zuma daughter, born of a different mother. Dudu was the daughter of Kate Zuma, Jacob's second wife, the one who had committed suicide in 2001. Dudu had stepped forward in 2006 to testify in her father's defense at the rape trial, and it was her testimony, punching holes in the account of her father's accuser, that had helped sink Khwezi's credibility.

In the current argument among siblings, it was three against Gugu. The other sisters backed Thuli, agreeing with her that Gugu's failure to name each one of them repeatedly, as seminal influences in her film work, had been a terrible breach of their fundamental code—*sisters first*. Gugu raised her hands, palms out. "*Forgive* me," she pleaded. Thuthu turned to me. "People ask who my best friends are. Here they are!" she said.

They took turns ferrying the food to the table, where Thuthu's step-brother, Vusi, was quietly doing his social studies homework. His round face was nearly lost in an oversize hoodie, and he raised his eyebrows at me in a gesture of male solidarity. Vusi was only thirteen years old, which meant that he was only six years old when his mother killed herself. He, too, was a Born Free South African.

I noticed that Vusi had been working on a watercolor painting of a rural village, which depicted shoeless children in the foreground. The painting made me think of Ndaba Mandela, who was a 100 percent city boy, too. I asked Vusi if he had based this painting on his memory of Nkandla. He pulled out his textbook, showing me the photograph that had inspired him. Rural life of the sort that had shaped his father's char-acter was a source of textbook study for Jacob Zuma's son. As soon as his sisters thumped their food down on the table, he beat a strategic retreat up the stairs.

Dudu said: "Nobody else really knows what life is like for us. But my *sisters* understand." They had been infants living in exile and youngsters during the early days after liberation, children of top ANC officials. Now they were part of an emergent black elite whose very existence was the firmest evidence that something fundamental had changed in South

Africa. Yet they quickly salted the conversation with details intended to disabuse me of the notion that they had led pampered lives. "I remember when we were young, we actually used to count five cents to try to get bread and milk," Dudu recalled. "[Even now] my friends are all like—why are you so broke? You can't afford to go to the *movies*?"[8]

Their mothers had pushed the girls from an early age to study hard, advising them to make their own way in top professions and not to count on men for their survival. There was this strong feminist influence for them, side by side with the influence of their father's conventional, patriarchal ideas.

In earlier conversations at the university and my house, Thuthu had begun describing her father as a *bicultural* person. Thinking of this, I suggested to the table full of Zuma sisters that nobody could really understand their father without spending time with him in Nkandla. "*Absolutely*," Gugu said before I had the question out, sounding a little like her father. I added, "But I don't think I have to travel to Nkandla to understand the four of *you*." They shouted, "Eee!" and began to talk over one another.

Gugu laughed so hard that she nearly slipped from her chair. "Take us to the Hilton and we'll be fine," Dudu said. The bad roads, dust, open fields, and country people of Nkandla were not their natural habitat, they admitted. They knew this fact about their identities disappointed their father. Zuma had told me that his children's first visit to the homestead had created a kind of culture clash. "When we went, they couldn't speak Zulu," he recalled. "The older girls spoke North London English. I took them to Nkandla and people said, '*Ninjani*.' They would say [mimicking the accent], 'Whut, whut, whut did they-ah *say*?'"

Gugu acknowledged this breach, and the unhappiness it had caused for her dad. "We always struggle a bit when we do go there," she said. "Also, we get crucified because we speak English—we speak *white*." The Zuma daughters spoke properly, with a city accent, and they had been raised to demand respect from boys. Whenever they arrived at the homestead, though, they felt that they were expected to accept a precipitous demotion in status. They traveled, in a matter of hours, from something like equality to a situation in which they felt placed completely under the thumb of the males.

"There are certain things that are expected of you when you're there that we didn't get taught," Gugu said. She moved away from the table as we pushed our plates away. Sweeping her hair behind her shoulders, she backed up, pretending to raise a service tray to her shoulder. Her sisters began hooting because of the way she tilted the make-believe server. They razzed her, saying she had surely already spilled the make-believe drinks.

"Don't look him in the eyes either!" Thuli warned. And Thuthu offered this correction: "Head *down* more!" As she approached, Gugu averted her glance from mine, offering a demure smile. It was prostration, a body shaped in the form of pure submission. Thuli commanded, "Go on all fours, bend those knees." Gugu kneeled, her shoulders sagging, an image of female compliance. "Then I must get down and hobble on my knees," she explained. "And then I can give you your jazz."

The sisters were no longer egging her on; they were no longer laughing. "It's a frustration of lots of people who grew up in our generation," Gugu said, sounding tired. "We come up in this Western world that preaches equality, and that anything is possible for you . . ." Thuli interrupted her sister then: "That preaches to us that guys can make their own *tea.*"

All of them laughed, and Gugu went on: "[In Johannesburg] it's understood that if I look you in the eye—that's good, I'm being confident, I'm being assertive. Suddenly you're there [in Nkandla] and expected to be something that's totally different." Thuthu nodded, remembering the time she had given up her chair for her *brother* when she hadn't even known she had one.

But, if the sisters felt out of sync because they were treated as quasi-white girls in Nkandla, they often felt out of place, too, in school, social, and business circles back in the city. They felt caught in a kind of limbo—

between South Africa's yesterday and the promise of a nonracial and non-sexist tomorrow. They described never feeling quite as *black* as they did in the neighborhood where the family kept a home in Cape Town.

"People have only become a little better at hiding what they think," Thuli put in. The stories spilled out then, of white girlfriends who laughed at their "cute" names, and boys who mentioned casually that they didn't smell like most black people. " 'You're not like other blacks'—we've all had this said to us!" Gugu reported, with an edge in her voice. "So it seems like you have to be white to be friends with white people." They wanted to succeed in the new society, but not at the expense of betraying their values in the country or bleaching their identities in the city. "There's an angry black contingent coming up that thinks it's not our job to teach every white person how to behave," Gugu went on.

From talking to white friends and their children in Cape Town and Johannesburg, I knew that well-meaning people on the other side of the line shared a sense of agitation about the apparent racial gulf among the Born Free generation. There was a deep expression of anguish, especially acute among white political activists who had worked side by side with blacks during the liberation struggle. So many of them felt pushed away by former black friends now, and were confused by the anger welling up from young blacks.

The next generation seemed even more segregated, socially, than the one before. A Jewish woman I knew, an antiapartheid progressive who had worked painstakingly to integrate her own company, was the mother of a teenage son. One afternoon she had unburdened herself to me after a strained exchange with a longtime black coworker: "I think, for us, it's like those people who complain about Jews who won't get over the Holocaust—who say, 'Why can't they let it *go*?' " she said. The legacy of apartheid was like that, she had decided. It intruded still, in devastating ways, into every crevice of social and cultural life.

It surprised me, when I introduced the subject of politics, to discover that none of the sisters placed much faith in the party their parents had worked a lifetime to build. "I'll always vote ANC, but, like, I just don't know . . . , " Dudu volunteered. She had spent time hanging out with leaders of the Youth League recently; they seemed, to her, like posers more interested in being seen behind the wheel of luxury cars than in creating a new kind of country.

"I feel the same way as you," Thuthu agreed. "I'll vote for the ANC, but I won't be an active member." The biggest complaint they had about the Youth League, and the party in general, was that the leaders had allowed the entire organization to become embroiled so fully in the feud between their father and the president. In their judgment, this was an abrogation of responsibility. "There's so much more the Youth League could be doing for young people!" Dudu cried. "All it's been is Zuma, Mbeki, Zuma, Mbeki—and I can't tell you what they've *done.*"

When I said this was a "generational complaint," Gugu nearly jumped out of her chair. "All this jazz the past few years has been a bit crazy," she complained. "They're trying to involve the rest of the country in this one battle, when we've actually got much bigger fish to fry—and you guys are squabbling about who's going to be the next president! That's not helping us in figuring out the things we need now."

Thuli jumped in. "It's *grown* people—grown people fighting!" she shouted, spreading her hands out as if intervening in a squabble. "Come on! Like, there is a country to govern, can't you just pull yourselves together?" It seemed like a logical question, all the more powerful since it had been expressed by offspring of one of the protagonists at the center of the confounding mess. Here was the generational divide that would get deeper, wider, and clearer as an all-out conflict between the top leaders of the ANC raged on.

16.

Orange Farm

In at least one key respect—its policy on HIV/AIDS—the ANC government pulled things together pretty well by the middle of 2007. On AIDS, the split between Zuma and President Mbeki, at the top, seemed actually to have improved prospects for a more concerted public health campaign to staunch the epidemic. This was true partly because of circumstance: the health minister had been sidelined by a serious illness. But it was also a consequence of the surprisingly energetic leadership on HIV by the new deputy president, Phumzile Mlambo-Ngcuka, who had replaced Zuma in 2005.

Behind the scenes, key figures in each camp—the deputy president and several ministers who supported Mbeki in the leadership contest, and the deputy minister of health, Nozizwe Madlala-Routledge, a Communist Party leader in the Zuma camp—were all agitating for a more robust effort. The secretary-general of the ANC, Kgalema Motlanthe, kept pressing for more action on AIDS from his office at Luthuli House.

The deputy president was a former schoolteacher who came to the post with a mixed record as minister of minerals and mines. But in the number-two spot she went swiftly about her business in areas where Zuma had not made much of a mark. Among other things, she inherited stewardship of the National AIDS Council, and used it as a bully pulpit to make noise about all of the things that remained to be done on prevention and treatment of HIV infection.

When the minister of health, Manto Tshabalala-Msimang, was sidelined by liver disease and went on medical leave in 2006 while awaiting a transplant, Mlambo-Ngcuka had the AIDS portfolio to herself. Activists celebrated when the health minister was shunted off for a long stay in a medical clinic. The country's comedians produced a flood of merciless skits portraying her as a broken-down drunk. Editorial writers noted that the minister elected to have her surgery in a private clinic, not in the public health system she had run.

There were even media reports that the minister had been jumped ahead of other patients awaiting available organs on a request by the president, a story Mbeki denied. Pieter-Dirk Uys, South Africa's acerbic performance artist, introduced a line in his performances expressing the hope that, in her case, "the liver would reject its host."

In the health minister's absence, in any case, Mbeki appointed Jeff Radebe, the minister of transport, to fill in. He and the deputy minister, Nozizwe Madlala-Routledge, who had been in a steady struggle with her boss over the department's lackluster approach to AIDS for years, swiftly repaired relationships with civil society. The Treatment Action Campaign's treasurer, Mark Heywood, was appointed deputy chairman of the National AIDS Council, and he began working closely alongside the deputy president. This was a sharp turnaround from the period when the two sides quarreled so bitterly in public. Just the year before, at the international conference, Heywood himself had been part of a demonstration urging the health minister's sacking. Now, a leader of TAC was close to the center of power in directing national AIDS policy.

At last, a coordinated response to HIV took shape. The nature of the change became clear in mid-March when a national conference was convened to unveil a new national strategic plan to manage the pandemic. Press spokesmen from TAC and the government, who had plenty of experience attacking one another in the past, were assigned to put out a joint release to announce the gathering. At a meeting room at the Birchwood Hotel near O. R. Tambo International Airport, health promoters from all over the country watched as leaders across the spectrum—from community health workers to business executives to government officials—issued an overdue call. "We aim to reverse the course of the epidemic in the next five years," acting minister Jeff Radebe pledged.

Zwelinzima Vavi, the trade union leader who had also been a steady critic of the Mbeki policy on AIDS, made his mixed feelings clear: "This marks a turning point in our new struggle. We shunned denialism and chest-beating claims. We regret we won't be able to return the thousands of lives that were wasted." His statement served as a direct criticism of President Mbeki, who had treated the illness as a manifestation of poverty alone. Now the trade union chief fashioned a new connection between the disease and economics. "Unemployment and AIDS form an albatross on the shoulders, in particular, of working-class communities," he said.

The union leader didn't take time to flesh out this notion, but everybody in the room understood what he meant. Where health care was less available, where people went hungry, where schools were bad, and where jobs couldn't be found, HIV spread largely unchecked. It was a disease that flourished in the nooks and crannies of vulnerability and thrived alongside social breakdown.

This was partly why the AIDS epidemic, like everything else in South African life, was so color-coded. By the middle of the decade, blacks had infection rates six times the rate among whites. In KwaZulu-Natal, Jacob Zuma's home province, the rates of HIV infection were far higher than anywhere else. The Western Cape, where per capita incomes were higher, had the lowest infection rate.

Wherever they lived, the disease hit the young particularly hard. Half of all mortality in the country was AIDS-related by the middle of the decade. Infection with HIV was the underlying cause of nearly three of every four deaths among young and middle-aged South Africans.

As the trade union leader left the podium, he turned to the next speaker, a dapper mining executive dressed in a sleek black suit and an eye-popping neon-pink tie. He was Patrice Motsepe, one of the country's few black billionaires, who looked a little nervous even before the union leader called him out: "Mr. Motsepe! You and our colleagues must come to the *party*!" Vavi shouted. "Money is not more important than people's lives."

As it turned out, the businessman had been trying to figure out how to openly discuss the realities of the sexually driven pandemic. He was the owner of a soccer team, Mamelodi Sundowns, so he started out by expressing his hope that men who had "multiple partners in multiple cities" could be educated, under the new national program, about the role they should play in halting spread of the disease.

The bishop who had offered an invocation at the start of the meeting was sitting to Motsepe's left. He and other officials on the dais began squirming a little in their seats. The businessman ignored them. He had, rather courageously, placed his finger on the nub of a significant challenge. Any effective prevention campaign against the fatal, sexually transmitted disease meant needing to discuss sex itself more openly. As I had discovered, over three years of travel around the country, the risks of HIV were only rarely discussed, even among close friends.

Ndaba Mandela, who had lost both parents to the disease, told me that he felt flummoxed by the number of young women who casually offered themselves to him, in the midst of the epidemic, for sex without a condom. "It's just the most obscene thing ever. This is ridiculous!" he said with fierce emotion. "The other day, I was having drinks with this guy and he said, 'You know, I was so pissed off the other day because this girl didn't want to have sex,'" he told me. "I said, 'Why?' He says, 'Oh, because I didn't have a condom.' So I was like, 'Why are you pissed off? *Good* for her! What is *wrong* with you?'" The resistance to use of condoms was widespread, even among his friends. "It's this obsession for sex that people have. How do you explain it?"[1]

The reaction of the other dignitaries to Patrice Motsepe's remarks demonstrated how dicey it could be, still, to try raising such a fundamental question. The businessman mentioned, for example, the dilemma of a friend of his, whom he described as a traditional leader from the Eastern Cape. This friend, Motsepe revealed, had expressed concern about how to keep his four wives safe from infection. He offered a brief digression about the history of polygamy among Xhosa-speaking traditionalists, explaining how local chiefs took wives from different clans in order to stitch the community together. Even now, it was a communally enforced standard that confounded traditional HIV-prevention approaches. "We have to be sensitive to various cultures," he added, glancing quickly to his left, where the bishop and the deputy president sat.

The deputy president waggled her head from side to side in an emphatic way. She cried out in mock distress, "Ay, Patrice! Patrice, Patrice, Patrice." He took stock then, and abruptly stopped talking. Turning to the bishop, bowing slightly, in an apologetic voice, he added, "I know, bishop: *One wife, one husband!*" Mlambo-Ngcuka led the hall in an emphatic round of applause. To me, it seemed like a moment of great potential had been squandered, when a prominent figure should suggest beginning a real discussion of sexual practices that were driving infection rates up but then should be shut down for doing so.

The deputy president had close-cropped curly hair and a pleasant, open, oval face punctuated on each side by large gold hoop earrings. Her sleek pantsuit was styled in shiny, brown-and-orange-patterned swirls. She looked like a model representative of the next generation of modern South African government officials—cosmopolitan, self-confident, and articulate. When she rose to take the microphone, she spoke in the style of an evangelical preacher, swaying from side to side. She called on everybody to join in the effort to create an "Africa that will be free of HIV and AIDS."

Placing the battle against HIV at the heart of the ANC's National Democratic Revolution, and casting it as a next stage in liberating the country, she called on those already infected to make "a personal pledge not to re-infect ourselves or infect another. . . . It's the most revolution-ary and most progressive act you can make for the future of our conti-nent." There was rapt silence in the hall when she added, "If you're HIV-negative, your revolutionary task is to stay negative."

This was the sort of clarity and passion that had been missing from the president's rare remarks on the subject, and from Zuma's speeches, too, for that matter. The new deputy president called on young people to delay their first sexual experiences, and then she turned to glance at the men on the platform. "The male sector has its job cut out for it," she said, raising her eyebrows. The latest survey on AIDS had shown the inci-dence of HIV infection leveling off overall among the young, which was surely good news. Yet the ongoing high levels of infection among teenage girls and young women was evidence that teenage girls, like the ones I had met at the Harriet Shezi clinic two years earlier, were especially vul-nerable because of their sexual involvement with older men.

Too many parents shielded the perpetrators of sexual violence and failed to protect vulnerable young girls from older suitors, Mlambo-Ngcuka added, with apparent bitterness. "What's good about being armchair revo-lutionaries?" she demanded. When she finished speaking, everyone on the dais and in the audience rose. They broke out in applause so thunderous that it showed how long the audience had been aching for leadership and support from the top in their struggle against the modern plague.

During a break outside the ballroom, Patrice Motsepe buttonholed Dali Mpofu, the CEO of SABC. Mpofu was Snuki Zikalala's boss, and he had been the target of insults for the lackluster performance of the public broadcaster on HIV. "Dali, you must get this right!" the business-man shouted, reflecting the views of so many people in the crowd. Mpofu looked grave, but he continued walking. On a little pedestrian bridge leading back to the parking lot, people long at odds with one another—organizers for TAC, health department officials, trade union activists, businessmen—created a happy cacophony. It was the sound of an overdue conversation.

The longtime communications wizard for TAC, Nathan Geffen, looked a little dazed at this tableau. He had been the organizer of TAC's message in its long, hard slog to get the government's attention. When I had spoken to him on the phone a few days earlier, Geffen had sounded cautious about what the meeting might accomplish. The fight against the AIDS epidemic in South Africa, sabotaged by President Mbeki's response to it, had unfolded like a never-ending nightmare. Now, it would take an enormous effort simply to make up for lost time. All of the pieces would have to fall into place just to move the country onto the launching pad of an effective national campaign to cork the epidemic. Standing across from the little bridge, Geffen shifted his weight from side to side and offered a shy grin. "Denialism has now been crushed in our country. That's the amazing thing that happened today," he said. "Denialism was forever crushed."[2]

What a remarkable turning point in the country's history. It was a breakthrough of enormous proportions. If South Africa could halt the spread of AIDS, it would break a pattern of apocalyptic thinking that came along with this modern plague. With the pandemic brought under control, South Africans might consider the possibility that other seemingly intractable problems—crime, social development, gender equity, and economic mobility—would also prove newly pliable.

Due west from the airport, and then straight south from the city along the N1 highway, lay Orange Farm. It was the sprawling informal settlement, about thirty-five miles from Johannesburg, where Gwendoline Dube lived. In communities like Orange Farm, people arrived all the time as migrants from traditional rural life of the kind the Zuma daughters had mentioned and Chief Mandla Mandela had celebrated. The trouble was that they then got trapped in what they had expected to be a short transition from the rural areas to more established neighborhoods, in Soweto.

In places like this, full of transience and so little work, the HIV rate was higher than anywhere else. Gwendoline was the teenager living with the disease whom I had met in the newly inaugurated teen group at the children's clinic two years earlier. I had tracked her down again when I moved to Johannesburg. We had lunch together once downtown, but I had been fishing ever since for an invitation to meet her family. Finally, I invited myself, because I figured the only way to understand the complicated challenge Gwendoline faced in staying healthy was seeing her in her own community.

The speakers at the national conference had sketched formulaic advice offered to a young woman like Gwendoline: steer clear of older men, focus on your studies, and safeguard your health. It seemed to me that if the war against AIDS that had been just announced had any possibility of making real headway it would have to resonate, in realistic terms, in poor communities like hers across the country.

Half of the population of Joburg lay in the city proper, but an equal number of people lived in the townships and informal settlements, where shacks were nearly stacked on top of one another. It took only about forty minutes to get to the central section of Orange Farm from the northern suburbs. The highway threaded through valleys of long uniform hills made up of massive mounds of gold-mine tailings squared off at the top.

You could chart class status crudely on the way from north to south—from the comfortable house around Zoo Lake, where Jacob Zuma lived, to the southernmost tip of the informal settlements. One way of expressing Gwendoline's plight was to note that, for her family, a move to Soweto would be a huge step up.

Orange Farm was the place where people who hadn't secured jobs or housing in the township to the north found shelter. The settlement was formed in the late stages of apartheid, around 1988, and more than 60 percent of its households lived below the poverty line, which meant subsisting on less than R840 a month (about $140).

Off the narrow dirt road on the way to Gwendoline's house, trees had long ago been chopped down for firewood. A few overflowing dumps provided the only break in the dusty, flat topography. I noticed a message inscribed on a large piece of metal, which advertised the services of Doctor Sithole at *Inyangas Own AIDS Clinic*. "The healers are confident," the sign read, "that they have their own 'vaccine' to cure the disease." Here was the sign that Gwendoline had passed every day on her way to school as she had begun treatment on antiretroviral medication.

There were approximately 350,000 people in makeshift homes set one next to the other, one-third of them without electricity and none with running water inside. Like others in the community, Gwendoline's mother eked out meager wages doing textile piecework, and her stepfather owned a pickup and occasionally found work in construction. The official unemployment rate in her area ran near 90 percent.[3] Her parents, then, were among the lucky few to have any money coming in. The cramped conditions, limited garbage disposal, and lack of a proper sewage system made it a poor place to live for someone like Gwendoline, who already suffered from a compromised immune system.

Estimates of the proportion of people living with HIV in her community ran as high as 80 percent. While I drove along the dusty streets to meet her, I tried to wrap my mind around this brutal statistic, ticking off the numbers as I passed people on the road: positive, positive, positive, positive, negative—then positive, positive, positive, positive, and only one negative again. It was this kind of sodden reality check that reproduced a form of apocalyptic thinking: how would the nightmare ever end?

That kind of thinking, of course, helped the virus, too. If the prospect seemed so hopeless, if the scale of the epidemic was too overwhelming, if it looked like everyone would eventually become infected no matter what they did, then there hardly seemed a point to denying yourself passing pleasures or taking the trouble to learn how to fight against the virus.

At the bottom of a hillock, Gwendoline lived with her parents and siblings in a three-room shack. The shack had concrete walls and was covered by a rusted tin roof. A stone carving of a mare and her foal was embedded in stucco near the front doorway. Inside, a small lounge showed off three ceramic dogs. Through a narrow doorway was a room that served as her mother's workroom and also her parents' sleeping area. There were two industrial sewing machines side by side, wedged into a small space at the foot of the bed. Off the common area was another space, set off by a makeshift door, where the girls slept. Across the way, an old storage crate had been converted into a dwelling for her stepbrothers.

On the day I visited, Gwendoline looked remarkably healthy, and noticeably more energetic than when I had seen her in the clinic in 2005. She had braided her hair and pulled it back off her face, revealing a heart-shaped silver locket at the spot where her clavicles met. Gwendoline was dressed in a lime-green shift and faded blue jeans. She felt far better these days, no longer experiencing side effects from her medications. Her appetite was strong again—perhaps "a little over strong," she added—and it was cheering to realize that she was well enough now that she could lapse into more prosaic worries, like the fear of putting on too much weight.

When she wandered off to speak with her brother, her mother offered me tea, and then settled in on the couch beside me. Teresa Dube was a genial woman in her mid-forties, with a pleasant face and a handsome brown felt bowler hat perched back on her head. Her shoulders were rounded, from long hours she spent at the large industrial sewing machines. Her hands were swollen from churning out the piecework.

Mrs. Dube allowed that Gwendoline was her most forceful child from her earliest days. She had taken on major household chores as an infant. "When she was six she was washing plates and cooking for the whole family," she recalled. Before her daughter fell sick, Gwendoline was the one her mother could count on for sisterly companionship. The fact that she had contracted HIV—what Mrs. Dube called "this thing"—was a memory that still made her flinch.

She regretted having sent Gwendoline off to live with her parents in Zimbabwe. At the time, she had thought it would be safer for a young girl there than in Orange Farm. When her own mother called one night to say the girl was ill, she had hurried straight away to fetch her. "I thought it was malaria or *what what*," she said. "I didn't suspect it could be *this thing*."[4]

All during the following winter, the girl had suffered from a terrible cough. She came down with one kind of influenza after another and eventually started missing school for weeks at a time. Painful pustules broke out across her lips. Gwendoline refused to go out in public or be around other kids during this period. At first, it hadn't occurred to her mother that her daughter might be suffering from AIDS.

When the nurse at the children's clinic delivered the news about Gwendoline's HIV test results, Mrs. Dube said that she felt knocked over by grief. Initially, she figured the diagnosis must mean that she was HIV-positive, too; she figured that her daughter had gotten the virus from her, at birth. It was a terror to imagine having inadvertently infected your own child. Then, at the nurse's prodding, the girl revealed the secret she had been keeping all along. It was difficult for Mrs. Dube to accept the idea that her own brother had raped her child and transmitted a fatal disease to her. "To think it's a child—just a *child*," she murmured.

When the news of the illness sunk in, Mrs. Dube considered taking her daughter to a traditional healer. Her own mother was a big believer in herbal remedies, and traditional medicine was the first line of defense for most South Africans. Lots of people she knew distrusted white doctors and white medicine. She also was aware that the health minister recommended good nutrition and lots of lemon, garlic, and African potatoes to slow progression of the disease.

But Mrs. Dube felt persuaded by the explanation of the doctor at Dr. Meyers's clinic, who had explained that her daughter was gravely ill and needed immediate treatment. Her T-cell count had fallen dangerously low, and her viral load was extremely high. "So my daughter and I talked, and we decided we had to try it," she recalled. They had scraped the money together to buy a watch—the first timepiece in the family—because the medication had to be taken precisely at the same time, twice a day. These decisions undoubtedly had saved Gwendoline's life.

There was a quick change in Gwendoline's physical condition once she got on the antiretrovirals. The results seemed miraculous, her mother said. Once the immediate danger passed, she said, her daughter had grown increasingly difficult to handle. "If you ask her the smallest question, she acts as if you are accusing her of something!" she complained. I was surprised to hear this report, because whenever Gwendoline mentioned her mother, she spoke of her the way Jonathan Persens had referred to his mother—as a miraculous, patient, Madonna-like figure. "Ay, it was affecting me how the child acted!" she added.

Mrs. Dube worried that her daughter was hanging out with older people, including older men, and that they would lead her astray. The mother had a theory: perhaps her daughter hoped to escape Orange Farm with the help of a rich man. She thought being HIV-positive made her more susceptible to the blandishments of men. "Gwendoline wanted a high, high life," Mrs. Dube continued. "Maybe she thought if she was up high like that, nobody would suspect her."

"*Suspect* her?" I asked. "Yes, of having *this thing*," she replied. Gwendoline had experienced considerable trouble concentrating on her studies, partly because she had missed so much school when she was ill. Now, she "stressed too much, she was *stressing*," her mother said.

Mrs. Dube beckoned me to the table across from the sofa, where there was a set of trophies Gwendoline had won for academic achievement in math and science. I remembered what she had told me, on the day we first met at the clinic, about her ambition to become a pilot *and* a doctor. When I mentioned this, her mother said, "I would like that for her, too! But if she fails her matric exam and can't become a doctor or lawyer, she will be terribly affected."

This was the first I had heard of Gwendoline's difficulties at school.

As for all South African schoolchildren, the matriculation examination at the end of the twelfth grade would determine whether she could go on to college and in which programs. The mother shook her head and settled her chin on an open palm. When I asked what she thought the matter was, she replied. "I think it's *that subject*. It's not the medication. I think it's the *idea* of it."

The clinic in far-off Soweto was the only place Gwendoline felt comfortable discussing her medical condition and the psychological effects of having the disease. In the neighborhood there was only a single woman who had spoken up publicly about being HIV-positive. Gwendoline hadn't told her siblings, and Mrs. Dube had not shared news of her daughter's conditions even with her husband.

Mrs. Dube supposed her daughter must feel quite lonely. "I feel guilty because I have not tested myself," she added. "I tried to talk to my husband, but he showed no interest. So, what's the use? He still will not agree to use a condom. He's so positive that he doesn't have it."

When Gwendoline returned to the house, her mother headed into the back room to work. We strolled around her community while she gave me a guided tour, heading down a rutted dirt road past the primary school where she had earned her trophies. Gwendoline filled me in on the gossip about the neighbors we passed—the married couples recently broken up because of affairs, the kids who had gone off to a university, the others who had dropped out of school and were just hanging around the neighborhood.

It was late afternoon by then, and a little breeze nudged the edge off the muggy heat. As we made a loop and turned to go back to the shack, Gwendoline blurted out some rather stunning developments. She had acquired a boyfriend since we last met, she told me. This was something I was forbidden to tell her mother.

The boyfriend was the kind of man her counselor at the children's clinic had warned her against: he was twenty-five, and Gwendoline was only seventeen. The imbalance in power, status, and money between young men and teenage girls was among the key factors fanning the rate of new infections among females.

I remembered how dismissive Gwendoline had sounded, in the support group session back at the clinic in 2005, when she spoke of other girls in her class who had gone off to service taxi drivers, schoolteachers, and local businessmen in exchange for clothes, food, and jewelry. She wanted me to understand that this boyfriend had approached *her*. She repeated it twice as if that made all the difference.[5]

Her boyfriend had been respectful and accommodating when she insisted on delaying sex. Gwendoline spoke of him in a respectful hush. But when she first revealed that she was HIV-positive, he had vanished for a few months. Then he had called and pleaded with her to take him back. He had agreed that they would practice safer sex, and lived up to the bargain. "So far," I said. She nodded.

We passed a set of shacks and cement brick homes, skirting an open rocky field. Gwendoline paused to point out the spot mid-field where she had seen a corpse a few days before. So many rapes occurred in the grassy spots between the rocks that she never set foot in the open field at night. Even in the daytime, she felt superstitious about crossing this space. So we tripped along its edges as she told me about the cascade of crimes. Here was the daily reality—the ubiquitous, powerful fear of assault that girls like Gwendoline carried with them all the time. Against that backdrop, the exploitive older suitor often looked more like a savior than scoundrel to the girls.

Risks ran high on every front. The chance of death by injury in South Africa was greater than elsewhere on the continent and nearly twice the global average, according to a recent study. Violence and accidental injuries were second only to unsafe sex in shortening lives, and they resulted in nearly sixty thousand deaths each year.[6] In its starkest terms, a young woman could choose her poison: slow death or something faster. I suggested to Gwendoline that it must bring some comfort to have a man willing to accept her and promise to provide for her. She nodded again, and looked away.

Gwendoline recently had been chosen to be health promoter in her twelfth-grade class. She figured that things would only improve if her fellow students spoke openly about the fear of rape or murder and the danger posed by HIV. But she hadn't revealed to her schoolmates that she was infected with the virus, even to the girls she considered intimates. Gwendoline shrugged when I asked why not. It wasn't a matter of shame, she insisted. This kind of revelation about "these things" just wasn't done.

With her final year of high school under way, she had grown more nervous about the big exam around which everyone's educational future revolved—the *matric*. Only extremely good scores, including in science and math, would give her a chance to study in a decent premed program and follow her dream of becoming a doctor. "You'll see—I'm going to surprise you," she said, lifting her head and poking her chin in my direction.

Gwendoline made a big fuss of seeing me off. She followed me up the road, power walking to keep the car in sight. Over the next few weeks, I would be traveling heavily, including to the national ANC conference in Polokwane to follow the unfolding political saga. And then, when the year was over, I would be returning home to Chicago. I watched her in my rearview mirror, and waved wildly out the window, feeling bereft. It seemed like an unforgivable betrayal to leave her behind.

One morning a few weeks after the visit with Gwendoline Dube in Orange Farm, I stopped by Melpark Elementary, the school a few short blocks from the house in Melville where I was living. There, I held another in a series of group interviews with young people, like those I had organized all over the country, about politics, race, sex, and life. These group conversations were intended to complement the periodic discussions with my small group of young informants whom I had gotten to know far more intimately—Ndaba Mandela, Thuthu Zuma, Jonathan Persens, Vunene Mabasa, Thomas Maree, and Gwendoline Dube.

During my visit to Orange Farm, Gwendoline had told me she was praying every night that Jacob Zuma would fail in his bid to become the president. This seemed a reasonable reaction in light of the rape trial, considering that Gwendoline was a young woman who had been sexually assaulted by an older relative. The interviews at the elementary school were my chance to look at the coming election from the point of view of other children.

Melpark was a public school and most of the children were bussed in from Soweto. A majority of them had parents who worked in the formal economy and could afford to pay the fees charged in a good public school, two big advantages they had over Gwendoline for becoming upwardly mobile in the new South Africa. The first thing the principal said to me when I arrived to speak with the kids, though, was that she felt certain I wouldn't get anything valuable out of them. "Oh, the *children*! They have no hunger for learning about politics!" she exclaimed.

The principal was a middle-class Indian woman originally from Durban, and she expressed the common view among the struggle-era generation that young people were profoundly unmotivated, ahistorical, self-absorbed, and apolitical. The minute I walked into the school's large auditorium, filled to its limit with Born Free adolescents, they upended all her belittling expectations.

Sixty girls and boys, brought up under the new democracy, listened closely to their teacher's introduction of me. Many raised their hands right away when I began asking questions, and they kept a lively debate going about the country's history and current politics for more than ninety minutes. Their teachers had to force them from the room back to their classes.

Only a few said their parents were active in the struggle to overthrow apartheid; most claimed loyalty to the ANC. They owed the party their freedom, they argued, and pointed to evidence they had seen for themselves, how social welfare grants had saved neighbors from hunger. They had witnessed public housing under construction and watched as the rapid increase in wages led to expanding numbers of middle-income families in their neighborhoods.

The children remained cautiously optimistic, and this reflected national generational trends. Through 2009, young South Africans would tell pollsters, by a margin of 57 percent, that they expected to be better off than their parents. This expectation of future social mobility helped bolster otherwise fraying fidelity to the ANC.

One boy, short and thin as a whippet, stood with his back ramrod straight and offered an exegesis about "this man, Jacob Zuma." He recited the narrative of Zuma as a hero who had been treated unfairly by President Mbeki. A girl on the other side of the room stood up. Equally brassy, she replied that Zuma had been accused of rape, and that he had funny ideas about women and HIV. They argued with one another in well-spoken volleys, revealing a sharp gender divide. Across the country, educated young women felt repulsed by what they had heard about Zuma's treatment of the much younger woman who had accused him of rape.

As the debate between Zuma's supporters and his critics grew more intense, many of the kids sat on their hands. Finally, several students raised both hands, as if they were victims of a stickup, and suggested that they wanted a third option. None were willing to consider an opposition party—not a single person mentioned the possibility of supporting Helen Zille's Democratic Alliance—but one after another called for a better range of choices from within the ANC.

This was a common complaint among young people from a wide variety of backgrounds in Johannesburg. The last time I had stopped in to see Ndaba Mandela, we discussed the widening split in the ANC. He said that his grandfather was deeply concerned about the state of the party and the Mbeki/Zuma division at the top. Nelson Mandela couldn't understand why the two top leaders were pursuing personal ambitions at odds with the best interests of the organization, his grandson said. "*Zuma?*" Ndaba added, sighing and shaking his head. "Zuma and Mbeki are causing the division with the ANC and are no longer part of the solution. They're part of the problem. . . . We need to find a third way."[7]

In this crowd of black kids from working-class families in the Melpark auditorium there was plenty of interest in a third option. One boy spoke up for Tokyo Sexwale, the wealthy businessman and former premier who was then spending substantial sums of his own money, in an American-style campaign, to build support on his own behalf; twenty-eight of the students raised their hands for the businessman. There were four votes for Cyril Ramaphosa, President Mbeki's onetime rival and the favored long shot among the intelligentsia. The remaining students broke by a wide margin in Zuma's favor, 25 for Zuma to 5 for Mbeki.

In smaller group conversations I held in a school meeting room through the afternoon, the students made connections between the turmoil that had embroiled the country's political elite and everything from persistent poverty in their neighborhoods to the prevalence of crime. When I asked whether the fight between Zuma and Mbeki supporters had a noticeable effect in their day-to-day lives, one student pricked the air with an index finger. "I think it all goes back to the matter of our leaders," Dimpho Ramalosa said. "First and foremost, our leaders don't respect each other. . . . They can't expect us to respect them if they don't even respect each other!"[8]

Dimpho was an intense, earnest boy who lived in the township community of Meadowlands, a neighborhood in Soweto that was a long bus ride away from the school. He felt lucky that his parents could afford the fees to send him to a better public school than he would find in his township. Boys his age were trapped in a bad cycle of poor schooling and limited opportunities that only became worse by the violent conditions in their neighborhoods, he argued. This was why he thought that the warlike language used by supporters of Mbeki and Zuma against one another was especially unwelcome.

He braced his forearms against the table, knitting his thin black eyebrows together while trying to work out an idea that had come to him. In years past under apartheid, he said, young black men who were down on their luck attributed their low stations in life to rank racism. If you were poor, the cause was obvious to everyone—it was the oppressors, the system. Now, he added, it was much harder to understand how some people's fortunes—like those of the businessman Tokyo Sexwale— soared while so many others continued to limp along at the bottom rung of society. When a man got turned down for a job these days, "people ask themselves, 'Is it because I'm black or because I'm dumb or because I don't have the right qualifications?'" Dimpho said.

This seemed like an elegant description of the crosscurrents of change, and doubt, that young people faced. The inability to advance in the celebrated, supposedly nonracial new democracy had generated a new and different kind of fury, especially virulent because it was borne of such uncertainty. "It's a matter of self-respect," he explained. Most of his childhood friends now smoked dagga, drank alcohol, and traveled around at night in search of sex with girls. "There's a bit of pressure," he admitted. "Your friends, when they're chilling, they're like, 'Let's go see those chicks.'" Proving that you were a man in this way was a mark of belonging. "You go from one zone to the other to force that girl to have sex with you, or rape her," he continued, glaring at the tabletop.

The only alternative to going along that he had figured out was to exile himself from the boys he had known since he was a toddler—which was quite painful—and to go through life feeling completely alone. "At the moment, I stay indoors a lot of the time," he said. Here was as poignant an explanation as I had heard from any expert or official about the conflating power of economic hardship, gender inequality, drugs and alcohol, and sexualized violence.

I asked the dozen other teens around the table whether they had experiences on a daily basis that made them fear becoming victims of crime, including rape. Every hand shot up. One adolescent named Lesego Motau, who was smaller than the others, had an open face punctuated with brilliant eyes the color of coal. She told the story of a neighbor girl, just two years older, whom she had known well. The friend had always preferred hanging out with boys. "She was a lesbian," was the way Lesego explained it. "So she was hanging out with only boys at her age." Her voice got a little shaky. "They raped this girl, and they killed her, and hid her in the bush." It was an especially intimate anguish for a thirteen-year-old girl: she knew both the victim and the perpetrators well.

"We're not being free!" Karabo Tserema put in. "You're too scared." She had a long, gorgeous face with a spray of incipient acne on her forehead. "The main thing is crime. That's why I say, 'You may love everybody, but trust no one.'" Like her classmates, Karabo spent much of her time after school and on weekends locked in her bedroom reading by herself. That was because she wanted to avoid the older men who cruised the neighborhood day and night. Just the day before, a man well into his thirties had accosted her. He had told her he would like to take her out on a date.

Karabo flexed her long fingers, giving her own half-grown body a glance and looking puzzled. "If we wear something bright, or beautiful, they think we are calling them," she said softly. "If we wear short skirts, they think we're cheap and we're asking them. Instead, we're just wearing it because we feel good the way we are."

These circumstances led most of the students to increasingly conservative conclusions about culture and politics. They all wanted tougher policing, longer sentences, and more severe and punishing conditions for convicted criminals. They had had it with the *tsotsis*, the thugs, roaming through their communities. They suspected that life was too cushy inside the country's prisons and not enough of a deterrent for repeat offenders. This tough-on-crime thinking spilled over to a more general critique of the post-apartheid culture of individual rights. In general, they figured that protection of these rights had gone way too far under the ANC.

Most of the kids believed that the culture of rights, trumpeted in the Constitution celebrated worldwide as the most progressive in the world, led to an expectation that anything went. In such a culture, they thought it would be harder to rein in criminals.

This general uneasiness about social standards led to a consideration of other kinds of restrictions. There was too much nudity allowed in advertisements, both the girls and the boys said; they wanted to know if I had seen the latest 50 Cent video "with all those naked women." The children also felt there was too much promotion of alcohol in the popular media. Cigarette companies passed out samples off the school grounds.

Most of them also cited the deleterious effects of American popular culture on their own lives. One boy asked if I could explain why *Law and Order* aired shows like the one he had seen about a group of boys who enforced discipline by sodomizing one another. Why did Americans sit still for the slick glorification of such degradation? He thought it was even more damaging to air such trash in the South African context.

They all agreed, without one dissent, that abortion was morally objectionable. Similarly, they felt that a law recently passed by Parliament to allow minors to terminate a pregnancy without consulting their parents was a travesty. Young people needed more guidance from the grownups, they argued. I must have looked startled because they all laughed. They were the first group of adolescents I had ever met anywhere who made an argument that they needed less freedom and tougher discipline.

"I want to raise the issue of children's rights," Sizwe Dube said with sudden force, and I thought he was ready to debate the other side. He was a tall boy with a wry smile. "I think the law influences what we do as children. Having these rights encourages us to do as we please," he argued. "I think the Constitution needs to go back and think about these rights. The only rights children need are the right to shelter, and education, and to be loved—and the others should be scrapped."

Here was an intimation of a trend that worried civil libertarians—an emerging skepticism about legal protections, individual rights, and the primacy of the courts and the Constitution. The other kids nodded their heads, and in this reactive expression there was a glimpse of future battles in South Africa over individual freedom and social responsibility.

"We say we are living in a democratic country. But are we living up to the name?" Sizwe asked. This was another version of the complaints I had heard from Jacob Zuma's daughters and the Mandela grandchildren, and it was similar to a query Gwendoline Dube had posed most recently. Gwendoline had latched onto the idea, when she was young, that it was possible to make anything of yourself—to become a doctor and pilot. But, these days, young South Africans were looking for the evidence that the dreams they had been encouraged to embrace could be achieved.

In its welcome shift on AIDS the ANC government had pledged to make up for lost time in protecting young South Africans. The day-to-day experience of young people, in the process of forming views that, in turn, would shape the country's future, demonstrated how progress on this one front had gotten thoroughly enmeshed with so many other urgent challenges.

17.

Nkandla

On a clear summer morning I awoke in Richard's Bay, the sprawling port city in KwaZulu-Natal province on the Indian Ocean. It was mid-November in 2007, and I was headed that morning to visit Jacob Zuma at his homestead, which lay straight inland on a rough four-hour drive from the coast. A month before the pivotal ANC convention, Zuma had decided to take a day off from his frenzied campaign and spend it at his ancestral home.

President Mbeki's advisors still believed they had the election sewn up. Zuma's supporters relentlessly kept up the pressure on local branches of the party, with overlapping sweeps on his behalf by organizers from the Youth League, Communist Party, Young Communist League, and the trade union federation COSATU. Provincial gatherings of ANC delegates all over the country were in the process of selecting representatives to the national conference. The makeup of these delegations would settle, once and for all, who would lead the ANC forward, Thabo Mbeki or Jacob Zuma.

The drive to Zuma's homestead took me past the Dlinza Forest, a lush stretch of impenetrable brush and tall trees, on through the sprawling town of Eshowe, with its new mall. From there, I headed into the hinterland of what once was the kingdom of Shaka, the legendary Zulu king. In the early nineteenth century Shaka conquered formerly scattered chiefdoms, creating a highly militarized society with as many as forty thousand soldiers in arms.[1] The king was responsible for establishing a cohesive Zulu identity in country marked by craggy mountains and deep ravines that lay between the Pongola River to the north and the Tugela River to the south.

It was Shaka's memory that the current king, Goodwill Zwelinthini, had invoked when he had danced on stage and declared his support of Zuma two years earlier. In advance of this trip, I had been reading more of Shaka's history. He was offspring of an unmarried mother, and he rose to power ahead of his more senior brothers largely on the basis of his strategic prowess. Shaka was the inventor of the short stabbing spear and devised effective methods of using them in close combat formation. The wars that Shaka had conducted had far-reaching, and quite unintended, consequences. During the *mfecane*, or time of troubles, Africans migrated north, west, and south to get out of the way, leaving large swaths of territory south of the Tugela River relatively unoccupied. In the 1930s, when Dutch-speaking emigrants began their Great Trek in the 1830s, away from British domination at the Cape, they had found it much easier to seize ample grazing land beyond the escarpment south of the Tugela because of the *mfecane*. By then, incidentally, Shaka was no longer leader—he had been assassinated in 1828, in the royal kraal, by two of his half-brothers. The country's history, it seemed, was full of stories of betrayal by men who had once considered themselves brothers.

My own trek inland was a swift passage, in just a few hours, from coastal bush to moist savanna, from the tropics to woodland. This meant leaving behind enclaves on the coast traditionally dominated by whites, and moving toward forested country where white people were always scarce. Past citrus groves and sugar cane plantations lay rolling green and tan hills dotted with wild honeysuckle and forest mahogany trees. There was Coward's Bush, where King Shaka reputedly put people to death for sport.

Further on lay the sad, poorly kept grave of King Cetshwayo, a less-well-known Zulu king who ended up aligning himself with the British but who was later betrayed by colonial authorities and banished to Cape Town. To the northwest was the Ncome River, known as Blood River by Afrikaans-speaking whites, which was the place where trekkers won a stunning victory over the Zulu Army in 1838, slaughtering an estimated three thousand warriors and losing not one fighter themselves.

Every turn in the road, it seemed, marked another epochal event in the centuries-old encounter between Europeans and Africans. The plot, in this case, was far more complicated of course, because of the internal divisions between English-speaking and Dutch-speaking colonizers and similarly shifting alliances between black communities in relation to the newcomers. Jacob Zuma's takeaway lesson from all this history, as he had already told me in the interview back in Johannesburg, had been that blacks were subjugated wherever they had allowed differences in language and culture to divide them.

The ride north and westward was a roller-coaster experience on narrow, poorly irrigated dirt roads that, every once in a while, crisscrossed newly bulldozed, unfinished, wide, and marvelously smooth boulevards. Finally, after a long climb on dirt roads colored deep red, uphill and around a sharp curve, was the thickly thatched collection of buildings that had caused Zuma so much political and legal trouble. His compound, and its finances, had been featured prominently in the trial of Schabir Shaik, and after hearing so much about it I expected something large and imposing; instead, the homestead looked like a rather modest group of dwellings enclosed by waist-high metal fencing.

There was a guardhouse and a large home at the top of the hill, where Zuma's senior wife lived. She was Sizakele Khumalo, the woman Zuma had fallen in love with as a teenager. Rondavels, the traditional circular huts, were scattered below the ridgetop across the side of a gently sloping hill. A younger wife, with whom he had had several children, lived in the rondavel just downhill from the main house. In the rest of them, various relatives resided, including one of his brothers. Verdant lawn stretching between rondavels had been cut recently. In the center stood the kraal, the traditional enclosure for animals in an African homestead.

The kraal was fenced in with interlaced tree limbs stripped of bark and buried to the hilt in the hard earth. An ox had been slaughtered right before I arrived. Its bloodied skin was still drying in the fierce midday sun. Four amputated hooves were clumped, all akimbo, in the center of the enclosure. Freshly slaughtered meat was carved out in strips.

Men were busy softening the meat with hammers and flat sides of their hatchets, readying it for the grill. Cast-iron pots had fires flaring beneath them. Off to the side were several dozen others smoking and chatting around two gigantic gourds of fermented home-brewed corn-based liquor, so-called Zulu beer.

Zuma greeted me, holding his hands out, palms up. He swiveled to gesture at the four corners of his place, opening his arms. Here, there was space enough to breathe, and walk, and think, he told me. "Why should someone be nervous here?" he said. He wore black slacks, white running shoes, and an elegant silk shirt with cream-and-coffee-colored patterns and big polished onyx-colored buttons.

Being back home clearly had inspired a burbling good humor in him. Zuma had a noticeable lift in his step. "Hau!" he shouted. Saying the word repeatedly allowed him another opportunity to explain that the meal was beef rather than horse, and, by implication, to make fun of the prissy prejudices of city slickers. "You can be sure of it, My Brother!"

Telling little jokes like this was also his way of steering the conversation away from other subjects.

There were two other signature habits I had noticed when he faced interlocutors. "Is that so?" was his most common expression whenever you told him anything. I realized that Zuma used the phrase to engage with people without actually giving anything away. He had cultivated the capacity to sound emphatic, validating the other person's feelings, without committing to any definite position himself. His other verbal tic was to hang back, keeping his own counsel, waiting until somebody made an argument he had generally suggested earlier; then, leaning forward, he would affirm his own point by saying, "*Absolutely!*" with great enthusiasm, appearing to be simply agreeing with his companion.

Zuma waved toward the valley below, poking his chin toward the mist-shrouded mountains on the other side of the river, a dun-colored waterway that cut in a lazy Z pattern. Above the river, steep trails slanted up to mountains that presented themselves in a natural series of terraces. "If we had more time, I'd like to show you those mountains," he said.

From the main house, with thatched roof and freshly painted stucco, you could see enormous, craggy bluffs through which he had herded goats and cattle as a boy. They were a quite mystical place, he assured me, "the land of honey and cobras." The bees up in those mountains produced honey that was extraordinarily fragrant when taken right out of the nest. The snakes were snouted cobra, long honey-colored, thick-bodied reptiles with enormous heads and extraordinarily potent venom known for the capacity to strike quickly.

Zuma said that the smell of the air, the feel of the soil, and the view of the jagged ridgetop in the distance brought him back to himself. "The environment is so calming here," he said.[2] "It's been nice to be here—far from the air pollution. Back to my roots."

The Tugela River, to the south, whipped through curlicues from west to east across the northern half of the province. The river meandered for more than three hundred miles, from the Drakensberg escarpment to its mouth on the Indian Ocean, its course marking a rough dividing line between territory once dominated by British colonial forces, to the south, and the traditional home villages of Zulu speakers.

I asked Zuma to say more about what the area meant to him as a person. "Remaining what I am, I remain true to myself," he said. It sounded like an aphorism he had worked out for me. He regularly navigated between the patriarchal style of village life in Nkandla and the hybrid, multilingual, globally inflected, and sexually free cosmopolitan vibe of a place like Johannesburg. Zuma came from King Shaka territory, but he operated most of the time in Brenda Fassie's Jozi. "I don't think I would want to look like an artificial person or pretend to be something else," he added.

I had been working my way through the recently released biography of Thabo Mbeki by Mark Gevisser, and Zuma's statement reminded me of Mbeki's admission that he had always felt so *disconnected*. Zuma said that he hadn't read the book, but seemed that he took every opportunity to present himself as someone who had remained *true to myself*, in contrast to his ex-comrade. "This," he said, gesturing toward the surrounding countryside, "makes me to be on my feet, on the ground, a South African who grew up in K-Zed-N who is a *Zulu* with *Zulu* traditions— *Zulu* values pushed into myself."

An assertion of his Zulu-ness seemed like a tricky matter, not least because ethnic pride had been so forcefully downplayed in ANC politics over the years. So-called tribal differences, of the sort that had been stirred up outside his court appearances, where male supporters wore T-shirts that said, "100% Zulu Boy," were anathema to older party stalwarts. Ever since colonizers and the apartheid regime had played on ethnic differences in the old days, party policy downplayed ethnic cleavages. And Zuma, having served as a negotiator between warring parties in neighboring Burundi, knew as well as anyone how explosions of interethnic tension had sabotaged postcolonial liberation movements elsewhere on the continent.

The much-celebrated election of 1994 in South Africa, after all, had been followed, a few months later, by the genocide in Rwanda. Ethnic divisions also had brought governments to the brink of breakdown in Kenya, the Sudan, and the Congo. From the late 1980s to 1994, more than ten thousand people had died in brutal clashes between followers of

the ANC and more traditional Zulus allied with the Inkatha Freedom
Party of Chief Buthelezi.

Before I could ask him about these points, Zuma continued on, as if
anticipating these objections. He said that his embrace of Zulu identity,
and of his sense of rootedness to his ancestral place, had allowed him later
to "become matured" more fully as a transformative agent in the country's history. He had the credibility—as a proud Zulu man inspired in the
first place by the Bambatha uprising—to persuade militants from both
camps to put down their pangas and knives in a common struggle. This
was because common people recognized their own experience inside him.

"My love of South Africa is not *gray*, it's not vague. It's very specific,"
he said. Even when we weren't discussing his rival, it didn't feel as though
Mbeki was far offstage. Zuma increasingly caricatured the president's
intellectualism as something unrooted from South African experience,
like abstract theory up in the clouds. Now, Zuma insisted there was no
contradiction between his assertion of ethnic pride and his role as a leader
in a nonracial democracy. "It's [also] in keeping with our Constitution—
unity in diversity," he added. "This is my [part in this] diversity."

As we talked, his junior wife placed their three-year-old daughter on
his lap. Nompumelelo Ntuli was a young, big-boned woman with a
round, cheerful face. I noticed that the eyes of the other women, as they
ferried food from the kraal to the kitchen, fixed on her when she arrived
back at the compound behind the wheel of a new BMW Zuma had
bought her. She carried herself confidently, more sure of herself around
the men than the other women. As he married progressively younger
women, Zuma had, in effect, set up the possibility of a generational clash
in his own home.

"This place made me who I am, how can I forget it?" he said, his
eyes on his child. Zuma offered his daughter a slice of grilled beef, but
then pulled it away each time she lunged for the food. Soon enough, his
young daughter figured out that she was supposed to hold out two
hands politely, and not grab. "If I can't identify with where I come from,

and begin to be too high flying, I'm like a South African who's floating in the air."

In a later discussion about the difference between his style of leadership and Mbeki's, I asked, "There's a difference between herding goats, you mean, and helping out at a store your mother owns [as Mbeki had when he was a child]?" He replied, "*Absolutely! That's* the point I'm making, yes." The line he drew between himself and the president was a refinement of the traditional distinction made between the *amagqoboka* and the *amaqaba*—educated modernizers, on the one hand, and the less educated traditionalists on the other. Zuma was throwing in his lot with the *amaqaba*, with this twist: his education in the *movement* had been the finishing school that had prepared him for the next challenge. "The style is certainly not the same," he went on. "And the background is not the same."

The second distinction Zuma drew concerned the roles each man had played during the struggle years, the action they had taken shaping the content of their character. "The experiences in the movement—much as we belong to the same movement—has not been the same," he went on. "Our backgrounds informed us. . . . I come from the poorest of the poor. Other people didn't necessarily come from the poorest of the poor."[3] Class background would be a trump card in his contest with the president.

Though Zuma described this brief return to the homestead as "quite calming," from what I could see he had little time to kick back. In the rondavel behind his senior wife's home, relatives and neighbors were waiting in a long and winding line to consult him. The area around Nkandla had been dominated for many years by followers of the Inkatha Freedom Party, and Zuma's neighbors still voted mostly for it. But in the national election campaign of 2004 he had led ANC efforts to vanquish Chief Buthelezi's forces once and for all, bringing Zulu speakers "home" to the ANC.

When he excused himself to meet with some of these people, I tagged behind. From outside the rondavel you could hear the murmur of a voice, followed by the rising and falling inflections of his reassurances. One of his brothers, passing by, said this was *Brother's* greatest strength— winning people over one by one. "Is that *so?*" he cried.

During a break from these chiefly consultations, we sat in plastic chairs on the porch of the main house. It was a one-bedroom ranch-style home with a large lounge and a small dining room. There was a large kitchen at the back, presided over by Sizakele Khumalo, the formidable, sharp-tongued woman in her sixties who was the unquestioned matriarch of Nkandla. When she crossed the threshold, he smiled at her. In the conversation we had had back in Johannesburg, he had whistled, long and low, when he mentioned her name, exclaiming: "Ten years she waited while I was in prison, and then fourteen years while I was in exile!"

Zuma considered MaKhumalo, as she was known, the embodiment of faithfulness. Unlike so many other exiled warriors, who had left lovers behind and never returned to them when liberation came, they had stuck by one another. "It's a love story really," he had murmured when we spoke of her months before. "Yes, a real love story."[4]

The next morning, I sat down for a talk with Sizakele Khumalo in the lounge of her home. She was dressed in a worn housecoat, looking a little unsettled by the prospect of her first interview. Zuma's younger brother, Mike, had agreed to serve as our translator, and I began by asking, as a kind of warm-up, what had led her to take notice of her future husband when they met for the first time.

Khumalo bolted upright and immediately challenged me: "*Phela uyena owaqala ukungibona,*" she began—"*He* noticed me first. A person does not just take notice of a man; he is the one who notices *you*."[5]

Clearly, I had gotten off on the wrong foot with Khumalo by implying that she had chased after Zuma. She told me that she had just turned seventeen when he started wooing her, and explained that he was put through the proper paces. Khumalo had received him courteously each time he walked two miles to see her, but she had offered little encouragement in the beginning.

"You don't see the person you love with the same eye that you use to look at other people," she said, studying me for signs that I knew the first thing about courting rituals. "It's not just one guy that would approach you but a dozen," she added. "Then the selection process begins. Whoever didn't speak to my heart got eliminated."

MaKhumalo didn't sound boastful when she said this, but rather like a mechanic explaining how pistons go up and down in a car engine. "With others, you try to place them in your heart but the heart will simply reject them," she said. But Zuma walked faithfully all the way to her home each weekend. "There was that one guy that just wouldn't take no for an answer," she went on. "You kept saying no and he kept coming back. I couldn't fight my feeling for him any more so I finally gave in and accepted him as a partner."

Directly over her shoulder was the only picture of herself on the walls of the main house. In the photo, her head was cocked toward Nelson Mandela, with her husband flanking the older man and looking uncomfortably stuffed into an overly tight suit. The occasion had been the construction of the first school in the area, a landmark event for both MaKhumalo and Zuma because neither had graduated from elementary school. Next to that picture was a folk artist's portrait of her husband over big block letters: "THROUGH THE BACK DOOR OR THE FRONT . . . I AM DEPUTY STATE PRESIDENT." It was the only explicitly political message anywhere in the house.

In the center of the wall, though, was a second photograph that caught my attention. It was a large portrait signed for Zuma by Atiku Abubakar, the former vice president of Nigeria. Abubakar had been ousted as vice president of Nigeria in 2006 after a fight with his long-standing comrade, President Olusegun Obasanjo. There was an eerie parallel, as if the South African leaders had mimicked their friends to the north. Thabo Mbeki had been relatively close to Obasanjo; Zuma, in turn, had worked closely with Abubakar.

The relationship between the two top Nigerian leaders had blown up a year after Zuma and Mbeki first came to blows. "When Obasanjo was after his blood, Mbeki was after my blood," Zuma would tell me later. They did exactly the same thing—those two.[6]

When Obasanjo, forced by term limits to leave the presidency, "retired" to party headquarters to continue pulling strings from there, Abubakar lost the entire game because he had allowed control of the party to slip away. He was even expelled from the organization. Zuma was determined not to make the same mistake, and that was why he had fought so hard to be restored to his position within the ANC. "Abubakar's party was still very fragile and was not able to defend him," was the way Zuma explained it. "On my side it was different. My party was very strong."

This part of her husband's life might as well have taken place on the far side of the moon for all MaKhumalo knew. "*Yebo, kona ngethuka, kodwa ukwethuka kwani . . .*," she murmured—"Yes, I didn't know anything, especially about his political involvements." She went on: "I only found out when he got arrested."

MaKhumalo spoke of Zuma's prolonged periods of absence as if they were mainly a test of her equanimity. "The thought of leaving him never crossed my mind," she volunteered. "I just gave in to the fact and hoped he will get out—hopefully alive." With a slight dip of the head, she acknowledged profound feelings of *intshezi*—loneliness—in his absence.

When she had heard, a decade after he was sent off to prison, that Zuma had been released from prison, her feelings were mixed. MaKhumalo felt both excited and fearful, she said. "I didn't know what to expect, he'd been away for so long. But eventually I got used to him again." She lifted her chin, smiling. "Obviously, a person ages, so he looked different. Considering the fact that he left here with nothing, it wasn't a shock that he came back empty-handed."

After he returned, MaKhumalo said she had pressed him, uncharacteristically, about his political involvements. He had pledged to her that his days in the movement were over, she recalled. This was also a lie, as she learned just eighteen months later when he was forced to skip across the border ahead of a likely arrest. "It was mentioned on the news," she reported, looking away. I suggested that it must have been quite a shock to discover in this way that her husband had fled into exile. "It really hurt my feelings," she admitted. "The whole thing caused me to think of what had happened before."

Over the years, she had heard from her husband infrequently, through secret couriers. "The only people I'd get frequent visits from were the police. Immediately I'd fear the worst," she continued. "Then I'd ask them if he's still alive and they'd say yes. The police would confiscate his letters." "*Kwakuba buhlungu mangabe engihlukumeza . . .*," she added. The police brought dogs and commanded them to attack her, but she took comfort from their visits because she figured the fact that they were still bothering her meant that Zuma was probably still alive.

She confirmed the stories her husband already had told me about how she had lost their baby shortly after his second disappearance and how she tried to cross into Swaziland to join him shortly afterward, but she didn't volunteer any other details. Was it a terrible experience? She paused, as if considering this question for the first time. "Yes," she said, rubbing her hands along the fabric of the couch.

MaKhumalo proved to be the model interviewee; she was direct, unstinting, and concise. I noticed that she passed up any opportunity to amplify on her own sorrows or play up her own quiet heroism. She shrugged when I said that it had been such a long wait while he was in prison, and then even longer while he was in exile when she could not be sure she would ever see him again. "It's inevitable that something like this could happen and not be emotionally disturbing," she said, looking at her hands.

She also confirmed that her husband had managed to get word to her, through a messenger, that he had met another woman while living in exile. It was Nkosazana Dlamini, she recalled, and in the message he had sent, he asked for her permission to take the woman as his wife. "I gave the go-ahead because we weren't together at that time, and if we were meant to be—we'll *be*," she told me. "I also didn't want him dying and not being there for his kids."

When Zuma finally returned from exile, her husband looked quite different. "Fat," she said, raising her eyebrows. Even so, she had felt over-joyed to welcome him back home. They had resumed their relationship, even though by this time he was also married to two other women, who would bear nine children between them.

Through the intervening years, MaKhumalo said that she felt con-tent to remain in Nkandla. At President Mbeki's inauguration in 1999, she was the woman among his many partners to accompany Zuma down the long red carpet. If she felt neglected, either because of his various marriages or because of his many affairs, she didn't say so.

Her husband's meteoric rise in the ANC and the country's politics clearly had taken her by surprise. If he wanted, now, to become president of the ANC and then president of the Republic of South Africa, she seemed quietly resigned, as she had been about so many of his other uni-lateral choices. "I'd like that for him," she offered softly.

When I told MaKhumalo that one of the reasons I had wanted to speak with her was that so little had been written about the price paid by the women who stayed behind, waiting for their warriors to return, her shoulders relaxed and she sank back into the couch. "That's beautiful," she murmured. Nobody else had ever bothered to ask for her point of view. Then she excused herself to get back to work. After all, the home-stead was a large operation and the hullabaloo caused by her husband's return meant there was a rather large mess to clean up.

On a trip to the area around Zuma's ancestral homeland a month earlier, I had caught up with him at a big rally in the nearby village of Nkandla proper. When he and the other key speaker of the day, trade union leader Zwelinzima Vavi, had entered the local stadium, a chorus erupted: "Tell us Mbeki, what have you done with Chris Hani?" The ubiquity of this song at Zuma rallies was a nasty piece of work. The implication of the lyrics, shamelessly promoted by the president's enemies, was that Mbeki was involved somehow in the 1993 assassination of guerrilla hero Chris Hani.

Hani was actually murdered, as had been well established in a criminal trial, by white supremacists, but since he had been a wildly popular man of the Left—an MK commander, unapologetic socialist, and longtime critic of Thabo Mbeki—it had become a common jab among Zuma supporters to tag Mbeki as a coconspirator in the assassination. This was the kind of ugly rumor that poisoned South African politics in 2007–2009. Zuma said nothing to the people singing, and likewise nothing to the organizers of the rally, and didn't say a thing to the crowd arrayed in front of him, when he spoke, to correct the record.

From another section of the audience came one in a series of lionizing stanzas: "Zuma's heart is so wide and clean / That he can hide under it / The bleeding that he did! / I cannot think of going to the IFP / Because your heart is so clean!" In the populist rhetoric that characterized his campaign, here was the operative overview reduced to two ditties: President Mbeki was an errant saboteur of the revolution and Zuma's history of suffering on behalf of the people cleansed him for the ascension.

The latter song especially stuck with me on the dusty drive out of the village. On my way back to the coast, I picked up three hitchhikers in a row. The first was an unemployed, and orphaned, twenty-two-year-old man who had finished high school but had no resources for college. The second was a mournful-looking teenager who had been forced to drop out of high school in eighth grade because his family couldn't afford the fees. He knew that education was supposed to be his passport out of poverty, but this solution was held just beyond his reach.

The third hitchhiker was a twenty-four-year-old named Wonderboy Mathenjwa. He was the son of a single mother who had managed to secure a spot in the first-year class at the University of Zululand. It was a remarkable achievement in a family where nobody else had gone to college. Mathenjwa had scraped together his first year's tuition with money raised by his uncle from neighbors in his home village, and he had studied hard by candlelight each night because he figured that he carried the expectations of his entire village on his shoulders.

On the way back to the coast, I turned off to the south in order to give him a ride all the way back to the university. It was a vast complex carved out of the forest near the town of Empangeni. Wonderboy had a broad forehead, almond-shaped eyes, and the wisp of a moustache dusting his upper lip. He wore faded blue jeans and a tan short-sleeved shirt with white thread spelling out "ROCKSTAR" across his chest. "I think Zuma will win," he predicted, when I told him where I had been. "Thabo Mbeki looked after the Xhosa people because he's a Xhosa. We think we need a Zulu guy in there. He'll make it better for us."

Wonderboy's own family had been stalwart supporters of Chief Buthelezi's Inkatha Freedom Party for generations. During the worst violence in the early 1990s, his mother had been forced to flee for her life when ANC-aligned militants rampaged through her village and burned her shack to the ground. But Wonderboy found himself supporting the leader of the party whose followers once tried to kill his mother because he felt certain that Zuma alone was capable of bringing development to the poverty-stricken region.

Lots of the other students felt similarly, he said, estimating that 90 percent of them were behind the ANC if it became a Zuma-led party. "People my age don't love politics," he cautioned. "Belonging to the ANC is sort of the style for youth today, though."

When I turned off the highway to drop him off on the campus,

Wonderboy invited me in. There was an impressive cluster of old class-rooms and new computer labs, and I got out of the car to peer through the windows. At the edge of campus he lived in a small, eight-by-eight-foot room in a row of similar hovels. The concrete walls were pock-marked and stained from where the rain had gotten in. White paint had peeled off in strips, curling at the ends. There was a single electrical out-let and a makeshift table with the *Oxford English Dictionary* stacked atop his assignments for the day.

Behind a small hot plate, on a small tray beside a single canister of rice, he had stashed cooking oil, curry powder, sugar, and salt. His stick of Mum deodorant and tube of Nivea body lotion were set on another plastic tray next to his cot. Wonderboy showed me the course of study he intended to pursue to become a social worker, which he had taken up because he believed the country urgently needed more social workers and community development specialists "because of all the dysfunction" that had come along with rapid political change.

When we walked around the campus to visit his friends, they all seemed in a relatively high state of anxiety. Most were barely scraping by in order to be able to continue studying. The young women we met mentioned casually that female students regularly turned to prostitu-tion to pay tuition; they also described a harrowing war between the sexes taking place on the campus, with Friday-night gang rapes, called "streamlining," a regular weekly event. Former lovers disappeared when-ever the girls they were dating fell pregnant.

When I related these stories to the young men we met, they gri-maced at what the young women had said. But they replied, as if defending the entire gender, that it was women who spoiled any pros-pect of romance or normal dating by hooking up with older men whose only attraction was that they had money.

The young men also ticked off the names of contemporaries back home who had not bothered to apply to university, but had become quickly wealthy instead through illegal businesses. The temptation to follow their example was fierce when the honest route to mobility was still quite narrow. "The ones who have the money are the ones who break the rules and steal," Wonderboy said. "They're the ones with the houses and the cars!"

In recent surveys of sexual behavior I had read, there was a suggestion that young women and men were beginning to delay the beginning of their sex lives in response to the AIDS catastrophe. This was a shift from the global pattern of ever-younger initiation into sexual relationships. It was also contrary to the conventional wisdom presented in the press.

When I mentioned these studies, Wonderboy looked somber. After a long, uncomfortable pause, he admitted a deep, penetrating fear of sex. He had seen sex lead to so many deaths. "I know that by waiting, I'm not losing," he added. "I'm gaining—gaining my days." His best female friend from high school had died of AIDS the year before. He said that she had knowingly infected men right before she died because she had felt angry, and betrayed, about her own condition. At the age of twenty-four, then, he had never made love. Wonderboy sometimes dated, just for show, he said, because that kept the other guys off his back. It allowed him to ward off untrue accusations that he was gay.

It occurred to me that this was the flip side of the fear of rape and the intense pressure to have sex early that had been described for me by boys and girls at the elementary school back in Johannesburg. Locking themselves in their rooms to read, under the circumstances, seemed like a perfectly healthy response. But seeing the sad expression on Wonderboy's face as he described the fear of sex he felt, and the loneliness that came with never dating, I also thought about the potential costs, individually and culturally, of sexual repression. All that energy, in adolescence and into the twenties, was being expended in holding back and canceling out the impulse to draw closer, date, court, and connect. What would be the consequences for this younger generation forced to respond to a fear of intimacy by killing off desire? Among young men, at least, some of the admiration they felt for Jacob Zuma was related to the fact that he had escaped their fate.

Back at Nkandla a month later, I spent much of the afternoon with Jacob Zuma's brothers down by the kraal. Joseph had been busy supervising preparations for the feast. He was older by a few months, offspring of the woman Zuma had called his "Elder Mother." From his appearance, though, you might have guessed that he was at least a decade senior. He towered over the other men but walked unsteadily in an old man's stoop. His hair was shot through with gray and his eyes were cloudy, crowded with cataracts.

Joseph attributed his health to years of manual labor at the Dunlop chemical plant in Durban. Respirators hadn't been provided in the years he worked there, he explained. He remembered that the dust often had been so thick inside the factory you could barely see. "When the bosses came in, they would come in white and go out looking black," he reported, laughing.[7]

When Jacob had returned to the village in 1990, he asked Joseph to come home and look after things for him. Joseph figured that this move had probably saved his life. Most of his friends who had remained working at the chemical plant were dead by now. "It was very bad," he said. "But my brother—he is very clever."

He spoke of his slightly younger sibling with unveiled awe. They had been raised in the same place, with the same opportunities, and yet somehow Jacob had risen to unimaginable heights. Joseph said that he had only come to fully realize how important his brother was when together they had visited the royal residence of the Zulu king, Goodwill Zwelithini, a year earlier. He had heard with his own ears the king promise that he would help swing the support of Zulu-speaking people toward the ANC if Zuma was chosen to lead the party. The king and the commoner had spoken together like equals—that was what astonished Joseph.

When the younger brother, Mike, joined us, they took turns trying to answer a question I kept posing: Why had this one sibling—among twelve children raised by two mothers—turned out so differently from all the rest? They shrugged their shoulders, looking puzzled. His brothers felt their sibling had distinguished himself from the start. They remembered that he had organized the other children to ask a neighbor who was literate to teach them how to write their own names. "He was a leader right away," Mike murmured. "He started to lead us, and tell us that we must go to school."[8]

There was something else he dredged up from his memory that drew my interest: it was the image of his brother working hard to master traditional Zulu stick fighting, called *ukuxoshisa*. Stick fighting was a central aspect of male bonding in traditional Zulu life. It was a means of containing conflict, but it was also a practice of physical discipline that involved maintenance of one's balance even when under attack.

Traditionally, Zulu boys went into the forest with their fathers at about the age of sixteen. They cut their own *induku* and *ubhoko*, striking sticks and blocking sticks. Sometimes the ends of these sticks were treated with *intelezi*—herbal extracts, cobra venom, or menstrual blood—to render the other fighter impotent.[9]

Mike remembered that Jacob had taken up the sport much earlier than normal. He had also fashioned a distinctive, unconventional, and stunningly effective style. Unlike the other boys, Mike said, his brother sometimes dispensed with the formalities. He would offer his opponents a smiling visage and avoid the traditional stances expected in the ritualized combat.

Ukuxoshisa was a test of quickness, balance, and misdirection. Winning blows were landed by whiplike motions involving a sudden flip of the wrist mid-strike and then ending in smacks to the head, torso, and legs of the opponent. These outside-to-inside maneuvers, which martial artists called "progressive indirect attack," were difficult to master.

Zuma had proved precociously expert. Sometimes, the young boy held his sticks casually, as if on a lark, as Mike remembered it. Occasionally he even turned away from his opponent to crack a joke with other kids standing around. When his opponent dropped his guard or joined in the teasing, though, Zuma would pivot swiftly and strike suddenly, sweeping his opponent off his feet.

Now I understood better why his friends considered Zuma's Zulu name, *Gedleyihlekisa*—the man who laughed while he endangered you— so appropriate. Stick fighting was essentially a form of combat in which one turned the fury of an adversary back against him. It was principally a test of balance and timing rather than brute strength. This seemed like a fair description of what Zuma had in mind for Mbeki—laying back, controlling his temper, feigning modesty, staying chill even as he prepared to wipe the floor with his comrade president.

When I asked the brothers about the broken relationship between Mbeki and Zuma, they expressed regret. "Mbeki doesn't come here," Joseph pointed out. It did seem strange that someone considered a life-long comrade for decades should never have visited the family.

Mike supposed that the row had something to do with their differences over Communism, but he wasn't sure exactly how. "The Boer government used to say we mustn't like the Communists—Communists are a bad thing," he offered, hesitating because he feared wandering out of his depth. "What we see now is those people—they're good, they're not bad," he continued. He believed that Mbeki didn't agree with this assessment.

"Until today, our mind is upside down at what you hear in the TV and the radio," Mike said, anger in his voice. "You see the face of the man *chancing* another man." He said that he had once visited Brother, as he referred to Jacob, in Johannesburg and had seen how easily Mbeki and Zuma used to move around one another. "I don't know what is happening now."

Whenever he criticized Mbeki in front of Jacob, though, he was sternly reprimanded. "Even now he don't talk bad about Mbeki," he reported. "Even now, he says, 'He's our president.'" The whole saga had left Mike feeling quite confused. "To us, he's enemy. But himself, he don't treat him as his enemy. He treats him as his brother, even today!"

As we talked, we could see Zuma ambling from one end of the compound to the other. He slipped away periodically for short side meetings with provincial officials and foreign businessmen. The businessmen included a mysterious Italian man who had dodged me when I asked him what he was doing in Nkandla. He had offered no name and hadn't even bothered to come up with a reasonable cover story.

The Italian businessman and a second group of visitors surrendered their cell phones when they went off to have private discussions with Zuma. This was a mark partly of Zuma's caution and also of his heightened sensitivity about conversations that involved money he was raising for the campaign. Not incidentally, it was also a reminder that so many people in South African politics, journalism, and judicial circles now figured, as a matter of course, that their conversations were being recorded.

"Why should you be a nervous person here?" Zuma had asked when we found ourselves together, sitting on the porch earlier that afternoon. Actually, there were many reasons for him to feel cautious. Earlier in the day he had learned from his lawyers that the National Prosecuting Authority was preparing to formally charge him again with bribery, corruption, and tax evasion.

Much of the president's Cabinet, many of them people Zuma had worked beside for decades, had spread out around the country in a final push within the party to end Zuma's career. They had been calling him corrupt, illiterate, a boor, and a rapist in meetings with the ANC rank-and-file. The chairman of the ANC, Mosiuoa Lekota, even had announced that any party member singing *"Awuleth' Umshini Wam',"* the ode that Zuma's supporters had appropriated on his behalf, must be mentally deranged.

It was down to the wire now in the branch-by-branch elections of delegates. Over the following weekend, provincial gatherings would offer a preview of what was likely to happen at the party's national conference. Text messages were coming in steadily on the cell phone belonging to Zuma's oldest son, Edward. Every once in a while another message would arrive, and he would walk over to whisper in his father's ear. In an aside, Edward Zuma said of Mbeki, "I know the president very well—he was always thick-headed." He believed that his father would prevail in provincial meetings in every part of the country, even in the president's backyard, the Eastern Cape. That eventuality would put the lie to the notion that Zuma was a regional or ethnic candidate.

Toward the end of our conversation on the porch that afternoon, I pressed Zuma on the kinds of changes he would make if he were placed in charge of the country. First, he said, rural development was key. It had been neglected in the Mbeki years, Zuma claimed. No one should ever have to drop out of school for lack of school fees, he added with an edge. I told him a little about Wonderboy's plight, and he leaned forward, growing suddenly animated.

He volunteered that toilets were important, too. He had studied up on a new technology that produced indoor units that used no water. Here, he felt certain, was something within the government's power to fix. The second thing he mentioned was the size of the homes built by the government under the Reconstruction and Development Program. "They're so small," he said, making his voice sound tiny, too. Entire communities had been designed without taking into account the size of African families. He thought there was something dehumanizing, un-African even, about the reduction of family life to tiny European-style nuclear family units in the informal settlements and townships. His ideas for reform of government were rooted in the vantage point of villages like Nkandla.

Near dusk, Zuma's brothers led him to the kraal. The skin of the ox slaughtered earlier in the day was still slick with traces of blood and viscera. Corn porridge had left yellowish streaks in the large cast-iron pots. On the grills only gristle remained. All the men had been served first, and now the women were eating and talking on the porch of a rondavel down below. The voices of the women were muted, carried on a slight breeze.

Two giant gourds were empty and tipped over; the homemade beer had been polished off. Zuma watched with a wry smile as the younger men tried to navigate across uneven ground, knock-kneed and tipsy. They sat on thin round logs to keep their pants from being soiled in the mud, listening to his brother's invocation.

Mike Zuma called on the intercession of the ancestors on behalf of Jacob Zuma. Traditional healers were already lined up across the country to canvass help from the spirit world in the campaign against Thabo Mbeki. On the day before, I had spoken to a local headman who had credited herbs and objects blessed by *inyangas*, or medicine men, for Zuma's victories so far. Powerful magical artifacts used on Zuma's behalf, called *muti*, had been provided to protect him.

When I had asked Mike about the particular *inyanga* widely credited with doing the job for his brother, he cautioned me that all sorts of people were now taking credit for his rise. "The story you heard is inaccurate," he had said stiffly. "It's inaccurate because it's the conversation with the ancestors that makes the difference—not the *inyanga* and not the *muti*."

There were blurts of shit where the animals had been dragged for slaughter. Zuma stood behind a wooden platter on which several bones of the oxen had been placed. Mike Zuma stepped toward the bones, opening his arms to the sky and calling on the ancestors for their help. "Thank you to God for this opportunity. For giving Jacob Zuma the chance to buy us this ox," he began in Zulu, addressing the heavens. "He always thinks about hungry people, homeless people . . ."

As he spoke, his brother's cell phone buzzed. Jacob Zuma glanced at the text, torn for a moment between the chance to communicate with the spirits and the more prosaic demands of the modern world. He bowed his head, arms crossed over the silk shirt. When Mike was done, Zuma wandered off to return the call. It was something important, apparently, but also secret. He summoned his driver, and the motorcade zipped away, carrying him back to Durban.

I stayed behind, to sleep overnight in the rondavel where Zuma had met with the mysterious Italian. The sun, a blazing blood-red orb, set behind the ridge. A light drizzle began. Darkness settled in, and sudden lightning strikes flashed across the valley. This was a kind of lightning I had never seen before. It seemed to move horizontally from ridge to ridge rather than vertically from sky to ground.

When I marveled at the sight, Mike Zuma claimed that this was how lightning always flashed in and out of these mountains. He said that rainbows did the same thing. I would see it in the morning, he promised. Rainbows in Nkandla spread along the ground rather than rising and receding into the distance, Mike claimed.

Thunder rumbled close by then. Were the ancestors applauding or were they upset? I could never get these signals straight: Friends some- times told me that when it rained like this in Johannesburg it meant the ancestors were upset about something—they were crying. But the same people, on different days, when things were going well in their lives, would say to me that the ancestors approved of them—because it was *raining*, wasn't it?

In the valley below, grazing land in the flood plain next to the milky river was dotted with thatched roofs. When the sun went down, stars lit up the sky. The rhythms of rural existence delivered a counterpoint to the busy syncopation of Johannesburg. It seemed natural to fall into con- versation about intercession by the ancestors here, the use of *muti*, the influence of *inyangas*, and the curious horizontal paths of lightning and rainbows.

Jacob Zuma, of course, was no true son of the soil of Nkandla. His brothers were. Zuma himself hadn't lived in Nkandla steadily since he was a child. He was as much a creature of Robben Island, Swaziland and Mozambique, Johannesburg, Cape Town, and Pretoria as he was of this village. He moved in and out of it, but he wasn't bound by its rules or limitations.

Mike Zuma told me, as we sat under the starlight, that on mornings when good things happened for his brother, rainbows jumped out from the base of the opposite hillside and shot in an arc across the valley. They rippled right along the ground through the compound. You could dance inside the bands of color, he said. "That's what had happened on the day Brother was acquitted of rape," he said. He swirled his arms around and lifted his legs, as though climbing back into the rainbow, shimmying around as he had done on that day.

The brothers told me that they understood how most smart observers still assumed that Mbeki, the educated, intellectual leader, would prevail over Brother, once a barefoot, uneducated boy. But Mike Zuma remembered vividly that sensation of walking inside a multicolored rainbow, and he expected another rainbow like it to come splashing across the meadow soon.

18.

Polokwane

Finally after a two-year buildup, the open and fiery confrontation between Thabo Mbeki and Jacob Zuma was on. It was December 16, 2007, and the drama unfolded on the soccer field of the University of Limpopo, outside Polokwane, a six-hour drive north from Johannesburg. Limpopo was the poorest province in the country, and home for the boys I had met in mid-2006 in Bungeni.

Holding the ANC national meeting in such an impoverished rural area was intended as a signal of the governing party's continued identification with the poor. But all you had to do was walk through the side entrance to the massive tent where the meeting was held to understand that something dramatic was happening.

South Africa's paramount leaders were sitting side by side on a huge dais beneath a gigantic banner that read, "BUILDING A CARING SOCIETY." Below that invocation was the tag line: "ADVANCING IN UNITY TOWARDS 2012." The slogans, and show of camaraderie onstage, were pure artifice.

Through thousands of delegates elected at the grass roots, the national conference would set the direction of the country for the next five years. There was a populist spirit running through the proposals that had been refined for consideration by the ANC National Conference, the party's highest policy-making body, with special attention paid to institutions the delegates thought were *untransformed*—the judiciary and the media. The key tension working its way around, beneath, and through these proposals, however, revolved around the two men at the center of the platform.

Flanking them on the far left was Communist Party leader Blade Nzimande, conspicuously reading from that morning's *City Press*, held up and out so the delegates could see the front-page story headlined, "MISTAKES I MADE—MBEKI." The health minister, who had recently returned to office after recovering from liver transplant surgery, turned to give Nzimande a sour look.

From the openings in the massive tent you could see bare, taupe-colored hills and a few mangy cows grazing in the distance. Rolls of razor wire topped the cyclone fences at the edge of the campus, and there were three more layers around the entrances to the university. Local police, presidential security, and army patrols were monitoring the perimeters and the dormitories, classrooms, and fields in between. There were rumors that Zuma's followers would march on the convention if he lost the balloting. One of his backers even bragged that the unruly scenes outside courtrooms hearing the cases against Zuma would be child's play compared to the insurrection that would break out if President Mbeki "stole the vote."

In a sense, the tight security was an indication that the president's men still held out hope that they would prevail in the balloting. One of Mbeki's close advisors said that I was about to see the difference between the Zuma forces, who were chanting and raising a hullabaloo, and the Mbeki people, who he said were far more disciplined and would simply, quietly, reelect their leader.

Outside the tent, several of Zuma's best-known supporters peered past the flaps. Mac Maharaj, the former minister of transport under President Mandela, was there. Mo Shaik, brother of Schabir and one of Zuma's closest allies, fiddled with his pipe on a walkway that ran between the university dorms. Ranjeni Munusamy, who had worked steadily for three years behind the scenes to build an image for Zuma as a responsible leader, worried her nails to their nubs while shuttling back and forth to the media room. Billy Masetlha, President Mbeki's former chief of national intelligence (the president had fired him), stumbled across the field behind the tent, toasting whoever happened by with an open bottle partly concealed in a brown paper sack.

The former deputy minister of health, Nozizwe Madlala-Routledge, made her way from one circle of anxious delegates to the next, speaking of the kinds of additional health interventions that might be possible under a Zuma administration. The president had sacked her earlier in the year for raising a stink over hospital conditions in the Eastern Cape. She was a reminder of all of the enemies the president had accumulated during ten years as president of the party. The mining billionaire I had seen at the launch of the new AIDS policy, Patrice Motsepe, made his way past her, greeting the majordomos of both camps, and making it clear he wasn't a diehard committed to either side.

Presidential advisor Joel Netshitenzhe, dressed in a blue nylon tracksuit and laden with a big stack of documents, hurried past. He was a strategic thinker about government and long-term social policy. When I had gone to see him in Pretoria numerous times over the past couple of years, he had always taken the long view of party history. Netshitenzhe liked slapping down the conventional wisdom, especially when it was based on the accounts of South African journalists. In our conversations, he had pooh-poohed the idea that Mbeki was autocratic or stifled free expression among those who worked beside him. These were misimpressions, he had said, repeated by ill-informed reporters.

When we had spoken a few months earlier, Netshitenzhe also had told me that Zuma was a long shot for the presidency. In a more recent conversation in his office at Union Buildings, he had seemed less confident. His hands shook when he held them out, and when he bent forward, I could see that his bald spot, once an inconspicuous circle just two years earlier, had enlarged to the circumference of a large orange. The internecine fight had clearly taken a toll on him.

The ANC, he remarked with a rueful tone, had never selected a "factional leader," and he implied that this was what Zuma had turned himself into, a thoroughly divisive force. He felt it "wasn't impossible, because nothing is impossible," that Zuma would prevail, but he also considered it exceedingly long odds.[1] Netshitenzhe also had dismissed predictions that his own name would turn up as a candidate on President Mbeki's slate for top positions. The conference would result in a mix of leaders being elected from varied factions, as one might expect in a normal democracy, he insisted. It would be contrary to the culture of the party for there to be rigid slates, he went on.

In the unlikely event that slate voting occurred, Netshitenzhe had thought that neither side would be allowed to sweep all six top posts, a key piece of business for the national conference. He had circled back, several times in this earlier conversation, to the value of collective leadership, and spoke of the kind of wisdom that emanated from the processes of collective decision-making, as though he was a scientist discussing emergent properties of a biological system.

By the opening session of the convention, it was clear from all discussions swirling around that there were only two fixed, divided slates of candidates—one put forward by Zuma acolytes and the other by Mbeki diehards. Netshitenzhe's name, in spite of his misgivings, had been put forward as the nominee for chair on the Mbeki list, which put him up against the current speaker of the National Assembly, Baleka Mbete. The clash of personalized politics that he had thought should be avoided in Polokwane had come to pass. Now, he was among the candidates at the intersection of the collision.

Inside the tent, his leader, President Mbeki, looked more elfin than ever up on the platform. He was a petite man, swallowed up in a rather large chair, dressed in a simple blue knit shirt and faded khaki pants. Looking out on the delegates from across the country, he raised his unruly white eyebrows as if surprised to find himself in such rowdy company. Mbeki had fourteen months left to serve in his second term as leader of the Republic of South Africa, so the stakes for him were exceedingly high. If he lost control of the party machinery now, his power as head of state would also begin to leach away.

The opening of the ANC's 2007 conference, then, was an unfolding nightmare for the president and his followers. On the floor there was a cacophony, the sound of a rebellion playing on and on. The insulting songs directed at him during the campaign were now shouted out in his presence. Thousands of voices refused to follow the script that had been written for them by him.

The delegates sang and chanted past the opening gavel, refusing to sit politely in their chairs so the convention could begin. This marked a sharp break from the previous fifty years of party history. As I had seen myself at the National Working Group meeting at the University of Pretoria two years earlier—when Mbeki was rebuked behind closed doors but praised when the media was allowed back into the hall—public sessions of party business were usually group professions of party discipline and solidarity.

Competition for the top jobs had never been so fierce or implicated in open and militant campaigning. The top positions within the ANC historically were held for long periods. When the apartheid regime outlawed the ANC, the party was led by just two leaders, Chief Albert Luthuli and Oliver Tambo. When the ban on the party was lifted in 1990, selection of the president typically involved discussion among a tight inner circle, with the decision heavily determined from the top.

When the ANC came above ground to operate legally again, top positions below the level of the presidency were contested, but party elders, including Mandela, intervened to discourage such competition. In 1992, when Thabo Mbeki and Chris Hani, the former guerrilla leader assassinated in 1993, gathered support for candidacies for the deputy president's position, the inner circle ordered both of them to stand down. Walter Sisulu, the ailing leader from Mandela's generation, was installed in the post in the name of unity.

In hindsight, this had been a lost opportunity to instill the habit of democratic decision-making. A head-to-head contest between Hani and Mbeki, with real political differences spelled out between them, might have accelerated the process of turning the organization into a more representative and democratically run political party. (Many of the elders, like Ebrahim Ebrahim, believed that in a fair contest Hani would have trounced Mbeki.)

The battle between Mbeki and Zuma, in other words, had forced long suppressed differences into the open and pressed the ANC to entertain more robust debate, internally and in public. The national conference of 2007 had jettisoned all the old habits. This was the point that businessman Tokyo Sexwale made to me when I bumped into him on the way to the tent. He had spent a considerable chunk of his own private fortune during the previous year trying to put himself forward as a "third way" compromise candidate for president. His campaign had fallen flat, widely excoriated within the party for having been conducted in the "U.S. style," stressing personality over ideological rigor.

Sexwale had served as premier of Gauteng province, the economic center of the country, before going into business. He was, in effect, the candidate of Joburg—suave, smart, cosmopolitan, and relentlessly au courant, as my snap survey of students at Melpark Elementary School a few months earlier showed. Ultimately, he had come across to delegates as too smooth, too Westernized, and too wealthy to be embraced by the party of the people.

In recent weeks, Sexwale had thrown in his lot with Zuma, even helping fund the final months of the campaign. "This is democracy at its finest," he told me as we approached the tent close enough to hear the roar of the crowd. "What we have right now is a division around leadership, and what is wrong with that? People are clamoring for change. They're demanding to be heard. Isn't that the nature of democracy?"[2]

Back inside the tent, up at the podium, party chairman Mosiuoa Lekota admonished delegates concerning what he called their boisterous, "uncomradely" behavior. Lekota had been elected chair of the ANC in 1997 as an independent reformer willing to criticize both Mbeki and Zuma. At the time, he was the darling of the Left, having come up in Black Consciousness circles as a student organizer. In the 1980s Lekota was a key leader in the United Democratic Front, the voice of the *inziles*—movement activists who had remained inside the country to fight for freedom. During the previous year, though, Lekota had spoken out in increasingly strident terms against Zuma's candidacy. His former allies had turned on him with a vengeance, criticizing him as a Mbeki toady.

Now he was getting a public comeuppance. From the first time Lekota smacked the gavel down in the opening moments of the conference right through to the end, you could tell he had lost the respect of his comrades and control of the crowd. When it was over, he would tell me he considered the rebellion "foreign to the ANC." He cautioned delegates that the flooring beneath their feet might collapse if they "made too much volume," so they tramped past the stage and jumped up and down.

From his seat on the stage, Zuma studied the chairman idly, the way a herder might track a goat. His supporters sang praise songs for Zuma loudly and shouted anti-Mbeki taunts throughout the proceedings. Delegates backing Mbeki mounted a counterdemonstration then, holding their hands up, palms in, with three fingers splayed to signal they were supporting his reelection for a third term. The Zuma forces jeered and rotated their hands in rapid circles, like fans at a soccer match who were signaling for a change of players.

In the late stages of the struggle against white rule, the ANC had broadcast appeals to its followers inside the country, calling on them to "make the country ungovernable." It seemed to me, now, that Zuma's supporters were registering the point that they could make the *party* ungovernable if Mbeki continued at the helm.

Twice, just when it seemed as though the convention was about to veer completely out of control, Zuma nodded his head in the direction of Secretary-General Kgalema Motlanthe. It was a slight gesture; you had to be looking closely at the two men to catch it. Zuma nodded, and Motlanthe rose to wave Lekota away from the podium. Both times, when Motlanthe replaced his "comrade chair" after politely asking for a moment at the microphone, the shouting died. The secretary-general spoke softly then and held himself with his trademark solemn dignity. Everyone hushed to hear him, the assembled four thousand party members jostling right back to order. It felt as though we were witnessing, in real time, the process of power flowing from one key leader to the next.

Mbeki sank a little lower in his seat, and Lekota, still the ANC chairman in name only, stood off to the side of the stage, twirling his arms like a band conductor who had fallen off the beat. Zuma glanced at Mbeki, checking to see whether his ex-comrade had gotten the point. When President Mbeki rose to offer his formal report to the convention, he seemed completely off kilter. Working his way through a forty-one-page address, he bowed his head to the text. It was a fairly encyclopedic recitation of everything the government had accomplished during the first thirteen years of democracy.

The president emphasized the strides made over the years in elevating the participation of women—30 percent at every level of leadership—and called for this conference to ratchet up to 50/50 parity going forward. He ticked off lots of numbers: there were forty-three women named to the Cabinet during his presidency, and four of nine premiers were female.

"The struggle to defeat patriarchy is central, an integral part of the National Democratic Revolution," he said. The unspoken subtext was that his candidate for deputy president was not Jacob Zuma this time, as it had been a decade earlier, but rather Nkosazana Dlamini-Zuma, the country's foreign minister and the ex-wife of his rival. Even in its late stages, the breach between the two leaders seemed like an intensely personal, even family affair.

Mbeki spoke, too, of the dream of an African Renaissance, warning that none of the revolutionary goals for which generations of martyrs had died could be achieved "unless the ANC remains strong and united." He warned that the party had been infiltrated by people who were simply out for "access to resources" and patronage, who would do anything to get contracts from the government "by hook or by crook."

There was a danger, he added, of people buying ANC membership cards and turning members of the party at the local level into a "captive group of voting cattle." Here, he clearly had in mind the promises of the trade union federation and Communist Party to flood the branches and pack local ANC meetings with workers and party members who supported Zuma. The president rebutted what he called "outright falsehoods about our leadership."

Sitting in the middle of the stage as Mbeki spoke, Zuma appeared to be speed-reading ahead a printed copy of the leader's remarks. When the president mentioned the "hoax emails" that had been passed around to make the case that there was a conspiracy against the deputy president, Zuma colored visibly. He still believed that many of the discredited emails were genuine.

Mbeki's address certainly seemed like a curious way to smooth divisions over or win back the affections of the crowd. Perhaps he had made a decision to say what was on his mind no matter how non-strategic it seemed. He plowed on then, highlighting the key areas where he thought his critics were manifestly wrong. The president offered an analysis of the destructive dynamics at work within the organization, but he sketched not a single new idea about the way forward. If the party was now full of members, as he claimed, with "limited consciousness," whose fault was that? He had been top leader of the ANC for more than a decade.

Toward the end of his speech, he quoted the Leninist nostrum "better fewer, but better." It was difficult to discern the relevance of this slogan of Vladimir Lenin in a multiparty democracy: was Mbeki actually suggesting that the ANC would become more effective by *shrinking*?

Their leader told ANC delegates that the party had "gravitated off its moral axis" because of riches available to officials in control of the government. But, then, who had been the head of the government all this time? Who had promoted and protected the corrupt commissioner of police, Jackie Selebi, who was seen on the first day of the conference lobbying for the president among arriving delegates? Who had pressed for the expensive package of military purchases that, through kickbacks and bribes, had done more to corrupt the political system than any other single act?

Toward the end of his address the president asked rhetorically, "What divides us?" It was an essential question, and he was prepared to go on, but just then several delegates shouted back, "*You!*" He looked up from his text then, his brows stitched together, looking startled. When he finished, the hall exploded into showy rival demonstrations. Members of the ANC were more divided than ever, and the National Democratic Revolution was about to devour some of its own.

Three days later, right before the results were announced, I broke away from the cordon of monitors placed around journalists covering the event, and wandered into the middle of the vast crowd of delegates. The casting of ballots the day before had been followed by an entire day and night of counting them, all by hand. Zuma's forces had insisted on the hand counting, saying they were fearful that Mbeki's operatives would tamper somehow with the computers ready for the tabulation. It was an odd reflex, playing into the ethnic-inflected stereotypes about Xhosa speakers being *too clever*.

The delegates were crammed shoulder-to-shoulder and hip-to-hip in cramped rows of plastic chairs, with narrow aisles between delegations. Everybody looked bleary-eyed and rumpled, punchy and tired. Right away, I noticed that the body language had shifted. The Zuma delegates carried themselves with a swagger, looking smug. The Mbeki supporters seemed more querulous, huddling together in their seats and chatting quietly. They crooned a lilting song in isiXhosa: "Thabo Mbeki—oooo, Thabo Mbeki—eeei! We are going there! Our Thabo is coming!" It sounded like a lullaby, not a tune for marshaling the troops.

There was a woman in the center of the Eastern Cape delegation holding up a handwritten sign: "JAIL IS WAITING / SHAME ON JZ," a reminder that Zuma's legal problems were far from settled. The delegate wore leather sandals, black stretch pants, and a red-and-black cotton sweater. "Fighting for freedom was not easy," she told me, pointing her finger at my notebook to make sure I took it down. "But when we got freedom, something went wrong. How do you go from good to bad in just ten years? Our country is going down, inside and in the eyes of the world. What will it be like for the children?" She turned in the direction of the KwaZulu-Natal delegation, raised her bottle of water, and mimed that she was washing her face with it. It was an insulting gesture, of course, to imply that the delegates could use a good cleansing.

A group of Zulu-speaking men wrapped in blankets tromped down in her direction, shouting insults. "Mbeki is too arrogant," one of them told me. "We don't want a Mugabe here." Another song broke out among the KwaZulu-Natal ranks: "Don't be afraid / Though the heart is pounding / So you must be cool / Take it like a man."

When Lekota came to the microphone to announce that the results were in, a massive cheer went up. The men behind me cried, "Bye-bye Lekota. Bye-bye!" As it turned out, it was not a close call. Zuma had beaten Mbeki for control of the ANC by a wide margin—2,329 delegates to 1,505, the exact reverse of what the president's operatives had expected. The announcement sparked pandemonium, which spread through the tent and onto the field outside. Delegates standing next to me vibrated as though in the midst of a religious experience, much like the feel and sound of the people gathered in Soweto's Mofolo Park who had celebrated so joyously South Africa's win in the competition to host the 2010 World Cup.

Every top official placed on the Zuma slate won by nearly the same margin, with some of the party's longest-serving comrades thoroughly humiliated along with the president. In balloting to select a new, and enlarged, National Executive Committee, some of the stars of Mbeki's Cabinet were returned—notably Trevor Manuel, minister of finance—but many others, like the banker Saki Macozoma, were summarily dropped.

Swathed in green and gold, the ANC colors, Zuma looked remarkably dour and studiously un-triumphant as his victory was sealed. When the hall exploded in a paroxysm of emotion, he remained seated, staring into the distance. It looked as though he suddenly felt the full weight of the victory fall upon him.

The new president glanced down and to his right, where his just-defeated rival sat in a heap on a hard metal folding chair. The other ex-officials were clumped together around Thabo Mbeki, who was still president of South Africa and the most powerful leader in Africa, but no longer in charge of the ANC. Mbeki sat splayed out across his chair like an umbrella broken by the wind. In the midst of pandemonium, I bumped into Ebrahim Ebrahim, Zuma's longtime friend and advisor. "I'm happy, of course," he said, looking distressed. "But it's no time to be gloating. It's not a complete victory because of what's happening to the party beneath the surface."

As delegates dispersed, a loop of film from a documentary began to play, over and over, on the massive screens set on either side of the dais. It was archival footage of Nelson Mandela in military khakis, training for the armed revolution. There were guerrillas marching, and then scrambling on their bellies in the dust, training their rifles on targets.

This was the visual coda, as it turned out, to the ANC national conference of 2007. It was obviously intended as a reminder of the spirit of sacrifice and revolutionary ardor once inspired by disciplined black commandos prepared to confront a militarized white regime. The elevation of Zuma reminded everybody of the enduring influence within the ANC of fighters from Umkhonto we Sizwe, the armed underground.

In elevating Mandela as its leader back in the 1990s, the party had, in effect, memorialized the contributions of an older generation who had spent much of their lives in prison. During the second presidency, key government posts had been heavily populated with representatives of an elite class of former exiles, like Thabo Mbeki. Now, with the ascension of Zuma, here was genuflection, in the closing images of the meeting, toward those who had been willing to risk their lives in armed combat.

Zuma would later tell me that this moment of victory felt quite bittersweet. His considerable pride in the achievement was mixed with profound sorrow as he vanquished Mbeki, he said. "I was actually feeling more for *them* than anything else," he added. "I wouldn't want my comrades to be humiliated like that. We could have avoided it for the sake of the organization."

There was a long pause when he said this. Then the new president of the ANC sounded, rather suddenly, angry. "Why the elections were so much, almost like *do or die*—what *for?*" he demanded, as if I would know.[3] This was precisely what I had been hoping that he would reveal to me. It was the question that would bedevil the country for the next several years.

The fact that Zuma himself seemed puzzled and posed the questions in this way—*do or die, what for?*—meant that he had already been forced to take stock of the considerable costs involved in his victory. It wasn't just the reputation of the ANC that had been battered in the fight between his forces and Mbeki's. There also had been serious collateral damage to the political culture of an emerging democracy.

Since I had driven so far north to attend the national conference, the minute it was over I drove on to Bungeni. I had set out to track down the kids I had met the year before, no easy feat. It was a breezy summer day with a cool bite to the air, and a relief to escape from the noisy tent. The roads were clear for one of those flat-out drives across undulating hills pocked with heartseed lovegrass, sturdy green shoots, and hairy golden crowns. Grassland opened up to stands of giant-leaf fig trees.

Outside Polokwane I caught a glimpse of an African golden oriole, with its elegant canary body and sleek ebony head. The call of the bird sounded like a human voice, saying, "Phew!" Over the previous several months, I had called around Limpopo to try to find Talent and Vunene, and had managed to reach the latter's mother. We arranged to meet in town because, as it turned out, it was Vunene's fourteenth birthday.

We found each other at the bustling Kentucky Fried Chicken outlet, which was where he had announced that he wanted to have a special birthday lunch. In just a year and half since I had seen him last, Vunene had filled out and shot up considerably. His lanky body now cleared his mother's shoulders. He wore a sleeveless yellow Nike T-shirt and white soccer shorts, carrying himself with a great deal of confidence.

His mother, Elizabeth, was a tall, full-bodied woman with a broad face and serious expression. She wore a black stretch nylon shift over blue jeans. Mrs. Mabasa had split up with her husband not long after I had met the boys, which led to a disruptive year for the children, so she felt happy that we were about to bid farewell to 2007.

Though she made a decent salary as a nurse, she told me, it was quite hard for her to support two children on her own. They were sharing a small concrete home with her brother and his extended family. The boys slept together in a single room, and it was difficult to set aside space in the house for Vunene to study. The tradeoff, she said, was that she could accumulate savings in rent that would allow her to send Vunene to a good school.

After lunch I followed the Mabasa family to their home and, once inside, I saw what she meant. When we entered the small house, we found her brother, wife, and other relatives were wedged into adjoining couches watching music videos in the small lounge. All of the tables and counters were covered with belongings. Children of various ages flowed in and out.

There wasn't any space to sit and talk, so Vunene led me outside, where we watched his neighbors chase a scrawny bull down a dirt lane. We followed them past a collection of rondavels with thatched roofs and flaking azure paint. In the gaps between homes were small gardens, where patches of cornstalks flourished.

A group of six men cornered the bull, flipped a rope around its neck, and tied it to a nearby tree. Vunene told me they intended to sacrifice it in honor of the ancestors. One of the men produced a revolver, placed it in the center of the animal's head, and pulled the trigger. Blood bubbled up out of the wound, and the animal bellowed but it didn't fall. So the man fired again. And again. Bullets slammed into the bull's brain, but instead of falling it lunged for the shooter, reared up, and pulled away, breaking the thick rope around its neck. The men scattered, and the bull galloped past us down the hill. A stunned posse trailed after the bull, cursing and complaining. "That *bull*!" Vunene said, in awe.

We wandered uphill in the opposite direction past a group of children playing in an orchard. "You know, when we met and you told us you came from America, we didn't believe you at first," he said. Vunene remembered the conversation in great detail, even the part of it where the boys had told me that President Mbeki had "a little bit of apartheid" and Comrade JZ, by contrast, "had no apartheid." I asked him what they had meant. "It means he's a good guy," he said slowly. "It means he's friendly to us—black, white, nobody's better. He treats everybody equally."[4]

This was a twist on what I thought I had understood. I had been telling others that having "a little bit of apartheid," and using the name of a historical period to describe an aspect of someone's character, meant that the boys had seen Mbeki as someone stuck in the past and still in the service of white people. Vunene's elaboration of what he and Talent had meant in using the phrase tilted the meaning toward a nonracial interpretation.

As Vunene talked on, it was clear that he had had little contact with whites. In fact, I was the first white person he had engaged in more than superficial conversation. The only Afrikaans-speaking whites he had met were teachers at his elementary school. He reported that they never showed prejudice toward the children. "They're good to us as learners," he said.

There was another topic he wanted to revisit from our earlier discussion, mentioning the wild stuff his friends had said about females. It wasn't right, he murmured. He had since learned, from his mother, that women deserved more respect. Perhaps, he thought, it was her struggle for equal treatment within the family that was part of the reason for the breakup between his parents. Vunene confessed that he longed to see them together again.

In his early teens still, Vunene had a rather sophisticated view of the trouble that happened between women and men. As the women became more powerful in workplaces and government ministries, he thought that the men were increasingly afraid they would "want to put the revenge to men." To him, this was retrograde thinking. He had pledged, in conversations with his mom, not to behave like a sexist bigot.

Vunene volunteered, unprompted, that he thought polygamy was wrong, not only as a matter of morality but also for practical reasons. "That would not be good for me," he explained, mentioning his right under the law to take multiple wives. "So you have one wife and you have kids with her. Then you have another wife and some kids. There will not be enough money to take care of all of them."

We passed by the Star Bar Lounge, its black-on-white sign sponsored by Castle Beer. It was the biggest shebeen in the village, and his mother had told me that she feared its possible influence on her son. She had spoken of the bar as if it were a sentient, malevolent, grasping monster.

Several older boys clustered in the doorway called out to Vunene, but he offered only a noncommittal wave. "When the sun goes down, they'll say, 'Come with us. You can arm yourself!'" It was my turn to look puzzled. "What are they really asking?" I said. "Oh," he replied, looking down. "They'll say, 'Let's go fuck some girls'—and we're too young to do that. Maybe they want to get me put under the alcohol." I took a long look at him; he had just turned *fourteen*.

Like the school kids I had interviewed in Joburg earlier in the year, Vunene avoided venturing out at night for fear of the temptations stretching up and down this narrow dirt lane. Up ahead, at the soccer field, his pals from the village were practicing. That reminded him of how his band of boys had told me the year before that they all wanted to be soccer players when they grew up. "I want to be a doctor now," he said. "Whilst I like soccer, if I was to become a star, I would drink, become addicted to drugs, smoking dagga and all that. I would not have a good future." If he became a doctor, on the other hand, he would be able to care for all of his neighbors suffering from HIV.

Vunene plunged right on, confiding that he worried all the time about his mother now. Would she be able to make it on her own? And wouldn't the stress grind her down over time? He had a tall forehead, big round eyes, large ears, and was quick with a blazing smile. At the moment, however, his smile had faded and his face was set like a mourning mask.

"I have to give my mother a prize for what she has done for me," he said. "If she died, nobody will be with me. I will be alone. My uncle turns his back; he never looks at me. With my mother, she will never turn her back." Like Jonathan and Gwendoline, he felt a deep debt to his mother that he wasn't sure he could repay.

When I asked, he said that he still enjoyed hip-hop, especially 50

Cent, Tupac, T-Pain, and Akon. He credited listening to the lyrics with helping him with his English. The more he understood these lyrics, the more troubled he felt about what the artists were trying to say, though. The songs were laced with profanity, sexual innuendo, and hatred of women. It was his deepening faith, and also his emerging pro-feminist attitude, that raised his objections to the tenor of the songs.

One night he had watched a movie set in America, and it showed children cursing, disrespecting their teachers, and jumping in and out of bed. "I want to say something to the American kids," he announced. "I see them in the movies, and it shows that when they go to school they don't pay attention. They are always bullying the teachers. I would like them to change."

When we got back to the house, Vunene's three-year-old sister came running toward us. She banged two small rocks together, examined my tape recorder, and asked if she could have it. Vunene instructed her to stay quiet because there was a question he wanted to ask me: What had I seen at Polokwane and what did I think it meant for a boy from Bungeni? I described how nasty the clashes had been and how President Mbeki and his supporters had been rousted. He shrugged his shoulders. "Well, at least something happened," he remarked.

Vunene pointed in the direction of a one-room shack that a friend of his was living in. The friend was forced in there alongside sixteen other people. "Jacob Zuma will give them a four-room house," he said, sounding quite confident. "Houses will be bigger." I asked what sort of organizing it would take to improve things in his village. He replied that the needs were all pretty basic—running water, shelter, lights. The ANC had promised these in three national campaigns so far.

At the end of our conversation, he looked puzzled when I mentioned that Zuma had ended the rally where we had first met by singing "*Awuleth' Umshini Wam'*." Vunene didn't know any Zulu words, as it turned out, so he had no idea what the song meant. When I told him that the lyrics glorified the power of armed struggle, and machine guns in particular, he looked startled.

"Zulus—I never heard about the life they live," he said slowly. Vunene had always assumed that Zulu speakers were more like Shangaan-speaking people than those who spoke isiXhosa. "Zulus and Shangaan boys both wear skins," he said. "Xhosas don't wear skins, they wear clothes." Zulu speakers like Zuma, in other words, were *amaqaba*, people in touch with the earth. Thabo Mbeki, by contrast, had been a stuck-up, Xhosa-speaking *amagqoboka*.

Vunene restrained himself from going on, because in the new South Africa, everybody was equal, right? He knew that ethnic divisions shouldn't matter—that was the official line. This romantic attachment to armed revolution that I had mentioned, though, was foreign to him. He wasn't alive when the liberation struggle was fought.

By this time, the sun was going down, so I gathered up my things. As I was leaving, I remembered to ask him the question I had been posing to every young person I met: "Do you feel free?" He smirked, smoothed his sweat pants, tapped his feet in the dirt, and leaned back against the rock. "Yes, of course," he said brightly. "Discrimination is all gone. A black child and white child, we all have the same advantages. We have the same education. We will go to the same university. They are friendly and we are friendly. . . . It will get better and better. We'll all end up being free."

His mother came out on the stoop then, and I snapped pictures of the three of them. Vunene's sister wore a handmade green skirt and a brown blouse with blooming red flowers. Their mother was caught in a relaxed pose in the reddish glow of the dying sun. The boy stood with impeccable posture. He was man of the family now.

As I bounced along the lane, leaving the village again, I thought of the difficult circumstances Vunene faced in the years ahead, and once again of all of the sacrifices his mother had made for him already. The battle back in Polokwane had been fought, supposedly, on his behalf. It wasn't clear, though, what either side in the ANC had to offer the poor, and the working poor, in a village like Bungeni.

In the face of Vunene's implacable optimism, it made me ashamed to feel so much doubt that the people's government would make a difference for him. I was moved by the fact that he still believed, with such utter confidence—unself-consciously and without irony—in full political, social, and economic liberation, and that he felt quite sure that it still lay within the country's reach.

19.

Mvezo

In a place like Mvezo, the remote outpost where Nelson Mandela was born, it was easier to remind oneself that so many South Africans still lived in rural or semirural surroundings. It was a long drive, on perhaps the worst road in the country, to reach the village when I went for the first time, in the autumn of 2007, to see Mandela's grandson consecrated as traditional leader there. Around the country, people were migrating from the most underdeveloped, poverty-stricken rural areas, like Bungeni, where Vunene Mabasa lived, or Nkandla, the home of Jacob Zuma, in the direction of the cities. Still, for the majority of Mandela's countrymen, life as it unfolded in Cape Town or Johannesburg was still as remote as the mischief caused by the upscale characters on installments of the soap operas *Generations* and *Isidingo*.

Hills rounded like half moons rolled on to the horizon. The Mbashe River threaded lazy curlicues in clefts between the hills. On the day before the Mandela celebration, I had attended a lavish birthday party in honor of Jacob Zuma at the International Convention Centre in Durban. There, it was smooth marble floors, cavernous expanses, bright lights, and the new business and government elite arrayed in all their finery; here it was dust, grit, tattered clothes, and the fresh air of the country. Sharp twists and turns led to precipitous climbs before I reached the stark beauty of the so-called Great Place.

Undulating lines of people, the just-risen sun at their backs, had begun walking early, streaming toward the village in hopes of catching a glimpse of their best-known native son. More than seventy years had passed since Nelson Mandela's father, headman of the Traditional Council of Mvezo, was summarily dismissed by a British colonial magistrate. The post of village chief had remained empty through the intervening years, according to the amaThembu king I consulted, who said that the people of the village had refused appointment of anyone but a Mandela.

This dismissal of Henry Gadla Mandela in the late 1920s was presented in Nelson Mandela's autobiography as a stark lesson in colonial oppression. In the younger Mandela's version of the story, his father, summoned by the magistrate, had refused to bow to British rule, supposedly sending back this reply: *"Andiza ndisaqula"*—I will not come, I am girding for battle.[1] The historical record produced a more complicated version of the story, including allegations that the elder Mandela had made illegal sales of land along the river.[2] In either case, ever since Nelson Mandela was released from custody in 1990, hopes flared periodically among the villagers that he would accept his father's inheritance and lead the council.

Mandela had been requisitioned to run the ANC and the country instead, however. Hope flickered again when he stepped down as president in 1999, but he argued that he was too old by then to take up the post. Next in line by customary law would have been his eldest son. Both his sons were dead, though—Thembi in a car accident while Mandela was on Robben Island, and Makgotho from complications of AIDS in early 2005. Now, Mandlasizwe—Makgotho's eldest son, Nelson's eldest grandson, and Ndaba Mandela's older brother—had agreed to be wrapped in the skin of a lion.

Here was the sign of a curious reverse migration to the one Nelson Mandela had made, from rural life to city lawyer to revolutionary hero.

392   AFTER MANDELA

The prospective traditional leader wasn't the only city dweller returning to rural homelands out of disappointment with the realities of cosmopolitan life. Though the predominant flow of movement within the country was toward the cities, a small number of people were coming *back* after they experienced terrible reverses in their lives—joblessness, illness, and victimization from crime—while in the big city.

Mandlasizwe, or Mandla, had grown up in Soweto and he had studied for a master's degree in political science from Rhodes University. He had budding business interests in China and the Middle East. Like his sister and brothers, Mandla was essentially a person shaped by Joburg's vibe, a cosmopolitan man. Still, he had decided to return to his grandfather's birthplace to assume a conservative, traditional role. In his autobiography, Nelson Mandela described Mvezo as "a place apart, a tiny precinct removed from the world of events, where life was lived much as it had been for hundreds of years."[3] Mandla, I soon learned, had arrived back at the family homestead with plenty of ideas about how the village would need to change.

A fierce wind blew through the gorges, rocking my car. I had stopped a few miles off the highway, and now the car was crammed with four old women in traditional dress and half-a-dozen children. It was so crowded that I could scarcely manage steering. Shifting gears was out of the question, so we trundled on in second.

The women's cheeks were dusted with reddish mud, a sign they were *amaqaba*, or Xhosa-speaking traditionalists. Pointing in the direction of the arriving *amagqoboka*, the civilized ones, my passengers laughed behind cupped hands. Luxury sedans careened past us, lickety-split up the hill. Around the bend a BMW 4x4 was parked akimbo at the side of the road, with two tires blown out. A little farther on, a brilliantly polished Mercedes revealed a popped hood and a plume of steam. The women murmured happily at the sight of the fancy car boiling over and the man in the fancy suit who had lurched out of the driver's seat to wave his arms madly over the engine.

At the end of the road, on the overlook at Mvezo, canvas tents had been set up to shield people from an unrelenting sun. In the middle of the clearing was a square platform adorned with lion and leopard skins. Lurking beside it were stick-thin dogs with whiplike tails.

Suddenly an army helicopter swooped past, landing on the top of a nearby ridge. When an oversized 4x4 pulled up, Nelson Mandela was visible in a passenger seat, with his face, fixed in a whimsical grin, pressed to the window. His grandsons—Mandla, the man to be honored on this day, and his younger brother, Ndaba—helped both their grandfather and his wife, Graça Machel, from the car. The young men were shirtless and garbed in traditional robes, with beaded bands around their heads and at their ankles. They followed the elders into the tent that had been raised for them.

A terrible wind kicked up, the dogs started yapping, and people stood to cheer for the father of their nation. Since the generator trucked in by the ceremony's producers had short-circuited, the sound system was also kaput. Only those of us standing right next to the stage could hear a series of speeches from struggle veterans and traditional leaders that opened the celebration.

Chief Mangosuthu Buthelezi, part of the royal delegation from Kwa-Zulu-Natal, gave an exhaustive account of his long relationship with the elder Mandela, complaining about how he had been disrespected by the ANC over the years. The younger Mandelas rolled their eyes: What did Buthelezi's long list of grievances have to do with this ceremony?

When Mandla was summoned forward, he looked wide-eyed. Thembu King Dalindyebo, a wiry, hyped-up middle-aged man with rows of beads around his neck, placed the lion skin across the young man's back. A cluster of old men, religious leaders and royalty, placed their hands over the lion to consecrate Mandla Mandela's ascendancy.

After the blessing was done, women in the crowd ululated in celebration. The brothers danced in the midst of a troupe of bare-breasted young women. Graça Machel joined them, taking the hand of Mandla's wife and leading her through the paces that had been, until this moment, intended only for the men.

Finally, it was time for the elder Mandela to speak. He was helped to his feet, but he insisted on walking under his own power to the stage. Mandela mounted the steps upright, wobbling all the way. As he passed by, you could see how frail he had become, at eighty-eight. Wind battered him from one side, and he headed in that direction, then it whipped at him from the other side and he faltered to the right.

He grinned into the gusts as he saluted the new *nkosi* of the Mvezo Traditional Council. Then Mandela murmured something in isiXhosa. His comment drew a shocked hush, followed by a sharp intake of breath from the people around me. "What did he say?" I asked a journalist standing next to me. "Now I can die in peace," he said, sounding stunned.

When the elder Mandela finished his remarks, he and Graça Machel greeted old-timers in the VIP tent while younger guests mounted the platform to approach the new chief on their knees. It was a gesture of intergenerational obeisance to traditional authority.

It was after the formal ceremony was over that I had followed the Mandela brothers down to an overlook near where their grandfather was born. Past a rocky ravine you could see stretches of fertile land lying fallow. That's when I noticed the image of a lion tattooed smack-dab in the middle of Ndaba Mandela's back, and tapped him on the shoulder to ask him a few questions.

His description of himself as "totally a Joburg boy" provided the opening for long conversations, spread over the following four years, about what it meant to be a member of South Africa's most famous family and a Joburger at heart. He seemed buoyant in the moment, and told me later how proud he thought his father would have been to see his sons together.

The new chief, on the other hand, looked somber, as if the weight of his new responsibilities suddenly had become quite clear. "The generators failed us today. But it was a wonderful ceremony anyway," he said. The new *nkosi* reported that there was no electricity in the village yet. He knew that it would be hard to convince the electricity supplier, Eskom, to install electricity way out in such a remote area. The road was abysmal, too. He noted that a number of VIPs had been waylaid by blown tires and ruined engines.

The new chief intended to revive small-scale agriculture in the area. He had already offered his neighbors the services of his own bull to generate new herds of cattle for people of the village. The headman of Mvezo imagined a new kind of village—a "place apart," perhaps, but also a rural precinct fully representative of new national aspirations. Mvezo would be more engaged in the wide world, and if Chief Mandela had his way, it would also be protected somehow from the more alienating aspects of modern life.

Between trips to Mveso, I stopped by the Mandela mansion in Houghton one morning, to speak with the two younger siblings of Ndaba and Mandla. They were the youngest sons of Makgotho, and like their older brothers they also had been fetched from Soweto at young ages to live with their older brothers in their grandfather's house. Andile and Mbuso, though, were from the Born Free generation, and they felt little connection to the homeland.

Ndaba had picked the two younger boys up at the home of an aunt, where they were living then, in Hyde Park, a high-tone neighborhood not far away. The three of them hunkered down on the couch, with Ndaba as a chaperone for our conversation. Mbuso, sixteen, was dressed in a red-and-white Fly Emirates soccer shirt, and Andile, thirteen, had his white Nike sweatshirt zipped all the way to his Adam's apple and was decked out in calf-length powder-blue jeans. The three of them, sitting side by side, made a striking tableau; Ndaba's resemblance to his grand-father was closest, but the two younger brothers could have been stand-ins for the Old Man in his teenage years as well.

I asked what it was like studying modern South African history when your own grandfather was at the center of it. Mbuso replied that he had been reading up on the history of the Black Consciousness Move-ment in school, and he told me that he admired its chief proponent, Steve Biko, more than anybody else. Biko, after all, had been the one to convince South African blacks to be proud of themselves, he said.

Mbuso Mandela didn't venture an opinion about the central role his grandfather had played in promoting a multiracial ethos so often at odds with black nationalist thinking. But he thought it was quite cool that when he was watching films in history class, and his grandfather came on screen, his classmates razzed him by saying, "Oh, Mbuso, you're now on TV!"[4]

It was clear, right from the start of our conversation, that, unlike their older brothers, the younger boys considered the apartheid period as something remote and strange, like ancient history. "It's weird. You never think that a human being could reach so low—that he could think someone who doesn't look like himself is scum of the earth," Mbuso offered.

When I had interviewed Ndaba earlier in the year he had spoken movingly of his ongoing struggle not to see white people as oppressors. There was no equivalent sense of grievance among the younger brothers. In this way, they sounded more like Vunene Mabasa, the boy who was their age from remote Limpopo province, than like their siblings. "I don't judge people based on the *past*," Mbuso volunteered. "I just look at the present, and see what happens now. Things have changed. Can't hold a grudge forever."

Next, I asked whether the boys considered themselves completely free then. Had all the bonds of the country's past been lifted from them and other young black people? They glanced at one another, trading small smiles. "South Africa has reached freedom," Mbuso said. "There's not really much you can't do except for smoking and drinking in public. You can go wherever you want, buy whatever you want, dress however you want. There's no discrimination, no judgment."

Ndaba looked increasingly discomfited by these answers. Andile, the younger brother, nodded. Neither of them had trace memories about life as young children in Soweto. They lived in the suburbs now, went to classes in an exclusive private school, and spent their weekends in the malls, like Rosebank, where Yfm was located and the polyglot urban culture of the new South Africa glossed over all that prior unpleasantness. Both boys confessed a complete lack of interest in the political battle roiling the country and rippling their grandfather's party from top to bottom.

When I asked whether they followed news about the ANC closely, they laughed. What did they think about Thabo Mbeki and Jacob Zuma? "My teacher was saying to us that if Jacob Zuma becomes president of the country, she will leave South Africa," Andile put in. Lots of other kids had been saying the same thing. He found it weird that the election of a certain person would motivate anyone to say they would leave their home country. What was that about? Besides, Andile had gotten to know Vusi Zuma, Thuthu's younger brother, in elementary school. Vusi seemed like a perfectly chill kid, and that seemed like a good and trustworthy measure of his father's worth.

The brothers were more heavily invested in trends in modern music, and were especially drawn to the songs of Lil Wayne and Young Jack. Politics had been the old family business, but their aunts and uncles were now engaged in various private enterprises. Mbuso thought his future lay in business administration; Andile hoped he could find a way in producing music.

The big ceremony they had attended with their grandfather, the one making their oldest brother chief of Mvezo, had been memorable, but they confessed that they hadn't understood much of what was going on because neither could speak isiXhosa.

Andile said that he had learned isiZulu as a first language, because his mother was Zulu speaking, but his older brother, Mbuso, had begun teaching him English when he was just five years old. In a single generation, then, the sense of rootedness in Xhosa language and Xhosa culture, celebrated so lyrically in Nelson Mandela's autobiography, had almost completely disappeared among his younger grandsons.

The way Mbuso talked about his identity reminded me of the children of Mexican immigrants whom I had gotten to know as a young reporter in the agricultural valleys of my native California. They often stopped speaking Spanish as soon as they started school, and you would often visit homes where the parents were fluent only in Spanish and the children understood only a fraction of what they said.

The difference here, of course, was that the Mandelas had not migrated across national lines. They had simply become urbanized. Theirs wasn't the classic story told of displacement and loss of language and culture caused by immigration, for they had filled the interstices of discarded identities with something new—a cross-cultural, cross-class, distinctly South African embrace of an emerging global identity.

"So when you think about your identity, do you consider yourself amaXhosa or not?" I asked. "No," Mbuso replied, matter-of-factly. Ndaba's eyes widened in disbelief. "You wouldn't say you were *Xhosa*?" he asked, with an edge of disapproval. Mbuso pulled his chin down and turned away from his older brother. "I didn't say anything," he protested. Ndaba glared at him. "The man asked you how you see yourself!" he exclaimed.

I interrupted, deflecting attention to Andile to try to ease the tension. "Say someone dropped from Mars and he asked who you were. What would you say about who you are and where you're from?" I was thinking of Jacob Zuma's introduction of himself on my tape: "I am Jacob Zuma and I come from Nkandla." Andile looked puzzled, but he replied, like a shot, "I would say, I'm Andile and I live in Hyde Park."

I pressed him a little further: Did the boys think of their oldest brother as a kind of repository of respect for their family's traditional life? "Xhosa is part of my heritage," Mbuso murmured, shifting in his seat.

"But I don't think it would be one of the first things I would say if someone asked me, 'Who are you?'"

At that point the door opened and their oldest brother came in.
Mandla and his wife, Thando, had arrived to visit with his grandfather
before embarking on a business trip to China. Chief Mandela was moving into the oil business in an arrangement that often took him to Beijing and the Middle East. Unfortunately, there had been an incident on
the way from the airport. His wife, traveling separately, was forced off
the road and rousted from her car at gunpoint. The car and all her lug-
gage were gone, just like that. It would be a scramble to replace her clothing in time for their departure the next day.

Being *nkosi* of Mvezo, and a Mandela no less, provided no immunity
from the daily reality of crime. The younger brothers rose and left the
room. They weren't about to discuss their tentative sense of belonging, in
Xhosa language and culture, in front of the sibling who had chosen, at
considerable effort, to spend the rest of his life reinventing it.

On Christmas morning, in the final week of 2007, I drove once more to
Mvezo, this time with my partner, Chengetayi, to see how the new chief
was faring. He and his wife had swapped lives rooted in Johannesburg
and Grahamstown for a rural existence after taking up his new role as
nkosi. In the intervening months, Ndaba Mandela had hinted several
times, in conversation, that the transition had proved harder than anyone expected for the new chief and his wife.

This time, as I drove out from the highway, there were no government ministers and royal visitors also lurching along the terrible road.
Instead, young women and little boys, barefoot, were hauling buckets of
water uphill. By the time I found the ridgetop and drove on to the overlook marked as Mandela's birthplace, the sun was blazing in a midsum-
mer sky.

Chief Mandela had been up since dawn to prepare for his first Christmas as village leader. A group of men had helped him slaughter seven sheep for a feast he was offering children from the surrounding area. Behind the five new rondavels built to accommodate Mandela's family, meat was cooking in huge metal pots over open fires.

Since I had seen him at his installation, the new *nkosi* had plunged with enormous energy into a new and complicated role. He had taken twenty children from the village to the Miss World competition in Beijing, and he also had chaperoned a delegation of teenage girls to the Reed Dance in Swaziland, where they engaged in the traditional ritual of being tested for virginal status.

The children who had accompanied him to China had traveled on an airplane for the first time. I thought of Jonathan's first flight, from Cape Town to Johannesburg, where he had met Nelson Mandela. None of the children from the village had ever left it before. "It was their first time seeing Chinese people," Chief Mandela said, smiling. "We went to see the biggest Buddha in the world. For them, it was the most amazing thing to see people worshipping another religion."

The girls who had gone with him to Swaziland—he referred to them as "our maidens"—wowed the Swazis with their singing, he reported. "It was about our maidens going to the Reed Dance, meeting the maidens there, and gaining an understanding of the cultural values in Swaziland, and having our kids teaching those kids what our values are on this side," he said.[5]

For all the pride he took in these accomplishments, though, the new chief was already deeply distressed by the enormous obstacles he had encountered in his efforts to bring change to Mvezo. He had made countless appeals to provincial and national officials to get help in widening the roads. There was desperate need for a health clinic. He had plans he wanted to pursue for nearby, low-tech economic development projects.

But Mandela felt that the provincial government officials had stone-walled him. He was left steaming with frustration that he had not been able to accomplish more in his first eight months. Now he said that he understood, firsthand, why traditional leaders felt so much bitterness toward the ANC and the Mbeki government. Since 1994, the focus of national policy had been concentrated on urban "nodes of development." Little had been attempted in areas like this one. "I feel I've been beaten," Mandela told me. "You tend to want to pull back and understand why certain things have not gone the way they should. You start afresh, as to what should be the way forward."

Chief Mandela wore a long-sleeved blue shirt and faded dungarees cinched by a studded brown leather belt. His face was creased with worry and a hint of sadness. At his investiture he had stood tall, with his shoulders thrown back. Now he hunched over, looking depressed.

About sixty children lined up across uneven ground to receive Christmas candy and a loaf of bread. Chengetayi and I helped distribute the bread. Mandela instructed the kids to sit on the slab near an enlarged photo of his grandfather in the traditional garb he had worn as he prepared to testify at the Rivonia Treason Trial forty years earlier. Then, Nelson Mandela had been about the age Chief Mandela was now. The grandson had closed the circle, bringing all of his inherited influence back to bear on the home village.

The children waited, jostling one another to receive their special meal. Ndaba, his brothers, and cousins arrived from their grandfather's in Qunu to help serve. Chief Mandela upbraided them for being late and put them to work right away. They fetched steaming mutton in paper bowls from the cooking pots down the steep hill, ferrying it up to the children. The young ones held their hands out, sitting wedged in, hip-to-hip, on the concrete slab. It was moving to watch the grandchildren of Nelson Mandela serving poor, hungry children a rare meal with meat at the birthplace of their grandfather.

Chief Mandela put on a canary-yellow sport coat. Behind us, women watched, many of them with infants strapped to their backs. The chief had insisted that parents drop their children off at the edge of the clearing and wait for them out in the field. Some villagers had refused to allow their kids to come because they disagreed with his decision to make it a feast for children only.

A light rain started, and the parents looked hungry, wet, and resentful. As the children dug into the meal, the *nkosi* helped the youngest ones settle their bowls in their laps. When adults called on the kids to bring the food uphill into the field to share, he waved them back into their seats. Mandela had upended tradition, trumping the power of the parents to apportion their family's rations.

By the time most of the kids had eaten their mutton, the misting rain had turned into a downpour. The storm shrouded the dying sun, casting the surrounding landscape into sudden darkness. On the outskirts of the village, you could see bonfires burning, and teenagers clustered around them.

Mandela told me of his disappointment that more teens hadn't shown up for the celebration. Now, as we left the Great Place, it became clear where the adolescents had been all this time, partying along the narrow, treacherous road.

On our drive past them, groups of older girls and young women danced toward the car, slipping and sliding in the mud. Wet clothing clung to their bodies, translucent in the headlights. "Take us, don't you want us?" one girl shouted at me, holding her arms out and pressing her breasts up against the side window. Another young woman shimmied toward the passenger side of the car, beckoning at my partner their desperate invitation, and that drunken call—*take us, don't you want us?*—haunted me all the way to Mthatha, the town where we were staying.

Early in the morning, on the day after Christmas, we made the muddy drive back out to Mvezo. The roads were clear of people. All the bonfires from the night before had been doused. Scattered remnants of charred wood were the only signs of the wild, roving celebrations that had taken place in the rain. It was overcast, and threatening gray clouds gave the impression of a sky brought low.

When we arrived at the Great Place, Chief Mandela was meeting with a dozen local residents in one of the large rondavels down below the ridge. These were the villagers who had been sent as delegates to the ANC national conference at Polokwane. They were mostly elderly men wearing blankets.

Each man took turns relating what had happened at the conference, all in rapid-fire isiXhosa. There was lots of laughter and even some acting out of the arguments during the discussions about policy and candidates, and lots of comments about the victory celebration afterward.

"They said, 'Madiba, we did exactly as you instructed us to do,'" Mandela said, turning to me. It struck me, then, that this use of the family's clan name, commonly reserved for Nelson Mandela, had been transferred in Mvezo to the new *nkosi*. "They said, 'We didn't compromise our votes,'" he continued. Mandela insisted that he had not influenced their votes, but only had warned them against the undue influence of others. The delegates should be true to the feelings of the members of local branches, the chief had argued. The net effect, of course, was to weigh in on Zuma's side since he had won 62 percent of the vote in a local ANC branch meeting.

Halfway through the political discussion, ceramic bowls were brought in. The bowls were filled with a charred delicacy, the brains of the sheep slaughtered to feed the children on Christmas Day. The brains were spongy and tasted salty. Mandela picked at his share, sitting and listening for more than an hour, as long as the elders wanted to talk. His head cocked, he nodded occasionally and interrupted to ask questions.

The outcome at Polokwane pleased him, because he had been rooting for Zuma. His grandfather, he told me, felt exactly the same way. It had been quite distressing for the elder Mandela to see the party in such disarray under Thabo Mbeki, he added. "My grandfather told me, 'I said

I would only serve one term as an example to the rest of Africa. I never in my lifetime thought that the ANC that I've been part of would want to discuss the issue of a third term.'" The effort by Mbeki to cling to power "had been troubling to him," the chief reported. The outcome in Polokwane, he assured me, had left the elder Mandela "happy to see that South Africa has become a mature democracy, you know, and that we were able to unpack the difficulties."

As the chief talked to the delegates recently returned from Polokwane, the cloud cover lifted. There was a bright, clear view of the valley below. The rises were covered with tall grasses, common saffron brush, broom cluster fig, and Cape ash. When his grandfather's father was chief, early in the last century, the family controlled the entire valley all the way to the horizon. Over the years, the land was divided up, sold, and resold. Reclaiming ownership had proved far harder than he had expected, Mandela told me.

The provincial government had placed procedural obstacles in the way. First, the premier offered to compensate current landowners, assessed the value at what Mandela considered inflated rates, and then failed to provide the money. Finally, King Dalindyebo had suggested to Nelson Mandela that he raise the funds needed for purchase of the land privately. Even after money raised by the elder Mandela was deposited in a bank, national and provincial officials put off approving transfer of the title, the chief said.

For the next three years, this issue would continue to fester. What Mandela had thought would be a quick and clean process of reclaiming family property turned into a long, hard, and complicated slog. Conflicts over boundary lines for the land eventually would place him at odds not only with government officials but also with significant numbers of his own villagers. Years later, residents of Mvezo would haul him into court, accusing their *nkosi* of dictatorial behavior and illegal land grabs as he pushed through his plan to build a luxury tourist resort near the village.

Inhabitants of Mvezo would accuse the chief, among other things, of fencing them out of traditional family burial grounds. At a community meeting in October of 2011, a reporter and photographer from the *Sunday Times* were held against their will for eight hours as Mandela accused them of trespassing and denounced the villagers challenging him in court. The chief made clear he considered the journalists agents of rebellion against him. "This is war. This is not time to fold our hands," Mandela was quoted as saying. "This is going to be a long weekend which calls for the slaughtering of a bull. The ancestors have brought these men to us."[6]

In the intervening years since his celebrated arrival as chief, the powers of his position—or perhaps, the *lack* of the kind of power he had anticipated—appeared to have taken Mandla Mandela off the rails. By then, even though I called and emailed Mandela regularly, we rarely managed more than a few words on the phone. He never responded in writing and skipped scheduled meetings. When I learned of the clashes in Mvezo in late 2011, it reminded me of how noble his plans had sounded three years earlier.

Even then, at the end of 2007, it was clear how important it was to Mandela to try to restore the kind of control over the village that his great grandfather had exercised before the colonial magistrate removed him in 1906. Many of the villagers in the area had deeds to parts of Mvezo that dated back to 1910, granted in the wake of the elder Chief Mandela's fall. The long delay in the recognition of his rights to control the surrounding lands the Mandela grandson put down to a lack of respect by government bureaucrats toward traditional leaders.

The younger Mandela's clashes with the bureaucrats led him to curious conclusions. In our conversation after Christmas in 2007, he predicted a coming confrontation of historic proportions between the ANC government and traditional leaders. "If you come to the core problems, the only real revolution that could emerge today in this country is out of traditionalism," he argued. "So the counterrevolution to ANC dominance lays upon the traditionalists. We have the masses, we have the people."

He interrupted himself, then, to call a group of passing teenage girls into the rondavel. They were stunningly beautiful young women dressed in short skirts and rayon blouses, with hair pulled back from their smiling faces. When their chief began talking, though, their smiles died and they bowed their heads. He rattled off a long rebuke. The young women thanked him for his advice about how to behave in the future, and took the leftover loaves of bread, backing out of the entryway.

"They were just caught up in those parties you probably saw," he explained, attributing the problem of the wild parties along the roadway to the influence of young men who lived in Johannesburg and Cape Town and returned to the home village only for the holidays. "They come three days before Christmas with money they've brought [home] and instead of being creative and assisting their families, they engage in these shebeens," he said.

Mandela had grown up in Johannesburg and spent a share of his young adulthood in shebeens himself. Now he sounded like a born-again prohibitionist. "They just engage in drinking!" he exclaimed. The holiday visitors retained a sense of belonging to Mveso, he noted, but the chief thought of them more as a kind of infectious agent. The young men had been "exposed to the Western lifestyle of urban culture," he complained. "They are not in touch with tradition, they are not in touch with custom."

I noticed that the chief's wife, Thando, had missed the feast the day before. It was disappointing, for me, because I had been looking forward to learning what the transition to rural life meant for her. When I asked if his wife was doing well, Mandela slumped in his seat. He acknowledged, a little mournfully, that she had decided to spend the holidays with her own family and confessed that life in Mvezo had come as quite a shock to her.

The two of them, after all, had begun their marriage as a modern couple. Their relationship had skidded up against old rules. Her identity in the small village had become circumscribed to that of the wife of a chief. "I've always loved this traditional lifestyle we lead. On her side, she's had a lot of sacrifices," Mandela remarked. "Being a modern woman: culture changes when you're out here." She was forbidden to wear pants in the village and was expected to cover her hair.

Mandela didn't mention a more significant source of tension, which I knew something about only because we had mutual friends. The subject was polygamy. It was expected of an *nkosi* in the Transkei that he would take multiple wives, stitching together varied families and clans in the area through marriage. Thando certainly wasn't ready to welcome other wives into the fold. "This whole friction is erupting out of modernity," Mandela explained, in a rather vague reference to arguments he had had with his wife on the subject.

It seemed to me that this was an updated version of the trouble many people had in reconciling the ways of the village with the ways of the city. Mandla Mandela, like Jacob Zuma, regularly shuttled between upcountry spots, where traditional authority held sway, and the most cosmopolitan settings in the country, where identity was mutable and diffuse. If you traveled frequently between villages like Nkandla and Mvezo to cities like Durban, Cape Town, and Johannesburg, it was hard to believe that Chief Mandela wasn't merely keening for the idea of a village already lost and longing for a way of life that had never been.

Anthropologists John Comaroff and Jean Comaroff, two South African scholars at the University of Chicago, had pointed out that this tension lay deep in the DNA of the new dispensation. The country's much-lauded Constitution included protection of human dignity, individual rights, and equal treatment, but it also promised a place of respect for traditional life characterized by what they called the chief-subject relationship.

"For many—perhaps most—South Africans, it is the *co-existence* of the two tropes, of citizen and subject, that configures the *practical* terms of national belonging," they had written.[7] When women in customary marriages were denied inheritance rights, when widows were punished because they refused to stay indoors for a year after the death of their spouse, when a woman in KwaZulu-Natal was killed for wearing trousers—and when both women and men accepted physical assault and rape as the appropriate response of a husband to a wife he felt was disobedient—these loosely intertwined strands of South African life came unraveled. Often, disputes rooted in these national contradictions ended up in courtrooms, and the trickiest cases to resolve involved the role of women.

By Christmas Day, 2007, this tension was starkly evident in Mvezo, even in the *nkosi*'s private life. Clashes over culture and power were bound to punctuate the second decade of democracy. It got Chief Mandela's back up, though, when people he knew from his old life decided that traditional ways were, at their core, oppressive of women. He launched, at great length, into a retelling of the history of the Thembu people, who had once been led by a queen.

"I've always said that men and women exist as parallel parties, like on a railway line," Mandela said. "No one is higher than the other, each are dependent on the other. You will never have things working right if the man and woman are not assisting one another. Once one becomes dominant, you find an oppressive system emerging."

Thando, as it turned out, would soon decide not to return to Mvezo. When she filed for divorce the following year, she accused her husband of having threatened and beaten her. The severity of the setbacks in the chief's personal life wasn't something Mandela addressed directly, but he acknowledged, in a more general way, that the obstacles he had encountered in his new role left him a little downcast.

As we talked into the afternoon, it seemed as though Mandela was struggling to reconcile the manifold sides of his identity—Soweto youngster, Rhodes University scholar, and global businessman—with this new role, as a traditional leader. It occurred to him, as we were talking, that you could succeed in the larger world, but in the process lose a special, fragile rootedness to your ancestral place.

Mandela's description of this quandary reminded me of his younger brother, the one who didn't consider himself part of the Xhosa culture. The twist, of course, was that the chief himself increasingly felt called on to play a larger role on the national stage. In 2009 he would get on the ANC party list and end up as a representative in the National Assembly. He looked toward trade with China as an element in underwriting the costs of development needed to lift more South Africans out of poverty. In order to deliver on promises he had made to the people of Mvezo at his investiture, the *nkosi* resembled his grandfather in at least one respect. In the end, Chief Mandela had decided that he must leave the village in order to save it.

PART IV

The End of Magical Thinking

(2008–2012)

Personality cults do not necessarily come from people like me. They come from different kinds of people, if you look at it historically. People who develop a personality cult are people who are too self-centered. I am a cadre of the ANC. I act on what the ANC instructs me to do.

—*JACOB ZUMA*
2009

Look, change must come from the bottom up. Otherwise, we're attacking the symptoms only, not the real underlying problems.

—*GUGULETHU ZUMA*
2010

Children in Mvezo, the birthplace of Nelson Mandela, line up in front of a portrait of him as a revolutionary hero. (*Douglas Foster*)

20.

The Globe

It was a crisp October day in 2008 when Jacob Zuma arrived in Washington, D.C., for his first trip to the United States since his election as leader of the ANC. I had last seen him the year before at the national conference in Polokwane. After the showdown there, where he had been dressed in casual clothes to oversee a populist rebellion in the governing party, it looked strange to see him now, all buttoned up in a conservative business suit. The new leader faced a challenge akin to Chief Mandela's—but on a significantly larger scale—having flown over the Atlantic to reassure American politicians, bankers, and potential investors that South Africa would be in good hands once he became head of state.

In essence, the leader was canvassing for help in buffering his country from the global financial meltdown that had just begun in the West. Zuma already had traveled to China, back in June, which was his first international foray as party chief. The order of these trips—first China, then the United States—revealed something about the changing power dynamics around the world. The United States was a highly indebted nation now and China the biggest holder of its notes.

Increasingly, as the years went by, Zuma began referring to Europe as "those small countries."[1] He figured that the Americans were only just beginning to come to terms with their declining share of world power, which he saw as an ongoing, inevitable slide.

Back home, there had been a stunning series of political developments. First, a judge threw out charges of corruption against him in a ruling that explicitly criticized Thabo Mbeki's administration for interfering in prosecution of his case. The National Executive Committee of the party met, instructing President Mbeki to resign as head of state seven months before the end of his term.

Mbeki had bowed to party discipline, making his final live appearance on national television in September 2008 to explain why he was stepping down. Sitting primly in an armchair, and flanked by the national seal on his right and the South African flag to his left, the departing president took the equivalent of a victory lap; he claimed credit for his role in resolving conflicts in six countries, including Côte d'Ivoire, Zimbabwe, and Sudan; and he reminded viewers of his belief in the indigenous cultural value system known as *ubuntu*, which amounted to respect of human dignity. It was an artful farewell. The ANC had installed its secretary-general, Kgalema Motlanthe, as a benchwarmer in the presidency until the election in 2009.

On the day President Mbeki was instructed to resign, I managed to reach Zuma by telephone at his home in Johannesburg. He told me that he had felt a bit sad to deliver the news of dismissal to his onetime friend. In a meeting between them, face-to-face, Mbeki "seemed okay," Zuma said. He figured the ex-president would survive the humiliation. "But then, you know that he did *much* worse to me," he added, making it clear how personal the breach had been.[2]

In remarks to supporters before Mbeki was forced to step aside, Zuma had sounded much harsher even as he counseled his supporters to temper calls for the president's ouster by saying it wasn't necessary to "beat a dead snake." In Washington, though, Zuma sang Mbeki's praises from the moment of his arrival. In his first public talk of the trip, at the Council on Foreign Relations, he referred to his old comrade as "his excellency," which left me thinking: which was it—snake or comrade or excellency?

When we had time to ourselves late the next evening, in his hotel room, I told him what the events of Polokwane had looked like from my vantage point. On the final day of the ANC National Conference the year before, I recalled that Zuma had appeared quite grim as I watched him on the dais after he won election as president of the party. "It was really disappointing. It was not a normal election victory," he admitted.[3]

In the months that followed, Zuma confided, he had held out hope that Mbeki and his supporters would "sober up" and get back to work in repairing the damage to the ANC caused by the schism. When the president did not show up at the annual celebration of the ANC's founding, on January 8, and excused himself from internal discussions with top party officials, Zuma signed off on this second public humiliation. As for his reference to Mbeki as a dead snake? "It was an accurate quote," Zuma said. "[But] I was only trying to say we don't need to be looking back. We need to look forward."

By the time I had caught up with Zuma on his American trip, he had already visited with the secretary of state, the deputy director of the FBI, and the outgoing president of the United States, George W. Bush. Ties between the Bush and Mbeki administrations had been correct if not particularly warm. Officials on both sides had made considerable efforts to ensure that their many differences—over AIDS, Zimbabwe, the Sudan, the World Court, and South Africa's pro-China votes in the UN Security Council—never swamped their common interests and remained controlled arguments among friends rather than consequential breaches.

"It wasn't necessarily a bad relationship," Secretary of State Condoleezza Rice would tell me years later. The Bush administration, much like the Clinton White House, had felt quite mystified and increasingly troubled by Mbeki's HIV policy. Rice said that Bush had been puzzled, too, by Mbeki's inability or unwillingness to influence Robert Mugabe, in neighboring Zimbabwe. "On Zimbabwe, Mbeki was just feckless," the former secretary of state recalled. "I remember meetings with President Bush where he [Mbeki] would tell us how he was talking to Mugabe. And he would get back to him [Bush] a few weeks later and say, as if anybody was surprised, that Mugabe hadn't lived up to his agreements. We thought Mbeki was being deceived by Mugabe."[4]

The Zuma visit provided a chance to take the new leader's measure face-to-face, and consider whether things could improve on these scores if he became head of state. The United States had no favorite in the intraparty struggle between the two men in 2007, Rice told me later. "It wasn't as if Mbeki had run the country that well. It wasn't as if he'd done an exemplary job," she added.

What had concerned the White House, as early as 2005, however, was the possibility that the fight for power between the country's two top leaders could erase all the gains made in South Africa since 1994. "Everybody felt that you had to have a stable South Africa and a stable Nigeria," Rice explained. "You needed those two anchor countries to be stable in order to ensure development in Africa. South Africa had seemed quite stable until then. It had a patina of stability anyway" until the split at the top. Naturally, a sustained, uncontrolled imbroglio between Mbeki and Zuma caught the administration's attention.

"The emergence of the Zuma-Mbeki rivalry demonstrated that there was a real problem that could affect stability," Rice continued. "You started to worry whether the political center is really going to hold. Is this the first step to things unraveling?"

In that sense, the visit by Zuma was quite reassuring, Rice added. He had impressed both the president and secretary of state with his quiet, soft-spoken style. "I remember thinking: He wasn't this crazy person. He's not what I expected," she recalled. "He seemed very focused on South Africa itself, on things like income distribution and inequality, economic policy. He was really rather sound in his approach. Of course, he was trying to make a good impression. He wanted to make sure that we understood foreign investment would be welcome."

The encounter had a rather different, even melancholy effect on Zuma. Seeing Secretary of State Rice and President Bush at the White House, during their twilight months in office, he caught himself mulling over the fact that the American leader, once so wildly popular with his people, was now so deeply disliked. Bush seemed more genial, and also smarter, than Zuma had expected. In the wake of the 9/11 terrorist attacks, the American leader had polled 90 percent support, but by the time Zuma arrived to meet with him, his approval rating was down to an all-time low of 25 percent.

Now, there was a good chance that the Democrats under Barack Obama would take the White House in the national election the following month. Here was another piece of evidence about how quickly a leader could fall after a long rise to the top, the same dynamic Helen Zille had mentioned in her comment about President Mbeki—"the more powerful you get, the quicker the wheel turns."

The trip to the United States provided a brief respite from ongoing troubles back home for the ANC's new chief. Behind the scenes, mostly out of the headlines, the arms scandal still festered. New revelations about the arms deals dribbled out as investigators for the British, German, and Swedish governments launched probes into bribery and corruption practices by major arms manufacturers. Among other things, German investigators focused on the effects of the global arms business on what they called "accountable democracy," which certainly included South Africa's part in the mess.

Andrew Feinstein, a former ANC member of Parliament turned whistle-blower, had continued to research the secret terms of the deals. After seven years of study, he had concluded that both Mbeki and Zuma were directly implicated in corruption related to the deals. As he looked back now on the chronology of events from the period when he had tried to investigate the deals as an ANC member of Parliament, he noted that Zuma had abruptly withdrawn his support for the investigation on the day he would have learned that a large payment was on its way to him through Schabir Shaik. From that day forward, Feinstein said, "[Zuma] treated me like the rest of the ANC treated me—like a leper."[5]

Two intrepid investigative reporters at the weekly *Mail & Guardian*, Sam Sole and Stefaans Brümmer, had continued gathering more details of corruption spawned in the arms deals. In 2008, they reported on the suspicious death a year earlier of a former agent of the National Intelligence Agency, Mhleli Madaka. Madaka had produced documents about a R30 million kickback, allegedly funneled to the ANC and to Zuma, and passed through the hands of President Mbeki, years earlier.

Richard Young, the businessman who had done his utmost to bring new details of corruption to light after his own company was sidelined in the contracts, called this "the society of mutual testicle holding." Like the journalists digging for more of the details, the businessman and arms deal gadfly expected that emerging splits between former comrades within the governing party would lead, at last, to more information leaking out.[6]

In Washington and New York, however, Zuma wasn't questioned at all about the arms deal. Everywhere he went, people were clamoring instead to ask about South Africa's *stability*. In his prepared remarks, the new ANC leader cast his election, and even the toppling of Mbeki, as signs of the country's maturity and resiliency rather than the reverse. "A few months ago we were visited by generals from other African countries who said, 'If this had happened anywhere else, there would have been a civil war,'" he said. At an appearance before the Press Club in Washington, he repeated his new mantra: "There is no need for panic. It is democracy at work."

Everywhere Zuma went, he lectured audiences about the long-standing reverence, within the ANC, for the principle of collective leadership. "We believe in collective culture, not in a one-man show," he kept insisting. Zuma began each talk by introducing the other officials accompanying him on the trip, among them Mathews Phosa, the new party treasurer; Siphiwe Nyanda, the former head of the military wing and the first head of the post-apartheid military in South Africa; Nomaindia Mfeketo, the former mayor of Cape Town; and Zweli Mkhize, ANC leader in KwaZulu-Natal who was increasingly touted as a possible future president.

In Zuma's hotel room, at the end of his second day in Washington, he slumped in the middle of a cream-colored couch, worn out but with his ear cocked to news bulletins on CNN. I began, perhaps unkindly, by asking for comment about Andrew Feinstein's version of events in the arms deal investigations, many of them detailed in his book *After the Party*.

"I supported the comrades in the committee to do the investigation," Zuma said, perking up. "I had a meeting with Feinstein and encouraged him [to investigate]." He summarized the steps he had taken to support a robust investigation in Parliament, and blamed President Mbeki for shutting these efforts down. It was Mbeki who had drafted a letter Zuma had signed ending the independent investigation Feinstein helped spearhead. "I couldn't tell [Feinstein], 'Look, this letter's not written by me,'" he murmured. ". . . I appreciate the fact that he said, 'But what happened? What must have changed Zuma?'"[7]

Now Zuma remembered this period, from 2000 to 2002, as one filled with several sets of unpleasant intrigue. When the director of the National Prosecuting Authority prepared a report for the president and Cabinet ministers shortly after the investigation was quashed, Zuma thought it odd that he wasn't briefed about the report. In 2003, he said, he felt compelled to release a statement in which he had insisted that he had never solicited a bribe or "used my public office to advance the private business interest of any person."

Zuma raised questions, at the time, about the "real motives" behind the probes of his finances and behavior. One of the characteristics of his defense, from then forward, was to concentrate on supposed bad motives by those who were behind his prosecution, as if they obviated conflicts of interest and corruption established at the sentencing of his close advisor, Schabir Shaik.

I asked, "Do you think you're going to have to deal with the arms deal scandal as president?"

"Well, I can't answer that question right now," he replied. "The problem is that there was an allegation made against me involving R500,000 from the French manufacturer. That opened up an investigation of me to this day. Now there's been allegations of huge sums of money that mention Mbeki."

"The thirty million," I put in.

He smiled. "There's no investigation [in that case], though," he said, as if this explained everything. He had been subjected to enormous pressure and ongoing inquiry; Mbeki had gotten off the hook.

"That, to me, is very strange," he went on.

Every time journalists asked Zuma about the case of corruption against him, he dodged the opportunity to provide details, or any careful accounting, by saying it was a matter in the courts and therefore he was prohibited from speaking of it. Now, the charges had been struck off the roll, so there was no good explanation for his refusal to answer questions.

"Can I just do the rude thing and ask this directly? I don't want to dance around it," I said. Zuma sank deeper in the couch, his eyes narrowed. He nodded. "Was there ever any quid pro quo of official actions taken in exchange for money?" I asked.

Zuma looked at me dead-on. "There was never anything of that nature," he replied, with an edge.

"In your official capacity, you never . . . ," I began, but he interrupted.

"There was *never* anything of that nature," he replied.

"Never a quid pro quo?" I repeated.

"Never, never, never, never," he said. He looked furious, and also a little exhausted. His eyes drooped. It was late, and he had an early start in the morning.

Still, who knew when I would see him again? So, I went at it from a different angle. "Is there anything, when you look back now, that you wish you'd done differently because it would *look* like a quid pro quo?"

Zuma squared his shoulders, glaring even more intensely now. "That was a very conscious relationship I entered into. We discussed it with Schabir a great deal. I'm clear about it. So there wouldn't be anything that I think we could have done differently," he said. "There was no ill intention of anything."

Here was another of Zuma's characteristic tics: when you asked about facts, or reasonable conjectures and political consequences of things he had done, he reassured you that his motives were quite correct. It reminded me of all the songs that had been sung around the country and in Polokwane, about his "clean heart," as if essentially good human beings were not transgressing all the time.

When I leaned in to ask another question, he cut me off. "If we were committing any crime, those files would not have been found in Schabir's office. There's no criminal that commits crimes and then puts it in the records," he said. "Even cash given to my kids in university—he was under instruction to record that. Why should I have done so if I was committing a crime?"

Zuma was implying that records used by the National Prosecuting Authority to build the case against him were actually a testament to this counter-narrative: if he had solicited a bribe, didn't I think he was smart enough to cover his own tracks? This seemed like an odd defense to mount for a man who soon would become president of a powerful, developing, modernizing middle-income country.

In a similar way, Zuma argued that the rape case was simply another piece of evidence, as if it was needed, of a long pattern of character assassination directed at him. "That was a staged thing!" he cried. Even now, with plenty of wreckage to be cleared still in the party and the country from the battles he had engaged, Zuma found no fault with his own behavior. He did not so much as admit that he had handed his enemies cudgels to use against him.

Stubborn adherence to a simple, grand narrative, in which he cast himself as the noble victim and never as the leader who had failed his movement or his people, had been his steady strength. "I felt, 'These people are dirty. . . . It's clear that they'll do anything,'" he told me, referring to the rape case.

"What was the effect on the rest of your life?" I asked, leaning back in my chair and expecting a long exegesis. He drove right to the point. "It was one of those things that, as a man, you have to go through," he replied.

Zuma reminded me that he had been convicted of subversion and spent ten years in prison as a result of an earlier betrayal from an informant within the ranks. "I knew, from that time, that the enemy is not only going to come across borders—the enemy can be within," he went on.

He said this offhandedly, but I found it chilling. It was so unreflective, conspiratorial, with no distinctions made between apartheid-era injustice and criminal investigations of top-level officials like himself operating in a new democracy. Here was a side of himself that Zuma had kept veiled in front of American policy-makers, journalists, and business people. It was a glimpse of the angry, emphatic, blinkered perspectives of the man who would soon be president of the Republic of South Africa, and would be charged with keeping the revolutionary vision of the ANC alive.

In Washington, Zuma needed no reminder, from me or anybody else, that decisions made in the far-flung citadels of world capitalism could radiate out to threaten the hope for sustained development held by his countrymen. His own political success, as leader of the governing party, hinged largely on decisions over which he had only marginal influence. Within days of the global financial meltdown in the fall of 2008, South Africa's currency weakened considerably as a result of errors made not in Johannesburg but in New York.

Third-world leaders, including the South Africans, had every right to feel indignant. The meltdown was caused by the profligacy of hedge fund investors and leaders of the largest financial institutions on Wall Street, yet it could negatively affect plans for everything from building new stadiums for the 2010 World Cup to job-training programs. Poverty alleviation relied on rising levels of foreign investment, access to credit, and much higher rates of economic growth. All of the country's hard-won progress was now at risk.

On his third day in the country, Zuma barnstormed across Wall Street, meeting privately with executives at Goldman Sachs and editors at the *Wall Street Journal*. Everywhere he went, the questions were the same: What would South Africa do about Zimbabwe? Would the integrity of the media and judiciary be protected? Would private property rights be respected under the new leadership? What would he do about AIDS?

He felt a rising sense of irritation at the repetitious nature of the queries, he confided. Americans seemed so parochial to him. He wondered why they raised questions about fraud only in the election in Zimbabwe. They didn't seem to know or care about recent stolen elections in Kenya and Nigeria. Why the clamor only for the protection of civil liberties and the formal trappings of democracy? Where was the concern for making social and economic justice real for the vast majority of the South African people? The only subjects his interlocutors raised with any enthusiasm, it seemed to him, were dictators, disease, and dystopia, the tired routine in any discussion about Africa in the West.

At the Harvard Club in midtown Manhattan, I tagged along when Zuma met with a small group of investors gathered to speak with him around a polished oak table. He was dressed in a conservative dark suit and traditional red power tie and looked a little wary. Zuma joined the scions of American capitalism like a high-level diplomat prepared for disarmament talks. Flanked by Mathews Phosa, Siphiwe Nyanda, and Phirwa Jacob Maroga, the newly appointed chief executive of the parastatal electricity colossus Eskom, he told the group that he welcomed "real engagement."

The first questioner from the American side was Frank Wisner, vice chairman of AIG, the insurance giant. He drove right to the central concern of potential investors: since the South African Left—the trade unions and Communist Party—had supported Zuma's candidacy for leader of the ANC against Thabo Mbeki, how would he "respond to pressure to change economic policy"? Wisner was a balding and open-faced man, soft-spoken but blunt as an interlocutor. He had served as ambassador in Zambia, Egypt, the Philippines, and India and was a former policy-maker in the Department of Defense.

The face-off between the two men—the longtime American official and the former guerrilla leader—was particularly poignant if you also knew that Wisner's father was among the founders of the Central Intelligence Agency and had participated in planning the anti-Communist overthrow of a democratically elected government in Guatemala in 1954. (Wisner himself would be placed at the center of world news several years later when he was sent to Egypt as an envoy of Secretary of State Hillary Clinton in a last-ditch effort to convince President Hosni Mubarak to relinquish power; he was repudiated by the Obama administration after being quoted as saying, "President Mubarak's continued leadership is critical.")

In the moment, Wisner cocked his round head, as if the angle might allow him to see this new leader of South Africa in a different light. "We are not going to change policy," Zuma replied, looking at the larger man straight on. Zuma did not blink, explaining for the umpteenth time that morning the principle of collective decision-making in the ANC. Government policy on private enterprise was long settled, Zuma insisted. It could not be altered by the shift from one national leader to the next.

The way Zuma spoke of party policy you might have thought the president of the ANC was nothing but a telegraph operator who faithfully transmitted consensus decisions to the world. The ANC's "Alliance partners" always participated fully in discussions about government policy, he conceded, but he added that the final say belonged to ANC officials. "In other words we need a balance here," he concluded.

Like leaders of other developing countries, Zuma already was used to being lectured by U.S. and European investors about the importance of unfettered markets and free trade. He previously had told me why this line of argument struck such a sour note. Investors like those in the room, after all, were responsible for the near meltdown of finance capital that threatened the rest of the world.

The company Wisner represented, AIG, had been pulled away from the brink of collapse, in the midst of the current credit crisis, by virtue of extension of $123 billion in emergency loans from the U.S. government. It hardly seemed as if he had much standing to argue against intervention by national governments to regulate markets. Others in the room were investors representing large hedge funds, which in the past three months had lost $180 billion in value, more than South Africa's annual budget.

Zuma gestured toward Phosa, Nyanda, and Maroga, explaining that they were businessmen capable of challenging the Communists and trade unionists within the governing alliance and prevailing in any fight over economic policy. It seemed telling that Zuma had not brought any of his chief supporters, the men centrally responsible for his survival as a political leader, along on this trip: Blade Nzimande of the Communist Party, Zwelinzima Vavi of the trade unions, Fikile Mbalula of the ANC Youth League, and Buti Manamela of the Young Communist League.

In his remarks to the investors, the ANC chief repeated what he had said to the secretary of state and president of the United States a few days earlier. He announced plans to revamp the entire educational system, emphasize skills training, and generate five million new jobs. Poverty alleviation efforts by the previous government had reached 12 million South Africans with social security grants, 8.3 million of them children, he reported. "But we want to create a developmental state, not a welfare state," he added, explaining that active intervention of the government was needed because the market still hadn't corrected for historic patterns of race and class bias.

Now Zuma was talking faster than I had ever heard him speak before. Usually, in English, he sounded a little halting and slightly stilted. He studied his own hands, as though wondering whether to share the unvarnished truth: there was a limited amount of time left to make visible, material progress before masses of people would get restive. "It would be a time bomb," he said softly. Everybody took a long look at him. He let the warning register.

In certain respects, at home, the global finance capital crisis provided a measure of vindication for the conservative macroeconomic policy President Mbeki had pursued from 1991 to 2008. It also raised an alarm for those advocating a more robust and interventionist policy by government, as I discovered six months later when I returned to South Africa for the 2009 national election campaign.

In the final weeks of the campaign, I drove out to Rivonia to a media briefing on the economy offered by the ANC. The briefing was held at Liliesleaf Farm, the historic site where leaders of the party underground once planned an armed revolution. Nearly forty years earlier, the quiet farm was the epicenter of revolutionary aspirations; on this day in March of 2009 it was the site for a sobering reexamination of the stymied effort to square the principles of the governing party's National Democratic Revolution with the exigencies of global capitalism.

At the briefing, Finance Minister Trevor Manuel argued that the national economic policy in the first fifteen years of democracy had aimed to protect the country from the "debt trap" so many other developing nations had fallen into. In this sense, it had been an overwhelming success; in his view South Africa had enjoyed balanced budgets and therefore had not ceded control of its national policy to outsiders.

The minister already had told his biographer that the example of Zimbabwe had been on his mind back in the late 1990s, when he had decided to impose heavy restraints on government spending at home. In Zimbabwe, large infusions of cash to leaders of the new nation from international lenders had driven up the national debt to unsustainable levels, encouraged graft, and entrenched a corrupt and autocratic leadership.[8] Minister Manuel, and President Mbeki, were determined to avoid placing South Africa's future in the hands of the World Bank and International Monetary Fund, a path that had also boomeranged on Latin American leaders a decade earlier.

In the burgeoning crisis of 2008 and 2009, low deficits and the accumulation of budget surpluses in South Africa served as partial buffers against the effects of the worldwide recession. The global economic contraction eventually hit South Africa hard, too, however. Nearly half of the country's economy was dependent on exports, and the global contraction revealed underlying vulnerabilities.

A large stockpile of iron ore sat unshipped at Saldanha Bay, north of Cape Town; vast supplies of manganese backed up in other ports. These were the visible reminders of the country's heavy dependence on trade in basic commodities. A once robust manufacturing sector, including domestic production of textiles, already had been crushed by the flood of Chinese imports.

Now China dominated manufacturing, India held the lead in service industries, and Latin America, led by Brazil, claimed a large proportion of agricultural production. It wasn't clear where the openings were, in the changing international system, for smaller, developing countries like South Africa.

Iraj Abedian, a banker and analyst, told the assembled journalists that there could be no significant expansion in the numbers of decent jobs without changing the terms of the game. The banker put his key concern this way: "Is not job growth the oxygen of a democracy? If we don't get growth, is the basis for democracy stable?" The banker thought that South Africa's future opportunities lay in the export of agricultural and mining technology and the sales of environmental retrofit devices to the rest of the continent.

Widespread stresses in the world's financial systems had exposed a web of unfair, unsustainable relationships at the heart of global capitalism. "You can't have China manufacturing everything and the United States consuming everything—on other people's savings!" the finance minister pointed out. "It just can't work."[9]

These fundamental problems had been largely ignored in the slapdash effort to stitch the first-world financial system back together. Shoring up the first-world financial institutions, as the Bush and Obama administrations had done, returned everybody to the starting point. The new terms, like the old ones, involved an unsustainable complex of relationships, from the vantage point of the developing world.

How could the South African government live up to its promises of lessening inequality and compensating for systemic patterns of racial discrimination? These constraints were more clearly visible in a place like South Africa, but the propulsive forces at the core of global capitalism also heightened economic and social inequality everywhere.

Journalists often wrote about the economy in developing countries as if every nation on the globe was headed toward—or, at least, wished to emulate—the same neoliberal destination, and as if every people longed for U.S. and EU standards of living. The deepening world economic crisis suggested a sharply different way of looking at the situation. Conditions in the countries of the north increasingly looked like those in the south, instead of the other way around.

If you followed this logic by turning the telescope in the other direction—looking at the developed world from the vantage point of the developing countries—it led to the unsettling possibility that the future of the world might be glimpsed more clearly from the so-called postcolonies than from the aging societies of the north.

This was the main thrust of an assertion by Jean and John Comaroff, South African scholars at the University of Chicago, who developed their argument in a series of papers and a book they had edited, *Law and Disorder in the Postcolony.* "It is as if the south, again reversing the taken-for-granted telos of modernity, is the direction to which point the signposts of history unfolding,"[10] they wrote.

The scholars noted evidence of this theme in the downsizing of government everywhere, in the rising rates of crime across the board, in the rampant corruption both whopper-sized and petty, and even in the ways the rule of law shrouded the oppressive effects of neoliberalism. "Postcolonies are hyperextended versions of the history of the contemporary world order running slightly ahead of itself," they argued. ". . . This is the ongoing present. It is history-in-the-making."[11]

By late 2011, world economic trends lent support to the Comaroff thesis. Suspicion settled in that growth rates above 4 percent were a thing of the past. Inequality bites; and it bit in the most pernicious ways in places still in recovery from historic traumas, such as the racialized oppression of apartheid.

A study by the Pew Research Center in mid-2011 showed that even in the highly developed north, the cost of the global economic contraction fell disproportionately on blacks and Latinos. Instead of becoming less racialized, inequality grew sharply more racialized in the United States during this period. A narrowing gap between American whites and minorities suddenly blew wide open; the median wealth of white households was twenty times that of black households, and more than a third of blacks in the country held zero or negative net worth.[12]

These were emerging common trends in uncommon circumstances; they suggested taking account of lessons to be learned, from places like

South Africa, about the persistence of racial bias built into the market-place. Here was another reason, this one rooted in self-interest rather than charity, for citizens in developed countries to pay closer attention to what was happening for the vast majority of people around the world.

In his inaugural address, back in 1999, Thabo Mbeki had described the state of the country, in anguished tones, as "*mahube a naka tsa kgomo*"— the dawning of the dawn, when only the tips of the horns of the cattle could be seen etched against the morning sky. Fifteen years later, the sun was up in South Africa and you could see the broad con-tours of its meaning—both what it had become and where it was headed.

South Africa had moved through at least three stages since its sup-posed liberation from apartheid—from a fraught handover of power under *Tata* Mandela, in the mid-1990s, to a new order under *Chief* Mbeki from 1999 to 2008, to this new post-apartheid/postliberation period under *Baba* Zuma—from Grandfather to Boss to Daddy. Each of the three leaders represented distinctive strands of the liberation move-ment: Mandela as an imprisoned elder; Mbeki as an exiled intellectual; and Zuma as a former guerrilla commander.

"*Wat verby is is verby,*" Nelson Mandela was widely reported to have said, in 1994. (Whether Mandela had actually said the equivalent of *The past is over, what's done is done,* the comment was so commonly cited because people desperately hoped that it could be so.) But, of course, the past was present still. In this perilous present, there were dynamics that Zuma needed to manage as president of the country, and he would have to do it with more finesse than he had ever had to exer-cise before in public life.

An autumn sun, blazing hot, drifted toward the horizon like a limp bal-loon. Just a week before the national election of 2009, people gathered early in the morning in the hill country of Limpopo, near the village of

Jane Furse. They were pressed together by the tens of thousands in a bowl of land between two cleared hillsides, a virtual sea of faces extended across the hilltop a quarter of a mile away. This was the way it had been for Jacob Zuma at mass rallies all over the country in the past several months as the campaign drew to a close. Suddenly, the helicopter carrying him swooped into view, and the place exploded. "Zuma!"

The ANC, the trade unions, and the Communists had swept across the country, unrolling a long-planned juggernaut of the kind South Africa hadn't seen since 1994. It was the most tightly organized campaign in the country's history, and the most expensive. Party leaders had raised the largest campaign treasury, much of it from foreign governments, large corporations, and super-wealthy members of the black elite. Under South African law, the sources of party funding did not have to be revealed publicly. So it was difficult for journalists to track what promises were being made in exchange for those contributions.

In her appearances around the country, Helen Zille, now leader of the opposition, regularly hit hard at the ANC's reputation for unseemly deals and slammed its leader. She cited the payments Schabir Shaik had made to Zuma—more than R4 million itemized in the charges drawn up against him by the National Prosecuting Authority—as "783 counts of corruption" and argued that this pattern of corruption in Zuma's career was one of many good reasons for voting against the ANC. (Soon though, the prosecuting authority would drop the charges of corruption, bribery, and tax evasion against Zuma.)

Later in the year, pollsters pinpointed the active campaign period, in early 2009, as the time when Zuma's personal popularity soared. In crisscrossing the country, he reassured South Africans of his leadership potential. During the rape trial in 2006, just 31 percent of black people had said they had "complete confidence" in Zuma, but this number jumped to 54 percent two years later. Masses of ANC supporters, wavering in their loyalties through the bitter split between Mbeki and Zuma, had flocked back into the party in response to the mass mobilization.

This trend, of a return to the fold for wavering supporters of the ANC, created a particularly difficult challenge for leaders like former party chairman Mosiuoa Lekota, who had broken off to form an alternative opposition party, Congress of the People (COPE). Young black people, in particular, began expressing broad and increasingly emphatic support for the ANC, for Zuma personally, and also for Julius Malema, the volatile and militant leader of the Youth League.

One of Zuma's closest confidants, Mo Shaik, felt that the defection of Mbeki allies to the new party had an unintended effect. "It galvanized the ANC like never before," Shaik had told me. "In a sense the formation of COPE was our 'Tora! Tora! Tora!' or Pearl Harbor. It caused the awakening of a sleeping giant." What Shaik meant was that the split by moderates aligned with Mbeki had put a serious scare into those left behind, and also freed party leaders to mount a much more explicitly left-leaning populist campaign.

Shaik, part of a network of former intelligence agents, would return to government after the election to head South Africa's Secret Service once Zuma took over. In 2011, he would also unceremoniously be fired from his post. He believed the success of a Zuma presidency would hinge on his ability to help rural masses of the kind who had turned out to see their leader on this day at campaign rallies around the country. "We've had massive disinvestment, both public and private, in agriculture. We have lots of land that could be redistributed, but its land that has fallen fallow," Shaik argued. "We're a net importer of food now! Once the farms shut down, there's massive movement of people into the urban centers. That's not sustainable."[13] Zuma's fate as a political leader, he believed, lay in what he could deliver in rural development.

Near the front lines of this particular crowd, close to the stage, I caught a glimpse of two young women holding a handmade cross, with Zuma's image and name at the top. The message, painted in unsteady letters, read, "BLACK JESUS." All across the country, the new leader had been greeted with similar expressions of adulation. Messianic allusions weren't part of the official campaign—cultish expressions of loyalty to individual leaders were supposedly verboten within the ANC—but Zuma had been making comments that implied a likeness to the suffering Christ ever since 2005.

I had been wondering, for some time, how deeply these intimations had landed with his public. So I made my way back into the crowd to speak with the woman who had painted the sign proclaiming a new black savior. She had a pleasant oval face and her hair was neatly braided. "He's the one! He's the one who will change things!" she cried. "*Big* change. He can do it!" I asked her why she thought Zuma would succeed where President Mbeki had failed. She shook the sign at me threateningly as if the answer was already written there. He was her savior, simple as that, she said.

The shirt Zuma wore was emblazoned with the image of Nelson Mandela. At his elbow as he walked out on stage was Julius Malema, the big-boned, pear-shaped young man who led the party's Youth League. The youth leader had pledged a cultlike devotion to the new leader, announcing that his supporters were prepared "to kill for Zuma." He regularly roiled the urban elites with his shoot-from-the-lip bravado, often antiwhite, anticoloured, and anti-Indian. Recently, he had denounced Zuma's enemies as spies and traitors, which were the kinds of epithets that led to possible execution during the struggle years.

"Long live Jacob Zuma, long live!" Malema chanted. "You must vote for the ANC! Or you will die from shock! We are burying [our opponents] alive!" he shouted, flashing a sly grin. He called on people not to fall for old, ethnic divisions. "We are people of Limpopo—not Shangaan, Pedi, or Venda [speakers]!" Malema assured listeners that the party was "closing a chapter of Mickey Mouse politics," a reference to both the former president's leadership and small stature.

Malema roused the crowd, in Sepedi, with his insistence that the Black Jesus had prevailed against all kinds of evil forces, including witch-doctors who had wanted "to kill Zuma!" "*Jwale re difithile boloyi Kwa*

Plolokwane, ke kafo Zuma a leng gona," he went on. ("Now, we have defeated witchcraft in Polokwane and that is why Zuma is here today.") He spoke of the ANC as an unstoppable force, and predicted that those who left the party would soon leave politics altogether because of their failing hearts. The crowd should learn from the example of these defectors, and embrace the fold. "If you are considering leaving the ANC, you must know that you are inviting hunger into your home," Malema threatened. "*Kamo gae mo, ho borutho, go-a tonya kantle,*" he continued. ("In this home of ours it is warm. It is very cold outside.")

Heroes of the struggle, including Chief Albert Luthuli, Oliver Tambo, Walter Sisulu, and Nelson Mandela, were all mentioned in the opening remarks, but nobody spoke openly of Thabo Mbeki, even though he had been head of the party and chief architect of postliberation politics. Now, the process of minimizing Mbeki's influence, and erasing memory of him at public events, was well under way.

The heaviest lifting in the electoral campaign had been accomplished by Zuma's allies already in government. In an effort that had proved especially effective in KwaZulu-Natal, the ANC had used its control of the provincial and the national government to arrange delivery of food parcels to far-flung communities. When these deliveries were made, entire departments of government officials traveled across the province to clear backlogs in requests for things like identity cards and applications for social grants. Long-stalled work on roads and bridges gave a taste of real overdue "service delivery."

This was how Zweli Mkhize, soon to become premier of the province, had explained the success of an effort he led: "We had mobile teams sent out to help people." People in far-flung communities, frustrated for so long by government inaction, were finally being taken seriously. "Once they have tasted it, they don't forget," he predicted.[14]

At the podium, before Zuma made his remarks, six women in skimpy nylon outfits colored ANC green and gold took the stage, showing plenty of skin. They gyrated to the up-tempo beat of reconfigured struggle songs. Party leaders sitting behind the dancers briefly fought the impulse to leer, but failed.

When the leader of the dancing group ducked behind the chairs to offer her hand, Zuma rose without any urging and boogied forward, crouching and swaying. His shoulders were rounded like the stick fighter he had once been, and he swayed, remarkably light and limber on his feet. Unlike Mbeki, who had always seemed pinched and closed off in the midst of the crowds, Zuma looked rested and happy dancing onstage.

The new leader couldn't speak Sepedi, the primary language of the crowd gathered before him. Most of his listeners could not understand English either. So the fine points of their leader's stump speech went right past them. He plowed through his remarks in English anyway, aiming them toward the cameras of the SABC.

His address reminded me of that fine, but largely unnoticed, speech I had heard Thabo Mbeki give in the Klein Karoo five years earlier. That's when Mbeki had seemed on top of his game as the most powerful leader on the continent. As it turned out, though, the forces that would topple him were already gathered and close at hand, including several of his own Cabinet ministers who would soon defect to the Zuma side. It was hard not to wonder if the same thing wouldn't happen to this leader, too.

"We must demonstrate that we are *different*," Zuma shouted to the crowd. His cheeks were drawn down in a pout. He admitted that there had been a few "shortcomings and gaps" during the first fifteen years of ANC government and bowed his head like a penitent, promising to correct the errors and crack down on corruption. "If some of us are corrupt, they must be dealt with!" he cried, which sounded especially awkward since he remained under threat of prosecution for receiving bribes himself.

Internal polling by the party revealed that most South Africans were more concerned about widespread corruption of a different kind, however. Their association with the word *corruption*, pollsters found, meant the kind of behavior they noticed among local councilors who were paid for a job they failed to do, or teachers who arrived late, and got drunk, and didn't teach, or mayors who gave government contracts to unqualified relatives.

When Zuma launched into a description of the planning commission he had proposed, and the "performance monitoring structure" he would establish once in office, you could feel the attention of the audience flag. "This is not play, governing the country!" he lectured. When his speech was over, the leader clenched his fists, arched his arms forward, hunched his body, and began to sing the struggle tune that had become an anthem among his supporters.

The crowd of people who had waited all day in the broiling sun to catch sight of him joined in, with enormous gusto. It sounded like a burst of relief, by both the leader and his followers, from a more complicated reality Zuma had just glossed over.

At the end of the rally, the leader shimmied his way down the gangway, hands up and palms outstretched. He skipped past me, lofted along by the cheers, and slid into a luxury BMW 4x4. Sirens wailed, and his entourage zipped off. The woman who had been holding the distinctive cross folded his portrait beneath her arm, the Black Jesus bending in two.

She looked suddenly downcast, as if her chance at redemption had vanished in the motorcade along with her hero. It struck me, then, that Zuma had failed to outline for her exactly what his government planned to accomplish on her behalf. What's more, he had said nothing at all about what she, and other people in the massive crowd, might accomplish for themselves—without his intervention or the efforts of government. For all the talk of empowering the people, and despite expressing a bias toward the poor, the ANC campaign as a whole was a rather wheedling, and disempowering, approach to building up people's experience of democracy in action.

In his long speech, Zuma had not even traced the distance from Nelson Mandela's promises in 1994 to Thabo Mbeki's proclamation in 1999 that the country was poised at "the dawning of the dawn," and on to the present moment. The overriding message of the campaign was an assertion of Zuma's own indispensability, and the indispensability of his party. The ANC had not structured its campaign to release, and direct, the vast latent organizing energy from the bottom up, which would be more characteristic of a great movement for social liberation.

The woman who thought of Zuma as a Christ-like figure had been left to trudge home past the scattering throng. She wandered through the dusty field to her shack, in a community in which people still emptied human waste into buckets and had no electricity. For the moment she held the image of her savior more firmly and hung onto a remarkably intense expression of quasi-religious faith in him.

When I caught up with the new leader a week later at Luthuli House, the ANC headquarters in Johannesburg, Zuma looked like a markedly different man. He seemed slightly shell-shocked by the pace of his campaigning and a little bloated. You could tell with a glance that he was a man of sixty-seven now.

His friends knew what the public hadn't been told: when Zuma got overly tired, he experienced drops in blood sugar from a health condition, chronic diabetes. I had seen this happen in the midst of his visit to the United States, at a reception at the South African ambassador's house. There, he had leaned back into the couch, the whites of his eyes showing, distant and not entirely cogent.

People who didn't know of his condition thought of these kinds of episodes as mere moodiness. The same thing had happened again at the end of our day rattling around Washington, when I had asked him directly about whether he had ever delivered a quid pro quo for the money Schabir Shaik had given him. It was clear that the rigors of the campaign, and the other demands of his life, including numerous ongoing romances, had pushed him near exhaustion. Now he seemed nearly ground to the nub.

"It has been enriching and exciting—at times very emotional," he replied, when I asked how he was doing. "When you come across the extreme enthusiasm and support of the poor people . . . you can't help feeling that these people need things to happen yesterday. You need to *move!*"[15] I reminded him of the trip to New York, where he had promised foreign investors that the party's economic policy would *not* change. At the time, he had seized on the difference between the sort of *changes* that might be upsetting to foreigners and a new phrase he had employed concerning *necessary adjustments*.

So I asked him, Were the changes he was suggesting out on the campaign trail "a matter of degree, or a matter of kind?" He shifted in his seat. "They could be both," he said, a pitch-perfect example of his reflexive instinct to split all differences right down the middle

His former comrades and current rivals, like former ANC chairman Mosivoa Lekota, were fanned out around the country to denounce Zuma, among other things, as a dishonest man, a rapist, and a Zulu-speaking chauvinist. The charge of chauvinism had his back up most of all. "There is no tribalism at all in Zuma. *None,*" he countered forcefully, when I told him Lekota had raised the issue with me in an interview. "People are trying to put a label [on me] that will not stick."

Zuma insisted that it was he who had done more than anyone else in modern South African politics to dampen ethnic tension. "Tribalism is a label used by politicians who are not very *matured,*" he added, stretching the last word out. In particular, he charged, "that man you are talking about"—as he referred to Lekota—had regularly raised the alarm about ethnic divisions in a disingenuous way. He warmed to the topic, claiming that it was Lekota rather than himself who had played on a sense of ethnic grievance, for example, by touting his election as chairperson of the ANC in 1997 as a victory for Sotho speakers. "He always talks about tribalism because it is in *him*," Zuma added. "He looks at things from ethnic, tribalist points of view. It is his problem, in his own *head*."

Zuma and his supporters had done plenty of damage on this score during their campaign against Mbeki in 2007, of course; the schisms he mentioned were inside more heads than Lekota's alone. Zuma's "fight back" against Mbeki had played into stereotypes of Xhosa speakers as clannish and conspiratorial, and Zuma's supporters had worn T-shirts announcing "100% Zulu Boy"—not 100% South African or 100% ANC.

When I switched angles, and asked if there was anything wrong with a political leader who took special pride in becoming the first Zulu-speaking president, he drew an interesting distinction. There was a difference between the understandable pride of his followers and the proper behavior of movement leaders, he remarked. "What I would not accept is people who are *matured*, who are *leaders*, to take that kind of pride. They can't," he said. "But you can't take it away from an ordinary person because their depth in politics is not that high."

He argued that people accusing him of being a tribalist were conflating this key distinction. "If you come from a particular ethnic group, these are your roots and that's where you come from, that's what you *are*. [If you] believe in your own culture, it doesn't mean you're a tribalist." Sometimes, because he identified himself as a person from Nkandla, he thought his critics had underestimated him. They had been victims of their own anti-Zulu bias, in his view. "Those who don't like it think you are stupid, you are backward," he said. "It's actually wrong. If you do your own culture, you are stupid, [while] if they do their own culture, they are clever. It shows how much they themselves have not matured to understand what a human being is all about."

Zuma only laughed when I asked about charges from Lekota and others that there was now a cult of personality around him. "Personality cults do not necessarily come from people like me. They come from different kinds of people, if you look at it historically," he told me. "People who develop a personality cult are people who are too self-centered. I am a cadre of the ANC. I act on what the ANC instructs me to do."

That's when I mentioned the handmade sign that had proclaimed him the "Black Jesus." He closed his eyes and smiled. I expected him to at least feign humility. After all, he had just denied any danger of a personality cult, and here was an early sign.

In the face of sacrilegious adulation, most politicians around the world would have sounded humble.

Instead, the new leader signaled acceptance of his supporter's outsize adoration. "It, to me, expressed the high expectations and, putting next to that, high expectations that this man, Zuma, can in fact meet those high expectations," he commented. "As you know, Jesus was an ultimate, the son of God brought here to help us. I think that this is what they think is going to be happening."

I wondered if he had any idea of how outlandish this sounded. "As a Christian," I said, before reining myself in. "You are a Christian, right?" I remembered both the sermon Zuma had given in an evangelical church before we met for the first time at his house in Johannesburg, and the ceremony I had seen him participate in with his brothers at Nkandla, in which the ancestors had been called on to help him triumph over Mbeki.

I thought, too, of all the other churches he had visited in the past five years. Zuma had a brilliant call-and-response relationship going with South African evangelicals. He observed me with brilliant neutrality, saying nothing. The lack of an answer to my question was a response of sorts: he would be whatever the moment required. Why should he be forced to make this a matter of either/or? He was the kind of character who preferred the conjunction *and*.

Zuma had woven a powerful narrative for himself that relied on a timeworn trinity—the rise, the fall through sin, and the rise again through redemption of a cleansed heart—and he would never give it up. It seemed to me that he had the kind of intuitive grasp of when to express himself with force and when it was in his interest, instead, to leave a blank slate upon which his followers could write their own varied and movable scripts.

The whole exchange led me to troll back in my memory to think about how assiduously he had nurtured the idea of Zuma-as-a-suffering-Christ figure, from his references in the 2004 campaign to the ANC ruling "until the Son of God returns," to mantra-like complaints of his suffering at the hands of a shadowy conspiracy and of his supposed "crucifixion by the media."

Zuma registered my reaction, leaning forward in his chair. "You talked to that woman with the sign? What did she say?" he asked. I thought back, remembering her uplifted, glowing expression. "She considers you a kind of savior," I replied. The woman clearly had taken the slogan quite literally.

He said, "It emphasizes the understanding of the people that here is this man who comes from the poorest of the poor, who has never forgotten us, who's been with us and for the first time we could have somebody at the decision-making who understands our plight and who's going to do something about it." The woman was "an innocent soul," he added then. Clearly, he considered himself the leader with the clean heart destined to lead a nation filled with innocent souls.

21.

The Prisoner

In the year between the campaign of 2009 and the World Cup of 2010, I often found myself stumbling through my days feeling as though I was living in limbo—teaching and residing in Chicago, sure enough, but preoccupied, most of the time, by what was happening half a world away. I was online when I wasn't in the classroom, and on Skype when I wasn't meeting with students. It was a strange kind of self-imposed exile within the ambit of a supposedly normal life.

The experience of being in the United States while dreaming of South Africa only amplified my sympathy for former exiles and freedom fighters forcibly kept from their home country. Many of them still had not returned fully to the new South Africa and fretted because they could not find the place they had longed to invent. "One cannot return to the same place as the same person," the Chinese writer Ha Jin had explained, in describing this kind of displacement. He pointed out that this was an ancient problem, faced even by Odysseus when he returns to Ithaca and "fails to recognize his own homeland."[1] Reading that passage one night, I thought: Ha Jin understands the tragedy of Thabo Mbeki.

In my case, I had flown readily back and forth for five years, and certainly recognized Chicago perfectly well after the year spent living in

Johannesburg. But I had emigrated almost entirely, in my imagination, to this other place I did not come from and where I would never belong. Even my dreams were filled with images of the high plains and golden grasses, and they were cast in that particular revealing angle of light above the escarpment.

The sounds of Simphiwe Dana in "Bantu Biko Street" came back to me while riding the El. When I was writing, I listened to Abdullah Ibrahim playing "Bra Timing from Phomolong" over and over again. On tape, I registered the urgent, insistent voices of hundreds of young people from interviews I had conducted. Each session of transcribing and listening to them all over again took me deeper into their points of view.

It was easy enough to keep track of five of my key informants—Gwendoline Dube, Ndaba Mandela, Vunene Mabasa, Thomas Maree, and Thuthu Zuma. They all had cell phones that worked most of the time. The void, while I was away, was Jonathan Persens, the homeless street kid who did not have a telephone, or Internet access, or a permanent address. Naturally, I worried more about him than the others.

What encouraged hope that he might survive was the fact that he had seemed to settle, by the end of 2007, on more reasonable expectations about what he might achieve in life. He no longer harbored dreams of becoming a rugby or hip-hop star. From two, brief conversations with Jonathan on the phone, I knew that he wanted to work with his hands. Above all other things, he still hoped to build a small bungalow for his mother and his sisters, bringing his family back together under one roof.

Jonathan wasn't alone in nurturing a dream of constructing a simple and fulfilling life. By the time of the national election in 2009, more than a third of South African children were not living in households with both biological parents. Nearly 64 percent of the country's children lived in poverty by 2008, which was down markedly from nearly 77 percent six years earlier, but still a stunningly large group.[2] This population of young people, almost two-thirds of South Africa's young, grew up in what amounted to an enormous incubator for social dysfunction and crime.

Since I had seen Jonathan last, I had been reading mountains of studies about young people and the links drawn between homelessness, drug and alcohol abuse, imprisonment, and violence in South African life. His story was my touchstone—the human face I referred to—as I read through the studies.

On the surface, it seemed perplexing that coloured people were imprisoned at a much higher rate than blacks and at ten times the rate of white citizens. On average, there were fewer coloureds than blacks in poverty, so the high incarceration levels were rooted, it seemed, in the gang history of the Cape Flats.

In early 2010, I had reread *The Number*, a gripping account of the Cape underworld by the journalist Jonny Steinberg; it helped explain how the long sentences in prison meted out to so many young coloured men had sealed their fates. "Prison is the great networking centre of criminal South Africa," Steinberg had written. "Spend four or five years of your life in the 26s, and wherever you go after that you will always find a brother with whom to do business. Prison has taken the illicit market to every village in the country."[3]

Jonathan came from the next generation of would-be gangsters, following in the footsteps of Steinberg's main protagonist. In our conversations, he had told me repeatedly that he intended to steer clear of any further involvement with contract crimes and the gangs, but when his job in the township ended because funding for the project ran out, he was thrown back on his own. Around the time of his birthday, in January of the New Year, Jonathan had thumbed a ride back into Cape Town. Stitching together scraps of information I could gather from a distance, I knew that he had returned briefly to the carpentry workshops at Salesian Brothers, but was thrown out of the program after getting embroiled in a nasty fight. Because he had turned nineteen, there weren't new shelters willing to take him in any longer. The Homestead took children in only until they were eighteen; Jonathan was now considered too old to be helped. After five years of struggling to take himself off the street, he was sleeping again in his old spot—in the ditch beneath the freeway.

One afternoon, when I rang through to the Homestead shelter from Chicago, he happened to be there, having stopped by to say hello to some of the younger boys. When he picked up the phone, Jonathan chatted with me as if we had spoken the day before. He presented a convoluted story about why he had been thrown out of the carpentry program— something involving the necessity of avenging a friend whose shoes had been stolen.

"I still gonna study woodcraft," he said. "I gonna still learn." Jonathan had gotten information from Gerald Jacobs about a new training program for welders; he figured this would be a good skill to have in the construction boom leading up to the World Cup. Every possible opportunity he mentioned sounded vaguely plausible, and there was an upbeat tone to his voice.

As I expected, he hadn't paid attention to politics during the intervening period at all. "Zuma? I don't follow it," he said, in response to a question from me. He had no report, either, about events closer to home, back in Atlantis. He had fallen altogether out of touch with his mother, sisters, and even his beloved granny.

When I pressed him about what he was doing since he was no longer in the carpentry workshop, he deflected the question. Jonathan had the habit of telling me bad news only if he could report on it in the past tense. He asked me to come fetch him for supper, so we could talk longer.

My heart dropped. I had to remind him that I was calling from Chicago. "Is it very far?" he asked. Yes, about thirteen thousand miles away, much farther than London, I told him. He urged me on: "Come fetch me tomorrow night then." I asked how he was surviving. There was another long pause. I could hear him take a long breath. "You must come here and I will tell you the truth then," he said. "When you come I will be talking to you for an entire day."

Activists from the liberation generation loved to complain about their children and grandchildren, dismissing them often, with a condescending shake of the head, as apolitical, ahistorical, and ungrateful youngsters. On the other hand, for what social, political, or economic breakthroughs—changes in the conditions of his own life—was a young man like Jonathan supposed to feel so grateful? Switch countries, and contexts, and it was the complaint of the older generation anywhere.

Struggle veterans claimed that young people were unaware of the sacrifices made for the free society created on their behalf. That wasn't the picture I had pieced together during six years of interviewing young South Africans from every socioeconomic group across the country. There was one thing, though, that nearly all young people I interviewed asked me to explain: Why did the elders—women and men my age and older—cling to power for so long? How had they gotten so set in their ways even while droning on about the need for revolutionary change? Why did they insist, even after they had run out of energy and new ideas, on carrying irrelevant business into the new age?

The short answer: they had been imprisoned, in a sense, by the party's ongoing electoral success. On the surface, the election results in 2009 had seemed a boon for the ANC, and for Zuma. The ANC had swept the national polls with 63 percent of the vote, falling short of the 69 percent won under Mbeki in 2004 but more than the margin of victory won under Mandela in 1994. Beneath the surface, pollsters found persistent signs of trouble among the young, though.

More than 70 percent of young voters polled by future*fact* in 2008 had announced that they intended to vote, but only 48 percent subsequently showed up at the polls a year later. Young people, in other words, were prepared to be engaged in political debate, but they were not inspired by the campaign. As it came to a close, the numbers expressing strong support for the ANC burgeoned, in large part only because the opposition parties had failed to address their concerns effectively.[4]

In the wake of the election, President Zuma followed through on his campaign promises, announcing an enlarged Cabinet in an effort to include representatives of the party's contending factions. He placed his oldest, closest allies in charge of police, national security, and intelligence agencies. Trevor Manuel, the former minister of finance, was named chair of the planning commission the new president had described during the campaign. Well-respected centrists took over key finance portfolios.

Early reviews, even by formerly critical editorial writers, were positive initially. Those who were close to Zuma reported that he had settled into his new job with confidence and a sense of purpose. "He's way more relaxed since the election," his daughter Thuthu said shortly after his inauguration. "He's less stressed. You would think he would be more stressed, given the responsibility he has now. But he's more at ease—yah—done with defending himself and now ready to start *proving* himself."[5]

Thuthu and her sisters had spent time on the campaign trail in 2009, both with their father and with their mother, Nkosazana Dlamini-Zuma, the Mbeki insider who had been retained in her ex-husband's new Cabinet as minister of home affairs. Thuthu thought that you had to get out amid those raucous crowds to grasp the ANC's ongoing hold on the loyalty of ordinary people.

In the northern province of Mpumalanga she had gone door-to-door with her mother. The conversations with villagers all boiled down to three things: poverty, corruption, and crime. She had campaigned, too, with her father in the Eastern Cape. "It was all kind of weird," she noted. The crowds surged forward, shouting chants of utter devotion to her father. "People were saying my dad was the Black Jesus—people actually *saying* this! People crying at the sight of him! It was insane."

His daughter began thinking of Jacob Zuma as two distinct beings—

her daddy, on the one hand, and the lionized icon worshipped "because he is president of the ANC." Julius Malema, the youth leader, had come along on the same tour, and Thuthu found him much smarter than she had been led to expect. She noticed that when Malema was present on the platform, if he wasn't scheduled to speak people clamored to be allowed to hear from him. Thuthu thought that the roar of the crowd for Malema was sometimes even louder than the cheering for her father.

Now that the campaign was over, she was happily returned to her anonymous life as a college student. She also had filed her application for a joint degree in anthropology and international relations and was dating someone seriously for the first time. Most of all, Thuthu was hoping to see the Zuma name in fewer embarrassing headlines. She had talked with her father, among other things, about his trip to Copenhagen, where he had helped salvage an agreement at the international conference on climate change. He had shown a new, more intense interest in environmental sustainability, taking pains to absorb the substantive details of the probable effects of drought and rising seas on South Africans. So far, though, the president's interest in climate change had not gotten as much attention as periodic revelations about his romantic liaisons.

Thuthu said that she had learned to screen most of it out, taking the headlines "with a pinch of salt." In the end, she believed the fixation on his sex life boiled down to widespread disapproval of polygamy. She framed the issue this way: everybody was so interested in the fact that her father continued to date, even though he had multiple wives, but how did they think a polygamous married man met and identified additional wives without courting?

Meanwhile, there were rifts within the Zuma family, some of them concerning ethically questionable business opportunities thrust at relatives of the new president. A nephew and several of his children were suddenly found on the boards of new companies with lucrative ownership shares they had neither bought nor earned.

There were political divisions among members of the family, lurking beneath the surface, too. For example, Thuthu's older sister, Gugulethu, was now a regular star on *Isidingo*, one of Africa's most popular soap operas. Unlike her sisters, she had not felt comfortable out on the campaign trail with her father. This was so, in part, because Gugu felt wary of the cultish passions invoked by ANC organizers during the 2009 election effort. "It was crazy. My dad was treated like a rock star," she had told me over the phone. "It all seemed very *pie in the sky*."[6]

Gugu had clashed with her father recently on a private matter as well. She had married Wesley Ncube, the son of Welshman Ncube, a leader of the opposition to Robert Mugabe in Zimbabwe, at the end of 2008. As part of bringing the two families together they had hosted two modern, perfectly pleasant ceremonies, one in Pretoria and the other in Cape Town. When it came to the traditional celebration of the marriage at her father's homestead, however, there was tension between father and daughter. Gugu said that she had gone to him in advance to discuss her reservations, and her father had agreed not to force her to wear freshly slaughtered animals or smear bile over her body. For her, the compromise was needed in order not to infringe on her own beliefs as an evangelical Christian.

When the wedding party had arrived in Nkandla, however, Gugu felt that she had been "totally ambushed" by her father. She was garlanded with bloody pelts and browbeaten into rituals that felt foreign to her. In the end, it had been her mother, the former minister of international affairs, who had been forced to negotiate a truce that allowed the ceremony to continue. "He becomes a totally different person in Nkandla," Gugu told me, sighing. "He's so different when he's there than when he's with us at home." It was skillful navigation between his two identities that had been the basis of his political success, though.

Thomas Maree was Thuthu Zuma's former classmate from Westerford High and lived not far away from the ditch where Jonathan Persens slept.

Like Thuthu Zuma, he found himself in a relatively upbeat mood in the wake of the national election. He was the son of Helen Zille, leader of the opposition, and in 2009 his mother had been elected premier of the Western Cape. In the matric examination, Thomas had scored well enough to be accepted to study economics and history at the University of Cape Town, where his father taught industrial sociology.

His studies, unlike Thuthu's, were not disrupted by the campaign, for the Zille/Maree offspring were not expected to participate. His mother had not asked her husband or children to accompany her as she crisscrossed the Western Cape in the search for votes. "She doesn't impose that on us," Thomas told me. "She likes to keep family and politics separate. Family means a lot to her, and when she comes home she wants to spend time with us here."[7]

As in her bid to become Cape Town mayor several years earlier, the campaign for premier seemed like a long shot. All of the country's provinces, as a result of the election in 2004, were governed by ANC leaders, after all, and the campaign juggernaut put together by the governing party was formidable. During the campaign, Zille had been the target of vicious attacks, but Thomas said he hadn't worried about her reaction because she was so tough and skilled at shrugging the nonsense off.

His only direct experience of the push-and-shove came when he attended a speech Julius Malema gave on the campus of the University of Cape Town, where he was studying. "That was quite scary because the Youth League has a lot of influence," Thomas reported. The youth leader's talk was stuffed full of hoary revolutionary rhetoric and he had called on students to roust "counterrevolutionaries" from their positions and "Africanize" South African institutions. When he was jeered, Malema accused the students who disagreed with him of being agents of a conspiracy to disrupt his address by Helen Zille.

As we talked about Malema's rise in power and influence, I reminded Thomas that we had both once listened, at a gathering of his friends back in 2007, as they invoked Jacob Zuma in a similar way, as a specter of looming apocalypse for the country. Thomas readily admitted that he had had a change of heart concerning the president himself. "It was an exaggerated fear," he said. The triumph of his mother's Democratic Alliance in the Western Cape offered hope for the emergence of a more robust multiparty system in South Africa.

"It's a great thing for democracy in this country, and South Africa has the healthiest democracy on the continent," he went on. "This shows the ANC doesn't have hegemonic control. It's a huge cultural shift my mother created, to allow people to question, for the first time, their loyalty to the ANC."

Thomas missed many of his closest friends, now scattered all over the world for college. Their messages and phone calls fanned his own wanderlust. He felt sure that, unlike most of them, he would make his career, and his life, inside the borders of South Africa. In the meantime, though, Thomas wanted to see more of the globe. He was not keen to travel to Europe or the United States. Instead, he wanted to see more of the developing world. "Once I graduate, I'd like to travel and experience other cultures," he added. "I understand my own culture better now. But it helps you to see it more fully if you get out of your comfort zone." He had his sights set on South America and Asia.

When I returned to South Africa in the middle of 2010, I made a purposeful series of visits around the country to see each of the young people who had helped me understand the challenges of the next generation. Jonathan Persens, as usual, was the toughest to track down. Whenever I called Cape Town, it seemed that he had retreated back to Atlantis; and whenever I reached his aunt's house in Atlantis I was told that he hadn't been spotted in his home community for ages. Finally, by the time I landed back in the

country in June, there was word that Jonathan had been busted for breaking into a car and hauled off to Pollsmoor Prison, the penultimate place
where Nelson Mandela was incarcerated before his release in 1990.

Pollsmoor Prison was also the setting of Jonny Steinberg's book *The
Number*, the account I had read of one gang leader's effort to get *out* of
prison. Jonathan, clearly, was headed in the opposite direction, behind the
walls of the country's most terrifying institutions. I remembered the fear he
had expressed about the 28s, the gangsters who "wanted your bum," as well
as all the times he had told me that he would do almost anything to stay out
from under other people's thumbs.

The rituals of gang membership, Steinberg had written, were "erected
to defend prisoners from two awful fates: becoming boys, and becoming
women." New members were inducted as so-called sex-sons, or *wyfies*. In
relationship to their warders, "they are told when to eat, when to sleep,
when to wash and when to brush their teeth. . . . Imprisonment is the most
infantilizing experience imaginable."[8]

I flew to Cape Town in July to inquire about the process of visiting
Jonathan. Pollsmoor was one of 239 prisons nationwide. When the ANC
came to power after the election of 1994, the prisons were already filled
to capacity, with 118,000 people behind bars. By 2010, there were even
more prisoners, 164,793 of them, which meant that South Africa's prisons were nearly 40 percent beyond the capacity.

The demography of the prison population revealed an astonishing
gender divide: only 2.4 percent of those imprisoned were women. It also
revealed a tragedy at work within the criminal justice system: 30 percent
of the mostly young men being held were awaiting trial, which meant
that nearly a third of the prison population had not been convicted of a
crime but were living inside institutions that functioned largely as
recruiting stations for the gangs. More than 54,000 people had been
swept into this system, waiting for a day in court.[9]

When I went looking for Jonathan inside the prison system, though,
nobody seemed to be able to locate him at Pollsmoor. A friend of his

reported having seen him escorted inside, but there was no record for a booking that had been completed under his name. Jonathan seemed to have offered a false name, as prisoners often did, and to have vanished entirely into the vast netherworld of prison life.

One afternoon, I met with one of his best friends to check the details of Jonathan's stories with someone else in his circle. The young man I met, outside the municipal swimming pools at Sea Point, told me that he was the one who had taught Jonathan how to *skarrel* in the first place. He bowed his head, and took credit, too, for having taught the younger boy how to stab and rob.

The friend said that he felt a little ashamed of having recruited his friend into such bad behavior. In the dying sunlight on a winter day, I read out sections of my manuscript that implicated both boys in the commission of crimes. The friend confirmed many of the relevant details and offered small corrections.

In general, he thought Jonathan had given me the truth about life on the streets, but he also thought of him as more of a reluctant participant in the assaults than the brash gangster he had portrayed in retelling the events to me. The friend volunteered that he himself had been trapped in a cycle of crime and desperation that had led him to sex work. It was important to him for me to understand, right away, the precise terms of what happened when he traded sex for money.

"I don't give him my bum, I put mine inside," he said, not blinking. He wanted me to know that he upheld standards and hung onto his pride. When we finished going over parts of the manuscript that had to do with Jonathan and himself, we shared dinner. As we were finishing, he announced brightly, "I heard that Jonathan got out of Pollsmoor today."

The next day, I canceled my appointments and haunted the places where Jonathan had hung out—in the food pantry for homeless people next to the cathedral, the gardens where several acquaintances reported having seen him, and the expansive lawns beside the National Museum where drunks and drug addicts often crashed during the day. I spent two days hunting for him.

On my last morning in Cape Town, that's where I found him at last. Jonathan was face down in the grass, splayed out as if he had been flung from a great height. I recognized him by the distinctive shape of the top of his head, where his curly hair whorled in an unhappy bunch. "Jonathan?" I asked. He turned over, blinked, recognized me, and asked how my trip back to South Africa had been so far.

Over fried chicken and Pepsi, Jonathan told me that he had been sent to prison for breaking into a car. Being in Pollsmoor was much different than he had expected, not nearly as scary. Prison was a kind of revelation to him, in fact. On balance, he was glad he was sent there, though. "I did get almost crazy there in prison. I did almost lose my mind," he allowed.

He was forced to fight every day to protect himself from assault, he said, but there was this compensation: he had met older men who accepted him, helped protect him, and offered to help him get ahead in life when they were released. "It's like a family," he said. "They were very, very good to me."

When I asked how he had been surviving on the street before he went to prison, he told me without any indication of shame that he had made his money by robbing tourists at knifepoint in the beautiful colonial-era gardens stretching from the far side of Parliament to the fashionable neighborhood at the base of Table Mountain. "It's so easy!" he exulted. "There are so many tourists with so much money!"

I asked if he did not feel the least bit sorry for his victims. "No, why?" he replied. I told him that during my last trip to Cape Town, during the election campaign the previous year, I had been mugged at gunpoint, and so I knew what it was like, and how terrible it felt, to be assaulted in this way. There was a long pause. "I guess if we were not friends, I would rob you, too," he said, sounding puzzled about why I had mentioned my experience on the wrong side of a gun.

Jonathan told me that his career as a robber had gotten much easier for him since he had begun smoking *tik*, the methamphetamine that was the focus of President Mbeki's trip to the Western Cape three years before. "It has helped me in my *work*," he insisted. When he took the drug, he said, he was freed from all spasms of conscience.

"It did blow my mind. It let me think about a lot of bad stuff. It let me think about it, and go into it. . . ." Now, the drug allowed him to do what needed to be done—robbing people, breaking into cars, fighting, robbing houses—without stressing over it. "I am not so nervous anymore," he added. "It's nice to rob. It's nice, really. It's almost as if you are in your own world. You don't feel anything. You don't even feel a little bit of pain."

I asked, "It's exciting?" And he said, "Very exciting. I want to rob a bank now." His new friends from prison, it turned out, had promised to include him in a fail-safe plan they had for pulling off a successful bank robbery when they got out of Pollsmoor.

Jonathan wanted to share with me an epiphany he had experienced during one long night inside prison. He had decided that he needed a big haul of money so he could set off in search of his father. "I have to find my dad first, and then everything would be okay for me," he said. "I got out of prison Monday, and this is Tuesday. So, I must find my dad."

This was mind-bending news because Jonathan had always told me his father was dead. I remembered Gerald Jacobs having said that every homeless kid had a big issue that had to be resolved before he would come off the streets. Jonathan had seen only a single photo of his father in his entire life.

He felt sure now, though, that his mother had lied when she had told him his father died of AIDS. If he could find his father, "then I would leave everything [behind]," he argued. It wasn't clear what he thought the long-lost dad could say to him, or do for him. "I *must* find him," Jonathan insisted.

With a meal under his belt, he seemed quite expansive. Jonathan was wearing a nice red nylon jacket that fell open, revealing that he had lost weight behind bars. He had a pair of new sneakers on. Jonathan sounded more cogent than usual. We took a stroll through the gardens, stopping to sit on a park bench.

I told him that Gerald Jacobs felt optimistic, even now, that Jonathan would get off the street for the last time and succeed in building a more normal life. "I still have hope," Jacobs regularly told me, like it was mantra, whenever I expressed doubts about Jonathan's future. I asked him directly: "Do you have the same hope?"

"No, not really," he told me, just like that. "I will try, but if I can't, I can't." There were two possibilities, Jonathan had decided—he might become a soccer trainer or a bank robber. He weighed the merits as though deciding between colleges he might attend.

There was a young people's soccer league in the city he had played in, and he had managed to work his way up to being the coach's assistant. Even in the middle of his crazy schedule as a thief, Jonathan endeavored to stay faithful to the team's schedule.

"If it worked out for you to be a soccer trainer[, what then]?" I asked. "Then I would not rob anymore, not hurt anybody anymore," he told me, sounding certain.

I pressed further: "If you were a betting man, and you were betting on how things were going to work out for Jonathan Persens, would it be that he was going to be a soccer trainer or would it be that he's most likely to become a bank robber? What do you think is the most likely end of the story?"

Jonathan looked at me, curled his lip, and looked down. "Bank robber," he said.

"Why?" I asked.

"Because there's a lot of money there!" He paused. "And to find my father."

By then, I was already late in setting off for the airport. It would take a flat-out race for me to make it now. I reminded Jonathan that we had known each other for three long years already. "I hope you'll become the soccer trainer," I told him. "Because I think it's more likely that you'll stay alive and have a good life [then]."

He averted his eyes. "That's what I want for you," I went on. Jonathan looked to his left, gazing off over my shoulder. I wanted to shake him and turn him upside down. I wished he would repeat what I had just said, and somehow come to believe in it.

In all the near miraculous turns in his life so far—his original decision to come off the street, the move to the shelter in Khayelitsha, his participation in the soccer team for homeless kids, his encounter with Nelson Mandela, the job he had taken in Atlantis—there had always been a sliver of hope in which I imagined his eventual redemption. After all, he had been the one to tell me, at the end of 2007, of his firm decision to leave his life of crime behind and that he wanted most of all to become a good man.

"Are you a good man?" I blurted out. Jonathan paused, set his chin, and considered me. He seemed to remember the conversation. In all of our previous talks, I think he had been calculating what I was prepared to hear and sometimes offered answers based on his assessment of my hopes.

"Not actually," he replied. "Not anymore." Here, boiled to its essence, was the most disturbing effect of Jonathan's inability so far to get real traction in acquiring a decent life, which had been promised to all in the new South Africa: he was no longer in a struggle with his own conscience. Before, he had always spoken like someone in a loud argument with himself about how to become a moral man, and how to protect his dignity while behaving in a dignified way toward everybody else. An older guy who knew Jonathan and also worked the gardens for easy marks arrived then. He swooped in on me, demanding money. "What are you telling this man?" he barked. I put away my camera and gathered up my things quickly. Jonathan offered me a firm, friendly handshake. "See you next time," he said.

22.

The Cup

Arriving back in South Africa in the middle of 2010 felt, at first, like walking into fantasyland. The World Cup competition, so long awaited, had taken over the country. The schools went into recess, and much of South Africa's normal political and corporate business was placed on hold, which was a much more pleasant form of limbo. From start to finish, there was an exuberant feeling of having beaten the odds. In every meaningful way South Africa had surpassed expectations, not only of its own citizens but of the tough critics among outsiders as well.

Getting all ten stadiums in nine cities prepared for sixty-four games of world-class soccer was no modest enterprise. Several stadiums rose from the ground up, and others had needed massive retrofitting to be ready for play. "Millions watched as we pulled off what many said we could not in a stadium they said we would never be able to build," was the way Danny Jordaan put it. He was the sports mogul and CEO of the local organizing committee who had been right at the heart of the enterprise.[1]

"People felt that South Africa would not do it," President Zuma admitted.[2] From the beginning, top officials had worried that if any number of things largely outside the government's control went wrong—

tourists were robbed or murdered, terrorists struck, or the lights went—the negative effects would be difficult to blot out. In certain respects, South African national dignity was at stake in the games.

Now, a week into the tournament, the critics had been proved wrong on every count. When the event opened on June 11, President Zuma announced that the Cup would "showcase Africa's potential to the world." In a stretch too far, he claimed the event would show that the continent "sings in the voices of many traditions and dances to the beat of our shared pulse."[3]

During the first week of competition, I had watched the games from my apartment in Chicago, tearing myself away from the screen only at the last minute to go off and teach at the university each day. The coverage on ESPN unspooled like promotional commentary from the South Africa Tourism Board. The buses worked; the new roads were smooth; the stadiums were soaring beauties; the systems for moving people from hotels to stadiums, and from city to city, were stunningly efficient. The distinctive horns known as *vuvuzelas* were always roaring.

Crime, organized and otherwise, had been brought under control, partly as a result of the government's hiring of forty thousand temporary security agents. By the end of the World Cup, more than three million fans would pass through the gates of the stadiums, only to be directed to their seats and watched over by more than eighteen thousand volunteers. It certainly surpassed the picture of what I had expected to happen six years earlier, when I watched the hosting rights granted to South Africa from the township park in Soweto.

Though I had seen this lionizing coverage from afar, I was not fully prepared for the sensation of national levitation that swept me up on my arrival. The ubiquitous World Cup slogan was "Feel it," and the song "Sign of a Victory" a ubiquitous anthem. On my first afternoon back in Jozi, three strangers approached me on the street—a domestic worker, a private security guard, and a street sweeper—to embrace me and thank me for coming.

Everywhere I went, longtime friends, even curmudgeonly types who had predicted disaster for the Cup back in 2004, struck unexpected patriotic poses. They wore the colors of the national team, flew South African flags from their car antennas, crowded into buses to get to games in the middle of the day, and reported a sense of cross-racial unity, and pride, in the nation's achievement. Several said that it seemed like the arrival of another miracle, just like in 1994.

"It meant the *world*," the trade union leader Zwelinzima Vavi told me when I stopped by COSATU headquarters to speak with him. He remembered the pandemonium surrounding the announcement that South Africa's bid to host the games had been successful, six years earlier. "To be honest, I never thought it could go so well." Vavi had served on the Local Organizing Committee, and he had seen popular support grow, across lines of race and class, until one night right before the games when hundreds of thousands of people showed up for a parade in Sandton. "When I saw that crowd, I could see Nelson Mandela's dream unfolding," he said. Across from where he was sitting in his office was the old poster of Mandela as a boxer that had been an iconic antiapartheid image. So many whites and blacks had been in that throng together. "The Freedom Charter told us that the country belongs to all who live in it. That was what we saw during the World Cup. . . . It would be a tragedy if we let that spirit slip out of our hands." The question that came to him next stopped him in his tracks: "Can we be so united behind other national goals?"

By mid-June, the South African team, Bafana Bafana, was already out of the competition, but not before famously holding Mexico to a 1–1 draw in the first game of the championship. African hopes for having a team from the continent in the quarterfinals transferred to Ghana. Local rooting for Ghana, like the excitement over the earlier but disappointed hopes for Côte d'Ivoire, Nigeria, and Cameroon, marked a welcome counterweight to an anti-immigrant furor that had swept through Johannesburg and Cape Town in 2008. Riots and murders of more than sixty African immigrants two years earlier had shocked the world and traumatized black newcomers to South Africa, including large numbers from Zimbabwe. It was African players who were being lionized for their prowess in the first two weeks of the World Cup. A pan-African spirit emerged; the question was whether it could be sustained, of course. Africans were presented not as competitors for jobs or as pimps, drug runners, and thieves—as Zimbabweans and Nigerians were often described by average South Africans—but rather as vehicles for the dream of continental uplift. It was something like a sports version of Thabo Mbeki's African Renaissance. In impromptu rallies, mobs of South Africans cheered on the team they had dubbed "Ghafana Ghafana," a linguistic embrace of trans-African pride.

South Africans were always among the most sports-crazed people on the globe, and now the whole country fell into a hyper-addicted swoon. As in every other aspect of national life, race still ran through it. In 1995, a year after he became president, Nelson Mandela suddenly had appeared in a stadium packed with fans, to cheer on the national rugby team, the Springboks. The team, predominantly white in a predominantly white sport, was supported fanatically by the country's minority white population. The new black president's unexpected appearance at the championship match came in the midst of other iconic gestures toward reconciliation and national unity, achieved mostly by fudging the old racial divides.

"Sport has the power to change the world," Mandela said at the time. ". . . It is more powerful than governments in breaking down racial barriers."[4] Now there was an opportunity to test this lesson in reverse—to see if whites would come out to join the predominantly black fan base for soccer. They did, in large numbers.

The world tournament provided a much-needed boost for Zuma, too. It also revealed weakening support for him as president, however. During his first year in office, the new president had moved quickly to put his stamp on national affairs. He had appointed a tough-minded team to monitor progress in implementing government policy and brought in a dynamic new minister of health, charging him with turning the tide in the fight against AIDS. Zuma surprised even longtime critics with his newfound mastery of international affairs. He drew close to U.S. Secretary of State Hillary Clinton and President Barack Obama.

At the UN Summit on Climate Change in Copenhagen in 2009 Zuma proved himself particularly helpful to the Americans. There he was the only African head of state among the small group of leaders—from Brazil, Russia, India, China, and the United States—who fashioned a face-saving final statement for the troubled conference.

"They respected him very much," reported Deputy Minister of International Affairs Ebrahim Ebrahim. "They were keen to see South Africa as part of the discussion." In a punishing schedule of world travel to global gatherings, President Zuma had tried to make it clear that South Africa would continue to punch above its weight. "We have been a bit reluctant to appear too [influential]," Ebrahim noted. "[Now] the feeling of the Western countries is that South Africa must push its weight around."[5]

As Zuma gained respect on the world stage, he lost ground at home. News of his unusual romantic life often undercut public recognition of any of his international achievements. Presidential sexual liaisons with young women were a tabloid editor's dream, and Zuma was a gift to the tabloids and satirical cartoonists that kept on giving. "He's like Mr. Bean," one of his aides said. She was a former admirer and close friend who had become wary of the way Zuma mixed personal pleasure with public business. The advisor said that the president seemed to be running the country the way he ran his private affairs—too much by the seat of his pants.

As if to underscore this point, on the day Zuma was flying back from the Copenhagen summit, the *Sunday Times* revealed in a front-page exclusive that he had fathered yet another child out of wedlock, this time with the daughter of a friend, one of the country's soccer moguls.[6] An old friend of Zuma's told me that even his closest friends were stunned. "There was disappointment in him. I thought he crossed the line too many times," the minister said. One of Zuma's own children put the matter more bluntly: "It's gone beyond culture and tradition now. People are not animals." In this conversation with Zuma's child, I suggested that since he had spent his twenties behind bars and much of his thirties and forties on the move as an operative of the party's armed wing, perhaps he engaged in so many affairs partly to make up for lost time. But his child believed that the recurrent scandals over his sex life revealed something nearly pathological about his attitude toward women. "It's like he thinks he's Hugh Hefner or something."

The public clamor that followed news of this newest mistress, and latest child, caught the president's advisors off guard. After initially insisting that his romantic life was a private matter, aides convinced him to issue a formal apology. On the bulletin boards of websites operated by major media houses, readers asked why multiple wives were not enough for him. Why, they asked, did the president also insist on betraying his own friends by bedding their daughters?

During the campaign, President Zuma had promised to promote "service delivery," ride herd on a sluggish government bureaucracy, and change the direction of the country. Behind closed doors, he also had promised top ANC officials that he would not embarrass the party again. Even die-hard supporters questioned his excessive risk-taking. Was it self-sabotage? Others wondered how he could keep track of targets and programs when he set aside so much time for courting.

Even in the midst of mostly positive coverage of the games, news of Zuma's private life kept intruding on his public role. The president seemed stung when his comrades didn't swiftly rally to his side this time, as they had before when he was criticized. His relationship with the ANC Youth League deteriorated already after a series of public exchanges with its leader.

Julius Malema, who earlier had pledged "to die for Zuma" and had appeared on countless stages with Zuma all across the country during the campaign, turned with a vengeance on his former idol. The Youth League leader announced, "In politics there are no permanent friends and no permanent enemies."[7] He implied that Zuma, in the way he had stifled internal political debate, was even worse as a party leader than Mbeki.

When the youth leader was brought up on discipline charges within the ANC, and then fined and sanctioned, the tension between the two former allies deepened. In mid-May, the Youth League announced a "One Boy/One Girl" campaign in the fight against HIV/AIDS, which never had been high on its agenda before. It was a bold blow aimed directly at Zuma. One of Malema's backers told a reporter, "South Africa will never win the battle against AIDS as long as we have a president who has more than one wife and even has a child out of wedlock."[8]

The schism between Zuma and Malema was presented, by journalists, largely as a tiff between the older leader and a more militant young stalwart, but there were strands of political disagreements worth noting. These disagreements revolved around Malema's contention that there should be more *Africans*—meaning blacks—among the party leaders placed in charge of economic and financial decision-making in the government. He pushed for nationalization of some of the country's mines, a call that had been raised at the party conference in Polokwane.

These policy positions staked out by the Youth League placed Malema and his allies at cross-purposes with the leaders of the trade union movement and the Communist Party. The three organizations were once fellow constituents of the pro-Zuma faction. Respected elders like Ebrahim Ebrahim worried about the consequences from this opening ideological breach. He characterized Malema's political stance as a radical lurch to the *right* on the part of the Youth League even though he wrapped his statements in populist terms.

"There is nothing socialistic about them," Ebrahim said, when I met him in his office at the ministry of international affairs and cooperation in Pretoria shortly after the World Cup. The deputy minister was worried that the direction of the Youth League signaled the emergence of an anti-Left perspective from "the new elitist middle class." He wasn't the only one who thought about potential dangers from a populist and militant faction with a right-wing, racialized twist and their potential to sow more divisions within the ANC.

In the following year, the split would widen further. Despite the efforts of his opponents within the ANC, Julius Malema was overwhelmingly reelected as president of the Youth League in 2011. He promptly signaled that he expected to continue playing an outsize role in party politics through the next national election in 2014. Implicated in a plan to replace Gwede Mantashe, secretary-general of the party, with the deputy sports minister, Fikile Mbalula (Malema's predecessor in the Youth League), Malema carried himself like a kingmaker. Zuma had only himself to blame; after all, he had treated Malema like a trusted confidant during the campaign.

In several years of close alliance with Malema, Zuma provided a regular, and quite elevated, platform for the younger man. During the 2009 campaign, Malema had insulted his political rivals, including ANC elders who had been allied with Thabo Mbeki, in the rankest possible terms. The president stood silently by. At the rally I'd seen at Jane Furse, Malema had played on fear, mocking traditional beliefs and presenting the Zuma forces as so powerful they could even vanquish witchcraft. He had predicted that the president's opponents would "die of fright," and warned residents that if they left the ANC it would be a cold and hungry world awaiting them. Even then, he had implied that he was the party leader's equal. "Whoever is thinking that we are supporting Zuma because we are fond of individuals is lying," he had proclaimed. What could be given, in other words, could also be taken away.

It wasn't only opposition leaders and frightened whites who were shaken by the rather sudden rise of Julius Malema as a major force in

South African politics. Those most concerned, in fact, were inside the Alliance, party structures, the trade unions, and the Communist Party. "I am looking for a more stable ANC. The worst sign, for me, would be if the Malema gang won power at the conference in 2012," trade union leader Zwelinzima Vavi told me one year later, in mid-2010. "Can you imagine if you were to have people who think like Julius Malema [take over the ANC]?" He thought corruption would flourish and the media would come under a sustained assault. "If they take over and replace the current leaders with *tenderpreneurs*, people in government only to accumulate wealth for themselves, and then they come out of the conference and do what Mbeki was doing, by closing the space for unions to operate . . . it may come to *break* honestly—I want to say this." A takeover of the party in this way "talks to the stability of the country," he went on. If Malema called the shots, "where will be the future of the country?" he asked. Then he provided a one word answer: "*Finished*."

Malema kept hammering at the idea of nationalizing the mines and seizing land from white owners on behalf of the black workers who labored upon it. He traced these demands back to the Freedom Charter of 1955, the party's seminal document outlining the movement values and objectives. The youth leader called on members of the ANC to become even more militant "economic freedom fighters" intent on transferring wealth from the white minority to the black majority.

In a manifesto at an organization conference in mid-2011, the youth leader posed a particularly pointed challenge to centrists in the party. "The ANC should never be an instrument that oppresses the people it is supposed to liberate. As things stand, the ANC is managing the state on behalf of those who own and control the means of production," he said, adding in the written version of the speech, "Political Power without Economic Emancipation is Meaningless."[9]

By then, it was quite clear that Malema had broken entirely with President Zuma. He praised former leaders of the ANC by name, but not the current officeholder. The youth leader called for regime change of a democratically elected government in neighboring Botswana, railed against the overthrow and killing of Qaddafi, and supported the uprising against the king of Swaziland, making it seem as if the Youth League had its own foreign policy.

Malema also criticized the pattern of "enriching a few families and individuals who are close to power," a thinly veiled attack on the sudden success in business by Zuma's children and other members of the extended family. He mentioned the "weak, directionless and visionless leadership" of the movement and demanded what he called a greater generational mix in party and government inner circles. "South Africa is a young nation, so those who lead the ANC and government should be younger," he insisted. On this issue, in particular, he hit a poignant and resonant note.

Months later, Malema and other top officeholders of the Youth League were suspended as members of the ANC, and stripped of their positions as a result. Malema crisscrossed the country, making increasingly incendiary speeches, defending his right to press his views. Although his suspension amounted to a reassertion of control over the party by its elders, especially Zuma, the move also threatened another schism. If the world economy continued to contract, and the possibility of achieving social equality through growth grew even dimmer, then calls for redistribution would surely gain support. The youth leader's generational complaint—that the older leaders of the ANC were out of step with the needs of young people in the country and hung on to power long after they had lost their revolutionary fervor—seemed incontrovertible now.

For the weeks of the World Cup, these hostilities were largely suspended. President Zuma did not engage with Malema publicly. After all, he had an international sports extravaganza to host, climate change to vanquish, an economy to revive. The celebration of the World Cup also coincided with new revelations in his less-than-private life that seemed wilder than the plots on *Isidingo*, the soap opera his daughter Gugu starred in. Each time a new scandal like this one broke, it weakened the president's ability to stand up to the youth leaders.

Just as the championship games began, the Zulu-language newspaper *Ilanga* carried a story that the president's fourth wife, Nompumelelo Ntuli, had cuckolded him with a bodyguard. She was the young woman I had met at Nkandla, the junior wife who had apparently been sent packing from his household after a tiff with a fifth wife, whom Zuma apparently had married in the midst of his campaign to become leader of the ANC in 2007. In the aftermath of these stories, the president's staff did everything they could to put his smiling face forward, positioning him as the busy chief executive of the country and host in chief of the beautiful games. As usual, it proved difficult to stanch the rolling tide of gossip, especially after the former bodyguard accused of having an affair with one of the president's wives died, an apparent suicide.

Through the online World Cup lottery the previous fall, I had bought tickets for me and my son, Jake, for Game 58, which turned out to be the battle between Ghana and Uruguay. It was our good fortune, for the match would determine which team went through to the quarterfinals. We attended two other games, and floated in the bubble of goodwill created by the Cup. This seemed like the key contest to observe in person because it was Africa's one remaining shot to shine.

After dusk, we walked from the bus stop along a low-lying ridge to Soccer City stadium, which was set in the midst of the northern edge of Soweto. It had been the first international soccer stadium in the country, built before the end of apartheid in the mid-1980s. The place was soaked in political and sports history.

I had been inside it five years earlier on Youth Day, to watch Thabo Mbeki make his annual address, and the place had looked rather worn. In preparation for the Cup, it had been treated to an artful conversion. Now, the stadium looked like a shiny calabash-shaped Leviathan prepared for liftoff.

We had seats close to the ceiling in the midst of a group of fans who had traveled by bus all the way from Accra. They were high on adrenaline, and plenty of beer as well. Ghana was ranked behind Uruguay, but from the roar of the crowd you could tell which team the audience favored. After all, Ghana had triumphed over the United States just a week earlier, dashing hopes for a better American showing. The fans awaited the next miracle.

From the outset, it was a fluid, beautifully played, riveting game to watch. The Black Stars, Ghana's team, had the younger, scrappier, more energetic players. The Uruguayans delivered a cooler, more strategic, and more defensively robust game. Three-quarters of an hour into it, Sulley Muntari, the bad boy of the Ghanaian team, took a long, powerful flyer into the corner of the net. His goal beat the whistle for halftime. The crowd of more than eighty thousand leapt to a spontaneous dance through the stands. If Ghana succeeded, it would be the first time in the history of the World Cup that an African team would play in the final four.

The Uruguayans struck back at fifty-four minutes. The score remained tied at 1–1 through the second half. Tension built in a way you could never fully experience from watching on television. In overtime, the Ghanaians were robbed of the prize. A nice solid header by the striker Dominic Adiyiah shot past the goalie, but it was blocked by a Uruguayan forward, Luis Suárez. The Uruguayan player used both hands illegally to deflect it—two "hands of death," as the move was called—which got him ejected; but under the rules of the game his illegal maneuver also robbed Ghana of the goal.

On the penalty opportunity, imposed as a result of the player's violation, the Ghanaian star player Asamoah Gyan, who had demonstrated such precision earlier in the match, narrowly missed his shot. The ball bounced off the top bar, and Gyan covered his face in shame. One of the fans from Ghana sitting behind us blurted out, "I have to leave now or I will have a heart attack!" Lurching to his feet, he clutched at his chest. Every one of us stood for the penalty shot, as if in a group prayer. It was good that our neighbor had shuffled off by then. In the shoot-out, the Uruguayans sewed up the game, 4–2.

The results of this game were accumulating testimony to superior skill and athleticism, but they were also commentary on the fulsome financial backing for the winning teams—exemplifying the political economy of sport. Too few poor communities in Ghana, or in South Africa for that matter, had decent playing fields; too few Africans, boys and girls alike, had access to shoes and balls and nets. Even soccer pointed up the enormous power of money in fielding a winning team. There was no escaping inequalities, even amid an uplifting extravaganza like the World Cup.

Everybody wanted to believe in the possibility of another miracle—South Africa pushing through to the round of sixteen or Ghana making it to the semifinals on behalf of the continent. Systematic differences established the odds, however. Though South Africans celebrated underdogs, and they adored the narrative of unlikely victories, the results of the World Cup said something sobering about the importance of long-term strategy, discipline, and national investment in identifying and developing talent.

When the games were over, the country's leaders spoke of the broad sense of social cohesion, across lines of color, language, ethnic identity, and geography, that deepened because of the World Cup. "The games created a sense that we have gotten over the hill. There's a huge degree of mutual acceptance, a sense of unity, a very strong sense of national pride and patriotism," Zweli Mkhize told me at the conclusion of the games. He was the Zuma ally whom I met for the first time on the president's trip to Washington. Now premier of KwaZulu-Natal province and among the most powerful politicians in the country, he was sometimes mentioned as a possible future president and, increasingly, as a potential Zuma rival.

"I would call it a blessing for the country," he added, when I caught up with him after the tournament ended. "[The World Cup] created a huge amount of excitement." He felt that the view of South Africa from *outside* the country had renewed a sense of self-worth and dignity among people *inside* it—much as the campaign against apartheid by global activists had encouraged a reassessment.

"The whole world was just looking at South Africa," was the way he explained this dynamic. "The country had progressed to the point where it could be trusted to that extent by the whole world."[10] The trick now, he had decided, was to get its citizens to use this experience of national triumph in order to shed the residue of so many traumas imposed by the country's history and to assume fully their identities as post-apartheid South Africans.

The day after the World Cup ended, following an orgiastic all-night celebration from the northern suburbs to Soweto, my son and I picked up Ndaba Mandela outside the home he shared with his grandfather. We had made several aborted plans to meet in the previous weeks, but there was such a blizzard of parties, celebrations, family events, and soccer games that Ndaba had to attend that we had not managed to connect. My son was flying back to California that evening, so we agreed to eat a meal together at last before we headed out to the airport.

After we picked up Ndaba and his girlfriend, Khomotso Faith Moloto, we headed off to a late lunch at the Mall of Rosebank. That was the place where Yfm, and the youth culture it represented, had its headquarters. By the middle of that year, Ndaba had taken a break from Cape Town and his job at Investec, the financial services corporation. He had wanted for so long to participate fully in the festivities, and to spend as much time with the gathered family as he could. Ndaba figured that bringing the World Cup to South Africa had fulfilled another dream of his grandfather's, a final symbolic triumph in a remarkable life, and he did not want to miss it.

For the Mandela clan the World Cup began with a terrible shock, though. There was an automobile accident after the opening ceremony in June that had cost the life of one of Nelson Mandela's favorite great-grandchildren. In the wake of that accident, the Old Man had spent more time than ever out of public view. He made an appearance at the closing ceremony, rolling through the stadium beside his wife, Graça Machel, and receiving a clamorous outpouring of emotion from the crowd.

There was a sense of the clock winding down now for Nelson Mandela. Preparations were well under way for the inevitable. It put people on edge, and led them to say inexcusable things. At lunch a few days earlier with a DJ who was a friend of ours, there was discussion around the table—as there often was now in South African social circles—about how frail the beloved former leader looked and how worried people felt about his health.

"Madiba must just *die* now," the DJ said, drawing a stunned silence from us. "He must just die!" He was actually an admirer of Mandela's; he wished him well, but he also thought that rising tension about his dying was getting harder to take. The DJ also thought that South Africans had developed an unhealthy dependency on Mandela, thinking of him as the magician who could manage the country's problems single-handedly no matter how badly others screwed the place up. Young South Africans were holding back from doing what they must do for themselves out of an expectation that the Old Man could somehow produce yet another miracle. "What, at the end of the day, are we all *waiting* for?" the DJ asked.

On the way to the mall, Ndaba had brushed aside all the swirling rumors of his grandfather's supposed decline. Sure, he was frail, as you would expect of a man of ninety-one, he said. "My grandfather is *fine*," he told us. When we got to the mall, and found a restaurant, and put our orders in, I asked him, "What's new in your life?" I hadn't seen him in more than a year, and it turned out there was much to report. He wasn't the best correspondent, and we mostly communicated through cryptic text messages on our cell phones.

I knew from those messages that his relationship with Khomotso had grown much closer. But now, he broke bigger news, smiling at me and placing a hand on her belly. "We're going to have a child, that's what's new," he replied. In the moment, I thought he was joking, because she still looked model thin. But Khomotso nodded, too, and on second glance I could see a little tuft at her waist.

I couldn't help remembering what Ndaba had told me about feeling cautious about romantic relationships with women because of how things had worked out for the men in his family. Ndaba had said, in a previous interview, that he planned to "try it," meaning marriage, only once.

Now, he seemed over the moon about the prospect of becoming a father. When his son arrived four months later, he was named Lewanika after a Zambian king. Ndaba told us that he was prepared for all other changes that would be required of him to be a superior dad.

Several months earlier I had sent him the chapters I had written about him, reminding him in an attached note about what he had told me, when we first met, concerning his grandfather's legacy, the seduction of bling-bling material culture in Joburg, and the importance of keeping the revolutionary values of the ANC alive. He grimaced, admitting that it was hard for him to feel much enthusiasm for the work he was doing at Investec in light of his politics.

As an intern at Investec, he was being groomed to become a rainmaker for the firm. The whole prospect of a career selling investment schemes to newly wealthy blacks made him nervous, especially when he was reminded of the warnings he had raised about the ways his friends had become imprisoned by the hunger for big money. In the midst of covering the campaign a year earlier, I had taken a break one night to have dinner with Ndaba. He hadn't volunteered much information about the new job. When I pressed him for details, and for a description of what exactly he was doing, he grew quiet. "It's, like, stealing from *pensioners*," he said, sourly.[11] Now, he was weighing the alternatives in a new way. He shrugged. "That's all still true, but I have a family to support now," he pointed out, as if arguing with himself.[12]

Ndaba's older brother, Mandla, had fashioned an identity for himself as *nkosi* of Mvezo, and also now as a member of Parliament increasingly known for controversial sexist and homophobic views. Ndaba had steered clear of politics, watching as the spotlight of public attention began to consume another Mandela. His hopes of securing a meaningful internship, or attending graduate school in the United States or Europe, had not led anywhere. From week to week, he wasn't sure which profession, on which continent, would be right for him.

Unlike most of his contemporaries, Ndaba was not forced to scrape by in the economic downturns sweeping across the world. There were a plethora of opportunities available to him, but he had not achieved liftoff in any one of them yet. He was looking for well-paid work, but he was also guided by the weight of his grandfather's legacy. Ndaba wanted the work to *mean* something. Overall, it had to be a force for good.

In the middle of the year, his wanderlust was reinforced when he traveled with a raft of cousins to New York, to take part in the celebration of Nelson Mandela's ninety-first birthday at a gala organized by the 4664 Campaign, to raise money for HIV/AIDS charities. Ndaba fell instantly in love with Manhattan. He thought everything he liked about Johannesburg was present in New York. On his return to South Africa, he didn't mention to his grandfather this yearning to move to Manhattan. The Old Man was often tired now, and his grandson did not want to say anything that would upset him. "I want to get out there in it, yo," he told me.

In the wake of the World Cup, his discomfort with being in financial services would only grow and he would part ways with the company. "Have you seen *Inside Job?*" he asked. "I definitely want to make the money, but I don't want to do it at the expense of my values—and my identity." After resigning from Investec, he would put more of his time into a new organization he had launched with several of his cousins, called the Africa Rising Foundation, a feel-good organization promoting South African music and entertainment and continental successes. By 2012, the foundation would adopt five schools in Soweto, including the high school in his old neighborhood, for help with the music curriculum. Here, it seemed to Ndaba, was a chance to hitch together his interest in culture and also give back to the community from which his family had come. "Look how we've developed as a nation, with all the investment in IT and infrastructure and finance," he said. "Compare it to how much we've put into education—it's *miniscule*. If we are to achieve progress and development, we have to invest in the leaders of tomorrow. That's key to South Africa's success. It's key to our progress, as a continent and as a people."[13]

He worked for a short period as the manager for Bongani Fassie, the talented and troubled son of the late Brenda Fassie, who was, in turn, the great singer who had died in the middle of my first trip to South Africa back in 2004. Ndaba found it was tough to break into event management in Johannesburg itself, though. Across the urbanizing areas in the Eastern Cape, he found a larger audience for live shows. He had put a white kid from East London who played *kwaito*, the music of urbanized black people, on stage. "That kid *killed*," Ndaba reported. "The attitude in Joburg is too bling-bling. I decided to promote our stuff outside—to get into the hearts of the people."

When we had finished eating, we drove Ndaba and Khomotso home. As I pulled to the curb, he said casually, "Won't you come in so you can see the Old Man?" I had seen Nelson Mandela at public events for more than six years, watching him come and go from the vantage point of Ndaba's room. We had never had an interview because by the time I arrived in the country, he had stopped granting them.

We spilled out of the car and trailed behind Ndaba through a side gate, meandering through the kitchen and into the cavernous living room where the elder Mandela was perched in an armchair. He wore a brilliant golden leopard-print silk shirt and flashed his trademark broad smile, saying, "It's nice that the young people still come around to see an old man even though he has nothing new to say."

The singer K'naan and an entourage with him came through the front door then, along with the photographer Joseph Peter, the creator of

The African Book of Happiness. Peter presented a hand-bound copy of the book to Mandela. He had been on a pre–World Cup tour with K'naan sponsored by Coca-Cola, and they had visited fifty-three countries in seventy-five days. The images in the book were celebratory, viscerally powerful expressions of joy.

Each of us said something stilted about how Mandela had inspired the work we were doing. I briefly mentioned his first tour of the United States in 1999, where I had heard him speak for the first time. He studied each person, nodding occasionally. It wasn't clear that he could hear any of it. Whenever his grandson spoke to him, I noticed he leaned over, cupped his hand, and spoke directly into the Old Man's ear.

Still, the elder Mandela demonstrated that he was fully in charge. When Ndaba popped up and moved around the room, the elder rebuked him: "Ndaba, *sit down* now. When you have guests you must sit, be calm, and *socialize.*" After about fifteen minutes, the Old Man's eyes turned a little glassy and his smile began to fade. There was a visceral sense of being in the presence of someone who had been nearly used up. Ndaba escorted us out of the house, and we all stood in the street together, star-struck. K'naan, in particular, looked like he had fallen into a religious reverie deep inside himself.

Two days later, I drove into Mary Fitzgerald Square. It was the massive brick-lined meeting place directly across from Museum Africa that anchored Newtown. Whenever I was in Johannesburg I found myself making arrangements to meet people around that square in my spare moments. It was a spot that served as a touchstone of sorts; from there, it seemed to me, you could imagine what South Africa might still become. Just across the Nelson Mandela Bridge from the University of the Witwatersrand, Newtown encircled a collection of cultural bulwarks. Surrounded by dozens of blocks in the Central Business District, where migrants from all over Africa were struggling to get a foothold, the district constituted a modest microcosm of the country's emerging urban style and culture.

Around the corner from the museum stood the venerable Market Theatre, where new South African playwrights launched the best new work. Across the square, the Bassline boasted a massive ballroom where hybrid jazz, pop, and hip-hop greats headlined regularly. At the Dance Factory, the most innovative choreography blending classical, global, and South African movement was regularly performed, such as the distinctive work of Gregory Maqoma, who was born in Soweto and was now recognized internationally as a singular dance talent.

Right under the freeway underpass on one edge of the square was an expanding network of businesses run by a young entrepreneur my son had gotten to know. He had grown up Soweto, but had reinvented himself as Osmic, the singular name he had given himself. Osmic, whom I had gotten to know through my son, was the son of working-class parents. You could tell you were entering a part of the square influenced by him because the struts and underside of the freeway were marked by splashes of bright colors, with one graffiti mural blending into another. Starting with nothing, but inspired by the imagery of American graffiti and hip-hop culture, he had moved from the township to the heart of the city to seize opportunities that would have been unimaginable to his parents' generations.

Sleeping little and working eighteen-hour days, Osmic had made a little empire, progressing from selling mix-CDs of international and local talent to distributing South African fashion labels. He also created a festival called "Back to the City," to commemorate National Youth Day. When his landlord rented his storefront out from under him, Osmic turned a previously abandoned storefront into a complex of music studio/retail space/art gallery, and then opened a nightclub to host South African and international music stars. He built a sound studio where friends from home could record music, and sold hip-hop clothing, sneakers, and music. Osmic's world was a presentiment of post-transition sensibilities.

Just across the way from his headquarters was the gigantic square. I had watched the beginning of the final World Cup game from there. What I liked about the square was that if you watched major events on the big screen mounted at one end of it, you were likely to find a beggar from the street standing on one side and a fashion designer from the emerging black bourgeoisie on the other.

A day after the tournament, the stage and screen were taken down and carted off. Detachable shiny metal restraining fences were stacked in piles one on top of another like cast-off scrap lumber. The tents for vendors, full of artwork and food at the base of the square, vanished, too. The square was revealed as a grimy and untended stretch of uneven stones, a barely recognizable palimpsest of the place that seemed so vibrant just a few nights before.

Outside the Market Theatre I met up with Gwendoline Dube, the young woman from Orange Farm who had been raped by her uncle as a teenager and was living with HIV, having been placed on treatment with antiretrovirals in 2004. When I was introduced to her the first time, in a children's AIDS clinic back in 2005, what struck me most of all was the outsize ambition she harbored. As a teenager, she had planned to become a pilot *and* a doctor. In the interim, because of poverty and poor grades, she had been forced to tailor those ambitions considerably. Today she was on a door-to-door search for employment of any kind. Like 75 percent of young black people looking for work, she hadn't found a job yet, and she had not been able to work in years.

Ever since I had moved back to Chicago in 2008, I had tried to keep track of Gwendoline by phone. That had proven difficult because her cell phone was often dead, she had little money to keep it operating, and the Internet café where she could access email was open only sporadically. Even when I reached her, she was loath to deliver bad news. When we finally had spoken about this in 2009, it was a terrible connection. "Hallooo! Hallooo! Hallooo!" she shouted down the line. Most of all, I wanted to know how she had done on her matriculation exam.

As it turned out, Gwendoline had scored poorly in math and science, and so the idea of going to medical school was totally scuppered. "I had that dream, yes," she said. "Now, it's gone."[14] She had enrolled instead in a course at a technological institute, to become a human resources manager, but soon dropped out because her mother could not pay the fees. Then, she had suffered a minor stroke and had been bedridden for several months. This was one of many things she had decided not to tell me over the telephone, and that I would learn only once I was back in the country.

Gwendoline had broken up with her boyfriend after discovering that he had betrayed her by secretly marrying someone else. She had deflected his eagerness for her to bear him a child, thinking she should defer until she had a profession and could support a family, and this was how he had repaid her. The ex-boyfriend had come back around, begging to continue seeing her, but Gwendoline stood firm, refusing to become his mistress. "No dating," she said briskly. "I don't want to date anymore—people hurting me, people leaving me."

A parallel drama had broken out between her mother and stepfather. Gwendoline's mom had found baby clothes in her husband's car, and this was how she had learned that he had taken up with another woman. The holidays had been especially difficult because her stepfather had moved home, bringing his younger lover along. Gwendoline thought that the baby looked eerily like a clone of him. It was hard for her, at first, to decide how to treat the child. "'Twas tough," she said. "But it's not the baby's fault." She figured that she and her mother—the two responsible women in the family—would now have to sort the whole mess out. This was what polygamy looked like, not for traditional royalty or presidents of the country but at the grassroots level, among the working class and the poor.

Gwendoline rarely responded to expressions of sympathy; she reacted as though acceptance of them would imply weakness. On the phone one night, she told me, "We just had bread for dinner," but then corrected herself swiftly—"I mean we had bread *and* tea." When I periodically told her that I was sorry about how things were turning out for her, she often responded crisply. "I'll be *fine*. I have my *health*." There was the bedrock proposition about the value of persistence and resiliency. Thanks to the efforts of thousands of activists, nurses, doctors, and public health officials, there were burgeoning numbers of young South Africans like her who were alive and otherwise would be dead and buried long ago. She had survived the AIDS epidemic, remarkably enough. Now she needed all her gathering strength to survive her survival.

I asked Gwendoline, "What did the World Cup mean for you?" "Eh— *nothing*," she replied, biting her lip. "They said there were supposed to be opening of new opportunities—hah hah! We were supposed to be having jobs in 2010. So, I'm just kind of *shocked*." The last time I had spoken to her, on the phone, she had told me she was enrolled in a human resources course of study at a technical institute. She loved her studies and felt called upon to pursue a career fighting for the rights of people "who were unfairly dismissed," she said.

Gwendoline had not shared the news, however, that she had been subsequently forced out of school when her mother ran out of money for the tuition. When I looked puzzled—after all, she had assured me recently on the phone that her studies were going *fine*—she murmured, "Sorry I didn't tell you before. I didn't want you to *worry*."

Beneath her arm Gwendoline had tucked fifteen, pristine, newly printed résumés and a collection of brochures from the Gauteng Travel Board, complete with listings for all of the World Cup concerts, cruises, and dances she hadn't had the money to attend. She thought that visiting these enterprises, fattened by the tourist boom begun during the World Cup, might provide good leads for her job search. These days, when she ventured into Joburg to look for work, she slept in a dingy one-room flat belonging to her cousin right downtown.

Gwendoline was dressed in blue jeans and a big, shiny-black faux-leather jacket, pulled tight against the cold. The coat had dramatic silver buttonholes and designs around the pockets that her mother had embroidered, using bright-red thread. Her hair was straightened, parted on the side and patted flat. When her face fell slack, gravity drew everything toward a quite mournful inverted U; when she smiled, thrusting her breasts forward, she looked sorted and businesslike. She set off at a brisk pace, with me trailing at a distance so my presence wouldn't complicate her job search.

Inside the doorway of Nikki's Oasis, I heard her ask in a clipped, proper tone, "Are there any *posts* available?" Before she could finish her sentence, the proprietor replied, "*No jobs!*" The cafe owner was an open-faced woman with a grim expression, and it was swiftly clear why she was so agitated. Business had been so poor during the World Cup, and even worse in the days since it had ended, that she had decided to close the restaurant entirely.

Here was a small piece of evidence of the kind of economic bust many feared might follow the boom instigated by the games. The World Cup created a temporarily booming economy, most of all for FIFA, the governing body of world soccer. FIFA had taken in an estimated $3.5 billion, and carried it tax-free out of the country.[15]

Far fewer foreigners had come to the games than had been predicted by the organizing committee back in 2008, and much of the foreign visitors' spending had taken place in the most exclusive hotels and restaurants in the whitest parts of town. Money still flowed in familiar patterns, in other words, as if capital itself discriminated on the basis of race and class.

Overall, there had been undeniable benefits for the country as a whole, including huge public capital investments in roadways and airports, and the installation of Next Generation Network, a massive upgrading of online capacity.[16] The promised boost in tourism didn't materialize in the months following the games, though, and a sustained influx of money and opportunity was needed if young people like Gwendoline were to get traction in the job market.

We crossed at the corner of the square, where a half-dozen signs pointed in so many happy directions—to the left the Artist Proof Studio, behind it Moving Into Dance, off to the right the Science Centre and the Workers' Museum—but these budding institutions weren't exactly relevant to her search. Gwendoline wasn't looking for an opportunity to make her mark as a painter, prove her artistry as a dancer, or show her familiarity with physics or history. She had not received an elevated education. Like the vast majority of black South Africans in their twenties, she was without work and had few skills.

She had begun to wonder, in fact, if there was any proper place for someone like her in the new South Africa. She had studied hard in a set of terrible schools, and she was prepared to make reasonable sacrifices in order to create a better tomorrow. It didn't seem like anybody was listening or would be willing to cut her a break, though.

Across an expansive lawn, frosted in brown from a midwinter freeze, lay the gutted-out remains of Shivava Café, which once was the preferred dive of black journalists, poets, and filmmakers. It was now out of business, too. On the other side of the street, there was a massive two-story building that once housed the Horror Café, where spoken-word performances were once staged. An outlet of the Italian cuisine chain Doppio Zero was an utter zero now—empty and locked. Gwendoline winced at the sight.

Her feet were aching, and there were as many shuttered places as open ones. The next restaurant she approached was a vibey place called Sophiatown, named after a nearby community that was once multiracial and thriving but had been bulldozed out of existence during apartheid and replaced by Triomf ("triumph" in Afrikaans). Near the entrance to the restaurant was a newly installed, hand-painted sign that read:

Remember

UBUNTU?

AFRIKA UNITE

Ubuntu, the word that means something like dignity, respect, empathy, and kindness all rolled into one, was written in large capital block letters tinted deep blood red.

Gwendoline was ushered to the bar to wait on word from the manager. Though she had done her best to project cheerful eagerness all the way up to the doorway, when she sat abandoned at the bar, with waitresses bustling by to serve afternoon customers, I noticed that her face fell slack.

It turned out that she was thinking, at that moment, of the sacrifice her mother was always making for her, and feeling a little weepy about it. Gwendoline apparently had promised herself that she wouldn't cry in front of me. She was thinking about the fact that, during the World Cup, rumors had swept through communities of African migrants that they would be attacked again as they had been in 2008 once the games were over. Her mother, who originally came from Zimbabwe, worried about how her family might be treated if there was another spasm of xenophobic violence.

Gwendoline had not felt vulnerable to attack in the mass rioting two years earlier, but she considered herself more of a target these days. Fluent though she was in Zulu, Gwendoline wondered whether the landscape had shifted beneath her feet while she wasn't paying attention. On this topic, she gave President Zuma high marks: he had been forceful and unequivocal from 2008 forward in arguing that anti-immigrant bashing was wrong, un-African, and counterrevolutionary.

When the restaurant manager finally joined her at the bar, he did his best to sound encouraging. He told her there weren't any jobs available in the cafe "at the moment," but asked her to return in a week to check again. She left, her head bowed and copies of the curriculum vitae clutched beneath her arm.

We perambulated in wider orbits around the square. Each new venue seemed less likely than the last. At Tasty Fried Chicken, a hole-in-the-wall fast-food outlet that promised *the Taste of Jozi* on Bree Street, people were streaming in, grabbing their orders, and pouring out again. Before she crossed the threshold, though, the manager shouted at her, "Nothing at the moment, Mama!" I flagged Osmic down, and he shook his head, too. "Wish I had something," he murmured. He urged her to come back to see him.

We made our way into the windswept plaza, which had been drenched in lights and packed with cheering crowds only a few nights earlier. Now all of the metal standards were stacked high on top of one another, waiting to be stored for the next public extravaganza.

Gwendoline sat on an upturned oil drum, and we watched tiny tornadoes of dirt whipping past. She had loved being a student and studying labor relations, she told me. Even in the wake of the breakup with her boyfriend, she had begun to imagine what it would feel like one day to have a more normal life—a job, a husband, a family.

"Hmm, my dream didn't come true," she added. "But I didn't want to lose hope." Now, she felt an electric charge of desperation. Her stepfather regularly beat her mother, and she thought it only a matter of time until she was beaten, too. The violence of the men in the family had a devastating resonance for her: her uncle had raped her, and the terrible intimacy of the crime of sexual assault within the family had left its mark, particularly in her distrust of men.

In the distance there was a massive advertisement for Nike shoes that showed a hunky white man in a pose of ecstatic triumph beneath a slogan that said, "Write your future." We stared at the image together. It looked like a kind of reproach, as if the marketers of Jozi's image thought that Gwendoline wasn't trying hard enough. It seemed to me that she had struggled rather valiantly to write her own future, but hadn't exactly been provided the needed implements.

Gwendoline had always been upbeat in my presence, insistent on doing whatever she could to contribute to her family and society. Now the breath had been knocked out of her. "My life, I don't really know," she said, scuffing her shoes on the faded bricks of the square. Her body rose and fell in soundless bursts of weeping as she turned away so that I wouldn't see.

Between bouts of crying, she whispered, "Every time I make goals for myself, they seem to be shattered down. So I don't make plans anymore." Gwendoline was twenty-two years old and she had no place to go. Finally, she could not hold her grief in any longer. "Oooo," she cried. "Ooo, oh." The wind caught the sound of her sorrow, swirled it around us in a ghostly way, and swept it to the south, out of Mary Fitzgerald Square.

23.

Liberated People

Less than a ten-minute drive from Newtown lay Johannesburg's equivalent of the City on a Hill, the sprawling campus of the University of the Witwatersrand. The Great Hall of the country's premier university, with its impressive Grecian columns and an expansive flight of steps, was perched near the peak of the ridge. Extensive lawns stepped down in a series of wide-open public spaces shaped like an oval. The oval was surrounded by classrooms, a first-rate library, and the student center. It was anchored by a pristine Olympic-sized swimming pool. This was the kind of place Gwendoline Dube once dreamed of attending, but she had never been inside the university gates. She knew that attendance in a place like this university worked like a key to open up opportunities in business, politics, medicine, and law in the global economy. Studying there had been placed far beyond her reach, though.

At the end of July, I met Thuthu Zuma and her sister, Gugu, for lunch on the campus. They were two of the president's daughters, and both of them had gotten to know Gwendoline through me. Thuthu had lent her clothes for her high school prom, and Gugu had gotten her help, through their mother's department, in acquiring a new official ID, without which she could not find a job or go to school. We had agreed to meet at the university because there was a meeting that afternoon about a planned anti-xenophobia rally that they wanted to attend. Ever since the attacks on African migrants in 2008, periodic panic over threats of new violence had swept through the communities of immigrants. Zimbabweans, in particular, were left in a high state of anxiety as the World Cup ended. In the days after the competition was over, the country's military and police forces flooded potential hot spots to put the lid on any new outbreaks.

Students at the university felt that a broad educative campaign including public demonstrations could extend the feeling of continental uplift and pan-African solidarity experienced during the games. The Zuma daughters were deeply committed to this cause. Gugu, after all, was now married to a Zimbabwean. She was dressed in a sleek lavender outfit, her hair flipped up in an elegant tuft, and had on large circular silver earrings and oversize sunglasses, which seemed appropriate for a star in *Isidingo*, among the most-watched soap operas on television.

Thuthu was also stylishly turned out. She had on a black-and-gray knit cap against the winter chill, chic black linen slacks, and a low-cut blouse beneath a cardigan, with two beautiful gold bracelets on her left forearm and a gold chain around her neck.

As we sat down to eat, she filled me in on personal news: she had begun dating the president of the Student Representative Council. He was Morris Mukovhe Masutha, the handsome and charismatic youth leader who had called the meeting we planned to attend. "Which is very weird," she said. "If I was the Thuthu of then [the period when we had first met in 2007], I would never even for a second consider dating someone like that!"[1]

She felt lucky that the young man had not known who her father was when they were first dating. Their initial courtship had been blessedly free of the pressure that came from being the president's daughter. When Morris periodically had informed her, in casual conversation, about what was happening inside his beloved ANC, Thuthu had pretended to be completely ignorant of politics.

One day when she first visited his room, though, she found it festooned with a poster of her father and his Cabinet. "That was so weird, too," she recalled. "You go to see your boyfriend and there's a huge picture of your *dad* on his wall." Morris also had posted cartoons by Zapiro, who regularly caricatured Jacob Zuma as a bulbous creature with a showerhead affixed to his scalp, a reference to the testimony he had given during the rape trial that he had showered after intercourse to protect himself from infection with HIV.

When Thuthu got agitated about seeing this depiction of her father, her boyfriend grew suspicious. She was always pretty cool, even when they disagreed about something. So, he googled her name and learned at last that she was the daughter of *that* Zuma. She thought it "nice to begin the relationship without that shadow."

This relationship was among a raft of many changes in her life since I had been away, not the least that her father had become head of state.

I had traveled to Pretoria the week before to see her at home with her mother, so we could finish fact-checking the chapters about her. I had also spent a long evening, over dinner and drinks, with Gugu in Melville. Both of them felt a little nervous about things they had said in interviews back in 2007 and 2008. They were true to the spirit of the interviews, though, and to their credit neither one asked me to change a word.

Since then, Gugu's feelings—about the campaign, the party, and the Youth League—had not altered much. She had been seriously disappointed by the apolitical, celebrity approach to the national election campaign. "A lot of people weren't really debating the issues. People just *like* him," she said, speaking of her father. "I really disliked what Julius Malema was saying. It seemed like people were not *thinking* anymore. The leaders were treated like superstars, and politics had become ridiculous."

In part, Gugu was influenced in this view by her marriage to Wesley Ncube, the son of a leader in the opposition party MDC in Zimbabwe. In neighboring Zimbabwe, of course, it had proved disastrous to rely too much on the party of liberation to protect civil freedoms. "The onus for liberation falls on that country's *people*," she said pointedly.

Thuthu's critique of the ANC, and its leaders, on the other hand, had softened quite a bit in the intervening years. "I'm a little bit more positive. Even my relationship with my dad has changed for the better— in the sense that I don't think I'm as hard on him as I was then," she reported. Thuthu was more engaged politically than before, and felt more optimistic about where the country was headed. After looking through the chapters of my manuscript about her in her mother's home in Pretoria, Thuthu acknowledged: "When I read it, I cringed a lot. It made me realize, I've changed a lot, and grown, and am really like 180 degrees different in some respects."

The main difference concerned politics, Thuthu went on. "Then I was very apolitical," she said. There had been a "bitter taste" in her mouth in the wake of the rape trial and corruption allegations against her father. Since then, she had taken her mother more explicitly as her model. Though Nkosazana Dlamini-Zuma had been defeated in a humiliating way at the balloting in Polokwane, she had ignored personal attacks on herself and had joined the new Cabinet, launching into the difficult work of reforming the Department of Home Affairs. Her mother's example instilled in Thuthu a desire to "work from within rather than criticizing from without," she went on. "I thought that if my mom can still have such love and passion and faith in the organization, who am I not to?"

Zuma's daughter felt more comfortable these days living inside her own skin, and much more settled about her own identity, quite apart from her parents. "I came out of a privileged background and went to a predominantly white school," she said. In retrospect, she thought the other black girls who had hurt her feelings in high school had been right to call her a coconut. "I was pretty much living the life of my white friends," she recalled. "I've now managed to redefine myself away from that coconut-ish environment, and also steer away from the crass materialism of the black elite, too, and navigate into something new."

Thuthu dreamed now about having the time and money to travel across Africa, doing community development work. Then she wanted to combine her interests in anthropology, sociology, and politics as a documentary filmmaker. It was a blessing, she added, that the campaign was over so she could get back to her studies.

Even the latest scandal in her father's personal life, concerning the child born to a woman half his age and not his wife, felt like no big deal. "There will never be anything worse than the rape trial for me and my family," she said, studying her hands. In all of our previous conversations, she had steered away from any discussion of the arrest and trial of her father on rape charges, back in 2006. The entire experience had left plenty of scars, the most significant of which was her ongoing, deep distrust of journalists. "It's his personal life! And he's now the president. He's not a dictator. He didn't say he must be president. He was *elected*. So the media need to respect that."

She echoed the view, popular in ANC circles, that "obviously, the media has an agenda and a very *crooked* one." There was a tendency among the emerging black elite, solidifying now it seemed to me, to exhibit great antagonism toward the media whenever black political and business leaders were embarrassed in the headlines. In the end, Thuthu pointed out, the onslaught of negative stories had not pushed her father out of politics. She didn't think the latest hoopla would dent his popularity much, either.

What lay beneath the superficial hoopla, Thuthu believed, was the question, and more than a little anxiety, among cosmopolitan people about the nature of polygamy. "It's a foreign concept to a lot of South Africans, especially urban people, and a lot of people all over the world," she went on. Since we had last spoken, Thuthu had talked about this with her father. She now understood his explanation of polygamy, she said, and accepted the idea that, in order to court additional wives, he would have to pursue new women. It came with the territory. She felt equally clear that this kind of relationship wasn't what she would ever accept for herself or her sisters—"not in a million years." It was not how she and her sisters had been raised. Thuthu thought of polygamy as a generational expression, likely to fade as her father's generation died off.

Her comment reminded me of a conversation over lunch with Thuthu and four of her friends in the spring of 2007. When they fell into a discussion about dating patterns and sex, a clear gender divide had emerged. She and another woman in the group had complained that the three men treated their lovers as disposable concubines rather than as human beings. "Why can't you treat your girlfriends the way you treat *us*—with respect?" Thuthu had lectured the men. They had smirked, averting their eyes. One of them had replied, "Because you're our *friends*."[2]

Thuthu later remembered this part of the conversation, too. "A majority of my male friends are very bad at relationships and they're not faithful when they're *in* them," she reported. "They're not necessarily advocates of polygamy, but their behavior is still a problem."

Thuthu did not think the next generation of South African women would put up with the inequality polygamy implied, or stand for being treated as disposable in one-on-one matches either. She felt that both were expressions of misogyny deeply embedded in South African culture, whether traditional or more modern. It would take generations to eradicate it. "There's no place for polygamy in modern-day South Africa, considering gender roles and how society progresses," Thuthu said. "But that doesn't mean that [when polygamy has disappeared,] I think people are [necessarily] going to have happy homes."

The three of us set off across the plaza, passing the Great Hall. Gugu was a spot-on mimic; she ran through a series of impressions, finishing with an eerily accurate portrayal of her father as he had explained why, despite an earlier pledge to serve only one term as president, he now felt called to put his name forward for a second five-year term.

The president's recent decision to "make himself available" for a second term had created divisions between current and former supporters. After all, the bargain between party insiders originally had been two terms for Mbeki, one for Zuma, and then a chance for a new generation of leaders to emerge. The Youth League had recently issued press releases in praise of both Tokyo Sexwale, the housing minister and a failed presidential candidate in 2007, and Deputy President Kgalema Motlanthe.

These signs of early positioning in competition for top positions in the ANC, which would not be decided until the end of 2012, caused a kind of mental whiplash; all you had to do was to change the names—Mbeki/Zuma to Zuma/Motlanthe—and the jockeying game at the top of the party seemed not to have changed much in the intervening three years. The Youth League poked fun at the current president and rallied support around his second in command; we had all watched this disruptive move before. So, just a year since Zuma's election as president of the country his leadership was being forcefully undermined from within.

In a lecture hall off the main oval, Thuthu's boyfriend brought the meeting of university students to order. It was a session attended by fifty organizers, including representatives of a Jewish youth group, to plan the anti-xenophobia march and rally scheduled for a few days later. Morris Masutha was a soft-spoken young man from a working-class family in Limpopo. He had worked through his own difficulties in navigating the cultural, social, political, and linguistic complexity of life in the university, having grown up in a poor Venda-speaking community. During his first year on campus, he said, he had not spoken a word in public for fear of revealing his accent. He recalled how he had spent endless hours simultaneously studying and improving his English. Now he was a respected leader, in part because he symbolized the social mobility that was possible in the new South Africa.

Masutha was dressed in blue jeans and a green shirt that advertised his membership in both the student group and the ANC Youth League. The shirt featured a picture of the slain martyr Chris Hani, an icon of the Left who had been murdered before the 1994 election. As it turned out, Masutha had been under considerable pressure on campus recently because he was part of a movement within the Youth League to oust

Julius Malema as leader. His chapter, like so many chapters of the Youth League nationwide, was caught up in a brutal internal fight over its controversial leader. "*Amandla!*" he shouted. "*Awethu!*" responded the crowd. Here was the movement's call-and-response ritual—"Power!" followed by the reassurance "To the people!" The traditional slogan pointed up the old question that nagged at a new generation of young militants: Were the representatives of the people in office now—but still not in power? Or was it simply that the wrong choices had been made about which comrades should be trusted in Parliament and the executive?

One of Masutha's colleagues called the outbreaks of violence that had periodically targeted African migrants a "colonial construction of foreigners"—meaning that he thought colonizing whites had always benefited from a divide-and-conquer strategy. Masutha, in turn, urged the students to think more deeply now about the "social markers" that led to the looting, assaults, and burning to death of black Africans back in 2008.

Someone protested from the crowd: "It's not *xenophobia* we face—it's *Afrophobia*!" After all, it was not white shopkeepers who had been attacked in the earlier rampages, but only black ones. "People here identify Africa as someplace else," another woman added. "They think of themselves as separate from the rest of the 'dark continent.'" Another speaker pointed out that the genocide in Rwanda, back in 1994, had begun just as the first democratic election was under way in South Africa; some of the people who had fled to South Africa in 1994 had been targeted a second time fourteen years later, right inside the supposedly enlightened country where they had sought refuge.

"Well, look, *poverty* is violent," someone countered from the audience. "And who are we marching *against* in this protest, exactly?" He went on to slam the ANC, and the Zuma government as well, for its failures to alleviate poverty. This was the cause of the attacks, he said, not some psychological problem in the culture, which is what the use of the word *xenophobia* implied. In the absence of a real program of revolutionary social and economic change, he asked, how could you expect people to do anything other than fight over scraps?

Thuthu whirled around to study her father's critic; Gugu shifted uneasily in her seat. She raised her hand halfway, as if not sure yet that she wanted to speak. When she was called upon, she said forcefully, "Look, change must come from the bottom up. Otherwise, we're attacking the symptoms only, not the real underlying problems." Her implication was that if young people continued to count too much on the party and government to solve systemic problems, they would accumulate disappointments and simply roll the problems onto the next generation. "Government will never emancipate us—emancipate us, mentally, I mean," Masutha responded.

From the ecstatic expectations inspired by promises made during the election in 2009, through to the month-long spectacle of the World Cup a year later, there had been lots of airy talk of more rainbows and miracles in South Africa. The emphasis had been on the supposedly exceptional quality of the South African national experience and the distinctive spirit of the people.

Now, these students seemed to understand that there was no sense in waiting any longer for the older generation to crack the complicated code involved in creating the conditions for national deliverance from the country's ills. They seemed to take a more realistic stance, understanding that nobody was going to lead them to the Promised Land. They would have to find the way on their own.

Earlier when I had asked Thuthu how well her father's administration had done so far, she had fallen silent for a moment. "At least the intention is there and steps are being taken to better the lives of the people," she had replied. "It's too early to say. We'll see." She had looked dubious, though. Her older sister, surrounded by students Thuthu's age, insisted on having them jettison their unrealistic expectations. Sweeping change of the kind the country needed now, she would tell me later, could only come from the bottom up—and from the young.

First thing on Sunday a week earlier, Vunene Mabasa had taken me to an early service at Basana Full Gospel Church. We were only a four-hour drive from that beautiful university meeting room in Johannesburg, but it felt like a world away from Jozi. Vunene was the youngest of the young people I had regularly visited over the years, so perhaps it should not have come as a surprise that he should be so unrelentingly optimistic. Still, it did surprise me, especially given how Gwendoline Dube was suffering, to find him as upbeat as ever.

Vunene was part of a circle of teenagers I had met at a Youth League rally in Bungeni in 2006 that had been designed to launch the "fight back" campaign on behalf of Jacob Zuma—his friend Talent was the one who had told me Zuma "had no apartheid" and Mbeki "had a little apartheid"—and he was the boy I had visited after the ANC National Conference in Polokwane back in 2007. Though Vunene came from the poorest part of the country, he had told me several times on the phone, in the intervening years, that he had witnessed the kind of uplift that had only deepened his sense of fealty to the ANC.

A year earlier, he had reported additional good news. His mother and father had patched up their differences and moved back in together. They were all living together, with his younger sister, in the same house again. "Oh, it's so good, Sir," Vunene had told me. His parents had managed to put aside money for school fees, and he had won pride of position as a striker on the soccer team in high school. "We will win the championship in February, Sir," he had assured me. When he wasn't on the field, Vunene reported, he was plowing through texts and workbooks each afternoon. "What I like is the mathematics—but it's *hard*—and life science, those are the best subjects. I still love school, Sir."[3]

In our periodic phone conversations, Vunene told me that the national elections and the inauguration of Zuma as president had been celebrated wildly in his village. "People were quite happy. It was like the election of 1994!" It struck me as funny that he should say so, since 1994 was the year that he was born and he could hardly claim to remember it. When I pointed this out, he laughed. It was what everybody in Bungeni had told him—that the country was "going *back* to 1994."

He had not attended any campaign rallies himself, even though one had been held near his village, because his time was increasingly taken up with church activities. Vunene had joined an evangelical sect. Each Friday, and much of each weekend, was devoted to worship. When I asked if he had a girlfriend, he told me, as if aggrieved, "In our church, we don't do that, Sir. We all go for the word of God here."

Though his religious faith was increasingly important to him, Vunene's belief in the ANC had not wavered. "Tar roads are being laid in my village right now, and many more people have water than last year," he said. In 2014, he would be eligible to vote for the first time, and he already felt ceratin of how he would cast his inaugural ballot. "The party I'm voting for in 2014 is the party that brought liberation and freedom and peace to our country," he announced.

Vunene was still living in the village of Bungeni and was in his next-to-last year of high school. He wore a long-sleeved, nicely pressed, white-and-gray-striped shirt tucked neatly into his faded-green khakis. It was a muggy winter morning, but the air was clear on the ridgetop we drove along to get to his church. There wasn't a single two-story building in sight. The church building was a simple rectangular clapboard construction set at the peak of a hill. In the valleys below, there were clusters of modest homes marked by puffs of smoke from wood fires.

In many ways Vunene Mabasa was a stand-in for all those who most needed to see the kind of radical change "from the bottom up" that Gugu Zuma had mentioned. He was a sixteen-year-old who expected to make his mark under the new dispensation, but he would need plenty of community support to succeed.

When I had seen him last, three years earlier, after the election of

Zuma as president of the ANC, he was a gangly boy of twelve, all elbows and knees. At the time, he reminded me of his ambition to become a doctor so he could treat the illnesses that cut short the lives of his friends and neighbors. Now, I noticed, he carried himself with the hint of a swagger. He was at that tipping point, in the process of claiming his identity as a man.

Vunene was a postliberation child who had lived through the Mbeki transition and reached adolescence during the Zuma interregnum. He still believed 100 percent in President Zuma and the ANC, with religious devotion, but these days he held even more firmly to his trust in a higher power. When I arrived the day before to stay with his family over the weekend, the first thing he had asked me was, "Would you go to church with me?"

Now we took our places on folding chairs toward the front of the hall in time for an opening hymn, "We Glorify Your Name," sung in overlapping choruses of Xitsonga and English. Members of the congregation wandered toward the pulpit, and wobbled back and forth in the aisles, palms turned toward the ceiling, calling out for divine intervention in no particular language. Vunene pointed skyward and raised his hands, calling on the Lord for help.

South Africans were among the most churchgoing people on the planet. This aspect of the social landscape was frequently given short shrift by secular journalists who lived in the cities. "You have to be on *fire* with Jesus!" the pastor beseeched his congregation. ". . . Be ablaze with Jesus," he continued, citing John 8:12. "We accept Jesus in order to be in communication with the Father." The purpose of the communication with the higher power, he explained, was to come fully into one's identity as one among "God's peculiar people." It struck me, then, that there were Christian correlatives for the kind of exceptionalism that marked the ANC's vision of its historic role in bringing its people to the promised land.

"You are not an ordinary person. Do not stoop down!" the pastor shouted. I thought of the expectation that party members should be completely situated among the people but also should never become infected, somehow, with greed, vice, or a consuming hunger for power like ordinary folk; this was precisely the way Thabo Mbeki had described the moral imperative of maintaining purity among party cadres. I remembered, too, that many top officials in the party, like Deputy President Motlanthe, were educated in religious schools and remained deeply dedicated to Christian faith.

"You have to live up to standards," the pastor continued. "Be a *blameless child of God!*" This reminded me of the distinction Zuma had drawn repeatedly in interviews with me between "matured" leaders and ordinary people. His description of the woman who had dubbed him *Black Jesus* as "an innocent soul" came back, too, illuminated from a different angle. I had been trying to work out why the leader thought it should be the business of a national leader in a secular, modernizing state to stoke up revolutionary fervor in party acolytes while praising the most highly victimized as passive vessels of the *innocent soul.*

"If you are not ablaze in Jesus," this pastor warned, "the devil will come and steal that light from you." It occurred to me how thoroughly the South African president and his advisors had adapted evangelical style and imagery in his fight-back struggle to lead the ANC, even promising that the party would "rule until Christ returns." In the end, the president had posed as a living martyr, attempting to redeem himself at every turn with public confession of his sins.

The underlying theme of the 2009 ANC election campaign had been to warn the population that if they were not ablaze with a passion for revolutionary transformation, the vision of turning the country into a nonsexist, nonracial society would be snuffed out. Part of the reason why rural provinces like this one had voted for the ANC by more than

80 percent was that he and the local leaders canvassing for the governing party had convinced voters that Zuma was their singular savior and that the Apocalypse—a slide back into the conditions of apartheid—still loomed as a current danger.

The pastor called up "all those who are sick"; half the people in the hall trudged to the front. Elderly women in traditional clothes, in bright head wraps, and much younger women and men, in jeans and cotton shirts, were ill from HIV, tuberculosis, malnutrition, parasites, and the flu. The pastor laid hands on their foreheads, assuring them that they would be "healed because you believe."

In the health clinics and hospitals in the area, HIV/AIDS programs were finally catching up with services offered in the rest of the country. The government's chief obstacles in taking on the AIDS pandemic were gone; Thabo Mbeki had retired from politics, and Manto Tshabalala-Msimang, the former minister of health, died after her new liver, transplanted in 2007, failed.

Vunene's mother was a nurse in nearby Elim Hospital. Over breakfast early in the morning, Elizabeth Mabasa had told me that medications for active antiretroviral treatment of AIDS were easily, widely available now. This had been a near miraculous change, she thought. The key problem she and her patients faced these days was that medications for so many other common ailments, including hypertension and diabetes, arrived more haphazardly. People were frequently dying from other preventable diseases, even from lack of antibiotics, as a result.

After church, we spent much of the rest of the day with Talent Mabunda and Matimu Mathebula, two of the boys who had been with Vunene when I first met him on the soccer field back in 2006. We sped around town so Vunene could point out the places he had lived before, and his old primary school. We stopped off in the mall for a big meal, and then returned to the same field where the boys and I had met originally.

The field was abandoned and overgrown, and we had to find protection in the stands against a sudden, fierce wind. When the guys stood together, chatting, it soon became clear that Vunene was the most stalwart ANC supporter in the group. The other boys felt quite skeptical of the governing party, drawn to the argument of the Young Communist League that there was a clash of class interests under way inside the governing party.

Like in 2006, Talent pointed at conditions in the surrounding communities and asked what exactly the government had accomplished that should draw their applause. Vunene protested: Paved roads, water, electricity. Talent replied: "They promised *work*."

In some ways, the difference of opinion between two close friends was rooted in the change Vunene had experienced in his own life. Talent's family was just scraping by, while Vunene lived in a newly built three-bedroom house with his parents and younger sister. Right outside the house was a large pile of sand outside the unfinished exterior walls because construction was still under way. The compound included a main house, a shed, two small, unattached rooms for visitors, and a few orange trees. The main house had large, unbarred windows and was painted an almond color. The pitched roof was layered in thick bright-red tiles.

Across the street, and down the lane, there were half-made homes with concrete blocks interspersed with more traditional circular rondavels. Traditional architecture was increasingly crowded out for more expansive modern homes.

Vunene's family wasn't wealthy, by any means, but they were surrounded by marks of progress. There was a television set in the living room, inside plumbing, electricity, and enough beds that nobody had to sleep in shifts or on the floor. There were two wage earners in the house, and his parents made up an intact family, which was relatively rare among his friends.

The Mabasa family, in fact, was an exemplar of the kind of sustainable development and upward mobility that President Zuma said he wanted for everyone. Talent and Vunene's other friends had not fared so well. They were living with single parents or their grannies, scrambling for decent meals.

On Sunday evening, Vunene and I sat out on the stoop together. "I've got my final president—the president of my *choice*," he told me,[4] considering the stars. It was a brilliant evening sky, the Milky Way presenting itself as a vibrant, creamy smear. "I have no worries because I think our government is trying to get up, to stand on its feet and pull up its socks," Vunene went on.

When he was younger, he recalled, he had been under the impression that Thabo Mbeki was the country's first black president. His friends had corrected him: no, the first president of the new South Africa, elected democratically by all citizens, was Nelson Mandela. Mandela, it seemed to him, had managed the nearly impossible.

Vunene didn't mention the intervening nine years of Thabo Mbeki's presidency. "My dad is owning a house because of what Mandela did for him—and did for me," he said. The night sky put him in a reflective mood. "Mandela is also an African hero. Go around Africa and look at all those countries that gained independence. This is the only country that won independence without *fighting*," Vunene pointed out.

The militant rhetoric of the election about the history of armed struggle, mass insurrection, and racial conflict hadn't made much of an impression on him. For Vunene, the postliberation child, his religious and political beliefs aligned perfectly. "Mandela is our hero here in South Africa," he said. "He's like Jesus. As they say, Jacob Zuma is Black Jesus. That means Nelson Mandela is *Extreme Black Jesus*."

Like his other friends, Vunene intended to join the party's Youth League. He had not been following the latest speeches by Julius Malema, in which the youth leader had revived the combative rhetoric of the struggle years and wasn't up to date on debates over Malema's call to nationalize some of the mines. He had not heard of controversies over comments Malema had made about whites, mixed-raced people, and Indians.

Vunene felt that the racial antagonisms of the apartheid era were completely *over*. This idea took a while to sink in, because so many of my other conversations, especially with members of the new elites, were so heavily freighted by considerations of race. Vunene thought, on the other hand, that South Africa was already a thoroughly nonracial place. "Do you think you have the same chance as a white boy from Cape Town to succeed?" I asked. I was thinking of Thomas Maree's friends back in Cape Town. "Yeah, it's an equal race," he said, smiling. "And I can even win it!"

He removed his glasses to clean them. "That white boy in Cape Town you are thinking of—he's *spoiled*," Vunene went on. My parents are sacrificing so I can be the richest person [yet] in this family. That boy there—his parents are already rich now. He will say, 'Oh, I don't have to study hard and work hard.'" The obstacles he had faced, and already cleared, in other words, had prepared him for competition with more privileged children.

Slowly, a general sense of multiracial cohesion seemed to have deepened in recent years. In a survey by future*fact* in 2009, 54 percent of respondents said they considered themselves *South African* first, ahead of racial or language identity; that was up from 46 percent who had answered in this way the year before. Only 7 percent of those surveyed identified themselves first by language, cultural belief, or religion in 2009. An additional 7 percent identified themselves foremost by race, and 30 percent simply called themselves *African*, which, for blacks, was a proxy for racial identity.

Asked in 2008 whether they agreed that "all people are my brothers and sisters and equals, regardless of their race, religion and political beliefs," 55 percent of respondents said they strongly agreed with the proposition. There was a leap upward in response to this critical question in 2009—to 64 percent.[5]

Under the brilliant night sky one year later, Vunene told me that his generation had a historic responsibility to push the country forward. That's why he hit the books diligently every afternoon and every night, allowing only little breaks for swapping tales about girlfriends with Talent and Matimu.

When I pressed him, he admitted that he had a romance going now. He kept his voice hushed because he hadn't informed his parents yet. Vunene imagined a long courtship with his girlfriend, with marriage as the goal at the end of his medical training. He figured that he would secure his first paid job, at the age of twenty-three or twenty-four, about eight years from now, and that was when he could afford to be married.

His optimism about the future, like the general upbeat expectations of his generation, rubbed up against stubborn facts. Nearly a third of black youngsters eighteen years and older were unemployed, while the unemployment rate for coloureds was 19 percent. For Indians, it was 12 percent, and for whites just 3 percent.[6] I had been looking through these statistics as I began to check back in with the young people I had met during the previous six years.

Among the young whites I had interviewed over the years, I found a sense of surprise at how well things had turned out for them. For example, the two young white men I had met in the Klein Karoo back in 2004 were living and working in Cape Town; after graduating from college, they had decided to stay in the country after all and secured well-paying jobs in spite of their earlier gloomy expectations. Though they voted for the opposition led by Helen Zille, and still distrusted the ANC intensely, they were thriving under the new dispensation.

For mixed-race and black young people outside the narrow band of the emerging black elite, though, the legacy of apartheid still meant the deck was stacked against them. The global economy that South Africa rejoined in the post-apartheid period was biased, in devastating ways, against the young: less than 30 percent of South Africans from the ages of eighteen to twenty-nine had a job.[7]

Vunene was among the lucky third of black South African children who had an employed parent in the household.[8] The implications of this simple fact were enormous: if at least one parent was earning a salary, the likelihood of children getting sufficient food and care, and being able to attend school regularly, was far greater. Here, too, the racial differences were stark: 94 percent of white children had an employed parent living at home, but only a small fraction of black children did. These were the results of systemic patterns of bias threatening to create yet another "lost generation" like the survivors of the struggle years. He wasn't alone in facing these daunting prospects with relentlessly upbeat expectations, though. In that same 2009 survey conducted by future*fact*, 57 percent of those who were questioned said they expected the standard of living for their children to be somewhat better or much better than their own. Vunene's calculus was simple, and it echoed the party's election manifesto: "Better education, and better schools, can make us have a better life," he said, before heading off to bed.

Early the next morning, on my last day in the village, I drove Vunene and his friends to school. On the way, he confessed, for the first time since he had begun speaking to me in 2006, that he was quite worried about getting adequately prepared for the matriculation exam looming ahead of him, in 2012. This was the same exam, of course, that had wrecked Gwendoline's ambition to become a doctor and pilot.

During the World Cup tournament, public schools had been shut down and a month or more of instruction time had been lost, which seemed like a strange decision by a government committed to creation of a "developmental state" in the service of a developing society. The educational needs of children had been sacrificed for an international spectacle and the honor of hosting it. Poor children in the worst schools had undoubtedly taken the biggest hit; they would suffer, this year's results would show, a dramatic dive in passage rates on the exam that determined where, and if, they could go on to college.

On the way to school, Vunene added a few other things to the list of obstacles to be overcome by students in rural schools. Among the most important was his dawning realization that the teachers in his high school, though well meaning, were often ineffective. School materials were generally presented in English, he pointed out, while his teachers conducted classes in Xitsonga. The students often found their translations garbled and nonsensical. "It makes confusion to each and everybody," he told me, and the other boys agreed.

At the big intersection near Merca's Supermarket and Hardware, right across from Mtchari's Electronic Repair, signs indicated that Bungeni lay behind us. The town called Tiyani loomed up ahead. We turned left off the paved road, sliding into a dirt thoroughfare thick with silt. Outside Vuk'uzenzeleguazeni Spaza Shop, across from Gwaleni Tyre Repair, "I'm Going to Love You for the Rest of My Life" blasted from a giant boom box.

On the rest of the drive out to their school, the boys told me about the second biggest problem they faced—the way male teachers led girl learners astray. The official line, from the government and school officials, was that young people should delay their sexual debut, limit themselves to a single partner, and practice safer sex. "But lots of girls at our school are having babies," Vunene reported.

One of these girls was a close friend of his. She was an excellent student whose grades had imploded after she became pregnant. "She was carrying a baby, and then she failed," he said, looking glum. The cause of this grand dysfunction was not the boy students, he insisted, but men "aged like my dad—or you. The man promises her money. [Or he says], 'I see you don't have a uniform. I'll buy you a uniform.'"

Among the older men who did "this nasty thing" were some of his own teachers. The fact that their instructors preyed on their own girlfriends created a fierce generational tension that wasn't conducive to learning. The other boys murmured angrily about how sexual predation poisoned the environment at school, and sometimes turned them away from learning.

When we arrived at Hluvuka High School, students were gathered for morning assembly in a clearing because no room inside would hold all of them. They were in school uniforms—powder-blue shirts over gray slacks—some of them pressed and new, others worse for wear. There were few backpacks or book bags needed; the availability of textbooks in public schools like this had been a recurrent problem.

The deputy principal told me that things were vastly improved under the new administration. His was a public school, but there were still required fees, and the amount had dropped recently, from R200 a month to R80. "Our biggest problem is absenteeism," he said. "And then, lack of parental involvement." He believed that parents who had never gone to school themselves were often clueless about the support they needed to offer their children if they were to thrive in school.

As Vunene and the other boys set off to join their friends in the middle of the crowd, they asked for a favor: Would I address this assembly of their peers? "The other students are curious, and want to hear from you," Vunene said. "Please, do it for me." Public speaking was not my forte; I was a journalist in part because I felt best equipped to ask questions rather than posing as an expert.

Suddenly, there were a thousand young South Africans, the age of the hundreds I had been interviewing all over the country, being told to quiet down and listen to prepared remarks of the distinguished visitor who had come all the way from the United States to address them. The teacher introducing me mentioned that I taught at an influential university and recently had spent time with President Zuma. Perhaps I would tell them all what I thought of the president?

"*Sawubona*," I said, and there was a murmur of response. "I live in Chicago," I began. "Who else comes from my home town—do you know?" The hand of a boy shot up: "Barack Obama!" he shouted. "Who else?" I asked. One of the girls jumped up and down. "I know—Oprah!" Endeavoring to explain myself, I told them that I had come to South Africa six years earlier full of so many questions. Among other things, I had wanted to figure out how a nation's people divided by race and class for so many years—ravaged by colonialism and apartheid, hit by the HIV/AIDS pandemic, and rocked by reintegration into the global economy—had made progress toward creating a visionary new kind of society.

It all came out in a kind of burbling mishmash. I said that I had spent time with President Zuma over the years, and was scheduled to spend more time with him in the following week. As much as I felt I had learned by interviewing the president and other leaders, though, I felt I had gotten much more from spending time in places like Bungeni, where the next generation of South Africans was busily taking charge of its own fate.

Believe it or not, I told the students, what they managed to accomplish in the surrounding villages would reverberate all around the world. If young South Africans seize the moment, and make progress toward the millennial vision of a new nonracial, nonsexist, egalitarian society, it would show the way for the rest of us. In the end, I said, Americans might aspire, in future years, to be more like *them*. There was a brief, stunned pause when I finished abruptly, out of words and out of breath, and then came a sustained and startling roar.

As I pulled away from Hluvuka High, I thought of how the rest of Vunene's day would unfold. He was privileged compared to most of his classmates, having dressed that morning in clean, pressed clothes. Vunene had the correct prescription in his new spectacles, so he could see well enough to read. He carried a five-rand note (less than a dollar) in his pocket. He had also been awake since five in the morning; there would be two breaks during the day so that by the end of lunchtime his money would be spent on food, and by three in the afternoon he would feel hunger beginning to gnaw at him. It was hard to keep the level of concentration he wanted on his studies when his stomach spoke up so forcefully, he had told me. In the community around him, there wasn't much reinforcement, save for the example of his own parents, for taking the path he had chosen.

During our talk the night before, Vunene had said that he knew little about the history of apartheid but he figured that Talent had been right to see that President Zuma "had no apartheid" whatsoever in his character. He felt certain, too, that he and his friends would never become infected with that particular illness. "Here in our country, they call us the Born Frees," he said proudly. "We *were* born free."

That was a proclamation that both heartened and also worried me. Like their elders, Vunene's generation would need to fight the powers-that-be in order to expand the ambit of their own freedom. The powers-that-be these days, though, were in control of the party of the people. For him and his friends, then, standing up for themselves would mean fighting against the assumptions of the elders in control of the ANC. After spending time again in Bungeni, I felt a dawning realization about why this would prove so difficult. Dust churned up from the roadway and spilled into the open windows as I turned south, again heading for a final series of interviews with the country's new leader. It was a long drive, on a collection of bad roads, to the highway that led me to Pretoria.

24.

The Leader

On my way to meet with President Zuma I was waylaid by security guards at Gate 10, an entrance to the vast government compound outside Pretoria known as Bryntirion Estate. Top government officials, including the president and Cabinet ministers, lived there in a bucolic, parklike setting with little traffic, no crime, clean air, and plenty of open space between the grand residences. No wonder they sometimes seemed cut off from the daily realities of the people they governed.

At the peak of the ridge was Mahlamba Ndlopfu, which means "New Dawn" in Shangaan, one of the country's indigenous languages. It was a gleaming white, Cape Dutch–styled mansion, built seventy years earlier by Dr. Gerrit Moerdyk, an architect who couldn't have foreseen in his wildest imagination that his masterpiece would be occupied one day by a once shoeless, uneducated goat herder from Natal. As the official residence for South Africa's head of state, the mansion had been placed purposely at the highest spot on the estate. When you drove past a remote-controlled gate on an empty boulevard to climb the steep drive, the president's house ruled the landscape in a way that reminded me of Hearst Castle.

When I had made the appointment to meet with the president, I expected to be summoned back to Union Buildings, where I had met ministers and aides to President Mbeki over the years. As it happened, though, the new leader conducted much of his business shuttling between three official residences, in Pretoria, Cape Town, and Durban. He had continued to operate, as president, much as he had done when he was running his insurgent campaign for control of the ANC out of his home in Forest Town.

Opposition politicians had objected to the cost of extensive renovations to the east wing of Mahlamba Ndlopfu, which had been undertaken so Zuma could place his top strategists to work inside the residence. There, they handled his schedule and communications strategy as well as the affairs of his multiple wives. The budget for maintaining the country's first family—which had meant only Thabo Mbeki and his wife, Zanele, during the previous presidency—soared under the new leader, with his three official wives, and counting, and two dozen children.

Mahlamba Ndlopfu was surrounded by tall trees and a botanical garden, which was a national heritage site. It had an extravagant foyer, a grand staircase, and a massive pair of drawing rooms, one of which I was ushered into on my arrival. The rooms were bordered by a huge living room that looked out on the gardens. From the window, you could see the Magaliesberg range, the craggy mountains with sheer quartzite cliffs formed billions of years ago. This mountain range was among the oldest in the world.

The Magaliesberg marked the line between the plateau to the south, which included Johannesburg and the surrounding area—responsible for producing half the gold ever mined in the world—and the subtropical grassland to the north, where I had spent the weekend with the Mabasa family. There was a campaign under way to have UNESCO (United Nations Educational, Scientific and Cultural Organization) declare an extensive section of the range a protected biosphere zone. It was home to mountain reedbuck, red hartebeest, sable antelope, and aardwolf. The most beautiful birds in the world nested there—tawny eagle, black cuckooshrike, yellow-fronted tinkerbird, and brown-hooded kingfisher.

While I waited for him, I could hear the president's distinctive laugh and the murmur of a story he was telling someone. There wasn't the kind of bustle you might have expected in the home offices of a head of state. No cars arrived in the driveway; no harried aides scurried past. The place had the laid-back vibe of Nkandla and the easygoing rhythm of the Zuma home back in Johannesburg.

Periodically, over the course of two hours as I waited, an assistant entered the room, wrung his hands, and apologized for the delay. He kept reassuring me that President Zuma was coming "shortly." Right at six o'clock in the evening, the president entered the room, greeting me with outstretched hands and a broad smile. He sat me down at the end of the formal banquet table to deliver the bad news: he wouldn't have time to talk to me after all.

There was a crisis involving a commission report on the status of traditional leaders in the country, as it turned out, and the secretary-general of the ANC, Gwede Mantashe, was on his way from Johannesburg, with a delegation of other top leaders, to meet with him. The Commission on Traditional Leadership Disputes report was a long-overdue attempt to clarify which traditional leaders and royalty around the country would have their authority honored. What a thorny mess the commission had been handed: its members were essentially given the task of disentangling relationships that implicated indigenous, colonial, and apartheid histories. Did a family line favored by a British magistrate have ongoing legitimacy as a traditional leader? How about royalty and local traditional leaders who had thrived largely through collaboration with the white regime?

Zuma would need to strike the right balance, in a final decision on commission recommendations, between the assertion of individual rights within a modernizing state, and the long-standing promises the ANC had made to traditional leaders. The exercise of broad authority in the former homelands by royals and unelected headmen, including

Mandla Mandela, was among the many conflicts that had been punted into the future during the democratic transition in the 1990s. Now, as the young Chief Mandela had told me, tensions were nearing a flash point.

President Mbeki had signed the Communal Land Rights Act in 2004. That new law had given traditional leaders greater control over land than they had enjoyed under apartheid. But the Constitutional Court had struck down the law in May of 2010. Traditional leaders worried that their power, in this case over control of land, was in the process of being stripped from them.

Back in 2007, I had interviewed an *nkosi* from KwaZulu-Natal, and so I had gathered a little insight about what was at stake in the fight from the point of view of traditional leaders. He had complained that nobody would take up the role of *nkosi* any longer given the shrinking value of the position; it was all *responsibility* with no real *authority*, he said.

Now, the commission, and the president, would decide which traditional leaders would have continued legal standing. Naturally, those who would be stripped of their authority were going to be furious, and since Zuma's base of support included traditional leaders in rural areas, the coming eruption needed his attention. "We must postpone, My Brother," the president said. "When do you go back to the States, eh?"[1]

It was Wednesday night, and I was scheduled to fly to Chicago the following Saturday. I mentioned, as my stomach fell, that for four months I had been asking for interview time with him in order to tie up so many loose ends. For five weeks I had been in the country, and nearly every day had been peppering his schedulers with increasingly emphatic entreaties. "Oh, it will be difficult now, My Brother," he said, looking cheerful.

At which point I blew a quiet gasket. "That's a shame," I replied. "Because it's your fault that I'm here." In the time we had spent together over the years, I had been the model interlocutor, endlessly patient. He had the power to let me in or, as Mbeki had done, freeze me out, and I felt grateful that he repeatedly had made time for me. Now, he was president of an enormously complicated country in need of his urgent attention, so I had felt a little abashed about demanding more of his attention.

The president pushed back from the table, looking startled. "*My* fault. How is it my *fault*?" I tapped at the list of fact-checking questions and thumped the thick manuscript on the table. I flipped through, showing him the blizzard of tabs attached to the most important points. There were close to fifty details, none that could be documented through other sources. I had already consulted his closest friends and advisors and had narrowed the list considerably with their help; but here were the marked-up questions only he could answer.

"You're always complaining about inaccuracies by journalists and telling me how academics have no clue about what really happens in the ANC or in your life," I said, angrily. "But here I've come thousands of miles just to make sure the account is correct. And you are unable to make the time for me, when I'm only trying to get the story right."

Zuma looked stung, unsettled, and more than a little surprised. Standing, he grabbed me by the elbow and pulled me across the hallway. He burst through a door into a room where his chief of staff, Lakela Kaunda, and chief spokesman, Zizi Kodwa, looked up from their work. They also looked quite startled. Kaunda said, "I am not here. I am a ghost," because she had made a series of unkept commitments to me.

The president began to lecture them, recalling that I had followed him around way back in 2006, and had interviewed him all through 2007. I had kept coming back over the years, he said, laughing. Then he repeated verbatim what I had said about the effort I had made in ensuring that my account was accurate. "He wants to make sure it's *correct*," Zuma said, as if this was the first time any journalist had done any fact-checking with him. "What can we do?"

He beckoned impatiently for a copy of his schedule. On Friday, two days later, he was scheduled to address a summit of farmworkers in Cape Town and fly to Durban. The president asked Kaunda to block out time on that day. I could travel with him, he promised, and he would make time for me after the speech, on the flight, and in the presidential residence in Durban afterward. "All night we can talk," he said. I could have however much time I needed until my own flight home on Saturday evening. "We will spend the whole night talking, My Brother," Zuma promised. "You can ask and ask, and we'll continue until the morning." And that was how I set off to spend my final days in South Africa with its new leader.

Our day together that Friday began outside Cape Town, in a VIP tent next to the hall where delegates of farmworker organizations from all over the country were meeting. Helen Zille, leader of the opposition and now premier of the Western Cape, was waiting to welcome the president. She had continued to slam the ANC and the government he led. When Zuma got out of his car, they embraced like old friends, though. Zille had led her party, the Democratic Alliance, to a dramatic increase in its national vote, up from 12 percent in 2004 to nearly 17 percent in 2009, and she had done so on the strength of a red-blooded blitz to "Stop Zuma." During the campaign, Zille repeatedly ripped into him as a flawed person and corrupt leader, denouncing the decision of the National Prosecuting Authority, made several weeks before the election, to drop its case against him on corruption, bribery, and tax evasion charges.

In the coming years, the Democratic Alliance would emerge as the essential minority opposition voice in Parliament, far outnumbered but steadily punching above its weight. Zille was a savvy politician, and she had also gone out of her way to develop a friendly personal relationship with the president. She knew that there was a fine line, in order to appeal to wavering traditional supporters of the ANC, between making acceptable criticisms of the black elected leader and creating the perception of disrespect toward the black majority who had put him there.

The premier perched on a couch, while Zuma took an armchair nearby. He confided that he had recently been forced to take a side trip to Tripoli, in order to try to talk Colonel Muammar al-Qaddafi, the leader of Libya, into taking a more reasonable stance about a set of important decisions ahead for the African Union. Zuma rolled his eyes and shrugged, cocking his head in a comic gesture, signaling that the matter was extremely delicate. Qaddafi was a difficult customer, after all. "We had to try to *contain* him," he said.

The following year, as a massive popular revolt threatened Qaddafi's rule, a UN-sanctioned NATO air campaign against Libyan forces would be launched, and Libya's leader would be indicted by the International Criminal Court in the Hague for war crimes. The South African leader got drawn into a long, ineffective campaign to mediate an end to the conflict that was widely seen as pro-Qaddafi.

The president's repeated trips to Tripoli, calls for NATO to stop the air strikes, and unsuccessful efforts to bring about a cease-fire placed South Africa in the strange position of seeming to side with a dictator while masses of people in the region—from Tunisia to Syria—were in open revolt against authoritarian rule in scenes that evoked memories of mass demonstrations against the white regime in the dying days of apartheid. Zuma placed his party and country on the wrong side in the Arab Spring.

From my conversations with young South Africans, though, I knew that there was considerable pressure from within the party that weighed on the other side. The intervention in the Libyan conflict by NATO, followed by the forcible overthrow and murder of Qaddafi, had left bitter feelings behind. In early 2012, Ndaba Mandela told me that many of his contemporaries celebrated Qaddafi for his longtime support of the fight against apartheid and felt quite perplexed that the South African government had not more effectively come to the dictator's aid. "It was sad for a lot of South Africans who knew the history," Mandela went on. "It was sad to see the Westerners bombarding us and none of us being able to stand up against them."[2]

In other ways, Nelson Mandela's grandson thought that the jury was out still on the value of Zuma's leadership. Two years after the World Cup, there weren't enough visible signs of progress, in his view. "It's more or less the same as when I met you back in 2007," he said. His son fussed at him in the background, demanding attention by grabbing at the phone. "That boy is so *stubborn*," he said. "He's going to be *trouble*." I reminded Ndaba that the boy came from a long line of troublemakers. "He comes by it honestly," I said.

Among his contemporaries, Ndaba added, "there's a little more positivity, partly due to the World Cup. Young people are a little more involved in shaping political opinion. It feels like it's *moving*, you see?" The endless internecine battles within the ruling party were not helping, however. "Having the likes of Julius Malema and our president—the most controversial leader we have had in the last 18 years—eish!" he exclaimed. "Then again, it's only Zuma's first term. In his second term, hopefully he shows us his value."

In the moment, Zille pulled closer to listen to the details of Zuma's meeting with Qaddafi. They chatted on as though the president wasn't already well behind schedule. When Zuma paused, the premier offered an anecdote about the ongoing struggle to clarify who were the legitimate traditional leaders in the Western Cape. "I met with a young man yesterday. He had blond hair and blue eyes, and yet he claimed to be the leader of the *San!*" she exclaimed. "Is that *so?*" Zuma replied, and they both broke up over the odd sorts of problems that you faced when you held power. An outsider happening on the scene might have thought they were long-lost friends instead of mortal political rivals.

As the new premier of the Western Cape, Zille was the favorite target of ANC spokesmen and the party's Alliance partners, especially in the trade unions. When she had named her provincial Cabinet in 2009, it was all male with only a single black representative. From the first day, there had been threats to force her out of office by making the province "ungovernable." The rhetoric, and the ANC strategy against her, led Zille to maintain strong doubts, still, about whether the governing party and Zuma himself were fundamentally committed to democracy.

Periodically, the president had issued reassuring statements about the government's respect for judicial independence and media freedom. But an ally and supporter, a judge from the Western Cape named John Hlophe, had attempted to lobby justices on the Constitutional Court in one of the appeal cases that involved Zuma, and the president had not criticized him for it. When Zuma disagreed with a subsequent judgment of the court, he reminded the justices, as if they were under some misimpression otherwise, that they "were not God."

Religious imagery kept popping up in Zuma's impromptu remarks— shades of his own status as the Black Jesus and his longtime prediction that the ANC would "rule until the Son of God returns." It worried plenty of others besides the premier that the new president didn't seem to respect meaningful distinctions between the interests of his party, the interests of the state, and the interests of the people. Would the ANC hand over power in a free and fair election? She did not feel entirely confident of the answer. That was surely the true test of an emerging democracy.

Soon enough, the president and premier crossed over to the hall together, mounting a long dais full of labor leaders, including trade union chief Zwelinzima Vavi. It struck me, immediately, that the relationship between the two men was no longer warm. All through 2007, I had seen them on countless platforms together—joking, complimenting one another, and behaving as fiercely protective allies. Now there was nothing but a perfunctory handshake.

Though Vavi had been expected to introduce the president, he was sidelined here for the honor. Two weeks earlier, I had stopped by trade union headquarters in central Johannesburg, and Vavi had assured me that relationships in general within the Alliance—the ANC, trade union federation, and Communist Party—were better than ever overall. When

I mentioned to him that I had seen Zuma in Washington, D.C., with Siphiwe Nyanda and Mathews Phosa, on his first trip to the United States after his election as leader of the ANC in 2008, he had smiled, looking into his open hands. "Well, I suppose he has *new* friends now," he had said softly.[3] "I don't really want to touch on the symbolism of being left out of delegations by the president," Vavi said. He didn't want to sound petty or egotistical. "There are moments when I feel: Wow, now the president is surrounded by new friends," he went on. ". . . Those new friends were never seen during the real difficult struggles. But we're leading a movement not in order to position ourselves so we can be close to the president. There were principles that we were defending."

The ANC, and the Alliance that included the trade union movement, were still "contested terrain," he murmured. He felt pleased that an industrial policy, one that included a robust growth plan, had been tabled for discussion by government, but it was action by Zuma's government, not talk alone, that would define the future of the relationship. He noted that he had criticized both the finance minister's budget speech to Parliament and the lackluster State of the Nation Address by President Zuma. "We have played the same role we did when Mbeki was in charge," he explained. Since Vavi had supported Zuma for the top job, some ANC leaders thought "we would be lackeys and endorse all the mistakes the leadership makes."

This amounted to a profound misreading of the role its leader thought the trade union should play, Vavi said. In sticking up for Zuma, as leader of the ANC, he had intended to strike a blow for workers and the poor, and stand forthrightly for an independent media, on the side of an autonomous judiciary, and against dictatorships in Zimbabwe and Swaziland. In the throes of the battle, he thought some people had misunderstood the proper position of the trade unions.

"When the rape case happened, we never jumped to the defense of the president," Vavi pointed out. "In the [recent scandal], with a child born out of wedlock, we just couldn't be quiet. We pointed out the dangers in that type of behavior. We have been extremely independent in our thinking. As a result, we have made lots of friends among people who are opposed to corruption and who want good morals to govern the state and organization. . . . We are a workers'organization, and we can't be seen to endorse things our members will find socially unacceptable. This movement belongs to the generations to come—not to ourselves."

As the president trudged through a long and dull address before the farmworker delegates, the trade union leader offered wide yawns, looking at his watch. "We have to pull together and work faster and harder to make change," Zuma said. These lines had lost their luster; they were invocations for a campaign, not a report on action taken by a sitting government. People all over the country, like Vunene Mabasa in Limpopo, were under the impression that Zuma's government had pulled together already.

The president ended with a more substantive appeal, saying that he had emphasized rural development during the campaign because the need for food security and a sustainable economy required it. On this point, the new president was undoubtedly correct. There would be no visible progress on housing, health, education, and the creation of decently paid jobs if the peri-urban areas and big cities continued to be inundated with burgeoning numbers of unskilled, uneducated, and increasingly desperate people flooding in from rural communities where no jobs were available.

From our earlier discussions, I knew that Zuma felt that there was also a cultural and even a moral aspect involved in rural development. He thought that young people in rural communities were less vulnerable to what he called "Western influences." He would tell me, later on this day, that the need to maintain a strong rural sensibility in the new South Africa required of the national government the creation of new, desirable jobs in fisheries, on farms, and in the timber industry so that fewer young people would migrate from rural to urban areas.

"As you develop the rural areas, I don't think there will be as much interest by the young people in migrating to the cities," he said. When I mentioned the initiatives of Mandla Mandela in Mvezo, and also the concern Mandela had expressed about losing young people to cosmopolitan ambitions, the president burst out: "That's the point! You wouldn't even know that Mandla grew up in Soweto by seeing him now!"

Zuma reveled over this twist in the Mandela narrative, as if he was personally responsible for it: the *nkosi* was a kind of reverse migrant, and he approved of the trajectory. "He's more country than people who grew up there now!" When I asked about whether any of his own children were likely to follow suit, he replied, "The younger generation, they have made it very clear. They are saying, 'Let us *discover* [for ourselves] who we are.'"

When the president finished speaking to the farmworkers, one of the organizers whispered in Zuma's ear. Everyone on the dais, except for Premier Zille, rose to sing the ode to the machine gun. He was president of the republic now, and the whole exercise looked halfhearted, like a threadbare lounge act. As Zuma finished dancing, we hustled out of the hall and into the waiting motorcade.

I was placed in a chase car behind the president's sedan and we tore out of the conference center and careened off at breakneck speed, sirens screaming and blue lights flickering. Once we reached the highway, the motorcade claimed multiple lanes, speeding up to 180 kilometers per hour and forcing startled drivers off to the shoulder. There were the sounds of brakes, and a dozen apparent near misses as the procession sped past Khayelitsha, the black township, and then Nyanga and Bellville.

These vast collections of poverty with booming populations were like blips on the windshield. I thought back to Limpopo, where I had once seen an old man in an ox-driven cart forced off the road by this kind of motorcade. We blasted onto the M3 highway toward Muizenberg, pulling off at the Newlands exit and barreling into the entrance to Groote Schuur, the government estate outside Cape Town.

The estate had been constructed more than a century earlier on the slopes of Devil's Peak. Down the slope to the right was the original presidential residence, designed in 1893 by Sir Herbert Baker for Cecil

Rhodes, the former prime minister of the Cape Colony. Rhodes was the one who had nurtured visions of establishing white rule in Africa "from the Cape to Cairo." His mansion was high Cape Dutch architecture, with verandas surrounded by colonnades and intricately carved gables.

Inside, fireplaces were flanked by Zimbabwe soapstone and souvenirs from Rhodes's time, including a writing table from Egypt and a stink-wood armoire. It was stunning to see this extravagant place for myself. I had read about the master bath, where an enormous tub fashioned from a massive piece of Paarl granite sported a brass spigot in the shape of a lion's mouth. Lounging in it, I imagined, it would be hard to think for long about village life back in Nkandla.

Once we arrived, it was hard to understand why we had hurried so reck-lessly to get to the mansion. I had imagined the president would be booked on the half hour with important meetings. From a casual observer's per-spective, it seemed as though he governed the country largely by wander-ing around. A call would come in requiring his urgent attention, or he would be summoned for an appointment with someone who had been nearly lost in the shuffle and was furiously trying to get through to him. You would hear the trademark phrase: *Is that so?* Skip a few beats. *Abso-lutely.* It didn't seem like the president's work patterns, or his intertwining of public and private life, had changed much since he became head of state.

When Zuma joined me for lunch, we began by working through some of the details I had wanted to confirm. At first, I felt a little wary about rais-ing all the questions in sequence, thinking that he might try to convince me to leave out the most controversial parts. He had not told anyone else, for example, about the plot he once helped hatch that would have involved the slaughter of civilians, back in Durban in the early 1960s. As I reviewed how this incident was portrayed in the manuscript, though, Zuma suggested only two slight alterations. "We did not *execute* [the plan]," he said. His other suggestion was to change a reference to the plotters as *boys* because the teenagers "were really young men rather than boys."

On the distinction between attacks on police or soldiers versus a plan that involved "butchering people"—which is how he had described it in the interview—he shrugged his shoulders. "We knew nothing about military science," the president explained. "Hmm. We were just looking at the whites." He paused, glancing at my digital recorder. "It was quite wrong," he went on. "Later, you realize how wrong we were. It wasn't different than what the PAC did, you know?"

Most of the discussion about the past placed the president in a reflective mood. When I tried to engage him on more recent rumblings within party circles about a campaign under way to replace him as leader of the ANC in 2012, he only smiled. The deputy president, Kgalema Motlanthe, the former secretary-general of the ANC, was apparently the preference of the Youth League.

The more the wheel turned, the more the fractionating impulse at the heart of the ANC wore on. It was clear that Zuma had failed in one of his prime objectives—unifying the party and the Alliance. On the eve of its centenary, the oldest and most revered liberation movement in Africa kept winning elections easily but seemed to have lost the plot in nurturing a broad-based bottom-up social movement.

Out on the veranda, where we were eating lunch, there was one question that turned Zuma snappish. It concerned his relationships with his wives and his children. In going back over the history of his marriages, I asked why he had never explained to his children when they were younger that he was married to three women and that they had stepbrothers and stepsisters. Why had he kept these overlapping circles of family relationships secret if he was so proud of his polygynous ways and perfectly settled on his own rectitude?

"Did you ever sit down with your children and simply explain who was who?" I asked. There was a long pause, and the president sank back in his chair, considering me with narrowed eyes. "You can't sit down the kids—what do they know? Hmm. That's not done with us," he replied, with an evident edge. "The kids don't understand. The kids are born in an environment. That's all." Zuma cleared his throat, as if I had attacked him. "You don't sit kids down and *talk* to them," he added, with rising force. "You sit down with your brothers or elders. The *children* grow up in a situation that is natural to them."

His answer led me to remember the explanation he had given me years earlier about how he had decided to take Nkosazana Dlamini as an additional wife while in exile, and how an ANC elder he had consulted advised him "to take manly decisions." Here was one of the rubs in his invitation, expressed earlier, for the next generation of South Africans, including his own children, to chart their own new direction. When push came to shove, in personal matters as in public life, the president remained firmly enmeshed in the idea that seniority, hierarchy, and patriarchal tradition trumped knowledge, innovation, or any number of generational grievances.

Another question I asked set the president off in an entirely different way. In our discussions during the three years since we had met, I periodically circled back to him on the origins of his dispute with Thabo Mbeki. The schism between them still seemed a little mysterious to me. Neither one of them was much of a risk-taker, and they both had excelled at the inside game—marshaling support, mediating differences, and advancing from within ANC circles through doggedness more than charismatic abilities.

Zuma always seemed wary about discussing this matter, except in opaque terms. He always reverted to vague references about shadowy figures around the former president who had conspired to sink him. Early on, the president had told me that tension with Mbeki began in the early days of the decade, when Zuma had asserted himself in his role as deputy president of the country. Later, he alluded to how few differences of any significance had marked his three decades of work alongside the man he kept describing as "more than a brother."

Now, as we reviewed the chronology together, Zuma revealed that he had not felt entirely sure—even as far back as the day he attended Thabo Mbeki's inauguration as president in 1999—what the new leader's intentions were toward him. "I *had* to be there. You couldn't have an inauguration without the deputy president of the party!" he said.

Yet he hadn't felt confident that Mbeki would name him to the Cabinet as deputy president of the country in 1999. "I had got the information that he'd talked to people and sort of hinted that he might not appoint me," Zuma revealed, studying his hands. This would have been so awkward for both men, but it occurred to me that it might have been a quite healthy development for the country. What if, back in 1999, the distinction between the party and the state had been drawn more firmly in this way? Phumzile Mlambo-Ngcuka's effectiveness in her brief service as deputy president, especially on HIV/AIDS, had served to reinforce the idea that you could have, in the second position in the executive, someone focused solely on government matters rather than a potential rival-in-waiting.

In any case, a core of party insiders who had seen Mbeki and Zuma as the essential pair—a balanced, complementary, workable duo—had prevailed in changing Mbeki's mind, according to Zuma. When the newly inaugurated president had consulted two powerful leaders about the possibility of choosing someone else, both warned him that he risked splitting the ANC if he chose someone else, Zuma recalled. "So, I knew that, in his mind, he had mixed feelings [back then]."

The roots of the tensions between the two men reached back even further, Zuma continued. As he finished eating, he traced the trouble all the way back to 1989. That was when he had been sent secretly, as part of a small delegation, back into South Africa to conduct "negotiations over negotiations." He now claimed that Penuell Maduna, the legal expert, had been sent by Mbeki mostly to keep an eye on *him*.

Maduna subsequently served as justice minister, and was aligned closely with Mbeki during the period when the corruption case against

Zuma was being pursued. In this account, Zuma maintained that he had been in charge, decades earlier, of Maduna's transition into exile. Back then, he had the duty of making an assessment of the kind of role Maduna should play in the movement.

"I did my assessment," Zuma recalled. "[Maduna] couldn't work in an underground situation," supposedly because he was a sieve for information, completely indiscrete, and couldn't be trusted with secrets. "So, we removed him from Swaziland," Zuma said. "I was part of those who said, 'This one can't work here.' They removed him from what we used to call internal work. He went on to become part of the legal committee of the ANC in exile—far away from sensitive things."

The clear implication was that the senior cadres always considered Maduna unreliable. Zuma was implying, of course, that from the moment of his return, the balance of power within the organization had begun to shift as the ANC called off guerrilla warfare and mass insurrection and turned its attention to sparring over legal distinctions in managing the negotiations that would lead to a transition to majority rule.

He was making the case, between the lines, that he had paid a price, with Mbeki and others, by ferreting out unreliable comrades and spies. In so many journalistic and scholarly accounts of the 1990s, Zuma was portrayed as Thabo Mbeki's muscleman within the organization, but Zuma pointed out that it was he, and not Mbeki, who was selected by an ailing Oliver Tambo to chair the ANC delegation in the first round of negotiations. Most outsiders had failed to understand these internal dynamics, he added.

It was against this backdrop, Zuma insisted, that he had attempted to pull away from national responsibilities in the early 1990s. He knew there were a slew of enemies waiting for revenge. When Zuma had tried, in the wake of the negotiations, to absent himself from any contest for national office, he said that he was pressed into service virtually against his will. "I'd gone back to the province by 1994. I wanted to pull away from the leadership for very good reasons of mine, which are confidential. Maybe when I'm a very old man I will write about it," he continued.

Tipped off that "some forces were worried about me," he wanted to signal clearly that he posed no threat on the national stage. He was willing to stay home in order to keep out of the line of fire, he said. "Then comrades came to me to say, 'Mandela is going to do one term.' Walter Sisulu, who was the deputy president, would not go into government. Naturally, Mbeki was going in," Zuma recalled. So the comrades insisted that Zuma stand for election as national chairperson of the party, with an eye to putting him in as deputy president in 1997.

"I tried again to say, no, no, no, no, no," he insisted, his voice rising. By then, a new amendment to the ANC's constitution prohibited officials from simultaneously holding top positions in the province and nationally. Here was an easy way out for Zuma, because he had no intention of dropping his commitment to the work in KwaZulu-Natal. In short order, though, the delegates had overwhelmingly passed what was called "the Zuma Clause," a one-person exception to the prohibition.

No wonder, it occurred to me now, that Zuma later expected to be treated with deference, including in relation to judicial judgments on criminal cases involving him. Right at the dawn of democracy, after all, he had been favored with an exception to the ANC constitution. His comrades had readily broken a rule that applied in an ironclad way to everybody else.

"This made people who were my enemies, even forces outside the party, even more worried," Zuma recalled. "They could see the move, and the mood, of the comrades with regard to my name. The comrades were ready to change the Constitution!" From that moment in 1994 until Mbeki sacked him as deputy president in 2005, Zuma said that he had withstood a high-level conspiracy to cut him down to size. He thought that everything that had happened, and nearly every criticism aimed at him, fit somehow into this grand narrative.

It was clear from the way Zuma told the story that he felt caught in a kind of half-baked triumph. He spoke of this history with the kind of bitterness that he normally attempted to hide. After the election of 2004, he said that he had wondered, once again, if Mbeki intended to dump him. "I knew that some people had been hatching plans to get rid of me," he recalled. "There was a plan hatched as early as 1990 that there must be character assassination against me."

I pressed him to tell me who had been behind these plots, and why the conspirators had targeted him. "For reasons known to me—by some forces for certain interests," he said, mumbling. "I knew that wherever I walked there were people lying in the bushes—there were snipers."

How odd it felt to be eating lunch and taking tea on the veranda of Cecil Rhodes's mansion with the most powerful person in the country, and to hear him lost in the weeds concerning the supposed conspiracy against him. The seeds of his supposed victimization, as Zuma told it, had been planted at the very moment of liberation.

"As a politician who took the trouble to understand politics, I've always known that people who have been with you in the same trenches will turn against you," he said. "There is nothing strange, nothing *surprising* . . ." He nodded, as a sign of recognition over the skirmishes we had had for years over my repeated suggestion that he might, like other people, occasionally be surprised by something.

"There's a song I composed during the time of the trials," Zuma volunteered. "It says, 'I am full of scars, which have been caused by the people I grew up with.' It's a Zulu song. Zulus understand it very well. . . . It's now part of my praise songs when I do the war dance in my village. It tells the story that people I grew up with, people I trusted, were the ones who [inflicted] these scars."

In the moment, you wouldn't have known that Zuma had prevailed in the battle against all these dark forces. Like with Mbeki, you couldn't be sure that the new president fully understood the nature of his own triumph or appreciated the full scope of his power. He was trapped by the difficulties of his past. By the tenor of his voice, you might have imagined that he was still engaged in the same longtime battle against supposed conspirators who he thought remained in the bushes, still laying in wait for him.

In my final weeks in the country, I made the rounds of friends and sources, intending to generate a clearer picture of what might happen next. At Luthuli House, I had a scrappy exchange with Gwede Mantashe, the secretary-general of the party, over the rightful expectations of the young. When I began one of our interviews by mentioning the plight of young people, like Gwendoline Dube in Orange Farm and Wonderboy Mathenjwa in Empangeni, who had been forced to drop out of universities in recent years because of tuition fees—Mantashe banged on the table between us as though I had insulted him.

"That university is not even a college in the true sense of the word," he said,[4] referring to the only university north of the Tugela, University of Zululand, where Wonderboy had studied. The ANC leader leaned forward to pursue his point. He demanded to know where in the world students could attend college tuition-free. "Not even in the United States does that happen!" he said.

It startled me to hear a left-wing leader of the ANC (he was also chairperson of the Communist Party) use my country as the standard for a policy in South Africa. Given the legacy of Bantu Education, and the difficulties the new government had faced in reforming the new, integrated educational system, I pushed back then, asking why it was acceptable for bright, motivated, committed students from poor families to be denied a college education for lack of funds. Wasn't overcoming this obstacle an essential part of the program to transform the country?

Mantashe launched into an explanation of the government's commitment to make all of the country's secondary schools "no fee" institutions, and to improve the quality of instruction. Now, 98 percent of young people between seven and fifteen years old were in school, he asserted. "But students come of the system ill prepared for work," he said, dolefully. "That's our biggest challenge."

When I asked about ongoing divisions in the Alliance—the ANC, the trade union federation, and the Communists—the ANC leader grumbled that "doomsayers always understate successes." He credited the current leadership, which included Zuma and himself, with having taken "an organization that was very divided" and successfully "moving it through that storm."

In the next breath he acknowledged that he was quite worried about the resurgence of turmoil within the ranks of the Youth League and clashes between the party and COSATU, the trade union confederation. "The Youth League is going through a silly season," he said. "There are young people with lots of energy just doing so many silly things!"

Given the scope and scale of problems for young South Africans, Mantashe seemed especially agitated about the grandstanding of Julius Malema, who was living a notoriously bling-bling life and throwing fancy parties while denouncing various elders for being insufficiently revolutionary. In particular, Malema had repeatedly denounced the Communists, including Mantashe, suggesting that he had a conflict of interest in holding top posts in both organizations.

The ANC chief also fretted aloud about recent public statements of trade union leader Zwelinzima Vavi. Vavi had recently warned, in the kind of language he had used in the Mbeki years, about the ongoing danger in South Africa of a slide into dictatorship. He had called publicly for the resignation of Siphiwe Nyanda, minister of communication, on grounds of corruption.

Mantashe said this kind of statement was "alien" to the culture of the ANC since he thought these sorts of differences should be raised privately, inside and between the organizations. "Trade unionism is not a political party," he went on. "It is not a social movement. It is focused on immediate gains and losses. . . . I have a problem with trade unionism that is destructive."

The ANC's secretary-general had begun our conversation by criticizing doomsayers, but he swiftly revealed, in the following ten minutes, just how seriously relationships were ruptured, including between those who had once been so fixedly aligned behind Zuma.

Earlier in the week, I had stopped by to see Joel Netshitenzhe, once a chief Mbeki lieutenant working in Union Buildings but now out of government for the first time in sixteen years. He was one of the few to survive in top-level positions through both the Mandela and Mbeki presidencies. I found his new office in the long stretch between Johannesburg and Pretoria, where a building boom in commercial and residential real estate continued.

The former Mbeki aide had established a think tank so he could continue his favorite activity—analysis of change in the country's political economy. Unlike many of his friends and comrades, he hadn't left the ANC in the wake of Mbeki's resignation. At the party conference in Polokwane, Netshitenzhe had lost his bid to become secretary-general of the party to Gwede Mantashe, but he had been reelected to the National Executive Committee, a key leadership forum.

"I was elected and felt I could not betray that trust," he explained, when I asked if he had considered bolting to COPE. He believed that the clash between forces at the national conference had been more a matter of personal differences than a disagreement over politics. "There were no ideological differences between the factions in Polokwane," he maintained.[5]

Netshitenzhe summoned up Namibian guerrilla leader Sam Nujoma's oft-quoted maxim—"You ride on the back of a crocodile if that's what it takes to get across the river"—in explaining why Zuma allies had turned against one another now. He argued that the Left, in supporting the crocodile called Zuma, hadn't advanced its progressive agenda in any meaningful way.

Trade union leaders and social democrats now found themselves in league with other Zuma supporters who thought "there is nothing wrong with siphoning off resources from the state through tenders," Netshiten-zhe maintained. It shocked him to find that young leaders should have become so thoroughly infected with these corrupt attitudes. "In the coalition that brought Zuma to power are people who are not progressive and are anti–working class," he went on.

As for the idea that the new leader had ushered in new openness within party structures—a position that Zuma aides kept pressing on me—he also demurred. The National Executive Committee meetings he had attended were still quite dysfunctional in several ways. "You go to a meeting now, and things are brewing all over the country," he said. "And we will meet for three days and nobody says anything about the elephant in the room—the state of the Youth League, for example."

He hinted that longtime party leaders, among them those who had supported Mbeki as well as Zuma, were biding their time and looking for a propitious moment for intervention. "The question in the year ahead was whether the ANC had the capacity for self-correction," the former Mbeki aide continued. "Is the capacity for self-correction inherent, or could more of it be encouraged? Who would do this work if more people were to leave?"

The first time I had spoken to him, six years earlier, during the national election of 2004, Netshitenzhe told me that the central challenge of the ANC government was "to get people to admit that the cart is 60 percent full rather than 40 percent empty." On a deeper level, though, he believed that restraint exercised by the governing party back then, undertaken "in the interest of reconciliation and stability," had ended up only diluting the drive for social redress and economic justice. "There are many radical things this government could have done," he pointed out.

Radical ends, what's more, could have been pursued through purely democratic means. He mentioned the idea of placing a public royalty on mineral extraction, for example. "[The ANC] could have raised with its constituency the possibility of nationalizing land or taxing whites at a higher level because of past privileges based on race. If questions like that had been put to a referendum, they would have passed overwhelmingly," he went on.

It was the restraint exercised by the Mbeki government, of which he had been an integral part, that had led to an unforeseen imbalance, in his view. "Whilst the leadership of the black community had restrained its constituency, to say, 'You can't get everything you want because of national needs,'" privileged whites had not gotten mobilized to express an equivalent commitment to a more equal society. Social redress and economic justice would require more of a sacrifice of their own narrow interests. Would whites be willing to sacrifice more in the national interest?

"On the basis of the election campaign, you would be inclined to say no," Netshitenzhe told me at the time, reflecting on the fact that whites overwhelmingly voted for the Democratic Alliance. Six years later, these stubborn patterns of political division and economic inequality remained daunting barriers to creation of the kind of society the ANC had promised. He thought that the populist, race-based appeals for redistribution of wealth, issued by the likes of Youth League leader Julius Malema, were the consequence of this imbalance.

One late night in winter on the outskirts of Pietermaritzburg, the capital of KwaZulu-Natal province, I also spent an evening with Zweli Mkhize, the premier who had been elected in the Zuma sweep of 2009. He was among the younger generation of ANC leaders and sometimes was punted as a possible future president. We met in the nature reserve where he lived, and talked beneath a brilliant night sky. I had just made a final circuit, from Durban to Nkandla to Empangeni and back again, and he was curious about whether the changes he had been working hard to make were visible on the ground yet.

The premier felt quite proud of what the provincial and national governments had accomplished in the first year of the new term. He was a medical doctor and had long chafed under former president Mbeki's

AIDS policies while serving as provincial minister of health. When Mkhize had taken office as premier the year before, he said, there were impossible queues for patients already quite sick from AIDS. The wait in those lines had been cut, the delivery of health care and social services had improved, and when President Zuma announced that treatment would be available once a patient's CD4 count fell to 350, not the old target of 200, "there was ululation all over this territory," he said.[6]

Premier Mkhize, like many others in the new government, was fixed intently on the complicated challenge of fulfilling campaign promises, even in the midst of an ongoing economic recession. In the wake of the World Cup, he said, "we are at the pinnacle of our national mood—in quite a state." He believed that his role, and the role of other leaders, was to channel this extraordinary enthusiasm in constructive directions.

After the internal party clash at Polokwane, a measure of reassurance was necessary, he believed. On balance, he thought Zuma had managed things brilliantly. "It was important for the ANC to restore faith in its ability to manage crises, to get over disappointment, and to absorb the shocks," he said. "Now the role of leadership is to move people out of that trauma." This is how he summed up the challenge: "We need to create a sense of revolution" in distinctly nonrevolutionary times.

Here, of course, was the rub: the global constraints, and the local lack of vision, had already sunk so many plans that had been announced in the Mbeki years. There were countless ambitions expressed on paper only. What if the previous decade of budget surpluses, and of 3 to 4 percent annual growth rates, was over? Even at those previous rates of growth, the gap between rich and poor had grown wider. The premier wanted to sweep away the legacy of apartheid and inspire a new revolutionary spirit among the young, all without tipping the country into civil conflict of the sort that had been skirted by the grand accommodation of 1994.

Twenty years earlier Nelson Mandela was released from prison, and he called on his countrymen to "seize this moment so that the process towards democracy is rapid and uninterrupted." Mkhize figured that the South African people, particularly the young, wouldn't wait forever for the kind of social and economic justice required in a true democracy. "It would be a fitting celebration, twenty years after Madiba's release, for us to take our next important steps," he insisted.

On the presidential jet, President Zuma and I watched Devil's Peak flit past. Table Mountain and Lion's Head vanished, too. The peninsula at the southernmost tip of the continent receded along with mile after mile of settled townships and the ramshackle informal settlements. From higher up, it all looked tranquil, peaceful, and innocent of the need for any remedy. As it happened, we were retracing, from the air, the same trip I had taken to the Klein Karoo six years earlier. Out the window was the Cape of Good Hope, where a historian had located "two great formative frontiers of the modern world; the physical one of the oceanic barrier to the east, and its concomitant one of the mind, global consciousness."[7]

In the years I had been coming to South Africa, it seemed to me that I had been watching the maturation of this border-crossing global consciousness. South Africa offered an addendum, in the dawning realization that political freedom, social justice, and economic liberty remained so firmly intertwined. None of them were separable any longer, if they ever had been. In the rapidly changing, ever-more globalized world, none of us would keep freedom long if the vast majority of people on the planet were denied their dignity.

In the past two decades a new experiment in social democracy had taken root in South Africa, and its survival exposed a third frontier—where there was a collision under way between the leveling impulse at the heart of global consciousness and the widening inequality driven by global capitalism. The experiment in nonracialism, antisexism, and egalitarian principles in one country, placed at the tip of the continent, would only succeed through extraordinary leadership and mass engagement from the bottom up, though. Survival of this historic experiment would require changes in the international economy as well.

As it turned out, this was the issue on President Zuma's mind as we flew out of Cape Town toward Durban. We were sitting across from one another, with a small table between us. Zuma seemed a bit on edge after the discussion we had had back in the presidential residence. He warmed to the new topic, though, saying that by establishing the National Planning Commission, and then placing a broad range of South Africans on it, his government had moved South Africa in the right direction. "We are developing an overarching plan for the country," he said.[8]

In community meetings around the country, and in the commission's own deliberations, the president discerned the possibility of constructive mass engagement. "We removed this culture of guiding things, as if it's only *us* who can do things," he said. I thought of the woman who had held up the sign calling him Black Jesus. His message to other top officials in the meantime was, "Don't fear. Be confident that people can make a contribution." His government had fallen out of touch with ordinary people, he admitted. Even though his predecessor had developed the notion of a commission of this sort, he took credit for making the whole operation more dynamic and relevant to the masses.

I asked Zuma how many of the goals identified so far by the commission could be achieved within the constraints imposed by global finance capital. "There's no country that can change the world on its own," the president acknowledged. That's why, he said, he had put so much emphasis on an expansion of trade with the rest of Africa and in "south-south trade" involving Russia, India, Brazil, and China.

"Europe is very worried about China in Africa," he acknowledged. "[But] it's *time* for China to come to Africa, because it's a huge developing country. You can't stop it." In intensive advocacy for emerging economies like South Africa's, at the World Economic Forum and at G8 and G20 meetings, Zuma had become increasingly convinced that European powers would play a diminished role on the continent. He alternately called them *old*, and *small* countries, and then noted that they were *shrinking*.

The global financial crisis, Zuma argued, had originated in the United States and Europe. In a sense, the world system had been saved by the buffering effect of developing countries. The response of emerging economies had saved the day. "We were the ones who'd stopped [the collapsing world system] halfway," he said. In Zuma's view, the Americans and Europeans were headed into a period when declining economic power would be followed by more limited political influence everywhere.

Everything from the operation of the UN to the rules of the World Bank and International Monetary Fund would be affected as a result. "You can't have people who are becoming *smaller* in terms of the economy having the last word on what must happen," he added, looking cheerful about this prospect. He knew that it would take fresh thinking to figure out the angles, and find all the possible openings in this new dispensation, for a medium-sized country like South Africa.

The president recalled a conversation he had once had with Mikhail Gorbachev at an event in Italy, when he had complimented the Russian leader for having put a stop to the Cold War. Zuma remembered asking Gorbachev, "What do you think we need now?" Gorbachev had told him that this was the question of the age—how to devise what he called "something in the middle" between capitalism and socialism.

"That is why I think South Africa is regarded by many in the world as a model to move towards," Zuma went on. Now, the South African leader felt a rising tide of pressure on his administration to "establish a real developmental state" in order to chart the proper path between two antiquated systems.

Within the movement, there was a debate, generations old now, about the nature of the so-called National Democratic Revolution. Was it an end in itself or rather a way station on the road to socialism? Zuma reminded me that the ANC remained a broad church, and included many Communists who took the latter view and businessmen who held to the former position. "That debate will always be there because that's the reality of class interests, national interests—*whatever*," the president remarked. He pointed out, however, that there were no contemporary socialist revolutions under way anywhere in the world. "The whole [socialist] system collapsed."

While we were discussing global matters, Zuma leaned into the conversation enthusiastically. When there was a pause, I shifted topics, asking him about turmoil within the movement. Youth League leaders had recently announced their "One Boy/One Girl" campaign, an unsubtle dig at his private life. The president had rebuked Julius Malema directly for having complained that he was "worse than Mbeki" in bottling up dissent.

Back at the presidential mansion in Cape Town, he had uncharacteristically gotten worked up, too, when I mentioned that several of his longtime comrades were upset with him for the most recent series of scandals in his personal life. These scandals undercut his effectiveness as a party and national leader. I asked if it was true that he had promised his comrades never to embarrass himself and the party again, as he had done during the rape trial in 2006. Zuma colored visibly and set his chin. He insisted that he had fulfilled his pledge; he had never again been accused of rape. "Is it not so?" he insisted. The stories that filled the tabloids since then were salacious renditions of the latest happenings in his romantic life, and he considered them gross and malicious invasions of privacy to which he was entitled.

These kinds of controversies were caused by "lack of political depth, and lack of understanding about how to handle things inside the organization—that's all," Zuma began. ". . . We are dealing with the matter of the youth. The ANC will certainly handle it." He spoke as if he had everything bottled up, completely under his control, but his voice betrayed him. At this point, he got so worked up that he swept his hand sideways, overturning his glass of water. The glass skidded across the table and water soaked my manuscript. One of his aides gathered up the pages and went off to iron them back into shape.

Sixty minutes into our flight, Zuma got equally agitated when I broached the subject of media freedoms. In more than four years of meeting with him, I had gotten used to evasions and challenges to the questions I raised. Before, though, he had presented disagreements in an even-keeled tone of voice, behaving as the endlessly *chill* person his daughter had described to me. When we started talking about media freedoms, though, there was an immediate chill.

We began by discussing the coverage of his latest romantic affair, and the resulting child. He chalked everything, even the publication of this story, up to "the continuous character assassination" he had stood up against for twenty years. Zuma felt unfairly treated by both the courts and the media. I figured this made him an unlikely candidate, as leader, to restrain the widespread anti-judiciary, and anti-media, tenor within the ANC.

There was a piece of legislation proposed by the governing party called the Protection of State Information Bill, which in itself was an Orwellian name for a draft law that included radical restrictions on investigative reporters. By the end of 2011, it would be rammed through the National Assembly and become an international public relations disaster for the ANC and South African government.

"Punitive new measures will make investigative reporting more difficult," I pointed out, pressing Zuma to explain why the ANC had moved forward on the legislation. The president considered me skeptically. I mentioned the proposed penalty of twenty years' imprisonment for revealing classified information or anything the government said was related to national security.

"Yes," Zuma said, suddenly roused to anger. "Why should people do so? I mean, state secrets are state secrets everywhere! What has happened in the United States? You don't do it? You can't undermine your country. You can't have a democracy that begins to be a danger to itself!"

The president cited, in particular, the damage to the American government from release of massive numbers of classified documents through

WikiLeaks. In the very next sentence he uttered, Zuma unintentionally confirmed my worry that his anti-media feelings were wrapped up in a rather impenetrable ball that included both political positions and personal pique. "A number of years ago, I was talking to editors," he went on. "[And I told them,] 'You are causing a problem for yourselves because you do not draw the line at personal, private things.' Instead of discussing matters of the country, they begin to talk about your personal life."

The president was clearly getting worked up. His press spokesman, who had been dozing for a while across the aisle from us, was fully awake now. He craned his neck so he could hear. It felt odd, and a little arrogant, to press on.

My relationship with Zuma until then had been as the respectful person who asked critical questions but didn't directly disagree with him. He was now the elected president in a democratic country, and I was quite aware that I hadn't been elected to anything. What's more, I felt conscious of my status as an outsider. Still, it would have felt profoundly dishonest, and a little cowardly, to say nothing more.

"Can I just engage you on this point?" I asked. President Zuma relaxed, and sat back in his seat, turning his palms up. "No problem," he said. So, I began by acknowledging that some of the reporting on private lives, in South Africa, as in the United States, troubled me deeply. I agreed that the tabloids often scummed up public life. I granted him this. But, then, I added that I had come of age in the era of the Pentagon Papers case—when highly classified documents had been published in spite of efforts by the U.S. government to block publication.

That massive leak had educated the American people about the underlying causes of the Vietnam War, I argued. This was the part of my history that informed my concern about the proposed restrictions on media in South Africa. It was dangerous, and undemocratic, to constrain journalism overall just because it sickened you to see the behavior of the tabloids.

"The only reason people didn't go to prison in the Pentagon Papers

case was because there's a provision in our law that allowed the newspapers to argue that the public interest in publication was greater than the
government's interest in withholding the information," I went on. "But
you don't have that kind of provision in the law you've proposed."

President Zuma nodded. "No, but I differentiate state secrets from
wrong secrets, like Americans going to kill Vietnamese," he said, leaning
toward me, looking for common ground. "That you can't treat as a state
secret. That must be leaked! If South Africa was involved in schemes to
undermine countries, attack people, leak that. *Siyabonga, Baba.* . . . You
can't exercise your authority by doing wrong things and hide [by saying]
it is a state secret. On that one, I totally agree."

For a moment, I thought we could bridge the divide that had opened
between us. The problem was the tendency of governments to classify information, and then reflexively strike at those whose job it was to inform the
public, I said. "But, what this country has just gone through, where you
yourself feel that people were using state intelligence agencies, police agencies, and even the judiciary in pursuit of a political agenda—that's where
the difficulty lies," I added. "Who is going to be allowed to decide whether
the information is in the public interest?" The president considered me
through unblinking eyes. "If there isn't a public-interest exception," I went
on, "that's where the balance shifts too far in the government's direction."

Now the president looked worn out. He had ceded ground already,
agreeing with me in a limited way, and yet here I insisted on stubbornly
pressing my points. "That's what I'm *saying*," he repeated. "If you take the
situation of Zuma/Mbeki, clearly there was an agenda. Leak that! Because
there is one person being persecuted."

Suddenly, it seemed to me, the terms of our disagreement had shifted,
from a discussion of means to one of ends. "If you find there is corruption
in tenders, leak it! It can't be a state secret if it *endangers* the state. To
me—that is the moral. When you leak a story, if I read it I should know
that it [the ill that is being exposed] is important and it is endangering
either the citizens or the nation," the president continued.

Here was the essential rub in the president's understanding of the way the media worked. Reporting was a messy, time-consuming, and often confounding process. The relevant question was who would decide if an exposé was important enough to warrant protection from retaliation by the state. The standard he had just articulated, if it prevailed, would have the effect of chilling freedom of speech and the press.

The plane bounced on the tarmac and taxied a short distance. From my point of view, Zuma had just sealed the argument. In essence, he was saying *he* would remain the judge of what were state secrets to protect and what were "wrong secrets." It certainly would not be left in the hands of judges to come to an independent assessment of the public interest. Here was where his own history blinded him to the essential values of the importance of an independent media, and an autonomous judiciary, in a modernizing democratic society.

After the plane taxied, I gathered my things, preparing to follow the president out of the plane. "We are *done*, n'eh," he said, not asking, raising both hands as if to push me away. "Done?" I asked, remembering his promise to work through the flight, and on into the evening, and all through the night if necessary, in order to answer any questions. The president had made it sound like a fine slumber party among friends.

Now, his press spokesman stepped in: "You are *done*." I thought of dozens of questions I would have asked earlier if I had known this would be the end of our time together. It struck me how much offense Zuma must have taken to my insistent defense of media rights after he had spent so much effort educating me about the wrongs the nation's media had done to *him*.

Zuma was normally a polite person who worked hard to keep his anger veiled. The veil had just slipped. He leaned toward me, saying coldly, "You got more time than you originally asked for, is that not so?" The president turned, without waiting for an answer and with no farewell, exiting the plane and hustling across the tarmac to his motorcade.

It startled me to have been so swiftly shifted to the discard pile, but our argument had at least allowed me a glimpse of his distress, surprise, and emotional upset—reactions he normally suppressed in order to keep the upper hand—had clouded his judgment.

It was nighttime, and it turned out that the hotels of the city were full because there was a big convention taking place in Durban. On the tarmac, I cooled my heels, thinking of whom I could call to take me in. During the six years I had spent chronicling Thabo Mbeki's fall from grace and Jacob Zuma's eventual rise to power, journalists had tended, too often, to present them as stick figures. Describing Mbeki as a brainy enigma and portraying his successor as a rather blunt force actually obscured the ways in which both of them were true expressions of the ANC's character. The progression from Mandela to Mbeki to Zuma was no mystifying devolution; instead, it was the logical outcome of the party's history.

By 2012, eighteen years after its leaders were vaulted into power in the first place, the African National Congress was no longer in transition. Transformation was still the buzz phrase, but the country's political transformation through its transition to democracy was finished. You could tell plenty about the party's deep-seated values from watching the leaders who had emerged from its ranks. President Zuma had managed a remarkable feat, pulling off one of the most amazing political comebacks in world history. He had done his level best in the past three years to knit his party back together, but in this he had largely failed. His ambition now was to be seen as the heroic figure who managed to ease the country into its post-Mandela, post-Mbeki, and even post-Zuma reality.

The president's main complaint about Thabo Mbeki had been that the former leader was ungrounded and spent too much of his time "up in the air." At the moment, Zuma was headed for King's House, the third magnificent presidential residence of the day. The mansion had a spectacular view of the harbor and a distinct feeling of *otherness*—of being in the world but not of it. When I last visited Nkandla, in the middle of 2010, MaKhumalo, his senior wife, told me that her husband seldom made it home to Nkandla anymore, having set aside the "land of cobras and honey" for more rarefied surroundings.

As his motorcade set off, the lights were coming up all over Durban and the vast harbor remained an inky void. It occurred to me that Zuma, the astonishingly resilient recent occupant of the presidency, was no proto-dictatorial figure, as opposition critics repeatedly warned. In the years since his election as leader he had managed several times, by firing close associates accused of malfeasance or corruption, to show that he was capable of shedding bits of his own history. Yet, on at least three essential counts—gender equality, media freedoms, and judicial independence—it was quite clear that the president could never be the nation's reliable guide.

Thabo Mbeki once had complained of his persistent sense of *disconnect* between himself, his land, and his people. Jacob Zuma had lofted himself into leadership by promising to *reconnect* South Africans with one another—from rural to urban, from poor to rich, from white to coloured to black, from local to global, from *amaqaba* to *amagqoboka*. This would remain the most urgent task in the years to come for whoever succeeded Zuma.

It would take someone from the next generation to see things from a fresh angle and in a different light. The time-honored chant in movement circles had always been *Mayibuye iAfrica*—Come back, Africa. All over the continent, people were searching for ways to light up the world by bending the trajectory of the human story toward economic, political, and social justice. *Ubuntu*, the profound recognition of individual and collective dignity, lay at the heart of the South African experiment. The ideal of a nonracial, nonsexist, egalitarian society at the southern tip of Africa lived on. Young South Africans would determine if that big idea, and everything it implied, would vanish, or yet prevail.

Coda

Freedom Day

On Youth Day, June 16, a national holiday in South Africa, there were rallies all around the country every year to commemorate the mass rebellion in 1976 known as the Soweto Uprising. On the thirtieth anniversary of the bloody clashes between students and soldiers that marked the beginning of the end for apartheid, I drove out to the township for consecration of a new memorial park to the heroes lost on that day. The official commemoration, involving top government officials, was moving enough, but what stuck in my mind even more vividly, even many years later, was a smaller event I stumbled across on my way out to Soweto.

An experimental dance performance, by the brilliant Soweto-born choreographer Gregory Maqoma, was being staged at the Apartheid Museum. The museum was located across from an amusement park on the way down the M1, south of Johannesburg. On one side of the road, there was a brilliantly conceived collection of exhibits detailing horrifying periods in the country's history, while across the way lay a carousel, blinking lights, arcade games, carnival shows, and a variety of rides. You could guess which parking lot was full on any given day, and which stood half empty.

At the entrance to the museum, visitors were handed tickets, as always, identifying them randomly by category—*Nie-Blanke* or *Blanke*. I was handed the card for *Nie-Blanke* this time, my identity set by random chance as a black person. It seemed like a corny gimmick at first blush, but it was actually eerily effective. Visitors parted in the entryway, cleaved into two separate groups. Whose identity—based on class, color, religion, language, or culture—wasn't an apparently random matter, in the end? Why then, such definitive, and often deadly, consequences?

The stream of people ahead of me entered through separate doorways for blacks and whites. We meandered up a wide walkway. At the top of the rise there was a 360-degree view through the haze, to Johannesburg proper on the north and informal settlements and the townships to the south. Along a low concrete wall a trio of musicians dressed in mourning black were already playing soothing strains of Bach on cello, violin, and bass. Directly in front of them, a line of young women and men, dressed in white dress shirts and black pants, swayed to the lilting rhythms.

Then, there was a sudden shift to the *toyi-toyi*, a hard-stamping, drumbeat dance of the revolution. It was a stiff-legged martial dance that evoked memory of decades of mass protests in the streets. In the new South Africa, *toyi-toyi* looked like a dated gesture, but the Bach felt a little out of place on a day for celebrating rebellion, too. Here was the many-sided nature of the post-trauma culture Maqoma was engaged in curating—what he called "artistic freedom that fuses mind, hearts, intellect, Armani suits, ball gowns and naked bodies."[1]

The young dancers replicated the motions with precision, as they had been taught in his studio; they were too young to have learned *toyi-toyi* in the streets. The uprising that the dancers were commemorating took place more than ten years before they were born. Key political figures regularly told me that young South Africans were ignorant of the recent past and needed to learn the lessons of history. But it wasn't entirely clear to me, on this day, what these youngsters really needed to know of long-ago events. What, in the end, were they supposed to make of them?

Thuthu Zuma, the daughter of two liberation heroes, had done her best to educate me about the gap that had sprung up, politically and culturally, between her parents' generation and her own. "They never told us much about it," she had told me. Perhaps that was partly because the elders also wondered, in their quieter moments, how relevant the history would be in helping shape the country's future.

The Soweto Uprising, like the residual heartache of prison, exile, and life underground, set the backdrop for this reconfigured country, but how should it inflect the contemporary struggle by young people to embrace their liberation and turn the end of an old system of oppression, somehow, into real freedom? The job of the next generation wasn't to kowtow to yesterday's victories, but to invent something seemingly new.

Inside the museum, the dancers and their choreographer swept past exhibits about colonial and apartheid history. Maqoma's troupe fused and fractured, all the while pushing ahead through one historical period to the next. The scene reminded me of that song I had heard, during my first week in Cape Town, from Johnny Clegg. "*Baleka Uzohaqwa!*" (Escape before you are injured!), he had crooned—beginning in Zulu, lapsing into English and coming back to Zulu again. "Same old human story / The saddest winds do blow / While we are trapped in the language of dark history," the song warned.

This museum underscored the lesson. It was an archive of the country's legacy of hatred butted alongside a powerful record of resistance and partial redemption. In front of an iconic photograph of a woman holding her starving children, the dancers' arms shot up in rapid sequence as if to embrace her. They also moved past images of the original Voortrekkers and indigenous San, then beneath thick-rope nooses and the etched names of freedom fighters who had been hanged during apartheid, and along a wall of photos showing the conditions for migrant gold miners.

The dancers paused in front of a video showing former prime minister Botha announcing in clipped defiance, "There is not one man/one vote in all of Africa!" Never would there be majority rule in South Africa,

Botha had protested. The former prime minister repeated himself, and the dancers left him behind, barking nonsense.

In a room dedicated to capturing the chaotic feel of the years of insurrection, they curved around the hulk of an old armored personnel carrier of the kind once used to occupy the townships. The tanks were installed opposite images of mass protest and brutal suppression. There was no sugarcoating: scenes of triumphant rallies, as the movement strengthened, led to footage of horrific violence, as contending supporters of the ANC and the Inkatha Freedom Party hacked one another to death. These murders were still undigested parts of South African political culture, partly because they had never fit neatly into the main narrative of the successful, and supposedly peaceful, overthrow of apartheid.

The dancers alternately pulled close to the images and pushed them away, seeming to protect themselves from the force of the violent imagery by sliding along the walls with their backs turned, and then moving sinuously on to the next space. In their own way, the musicians and dancers of this piece, called *Rhythm Colour*, were acting out one of the enduring puzzles of the human story. This was the mystery that had fired my imagination ever since my first visit to South Africa in 2004: how some people managed to escape from history's grasp and why so many others remained so deadeningly swamped by the past.

The choreographer hadn't suggested that you could escape through denial or ignorance. Maqoma himself was a child of Soweto, after all. His series of performances often touched on the effects of violence, including the kind of death-by-drowning torture used by apartheid-era agents of the regime. Maqoma's dances juxtaposed fluidity and the sudden shock borne by bigotry—communicated, in this performance, with a slap, a push, a blow, and then the dehumanizing spectacle of a canvas sack placed over someone's head. In an earlier performance I had seen by him, he had danced a critique of the national obsession with the black body. In the theater version of *Rhythm Colour*, a disembodied voice proclaimed, "I am that body."

At an anteroom close to the entrance of the museum, those of us in the audience circled back to watch as each of the dancers fell, one by one. When they were all laid out, seemingly finished off, it was an eerie homage to the protesters at Sharpeville in 1960 and Soweto in 1976, where so many protestors had been slain, having been shot in the back. Each dancer fell; but each eventually was also resurrected. "I do not see the end," a voice intoned. "But I see the light." The message, implicit in the dance, was that nobody would find freedom without standing up to fight for it.

One by one the young people revived, stood, and leaned down to offer a hand to the next one. Half of South Africa's population was so young—nearly 40 percent were eighteen and under—and Maqoma was making an artful case that it was creative improvisation by them that would shape the country's future. In the years that followed, whenever I thought of the young people who had allowed me so deeply into their lives, I would be reminded of these dancers as they moved through the artifacts of apartheid on Youth Day.

At the end of the performance, the young dancers raised their hands in clenched fists, then opened them as if prepared to catch whatever would come their way. They swiftly changed out of their dress clothes into jeans and jerseys, and shifted from performance visage—intense, anguished, searching—into the more varied, hang-loose rhythms of real life. They looked smaller when they stopped moving, right-sized now and no longer the objects of attention who were expected to deliver a cogent message for the rest of us.

They were young, and stunning-looking, and eager, and restless. Turning their backs on the exhibits, skirting the questions being directed their way, they walked across the long brick path to the entrance of the museum, laughing and poking one another, and headed off in a rush toward home.

Acknowledgments

In reporting and writing *After Mandela*, I owe a lifelong debt to two beloved mentors: John H. Schaar, the late political theorist who taught me how to think about authority, community, political participation, and democracy; and Roger Wilkins, the wise scholar and loyal friend who showed me, over the years, so many ingenious ways of crossing lines of race, ethnicity, culture, and language in the search for deeper understanding across those lines.

For steady support on this project, from start to finish, I am indebted as well to two masters of the craft, Adam Hochschild and Alex Kotlowitz. For his kindness, friendship, and wisdom, Edwin Cameron, a justice of the Constitutional Court of South Africa, deserves special mention. Though not quoted in these pages, he offered acute criticism and valued counsel throughout.

In the end, it was the experience of young South Africans, from cities and villages alike, who most influenced the overall shape of the narrative. Groups of teenagers in Cape Town, Johannesburg, Bungeni, and the University of Zululand welcomed me and allowed me to hang out for days on end, even at the most inconvenient times, on repeated visits.

These teens were full of surprises, often upending my assumptions and complicating the work in ways that always made it sharper. They were willing to crack open their own thinking about everything from politics to sex, even when the traumas were recent and the memories were fresh. Polling data, provided by Jos Kuper at future*fact*, helped place the group and individual interviews in broader context.

The responsiveness, warmth, and understanding of six key individuals made my job much easier. In many ways, this is their book. These were the young people who allowed me to keep returning for repeated observation and interrogation during the past five years: Gwendolyn Dube from Orange Farm, Vunene Mabasa of Bungeni, Ndaba Mandela from Johannesburg, Thomas Maree of Cape Town, Jonathan Presens from Atlantis, and Thuthukile Zuma, daughter of the president.

In early 2012, Thuthu Zuma moved to Paris for the year. Her older sister, Gugulethu Zuma, offered me critiques of the government and governing party, at some risk of criticism to herself. Many of President Zuma's other children, like the grandchildren of Nelson Mandela, were quite forthcoming, and they deserve credit, too, for their frankness, which carries a risk given their prominence.

An expression of deep appreciation is also due to my students from Medill School of Journalism at Northwestern University, who shared their enthusiasm and curiosity with me as they undertook internships at South African media outlets from 2004 to the present. Students who worked with me as research assistants include Sarah Collins (the master transcriber), Fui Tsikata, and Tanveer Ali.

Both in Johannesburg and Chicago, I drew on the expertise of translators who checked materials and interviews, including Mbongeni Mtshali and Wonderboy Mthenjwa in isiZulu and Lesedi Ntsane in Sepedi. During the year of reporting in Johannesburg, and through much of the drafting of this manuscript in Chicago, I was also lucky to have the research assistance, and support, of the Zimbabwean exile Chengetayi Chando.

A special shout out of gratitude is owed my stellar colleague and former dean, Loren Ghiglione. He entrusted me with the school's South Africa Teaching Media program, which he invented back in 2003, and without his support this project would never have begun. Associate Dean Mary Nesbitt worked hard to accommodate my travel needs. My faculty mentor in the tenure process, Jack Doppelt, helped me navigate competing obligations in teaching and writing, and without him I might have given up one or the other. Many colleagues at the school sacrificed to cover for my long absences from 2004 to 2007, and I remain especially thankful, in particular, for the friendship and quiet, sustained cheerleading of Charles Whitaker.

During the year I lived in Johannesburg, Anton Harber welcomed me at the University of Witwatersrand Journalism Program, providing the essential props for any journalist—an office, telephone, Internet access, and a supportive environment in which to pursue the work. He and his wife, the talented producer Harriet Gavshon, repeatedly took me and my family in, including during the heady weeks of the 2010 World Cup. Thanks, on this score and so many others too, to Elizabeth Barrett.

For their accessibility, I am especially grateful for the cooperation of many government officials, including President Jacob Zuma, Deputy President Kgalema Motlanthe, Deputy Minister of International Relations Ebrahim Ebrahim, Premier Zweli Mkhize of KwaZulu-Natal province, former head of government communications Joel Netshitenzhe, former presidential spokesman Bheki Khumalo, and former national security operative Mo Shaik.

At the African National Congress, Steyn Speed and Moferere Lekorotsoana helped thread requests for information and interviews with then Secretary General Kgalema Motlanthe and current Secretary General Gwede Mantashe. They made themselves available to explain the logic of party decisions and the terms of its policy debates.

At the trade union federation COSATU, its leader, Zwelinzima Vavi, and spokesman Patrick Craven were always responsive and accessible.

Buti Manamela, leader of the Young Communist League, offered background on the role of his organization in the campaign on behalf of Zuma, and Fikile Mbalula, the former president of the ANC Youth League, offered similar perspective from his vantage point.

Helen Zille, now premier in the Western Cape and leader of the opposition, often made time for me, even when it was difficult to do so, and Robert McDonald, her former press aide, offered extensive background and made the schedules work.

Scholars and writers who contributed in profound ways to my understanding of the country include Antony Altbeker, Adam Ashforth, Edwin Cameron, Jean Comaroff, John Comaroff, Rodney Davenport and Christopher Saunders, Mark Gevisser, William Merwin Gumede, Sean Jacobs, Xolele Mangcu, Achille Mbembe, Liz McGregor, Noel Mostert, Nicoli Nattrass, Njabulo Ndebele, Sarah Nuttall, Jeremy Seekings, Crain Soudien, Allister Sparks, Leonard Thompson, and the astonishing Jonny Steinberg.

In reporting on the HIV/AIDS pandemic, I would have been considerably less sure of my footing without the guidance of many stellar experts, including the staff of Health-e, Dr. Ashraf Coovadia, Kerry Cullinan, Laurie Garrett, Nathan Geffen, Jillian Green, Dr. Ashraf Grimwood, David Harrison, Mark Heywood, Claire Keeton, Tamara Kahn, Dr. Tammy Meyer, Sipho Mthati, Sue Roberts, and Dr. Francois Venter.

Among the most serious debts I owe, of course, are to three generations of South African journalists—those who incurred heavy personal and professional costs for speaking truth to power during the apartheid era; the next set, who kept at it through the tumultuous and invigorating transition to democracy; and the current practitioners, who labor on to make sure that the promise of good journalism pays off for citizens of a much-changed country. As proven by the ongoing bitter fight over the proposed Protection of State Information Bill, the struggle to create space for truly independent media remains contested terrain, and this is a more crucial "site of struggle" than ever.

Journalists who went out of their way to help along the way include, first and foremost, Angela Quintal. For willingness to entertain so many pesky questions from an outsider, I remain grateful to Karima Brown, Stefaans Brummer, Paddi Clay, Patrick Conroy, Kerry Cullinan, Paula Fray, Jillian Green, Ferial Haffajee, Zenzile Khoisan, Fred Khumalo, Mondli Makhanya, Justice Malala, Ranjeni Manusamy, Jimi Matthews, Cyril Mdlala, Zingi Mkefa, Moshoeshoe Monare, S'thembiso Msomi, Wisani wa ka Ngobeni, Judy Nwokedi, Joe Thloloe, Beauregard Tromp, Mathatha Tsedu, Tony Weaver, Chris Whitfield, Moegsien Williams, and Snuki Zikalala.

My literary representative, David Black, took on this project when nobody in his right mind would have counted on its success. I owe him more than a writer ought to admit. He led me to Robert Weil, at Liveright and W. W. Norton, who signed a contract for the book after a single weekend of reading. Assistant editor Philip Marino worked alongside me productively during the long months required for pressing the book into its proper shape.

My family made it possible to complete the journey, particularly Jacob Foster and Sandile Hlatshwayo, who shared every step of this adventure with me. Anne Lamott read every word more times than either one of us can remember.

It should go without saying that this work would be far weaker without the encouragement, collaboration, argumentation, guidance, and criticism only hinted at in the acknowledgments above. The obligatory, but important, disclaimer also applies: I alone bear the burden for any mistakes, omissions, distortions, or missteps visible in these pages.

Notes

OVERTURE: *BALEKA UZOHAQWA!*

1 Interview with the author: Gavin Jacobs, Cape Town, June 1, 2004.
2 Mandela, *In His Own Words*, 62.

CHAPTER 1: THE CHIEF

1 Giliomee and Mbenga, *New History of South Africa*, 40.
2 Mostert, *Frontiers*, 22.
3 Ibid., xv.
4 Thompson, *History of South Africa*, xix.
5 Mostert, *Frontiers*, 77.
6 Mandela, *Long Walk to Freedom*, 9.
7 Mbeki, *Africa, Define Yourself*, 297.
8 Sparks, *Beyond the Miracle*, 256.
9 Gevisser, *Thabo Mbeki*, 662.
10 Waldmeir, *Anatomy of a Miracle*, 261.
11 Gumede, *Thabo Mbeki*, 49–52.
12 Hadland and Rantao, *Life and Times of Thabo Mbeki*, 85.
13 Green, *Choice, Not Fate*, 381.
14 Sparks, *Beyond the Miracle*, 16.
15 David Goodman, "Witness to the Dawn," *MotherJones.com*, June 29, 1999, 1.
16 Thabo Mbeki, "The Full Meaning of Liberation," address at his inauguration, Pretoria, June 16, 1999, seen on the South African government website and also included in Mbeki, *Africa, Define Yourself*, 26.

17 Nelson Mandela, inaugural address, May 10, 1994, available at http://www
.youtube.com/watch?v=grho3Njzc, and in Nelson Mandela, *In His Own
Words,* 68.

18 Gevisser, *Legacy of Liberation,* 265.

19 Mbeki, *Africa, Define Yourself,* 27.

20 Interview with the author: Bheki Khumalo, former press secretary to President Thabo Mbeki, Johannesburg, September 2, 2008.

21 Joel Netshitenzhe, *Towards a Ten Year Review, Synthesis Report on Implementa-
tion of Government Programmes.* Policy Coordination and Advisory Services,
The Presidency, October 2003.

22 Thabo Mbeki, *Castro Hlongwane, Caravans, Cats, Geese, Foot and Mouth and
Statistics: HIV/AIDS and the Struggle for the Humanisation of the African,*
March 2002. Available at: http://www.virusmyth.com/aids/hiv/ancdoc.htm.

23 Feinstein, *After the Party,* 124.

24 Interview with the author: Condoleezza Rice, Stanford, CA (telephone), June
21, 2011.

25 Interview with the author: Joel Netshitenzhe, Pretoria, September 6, 2007.

26 Interview with the author: Bheki Khumalo, Johannesburg, August 1, 2007.

CHAPTER 2: THE THIEF

1 World Bank, *World Development Report 2007,* 4.

2 Interviews with the author: Jonathan Persens, Cape Town, February 26, 2007;
Khayelitsha, July 23, 2007; and Atlantis, December 2, 2007. All quotations
from Persens are from these interviews unless otherwise noted.

3 Duiker, *Thirteen Cents,* 35.

4 Watson, *Brick by Brick,* 13.

5 Bray et al., *Growing Up in the New South Africa,* 1.

6 Altbeker, *Country at War with Itself,* 119.

7 Ibid., 37.

8 Margaret Keenan, "The Proliferation of Firearms in South Africa, 1994–
2004," unpublished, Oxfam Canada, April 30, 2005.

CHAPTER 3: THE RIVAL

1 Interviews with the author: Jacob Zuma, Johannesburg, April 7, May 25, and
August 8, 2007; Nkandla, November 21, 2007; Washington, DC, October
22, 2008; Luthuli House, Johannesburg, March 23, 2009; Cape Town and in
flight to Durban, July 31, 2010. All quotations from Zuma are from these
interviews unless otherwise noted.

2 Interview with the author: Mosiuoa Lekota, Cape Town (telephone), March
16, 2009.

3 Interview with the author: Blade Nzimande, Johannesburg, April 4, 2007.
4 Interview with the author: Zweli Mkhize, Washington, DC, October 23, 2008.

CHAPTER 4: THE CHRONICLERS

1 Interview with the author: Chris Whitfield, Cape Town, March 30, 2004. All quotations from Chris Whitfield are from this interview unless otherwise noted.
2 Tyson, *Editors under Fire*, 26–27.
3 African National Congress, *Submission to the Human Rights Commission*, April 5, 2000. Available at http://www.anc.org.za/show.php?id=2674.
4 Interview with the author: Tony Leon, Cape Town, May 31, 2004.
5 Interview with the author: Joseph Aranes, Cape Town, April 1, 2004.
6 Interview with the author: Murray Williams, Cape Town, June 29, 2004.
7 Interview with the author: Zenzile Khoisan, Cape Town, July 1, 2004.
8 Interview with the author: Moegsien Williams, Johannesburg, May 21, 2004.
9 Ndebele, *Fine Lines from the Box*, 213.
10 Ibid., 217.

CHAPTER 5: THE DOCTOR

1 Interviews with the author: Dr. Ashraf Grimwood, Cape Town, March 26, March 29, April 7, and May 31, 2004. All quotations from Grimwood in this chapter are from these interviews unless indicated otherwise.
2 Sontag, *Illness as Metaphor and AIDS and Its Metaphors*, 114.
3 Ibid., 115.
4 Shilts, *And the Band Played On*, xxii.
5 Ibid., xxiii.
6 Interviews with the author: Counselors at LifeLine, Johannesburg, July 20, 2004.
7 Interview with the author: David Harrison, Johannesburg, May 17, 2004.
8 Interview with the author: Sister Sue Roberts, Johannesburg, July 20, 2004.
9 Interview with the author: Ursula Maynier, Johannesburg, July 20, 2004.

CHAPTER 6: THE CITY

1 Pinchuck et al., *Rough Guide to South Africa, Lesotho and Swaziland*, 581.
2 Ruth Bhengu, "Romance," in Holland and Roberts (eds.), *From Jo'burg to Jozi*, 44.
3 Christopher Hope, "Jo'burg Blues," in Holland and Roberts (eds.), *From Jo'burg to Jozi*, 116.
4 Adam Roberts, "From Jo'burg to Jozi," in Holland and Roberts (eds.), *From Jo'burg to Jozi*, 9, 10.

5 Rian Malan, "Jo'burg Lovesong," in Holland and Roberts (eds.), *From Jo'burg to Jozi*, 155.
6 Achille Mbembe, "Why Am I Here?" in McGregor and Nutall (eds.), *At Risk*, 168.
7 Ibid., 161.
8 Ibid., 170.

CHAPTER 7: THE GRANDSON

1 Interviews with the author: Ndaba Mandela, Mvezo, April 16, 2007, and Johannesburg, April 26, May 21, June 21, and September 8, 2007. All quotations from Ndaba Mandela are from these interviews unless indicated otherwise.
2 Lodge, *Mandela*, 225.
3 Ibid., 203.
4 Mandela, *Long Walk to Freedom*, 548.
5 Ibid., 571.
6 Ibid., 447.
7 O'Malley, *Shades of Difference*, 17.
8 Deborah Posel, "A Matter of Life and Death," in McGregor and Nutall (eds.), *At Risk*, 52.

CHAPTER 8: INSIDE

1 Editorial, "Pressing Needs," *Business Day*, May 3, 2005, 16.
2 Trevor Manuel, Minister of Finance, February 23, 2005. Available at http://www.dfa.gov.za/docs/speeches/2005/manue0225.htm.
3 Evans Maluleke, "Wild Chicken Chase," *Daily Sun*, April 19, 2005, 5.
4 "Hugh Battles Foreign Culture," *Daily Sun*, April 7, 2005, 21.
5 Bonny Schoonakker, "Ugly Feud Erupts over Mandela Money," *Sunday Times*, April 10, 2005, 1.
6 Shaun Smillie and Kevin Ritchie, "Madiba Obsessed with Money, Claims Ayob," *Star*, July 11, 2005, 1.
7 Interview with the author: Moegsien Williams, Johannesburg, April 20, 2005.
8 Liz McGregor, "Who Killed the Rain Queen?" in McGregor and Nuttall (eds.), *At Risk*, 20.
9 Judge Hilary Squires, "The State versus Schabir Shaik and 11 Others," Judgment 31 May 2005. Available at http://www.polity.org.za/article/the-state-versus-schabir-shaik-11-others-judgment-may-2005-2005-06-09.
10 Holden, *Arms Deal in Your Pocket*, 29.
11 e.tv, Live broadcast of the Shaik verdict, June 1, 2005.
12 Jovial Rantao, "Zuma Must Act Honourably," *Star*, June 3, 2005, 16.

13 Vicki Robinson, "Exclusive: Zuma on His Future," *Mail & Guardian*, June 17, 2005, 2.

14 Ray Hartley, "The End of a Friendship," *Sunday Times*, June 19, 2005, 4.

15 Interview with the author: Bheki Khumalo, Johannesburg, July 17, 2007.

16 Gugu Sibaya, "I Will Fight, Zuma Talks Tough as Zulu King Zwelinthini Backs Him," *Sowetan*, June 8, 2005, 1.

17 Xolela Mancgu, "Mbeki's Actions Give Conspiracy Theorists Plenty to Chew On," *Business Day*, June 23, 2005, 12.

18 Interviews with the author: Thuthukile Zuma, Johannesburg, April 26, July 26, July 30, October 28, and November 18, 2007. All quotations from Thuthukile Zuma are from these interviews unless otherwise noted.

19 Thompson, *History of South Africa*, 248, quoting a report from the South Africa Institute of Race Relations.

20 Interview with the author: Thuthukile Zuma, Johannesburg, July 15, 2010.

21 Thabo Mbeki, "Statement of the President of South Africa, Thabo Mbeki, at the Joint Sitting of Parliament on the Release of Hon Jacob Zuma from His Responsibilities as Deputy President," National Assembly, June 14, 2005. Full text available at http://www.sahistory.org.za/dated-event/president-thabo-mbeki-sacks-deputy-president-jacob-zuma.

22 Moshoeshoe Monare and Jeremy Michaels, "The Emasculation of Zuma," *Star*, June 21, 2005, 1.

23 Interview with the author: Zwelinzime Vavi, Johannesburg, July 16, 2010.

24 Vukani Mde, "Scorned 'Populists' Parodied at SA's Own Peril," *Business Day*, July 5, 2005, 9.

25 Political staff, "Sacked Zuma Urges ANC Unity as Youth Rally against Mbeki," *Business Day*, June 17, 2005, 1.

26 Sipho Khumalo, "Zuma's Court Battle Begins," *Star*, June 30, 2005, 3.

27 Marianne Merten, "A Winter of Discontent," *Mail & Guardian*, May 27, 2005, 5.

28 Interview with the author: Jo-Jo Tsheola, Soweto, March 27, 2005.

29 du Preez Bezdrob, *Winnie Mandela*, 220.

30 "Report on the National and Provincial Elections, 2004." Independent Electoral Commission, 2004. Available at http://www.ied.org.za.

CHAPTER 9: OUTSIDE

1 Interviews with the author: Jonathan Persens, Cape Town, February 26, 2007; Khayelitsha, July 23, 2007; and Atlantis, December 2, 2007. All quotations from Persens are from these interviews unless otherwise noted.

2 Sontag, *Regarding the Pain of Others,* 18.

3 Bray et al., *Growing Up in the New South Africa*, 323.

4 Soudien, *Youth Identity in Contemporary South Africa*, 17.

5 Joel Netshitenzhe, Presentation before the National Youth Commission of South Africa, June 7, 2006.

6 Interviews with the author: Gerald Jacobs, Cape Town, January 29 and November 30, 2007.

7 Interview with the author: Ciko Thomas, Johannesburg, November 26, 2007.

8 Interview with the author: Ndaba Mandela, Johannesburg, May 21, 2007.

9 John Hennion, filmmaker, from outtakes of his unfinished documentary about street children in Cape Town. More about his project is available at www.capetownstroller.com.

CHAPTER 10: UPSIDE DOWN

1 Laurie Garrett, "Rage over 'Poison' as AIDS Treatment, South African's Fears Disputed by Others," *Newsday*, July 8, 2002.

2 SAPA, "AIDS Is God's Challenge: Tshabalala-Msimang," March 31, 2003. Available at http://doh.gov.za/show.php?id=528.

3 "Manto Sticks to Her Guns," *Star*, June 30, 2005, 6.

4 Gumede, *Thabo Mbeki*, 149.

5 Interview with the author: Nomawonga Sylvia Mtshizana, Soweto, July 25, 2005.

6 Interview with the author: Tammy Meyers, Soweto, July 25, 2005.

7 Interview with the author: Gwendoline Dube, Soweto, August 2, 2005.

CHAPTER 11: ON THE AIR

1 Interviews with the author: Snuki Zikalala, Johannesburg, June 28 and July 7, 2005. All quotations from Zikalala in this chapter are from these interviews unless otherwise noted.

2 Interview with author: Tony Leon, Cape Town, May 31, 2004.

3 Guy Berger, "What Makes Snuki Tick," *Converse*, April 28, 2004. Available at http://mg.co.za/Content/13.asp?=7157&area=/insight_columnists.

4 McGregor, *Khabzela*, 94.

5 Ibid., ix.

6 Nkosi, *Mandela's Ego*, 158.

7 Interview with the author: Sanza da Fanatik, Johannesburg, June 26, 2006.

8 Interviews with the author: Jimi Matthews, Johannesburg, June 21 and 22, 2005. All quotations from Matthews in this chapter are from these interviews unless otherwise noted.

9 Interview with the author: Dumisani Nkwamba, Oudtshoorn, April 3, 2004.

10 Hopewell Radebe, "SABC Is the New Enemy of Freedom, Vavi Says," *Business Day*, June 29, 2005, 1.

CHAPTER 12: ON THE GROUND

1 Interview with the author: Jacob Zuma, Washington, DC, October 23, 2008.
2 Interview with the author: General Siphiwe Nyanda, Washington, DC, October 23, 2008.
3 Gordin, *Zuma*, 125.

CHAPTER 13: CAPE TOWN

1 Interviews with the author: Helen Zille, Cape Town, June 2, June 20 (telephone), and August 16, 2007. All quotations from Zille are taken from these interviews unless indicated otherwise.
2 Interview with the author: Saki Macozoma, Johannesburg, December 5, 2007.
3 "Tik, Memory Loss, and Stroke," *Science in Africa*, June 2005, 2. Available at http://scienceinafrica.co.za/2005/june/tik.htm.
4 Interview with the author: Ebrahim Rasool, Khayelitsha, July 21, 2007.
5 Book Launch, Presidential Guest House, June 22, 2007.
6 Roberts, *Fit to Govern,* 67.

CHAPTER 14: ATLANTIS

1 Interview with the author: Jonathan Persens, Khayelitsha, July 23, 2007.
2 Interview with the author: Thomas Maree, Cape Town, December 3, 2007.
3 Interview with the author: Jonathan Persens, Atlantis, December 2, 2007.
4 Interview with the author: Susan Persens, Atlantis, December 2, 2007.

CHAPTER 15: JOHANNESBURG

1 Interview with the author: Joel Netshitenzhe, Pretoria, August 6, 2007.
2 Interview with the author: Saki Macozoma, Johannesburg, December 5, 2007.
3 Interview with the author: Jacob Zuma, Johannesburg, May 25, 2007. All quotations in this chapter are from this interview, and another at his home on August 8, 2007, unless indicated otherwise.
4 Interview with the author: Ebrahim Ebrahim, Johannesburg, October 3, 2007.
5 Truth and Reconciliation Commission Final Report, as quoted in Gordin, *Zuma*, 35.

6 Interview with the author: Jacob Zuma, Cape Town, July 30, 2010.

7 Interview with the author: Blade Nzimande, Johannesburg, April 4, 2007.

8 Interview with the author: Thuthukile Zuma, Gugulethu Zuma, Duduzile Zuma, and Nokuthula Zuma, Johannesburg, October 28, 2007.

CHAPTER 16: ORANGE FARM

1 Interview with the author: Ndaba Mandela, Johannesburg, September 8, 2007.

2 Interview with the author: Nathan Geffen, Benoni, March 14, 2007.

3 Brodie, *Joburg Book*, 314.

4 Interview with the author: Teresa Dube, Orange Farm, December 13, 2007.

5 Interview with the author: Gwendoline Dube, Orange Farm, December 13, 2007.

6 Mohammed Seedat et al., "Violence and Injuries in South Africa: Prioritizing an Agenda for Protection," *Lancet*, 374 (9694): 1011–1022, 2009.

7 Interview with the author: Ndaba Mandela, Johannesburg, September 8, 2007.

8 Interviews with the author: Dimpho Ramalosa, Karabo Tserema, Sizwe Dube, and other students, Melpark Elementary School, Johannesburg, November 16, 2007.

CHAPTER 17: NKANDLA

1 Thompson, *History of South Africa*, 83–87.

2 Interview with the author: Jacob Zuma, Nkandla, November 21, 2007.

3 Interview with the author: Jacob Zuma, Luthuli House, Johannesburg, March 23, 2009.

4 Interview with the author: Jacob Zuma, Johannesburg, May 25, 2007.

5 Interview with the author: Sizakele Khumalo, Nkandla, November 22, 2007.

6 Interview with the author: Jacob Zuma, Cape Town, July 30, 2011.

7 Interview with the author: Joseph Zuma, Nkandla, November 21, 2007.

8 Interview with the author: Michael Zuma, Nkandla, November 21, 2007.

9 Marie-Helen Coetzee, "Zulu Stick Fighting: A Socio-Historical Overview," *Inyo: Journal of Alternative Perspectives*, September 2002.

CHAPTER 18: POLOKWANE

1 Interview with the author: Joel Netshitenzhe, Pretoria, September 9, 2007.

2 Interview with the author: Tokyo Sexwale, Polokwane, December 16, 2007.

3 Interview with the author: Jacob Zuma, Washington, DC, October 22, 2008.

4 Interview with the author: Vunene Mabasa, Bungeni, December 21, 2007.

CHAPTER 19: MVEZO

1 Mandela, *Long Walk to Freedom*, 7.

2 Smith, *Young Mandela*, 25–30.

3 Mandela, *Long Walk to Freedom*, 3.

4 Interview with the author: Andile Mandela and Mbuso Mandela, Johannesburg, November 17, 2007.

5 Interviews with the author: Mandla Mandela, Mvezo, December 25 and 26, 2007. All quotations from Mandela are from interviews on these two days unless indicated otherwise.

6 Staff writer, "Mandla Mandela the 'Dictator,'" *Sunday Times,* October 9, 2011. Available at http://www.timeslive.co.za/politics/2011/10/09/mandla-mandela-the-dictator.

7 John Comaroff and Jean Comaroff, "Reflections on Liberalism, Policulturalism and ID-ology," in Robins (ed.), *Limits to Liberation after Apartheid*, 34.

CHAPTER 20: THE GLOBE

1 Interview with the author: Jacob Zuma, Durban, July 30, 2010.

2 Interview with the author: Jacob Zuma, Johannesburg (telephone), September 20, 2008.

3 Interview with the author: Jacob Zuma, Washington, DC, October 22, 2008.

4 Interview with the author: Condoleezza Rice, Stanford, CA (telephone), June 21, 2011.

5 Interview with the author: Andrew Feinstein, Washington, DC (telephone), February 27, 2010.

6 Interview with the author: Richard Young, Cape Town (telephone), February 15, 2010.

7 Interview with the author: Jacob Zuma, Washington, DC, October 22, 2008.

8 Green, *Choice, Not Fate*, 544.

9 ANC Briefing on the Economy, Rivonia, March 29, 2009.

10 Comaroff and Comaroff, "Law and Disorder in the Postcolony," 40.

11 Ibid., 41.

12 Paul Taylor, Rakeesh Kochhar, Richard Fry, et al., *Wealth Gaps Rise to Record Highs between Whites, Blacks, and Hispanics* (Washington, DC: Pew Research Center, July 26, 2011).

13 Interview with the author: Mo Shaik, Pretoria, March 26, 2009.

14 Interview with the author: Zweli Mkhize, Pietermaritzburg, March 30, 2009.

15 Interview with the author: Jacob Zuma, Luthuli House, Johannesburg, March 23, 2009.

CHAPTER 21: THE PRISONER

1 Jin, *Writer as Migrant*, 66.

2 Katharine Hall, *Income and Social Grants—Children Living in Poverty* (Cape Town: Children's Institute, July 2010). Available at http://www.childrencount. ci.org.za.

3 Steinberg, *The Number*, 61–62.

4 Jos Kuper, *Politics and Accountability*, future*fact*, personal communication, February 17, 2010. Data are from surveys on economic issues and political issues conducted annually since 1998 based on a sample ($N = 2,500$) of respondents age fifteen years and older throughout the country.

5 Interview with the author: Thuthukile Zuma, Johannesburg (telephone), July 5, 2009.

6 Interview with author: Gugulethu Zuma, Johannesburg (telephone), February 16, 2010.

7 Interview with the author: Thomas Maree, Cape Town (telephone), November 11, 2009.

8 Steinberg, *The Number*, 219.

9 South Africa data, World Prison Brief, International Centre for Prison Studies, University of Essex, Colchester, UK.

CHAPTER 22: THE CUP

1 Danny Jordaan, "Weep No More, SA," *City Press*, June 27, 2010, 25.

2 Interview with the author: Jacob Zuma, Cape Town, July 30, 2010.

3 Rich Mkhondo, "Don't Drop the World Cup Ball," *Star*, July 28, 2010, 15.

4 John Carlin, *Invictus, Nelson Mandela and the Game That Made a Nation* (New York: Penguin Books, 2009), 4.

5 Interview with the author: Ebrahim Ebrahim, Pretoria, July 7, 2010. All quotations in this chapter from Deputy Minister Ebrahim are from this interview.

6 "Zuma's Love Child," *Sunday Times,* January 31, 2010, 1.

7 Carien DuPlessis and Xolani Mbanjwa, "Now It's a Showdown," *Cape Times*, April 12, 2010, 1.

8 Mzilikazi Wa Afrika and Moipone Malefane, "Malema's Followers Turn on Zuma," *Sunday Times*, May 16, 2010, 1.

9 Julius Malema, *24th National Congress: Political Report*, Midrand, June 16, 2011. Available at http://www.ancyl.org.za/show.php?id=8031.

10 Interview with the author: Zweli Mkhize, Pietermaritzburg, August 3, 2010.

11 Interview with the author: Ndaba Mandela, Johannesburg, March 30, 2009.

12 Interview with the author: Ndaba Mandela, Johannesburg, July 12, 2010.

13 Interview with the author: Ndaba Mandela, Johannesburg (telephone), January 28, 2012.

14 Interviews with the author: Gwendoline Dube, Orange Farm (telephone), September 17, 2008, and September 26 and December 10, 2009.

15 Peter Delonno, "World Cup Adds to GDP and Image," *Business Report*, July 12, 2010, 1.

16 Grant Thornton Strategic Solutions, "SA 2010 World Cup: A Year in Review," July 21, 2011.

CHAPTER 23: LIBERATED PEOPLE

1 Interview with the author: Thuthukile Zuma and Gugulethu Zuma, Johannesburg, July 28, 2010.

2 Interview with the author: Thuthukile Zuma and her friends, Johannesburg, July 30, 2007.

3 Interview with the author: Vunene Mabasa, Bungeni (telephone), October 1, 2009.

4 Interview with the author: Vunene Mabasa, Bungeni, July 18, 2010.

5 Jos Kuper, *Politics and Accountability*, future*fact*, personal communication, February 17, 2010. Data are from surveys on economic issues and political issues conducted annually since 1998 based on a sample ($N = 2,500$) of respondents age fifteen years and older throughout the country.

6 Debbie Budlender, "Unemployment and Children's Well-Being," in Graham (ed.), *Inheriting Poverty?*, 4.

7 Ibid., 7.

8 Ibid., 18.

CHAPTER 24: THE LEADER

1 Interview with the author: Jacob Zuma, Pretoria, July 28, 2010.

2 Interview with the author: Ndaba Mandela, Johannesburg (telephone), January 28, 2012.

3 Interview with the author: Zwelinzima Vavi, Johannesburg, July 16, 2010.

4 Interview with the author: Gwede Mantashe, Johannesburg, July 16, 2010.

5 Interview with the author: Joel Netshitenzhe, Johannesburg, July 6, 2010.

6 Interview with the author: Zweli Mkhize, Pietermaritzburg, August 2, 2010.

7 Mostert, *Frontiers*, xv.

8 Interviews with the author: Jacob Zuma, Cape Town, in flight, and Durban, July 30, 2010.

CODA: FREEDOM DAY

1 Gregory Maqoma, "African Contemporary Dance?," in *Proceedings of 7th Jomba! Contemporary Dance Conference*, 2004, 24. Available at http://google .com/books/about/African_contemporary_dance.html?id=bpA7AQAAIAAJ.

Selected Bibliography

Abdool Karim, S. S., and Q. Abdool Karim (editors). *HIV/AIDS in South Africa.* Cambridge, United Kingdom: Cambridge University Press, 2005.

Adebajo, Adekeye, Adebayo Adedeji, and Christopher Landsberg (editors). *South Africa in Africa: The Post-Apartheid Era.* Scottsville, South Africa: University of KwaZulu-Natal Press, 2007.

Adhikari, Mohamed. *Not White Enough, Not Black Enough: Racial Identity in the South African Coloured Community.* Athens: Ohio University Press, 2005.

Africa Remix: Contemporary Art of a Continent. Johannesburg Art Gallery, 2007.

Allen, John. *Rabble-Rouser for Peace: The Authorized Biography of Desmond Tutu.* London: Free Press, 2006.

Altbeker, Antony. *A Country at War with Itself: South Africa's Crisis of Crime.* Cape Town: Jonathan Ball, 2007.

Ansell, Gwen. *Jazz, Popular Music and Politics in South Africa.* New York: Continuum, 2005.

Arndt, Corinna. *Managing Dissent: Institutional Culture and Political Independence in the South African Broadcasting Corporation's News and Current Affairs Division.* Unpublished thesis, University of Cape Town, 2007.

Ashforth, Adam. *Madumo: A Man Bewitched.* Cape Town: David Philip, 2000.

Ballard, Richard, Adam Habib, and Imraan Valodia. *Voices of Protest: Social Movements in Post-Apartheid South Africa.* Scottsville, South Africa: University of KwaZulu-Natal Press, 2006.

Barnett, Tony, and Alan Whiteside. *AIDS in the Twenty-First Century: Disease and Globalization.* New York: Palgrave Macmillan, 2002.

Barratt, Elizabeth. *Choosing to Be Part of the Story: The Participation of the South*

African National Editors' Forum in the Democratising Process. Master's thesis, University of Stellenbosch, 2006.

Barratt, Elizabeth. *Part of the Story: 10 years of the South African National Editors' Forum.* Johannesburg: SANEF, 2006.

Biko, Steve. *I Write What I Like.* Johannesburg: Picador, 1978.

Bizos, George. *No One to Blame?* Cape Town: David Philip, 1998.

Bond, Patrick. *Talk Left, Walk Right: South Africa's Frustrated Global Reforms.* Scottsville, South Africa: University of KwaZulu-Natal Press, 2004.

Bray, Rachel, Imke Gooskens, Lauren Kahn, Susan Moses, and Jeremy Seekings. *Growing Up in the New South Africa: Childhood and Adolescence in Post-Apartheid Cape Town.* Cape Town: Centre for Social Science Research, 2008.

Brodie, Nechama (editor). *The Joburg Book: A Guide to the City's History, People and Places.* Johannesburg: Pan Macmillan South Africa, 2008.

Brown, Duncan. *To Speak of this Land; Identity and Belonging in South Africa and Beyond.* Scottsville, South Africa: University of KwaZulu-Natal Press, 2006.

Bull, Chris (editor). *While the World Sleeps: Writing from the First Twenty Years of the Global AIDS Plague.* New York: Thunder Mouth Press, 2003.

Butler, Anthony. *Cyril Ramaphosa.* Johannesburg: Jacana Media, 2007.

CADRE (Center for AIDS Development, Research and Evaluation). *What's News: Perspectives on HIV/AIDS in the South African Media.* Johannesburg: CADRE, 2002.

Calland, Richard, and Paul Graham (editors). *Democracy in the Time of Mbeki.* Pretoria: Idasa, 2005.

Camay, Phiroshaw, and Anne J. Gordon. *Evolving Democratic Governance in South Africa.* Braamfontein, South Africa: CORE (Co-operative for Research and Education), 2004.

Cameron, Edwin. *Witness to AIDS.* Cape Town: Tafelberg, 2005.

Campbell, Catherine. *Letting Them Die: How HIV/AIDS Prevention Programmes Often Fail.* Bloomington: Indiana University Press, 2003.

Chipkin, Ivor. *Do South Africans Exist? Nationalism, Democracy and the Identity of "the People."* Johannesburg: Wits University Press, 2007.

Chirambo, Kondwani, and Mary Caesar. *AIDS and Governance in Southern Africa: Emerging Theories and Perspectives. A Report on the IDASA/UNDP Regional Governance and AIDS Forum April 2–4, 2003.* Pretoria: Idasa, 2003.

Coetzee, Erika, and Judith Streak (editors). *Monitoring Child Socio-Economic Rights in South Africa: Achievements and Challenges.* Pretoria: Idasa, 2004.

Coetzee, J. M. *African Compass: New Writing from Southern Africa.* Cape Town: New Africa Books, 2005.

Coetzee, J. M. *Age of Iron.* New York: Penguin Books, 1990.

Coetzee, J. M. *Disgrace.* New York: Viking, 1999.

Cohen, Jon. *Shots in the Dark: The Wayward Search for an AIDS Vaccine*. New York: W. W. Norton, 2001.

Comaroff, Jean, and John L. Comaroff. "Reflections on Liberalism, Policultural-ism, and ID-ology: Citizenship and Difference in South Africa." *Social Identities*, 9(3): 445–474, 2003.

Comaroff, John L., and Jean Comaroff. "Criminal Obsessions, after Foucault: Postcoloniality, Policing and the Metaphysics of Disorder." *Critical Inquiry*, 30(4): 800–824, 2004.

Comaroff, John L., and Jean Comaroff. "Law and Disorder in the Postcolony: An Introduction," in John L. Comaroff and Jean Comaroff (editors), *Law and Disorder in the Postcolony*. Chicago: University of Chicago Press, 2006.

Cooper, Frederick. *Africa since 1940*. Cambridge, United Kingdom: Cambridge University Press, 2002.

COSATU (Congress of South African Trade Unions). Fourth Central Commit-tee. Executive Summary. Johannesburg, 2007.

COSATU. *The NDR and Socialism, The NDR and Capitalism: Key Strategic Debates*. Discussion document for the Fourth COSATU Central Committee, September 17–20, 2007.

Crawford-Brown, Terry. *Eye on the Money*. Cape Town: Umuzi, 2007.

Cronin, Jeremy. *More Than a Casual Contact*. Cape Town: Umuzi, 2006.

D'Adesky, Anne-Christine. *Moving Mountains: The Race to Treat Global AIDS*. London: Verso, 2004.

Dangor, Achmat. *Bitter Fruit*. Cape Town: Kwela Books, 2001.

Davenport, Rodney, and Christopher Saunders. *South Africa: A Modern History*. 5th ed. Hampshire, United Kingdom: Macmillan Press, 2000.

Department of Health, Republic of South Africa. *An Assessment of the Implemen-tation of the HIV and AIDS and STI Strategic Plan*. Pretoria, 2007.

Duiker, K. Sello. *The Hidden Star*. Cape Town: Umuzi, 2006.

Duiker, K. Sello. *The Quiet Violence of Dreams*. Cape Town: Kwela Books, 2001.

Duiker, K. Sello. *Thirteen Cents*. Cape Town: David Philip, 2000.

du Preez, Max. *Pale Native: Memories of a Renegade Reporter*. Cape Town: Zebra Press, 2003.

du Preez Bezdrob, Anné Mariè. *Winnie Mandela: A Life*. Cape Town: Zebra Press, 2003.

Ebrahim, Noor. *Noor's Story: My Life in District Six*. Cape Town: District Six Museum Foundation, 1999.

Editorial. "The Fundamental Challenge We Face Is to Sustain a Full-Scale AIDS Response over At Least Another Generation " *Lancet*, 368(9534): 423–552, 2006.

Engel, Jonathan. *The Epidemic: A Global History of AIDS*. Washington, DC: Smithsonian Books, 2006.

Epstein, Helen. *The Invisible Cure: Africa, the West, and the Fight against AIDS*. New York: Farrar, Straus and Giroux, 2007.

Ewing, Deborah. *Report on the Children's Participation Component of Monitoring Child Socio-Economic Rights in South Africa*. Pretoria: Idasa, 2004.

Feinstein, Andrew. *After the Party: A Personal and Political Journey inside the ANC*. Cape Town: Jonathan Ball, 2007.

Fredricksen, George M. *Black Liberation: A Comparative History of Ideologies in the United States and South Africa*. Oxford, United Kingdom: Oxford University Press, 1995.

Garrett, Laurie. *The Coming Plague: Newly Emerging Diseases in a World Out of Balance*. New York: Penguin Books, 1994.

Gevisser, Mark. *Thabo Mbeki: The Dream Deferred*. Cape Town: Jonathan Ball, 2007. (An updated, and abbreviated, version of this book was published in the United States, as *A Legacy of Liberation*, in 2009.)

Giliomee, Hermann, and Bernard Mbenga Bernard. *New History of South Africa*. Cape Town: Tafelberg, 2007.

Global Fund. *Investing in Impact: Mid-Year Results Report 2006*. Geneva: Global Fund, 2006.

Gobodo-Madikizela, Pumla. *A Human Being Died That Night*. Boston: Houghton Mifflin, 2003.

Goodman, David. *Fault Lines: Journeys into the New South Africa*. Berkeley: University of California Press, 1999.

Gordimer, Nadine. *The House Gun*. New York: Penguin Books, 1998.

Gordimer, Nadine. *July's People*. New York: Penguin Books, 1981.

Gordimer, Nadine. *Jump*. New York: Farrar, Straus and Giroux, 1991.

Gordimer, Nadine. *Loot and Other Stories*. New York: Penguin Books, 2003.

Gordin, Jeremy. *Zuma: A Biography*. Cape Town: Jonathan Ball, 2008.

Govender, Pregs. *Love and Courage: A Story of Insubordination*. Johannesburg: Jacana Media, 2007.

Gow, Jeff, and Chris Desmond (editors). *Impacts and Interventions: The HIV/AIDS Epidemic and Children of South Africa*. Scottsville, South Africa: University of Natal Press, 2002.

Graham, Paul (editor). *Inheriting Poverty? An Economic Research Agenda for Realizing the Rights of Children*. Cape Town: Idasa, 2006.

Green, Pippa. *Choice, Not Fate: The Life and Times of Trevor Manuel*. Johannesburg: Penguin Books, 2008.

Gumede, William Merwin. *Thabo Mbeki and the Battle for the Soul of the ANC*. Cape Town: Zebra Press, 2005. (An updated edition if this book, under the same title, was published in London: Zed Books, 2007.)

Hadland, Adrian (editor). *Changing the Fourth Estate; Essays on South African Journalism*. Cape Town: HSRC Press, 2005.

Hadland, Adrian, and Jovial Rantao. *The Life and Times of Thabo Mbeki.* Rivonia: Zebra Press, 1999.

Haffajee, Ferial (editor). *The Book of South African Women.* Johannesburg: Mail & Guardian, 2006.

Harrison, Philip. *South Africa's Top Sites: Struggle.* Cape Town: Spearhead, 2004.

Heunis, Jan. *The Inner Circle.* Cape Town: Jonathan Ball, 2007.

Hoad, Martin, Karen Martin, and Reid Graeme (editors). *Sex and Politics in South Africa.* Cape Town: Double Storey Books, 2005.

Hochschild, Adam. *The Mirror at Midnight: A South African Journey.* London: Viking, 1990.

Holden, Paul. *The Arms Deal in Your Pocket.* Jeppestown, South Africa: Jonathan Ball, 2008.

Holland, Heidi, and Adam Roberts. *From Jo'burg to Jozi: Stories about Africa's Infamous City.* London: Penguin, 2002.

Hunter, Susan S. *Who Cares? AIDS in Africa.* New York: Palgrave Macmillan, 2003.

International AIDS Society. *Annual Report 2005.* Geneva: International AIDS Society, 2005.

Jacobs, Sean, and Richard Calland. *Thabo Mbeki's World: The Politics and Ideology of the South African President.* Scottsville, South Africa: University of Natal Press, 2002.

Jin, Ha. *The Writer as Migrant.* Chicago: University of Chicago Press, 2008.

Johnson, Shaun. *Strange Days Indeed, Tales from the Old, and the Nearly New South Africa.* London: Transworld, 1993.

Keegan, Margaret. *The Proliferation of Firearms in South Africa, 1994–2004.* Commissioned and funded by Oxfam Canada. Ottawa: Gun Free South Africa, 2005.

Khumalo, Fred. *Bitches' Brew.* Johannesburg: Jacana Media, 2006.

Khumalo, Fred. *Seven Steps to Heaven.* Johannesburg: Jacana Media, 2007.

Khumalo, Fred. *Touch My Blood; The Early Years.* Johannesburg: Umuzi, 2006.

Kinsella, James. *Covering the Plague: AIDS and the American Media.* New Brunswick, NJ: Rutgers University Press, 1989.

Kok, Pieter, Derik Gelderblom, John O. Oucho, and Johan van Zyl (editors). *Migration in South and Southern Africa: Dynamics and Determinants.* Cape Town: HRSC Press, 2006.

Krog, Antjie. *A Change of Tongue.* Johannesburg: Random House, 2003.

Langa, Mandla. *The Lost Colours of the Chameleon.* Johannesburg: Pan Macmillan, 2008.

Lelyveld, Joseph. *Move Your Shadow: South Africa, Black and White.* New York: Penguin Books, 1985.

Levine, Laurie. *Traditional Music of South Africa.* Johannesburg: Jacana Media, 2005.

Lodge, Tom. *Mandela: A Critical Life*. Oxford, United Kingdom: Oxford University Press, 2006.

Lodge, Tom. *Politics in South Africa: From Mandela to Mbeki*. Bloomington: Indiana University Press, 2002.

Luirink, Bart. *Moffies: Gay Life in Southern Africa*. Cape Town: David Philip, 1998.

Madondo, Bongani. *Hot Type: Icons, Artists and God-Figurines*. Johannesburg: Picador Africa, 2007.

Mandela, Nelson. *From Freedom to the Future: Tributes and Speeches*. Cape Town: Jonathan Ball, 2003.

Mandela, Nelson. *In His Own Words*. New York: Little, Brown, 1994.

Mandela, Nelson Rolihlahla. *Long Walk to Freedom: The Autobiography of Nelson Mandela*. Boston: Little, Brown, 1994.

Mangcu, Xolela. *To the Brink: The State of Democracy in South Africa*. Scottsville, South Africa: University of KwaZulu-Natal Press, 2008.

Mangcu, Xolela, Gill Marcus, Khehla Shubane, and Adrian Hadland (editors). *Visions of Black Economic Empowerment*. Johannesburg: Jacana Media, 2007.

Marinovich, Greg, and João Silva. *The Bang-Bang Club: Snapshots from a Hidden War*. London: Basic Books, 2000.

Mashabela, Harry. *A People on the Boil, Reflections on June 16, 1976 and Beyond*. 30th anniversary edition. Johannesburg: Jacana Media, 2006.

Massie, Robert Kinloch. *Loosing the Bonds: The United States and South Africa in the Apartheid Years*. New York: Doubleday, 1997.

Matlosa, Khabele, Per Strand, and Ann Strode. *The Impact of HIV and AIDS on Electoral Processes in South Africa. Preliminary Research Findings by the Governance and AIDS Programme (GAP)*. Pretoria: Idasa, 2004.

Mbeki, Moeletsi. *Architects of Poverty; Why African Capitalism Needs Changing*. Johannesburg: Picador Africa, 2009.

Mbeki, Thabo. *Africa, Define Yourself*. Cape Town: Tafelberg, 2002.

McGregor, Liz. *Khabzela: The Life and Times of a South African*. Johannesburg: Jacana Media, 2005.

McGregor, Liz, and Sarah Nuttall (eds). *At Risk: Writing On and Over the Edge of South Africa*. Cape Town: Jonathan Ball, 2007.

Mda, Zakes. *Fools, Bells and the Habit of Eating*. Johannesburg: Wits University Press, 2002.

Mda, Zakes. *The Heart of Redness*. New York: Picador, 2000.

Mda, Zakes. *The Madonna Excelsior*. New York: Farrar, Straus and Giroux, 2002.

Mda, Zakes. *Sometimes There Is a Void*. New York: Farrar, Straus and Giroux, 2012.

Mda, Zakes. *Ways of Dying*. Oxford, United Kingdom: Oxford University Press, 1991.

Meldrum, Andrew. *Where We Have Hope: A Memoir of Zimbabwe.* London: John Murray, 2004.

Meredith, Martin. *Diamonds, Gold and War: The British, the Boers and the Making of South Africa.* New York: Simon and Schuster, 2007.

Meredith, Martin. *Our Votes, Our Guns: Robert Mugabe and the Tragedy of Zimbabwe.* New York: PublicAffairs, 2002.

Modisane, William Bloke. *Blame Me on History.* Johannesburg: Ad Donker, 1963.

Mostert, Noel. *Frontiers: The Epic of South Africa's Creation and the Tragedy of the Xhosa People.* New York: Alfred A. Knopf, 1992.

Mpe, Phaswane. *Brooding Clouds.* Scottsville, South Africa: University of KwaZulu-Natal Press, 2008.

Mpe, Phaswane. *Welcome to Our Hillbrow.* Scottsville, South Africa: University of Natal Press, 2001.

Mulemfo, Mukanda M. *Thabo Mbeki and the African Renaissance.* Pretoria: Actua Press, 2005.

Nattrass, Nicoli. *The Moral Economy of AIDS in South Africa.* Cambridge, United Kingdom: Cambridge University Press, 2005.

Nattrass, Nicoli. *Mortal Combat: AIDS Denialism and the Struggle for Antiretrovirals in South Africa.* Scottsville, South Africa: University of KwaZulu-Natal Press, 2007.

Ndebele, Njabulo S. *Fine Lines from the Box: Future Thoughts about Our Country.* Cape Town: Umuzi, 2007.

Ndebele, Njabulo S. *Fools and Other Stories.* Johannesburg: Picador, 1983.

Niehaus, Isak. *Witchcraft, Power, Politics: Exploring the Occult in the South African Lowveld.* London: Pluto Press, 2001.

Nkosi, Lewis. *Mandela's Ego.* Cape Town: Umuzi, 2006.

Nuttall, Sarah. *Entanglement: Literary and Cultural Reflections on Apartheid.* Johannesburg: Wits University Press, 2008.

Nyatsumba, Kaizer. *All Sides of the Story.* Cape Town: Jonathan Ball, 1997.

O'Malley, Padraig. *Shades of Difference: Mac Maharaj and the Struggle for South Africa.* New York: Viking Penguin, 2007.

Padayachee, Vishnu (editor). *The Development Decade? Economic and Social Change in South Africa, 1994–2004.* Cape Town: HRSC Press, 2006.

Pinchuck, Tony, Barbara McCrea, Donald Reid, and Greg Mthembu-Salter. *The Rough Guide to South Africa, Lesotho and Swaziland.* London: Penguin, 2002.

Pogrund, Benjamin. *How Can Man Die Better: The Life of Robert Sobukwe.* Cape Town: Jonathan Ball, 1990.

Race Relations Survey. Johannesburg: South African Institute of Race Relations, 1987.

Ramphele, Mamphela. *Laying Ghosts to Rest: Dilemmas of the Transformation in South Africa*. Cape Town: Tafelberg, 2008.

Rapola, Zachariah. *Beginnings of a Dream*. Johannesburg: Jacana Media, 2007.

Reproductive Health Research Unit (RHRU). *HIV and Sexual Behaviour among Young South Africans: A National Survey of 15–24 Year Olds*. Johannesburg: Health Systems Trust, 2004.

Roberts, Adam, and Joe Thloloe (editors). *Soweto Inside Out, Stories about Africa's Famous Township*. London: Penguin Books, 2004.

Roberts, Ronald Suresh. *Fit to Govern: The Native Intelligence of Thabo Mbeki*. Pretoria: STE Publishers, 2007.

Robins, Steven L. *Limits to Liberation after Apartheid: Citizenship, Governance and Culture*. Oxford: James Currey, 2005.

Ross, Robert. *A Concise History of South Africa*. 2d ed. Cambridge, United Kingdom: Cambridge University Press, 1997.

Russell, Alec. *Bring Me My Machine Gun: The Battle for the Soul of South Africa from Mandela to Zuma*. New York: PublicAffairs, 2009.

SADC (Southern African Development Community). *Expert Think Tank Meeting on HIV Prevention in High-Prevalence Countries in Southern Africa: Report*. Gaborone, Botswana: SADC, 2006.

Sampson, Anthony. *DRUM: The Making of a Magazine*. Cape Town: Jonathan Ball, 2005.

Sampson, Anthony. *Mandela: The Authorized Biography*. New York: Alfred A. Knopf, 1999.

Schreiner, Olive. *The Story of an African Farm*. Johannesburg: Ad Donker, 1975.

Seekings, Jeremy. *The UDF: A History of the United Democratic Front in South Africa 1983–1991*. Cape Town: David Philip, 2000.

Sergeant, Barry. *Brett Kebble: The Inside Story*. Cape Town: Zebra Press, 2006.

Serote, Mongane Wally. *To Every Birth Its Blood*. Johannesburg: Picador, 1978.

Shaw, Gerald. *The Cape Times: An Informal History*. Cape Town: David Philip, 1999.

Shilts, Randy. *And the Band Played On: Politics, People, and the AIDS Epidemic*. New York: St. Martin's Press, 1987.

Shisana, O., T. Rehle, L. C. Simbayi, et al. *South African National HIV Prevalence, HIV Incidence, Behaviour and Communication Survey, 2005*. Commissioned by the Nelson Mandela Foundation. Cape Town: HSRC Press, 2005.

Shoumatoff, Alex. *African Madness*. New York: Alfred A. Knopf, 1986.

Shukri, Ishtiyaq. *The Silent Minaret*. Johannesburg: Jacana Media, 2005.

Sisulu, Elinor. *Walter and Albertina Sisulu in Our Lifetime*. Cape Town: David Philip, 2002.

Slabbert, Frederik van Zyl. *The Other Side of History: An Anecdotal Reflection on Political Transition in South Africa*. Cape Town: Jonathan Ball, 2006.

Slovo, Gillian. *Every Secret Thing: My Family, My Country.* London: Virago, 1997.

Smith, David James. *Young Mandela: The Revolutionary Years.* New York: Little, Brown, 2010.

Sontag, Susan. *Illness as Metaphor and AIDS and Its Metaphors.* New York: Picador, 1990.

Sontag, Susan. *Regarding the Pain of Others.* New York: Picador, 2003.

Soudien, Crain. *Youth Identity in Contemporary South Africa: Race, Culture and Schooling.* Claremont, South Africa: New Africa Books, 2007.

South African Human Rights Commission. *Faultlines: Inquiry into Racism in the Media.* Johannesburg: South African Human Rights Commission, 2000.

Southall, Roger, and John Daniel. *Zunami! The 2009 South African Elections.* Johannesburg: Jacana Media, 2009.

Sparks, Allister. *Beyond the Miracle: Inside the New South Africa.* Chicago: Chicago University Press, 2003.

Sparks, Allister. *The Mind of South Africa: The Story of the Rise and Fall of Apartheid.* Cape Town: Jonathan Ball, 1990.

Sparks, Allister. *Tomorrow Is Another Country: The Inside Story of South Africa's Negotiated Settlement.* Cape Town: Jonathan Ball, 1995.

Steinberg, Jonny. *Midlands.* Cape Town: Jonathan Ball, 2002.

Steinberg, Jonny. *Notes from a Fractured Country.* Cape Town: Jonathan Ball, 2007.

Steinberg, Jonny. *The Number.* Cape Town: Jonathan Ball, 2005

Steinberg, Jonny. *Sizwe's Test: A Young Man's Journey through Africa's AIDS Epidemic.* New York: Simon and Schuster, 2008

Stiebel, Lindy, and Liz Gunner (editors). *Still Beating the Drum: Critical Perspectives on Lewis Nkosi.* Johannesburg: Wits University Press, 2006.

Stine, Gerald J. *2005: AIDS Update.* San Francisco: Pearson Education, 2005.

Stober, Paul, and Barbara Ludman (editors). *The Mail & Guardian A–Z of South African Politics.* Johannesburg: Jacana Media, 2004.

Thompson, Leonard. *A History of South Africa.* New Haven, CT: Yale University Press, 2001.

Thompson, Leroy. *Dirty Wars: Elite Forces vs the Guerrillas.* London: David and Charles, 1988.

Tleane, Console, and Jane Duncan. *Public Broadcasting in the Era of Cost Recovery: A Critique of the South African Broadcasting Corporation's Crisis of Accountability.* Johannesburg: Freedom of Expression Institute, 2003.

Treatment Action Group. *What's in the Pipeline: New HIV Drugs, Vaccines, Microbicides, HCV and TB Therapies in Clinical Trials.* Cape Town: Treatment Action Group, 2006.

Tutu, Desmond Mpilo. *No Future without Forgiveness.* London: Rider, 1999.

Tyson, Harvey. *Editors under Fire.* Johannesburg: Random House, 1993.

UNAIDS (Joint United Nations Programme on HIV/AIDS). *Report on the Global AIDS Epidemic: Executive Summary. A UNAIDS 10th Anniversary Special Edition.* Geneva: UNAIDS, 2006.

UNICEF South Africa. *Saving Children, Enhancing Lives: Combating HIV and AIDS in South Africa.* 2d ed. Pretoria: UNICEF South Africa, 2006.

Uys, Pieter-Dirk. *Funigalore: Evita's Real-Life Adventures in Wonderland.* London: Penguin, 1995.

van Niekerk, Marlene. *Triomf.* Cape Town: Jonathan Ball, 1994.

van Onselen, Charles. *The Small Matter of a Horse: The Life of "Nongoloza" Mathebula, 1867–1948.* Pretoria: Protea Book House, 2008.

van Zyl, John (editor). *Community Radio: The People's Voice.* Johannesburg: Sharp Sharp Media, 2003.

Vladislavic, Ivan. *Portrait with Keys: The City of Johannesburg Unlocked.* New York: W. W. Norton, 2009.

Waldmeir, Patti. *Anatomy of a Miracle: The End of Apartheid and the Birth of a New South Africa.* New York: W. W. Norton, 1997.

Walker, Liz, Reid Graeme, and Cornell Morna. *Waiting to Happen: HIV/AIDS in South Africa.* Boulder, CO: Lynne Rienner, 2004.

Wa Thiong'o, Ngugi. *Decolonising the Mind: The Politics of Language in African Literature.* London: James Currey, 1986.

Wa Thiong'o, Ngugi. *Matigari.* Portsmouth, NH: Heinemann, 1987.

Watson, Wendy. *Brick by Brick: An Informal Guide to the History of South Africa.* Claremont, South Africa: New Africa Books. 2007.

Willan, Brian. *Sol Plaatje: South African Nationalist, 1876–1932.* London: Heinemann, 1984.

World Bank. *World Development Report 2007. Development and the Next Generation.* Washington, DC: World Bank, 2006.

World Health Organization. *Towards Universal Access by 2010: How WHO Is Strengthening Health Services to Fight HIV/AIDS.* Geneva: World Health Organization, 2006.

Index